Copán

Publication of the Advanced Seminar Series
is made possible by generous support from
The Brown Foundation, Inc., of Houston, Texas.

**School of American Research
Advanced Seminar Series**

George J. Gumerman
General Editor

Copán

Contributors

Ricardo Agurcia Fasquelle
Asociación Copán, Copán, Honduras

E. Wyllys Andrews
Middle American Research Institute, Tulane University

Ellen E. Bell
Department of Anthropology, Kenyon College

Cassandra R. Bill
Middle American Research Institute, Tulane University

Barbara W. Fash
Peabody Museum of Archaeology and Ethnology, Harvard University

William L. Fash
Peabody Museum of Archaeology and Ethnology, Harvard University

Matthew G. Looper
Department of Art and Art History, California State University, Chico

Julia C. Miller
Department of Anthropology, University of Pennsylvania

Linda Schele
Department of the History of Art, University of Texas, Austin

David W. Sedat
University of Pennsylvania Museum of Archaeology and Anthropology

Robert J. Sharer
University of Pennsylvania Museum of Archaeology and Anthropology

Rebecca Storey
Department of Anthropology, University of Houston

David Stuart
Department of the History of Art, University of Texas, Austin

Loa P. Traxler
University of Pennsylvania Museum of Archaeology and Anthropology

David Webster
Department of Anthropology, Pennsylvania State University

Copán
The History of an Ancient Maya Kingdom

Edited by E. Wyllys Andrews and William L. Fash

School of American Research Press
Santa Fe

School of American Research Press
Post Office Box 2188
Santa Fe, New Mexico 87504-2188
www.sarpress.org

Director: James F. Brooks
Executive Editor: Catherine Cocks
Manuscript Editor: Kate Talbot
Design and Production: Cynthia Dyer
Proofreader: Marjorie Pannell
Indexer: Ina Gravitz

Library of Congress Cataloging-in-Publication Data:

Copán : the history of an ancient Maya kingdom / edited by E. Wyllys Andrews and William L. Fash.—1st ed.
    p. cm. — (School of American Research advanced seminar series)
    Includes bibliographical references and index.
    ISBN 1-930618-37-9 (cloth : alk. paper) – ISBN 1-930618-38-7 (pbk. : alk. paper)
1. Copán Site (Honduras) 2. Mayas—Honduras—Copán (Dept.)—Antiquities. 3. Maya architecture—Honduras—Copán (Dept.) 4. Maya scupture—Honduras—Copán (Dept.) 5. Inscriptions, Mayan—Honduras—Copán (Dept.) 6. Copán (Honduras : Dept.)—Antiquities. I. Andrews, E. Wyllys (Edward Wyllys) II. Fash, William Leonard. III. Title. IV. Series.

F1435.1.C7C67 2004
972.83'84'01—dc22   2004017173

Copyright © 2005 by the School of American Research. All rights reserved.
Library of Congress Catalog Card Number 2004017173
International Standard Book Numbers 978-1-930618-37-4 (cloth); 978-1-930618-38-1 (paper).
First edition 2005. Third paperback printing 2021.

Cover illustration: Stela N, north side detail. Court of the Hieroglyphic Stairway, principal Group, Copán, Honduras. Photograph © 1995 by Barbara Fash.

Contents

	List of Figures	ix
	List of Tables	xii
	Preface	xiii
1.	Contributions and Controversies in the Archaeology and History of Copán *William L. Fash and Ricardo Agurcia Fasquelle*	3
2.	Political Ecology, Political Economy, and the Culture History of Resource Management at Copán *David Webster*	33
3.	Toward a Social History of the Copán Valley *William L. Fash*	73
4.	Iconographic Evidence for Water Management and Social Organization at Copán *Barbara W. Fash*	103
5.	Early Classic Royal Power in Copan: The Origins and Development of the Acropolis (ca. A.D. 250–600) *Robert J. Sharer, David W. Sedat, Loa P. Traxler, Julia C. Miller, and Ellen E. Bell*	139
6.	The Evolution of Structure 10L-16, Heart of the Copán Acropolis *Ricardo Agurcia Fasquelle and Barbara W. Fash*	201

Contents

7. A Late Classic Royal Residence at Copán   239
   E. Wyllys Andrews and Cassandra R. Bill

8. Health and Lifestyle (before and after Death) among the Copán Elite   315
   Rebecca Storey

9. Seats of Power at Copán   345
   Linda Schele and Matthew G. Looper

10. A Foreign Past: The Writing and Representation of History on a Royal Ancestral Shrine at Copan   373
    David Stuart

11. Issues in Copán Archaeology   395
    E. Wyllys Andrews and William L. Fash

References   427
Index   479

Figures

1.1	An aerial view of the Copán Valley, looking east	5
1.2	The Principal Group of Copán, 10L quad	7
1.3	Map of the urban core of ancient Copán	13
1.4	The Copán Sculpture Museum	24
2.1	Survey zones, sites, and major physiographic features, Copán Valley	40
2.2	The Copán population by period	43
2.3	A raw simulation of the Copán population through time	44
2.4	A population reconstruction for the Copán polity	46
2.5	An elite structure along the northern edge of Las Sepulturas zone	48
2.6	Raw obsidian-hydration dates from Copán Valley sites	51
3.1	A map of the Copán pocket of the Copán Valley	77
3.2	A schematic east-west cross section of Structure 10L-26	81
3.3	The Motmot floor marker	82
3.4	A plan map of the Acbi-phase courtyard in Group 9N-8	89
4.1	An Indigo Structure mask	117
4.2	*Tun* motifs from Copán	118
4.3	Quatrefoil motifs from Copán	120
4.4	Half-quatrefoil motifs from Copán	121
4.5	Water-lily headdresses from Copán	124
4.6	Figure with maize headdress, Las Sepulturas	125
4.7	Four possible *sian otots* near the site core	127
4.8	Structure 10L-22A; sculpture, structure 10L-32; vessel	128
4.9	Water-lily serpents from Copán	130
5.1	Perspective reconstruction of the Copán Acropolis	141
5.2	Preliminary plan of the Early Classic Acropolis	154
5.3	Hunal Structure	159
5.4	Yehnal Structure: *K'inich Ajaw* mask	167

FIGURES

5.5	Margarita Structure: emblem of K'inich Yax K'uk' Mo'	169
5.6	Motmot marker: founder portraits	170
5.7	Margarita Tomb: perspective drawing	172
5.8	Xukpi Stone: hieroglyphic text	172
5.9	Stela 63	175
5.10	Preliminary plan of the Early Classic Acropolis, Time Span 4	178
5.11	Preliminary plan of the Early Classic Acropolis, Time Span 3	183
5.12	Preliminary plan of the Early Classic Acropolis, Time Span 2	187
5.13	Ante Structure	188
5.14	Ante Step	188
6.1	Cross section of the Copán Acropolis	203
6.2	Rosalila Structure, inside structure 10L-16	205
6.3	Floor plan of Rosalila's lower level	206
6.4	Incense burners from Rosalila	208
6.5	Hieroglyphic step of the Azul Substructure	209
6.6	Termination offering inside Rosalila	210
6.7	Buried terraces of Purpura	211
6.8	West side of Structure 10L-16	212
6.9	Plan of Structure 10L-16	213
6.10	The west room of Structure 10L-16	215
6.11	Jaguar cyst behind Altar Q	216
6.12	Pedestals and sculpture found under Altar Q	216
6.13	Full-scale replica of Rosalila	218
6.14	Reconstruction drawings of Rosalila	219
6.15	Mask of the Sun God on the Azul Substructure	220
6.16	Sun God and Bird	223
6.17	Central Sun God mask	225
6.18	Solar cartouche	227
6.19	Turbaned niche figure	228
6.20	West side of Structure 10L-16, drawing	231
6.21	Skull rack (*tzompantli*)	233
6.22	Reconstruction of the vision serpent bench	234
6.23	Sculpture motifs from Structure 10L-16	235
6.24	Altar Q in the sculpture museum	236

Figures

7.1	Plan of Group 10L-2, Late Classic period	241
7.2	Structure 10L-34 after consolidation	248
7.3	Small vaulted crypts in Structure 10L-238	250
7.4	Miniature double-headed jaguar throne	251
7.5	Structure 10L-32	254
7.6	Structure 10L-32	255
7.7	The sculpture of Structure 10L-32	256
7.8	Vaulted tomb in Structure 10L-32-2nd	259
7.9	Structure 10L-30 from the southwest	261
7.10	Structure 10L-33	262
7.11	Structure 10L-31	266
7.12	Structure 10L-29	267
7.13	Structure 10L-29	268
7.14	Structure 10L-41	270
7.15	Structure 10L-41A, Cache 1	273
7.16	Structure 10L-41, construction phases	276
7.17	Reconstruction of sculpture placement on Structures 10L-41B, C, and D	277
7.18	Structure 10L-43	281
7.19	Altar F'	286
7.20	Round altar from Structure 10L-30	287
7.21	Fragment of a broken rectangular altar from Structure 10L-32	289
7.22	Half of a round altar from Structure 10L-29	290
8.1	Stingray spines, Burial XXXVII-5	321
8.2	Patellar surface of Burial XXXVII-4	325
8.3	The maxilla of Burial XXXVII-10	329
9.1	Impinged-bone allographs	347
9.2	/ki/ allographs	348
9.3	Contexts of *pib' il nah* and *kunil* from Palenque	348
9.4	References to seats/platforms and *kunil* at Palenque	350
9.5	Contexts of the impinged-bone at Tikal	351
9.6	Polychrome ceramic vessel	352
9.7	Sky– and earth–impinged-bone collocations	353
9.8	Reference to a seat/platform in text and image of Quiriguá Stela D	355
9.9	The impinged-bone in references to warfare	356

FIGURES

9.10	Toniná Monument 122	357
9.11	Tamarindito Hieroglyphic Stairway 2, step 3, D2–P2	357
9.12	References to early seats/platforms at Copán	359
9.13	Copán Altar T, detail	359
9.14	Copán Altar U, D1–D3	360
9.15	Copán Stela J, east text, 20–30	361
9.16	Copán Motmot marker	363
9.17	Copán Papagayo Step, side	364
9.18	Copán Stela 2	366
9.19	Copán Stela 12, C13–D14, E1–F3	368
9.20	Copán Stelae 10 and 13	369
9.21	Copán Stela 13 Altar	370
10.1	Structure 10L-26 in 1987	375
10.2	Photograph of 1895 excavations at Structure 10L-26	379
10.3	Dedicatory statements from the Hieroglyphic Stairway	381
10.4	The accession record of K'inich Yax K'uk' Mo'	384
10.5	Sections of the Hieroglyphic Stairway	386
10.6	Three parallel passages, Temple Inscription, Structure 10L-26	388

Tables

3.1	Final-Phase Copán Acropolis Buildings	95
5.1	Radiocarbon Dates	143
5.2	Obsidian-Hydration Dates	144
5.3	Copán Dynastic Sequence and Architecture	152
7.1	Chronology of Group 10L-2, Copán	245
8.1	Skeletal Indicators of Stress in Elite Burials at Copán	337

Preface

Seven seasons of intensive archaeological fieldwork by the Copán Acropolis Archaeological Project (PAAC) came to an end in 1994. The advanced seminar on Copán was held that October at the School of American Research. Limited excavations, exposure of burials, consolidation of buildings investigated by the PAAC, analysis, and work on the new Sculpture Museum were to continue, but that year seemed an appropriate time for us to gather the results of this research and consider them in a setting conducive to extensive discussion about the rise and fall of this distinguished Maya kingdom.

Only once before has an SAR advanced seminar concentrated exclusively on one site. The study of Chan Chan, published in 1982, followed years of survey and excavation in this huge urban compound on the north coast of Peru. Numerous earlier SAR seminars on various aspects of ancient Maya civilization provided an enormously productive backdrop and incentive for looking at broader problems through the venue of one particularly well-studied kingdom. A natural follow-up on the Copán session was the 1999 advanced seminar on the great Maya metropolis of Tikal, published in 2003.

At Copán, investigations and consolidation beginning in the late nineteenth century were carried out by A. P. Maudslay, Harvard University, the Carnegie Institution, and the Honduran Institute of Anthropology and History. Since 1975, research by Honduras, Harvard, Penn State, and other institutions has continued almost every year at the site center, in the immediately surrounding valley, or along the much more extensive Copán River drainage. This research has run the gamut of investigation, from the largest public buildings to the simplest dwellings, from the mundane artifacts of daily subsistence to the elaborate possessions of the rich and powerful, from food production, land use, and water control to art, writing, and astronomy. Through these decades of investigation, the differing scales of research and theoretical

PREFACE

orientations have given our understanding of the ancient Copanecos a fullness that is perhaps surpassed at no other ancient Maya city. For this reason, a seminar on one Maya city seemed worthwhile.

Half of the ten participants were co-directors of the PAAC, which concentrated on conservation, excavation, and interpretation of architecture and sculpture on top of, inside, or adjacent to the Acropolis, at the center of Copán. Bill Fash, initiator and overall director of the project, had concentrated for nearly a decade on Structure 10L-26, the Temple of the Hieroglyphic Stairway, and its antecedents, as well as the adjacent ball court and Structures 10L-22 and 10L-22A. Barbara Fash was responsible for analysis and coordination of the architectural sculpture and for the conception of and exhibitions in the Sculpture Museum, which was completed in 1996. Ricardo Agurcia had worked on Structure 10L-16 and its predecessors, including the uniquely preserved Rosalila temple. Bob Sharer had directed excavations in a multitude of buildings on the east side of the Acropolis, and Will Andrews worked in Group 10L-2, a Late Classic elite compound off the south side of the Acropolis. Linda Schele and Dave Stuart were the Copán epigraphers at the seminar, although many others have contributed to understanding the extensive written record there.

Dave Webster, co-director of the second phase of the Proyecto Arqueológico Copán (PAC II) and of more recent excavations, brought a view from excavations and survey outside the Acropolis. Rebecca Storey, who served as the skeletal biologist for PAC II, also contributed a comparative perspective from her research in the Las Sepulturas group. Grant Jones used his knowledge of the late Maya Itza kingdom to consider aspects of the Classic polity.

All the participants except Grant Jones have contributed to the current volume, often in combination with other authors participating in the research about which they write. After Linda Schele died in 1998, Matt Looper generously took the paper she had written for the 1994 seminar and turned it into the chapter published here.

The seminar gave us a stimulating week, providing a unique opportunity to examine complex issues in ways that would otherwise have been impossible. As always at SAR seminars, the papers were prepared and circulated in advance, and we discussed them and many related issues. These conversations proved constructive as differing perspectives dovetailed, partially overlapped, or remained in conflict. Sometimes the discussions produced new insights. Perhaps the most exciting was Dave Stuart's realization that a personage on two or more monuments in Group 10L-2 was not a heretofore unknown noble named *Chak*, but rather a supernatural patron. This meant that the human protagonist on these monuments and in this group of buildings was none other than Yax Pasaj, the sixteenth and final ruler in the Copán dynasty. Linda Schele immediately agreed with Stuart. This discovery enabled us to fill in a totally new dimension of the final ruler's life and to link a Late Classic Copán king to his residential neighborhood.

Interpretation of ancient Copán's history, despite all the work that has been done, is still in its youth. We understand far more about this site and its external relations than was possible a generation ago, but as the following pages show, we know frustratingly little about many important questions, such as the relationship of ancient Maya social groups to the land that sustained them, or the nature of Copán's changing ties to the surrounding Maya and non-Maya groups. Even on certain matters of chronology, so crucial to understanding the chronicle of the ancient city, we could sometimes not reach consensus. The issues on which we could not completely agree appear in some of the chapters and are underscored in the concluding chapter of the book.

The names of Maya rulers at many sites have changed as scholars have discovered how to read their Maya names as they would have been spoken. The somewhat confusing result is that one king may have several names in the literature. Here we have tried to use the names given in the 2001 edition of Bill Fash's *Scribes, Warriors and Kings* (see also *Chronicle of the Maya Kings and Queens: Deciphering the Dynasties of the Ancient Maya* by Simon Martin and Nikolai Grube, 2000). We also refer to them as *Ruler 1*, *Ruler 2*, and so on.

We are grateful to Doug Schwartz and to the staff of the School of American Research for their hospitality, constant concern for our comfort, wonderful sustenance, and, most important, the opportunity to share this stimulating week. More recently, Richard Leventhal supported our efforts to see this into print, as have, at various times, Joan O'Donnell, James Brooks, and Catherine Cocks. We are deeply in debt to two anonymous reviewers, who made extraordinarily thoughtful and helpful comments about all the chapters, suggesting

Preface

arguments, topics, and directions we considered for the volume as a whole. Following their lead, we extensively revised parts of the volume. And finally, we thank Kate Talbot, who did a fine job of editing the volume.

Most of all, we thank the seminar participants for their patience and their willingness to revise chapters, often more than once. We hope that the greater richness and depth provided by more recent analyses and new insights make up in small part for the long time that has passed since the seminar.

We dedicate this volume to the memory of Linda Schele, who contributed so much to the understanding of Copán and to the people around her, and to Gordon R. Willey, who was the architect of all the research at Copán in the past thirty years.

Copán

1

Contributions and Controversies in the Archaeology and History of Copán

William L. Fash and Ricardo Agurcia Fasquelle

The Classic Maya kingdom of Copán has enriched and enlivened scholarly debate on a host of anthropological issues since the mid-nineteenth century. Best known for the abundance and great artistry of its stone sculpture, Copán reached its apogee during what scholars refer to as the Classic period (A.D. 250–900) of Lowland Maya civilization. Its settlements, architectural history, and hieroglyphic inscriptions attest that this southeasternmost Maya state peaked during the historically documented dynasty that reigned from A.D. 426 to 822. Copán has provided fertile ground for productive theoretical debates on issues as diverse as state formation, urbanism, sociopolitical organization, economic specialization, the relative merits and strengths of historical texts and archaeological data, architecture and space, warfare, the Classic Maya collapse, and the possibilities for linking archaeology, epigraphy, and iconography in Mesoamerican studies. As Joyce Marcus (2004:372) noted recently, the Copán case has transcended its region: "One need no longer be a Mayanist to find the Copán story compelling. It is now one of the most detailed archaeological examples of secondary state formation in the prehistoric world."

WILLIAM L. FASH AND RICARDO AGURCIA FASQUELLE

The abundance of Copán's carved stone monuments has privileged the study of its hieroglyphic inscriptions and pictorial sculpture ever since ancient Maya ruins became an object of search, and research, in the early nineteenth century. The diversity and sheer numbers of its inscribed texts have made Copán the origin or the litmus test for a number of hieroglyphic decipherments. Its inscriptions are so well known by relevant specialists and so frequently scrutinized in the literature that Copán has one of the best-documented dynastic histories of the ancient world. The resulting historical data provided an important context for the evaluation of competing anthropological models of sociopolitical organization and evolution (Marcus 1992a, 1993, 2004). Such formulations have been examined both on the basis of the inscriptions alone (Marcus 1976; Stuart, chapter 10 in this volume) and by testing via independent archaeological data (Aoyama 1999; Sanders and Webster 1988; Webster, chapter 2 in this volume).

Field archaeologists are skeptical of political pronouncements on public monuments at ancient sites, and Mesoamericanists are no exception (Marcus 1974, 1992b). Much research has been devoted to illuminating the social and economic contexts of the claims made by ancient Maya rulers, through concerted archaeological investigations both within and outside their royal precincts. The Copán research has contributed strongly to this effort, with extensive settlement surveys, household archaeology, and specialized studies of architecture, artifacts, and osteology (Storey, chapter 8 in this volume). Even within the valley research, however, controversies continue with regard to the population's size and heterogeneity (fueling debates on its degree of urbanization), the degree of economic specialization (enlightening discussions of ranked versus stratified societies), and, most hotly contested of all, the nature and timing of the so-called "Classic Maya collapse" (T. P. Culbert, ed., 1973). In particular, how many people remained in the Copán Valley (figure 1.1), and for how long, after the fall of centralized authority in the early ninth century A.D.?

At its peak, the population of the kingdom of Copán numbered at least twenty thousand, with marked status differences (whether ranked or stratified; see Webster, chapter 2 in this volume) between its households. At its height, the hegemony of its royal line extended over an area of at least 250 km². Most of the populace consisted of commoners

FIGURE 1.1
An aerial view of the Copán Valley, looking east. The Principal Group, or royal compound, lies in the forested area in the center of the alluvial bottomlands. (Photograph by B. Fash in 1977)

engaged in agricultural pursuits, but excavations show that many of them practiced part-time craft specializations as well (Abrams 1987). The case of the chipped-stone industry indicates that state sponsorship of full-time craftsmen also took place (Aoyama 1999). Among the nobility, numerous citizens distinguished themselves as scribes, sculptors, ballplayers, administrators, warriors, councilors, and rulers. This volume is fundamentally devoted to understanding the origins and development of this remarkable city and the forces that eventually brought about its end. To that purpose, the authors pursue their distinct approaches and specialized studies within the larger framework of paradigms and questions that have shaped Maya and Mesoamerican archaeology for the past 150 years.

The advanced seminar on Copán both built upon and reflected the contributions of previous School of American Research seminars, such as the rise (Adams 1977) and the fall (T. P. Culbert, ed., 1973) of Classic Maya civilization, lowland Maya settlement patterns (Ashmore

1981) and political history (P. Culbert 1991), and the nature of late Lowland Maya civilization (Andrews and Sabloff 1986). While the Classic-period inscriptions played a large role in scholarly understanding of political history and relations between centers, Maya archaeology—like the broader field of Mesoamerican archaeology—continues to be characterized by a diversity of research interests and agendas. The interest in settlement patterns and its logical extension into household archeology have provided Mesoamericanists with remarkable opportunities to study all segments of ancient society.

In Copán, attention was focused on the settlements outside the city center or "site core" (figure 1.2) as far back as the early twentieth century by the pioneering epigrapher Sylvanus Morley (1920). The residential zones surrounding the royal compound have been the focus of continual archaeological research projects since Gordon Willey's Copán Valley research began in 1975. Willey's settlement mapping (Leventhal 1979, 1981; Willey and Leventhal 1979) and household archaeology (Willey, Leventhal, and Fash 1978; Willey et al. 1994) opened new vistas onto the organization of society that have been pursued through diverse specialized studies in a variety of research projects in the valley that show no signs of abating.

As in all of academe, much of Maya archaeology has been sharply divided between scholars pursuing scientific approaches and those pursuing humanistic approaches (Marcus 1995). In Copán, there certainly have been strong players in each camp over the years. Nonetheless, Willey's (1980) vision of pursuing a holistic view of Maya civilization has come to fruition in Copán, where recent research is viewed as "a model of multidisciplinary integration" (Marcus 2003b:94). Willey's project was also important in leading the charge to incorporate the study of hieroglyphic inscriptions found at elite residential sites into the broader study of their inhabitants' lifeways. The abundance of such inscriptions in the Copán Valley, combined with the fruitful nature of conjoined studies of written history, art, and archaeology, have led to an excavated sample that is biased toward elites. Although household archaeology and survey of smaller sites in the valley have been extensive compared to many other Mesoamerican settlement zones (Webster, chapter 2 in this volume), our understanding

CONTRIBUTIONS AND CONTROVERSIES

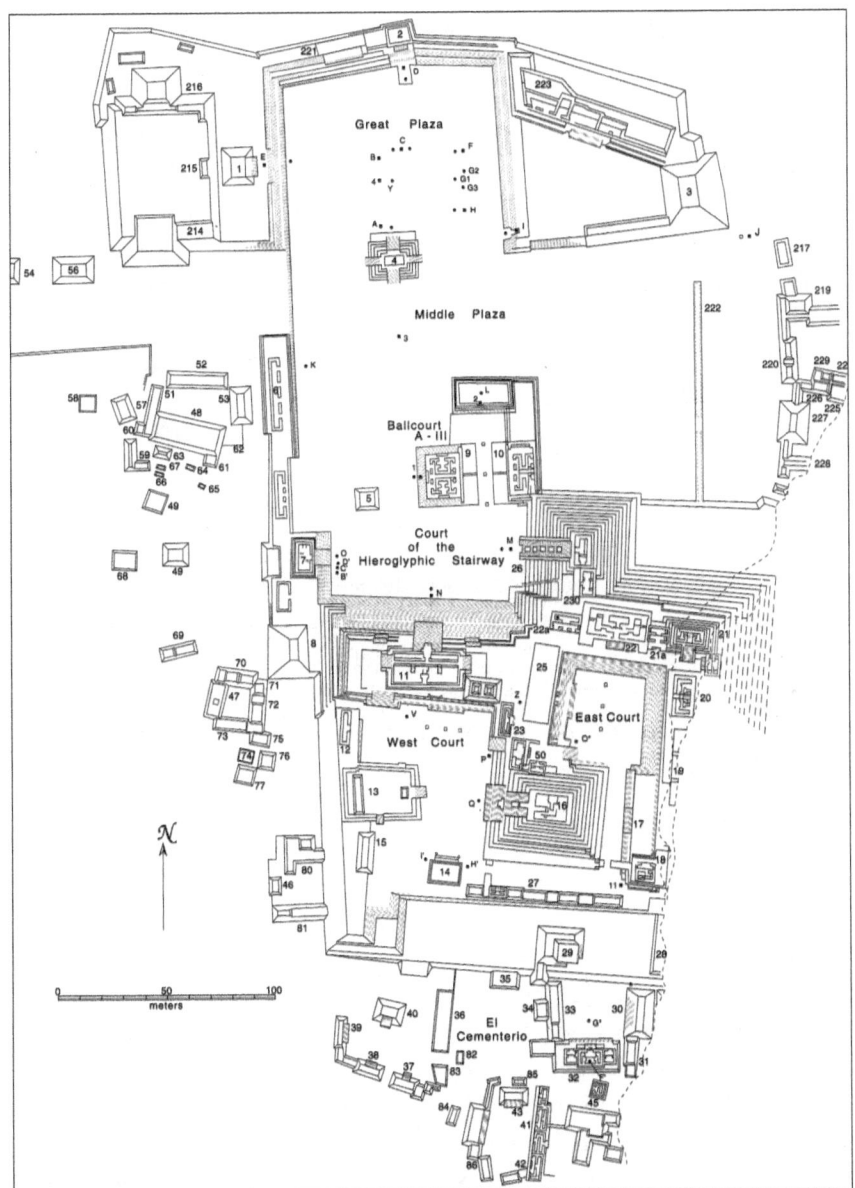

FIGURE 1.2
The Principal Group of Copán, showing structures in the 10L quad of the valley map (after W. Fash 2002).

of Copán's history is heavily weighted to the lifestyles of the rich and famous. The many strengths of the Copán data on elites are reflected in this volume but are also balanced by a wide array of information on the evolution of complex society in Copán presented in several chapters in the book (chapters 2, 3, 4, 8, and 11).

This introduction provides background on the origins and development of scholarship on Copán and on the forces that brought about the production of this book and many others. Increasingly, the social context of archaeology is seen as a key element in the questions asked, the methods employed, and the results obtained by its practitioners. We hope that this brief review can serve as a framework that will be useful for historians of the larger discipline, as well as those interested in why the Copán research—and the larger field of studies of the ancient Maya and Mesoamerica—has taken the course leading us to where we are in 2004. For the interested reader, more detailed descriptions of the various projects and players on the stage of Copán studies can be found in W. Fash 1991 and Webster 1999. The conclusion of this introduction broadly outlines, for the non-Mesoamericanist reader, our present understandings of ancient Mesoamerican culture history and cultural process at Copán and serves as a baseline for the more detailed and specialized treatments that follow.

CHANGING TIMES, QUESTIONS, AND DEBATES IN COPÁN STUDIES

The ruins of Copán were among the first ancient Mesoamerican sites to attract the attention of Western travelers, scholars, and the European-American public in what Willey and Sabloff (1993) refer to as the "Period of Exploration and Discovery." The first was the 1576 visit of Diego García de Palacios, who managed to secure a Maya codex ("the only one in the region"), as well as the local wisdom that the ancient city was built by a single ruler from Yucatán. The story was that this "outsider king" eventually became disgruntled with the local people and returned to his homeland. It was García de Palacios who recorded the local name *Copán* for the abandoned ruin, a designation by which it has been known ever since. Explorations by the colorful Irishman John Gallagher (a.k.a. Juan Galindo) and the famous team of John Lloyd Stephens and Frederick Catherwood in the 1830s brought the site to the attention of a broad readership (Stephens 1841). Stephens' assessment that the Maya ruins were built by the ancestors of the Maya still living in the region was hotly debated, with many "scholars" trying to ascribe them to Old World peoples and cultures instead (Willey and Sabloff 1993). Thereafter, Alfred Maudslay (1889–1902) made a signal contribution to the study of ancient Maya art and hieroglyphic writing by publishing detailed drawings of the stelae, altars, and architectural sculpture of Copán and numerous other lowland Maya sites. Maudslay also participated in one of the four Copán expeditions of the Peabody Museum of Harvard University in the early 1890s.

Conducting the first institutional exploration of the site with the authorization of the Honduran government, the Peabody investigators carried out excavations on Structures 10L-4, 10L-26 (with its Hieroglyphic Stairway), 10L-32, and 10L-41 in the Principal Group and the first excavation of a house-mound (Structure 10L-36) in Maya archaeology. The interest in the valley and its archaeological remains translated into the first map (Gordon 1896) and the discovery of ancient burials in caves (Gordon 1898), presaging further interests in this direction in years to come. The Peabody investigations inspired a Harvard graduate student by the name of Herbert Joseph Spinden (1913) to undertake a thesis that would eventually be published as *A Study of Maya Art*. Spinden's insights on Maya art were brilliant, but it was his concern with chronology that established the systematic cross-checks on chronology that have characterized Maya archaeology and history ever since.

The advances in Gordon's (1902) decipherment of the dates on the Hieroglyphic Stairway and other stelae, and in the chronological studies by Spinden, were to be enhanced by Sylvanus Morley (1920) in his massive tome, *The Inscriptions at Copán*. Morley was fascinated by the dates in the texts, which became a virtual obsession for him and other Mayanists during a time when chronology building was the central focus of American archaeology (Willey and Sabloff 1993). Morley (1920:402), however, was prescient in hoping that "we may possibly look forward with some degree of confidence to finding...place-names, personal-names, and signs of generalized meaning, by the aid of which we will eventually be able to fill in the background of Maya history as successfully as we have already constructed its chronological framework." This statement shows that the larger concern was to get beyond the dates to the history of the people and places associated with the chronological and astronomical data inscribed in the texts.

Beginning with the efforts of the Carnegie Institution of Washington in the 1930s and 1940s, a number of patterns were established in the investigation and conservation of Copán and other Maya sites. These patterns have helped shape attitudes, priorities, and actions in Maya archaeology from that day to this. First, the government of Honduras assumed an active role in the work, paying for the workers and helping to set the agenda for the restoration work (then called "repair") and investigations. Second, conservation became a major focus of the efforts, not only to save the monuments for the future but also to create a stronger sense of national identity. More pragmatically, the restoration work, the construction of an airstrip, and the building of a modest visitors' center at the site, as well as a museum and fountain on the town square, were intended to literally pave the way for increased tourist visitation and revenues. Finally, complementing the investigation and conservation of the site's civic-ceremonial center (the Principal Group), mapping and excavation in the surrounding settlements were undertaken to provide a broader perspective on the ancient city's history.

A plane-table and allidade map by John Burgh appeared in the frontispiece of John Longyear's still widely consulted Carnegie Institution volume *Copan Ceramics* in 1952. Longyear laid out the chronology of the valley's human occupations, tying the Classic-period sequence to the inscriptions and datable architecture in the Principal Group. He also confirmed Morley's earlier assessment that non-Maya populations occupied the valley before the bearers of the "stela cult" arrived. Both Morley and Longyear believed the latter to have come from the central Petén, most likely the area around Tikal. Thus, Copán has always been thought of as a cosmopolitan, multiethnic site, beginning at least with the arrival of people from the central Petén ca. 9.0.0.0.0 (A.D. 435).

Students of the Maya will forever be indebted to the brilliant artist, architect, and scholar Tatiana Proskouriakoff, another key member of the Carnegie team in Copán and beyond. Her compelling renderings of the Copán Principal Group (Proskouriakoff 1946) continue to inspire all who behold them. On the intellectual front, her insights into the history and derivation of Copán's artistic style (Proskouriakoff 1950) and its sacred geography and dynastic history (Proskouriakoff 1973) continue to provoke fresh ideas and approaches.

Jesús Nuñez Chinchilla was the next archaeologist—and first Honduran—to direct fieldwork in Copán, having trained at the Escuela Nacional de Antropología e Historia in Mexico before becoming the director of the Instituto Hondureño de Antropología e Historia (IHAH) when it was founded in 1952. He conducted a series of excavations in the Copán Valley, including a mountain shrine with jade offerings (Nuñez Chinchilla 1966). His successor as director of the IHAH, Dr. J. Adan Cueva, made Copán a national project and a symbol of Honduran identity. Himself a Copaneco, Dr. Cueva had trained, practiced, and taught as a physician in Tegucigalpa, but he never lost his love for the ruins of Copán and his hometown. His vision and strategy for Copán's development placed scholarship and conservation before, and as a permanent check on, economic development.

Dr. Cueva invited Gordon R. Willey of Harvard University to Honduras, asking him to design a long-term plan of "protection" and investigation for the ruins. In turn, Willey invited Robert Sharer and William Coe from the University of Pennsylvania Museum of Anthropology and Archaeology, at that time working just across the border at Quiriguá, Guatemala, to join him in formulating that research and conservation design. They drew up a plan, and it graced the pages of the very first issue of the IHAH journal, *Yaxkin* (Willey, Coe, and Sharer 1976). Mapping all the archaeological features in the Copán Valley served as a necessary first step to any kind of infrastructure development. The conservation and consolidation of the great river cut of the Acropolis and other important monuments were also key aspects of the long-term management plan.

The Willey, Coe, and Sharer study has served as the blueprint for most of the subsequent archaeological investigations in Copán. It envisioned a broad-gauged, multidisciplinary research program that would investigate Maya society from the ground up, with settlement surveys and household archaeology in the residential areas as the key to understanding the populace as a whole. A renewed attack on the inscriptions and imagery in the stone monuments was to be complemented by studies of the architecture in the royal precinct, particularly in the long river cut into one side of the Acropolis. Willey himself got the plan underway, beginning a settlement pattern survey with his graduate student Richard Leventhal in 1975. Willey and Leventhal started the detailed instrument mapping of the valley settlements and the excavation of a sampling of sites in the following two seasons (1976 and 1977). Leventhal's doctoral research on the settlement patterns at Copán laid the groundwork for all subsequent research on the topic (Leventhal 1979, 1981). As in the rest of Mesoamerica, the broad theoretical and ecological concerns of the settlement pattern study pioneered by Willey in the Virú Valley of Peru (1953) and subsequently in the Maya area (Willey et al. 1965) brought a wealth of new questions and a much broader understanding of Copán's archaeology and history. Willey and Richard Leventhal devised a typology of the housemound groupings (into categories 1–5, with the Principal Group being the only Type 5 site) to reflect the social classes of their respective occupants (Willey and Leventhal 1979).

Subsequent excavations of test probes throughout the valley and of entire households by Willey, Leventhal, and William Fash (Willey, Leventhal, and Fash 1978; W. Fash 1983a; Willey et al. 1994) and in the Honduran government–sponsored Proyecto Arqueológico Copán, or PAC (directed by Claude Baudez during its first phase, from 1978 to 1980 [Baudez, ed. 1983; W. Fash 1983b, 1983c], and by William Sanders from 1980 to 1984 in PAC II [Sanders, ed., 1986, 1990]), confirmed that the Willey and Leventhal site typology accurately reflects social status. Roberto Reyes Mazzoni, a Honduran economist and archaeologist trained in Mexico, had been instrumental in formulating the first phase of the PAC and acquiring funding by the Central American Bank for Economic Integration, conceiving the PAC as a training ground for Central American archaeologists of various nationalities. Honduran, Guatemalan, and Nicaraguan students participated in the project, and dozens of local townspeople were trained in various archaeological jobs.

In the first phase of the PAC, Claude Baudez assembled an international, interdisciplinary team to pursue all the facets proposed in the Willey, Coe, and Sharer plan, adding a few new elements. Ethnographic

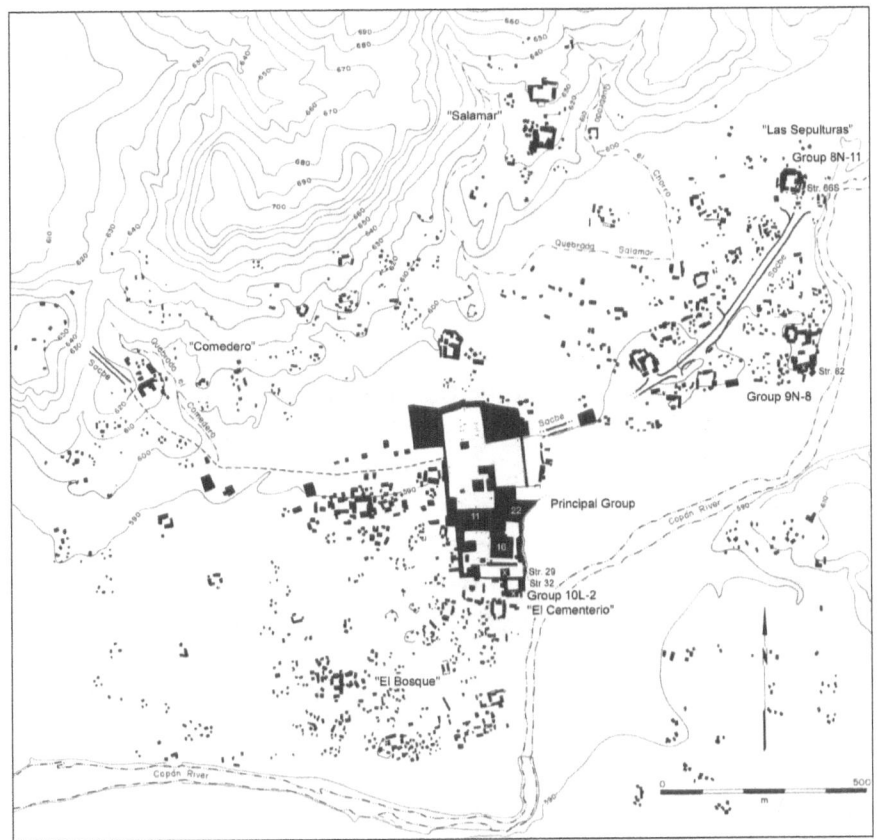

FIGURE 1.3
Map of the urban core of ancient Copán, comprising all the structures within 1 km of the center of the Principal Group, Ballcourt A-III (after W. Fash 2001, figure 96).

research and ethnohistoric research on the Copán region were important new components to the work. While Baudez continued the Harvard program of mapping the Late Classic (A.D. 600–900) visible remains (figure 1.3), he also sought to investigate a new realm of the valley's occupation: the buried remains of earlier settlements. This was to be accomplished by testing the areas between the superficially visible remains through a variety of statistically based sampling methods of physical *space*, rather than relying on investigations of visible *mounds*, or mound-groupings, as done previously. The various sampling methods did locate major Preclassic deposits that well served Baudez's project ceramicist, René Viel, in his efforts to expand and revise Longyear's ceramic sequence (Viel 1983, 1993a, 1993b). The valley research conducted under Baudez's direction demonstrated that the bottomlands were the first and always the most intensively settled, followed by the adjacent piedmont and lower slopes. Only in the final years of the Classic period was there sparse habitation on the uppermost slopes of the hills and mountains that delineated the edges of what Willey and Leventhal defined as the Copán "pocket" of the larger Copán Valley system (W. Fash 1983b, 1983c).

The detailed analysis of the Copán region's physical environment and human ecology has greatly broadened our understanding of the rise and fall of this Classic Maya realm, as well as the occupations before and after its glory days. Begun under Willey's project, with a team of geographers and other natural scientists directed by the cultural geographer B. L. Turner II, this group continued its work under the subsequent Honduran government PAC I project, incorporating specialized studies of flora, rainfall patterns, geology, river geomorphology, soils, pollen, agricultural technology, and deforestation (Turner et al. 1983).

Baudez' project also made strong contributions to the renewed study of the royal precinct. In the Great Plaza area, Cheek (1983a, 1983b) was able to piece together a detailed and useful construction history for this most public part of the Principal Group, including the Late Classic Structures 10L-2 and 10L-4. His work complemented the epigraphic research on the monolithic and architectural monuments entrusted by Baudez to Berthold Riese (1986, 1988) and the iconographic research of those same monuments commenced by Marie-France Fauvet and subsequently completed by Baudez himself (Baudez 1985, 1988, 1994). Further enhancing these investigations, Jorge Guillemin and Juan Antonio Valdés began the documentation and preliminary tunneling of the Acropolis Cut, which had been envisioned as part of the Willey, Coe, and Sharer proposal. Upon Guillemin's untimely death, Marshall Becker (1983) continued this work, providing an initial glimpse into the complexities of the Acropolis's architectural sequence. In this way, working outlines of the ruling dynasty's political history, the Principal Group's architectural history, and the valley's settlement and ecological history were, as a whole, laid out in the first phase of the PAC.

Turner and his colleagues' work served as a base for continuing ecological research during William Sanders' PAC II. This incorporated the study of demography and disease, which were reflected in the human skeletal remains recovered from excavations conducted throughout the Copán Valley (Storey, chapter 8 in this volume). Sanders' vast experience in settlement survey and settlement history in the Basin of Mexico (Sanders, Parsons, and Santley 1979) and the Valley of Guatemala (Sanders and Michaels, eds., 1977) and his broad anthropological perspectives were among the many reasons he was selected to direct this second phase of the Honduran government project, financed by the World Bank and administered by the IHAH. Sanders decided to expand the settlement survey to a much larger realm under the direction of David Webster, insistent that Mayanists do archaeological survey on too small a scale to give a complete picture of human settlement and resource exploitation on a regional frame of reference (Sanders, ed., 1986; Webster and Freter 1990a, 1990b).

Continuing and expanding upon the Harvard/PAC I interest in soils (Wingard 1988), pollen and botanical studies (Abrams and Rue 1988; Rue 1987), and agricultural technology (Sanders, Webster, and van Rossum 1992; Webster, chapter 2 in this volume), Sanders also brought in new methodologies. These included studies of energetics (Abrams 1994) and obsidian hydration, to refine the dating of valley settlements (Freter 1992; Webster and Freter 1990a, 1990b). The obsidian-hydration dating and the pollen and soils research have prompted Sanders, Webster, and their former students to propose that Copán's decline or "collapse" was not sudden at all. Their dating of settlements outside the royal compound indicates that the abandonment of the valley was a long process, drawn out over several centuries following the end of dynastic rule (Freter 1992; Webster 1999, 2002, and chapter 2 in this volume; Webster and Freter 1990a, 1990b; Webster, Freter, and Gonlin 2000). Again, chronology became the focus of significant debate in Copán research, with the obsidian-hydration dating placing the end of occupation in the valley much later than the traditional view of the city's decline espoused by such scholars as Longyear (1952), W. Fash (1983b, 1983c), and Viel (1983, 1993a, 1993b).

Debating the Classic Maya Collapse in Copán

Few subjects in Mesoamerican archaeology have captivated both scholars and laymen more than the decline of Classic Maya civilization (T. P. Culbert, ed., 1973). Factors as diverse as ecological degradation, droughts (deMenocal 2001; Gill 2000; Haug et al. 2003; Hodell, Curtis, and Brenner 1995; Hodell et al. 2001), disease (Shimkin 1973), changing commercial systems (Andrews and Sabloff 1986), warfare (Webster 1977, 1998a, 1998b), and the inability of Maya kingdoms to restructure their social systems for larger polities (Demarest 1992a, 1992b; W. Fash 1983b; Webster 1998b) have all been posited as important components—either alone or in combination—in the decline and abandonment of the large centers throughout the southern Maya lowlands in the ninth century A.D. Much productive research in Copán has focused on the ecological overshoot model (Webster, chapter 2 in this volume) and elite competition and structural defects (W. Fash 1983b; Webster 1998b). The relative weight of each purported factor varies greatly across the Maya lowlands, as do the timing and duration of the decline.

One of the most engaging aspects of the revised chronology for the supporting population's decline was that the obsidian-hydration dating held out the possibility of life histories for individual households in the Copán Valley. The prospect of firmly establishing the dates of occupation and use of each household within spans of decades instead of centuries would have allowed a much better understanding of the supporting population's life, times, and roles in shaping events. In many ways, this quest was not unlike Morley's earlier hope that scholars would eventually decipher the names of people and places recorded in association with dates, as indeed they have. The fundamental difference is that the texts tell us only about a minute percentage of the population, whereas obsidian tools are found in every household in Copán and thus hold the potential to provide chronological frames of reference for each and every one of them.

As with all innovations, the new schema aroused considerable skepticism. While the senior author embraced the new possibilities inherent in the method and the argument for a longer decline in the valley (W. Fash 1991:174), he and other colleagues were less persuaded by other initial results of the new method. In addition, the discovery and meticulous documentation of an Early Postclassic village just to the south of the Copán Acropolis by T. K. Manahan (1995, 2000, 2002a, 2002b) have brought renewed vigor to the question of the timing and nature of the valley's abandonment after the collapse of centralized rule. This continues to generate considerable debate, with two distinct views on the subject well represented here in chapters 2, 7, and 11. Likewise, the dating of the valley's visible mounds to the Late Classic and Postclassic, which led Webster and Freter (1990a, 1990b) to assert that no earlier occupations in the valley were of any consquence or significance, has also inspired productive scholarly exchanges (W. Fash and Sharer 1991; W. Fash and Stuart 1991).

The Rise of Copán and the State

Morley and Longyear's early assertions that the Classic Maya tradition "arrived" in the Copán Valley ca. A.D. 435 came under renewed scrutiny as a result of the new chronological approach provided by the obsidian-hydration studies. Particularly provocative was Webster and Freter's (1990a) claim that the records of Early Classic kings in Copán's inscriptions and on the four sides of the king's list carved on Altar Q were those of "putative kings," recorded by later rulers to give a fictive, longer history and genealogy to what was essentially a Late Classic phenomenon. The intensive excavations of the Acropolis have demonstrated that those Early Classic rulers undertook significant constructions from the early fifth century onward (see chapters 3, 5, 6, 9, and 10), laying that particular issue to rest.

Nonetheless, the processes and timing of the state's formation in Copán continue to be debated. This ties into larger anthropological debates regarding what criteria best allow us to define and demonstrate a state level of sociopolitical organization. Most states are centered in cities, making the definition and establishment of urban society part and parcel of the discussion. Sanders and Webster (1988) produced a masterful study of the Mesoamerican urban tradition; size and economic heterogeneity were the foremost criteria for the definition of urban societies. There, and in Webster's chapter 2 in this volume, they assert that even during its apogee in the late eighth and early ninth centuries A.D., Copán had many features more in line with ranked societies than stratified societies. W. Fash (1983b) argued that a state level of society was achieved in the seventh century A.D., and more recently Marcus (2003a, 2004) suggests that the founder of the Copán dynasty established a secondary state there in the fifth century A.D. Clearly, this is another issue in which the Copán data are useful for such scholarly considerations, with several chapters in the present volume providing much grist for the mill.

The Reliability of the Historical Record

The controversy regarding the degree to which the inscriptions and pictorial sculpture commissioned by Mesoamerican rulers do, indeed, constitute a reasonable representation of historical events (leaving aside questions of ultimate truth) is an ongoing and lively debate in historiography and, more broadly, archaeology. Marcus (1992b) has masterfully evaluated the social and political context in which Mesoamerican writing systems evolved, concluding that for the Maya and other Mesoamerican societies, the public monuments contained a mixture of history, myth, and propaganda. It hardly seems novel that we should question the pronouncements of public figures, particularly those in positions of relative weakness rather than strength (Marcus 1974). Yet the decipherment of the Classic-period inscriptions at Copán and other Maya centers is now providing us with the opportunity to check and cross-check the claims of rival rulers in the many conflicts that played out on the stage of ancient Maya history (Martin and Grube 2000; Schele and Freidel 1990; Sharer 2004).

During the early days of the epigraphic revolution in Maya studies (1959 to the present), there were many more skeptics of the inscriptions than true believers among the ranks of field archaeologists. Some groused that the epigraphers were constantly changing their minds about how to read particular glyphs. Their more even-tempered colleagues pointed out that the epigraphers were right to revisit their readings responsibly with the same frequency and dedication as field archaeologists revising their population estimates and dates for ceramic phases. Many archaeologists admired and had confidence in their epigrapher colleagues' abilities to read the texts but simply could not bring themselves to agree that the inscriptions could be accepted at face value, given that these constituted "winner's history." The value of providing checks and counterchecks on the content of historical records became increasingly apparent to Mesoamericanists, and the questioning of such records has led to ethnohistorical (Gillespie 1989) and archaeological (Webster and Freter 1990b) revisionism.

Copán was to play a valuable role in this debate because a strong database in the archaeology of the supporting population nicely balanced the abundance of the inscriptions and iconography. The PAC and subsequent Pennsylvania State University research in the valley, directed by David Webster, provided one set of checks on the inscriptions' content in the mid-1980s. It remained to test the historical and iconographic registers with new conjoined investigations in the royal precinct. The most pressing issue at that time was to identify the consequences of the defeat in A.D. 738 of the Copán ruler XVIII Jog (also known as "18 Rabbit" and now as "Waxaklahun Ub'ah K'awil") by the sovereign of Quiriguá, Cauac Sky (now "K'ak' Tiliw"), in each of those kingdoms.

This question tied Copán into the larger issue of the causes and consequences of Maya warfare (Webster 1977), making the question pertinent to larger anthropological concerns than just the culture history of this particular realm. One project set out to test this particular historical event, with a renewed investigation of both the archaeology and the epigraphy and iconography in the Principal Group. Besides testing the veracity of this historical account from the perspective of the Copán inscriptions and archaeology, this new effort sought to ascertain the role of ideology in forging cultural cohesion at Copán following the purported sacrifice of its thirteenth ruler (W. Fash 1988).

THE STUDY OF IDEOLOGY AND HUMAN AGENCY IN THE ANCIENT HISTORY OF COPÁN

Gordon Willey's larger research interests left another legacy that played a role in the direction taken by the archaeology of Copán: his conviction that ideology played a key role in culture history and that it could be productively investigated and analyzed in the archaeological record (Willey 1962, 1976). This view has subsequently been applied with success to the archaeology of the ancient Maya on both local and macroregional scales (Demarest 1992a, 1992b; Freidel, Schele, and Parker 1993; Schele and Freidel 1990). In Copán, the first project directly focused on this aspect of the archaeological record was the Copán Mosaics Project (W. Fash 1988). As a direct result of the work in elite residential sites in the urban ward on the east side of the Principal Group (known as "Sepulturas"), William Fash, Barbara Fash, and Rudy Larios developed a collaborative relationship born of a keen sense of the need for the long-term conservation of architectural sculpture and an understanding of how much potential existed for its study (Larios and Fash 1985). They subsequently formed the Mosaics Project in 1985 to preserve the architectural sculptures that lay strewn about the Principal Group. This project sought to describe and explain ideological adaptations within the context of the social, economic, and political forces that had been documented for eighth-century Copán.

The "great divide" between scientific and humanist approaches to the study of Maya archaeology referred to by Marcus (1995) has, of course, played more broadly in Mesoamerica as well. For every major city, seemingly, there have been those who have taken the materialist position to explain its rise to prominence, counterposed—if not necessarily balanced—by those who have sought to place ideology in the causative role. For Teotihuacan, Sanders (1956) and Price (Sanders and Price 1968) used cultural materialism as their theoretical framework for explaining the rise of urban life (and "civilization") in Mesoamerica at Teotihuacan. The landmark Basin of Mexico volume (Sanders, Parsons, and Santley 1979) made a compelling case for this theoretical perspective's strengths in describing and explaining the evolution of complex society and states in the region that produced the two largest and most powerful polities in ancient Mesoamerica. This paradigm was countered by the one espoused by René Millon (1981), who argued for the primacy of ideology in the formation of the Teotihuacan city, state, and civilization. His arguments were based on the religious ideas and social mores expressed in the murals of the early city and in the cave beneath the Pyramid of the Sun. Similarly, Arthur Demarest (1986) argued for the primacy of ideas and human agency in the formation of the Triple Alliance, in the wake of what he referred to as the "transformational crisis" of the war with the Tepanecs. The same division between materialists and ideationists, of course, exists in Maya studies. Whereas many scholars emphasize such factors as soil fertility and drainage, natural communication corridors, and other environmental factors to explain the ascendance of sites like

Tikal and Calakmul, others prefer to put ideas in causative roles.

The intellectual agenda for the Copán Mosaics Project research was to describe and explain ideological adaptations by the final four rulers of Copán, via their expression in art, texts, and architecture, in response to the increasing ecological and political problems that the PAC I and II projects had documented in a variety of databases (W. Fash 1988; W. Fash and B. Fash 1990). Larios was the architectural master, William Fash provided expertise on ceramics, dating, and stratigraphy gleaned from his research in household archaeology in the valley, and Barbara Fash lent her keen eye to the recognition and refitting of the blocks of fallen architectural sculpture that gave the project its name and motivation. Linda Schele and David Stuart joined the project to engage in a renewed attack on the hieroglyphic inscriptions at Copán.

The project focused on explaining the political and ideological strategies of each ruler, based on our reconstruction of the historical events and context in which he acted. The ideological strategies were believed to be reflected in the historical records and archaeological remains of royal rituals, the dates chosen for the rituals, the iconography of buildings and freestanding monuments, and the names given to the buildings and monuments. We hoped to reach the level of individual action, and agency, in ancient Copán through the conjoined study of its archaeology and history (for comparison, see Flannery 1999).

The interplay of ideas on this project was open, frank, occasionally sharp, and always challenging. No data point or argument was sacred, and in the exchange among peers, each scholar learned much more about the other fields. The occasions when data or perspectives differed—at times, dramatically—challenged us all the most. Often, project members found themselves teasing out solutions that none could have anticipated when the discussion began. Schele and Stuart's collaborations resulted in the series of brief field reports on epigraphy called the *Copán Notes*, which helped enormously in fostering the exchange of information and ideas among the research team members. Several chapters in the present volume reflect that interdisciplinary collaboration, which is now something of a standard operating procedure in lowland Classic Maya archaeology.

The Mosaics Project expanded to incorporate the Hieroglyphic

Stairway Project in 1986, which then was incorporated in the more ambitious Acropolis Project. In 1988, the senior author founded the Copán Acropolis Archaeological Project (*PAAC* in Spanish), with funding from the United States Agency for International Development (USAID), and directed it for its eight-year duration, through 1996. The project was administered through the IHAH, that is, through the central Honduran government, following in many ways the precedent and structure of the earlier Carnegie and PAC projects. Most Maya projects directed by the United States had been run by a single institution, such as the Peabody Museum, the Carnegie Institution of Washington, the University of Pennsylvania Museum of Archaeology and Anthropology, and the Middle American Research Institute of Tulane University.

For the PAAC, Fash sought to bring in colleagues from institutions traditionally involved in Maya archaeology, universities representing solid traditions of scholarship in the field and producing renowned publication series. These were Robert Sharer, of the University of Pennsylvania Museum of Archaeology and Anthropology, and E. Wyllys Andrews V, director of the Middle American Research Institute (MARI) of Tulane University. Bob Sharer's (and the University Museum's) experience with investigating complicated architectural sequences in the Maya area made him the natural choice for the investigation of the Copán Acropolis Archaeological Cut (el Corte Arqueológico) and its related buildings in the untouched earlier levels of the Acropolis, to the west of the Corte. Will Andrews was asked to investigate the elite residential area on the south flank of the Acropolis, given his (and MARI's) long trajectory of investigation of Maya architecture in the northern Maya lowlands, as well as his familiarity with ceramics of the southeastern Mesoamerican zone. In this residential complex, the nineteenth-century Peabody Museum project and Carnegie investigators had investigated several of the largest buildings but had never backfilled them, resulting in serious conservation problems that could be addressed only after recovering the pertinent archaeological and architectural data. The third US-based institution to become a partner in the Acropolis Project was Northern Illinois University, which provided strong support to the Fashes on many levels from 1984 to 1994. The example of combining institutions and investigators on large-scale projects has been emulated at many major Maya sites and has proven just as effective as in the Acropolis Project. Such collaborations are now so commonplace that our graduate students view them as the norm instead of the exception, as if things have always been done this way in Maya archaeology.

The Acropolis Project, like its parents and predecessors the Mosaics and Hieroglyphic Stairway projects, also continued to draw upon the tremendous talents and insights provided by Rudy Larios and the project epigraphers, Schele and Stuart. Over the years, the epigraphers engaged in much fruitful collaboration with their colleagues Grube, Lounsbury, Houston, and Fahsen. The interchange between scholars working on the hieroglyphic texts, the iconography on artifacts and architecture, and the excavations that uncovered them, as well as so many other features and datable materials, was intense and highly productive. In turn, the constant comparisons and exchange of data from excavations on various parts of the Acropolis, excavated by different research teams, was stimulating and enormously beneficial to the larger enterprise. More than thirty graduate students participated in the Acropolis Project and kept their professors up to date. In many cases, these same students conducted primary research for their dissertations, just as on the earlier Harvard, PAC I, PAC II, and Pennsylvania State University settlement survey projects.

Ricardo Agurcia Fasquelle constituted the other key element of this enterprise, having worked on the PAC I valley survey, mapping, and excavation program and having served as the subdirector and representative of the IHAH on the PAC II project and subsequently as the director of the IHAH. Agurcia was deeply committed to Copán and its cultural and natural patrimony, and he became the co-director and IHAH representative on the Acropolis Project in 1989, remaining so until its work was completed in 1996. Our collaboration also resulted in the formation of the Copán Association for Pre-Columbian Studies in 1990, a nonprofit organization designed to champion conservation issues and projects across the country and promote the dissemination of scientific and humanistic research to the people of Honduras and beyond. The Copán Association was the executor of another outgrowth of the Acropolis Project, namely, the construction of the Copán Sculpture Museum, completed in 1996 (figure 1.4). Because the governmental apparatus was notoriously slow and cumbersome, the

FIGURE 1.4
The Copán Sculpture Museum, view from the second story, looking north. (Photograph by R. Frehsee)

realization of this dream, first conceived by Barbara Fash but quickly seized upon by all who heard it, would likely never have occurred were it not for the administrative skills of Agurcia and his board of directors. The association was empowered to oversee the project design and supervise the construction (W. Fash and Agurcia Fasquelle 1996; W. Fash and B. Fash 1996; W. Fash et al. 1996). Today, the museum stands as a testimony to the artistic and architectural genius of the ancient people of Copán and to their nuanced expressions of the importance of religion and human agency in constructing that legacy.

In the meantime, René Viel joined his University of Queensland colleague Jay Hall in the 1990s to begin several research ventures in the Copán Valley that have continued to provide important new information. Among these are projects that strongly focus on documenting changes in the physical landscape of the valley bottomlands through a variety of subsurface sensing techniques (Hall and Viel 1994, 2004) and make a concerted effort to broaden and deepen our understanding of Copán and its development during the Preclassic period (Viel 1999a). Likewise, Viel's study of the ceramics, the social factions, and the iconography of public portraiture on Altar Q and Structure 10L-11 has led to the formulation of a provocative new model for the political structure of the ancient kingdom of Copán (Viel 1999b). Robert Sharer engaged the physical anthropologist Jane Buikstra to study the strontium and DNA aspects of the Copán Acropolis skeletons (Buikstra et al. 2004), just as Hall and Viel had undertaken with the valley material, as well as other former students of Sanders and Webster (Whittington 1989, 1999; Whittington and Reed 1997). In the late 1990s the IHAH commenced a new phase of the conservation efforts with the formation of the PICPAC (Proyecto Integral de Conservación del Parque Arqueológico de Copán), first under the direction of George Hasemann and then, following Hasemann's untimely passing, under Seiichi Nakamura. Also, the IHAH founded the Hieroglyphic Stairway Conservation to engage the Getty Conservation Institute in the conservation of that monument, with Barbara Fash serving as director from 1999 to 2002.

At this writing, a new wave of research and conservation projects has begun under the overall direction of Agurcia and the IHAH. These will, no doubt, bring surprises and unprecedented confirmations and contradictions of varying data sets as the archaeology of Copán commences a new chapter in its cultural history in the twenty-first century. Conservation is the credo of the projects we have directed or participated in over the years, with Copán serving as the inspiration and setting for the Declaration of Copán. Signed in 1993 by the heads of state of the five nations with Maya archaeological remains, this document provides a charter for conservation and responsible development in the region. Scholars and local communities must hold their respective central governments accountable for observing the spirit and the letter of that charter. In Copán, economic returns on investment in infrastructure and archaeology have been so impressive that the central government now finds its authority over the ruins contested by both the Ladino and indigenous segments of the local community. Their competing claims for ownership of the ruins may play a significant role in the formulation and execution of conservation and research projects in the Copán Valley in the twenty-first century.

William L. Fash and Ricardo Agurcia Fasquelle

A BRIEF SYNOPSIS OF CULTURE HISTORY AND CULTURAL PROCESS IN CLASSIC-PERIOD COPÁN

In what follows, we briefly outline the past 175 years of Copán research in order to contextualize the issues that are examined in greater detail in this volume. References to the specialized literature on all these topics can be gleaned from each chapter and are not cited in the remainder of this introduction. Instead, we direct the reader to the appropriate chapters where a particular facet is discussed in most detail.

By 1000 B.C., sedentary village agriculturalists in the Copán Valley began constructing large, elevated, stone platforms for their houses and burying their dead beneath the house floors, along with ceramics and jade offerings that signal their participation in the larger Mesoamerican exchange systems of the Early Formative Horizon (W. Fash 1982, 2001). By A.D. 250–400, Copán was home to a vibrant community that had expanded into all the physiographic zones in the Copán pocket and the larger Copán Valley (W. Fash 1983c). The valley and its growing population provided economic opportunities that, apparently, attracted the attention of the larger, more urbanized Maya communities to the west and the north. In the early fifth century A.D., an interloper, a "Lord of the West" (Stuart 2000), came to change the course of history in this idyllic and fertile setting.

The regal-ritual center known today as "the Acropolis" was founded by a foreigner named *K'inich Yax K'uk' Mo'* in the hieroglyphic texts. The city's later inscriptions state that he "arrived" in December of A.D. 426, some three days after he first grasped the insignia of rulership (*K'awil*). Subsequent retrospective histories of this "outsider king" state that he practiced royal rituals ten years before the famed "arrival" date, in A.D. 416, but do not stipulate where those actions took place (W. Fash 2001, Stuart 2004). Several hieroglyphic texts refer to him as a "Lord of the West," and the analysis of his bone chemistry reveals that he was not a native of the Copán Valley (Sharer et al., chapter 5 in this volume). Present evidence indicates that he probably passed his childhood and adolescent years in the central Petén, in the region of Tikal. He was buried in a building (known as "Hunal Structure") whose substructure sported the *talud-tablero* facade associated with Teotihuacan. In later portraits, he is depicted in the garb of a Teotihuacano, complete with Tlaloc (Storm God) goggles over his eyes. The form and decoration of his funerary temple, as well as his Late Classic portraits and glyphic titles, show that he wanted to be remembered, and his successors wanted him to be remembered, as having affiliations with the great urban center of Teotihuacan in the Basin of Mexico (W. Fash and B. Fash 2000; Stuart 2000, 2004, and chapter 10 in this volume).

The original nucleus of the Acropolis included three buildings (including Hunal) grouped around a central courtyard, as well as ancestral versions of Structure 10L-11 and of the dynastic temple (Structure 10L-26) that was later to carry the famed Hieroglyphic Stairway, and the ball court to the north (W. Fash, chapter 3, and Sharer et al., chapter 5 in this volume). An inscribed floor marker in association with the first constructions of the ball court and Structure 10L-26 bears an important early text and portraits of the founder of the Classic dynasty and his son and successor, Ruler 2 (W. Fash, chapter 3, and Schele and Looper, chapter 9 in this volume). Succeeding his father in the office of *K'ul Ajaw* (Holy Lord) of Copán in A.D. 437, Ruler 2 immediately embarked upon an ambitious building program, creating a series of buildings and associated art and inscriptions in Early Classic Maya style.

Over the ensuing four centuries, the successors of K'inich Yax K'uk' Mo' rebuilt the Acropolis and its constituent buildings and courtyards many times over. Particularly grandiose construction projects were undertaken by Rulers 7 (Waterlily Jaguar), 10 (Moon Jaguar), and 12 (Smoke Imix God K). Hunal Structure was the centerpoint for all subsequent versions of the Acropolis, but the larger civic-ceremonial center of which it formed a part included temples, administrative buildings, a ball court, and the royal residence, ever more grandiose and elaborate with each passing sovereign. Two of the most ornately embellished structures investigated to date, Ante Structure and the famous Rosalila, the latter standing above the successors to Hunal and the tomb of the founder (Agurcia Fasquelle and B. Fash, chapter 6 in this volume), were built during this era. Rosalila, its predecessors, and its successors bear the first ruler's name and religious symbolism in their façade sculptures, modeled in stucco in the case of Rosalila and its predecessors and in stone perhaps as early as the reign of Ruler 10.

Reigning in the glory days of the Copán kingdom, Ruler 12 was in power longer than any other king in the city's history, from A.D. 628 to 695. At this time, the Acropolis was the center of a vast and complex domain, with more architects and sculptors in its employ than ever before. A new, high-relief sculpture style was being employed on building façades, decorated with tenoned mosaic stone pieces. Ruler 12 also commissioned more stelae and altars than any other dynast, including a set of six stelae erected at selected spots throughout the valley in A.D. 652 to do homage to the sacred geography and the role of the king and his ancestors (especially K'inich Yax K'uk' Mo', named on two of the stelae) in rituals designed to maintain order in the secular and supernatural worlds. Shortly before A.D. 652 he oversaw the installment of a ruler at the site of Quiriguá, located 70 km to the northwest, as recorded on the latter's accession monument (Quiriguá Altar L). This statement implies that Copán's twelfth ruler held sway over dominions both far and near to his regal-ritual center. This king's death was marked by the construction of one of the largest tomb chambers in the Maya area, stocked with hundreds of offerings in ceramics, shell, jade, and perishable materials such as wood and gourds. Atop his grave, his son and successor, Ruler 13, built Esmeralda Structure, which bore the first Hieroglyphic Stairway and references to the death and burial of Ruler 12 (Stuart, chapter 10 in this volume). Esmeralda was soon to be covered by the final version of Structure 10L-26 and the larger, more grandiose version of the Hieroglyphic Stairway visible at the site today.

Ruler 13, Waxaklajun Ub'ah K'awil, took the high-relief sculptural tradition initiated in his father's reign to new heights in his own architectural masterpieces, Structure 10L-22, the first version of the Hieroglyphic Stairway (Stuart, chapter 10 in this volume), and the final version of the Copán ball court. He is best known, however, for the exquisite, nearly full-round stelae he erected in the Great Plaza. Each of these commemorate important rituals he performed to mark the passage of the Period Endings in the Long Count calendric system that occurred during his reign (A.D. 695–738). The dominion Copán held over Quiriguá came to an abrupt and violent end in 738, when Waxaklajun Ub'ah K'awil was captured in battle and beheaded by his counterpart from Quiriguá, K'ak' Tiliw (Two-Legged Sky, or Cauac Sky). His death was viewed at Copán as heroic martyrdom, where the second and final version of the Hieroglyphic Stairway text records that he was killed on that fateful day "with his flint [weapon], with his shield." The text of the final version of the stairway, dedicated by Ruler 15, K'ak' Yipyaj Chan K'awil, thus constitutes a "loser's history" of Ruler 13's death, providing us with a check on the accuracy of the claims of K'ak' Tiliw of Quiriguá. The Copán dynasty weathered this storm and was to prosper for nearly a century after the loss of Waxaklajun Ub'ah K'awil. All his architectural and sculpture monuments in the Great Plaza were maintained, rather than displaced or built over, by the city's last three rulers.

It is thought that his successor, Ruler 14 (K'ak' Joplaj Chan K'awil), responded in an innovative manner to the humiliating loss of this great patron of the arts. Rather than continue in the tradition of erecting stelae and altars in his own honor, this ruler built a new and highly decorated version of the council house, Structure 10L-22A, in which he portrayed each of the nine council members seated above toponymic hieroglyphs that named the wards or places each of them represented in the deliberations that took place there (B. Fash, chapter 4 in this volume). The building is labeled by ten large mats that gave its name, *popol nah* or *popol otot* (translated as "Mat House," "Council House," or "Community House"). Such buildings (and the institution of the council) were cited in Maya dictionaries and other documents of the Colonial period, indicating that they survived the vicissitudes of the conquest. In front of the council house was a dance platform (dance is frequently mentioned in conjunction with the council house in Colonial documents) and a food preparation area (feasts were offered immediately after the convening of the council). The kingdom subdivisions represented by the toponyms may have been organized by water management districts similar to those of the living Maya and of Southeast Asia (B. Fash, chapter 4 in this volume). However successful this building and the consensus it sought to maintain, Ruler 14 reigned for only eleven years (A.D. 738–749) and did not erect any other monuments, as far as is known.

Ruler 15 completed the magnificent Hieroglyphic Stairway and temple of Structure 10L-26 in A.D. 757, extolling the achievements of all his predecessors in office and placing his own portrait (Stela M) squarely in front of the stairs at its base (W. Fash, chapter 3, and Stuart, chapter 10, in this volume). This is the longest pre-Columbian hieroglyphic text to survive the Spanish conquest, detailing the life histories of the first fifteen kings and portraying them in grand style as powerful warriors bearing lance and shield. The text in the temple at the pyramid's summit bears two forms of writing, in parallel columns (Stuart, chapter 10 in this volume). One is presented in Classic Maya "full-figure" style, but the parallel text (the first in each pair of columns) relays the same information in a glyphic style that incorporates elements from central Mexican (that is, Teotihuacan) iconography and picture writing. This monument and earlier ones at this locus refer to the place of the bullrush (ancient Tollan). Both this text and the Teotihuacan-derived iconography displayed on most of the ruler portraits on the stairway and temple also serve to highlight the affiliations this Maya dynasty enjoyed with the great metropolis of the west. Ruler 15 also commissioned Stela N, placed at the base of the nearby Structure 10L-11, portraying himself on the south side and Ruler 14 on the north side.

After Ruler 15's death, the last great king of Copán, Yax Pasaj Chan Yopat (Newly Dawned), ushered in a new era in the city's history. During his early years in power, this sovereign created some of the largest and most imposing architectural monuments in the Maya world in the final versions of Structures 10L-11, 10L-16, and 10L-21A, as well as an elaborate personal residence on the south flank of the Acropolis (Andrews and Bill, chapter 7 in this volume). These were adorned with abundant façade sculptures and hieroglyphic texts. Structure 10L-11 had some of the largest and most elaborate façade sculptures ever carved in ancient Mesomerica, as well as numerous inscriptions in its eight temple panels, in the Reviewing Stand text on the West Court side, and in an outset sculpture panel on the side of the Hieroglyphic Stairway plaza.

During the middle and later years of his long reign (A.D. 763–ca. 822), Yax Pasaj was content to dedicate a series of small stone sculptures in the form of altars, stone censers, and circular bases for censers with inscribed dates. These marked the passing of the Period Endings and the ceremonies he performed on those occasions. His name also appears on a series of inscribed benches or thrones in the domiciles of the patriarchs of noble families who lived in the Type 3 and Type 4 elite residences in the valley. The abundance of these and other sculpture monuments in so many palatial noble quarters has led the senior author to suggest that the dynasty may have ended because the number of political posts available was limited (recall the nine places represented in the council house) vis-à-vis the much larger number of men who sought to occupy those positions of power and influence (W. Fash, chapter 3 in this volume).

The political problems caused by an elite class that had burgeoned during four centuries of dynastic rule, as well as the breakaway of Quiriguá and other formerly subsidiary centers, resulted in the loss of vital tribute to the kingdom precisely when it was most in need. By building the city center in the middle of the best farmland, the dynasty's founders inadvertently created an enormous problem for future generations, for by the eighth century A.D. the city covered all the best agricultural fields. This forced agriculture up into the adjacent piedmont, which residences also took over as the population rapidly expanded. Eventually, the maize, beans, and squash that had always formed the mainstay of the diet had to be cultivated on thin, upland slopes. These were quickly washed away in the massive erosion in the late eighth and early ninth centuries A.D., indicated by various kinds of evidence (Webster, chapter 2 in this volume). Elliot Abrams (1994) has demonstrated that the valley's deforestation resulted primarily from the need to secure cooking fuel for the city's hearths. With each passing year, the city was less able to provide its own food, fuel, and potable water.

Archaeological evidence indicates that the years following Yax Pasaj's death saw numerous destructive actions in the temples, palaces, and monuments of the royal line (Andrews and Bill, chapter 7 in this volume). Yax Pasaj's private ancestral shrine (Structure 10L-29) was burned and toppled, as was his funerary temple (Structure 10L-18), and the council house (Structure 10L-22A). Fragments of human bone, jade beads, and an inscribed marble vessel from the tomb of Structure 10L-18 suggest that Yax Pasaj's tomb was looted and then ransacked. The offering caches found inside the sculpture panels on the stairways of Structures 10L-11 and 10L-16 were also looted, and some of their sculptures were rolled down the stairs. Many families residing in the urban core continued to live there for another generation or two, but by the mid-tenth century the valley was abandoned (Andrews and W. Fash, chapter 11 in this volume). A group of immigrants from the west or south built a modest village in the shadow of the Acropolis ca. A.D. 975, scavenging the last king's funerary temple for sculptures and other nearby buildings for their house foundations and an occasional household shrine as reminders of the glory that had been. Within a century, they, too, were gone. The valley held no other significant occupation until well after the first Spanish description of Copán (and the first mention of it by that name), penned by Diego García de Palacios in 1576.

2

Political Ecology, Political Economy, and the Culture History of Resource Management at Copán

David Webster

This chapter investigates relationships among economy, society, and politics in the Classic Maya Copán polity of western Honduras.[1] More succinctly, it explores the management of agrarian economic transactions and exchanges between Copán's commoners and elites, as conditioned by limiting factors inherent in their environment and by their own population and agricultural history—what we can broadly envision as political ecology and political economy. Of greatest concern is the mature Classic period (approximately A.D. 600–800), when the Copán polity reached its maximum scale and complexity, although preceding phases of growth and subsequent phases of decline are also included.

The first part of this chapter evaluates the degree of fit between two related models that have emerged from Copán research since 1975. One consists of a varied set of demographic and settlement interpretations assembled over many years. I call this the "settlement model." Here I provide only a very brief overview of this model, and the methods used to assemble it, because its various elements have been extensively published (W. Fash 1983b; W. Fash and Long 1983; Freter 1988, 1992,

1994; Webster 2002; Webster and Freter 1990a; Webster, Freter, and Gonlin 2000; Webster and Gonlin 1988; Webster, Sanders, and van Rossum 1992). The second is a historical simulation of agricultural strategies and productivity (Wingard 1988, 1992, 1996) that I call the "soil model." More restricted but crucial research results from studies of palynology, skeletal material, paleonutrition, and erosion are also discussed where pertinent.

In the second part of the chapter, I explore the managerial implications of these models, using reconstructions of Copán's political structure, dynastic history (W. Fash 1991; W. Fash and Stuart 1991), and subroyal elites (Andrews and Fash 1992; Sheehy 1991; Webster 1989a; Webster, ed., 1989; Webster, Freter, and Gonlin 2000). Soil, settlement, and political models have, to a great extent, been developed independently of one another, and the goodness of their fit can now be explored. This juxtaposition of models, albeit less complex, is very similar to recent ones from the American Southwest evaluated by Jared Diamond (2002).

MANAGERIAL ISSUES AND MAYA ECONOMIES

Studies of the elite managerial dimensions of ancient Maya economies, especially of the agrarian economy, are rare, despite Wiseman's (1983b:178) observation long ago that such management "is one of the most substantive, and yet most intractable, issues facing Lowland Maya archaeology today." Most studies focus on how labor must have been recruited and managed to create temples, palaces, and other accoutrements of large royal centers (for example, Abrams 1994) or on the production and exchange of nonfood items, particularly among Maya elites themselves or with foreigners (for example, Sharer 1977:538). When management of the agrarian economy is discussed in passing, it is usually from the perspective of intensive production systems such as terraces or drained fields and the redistributive systems required by such localized production (for example, P. Culbert 1988:73, 92). Timothy Murtha's (2002) detailed analysis of the managerial implications (among other things) of the famous terrace systems at Caracol provides an excellent model for managerial studies of Maya agrarian economies.

The general lack of attention to agrarian managerial issues is puzzling because some reconstructions of Maya subsistence emphasize intricate, highly patterned (that is, highly "managed" in some sense), agricultural landscapes (Fedick 1996; Pohl, ed., 1990; Turner 1983; Wiseman 1983b). Several assumptions seem responsible for it:

1. Maya agricultural practices required only simple technology, small labor forces, and minimal organization. Cultivation, in essence, was a traditional, nondynamic, domestic enterprise inherently requiring little management.
2. The dispersal of Maya producer residences made management difficult.
3. Food energy was redistributed in very simple ways: Most was consumed by the households of the producers, and some was transferred to consumers, mostly elites, in the form of tax or tribute.[2] Elites mainly managed redistribution, not production (Freidel 1981).
4. There was little economic interdependence in Maya society except for the reliance of consumers on producers.
5. Production and redistribution were collective enterprises controlled by elites primarily through sanctification and rituals that emphasized collective action rather than competition.
6. Maya commoners were a passive social element. Change mainly occurred at elite levels, and impetus for change was from the top down rather than the bottom up.

The notion of a primarily domestic economy of producer Maya households, largely ignored by elites, is probably a reasonable idea at the lowest levels of decision making: how to acquire and maintain the necessary tools, how to produce crops on available plots of land over the short run, and how to recruit and deploy labor. But rapid transformations in the relationships between farmers and their landscape also created problems not easily resolvable on the producer level. These include

1. Retention and transmission of rights to land and other necessary resources by commoner producing units

2. Establishment of new households and new rights when segments of producer households had to move and adjust to new productive strategies

3. Jealousy and competition among farming households over increasingly differentiated productive landscapes and redistribution of their products

When these concerns are compounded by the elites' energetic and labor demands and their strategies of political manipulation and status rivalry (see Webster 1998b, 1999), the necessity of management becomes more obvious.

Farriss (1984:3), relating the Maya to small-scale, hierarchical, agrarian societies in general, portrays them as living in "a world that they, lacking the means to transform, have had to take largely as they find." My own position is different. Despite my agreement with some of the preceding assumptions, I believe that Maya farmers at Copán, wittingly or not, caused dynamic transformations of their agrarian environments. These transformations posed managerial opportunities and stresses for Maya elites and commoners alike and affected all levels of society. Both commoners and elites had to adapt to rapid changes in population size, distribution, and agricultural productivity. The system was ultimately unable to withstand the stresses of such changes, resulting in a gradual collapse and decentralization of the polity.

In many respects, what follows is a more focused and informed update of an earlier paper (Webster 1985), stimulated by several issues that have become clearer about Copán since 1985:

1. The size and distribution of the Copán population and the changes in these through time

2. The internal variability of Copán settlement and the partitioning of the Copán population into social segments of different ranks

3. The diet of Copán's inhabitants and the physiological characteristics plausibly related to dietary factors

4. Details of the distribution, productive capacity, and stability of major agricultural soils, erosion, and vegetation history

5. The polity's dynastic history as revealed by iconography, inscriptions, and architectural stratigraphy

As a result of these new insights, Copán presents a unique opportunity to explore when, how, and under what conditions the Copán elite might have intervened in the agrarian economy and how this intervention affected commoners and elites alike.

THE AGRICULTURAL BASE OF THE COPÁN ECONOMY: COMPARISONS AND IMPLICATIONS OF THE SOIL AND SETTLEMENT MODELS

A basic assumption of this chapter is that for the Maya, as for other New World preindustrial agrarian societies, the most fundamental economic activity is, as Farriss (1984:3) notes, "wresting a living from the soil by largely unaided human effort." Another is that the Copán polity's subsistence economy at all times was largely self-contained, in the sense that there were no significant flows of food energy into the polity from distant sources, nor exports to distant places. It is taken for granted that elites had a fundamental stake in the flows of food energy, either directly or in the form of labor: "At the most elementary and general level, political power is universally perceived as the ability to control energy" (Trigger 1990:125). Finally, I assume that climatic and landscape conditions after about A.D. 1 and especially after A.D. 400 roughly approximated those of the present. I say "roughly" because we know that many changes did occur.[3] Some of these were human-induced transformations, such as the erosion discussed below. In addition, recent research by René Viel and his colleagues suggests different soil and hydrographic conditions on the floor of the Copán pocket in Late Preclassic times (Viel, personal communication 1997). My own observations of sediments underlying Group 8N-11, tested by Penn State projects in 1990 and 1997 (Webster et al. 1998), suggest that the river flowed at a much higher level at this time and that drainage of the valley floor was much more immature.

Two sets of information now make building plausible models of Copán's subsistence agriculture much easier than was possible in 1985: we have better insights into the Copán diet and better information about soils, their productivity, and their sustainability.

Diet

Information concerning diet comes from the work of David Lentz (1991), Mary Pohl (1994), John Gerry (1993), and David Reed (1994, 1997, 1998). From macrofossils in Copán soil samples, Lentz identified a range of plant foods, including maize, beans, squash, bottle gourd, *chayote*, avocado, *coyol*, *nance*, possibly *zapote*, and several minor wild species. Although macrofossil preservation is not particularly good at Copán, maize shows up in many contexts. For example, it was present at five of seven rural farmsteads extensively excavated in 1985–1986 (Gonlin 1993; Webster and Gonlin 1988). Pohl provides a list of fauna from a small sample of vertebrate bones that mostly date after A.D. 600, and she suggests that deer contributed significantly to the diet.

Reed has calculated carbon and nitrogen isotope content in bone collagen samples from ninety Copán skeletons excavated at sixteen sites dating to the Acbi-Coner phases (some plausibly fall as late as the twelfth century or later). His sample is stratified by age, sex, commoner-versus-elite contexts, and rural-versus-urban (Copán urban core) location. Even though some variations exist within this sample, the overall picture is very consistent and supports Gerry's earlier findings. Carbon^{-4} pathway plants, almost certainly maize, constituted 62–78 percent of the ancient Copán diet. Gerry and Krueger (1994) analyzed carbon isotope content of apatite bone samples for human and faunal samples from seven Maya centers, including Copán. They calculated a 55 percent mean caloric contribution of maize to these populations' diets, with Copán at the high end of the range at 59 percent. Reed's sample is larger than theirs and incorporates people with a wider range of statuses, one possible reason for his somewhat higher values.

These studies strongly support the conclusion that for ancient Copánecos, as for ethnohistorically and ethnographically observed Maya populations (including the local Chorti studied by Wisdom [1940]), maize was the basic staple, almost certainly heavily supplemented by beans. It accounted for 60 percent or more of caloric intake, even though a variety of other plant foods were available and eaten. Heavy reliance on maize plausibly contributed to the infirmities detected by Storey (1992, 1997) and Whittington (1989) in the large skeletal samples they analyzed. Animal food, including deer, apparently contributed only sparsely to the diet. At Copán, such a pattern seems to apply to people of all ages, sexes, and social ranks. This strong inference, along with the certainty that human muscles accomplished most of the work, greatly simplifies the calculations of agricultural demand, productivity, and population that follow.

Soils and Productivity

Wingard (1992, 1996), building on earlier ecological studies (Rue 1987; Turner et al. 1983) and his own interviews with modern farmers at Copán (Wingard 1988), took more than two hundred soil samples from a large area of the Copán Valley that overlapped significantly with regions already surveyed by archaeologists. Analysis of these samples enabled him to produce a generalized soil map covering more than 200 sq km. He then simulated the valley's agricultural and population history, using a complex EPIC (Erosion/Productivity Impact Calculator) program. His study was "undertaken to ascertain if a direct link could be established between ecological variables, in particular soil erosion and nutrient depletion, and population growth and decline at Copán, Honduras" (Wingard 1996:208).

The Soil Model and Its Implications

On a descriptive level, Wingard's research delineates the most significant, natural limiting factors on agricultural production in the Copán region. First, some 84 percent of the upland landscape consists of recent soils (inceptisols) of generally moderate or low fertility. In general, upland soils (as well as some low-lying ones) tend to be highly acidic and deficient in phosphorus, and more than half show low cation-exchange capacity, which would inhibit nutrient availability. In addition, distribution of the best soils is very patchy and limited. The five major alluvial pockets of the Copán drainage in Honduras (figure 2.1) have very restricted amounts of comparatively flat soils on or near the valley floor: Copán pocket = 1,300 ha; Rio Amarillo East = 600–700 ha; Rio Amarillo west, El Jaral, Santa Rita < 200 ha each. The most fertile soils (entisols and mollisols) cover only 15 percent of the area of the soil map and are especially common on active alluvium, old alluvial terraces, and the gently sloping foothills immediately above them. Fully 75 percent of the mapped soil region has slopes greater than 8 percent, and 40 percent has slopes in excess of 16 percent. It is not surprising

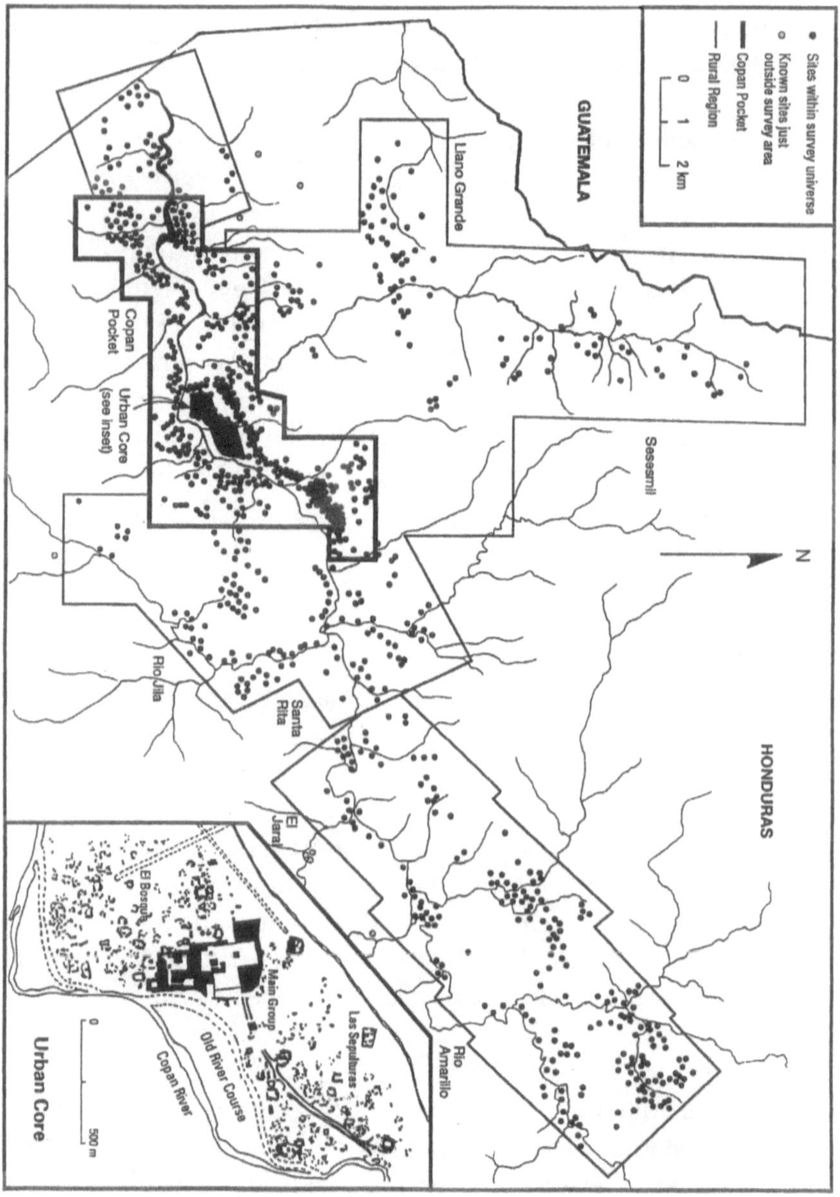

FIGURE 2.1
Survey zones, sites, and major physiographic features of the Copán Valley. (Map by A. Freter)

that Wingard found erodibility and nutrient depletion to be the most powerful causes of decline in agricultural productivity.

These findings amply reinforce and add detail to what was known long before—the most fertile and stable soils in the region are the comparatively flat, active or recent alluvium distributed in noncontinuous pockets of extremely limited size. One of these, the Copán pocket, is by far the largest. More extensive upland soils on steep slopes are generally less fertile and always subject to erosion.

More important is Wingard's simulation of subsistence agriculture and population based on these findings, which incorporated and explored several assumptions long held by Copán researchers:

1. Agricultural populations initially settled on or near old or recent alluvium.
2. Population was heaviest and most stable in the Copán pocket.
3. The population completely filled deep, fertile, low-lying soil zones before colonizing less fertile, more fragile upland zones.
4. Settlement units in upland zones appeared later than on valley floors and were more short-lived.
5. Upland settlement and cultivation caused severe deforestation and erosion.
6. The presence of low-lying, deep soil zones buffered the effects of catastrophic erosion and consequent declines in productivity and population, and the valley was always able to sustain a reasonable population.

Wingard's results are methodologically significant because they are calculated from data essentially independent of those used in the parallel model of population history derived from settlement research, which we will review shortly. Most important, they are independent of the hydration dates central to the establishment of the settlement curve.[4] He also created his soil simulation in virtual ignorance of our own settlement simulations and our field documentation of erosion. We, in turn, did our simulations in general ignorance of his work. Although both soil and settlement models are subject to many errors, the close agreement between them (see below) suggests that such errors are small and tend to cancel each other.[5]

Components of Wingard's simulation, apart from the soil data, include a seed population of 1,000 people at A.D. 0 that increases at specific rates, 60 percent dietary contribution of maize (virtually identical to the proportion later experimentally calculated by Gerry and Krueger, cited above), and maize productivity estimates. Population growth is accommodated by five management strategies (management here refers to productive strategies of farmers rather than elite control) and by extensification (the extension of an existing strategy to new areas) and intensification (reductions of fallow, double-cropping, and irrigation). Farmers switch sequentially from one strategy to another as the capacity of the preceding one is reached (Wingard recognizes that this artificial property of the program masks the significant chronological overlap among strategies that must have occurred in the past).

In essence, the soil model reflects choices that maize farmers would optimally have made, given previous constraints on land occupied and degraded under successive management strategies. No influence in the exercise of their choices by political or social factors is assumed. Obviously, such influences did occur. Departures from soil model expectations in the reconstructed settlement history provide one window onto what such interference was like.

Wingard's main conclusions (figure 2.2) are as follows:

1. The seed population initially used a long-fallow strategy on the alluvial-foothill soils of the Copán pocket, which filled in to capacity at 3,000 people by the end of the fourth century. By about A.D. 575, this strategy had been extended over all other alluvial pockets, reaching capacity at about 5,000 people. A switch to a medium-term fallow system then occurred.

2. By about A.D. 650, the medium-term fallow strategy on the alluvial-foothill soils reached its capacity throughout the Copán Valley at a population level of just over 6,000 people.

3. An annual (permanent) wet-season cropping strategy was then established on the valley floor, supporting at capacity 6,400 people by A.D. 675.

4. Hillside soils were colonized at about A.D. 650–675 and then went through the same processes of extensification and intensification outlined for the valley floor. Hillside cultivation was a

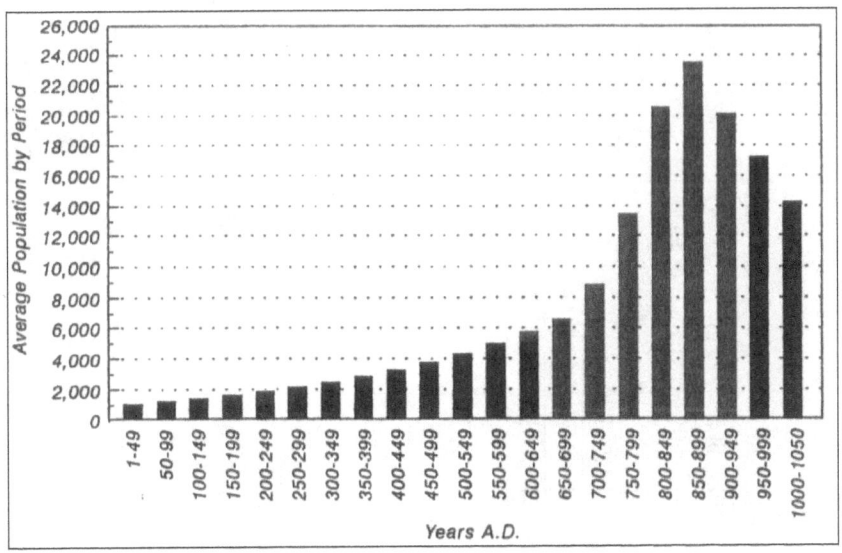

FIGURE 2.2

The Copán population by period. Wingard's estimate of this sequence of population levels is based mainly on maize productivity. Maize is assumed to make up 60 percent of the per capita diet in his simulation. The jump in population after A.D. 1000 is based on the assumption that some classes of soil regained fertility. If this assumption is incorrect, the population probably continued to decline. (Histogram constructed by Webster from figures provided by Wingard)

very destructive process. About 120 sq km was deforested for agriculture between A.D. 650 and 800, and between A.D. 700 and 800 "the Copán Valley probably experienced a rather massive erosional event" (Wingard 1992:182). Maize production outside the Copán pocket exceeded that within it sometime around A.D. 700–750. By A.D. 800 the valley had a total population of about 14,000 people, and all soils were either in permanent cultivation or exhausted and lying fallow.

5. Land throughout the alluvial and foothill zones was then double-cropped annually, supporting 20,000 people by A.D. 850–900. Assuming that irrigation was applied to areas of less than 5 percent slope in the Copán pocket, about 22,000 people could have been supported by this time.[6] Neither of these levels was sustainable, however, and population declined after A.D. 900.

Time Period	Urban Core	Copan Pocket	Upper Main Valley	Lower Main Valley	Sesesmil Valley	Jila/Mirasol Valleys
400–449 A.D.	627 (100%)	0 (0%)	0 (0%)	0 (0%)	0 (0%)	0 (0%)
450–499	683 (66.6%)	38 (3.7%)	0 (0%)	0 (0%)	105 (10.2%)	200 (19.4%)
500–549	968 (69.8%)	38 (2.7%)	0 (0%)	0 (0%)	200 (14.2%)	200 (14.2%)
550–599	1024 (52.5%)	38 (1.9%)	83 (4.3%)	0 (0%)	380 (19.5%)	424 (21.8%)
600–649	2519 (45.6%)	1312 (23.8%)	393 (7.1%)	48 (0.9%)	452 (8.2%)	796 (14.4%)
650–699	4368 (41.9%)	2973 (28.5%)	1028 (9.9%)	48 (0.5%)	593 (5.7%)	1416 (13.6%)
700–749	5910 (39.4%)	5642 (37.6%)	1158 (7.7%)	150 (1%)	629 (4.2%)	1520 (10.2%)
750–799	11828 (42.6%)	10627 (38.3%)	1739 (6.3%)	341 (1.2%)	902 (3.3%)	2316 (8.4%)
800–849	10261 (40%)	10159 (39.6%)	2021 (7.9%)	436 (1.7%)	885 (3.4%)	1894 (7.4%)
850–899	9736 (36.9%)	10227 (38.8%)	3050 (11.6%)	534 (2%)	780 (3%)	2054 (7.8%)
900–949	4276 (28.9%)	6031 (40.8%)	2240 (15.1%)	414 (2.8%)	622 (4.2%)	1238 (8.4%)
950–999	3262 (26.9%)	4939 (40.8%)	2239 (18.5%)	328 (2.7%)	424 (3.5%)	924 (7.6%)
1000–1049	1679 (21.8%)	3069 (39.9%)	2037 (26.5%)	243 (3.2%)	260 (3.4%)	410 (3.4%)
1050–1099	751 (19.7%)	1207 (31.7%)	1325 (34.7%)	86 (2.3%)	86 (2.3%)	358 (9.4%)
1100–1149	472 (24.4%)	688 (35.6%)	486 (25.2%)	0 (0%)	66 (3.4%)	220 (11.4%)
1150–1199	413 (39.3%)	505 (48%)	133 (12.7%)	0 (0%)	0 (0%)	0 (0%)
1200–1249	284 (43.3%)	239 (36.4%)	133 (20.3%)	0 (0%)	0 (0%)	0 (0%)
1250–1299	42 (26.1%)	119 (73.9%)	0 (0%)	0 (0%)	0 (0%)	0 (0%)

FIGURE 2.3
A raw simulation of the Copán population through time, derived from settlement data for various parts of the Copán Valley.

6. By A.D. 1000 population had declined to A.D. 800 levels, with some soils recovering lost fertility. Reasonable levels of productivity would always support some occupation.

Comparison of the Soil and Settlement Models

Let us now consider how this soil model compares with the settlement model, which, as already noted, has been well published. Comprehensive and slightly varying summaries include those of Freter (1988, 1992, 1994), Webster and Freter (1990a), Webster, Sanders, and van Rossum (1992), Webster (1999), and Webster, Freter, and Gonlin (2000). The Webster, Sanders, and van Rossum presentation is emphasized here for comparative purposes. Readers should review the original paper for details, which are summarized in figures 2.3 and 2.4.[7] Of particular comparative concern are three dimensions of population change: chronology, scale, and distribution.

Chronology and Scale

The two independent methods of calculating peak population yield remarkably similar figures—22,000 (soil model) and 27,753 (settlement model). Three factors are mainly responsible for the discrepancy: the settlement calculation algorithm extrapolated population for an area larger than Wingard's mapped 200-sq km soil zone, it deliberately simulated maximal population figures, and finally, some sites may not have been year-round habitations (more about this below). I believe that Wingard's lower estimate is the more reliable. It falls squarely within the range of 18,000–24,000 people suggested by Freter and me (Webster and Freter 1990a) in an earlier simulation and agrees extremely well with Fash's (1983b) estimate for the Copán pocket, always the demographic core of the polity.

Wingard's maximal population estimate corresponds to a reasonable overall peak density of 110 people per sq km. Densities of this magnitude are far more convincing than those projected for the core Tikal polity, which at 265 people per sq km are, in my opinion, neither reachable nor sustainable.[8] Still, the Copán figure is very respectable in light of later Maya densities. For example, during the contact period, the Mani polity in northern Yucatan had on the order of 10–20 people per sq km.[9]

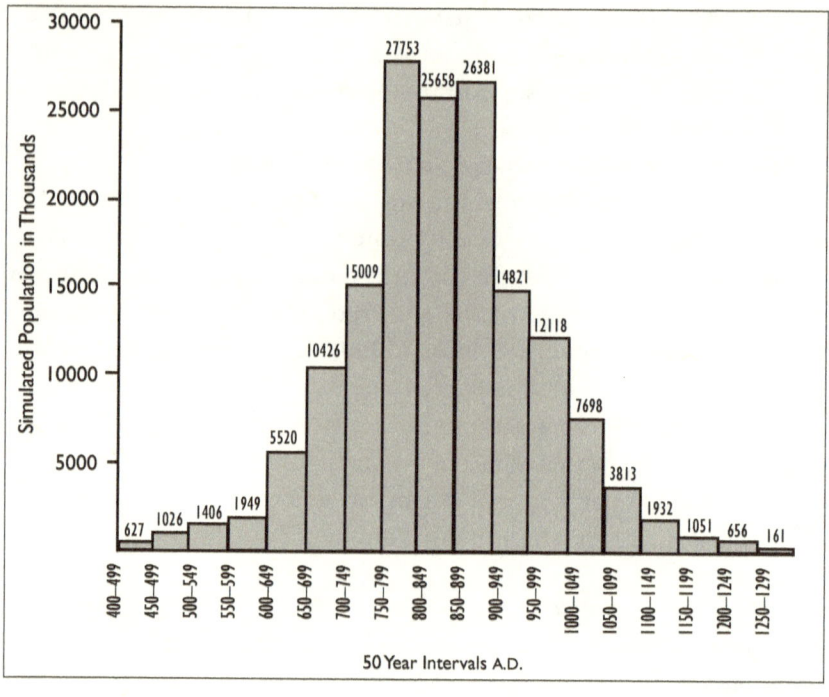

FIGURE 2.4

A population reconstruction for the Copán polity from the settlement model. The population before A.D. 600 was undoubtedly higher than that shown in the histogram.

Wingard's population peaks at A.D. 850–900; the settlement-derived peak is shown at A.D. 750 (see figures 2.3 and 2.4). Note, however, that three very similar high estimates in the latter extend to A.D. 900. The variability among them is just as likely an artifact of the simulation as actual population change (Webster, Sanders, and van Rossum 1992:189). In effect, the peak could have occurred at any time between A.D. 750 and 850. Put another way, a rough demographic plateau exists between A.D. 750 and 900. Again, agreement is good.

This outcome is especially crucial because it supports one of the core assumptions of the soil simulation—rates of population increase. Obviously, Wingard's built-in rates drive his simulation; in conjunction with other components, they ultimately determine the timing (although not the size or location) of the peak population. In the settlement model, by contrast, the rate of population growth and the peak are derived products from completely independent data, not assumed. Rates of growth are rapid in both models and cause the correspondingly rapid shifts in management strategies and associated environmental problems in the soil model.[10]

Close agreement between the two models suggests that Wingard's assumed rapid rates of increase are accurate in order-of-magnitude terms. Processes of environmental transformation could be slowed down by greatly decreasing the size of the seed population or by decreasing the rates of growth. The seed population estimate of 1,000 people at A.D. 0 is certainly reasonable, however, given available archaeological evidence. Decreasing growth rates would produce a much later peak, but this is unacceptable—all previous estimates of the timing of the Copán population peak, from all lines of evidence, place it in the A.D. 750–900 range. No one, so far as I know, thinks that 22,000 people is an unreasonably high peak estimate (in fact, the contrary is the case).

Wingard predicts the rapid colonization of upland areas during the last half of the seventh century. In the settlement model, this process should begin about fifty years earlier, and uplands would fill in faster because population increases more rapidly.

Large-scale erosion certainly occurred at Copán as a result of upland cultivation. Excavations carried out by the PAC I ecological survey, by Freter in her valley test pitting, and by Wingard during his soil testing all encountered buried soils. The best evidence about timing comes from the urban core's northern zone, where buried Conerphase structures were excavated during PAC I by Boyd Dixon and later in 1989 by me (figure 2.5). The latter excavation revealed that 2.3 m of colluvium from the northern foothills accumulated around an impressive building of Type 4 scale that was probably built sometime after A.D. 750. Two obsidian-hydration dates of A.D. 792 and 819 (each with a one-sigma error factor of seventy years) come from samples predating this erosion event, which therefore could have begun as early as A.D. 722 or as late as A.D. 862. Either limit reasonably reflects the settlement peaks of both soil and settlement models, but the former is most consistent with Wingard's prediction of an eighth-century erosion event. Settlement model population estimates imply somewhat earlier large-scale erosion.

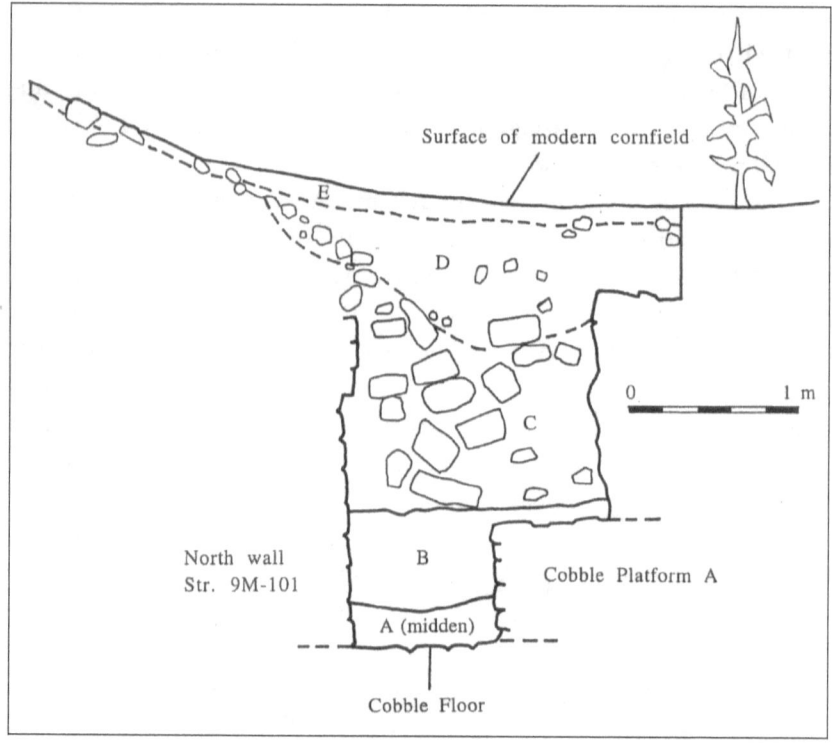

FIGURE 2.5

An elite structure along the northern edge of Las Sepulturas zone at Copán was deeply buried by soils eroding from the hills along the north edge of the Copán pocket. Two obsidian-hydration dates of A.D. 792 and 819 from the Level A artifact-rich midden should date the beginning of this episode of erosion. Level B is fine yellow clay washed into the corridor by hillside erosion. Overlying levels are collapse debris from Structure 9M-101 (C), collapse debris mixed with silt (D), and humus (E).

Both models agree that population decline begins at about A.D. 900, but in the soil model there is no population plateau as shown for the period between A.D. 800 and 900 by the settlement model. The rate of decline is also less steep in the soil model. Wingard did not simulate the process of population decline past A.D. 1050 (see figure 2.2), but at that time he postulated that some previously abused soils began to recover fertility, hence the spike of increase shown at the end of his population reconstruction. Had his simulation continued, the decline would have been interrupted and population stabilized, at least for a time. The settlement model, by contrast, shows a continuing and rapid decline.

Initial interpretations of Rue's (1987) sediment core indicated, on the basis of two uncalibrated radiocarbon determinations, virtually complete deforestation at about A.D. 900 and signs of arboreal recovery by A.D. 1200. Calibrated one-sigma ranges of these same determinations are A.D. 1022–1177 and A.D. 1303–1413, suggesting even later forest clearing than he originally envisioned. These dates are not directly from artifacts or human skeletal material, but they unquestionably relate to striking anthropogenic alterations of the landscape and strongly suggest the surprisingly late practice of extensive cultivation.

Deforestation is consistent with both soil and settlement models. Recovery could fit either but is more consistent with the settlement model. Both the settlement and soil models predict an extended period of demographic decline, consistent with the obsidian-hydration chronology established for the region (Freter 1988; Webster and Freter 1990a; Webster, Freter, and Rue 1993). In the soil model, decline would be even slower, and a population of some reasonable size would remain present—in other words, there would never be the complete (albeit gradual) demographic collapse that the settlement model shows.

Distribution

The soil model has two spatial dimensions. One is extension beyond the alluvial and foothill zones of the Copán pocket to other parts of the valley. The second, partly overlapping dimension is vertical—colonization of upland zones of increasing elevation, where soils are generally less fertile and stable. Comparison of the vertical spatial expectations of the two models can be made only in a loose sense because distribution of sites—especially in terms of altitude—will only generally reflect the soil predictions. For example, some producers might have relocated their households on newly colonized, marginal upland soils, as expected. Other people, however, might have farmed such soils but continued to live on or near the valley floor, blurring the spatial distinction between management strategies.

Wingard's initial population is in the Copán pocket because he placed it there based on existing archaeological evidence and assumptions about the choices early agriculturists would make.[11] Note, however, that had he planted his seed population elsewhere, say, in intermountain alluvial pockets of the tributary Sesesmil Valley, it would quickly have overrun the productive capacities of these small zones and colonized the Copán pocket, which thereafter would have rapidly developed the greatest demographic and productive weight in the system anyway. Overall, the simulation would not look much different.

According to Wingard's model, all alluvial and foothill soils in the valley were utilized on a long-fallow basis by A.D. 575. Consequently, the settlement model should show expansion into nonpocket zones between A.D. 400 (when the Copán pocket is filled to capacity) and A.D. 575. In fact, it does. Thirty percent of the population is in these areas as early as A.D. 450–499 and rises to 41 percent by A.D. 575. By A.D. 675, settlement should be even heavier throughout all the alluvial-foothill lands under a permanent cultivation regime. The settlement model does show an absolute increase in nonpocket areas, but a percentage reduction vis-à-vis the pocket to 24 percent from the earlier 41 percent, indicating more concentration of population there than predicted.

Hillside cultivation begins in the soil model about A.D. 650, and uplands throughout the valley are heavily utilized by A.D. 700–750. By the latter date, maize production outside the Copán pocket exceeds that within, so outlying populations should be greater than 50 percent of the total if people are living near the lands they cultivate. The settlement model (optimally reliable at this point) does not conform to this spatial expectation. Growth in the pocket outstrips all other regions combined, which collectively have only 23 percent of the population. Webster, Sanders, and van Rossum (1992:193) earlier noted the lack of congruity between productive capacity and the spatial distribution of the population.

We have not yet simulated population variation by altitude. An indirect proxy for population is, however, available in the distributions of raw obsidian dates by altitude (figure 2.6). A few upland dates are early, but remember that there are upland pockets of alluvial and foothill land. Heavy upland colonization of zones at elevations of >750 m appears just when it should, between roughly A.D. 600 and 700.

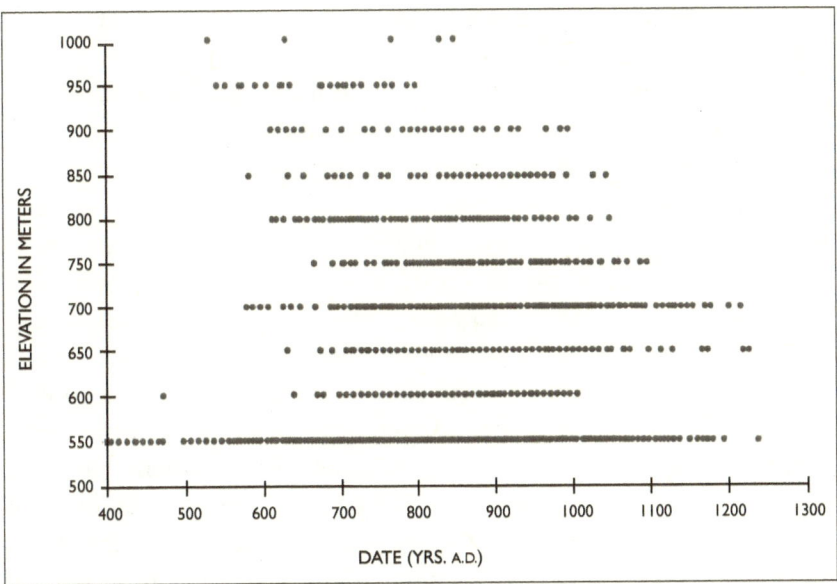

FIGURE 2.6

Raw obsidian-hydration dates from Copán Valley sites, arranged by elevation. Each array is shown at the base of the 50-m interval to which it pertains.

According to the soil model, widespread erosion of upland zones resulted in population declines in higher elevations at about A.D. 750–800. In the settlement model, dates conform reasonably well to this expectation at 900 m and above, but at intermediate elevations these tail off later than predicted, or about A.D. 900–950. On the other hand, the expectation that upland sites were generally founded later, had shorter occupations, and were abandoned earlier than valley floor sites is strongly supported by Paine's (1996) statistical study of occupational life spans of sites with five or more dates (see also Paine and Freter 1996; Paine, Freter, and Webster 1996).

Double-cropping of the valley's alluvial and foothill lands, supplemented by irrigation in the Copán pocket, temporarily took up the slack in the soil model, resulting in the peak population of 22,000 at A.D. 900. Continued heavy population is predicted throughout the valley, in contrast to the settlement model, which still shows only 24 percent outside the pocket at that time. After A.D. 900 the outlying population increases, exceeding that of the Copán pocket at about A.D. 1050–1100.

As noted above, Wingard terminated his simulation at A.D. 1050, estimating the population of his 200-sq km section of the valley at that time at about 14,000, which assumed a new episode of growth because of the postulated recovery of previously degraded parts of the landscape. Only 3,800 people are calculated for that time by the settlement model, which also shows that until A.D. 1150 population remained respectable outside the Copán pocket, then collapsed abruptly, except in the upper main valley. If the presumption of recovery of soil fertility were eliminated from the soil simulation, Wingard's terminal population estimate would be much more congruent with that of the settlement reconstruction. Interestingly, Wingard's model predicts an even larger and more temporally extended post–A.D. 900 population than that derived from settlement (consistent with Rue's calibrated radiocarbon dates). He offers the best quantification available in support of the long-held idea that while loss of agricultural productivity can explain the decline of the Copán population, it cannot explain its disappearance. Various early critics of ecological explanations of the Classic Maya collapse, we should remember, felt that the apparent suddenness of the collapse suggested nonenvironmental causal factors. For example, Kidder (1950:9) asserted that "had there taken place a gradual washing away of soil or the choking of arable land by grasses, their effects should only gradually have made themselves felt and have led to a much longer and slower decadence than seems to have gone on." At Copán, both soil and settlement models independently predict just such a gradual decline, although they suggest somewhat different patterns for it.

Evaluation

One can evaluate this set of comparisons from either the "glass half-empty" or the "glass half-full" perspective. I obviously prefer the latter. Although there are certainly differences, the degree of fit between the two independent models, each subject to many internal errors and simulation distortions, is quite remarkable, as Wingard (1996) also repeatedly notes. Overall rates of population increase (assumed in advance for the soil model, derived in the settlement model) are very similar, as are timing and scale of the peak population. Both models feature a single, accelerating growth curve with a downturn at the end of the Late Classic. The settlement model well reflects initial upland colonization.

Principal differences are the much greater demographic gravity of the Copán pocket population than predicted by the soil model, the slower decline of population in the soil model, and the failure of the settlement model population to stabilize at some reasonable level after A.D. 1050, as the soil model predicts. Differences may be due to errors. I believe that they are much more likely due to political management, interference, and competition, as we shall see shortly.

Our quantitative assessment of agricultural and settlement processes is, of course, highly abstract and impersonal. The soil model, in particular, masks the human realities behind the very dramatic and often stressful choices individuals or groups had to make. People did not automatically and without friction choose to work harder for less on hillsides rather than cultivate the deep soils of the valley floor. Farmers did not willingly shift to permanent cultivation, with its declining yields, if other options remained open. They did not fail to appreciate the increasing productive diversity and risk that advantaged some and disadvantaged others. They could not help but find the extremely rapid changes that sometimes occurred over as few as one or two generations disruptive. The emergence of elites or their managerial roles cannot be understood without attention to these stresses.

Maya farmers at Copán certainly did not lack the power to transform their world, nor did they passively take it as they found it. On the contrary, their agricultural activities and population growth produced a cascade of transformations in the agrarian economy and associated settlement, some of which were extremely rapid and had important sociopolitical effects.

ELITES, DYNASTIC HISTORY, AND THE MANAGEMENT OF THE COPÁN ECONOMY

Before exploring possible patterns of management, we must consider one unresolved issue fundamental to it: To what degree was the mature Copán sociopolitical system characterized by stratification as opposed to ranking?

That there was a wide range of sociopolitical arrangements among Classic Maya polities in the eighth century A.D. seems clear. I suggest that one of two very basic, contrastive models of sociopolitical organization characterizes the eighth-century Copán Maya. Although other models are possible, the ones discussed below allow us to envision various dimensions of fictional and status rivalry.

The lineage model emphasizes lineage organization (Sanders 1989). It envisions most or all members of a regional polity such as Copán as belonging to large, internally ranked kinship groups that had important corporate functions. Most significant among these, from our perspective, were corporate access to resources and the potential of lineage members to act cohesively in their own political interests—in other words, as political factions. High-ranking individuals within maximal lineages collectively constituted a kind of elite but were not necessarily linked by strong consanguineal kin connections to a central royal descent line, although they might be by marriage. A royal lineage ranked higher than the rest. Lineage heads managed the resources of their lesser relatives, who, in turn, formed their natural political constituencies.

In the lineage model, kinship ranking predominated as a structural principle for the society as a whole, not just for elites. The presence of a prestigious royal lineage created a dimension of weak stratification. Lineage heads and their close relatives and retainers collectively formed an emergent elite that shared codes of comportment, values, knowledge, tastes, and status symbols distinguishing them from lower-ranked people. This feature was intensified to the extent that they intermarried with one another or with the royal line. Considerable political tension is implicit. Kin groups were potential competitors with one another and, singly or collectively, with the royal lineage. Finally, lineage heads constituted a faction with internal interests that might conflict with those of the royal line, but also with the interests of their own, lower-ranked kinfolk.

As its name implies, the Hawaiian model derives from the ethnohistoric and archaeological record of the Hawaiian archipelago, which supported the most complex Polynesian political systems in the late seventeenth and early eighteenth centuries (Kirch 1984; Webster 1998b). A fundamental feature of Hawaiian society was its division into two distinct segments. At the top was a small segment of people (percentage uncertain), collectively called *ariki*—potential players in the highly competitive games of political maneuver and succession in the several competing island polities. Ariki status was defined genealogically within the framework of conical clan organization, ideally reflecting degree of relationship to central, royal lines.

A second, much larger segment consisted of people who were essentially commoners (collectively, *manahune*), the basic producers of the Hawaiian system who were of little or no direct political consequence. Although linked to ariki by vague concepts of very distant shared descent, commoners were effectively separated from them by a profound social gulf. Commoner families seem to have had very short genealogical depth and no significant corporate functions. Communities of commoners were defined by co-residence and attachments to notable individuals. Linking ariki and commoners were various minor elites and managers.

Paramounts were "owners" of the productive landscape in the sense that they asserted dominant rights of disposal over commoner lands, their products, and populations. Use-rights to land were delegated by paramounts and were retained by commoners through residence and contributions of labor (Earle 1978:148). Large numbers of commoners were sometimes moved on the landscape by paramounts for political purposes. Labor and goods supported elites and their establishments and were redistributed to attract and retain supporters in a political environment of intense status rivalry. Little or nothing flowed back down to commoners.

General features of the Hawaiian model potentially applicable to the Copán Maya include

1. Well-developed social and economic stratification, with political power heavily concentrated in the hands of the highest-ranked stratum

2. Formal state institutions feebly, if at all, developed

3. Elites internally defined by internal kinship ranking

4. A large commoner population that was very atomistic in terms of its own kin organization and lacked significant corporate functions

5. Little economic interdependence among commoners

6. Appropriation of goods and services by elites

Both the lineage and Hawaiian systems are politically centralized under paramount ruling lines, and both are internally segmented into politically potent factions, but in dramatically different ways.[12] A major difference is that in the lineage model, leaders have natural constituencies: authority over others of lesser rank is not entirely or even partly delegated by the king. These constituencies share corporate interests and resources and include people in the lowest social ranks, who are by no means politically marginalized or isolated. Elite competitors for political advantage depend on lesser kinspeople for political support. Because the latter have corporate interests as producers, another dimension of competition is among producer corporate groups. Their own elites and others must respond, or "manage," such potential competition, which they can do in both system-serving and self-serving ways. Leaders are thus subject to bottom-up political pressures and expectations.

Competition is also inherent in the Hawaiian model, but the effective political factions are on the elite level only. Another great segmentary gulf exists, however, between elites and commoners. Although the latter are politically quiescent and disorganized, they do constitute a potentially troublesome social component because they are so numerous, and because they lack meaningful links to elites.

In both models, a small segment of consumers is energetically underwritten by a large mass of producers, but, again, there is more continuity between them in the lineage model, making it difficult to differentiate strictly between elites, on the one hand, and commoners or peasants on the other. In both models, important positions were inherited, and status rivalry was aggravated by growth of elite populations and by politically advantageous elite marriages, which created genealogical ambiguities in access to offices and titles.

These models are by no means mutually exclusive. In fact, I assume that some Maya systems dominated by ranking evolved into ones with more stratification and that this process operated at Copán. The issue is how far this process went and its relationship to the Copán economy, because each model has different economic and political implications.

ELITE CULTURE HISTORY AND AGRARIAN MANAGEMENT

We can now synthesize a generalized soil/settlement model and what we know about elite culture history. For the sake of simplicity, I structure the discussion by recorded rulers' reigns. The intent is to (1) identify the contexts in which elite management might have occurred, (2) detect possible evidence for it, and (3) see whether plausible linkages exist between elite culture history and transformations in the agrarian economy.

Motives and goals for elite management of Copán's agrarian economy are clear. As consumers, elites had to ensure effective, direct flows of food energy to support their establishments. Indirect flows in the form of situational labor were also required. Such flows were not only necessary for maintenance, but also provided fuel for status rivalry. Access to the products and labor of others was thus the most potent political resource, and maintaining or enlarging such access was the primary political concern of royal and elite factions alike. Demands for products and labor were not static, but changed as consumer groups became larger and more numerous, more differentiated from commoners, and as status rivalry among them intensified. Management motives and goals were, in turn, conditioned by changes in agricultural productivity and strategies, the size of the producer population, and real or potential competition among producers for land.

Although I cannot develop the topic here, I do not envision elite management only in collective terms. Indeed, as the Copán resource base deteriorated, status rivalry may well have involved management prerogatives.

Possible irrigation in the Copán pocket aside, Copán elites do not seem to have initiated or managed capital productive improvements to the agricultural landscape. Scrutiny of aerial photographs and ground surveys have turned up no signs of drained fields, for which there is little potential in the Copán Valley anyway, at least by Classic times. Terraces do occur, but in very restricted and spotty distributions, and their dating remains unknown.

Two possible reasons ancient farmers failed to use terracing come to mind, given the obvious difficulties they experienced with erosion. First, upland soils at Copán tend to be infertile compared to similar soils elsewhere in the Maya lowlands proper, where they often constitute the principal agricultural resource. They are also highly unstable. Terracing of such uplands, especially when already damaged by erosion, was probably not worth the effort. Interestingly, the most impressive ancient terraces on steep hillsides that I have seen are on patches of unusually good soils weathering from limestone bedrock. Another possible reason is landholding patterns. Farmers without secure access to particular landholdings might have been reluctant to invest labor in capital improvements. Such a pattern is most consistent with the stratified model, which allows more arbitrary dislocation of producers from their fields.

More revealing is that Copán's elites seem to have been either uninterested in dictating or unable to manage the widespread construction of terracing or other landscape alterations that would have stabilized or increased productivity.

The First Ten Reigns

As long as the Copán population was small enough to practice long-fallow cultivation on the high-quality soils of the Copán pocket, with perhaps a few people scattered elsewhere around the valley, there was little necessity for management. Productivity was not highly varied, and potential for social distinctions based on differential access to resources was low. The pocket filled to capacity by about A.D. 400, and both soil and settlement models support sizable population expansion into nonpocket areas between A.D. 400 and 575. This period coincides with the establishment of the Copán dynasty and the careers of its first ten rulers. We know almost nothing about subroyal elites at this time, although important people seem to have been living at Group 9N-8 in what later was to become Copán's urban core (W. Fash 1991).

Labor on a modest scale was expended on Main Group constructions (Sharer, Miller, and Traxler 1992), and Christine Carrelli (1997) has been working on energetic calculations, adopting and adapting methods developed by Abrams (1994). Whatever the details of political organization, elites seem not to have been very demanding, meddlesome, or competitive, nor was competition among commoners a significant problem. The main elite management concern was the maintenance of relationships with the few commoners residing outside the Copán pocket and access to whatever small contributions to elite sustenance and enterprises were required from them.

The Reigns of Butz' Chan (K'ak' Joplaj Chan K'awil, Ruler 11) and Smoke Imix (Ruler 12)

During the next seventy-five years, population increased very rapidly, forcing adoption of medium-fallow strategies on prime lands and probably initial cultivation of less fertile and stable uplands. This period, incorporating all or parts of the reigns of the eleventh and twelfth rulers, Butz' Chan and Smoke Imix (A.D. 578–695), would have presented the first major managerial challenges and opportunities. The decline of per capita maize production and squabbling among producers over prime lands began to have effects. Annual cropping on the valley floor closely identified some producers with very restricted parts of the landscape. More restricted rights to land may have been asserted, requiring effective management to sort out conflicting claims and keep competition within acceptable limits.

On the other hand, there were many more producers, so elite food and labor requirements could still be satisfied with small, per capita, producer contributions. If the increasing labor pool could be effectively tapped, elite constructions could reach unprecedented size. A prediction is that when accurate energetic investments are possible on a reign-by-reign basis, activity at the Main Group will be more ambitious than before for this period; the same will be true at some subroyal elite establishments in the urban core and elsewhere.

At this time, we detect the first clear evidence of meddling. The population should expand much more heavily beyond the Copán pocket than it does. Certainly there are no external obstacles to such expansion, as there may have been elsewhere in the Maya lowlands where contentious polities were closely juxtaposed. Unusual concentrations within the pocket probably reflect efforts by kings or elites to keep producers within a few kilometers (almost literally within visual distance) of the urban core. Moreover, settlement evidence from the upper Copán River in Guatemala (Murdy 1991) strongly suggests that people living there were deliberately moved into (or were attracted to) the core of the Copán polity about the time of the Acbi-Coner transition, which Viel (1993a, 1993b) has now shifted to A.D. 600–650. All this makes it much more probable that the valley stelae erected by Smoke Imix in A.D. 652 were, as long suspected, statements of political domination of an essential core territory and population, although not of the whole polity.

Smoke Imix appears to have been an unusually strong king compared to his predecessors and may have traveled as far afield as Quiriguá to participate in rituals. During his reign, other changes occurred, such as the widespread adoption of Copador polychromes and other ceramic markers of the Coner ceramic phase, that are conspicuous but difficult to tie to political events. Possibly, they reflect in-migration of new population elements from elsewhere on the southeastern Maya frontier. Here the A.D. 590 eruption of Loma Caldera in El Salvador (Sheets 1992), where Copador appears early in household contexts, might be significant. (Paine's [1996] statistical analysis, however, reveals that the patterns of demographic growth in the settlement model do not require in-migration but are perfectly feasible in terms of the local population's intrinsic fertility.)

Unfortunately, we still lack information about subroyal elites for this period, so we do not know how these changes reflect royal initiatives, or those of elites more broadly. The royal role is highly conspicuous, suggesting considerable political centralization and stratification consistent with the Hawaiian model, but this may be just an illusion. On the other hand, negative evidence is also suggestive: I know of no major, nonroyal, elite groups in the Copán urban core or elsewhere that have significant masonry architecture before A.D. 650.[13] If subroyal elites were politically important, their power seems minimally expressed by labor expenditures on their own establishments.

The Reigns of Waxaklajun Ub'ah K'awil (Ruler 13) and K'ak' Joplaj Chan K'awil (Ruler 14)

The century between A.D. 650 and 750 was extremely dynamic according to both soil and settlement models. Early in this period, Smoke Imix still dominated events, followed by Waxaklajun Ub'ah K'awil and his successor, K'ak' Joplaj Chan K'awil. Population rose at its most rapid rate, expanded heavily into uplands, and may have peaked by the end of the period. Erosion on a large scale probably began. Managerial challenges included dampening the effects of competition over an increasingly unproductive and differentiated agricultural landscape, keeping control over the most valuable parts of it, redistributing food to correct production shortfalls, and controlling households that were more distant and whose locations frequently shifted.

Opportunities existed as well. However much general per capita production fell, there were more people than ever before, and their collective efforts allowed construction on an unprecedented scale, especially during the reign of Waxaklajun Ub'ah K'awil. Many anthropologists and geographers have noted that as population grows and land use intensifies, access to land becomes more restricted. This process probably began in the late seventh century as permanent cultivation replaced shifting cultivation, but eighth-century Copán provided an even more potent environment for it, resulting in increasing stratification and conflicting claims over prime lands. Effective management of apportionment and extension of land rights and adjudication of disputes became critical.

Even though elite establishments outside the Main Group certainly existed by this time, we are just beginning to understand their sociopolitical implications. Activities of subroyal elites are still, from our perspective, eclipsed by those of powerful rulers, particularly Waxaklajun Ub'ah K'awil, perpetuating the impression of power concentrated at the center.

The Reigns of K'ak' Yipaj Chan K'awil (Ruler 15) and Yax Pasaj Chan Yopat (Ruler 16)

By A.D. 750, Wingard estimates, more than 50 percent of the polity's maize requirements had to be obtained outside the Copán pocket. Continued heavy concentration of population in the pocket was almost certainly, in part, due to elite management decisions, which reflect heavy political motives at the expense of more rational distribution of population vis-à-vis resources. One solution to the local deficits caused by such concentration would have been for a regionally powerful Copán state to have imported maize from distant subordinate centers, as would be possible under the "Big-polity" model that some Mayanists advocate (for example, Marcus 1992a). I believe that such a model never applied at Copán and that bulk food-energy transfers over distances greater than 30–40 km were unfeasible. Even if such transfers were possible, political developments rendered them unworkable. Most important, whatever "control" Copán had over the Motagua Valley was abruptly terminated in A.D. 738 with the inglorious demise of Waxaklajun Ub'ah K'awil at the hands of the Quiriguá ruler Cauac Sky.

Another potential solution was to export labor from the Copán pocket to other parts of the valley to make up the deficit. Under this scenario, many nonpocket sites, particularly in the upper valley, would have been heavily occupied only on a seasonal basis. Given Wingard's calculations, I think that this very likely occurred. The effect, as already noted, would make the settlement model overestimate the peak population because permanent occupation is assumed for outlying sites. Such transitory residence is also consistent with the paucity of burials in outlying small sites of this period.

Management was required for establishment and maintenance of new, distant residences and other facilities, the organization of seasonal movements of labor to and from them, the collection of all-important elite and royal food subsidies, and the recruitment of labor for large Main Group projects such as Structures 10L-26, 10L-11, and 10L-16. Above all, new mechanisms would have been necessary to redistribute resources from the outlying parts of the valley to the core population.

By A.D. 700–750 there is compelling evidence for the existence of multiple subroyal elite establishments, mainly in the Copán urban core. According to the lineage model, the elites who lived in these groups were heads of corporate kin groups, their increased prominence, in part, derived from crucial managerial efforts to advantage their producer-kin and at the same time promote themselves. In the Hawaiian model, they would be elites whose authority was delegated by the ruler. In either case, they were emerging as a powerful factor in Copán politics. Interestingly, comparatively few elite establishments are found outside the Copán pocket. Apparently, outlying production could be arranged in the absence of many outlying administrative nodes of impressive size. Elite concentration in the Copán pocket can be seen as a royal ploy to control them, a pattern consistent with the stratified model. On the other hand, it might also reflect the political advantages of being near the royal court and the largest zone of prime lands.

By about A.D. 750–800 the polity was in severe trouble. Internal political squabbling was intensified by the lowered prestige of the royal dynasty after the Waxaklajun Ub'ah K'awil debacle and by the disruptive bottom-up pressures caused by a heavily eroded and deforested core environment in which double-cropping placed a heavy load on producers. Most of the burials examined by Storey (1992, 1997, chapter 8 in this volume) and Whittington (1989) probably derive from the eighth century or later. The demographic and pathological patterns detected in this sample, including the high mortality and frequency of morbidity indicators in subadults, high frequency of infections throughout life, probable chronic iron-deficiency anemia, and endemic diseases such as tuberculosis and pellagra, are consistent with a population assailed by environmental stresses. The gross patterns in the demographic reconstructions for the eighth and ninth centuries almost certainly mask the kind of recurring, short-term mortality crises detectable wherever good demographic data exist for complex nonindustrial societies (Flinn 1981; Livi-Bacci 1997).

Even as general well-being deteriorated, subroyal elite establishments emerged as large and impressive places, boasting their own high-quality masonry buildings and, significantly, iconography and inscriptions as well. Whether elite consumers were more numerous than before is unknown, but they certainly used labor more conspicuously and thus placed additional demands on the production system. An ominous portent was the eroded soil from uplands that literally began to bury some of these elite compounds in the northern Las Sepulturas zone almost as soon as they were completed.

In the Hawaiian scenario, subroyal elites were formerly dependent managers now asserting their own interests and competing with one another. In the lineage model, they would be upstart lineage heads increasingly aping the prerogatives of a declining royal dynasty. In either case, elites competed with one another and with the royal dynasty for a now very limited set of prime resources while still somehow managing to keep most people resident in the Copán pocket and imports flowing in from other parts of the valley. Under these circumstances, managerial roles became objects of competition.

By this time, if not before, elites probably had to oversee the redistribution of some foodstuffs among producer households because unpredictable domestic shortfalls must have become very common. The physiological and demographic patterns detected in Copán burials are consistent with stresses related to poor diet. Elites also faced the increasingly vexing problem of luring back laborers seasonally sent to more lightly settled and productive parts of the valley to make up the pocket deficits, which were larger than ever. Marked economic stratification and its sociopolitical concomitants, if they ever emerged at Copán, did so at this juncture, creating new managerial problems as demands of elite proprietors for food and labor increased and land-poor producers became extremely hard-pressed. If irrigation were adopted, as Wingard and I (Webster 1992) have speculated, it probably was applied on a very limited basis to the flat, prime lands of the western Copán pocket. This strategy would not have made up for much of the productive shortfall but would have exacerbated the differential productive capacity of the landscape, intensifying stratification and competition. If high-ranking proprietors of irrigated plots switched them over to production of nonsubsistence commercial crops such as tobacco (the pattern today), even more stress was generated, complicating agrarian management still further.

Decline

This is the most controversial part of the sequence, although the least important from the managerial perspective. We cannot review here the complex issues and debates about Copán's postdynastic population history, but a few comments are necessary. Everyone agrees that sometime during the interval of A.D. 800–825, Copán's royal dynasty experienced a crisis and collapsed (W. Fash and Stuart 1991; Stuart 1992, 1993) and that about the same time, some elite establishments were either abandoned or about to be (Andrews and Bill, chapter 7 in this volume; Andrews and Fash 1992). According to René Viel's (1983) original ceramic scenario, all elites effectively lost power about this time, followed shortly by the wholesale decline of the regional population by about A.D. 850–900, ending the Coner ceramic complex. Viel (1993a, 1993b) later refined his reconstruction of decline. Concerning the end of the polity, he noted that "the fall of the centralized order does not necessarily mean the end of life at Copán. A progressive decline is a more likely model than a sudden death" (Viel 1993a:17). He identified an Epiclassic facet of Coner in which Coner types were mixed with Fine Orange Pabellón Modeled Carved ceramics and dated it from A.D. 800 to about A.D. 950. He believed that it was then replaced by a Postclassic Ejar complex, defined by Fine Orange Pabellón Modeled Carved ceramics, as well as by San Juan and Tohil Plumbate and other minority types. Of Ejar generally, he remarks that it is "a heterogeneous assemblage including anything obviously post–A.D. 800 and non-Coner" (Viel 1993a:17).

For the post–A.D. 800 period, late-facet Coner and Ejar are defined by Viel on the basis of an extremely small collection of imported or rare types (number of sherds = 441 [Viel 1993b: 121]) that are not part of any larger Coner or Coner-like complex, although they can co-occur with Coner types before A.D. 950. He thinks that no Coner ceramics were made after that date, and the Plumbate (or Postclassic) facet of Ejar does not extend beyond A.D. 1000. The Postclassic Ejar complex is thus a kind of grab-bag association of chronologically late types that has no implications for whatever kind of household assemblages might have been in use. If such assemblages existed, they have no ceramic visibility in the 1993 scheme and, by definition, did not include Coner types. Although Viel does not say this in so many words, the implication of his 1993 sequence is that the Copán Valley was essentially depopulated by A.D. 950—not a significantly later date than that given in his original 1983 reconstruction of events.

Our settlement model indicates a very different picture of decline. Viel's 1993 sequence and Braswell's (1992) objections to the contrary, some elites survived at Copán long after the royal collapse, and population wound down gradually after A.D. 900 (Sheehy 1991; Webster et al. 1998; Webster, Freter, and Gonlin 2000; Webster, Freter, and Rue 1993). The decline occurs more rapidly in the settlement model than in the soil model. New support for such a demographic decline and long use of Coner or Coner-derived household assemblages comes from a recent set of concordance experiments that compared hydration dates and accelerator mass spectrometer (AMS) determinations from human bone collagen, with excellent results (Webster, Freter, and Gonlin 2000; Webster, Freter, and Storey 2004). One of these experiments, for example, produced five AMS dates that show late occupation at a well-excavated rural site with a Coner or Coner-like assemblage that entirely lacked Ejar sherds.[14] Sites with non-Coner or Coner-derived domestic assemblages may, of course, exist in the Copán Valley. If they do, however, they are few in number and coexist with plenty of small sites that carried on the broader Coner ceramic tradition and that have yielded no traces of Ejar ceramics. Our detection of late occupations at Copán merely confirms and adds detail to what archaeologists have long postulated for other parts of the Maya lowlands: that populations remained in many regions for a considerable time after dynastic rule collapsed (Demarest, Rice, and Rice 2004; Sharer 1977:532).

In important respects, however, the revised postdynastic ceramic patterns detected by Viel support our own demonstration that many elite-rank residences remained in use long after the royal collapse. Deposition of imported ceramics and other valuable exotic objects in ritual contexts in the Copán Main Group and urban core strongly suggests the continued presence of highly ranked individuals or groups who maintained contacts with trading partners in distant regions and who retained ancestral or other ritual associations with the great monuments and buildings of dynastic times. I think that this scenario is much more convincing than one involving only "foreign" visitors to an otherwise depopulated valley.

Returning to the settlement model, population in the Copán pocket continued to outweigh that in all other areas combined until A.D. 1050, a pattern consistent with the productive potential of the prime soils even when degraded, but also with lingering elite manipulation, competition, and management. At about that time, roughly half the total population of the valley resided outside the pocket (the largest such dispersal since the mid-sixth century), so central mechanisms of elite control appear to have broken down entirely. Much outlying population coalesced around the modest center of Piedras Negras, which seems to have been founded or, at least, to have grown remarkably after A.D. 1000 and to have dominated, for a short time, a small up-valley polity as far away from the Copán pocket as possible.

By the fourteenth century, we have only the scantiest indications of settlement anywhere, and forests were regenerating. This pattern of continued decline, as noted above, is contrary to the expectations of the soil model, but I believe that if it were incorrect, we would have many more late dates because the latest settlement phases are easiest to sample (although they might be so few that they are difficult to find). Political insecurities and better opportunities elsewhere probably caused most inhabitants of the Copán Valley to leave, but in such small numbers over several generations that the process would probably be archaeologically invisible in the colonized regions.

SUMMARY

T. Patrick Culbert (1988:100), reviewing the Classic Maya collapse, concluded that we can make up any scenarios we like, because we lack precise data. However true this might be for other Maya polities, it is, happily, no longer so for Copán, and not just for the period of the collapse. Whether the preceding reconstruction of Copán culture history and process meets Culbert's criterion of precision is less important than that we know, with reasonable accuracy, the main outlines of what, where, and when things happened and on what scale. Quibbles over details aside, something very much like the processes described above happened at Copán.

There is reasonably good fit among the soil and settlement models and the known dynastic/elite culture history, and these, in turn, accord well with ancillary information from studies of burials, diet, fossil pollen, and erosion. That these largely independent lines of evidence agree by chance is astronomically improbable. We can infer from them the basic outlines of elite management strategies (or lack of them) and the anthropogenically induced environmental processes against which they were played out. Considerable demand for hands-on elite management of the agrarian economy existed, and it increased through time. While households probably organized day-to-day production, other issues, such as access to land, competition over it, and increasingly restricted claims to it, certainly could not always have been sorted out on the domestic level alone. Management was thus highly focused on the social relations of domestic producing groups to land, to one another, and to elite groups and on the redistribution of food resources. Increasing crop insecurity and productive variability eventually caused uncontrollable shortfalls in some producer units, and the capacity to manage these by reciprocal exchanges among producer households was exceeded. Elites had to manage crucial components of this dynamic system to maintain and increase their own perquisites, and seemingly did so with little regard for the long-term stability of the productive infrastructure.

Population growth was at the root of these ecological transformations and their consequences, a conclusion accepted by all seminar participants. Why population growth occurs in preindustrial societies remains a hotly debated evolutionary issue. The dramatic increases at Copán after A.D. 600 are deceptive, we should note, because as Paine (1996) has shown, the increments of absolute change are products of essentially the same general fertility rate throughout the growth part of the sequence. For our present discussion, the reasons are immaterial. The fact is that such growth did occur, and occurred rapidly, as all Copán researchers agree. All the soil and settlement simulations do is measure its scale and timing, which, in turn, imply demographic processes and consequences. The models do not consider stochastic (and, to some degree, density-dependent) productive shortfalls and variability resulting from drought, storms, crop diseases, or other uncontrollable events, nor deficiencies in essential nonfood resources, such as building materials. How destructive such events can be was illustrated by Hurricane Mitch in 1998, and, of course, the ancient population would not have been buffered against a hurricane's worst effects by resources from outside the regional system, as the modern Copañecos fortunately were during that crisis. Shortfalls and mortality associated with such ancient disasters would have further exacerbated already powerful economic and political stresses.

As for the contrasting models of ranking and stratification presented, each is consistent with some of the patterns observed. I think that the lineage model is most plausible, with the proviso that between A.D. 700 and 800, ranking came under great stress as elites controlled and competed for resources more directly. In other words, both on the royal and subroyal elite levels, economic stratification was stronger then than at any previous time. Some management decisions, such as the heavy concentration of population in the Copán pocket, made the polity more fragile in the long run. Survival of some elites after the royal collapse seems to me more consistent with the lineage than with the Hawaiian model.

Elite demands certainly increased, in an absolute sense, as the agrarian crisis intensified. In my earlier paper (Webster 1985), I calculated that the surplus production of food energy necessitated by such demands would not, by itself, have produced heavy stress on producers, and I see nothing in the new information that would change this view. The effect of labor impositions, particularly for construction and maintenance of large structures, is an empirical issue yet to be addressed by systematic quantification. Preliminary work by Abrams (1994) and Webster and Kirker (1995) suggests that such demands at Copán were not as heavy as often envisioned.

In one of the few considerations of the agrarian dimensions of the Maya political economy, Turner (1983:115) pointed out that "it is difficult to envision how political economy can be deduced or understood from agricultural features, ecology, or crops per se. Indeed, while agriculture is strongly influenced by the political economy, there is no established relationship between agricultural type or levels of input and output and the political economy....For these reasons, Mayanists have avoided statements on political economy as related to agriculture."

I agree with Turner so far as he goes here. But the larger question is how much we can infer about the political economy if, in addition to such basic knowledge, we have detailed information about transformations in settlement, population, and agricultural history, as well as political history. The lesson from Copán is that we can reasonably infer a good deal.

Short of unexpected epigraphic revelations, we may never know in detail "the degree of control the elite exerted on the farming units, how decisions were made, how labor was organized, how production was distributed, the level of control of agricultural trade and the benefits derived from the farming units. Could Maya farmers trade or market surplus beyond that taken/given to the elite? Did farmers own their land or have inherited access to it? Were elite 'taxes' fixed or not? Were cropping decisions controlled by communities? What did the farmer gain by supporting the elite, or did they gain?" (Turner 1983:120). We certainly can, however, discern the main outlines of some of these things and identify some of the probable managerial stresses on commoners and elites alike, along with the constraints on and consequences of the decisions they made.

Consider the following hopeful and harmonious view in light of the preceding discussion:

> The Maya conceived of survival as a collective enterprise in which man, nature, and the gods are all linked through mutually sustaining bonds of reciprocity, ritually forged through sacrifice and communion. This collective enterprise, provided the organizing principle of Maya society, incorporating the individual in widening networks of interdependence from extended family through community and state and ultimately the cosmos. The elite directed this enterprise in all its aspects. Above all, they ensured the flow of offerings and benefits between society and the sacred order, and thus the survival of both. (Farriss 1984:6)

However accurate this state of affairs might be for the contact-period Maya, it is clearly not so for Classic Copán. If collective enterprise backed by sacred sanctions could have stabilized the effects of the dynamic transformations of the Copán environment, the Maya would indeed have achieved something unique in the comparative history of ancient complex societies. To the extent that faith was focused on a sacred sustaining order ensured by the rituals and constructions of kings, its plain inefficacy may have indirectly caused the collapse of the royal dynasty (see Webster [1995, 2002] and Sharer [1977] for discussions of the possible effects of attempts to manage agrarian crises ritually). Stuart (1993:336), referring to widespread political instabilities, says, "In my view, the whole Late Classic sees a single, long-term demise of the institution of southern Lowland Maya rulership." I think that his comment is especially pertinent to Copán after the reign of Smoke Imix.

My own view is that competitive stresses resulting from processes of rapid agrarian change at Copán, especially after A.D. 600, resulted in increased social, political, and economic differentiation. These stresses were not entirely manageable by producers. They required significant levels of elite intervention that involved far more than ritual maintenance of the "sacred order." Active political management of the agrarian economy, in part, served to dampen stresses but also created new ones because elites meddled for their own self-serving purposes. Agrarian management helped parlay elites into positions of greater power, but in the end, neither their management of the political economy nor their rituals could withstand the Malthusian agrarian transformations occurring from the bottom up.

Notes

1. Except for a few updated citations, the addition of some quotes, corrections or alterations suggested by reviewers, and two somewhat expanded sections on chronology and diet, this paper remains substantially as written in 1994. My apologies to any colleagues whose more recent work is insufficiently cited, evaluated, or otherwise acknowledged. I did not have the revised chapter by William Fash in this volume until June 2003 and have made no attempt to evaluate it in light of my own.

2. I use here the distinction between producers (individuals or social groups who produce food energy) and consumers (individuals or social groups who consume but do not produce food energy). No absolute hierarchical implication is implied, but producers are predominantly members of low-ranked farming households, and consumers are predominantly privileged or elite people. See Webster (1985) for a more detailed discussion.

3. See Webster (2002) for a discussion of megadrought—the most recently fashionable, extraneous climatic explanation.

4. See Wingard (1996) for his own evaluation of the independence of the simulations.

5. See Wingard (1992:152–159 and 1996:221–223) for a thoughtful evaluation of possible errors.

6. As far as I know, there is no direct evidence for valley-floor canal irrigation in Classic times from any context. Many tributary streams today are strictly seasonal and do not provide dry-season water. Small gravity-flow irrigation systems, however, do exist around the town of Copán and other parts of the Copán pocket, watered by perennial streams such as the Sesesmil and Titichon. Wingard includes an irrigation component in his model because it is technologically and environmentally feasible, because it is used today, and because it is a logical (if localized) adaptation to ancient productive shortfalls using less intensive systems. Substantial reductions in population estimates would result if irrigation were removed from his model.

7. Summary data are from Webster, Sanders, and van Rossum (1992). Because of difficulty in sampling early sites, the simulation produces some absurdities, such as the absence of population in many parts of the valley between A.D.

400 and 500. As noted in the 1992 article, we believe that the population for this interval is undercounted and should be on the order of 4,000–5,000 people.

8. This is my estimate, calculated from the presentations of P. Culbert (1991) and T. Culbert et al. (1990).

9. Using the A.D. 1549 tax lists, Ralph Roys (1957) estimated the population of the Mani province to be minimally 32,500 people. My colleague William T. Sanders later reconstructed the pre-Conquest population for Yucatan (and other parts of Mesoamerica) using this and other ethnohistoric documents (Sanders 1972). Although he did not publish all his estimates, his figure for Mani is 60,000 (personal communication to Webster), from which I calculated the densities given. These densities are presented as a range because it is unclear what portion of the population occupied that section of Mani territory lying south of the Puuc range. Sanders estimates that densities for Yucatan as a whole were in the neighborhood of 15–25 people per sq km.

10. The rates of population increase detected by settlement research and simulated by Wingard are rapid, but not unusually so for preindustrial populations over short periods of time. They suggest, but do not require, migrations into the surveyed zones, because they are within the limits of the intrinsic fertility of the valley's inhabitants. I, personally, suspect that they result from a combination of in-migration of people attracted by a stable dynasty and the reproductive capacity of a high-fertility, high-mortality indigenous population.

11. A recently analyzed sediment core from the Aguada Petapilla strongly suggests the presence of at least part-time, maize-using horticulturalists by 2000 B.C. or before (see Webster, Freter, and Gonlin 2000).

12. A related possibility that incorporates aspects of both these schemes is the "house model" derived from Levi-Strauss, which, I think, probably has great utility at Copán (for example, see Gillespie 2000).

13. By significant, here I mean buildings with high, stone-faced substructures and with superstructures of well-cut masonry bearing heavy vaulted or beam-and-mortar roofs. Their absence is probably not a sampling problem because many buildings in the urban core have been thoroughly trenched by several projects.

14. The calibrated one-sigma intervals are A.D. 646–768, A.D. 687–873, A.D. 883–997, A.D. 985–1029, and A.D. 1278–1411. All were run at the University of Arizona AMS Laboratory as part of a blind test against a set of twenty-seven hydration dates, whose collective one-sigma span (adjusted to the same 1950 baseline as the radiocarbon dates) is A.D. 756–1060. Note how congruent the late dates in the AMS series are with the calibrated dates from Rue's pollen core.

3

Toward a Social History of the Copán Valley

William L. Fash

The roles and aspirations of "people without history" are among the most important yet intractable forces to discern from the archaeological record. The study of the Mesoamerican past, including the Lowland Maya of the Classic period, now routinely incorporates—while critically evaluating—significant historical data. Anthropological archaeologists working in this part of the world currently make careful and considerate use of this expanding source of insights and information in pursuing the challenging task of reconstructing the goals and actions of the major players whose tales have survived to the present day. The more daunting task is to reconstruct the perspectives and dynamics of those who were not privileged to enter the historical record, crucial though their role may have been in creating it. Within the Maya realm, the abundance of both hieroglyphic texts and recent multidisciplinary research projects has yielded glimpses into the history and ambitions of the noble class. Household archaeology and settlement surveys now provide us with insights into the ethnic background, roles, and motivations of the tens of thousands of people who came to call the Copán Valley home in the three millennia preceding European contact. Here I would like to present some new ideas and observations about the social context in which Classic Maya kingship developed, flourished, and declined in the Copán Valley. In keeping with my previous contributions, I seek here to explain the developments in the dynastic center from the perspective of the supporting population, vis-à-vis its development in size and complexity through time and space.

In recent decades, scholars have demonstrated that political units of numerous sizes and levels of inclusivity existed side by side in complementary and often conflicting ways throughout the Maya lowlands from the Late Formative period onward. These ranged from the largest and most powerful states, such as Tikal and Calakmul, to smaller yet still powerful kingdoms, down to minor centers and hamlets. This view has been most thoroughly developed by Joyce Marcus (1992a, 1993), whose "dynamic model" was informed by analysis of ethnohistorical, archaeological, and epigraphic materials. Marcus follows Ralph Roys' (1957) division of Maya sociopolitical entities into three types and encourages us to look at the kinds of interaction and degrees of inclusivity of the parties involved through time and space. To interpret the archaeological data, given our inability to observe directly those interactions and the social structures that generated and helped to shape them, we are best served by using analogy with living or historically documented cultures at the same level of sociopolitical integration and inhabiting a similar ecological setting (Shimkin 1973). In this vein, Arthur Demarest (1992b) has made a compelling case for structural similarities between Classic Maya states in the southern lowlands and the Negara or "galactic polities" of Southeast Asia.

Both the dynamic model and the galactic polity model retrodict a pattern of cyclicity in the growth and decline of states, beginning with a relatively rapid, initial nucleation and centralization of power in a primary center and followed by a rapid expansion in territory and political control. Thereafter, a period of relative stability (of variable duration) occurs, which eventually deteriorates when the elites of secondary centers that were originally established or co-opted by the capital begin to exert their independence and finally break away from the primary center. After many secondary and tertiary centers sever ties with the old capital, its fortunes decline abruptly and its role as the political center is terminated, to be taken up by the region's most resourceful and powerful center(s). The Negara kingdoms of Bali were called "theatre states" by Geertz (1980), who noted that royal power was based on elites' control over ideological resources and their ability to "make inequality enchant." Material assets such as land and portable wealth were not under the ruler's direct control, so he could not use these to impose his will on competing nobles. The ruler and his royal precinct, or "regal-ritual city" in the useful construct of Richard Fox (1977), were therefore potentially vulnerable to usurpation of royal power by upstart nobles or even outsiders. These models provide a useful framework for describing and explaining the social history of the Copán kingdom. The case made here is that noble households in the valley replicated, on a smaller scale, the organizational structures and rationales for rulership of their paramount lords. This symbolic representation and its underlying political aspirations created a structural redundancy and social friction that eventually, in my view, weakened and divided the kingdom.

In a compelling analysis of the Colonial-period Maya, Nancy Farriss (1984:138) concluded that the integration of communities into states depended on elite relations of trade, as well as alliance and warfare, all made without reference to the mass of the population. Such alliances between the Maya royal lineages—or "houses," if one prefers not to link noble households to particular lineages (Gillespie 2000; Joyce and Gillespie, eds., 2000; for comparison, see Carsten and Hugh-Jones, eds., 1995)—and the limits of the area they could effectively control created a highly fluid political landscape. Among the indigenous, complex societies of Southeast Asia, the resources to underwrite independent action on the part of a ruler came not just from the pyramid of politicoeconomic relations within the polity, but also from controlling the supply of nonsubsistence goods from outside the system (Demarest 1992b; Tambiah 1977:86). In what follows, I seek to identify some major players in the social history of the Copán Valley and their role in shaping the trajectory of this remarkable kingdom, as reconstructable from current historical, iconographic, and archaeological evidence. This chapter relies most on the intensive and extensive excavations of specific sites to complement the results obtained from the valley testpitting programs that provide the bulk of the data for the settlement model and soils model discussed in chapter 2 by David Webster. I draw upon my own and others' investigations in the valley and my diachronic investigations of the northern end of the Acropolis, specifically, the main ball court and Structures 10L-22, 10L-22A, and 10L-26.

THE ORIGINS OF INEQUALITY IN THE COPÁN VALLEY

As noted in the first two chapters, the overall occupational history of the Copán Valley has been the subject of intensive and extensive excavation programs and ecological research since the mid-1970s (W. Fash 1983a, 1991; Freter 1992; Hall and Viel 1994, 1998, 2004; Manahan 2000, 2002a, 2002b; Viel 1999a; Webster 1999; Webster and Freter 1990a; Webster, Freter, and Gonlin 2000; Webster, Sanders, and van Rossum 1992; Willey and Leventhal 1979) and is framed for us within larger questions of resource management in Webster's chapter 2 in this volume. As in most discussions of this nature in archaeology (Teotihuacan being but one example that comes to mind), debate continues regarding the size of the resident population during the Early Classic period in Copán and the time it took for the valley to be depopulated after the political collapse of the center about A.D. 822 (W. Fash, Andrews, and Manahan 2004; W. Fash and Sharer 1991; Manahan 2002a, 2004; Webster 2001, chapter 2 in this volume; Webster and Freter 1990a, 1990b; Webster, Freter, and Gonlin 2000). The material remains of the Early and Middle Formative occupations in the Copán Valley conform to what E. Wyllys Andrews (1990) considers to be the non-Maya neighbors who peopled the southern part of the Maya area. The jades and vessels with Early Formative Horizon incised designs associated with the burials found in the author's deep excavations of Group 9N-8 (figure 3.1, #2; W. Fash 1982; 1983b:volume III, 1991, 2001; W. Fash, Agurcia Fasquelle, and Abrams 1981; Sharer 1989) and the ceramics discovered by George B. Gordon in his Cave 2 (Gordon 1898) evince considerable artistic and iconographic sophistication, in keeping with the cultural developments in Mesoamerica more broadly at that time (Flannery and Marcus 1994; Sharer and Grove 1989). They are, however, not associated with monumental architecture or art that would reflect significant levels of sociopolitical integration.

The extensive test-pitting programs conducted in the Copán Valley in the late 1970s and 1980s did not locate evidence for large settlement

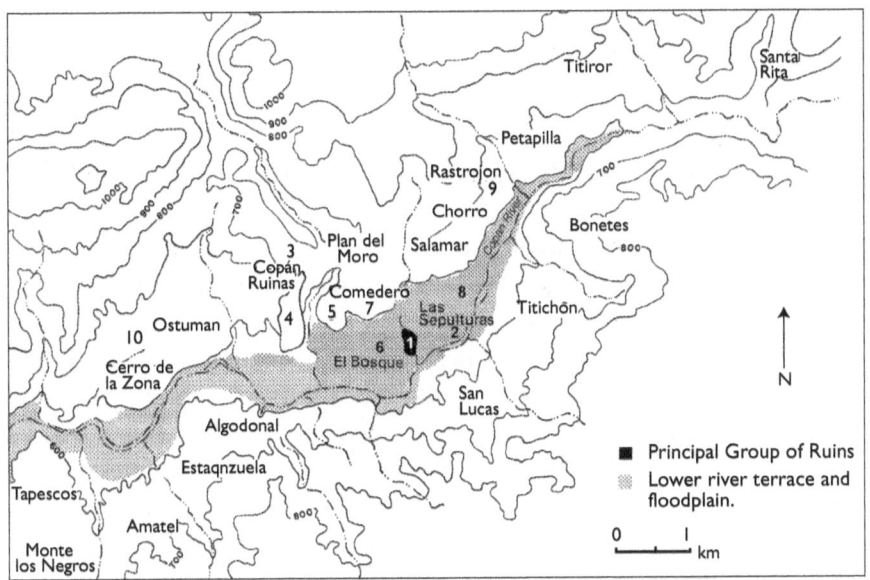

FIGURE 3.1

A map of the Copán pocket of the Copán Valley with modern local place names and locations of sites mentioned in the text: (1) the Principal Group, (2) Group 9N-8, (3) Cerro de las Mesas, (4) the site of the modern town (Morley's Group 9), (5) Group 9J-4 (Cerro Chino), (6) the densely settled urban ward west of the Principal Group, (7) Group 9J-5, (8) Group 8N-11, (9) Rastrojón, (10) Ostumán. (Drawing by B. Fash, based on the original published in Willey, Leventhal, and Fash 1978)

units, or any public architecture, for the Middle or Late Formative periods. The Middle Formative populations seem to have made use of all the valley's physiographic zones. For the Late Formative, the few recovered traces of occupations were concentrated in the area of what would later become the Principal Group, in the center of the broadest expanse of alluvial bottomlands (W. Fash 1983b, 1983c). This finding prompted us to posit that a decline in population occurred at that time, vis-à-vis the more widely distributed remains (including domestic architecture and burials) of the Middle Formative period (W. Fash 1983a, 1991). Recent research in the area north, west, and south of the Principal Group by Jay Hall and René Viel of the University of Queensland shows that both the physical landscape and the human population were more complex during the Late Formative than previously thought (Hall and Viel 1994, 1998, 2004; Viel 1999a; Viel and Hall 1997;).

During the Bijac phase (dated A.D. 100–400 by Viel [1983a, 1993b]), ceramics, architecture, and burials found in the area of the Principal Group are complemented by occupations documented from all the physiographic zones of the Copán pocket. Offerings found with subfloor burials in a large platform revealed in the broad horizontal exposures of Patio A at Group 9N-8 (W. Fash 1983b:volume III, 1983c, 1985, 1991) indicate that members of the resident population in the urban core participated in long-distance exchange networks. Likewise, Charles Cheek's investigations of the Great Plaza area (Cheek 1983a, 1983b) showed that public architecture was constructed and used at that locus in Bijac times, and also recovered elite craft goods deriving from other regions. Excavations conducted in 2000 by Harvard University on the summit of the Northwest Platform, located directly west of Structure 10L-1 and the Great Plaza, encountered a potbelly sculpture similar to the one found in the substela cache beneath Stela 4. Previous probes to the west of the platform by Viel and Hall had uncovered significant Formative deposits less than a meter below the present ground surface, indicating that the Northwest Platform may yet yield deeply buried Formative remains. The platform itself is 10 m high, 30 m wide, and 80 m north-south, making it the second largest construction mass in the Copán Valley after the Acropolis.

The boulder sculpture found on the summit of the Northwest Platform, toward its southern end, is of the potbelly tradition seen in the southern Maya area during the Late Formative period (Demarest 1986; Parsons 1986). Other potbelly sculptures have been found in substelae caches under Late Classic monuments in the Great Plaza and the valley (Parsons 1986). These decidedly non-Classic Maya sculptures, as well as the non-Maya affiliations of the Late Formative and Protoclassic ceramics in the Copán Valley, suggest that the resident population continued to be non-Maya, precisely as suggested long ago by Sylvanus Morley (1920) and John Longyear (1952). It seems to me that present evidence is in keeping with a chiefdom level of sociopolitical integration for the valley in the Late Formative and Protoclassic periods.

The discovery of another potbelly sculpture serves to remind us of the early date of 8.6.0.0.0 10 Ahau 13 Ch'en (A.D. 160) cited on three of the Classic-period monuments from Copán: Stelae I, 4, and 17 (Schele and Freidel 1990). Stelae 4 and I were erected in the Great Plaza less than 100 m from the Northwest Platform, and Stela 4 had a potbelly sculpture cached beneath it. The text from Stela I also refers to a variant of the Copán emblem glyph in association with a date some two hundred days after the 8.6.0.0.0 Period Ending date (Schele and Freidel 1990; Stuart 1992, 2004). Some skeptics had dismissed these references as later constructions of a glorious past by the Late Classic rulers, with no supporting evidence in the archaeological record. However, the Preclassic deposits and potbelly sculptures in the vicinity of the Northwest Platform mean that these textual references can no longer be regarded as mere fictions of later kings. Particularly intriguing is that the ancient name of the Copán community (later kingdom), as recorded in its emblem glyph, may predate the arrival of Maya speakers in the Copán Valley.

THE ESTABLISHMENT OF A NEW ROYAL CENTER AND ITS CONSEQUENCES IN THE COPÁN VALLEY

The long-term program of conservation, documentation, and investigation of Copán Structure 10L-26 and its Hieroglyphic Stairway has provided direct archaeological evidence regarding the establishment of the Classic Maya tradition in the Copán Valley. Excavations inside this building's pyramidal core were conducted to test a series of predictions derived from archaeological investigations in the Copán Valley, as well as epigraphic studies of the inscriptions from the Principal Group (W. Fash 1988; W. Fash et al. 1992; Williamson 1996, 1997). These investigations have documented the use of this sacred space through time, beginning with the first constructions in the early years of the fifth century A.D. One primary objective of the archaeological investigations of the Early Classic buildings buried inside Structure 10L-26 was to determine whether the historical accounts regarding the Early Classic Copán rulers (and other Late Classic texts), which were carved in stone on the Hieroglyphic Stairway, could be evaluated in light of independent archaeological data at this locus. Taken together, the Structure 10L-26 and other Acropolis Project investigations (Sharer at al., chapter 5 in this volume) have helped to confirm the existence of the individual referred to in the city's annals as the "founder" of Copán's Classic-period dynasty. They have also provided evidence of his role and contributions in the foundation of the regal-ritual center that dominated the Copán region during the fifth to early ninth centuries A.D. Clearly, this "outsider king" (compare Gillespie 1989) had an enormous role in shaping the perception of Copán in the eyes of his contemporaries and later generations.

The Structure 10L-26 tunnel investigations uncovered the remains of the two earliest buildings constructed at this locus, constructed atop sterile alluvium (figure 3.2). The first one was given the field name Yax, in keeping with our interpretations of its antiquity and the name of the dynasty's founder. Its subfloor leveling fill contained green obsidian imported from central Mexico (Aoyama 1999) and ceramics dated by Viel to the end of the Bijac phase (ca. A.D. 400). Yax Structure's immediate successor, given the field name Motmot Structure, made use of Yax's stairway on the west side of the building and apparently followed but enlarged the former's floor plan (Williamson 1996). Both these early buildings carried stucco decorations on their substructure façades, but the dismantling of Yax Structure at the time of Motmot's construction resulted in the demolition of most of the first building's stucco adornments. Motmot's substructure was built with large apron moldings in the tradition of the Classic central Petén heartland, with two sky bands each on the east and west sides and a large G-1 deity head mask as the main element of a large outset panel on the center of the eastern (back) side.

A large, carved floor marker placed 3.5 m due west of the front stairway of Motmot Structure was uncovered in 1992 (figure 3.3) and has been referred to as "the cornerstone of Copán" (Stuart and Stuart 1993:36). The decipherment of the Motmot marker text and the interpretation of its accompanying imagery have been a subject of considerable interest and are detailed elsewhere (W. Fash 2002; W. Fash, B. Fash, and Davis-Salazar 2004; Stuart 2004, chapter 10 in this volume). Happily, the archaeological data help to illuminate its text and iconography. The dating of the floor marker and its associated floor corresponds to the time of its dedication, on or near the Period Ending 9.0.0.0.0 (A.D. 435), and supports Stuart's conclusion that both the founder and his son and successor (Ruler 2) participated in the rituals

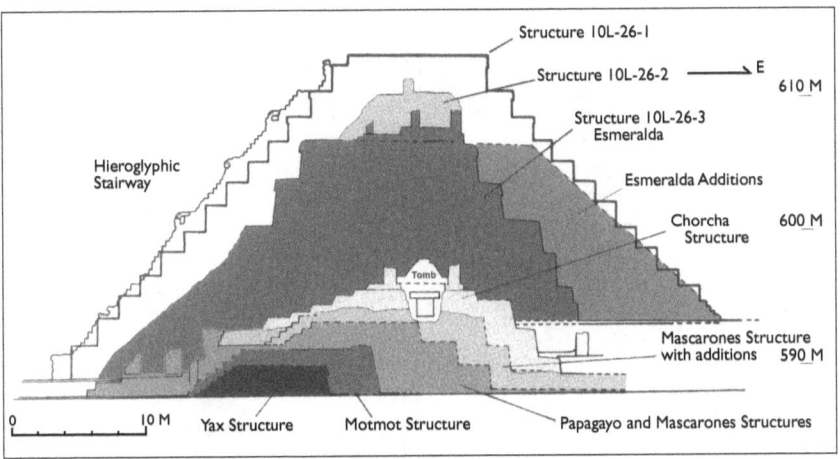

FIGURE 3.2

A schematic east-west cross section of Structure 10L-26, showing buried architecture partially uncovered in tunnel excavations. (Based on investigations by the author, Richard Williamson, Rudy Larios, Fernando López, Karla Davis-Salazar, Barbara Fash, and Joel Palka; digital version by Barbara Fash, based on an ink drawing by Fernando López)

associated with the monument and the series of offerings found directly beneath it. The tied deer hooves and "lancet" verb have an archaeological correlate in the skeleton of a deer that was found with bound legs, beheaded and burned, atop the capstones of the cylindrical tomb that the floor marker was positioned above. We can associate the "4 sky" reference in the text with the building on whose central axis the floor marker was placed, because Motmot Structure had four sky bands modeled in stucco, two on the front side and two on the back. The dedication of the "numbers tree" is surely a reference to the floor marker itself, naming the object on which the text occurs, as the Copanecs were so fond of doing (Stuart 1992, 1997). The "fire entering" verb corresponds to the re-entry and burning of the contents of the cylindrical cist, documented during the investigations. The lower leg bones of the young adult woman placed in the burial chamber were found still completely articulated and in situ on a reed mat on the floor of the tomb, indicating that they were undisturbed since their original placement. The upper leg bones and remainder of the skeleton were

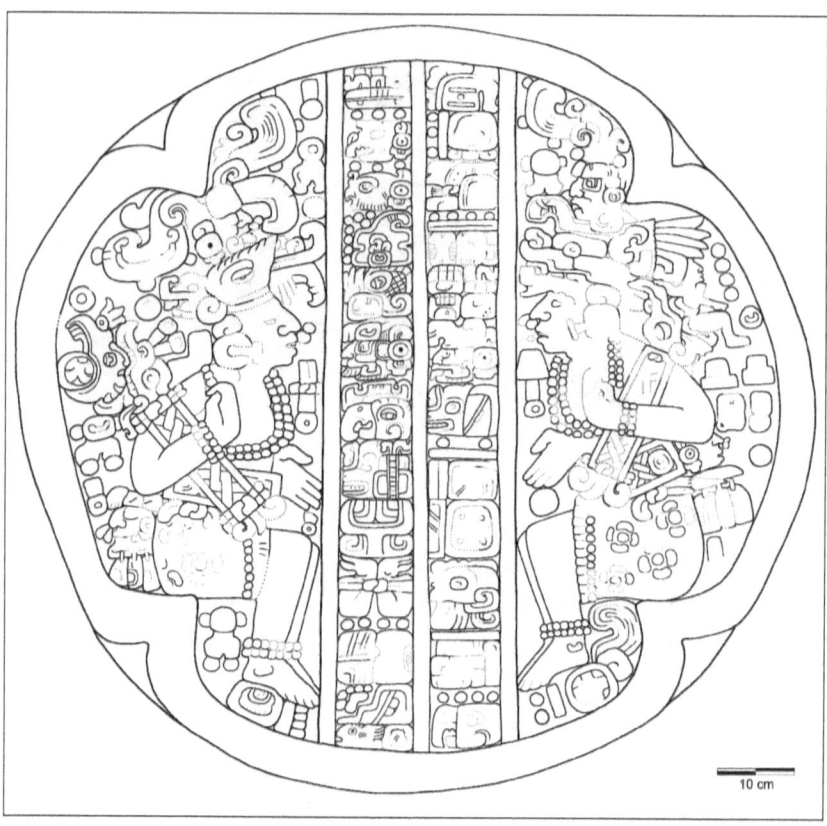

FIGURE 3.3

The Motmot floor marker. (Drawing by B. Fash)

found jumbled and burned and intermixed with the eleven ceramic vessels, disarticulated puma skeleton, turtle shells, and other offerings found inside the cist. This would correspond with the fire-entering event recorded in association with the baktun completion.

The "4 macaws" glyph at the end of the text can be associated with the four large stucco macaws that adorned the substructures of Ball Court I (W. Fash and B. Fash 1996), which shares the stucco floor into which the marker was set, and was therefore dedicated at or before the same time. It also bears noting that the numerous crocodile scutes found atop the capstones of the cylindrical burial chamber suggest that a crocodile skin was laid over the chamber's roof and burned before the deer carcass was placed there. This is in keeping with the much later Altar T of Copán, but more importantly with the building that immediately succeeded and encapsulated Motmot Structure. Pagagayo Structure was decorated with modeled stucco depictions of crocodiles, which formed the base of the decoration on the two sides of the building's entablature that survived (W. Fash 1988). Placed inside Papagayo Structure was Stela 63, whose text refers to the 9.0.0.0.0 Period Ending rituals performed by K'inich Yax K'uk' Mo' and also cites his son and successor, who was responsible for both the building and the stela. Thus, even the later monuments at this locus tied in both contextually and conceptually with the floor marker text and associated material remains of its attendant rituals, designed to mark the nascent Copán dynasty's celebration of this momentous date in Maya history and to sacralize permanently the place where the marker stood.

The cylindrical burial chamber beneath the Motmot floor marker is unique in the corpus of burials in Copán, which now exceeds seven hundred. However, it is remarkably like contemporary burial pits in Teotihuacan, where high-status individuals were placed in cylindrical pits of this same size, with ceramics and other offerings, and then deliberately burned (Manzanilla 1993; Serrano Sánchez 1993). Likewise, the aforementioned green obsidian in the fill of Yax Structure, the presence of a tablero on the platform on which Papagayo Structure was built (field name *Gran Corniza*), the talud-tablero structure in which K'inich Yax K'uk' Mo' was buried in the nascent Acropolis to the south (Sharer et al., chapter 5 in this volume), the abundance of Thin Orange and Teotihuacan-style vessels in the founder's tomb, as well as in that of the woman Sharer and his colleagues identify as the founder's wife (and mother of Ruler 2 [Bell, Canuto, and Sharer, eds., 2004]), the Tlaloc Warrior buried due west of Margarita Structure, and Burial V-6, located just north of Papagayo Structure (Cheek 1983a), all evince active exchange links with Teotihuacan. The feathered-serpent heads on the Ball Court I stucco macaws were direct copies of the numerous examples then visible at Teotihuacan (W. Fash and B. Fash 2000). Likewise, the temple text of the final-phase version of Structure 10L-26 (Stuart, chapter 10 in this volume), as well as the vast majority of the seventh-century Acropolis façades (B. Fash 1992a), emphasize ties to Teotihuacan.

The evidence indicates that an important source of power for the first rulers of the dynasty portrayed on Altar Q, as for their counterparts in other regions of Mesoamerica, was their ability to obtain goods, services, and ideas from elites outside their domain. This finding is in keeping with the patterns documented for the Colonial and Postclassic Maya and for the Negara and other Southeast Asian theatre states (Geertz 1980; Tambiah 1977). In her work on the acquisitiveness of aristocratic elites in ancient Panama, Mary Helms (2000:156) has explored why "the aristocratic elite desires and requires such tangible products with considerably greater intensity than commoners do and strives therefore to acquire greater quantity or greater quality of such goods than is permitted to other members of society." It also accords with the conclusions of Schele and Freidel (1990) and Demarest and Foias (1993) regarding the interactions between aspiring Early Classic Maya elites and the great capital of Teotihuacan. In their view, those nascent royal lines sought to enhance their status by obtaining goods, services, ideas (including strategies of war [for comparison, see Schele and Freidel 1990]), and the trappings of success from emissaries of the archetypal city of central Mexico.

In the case at hand, following the death of Ruler 1, his successors shifted the emphasis to Classic Maya architectural styles and dynastic monuments, at the Structure 10L-26 locus and the rest of the Acropolis that has been investigated thus far by Sharer and his colleagues. Nonetheless, the ties to central Mexico were not forgotten; they were to become a central focus of religious and historical propaganda in the last half of the eighth century A.D. (B. Fash 1992a; Stuart, chapter 10 in this volume). For the duration of the Early Classic, however, the emphasis was on creating a ruling court in the Classic Maya tradition. The question that comes to mind is how such a foreign, Petén-derived cultural tradition could prosper, indeed thrive, in the context of what the material record indicates was a non-Maya population beyond the southeastern geographic limit of the southern Maya lowlands.

The PAC I test-pitting programs documented a significant increase in population size and complexity during the Acbi phase (originally dated A.D. 400–700 by Viel [1983], but now considered more likely to end between A.D. 600 and 650 [Viel 1993a, 1993b; for comparison, see Andrews and Bill, chapter 7 in this volume]). This development can be seen in several categories of data from the excavations in the valley: First, by the greater numbers of ceramics recovered from the test excavations in each physiographic zone. Second, by the increase in the number of primary contexts (including burials and architectural features) encountered in those same probes, including on the mountaintop redoubt of Cerro de las Mesas, 1 km north of the modern town (see figure 3.1, #3). Third, by the documentation of an elaborate Acbi-phase architectural compound at Group 9N-8 (see figure 3.1, #2), whose plaster plaza floor connected three differentiated structures, one of which had a richly furnished grave (Burial VIII-36). Fourth, by the fact that the area presently occupied by the modern town (see figure 3.1, #4) seems to have served as the seat of power for a royal line that predated the arrival of K'inich Yax K'uk' Mo', to judge from the references to the earliest *ajaw* and other titles found there (Stuart 1992), as well as the abundant and diverse archaeological remains from the Bijac and succeeding Acbi phase buried at that locus (Galloy 1993). Fifth, by the abundant evidence for Acbi occupations in the forested area to the west of the Principal Group (see figure 3.1, #6) recovered during the PAC I settlement history excavations. Finally, as just seen, by the fact that the area we refer to as the "Principal Group" has an unprecedented burst of construction activity, accompanied for the first time by in situ dynastic sculpture monuments containing both inscriptions and pictorial imagery (Sharer et al., chapter 5 in this volume).

Recent investigations in the Río Amarillo Valley have shown that a number of important early settlements existed in the area to the east of the Copán pocket as well. Mapping and excavations by William Saturno at the site identified by Morley (1920) as "Río Amarillo," known in the more recent literature as "La Canteada" (Pahl 1977, 1987), have shown that Early Classic fills (Saturno 2000) underlie the main architectural complex there. Likewise, investigations conducted by Marcello Andrea Canuto (2002, 2004) at the site of Los Achiotes have also produced abundant Chabij- and Bijac-phase ceramics of the Late Formative and Protoclassic periods. The public architecture at these sites is modest in comparison to major Late Classic sites, but nonetheless of significant size and elaboration, including a ball court at the site of Los Achiotes (Canuto 2002, 2004; Canuto and McFarlane 1999). These sites thus evince a larger and more complex resident population in this valley ca.

A.D. 400 than had been attributed to it solely on the basis of the extensive test pitting of surface mound sites. Canuto (2002, 2004) suggests that the residents of the nearby site El Raizal were drawn into the Copán hegemony early in the sixth century A.D. as part of a deliberate policy "seeking both control and representation within the polity to the detriment of local identity and autonomy" (Canuto 2004:49). This strategy was complemented by one of deliberate nucleation of people from the rural areas into the area surrounding the royal precinct, to judge from the significant population upswing in the Copán pocket noted by the PAC I test-pitting program. It may also explain why the hilltop site of Group 9J-4 (Cerro Chino), located 1.2 km northwest of the Principal Group within the Copán pocket (see figure 3.1, #5), was abandoned toward the end of the Bijac phase (Carballo 1997). This site is similar in layout and configuration to Los Achiotes and may represent the same ethnic group (Canuto 2004).

The small size of the sample we currently control means that we will probably continue to debate the number of people who inhabited the Copán Valley during the fifth century A.D.. The points I would like to emphasize regarding the origins of the Copán polity as a Classic Maya dynastic center from A.D. 426 to 500 are the following:

1. Population increased in the Copán Valley over the preceding century, as seen by the numbers and diversity of occupational remains recovered from all physiographic zones in the PAC I test-pitting program, which was not biased to surface mound features.

2. The elaboration and complexity of the architectural features, burial chambers, and associated burial furniture increased significantly, in both the site center and the one large, elite residential complex in the valley that has been thoroughly excavated.

3. Dynastic monuments were being erected in at least two loci in the Copán pocket (the Principal Group and the locus of the modern town), indicating programs of formal political propaganda, the tracing of descent and legitimization of authority, and associated religious rituals for the residents of at least two elite residential zones in the valley.

4. The volume, elaboration, and, above all, rapidity of sequent constructions in the site core, specifically at the loci of Structure 10L-26 and the ball court (see above) and the nucleus of the central part of the Acropolis (Sharer et al., chapter 5 in this volume), reflect the ability to conscript labor for the edification of ever more imposing works of art and architecture. These public works were designed to enhance the prestige and power of the royal household, whose palaces and temples were the centerpiece and primary manifestation of its exalted status.

All these characteristics of fifth-century Copán are in keeping with the expectations of Marcus's dynamic model and the related growth pattern documented by Tambiah for galactic polities and by Geertz for the Negara, which served as the inspiration for Demarest's (1992b) model. In the regal-ritual center, a number of recent findings have illuminated the nature of the ceremonies used to sanctify the ruling line and its monuments. The material remains of sacred rituals and the forms and decoration of public architecture in the center were soon to be replicated by the supporting nobility in the Copán Valley.

REPLICATION OF THE ROYAL COMPOUND AT ELITE SITES IN THE COPÁN VALLEY

The founding of a new royal center by K'inich Yax K'uk' Mo' coincided with the construction of elite residences in other parts of the Copán Valley. Sadly, precious few contexts of this time period have been fully excavated and exposed in the Copán region because most valley-focused research designs have concentrated on the Late Classic apogee and its aftermath (Webster, chapter 2 in this volume). One exception to this rule was the broad horizontal excavations I designed and directed to uncover the earlier occupations beneath Plaza A of Group 9N-8 (W. Fash 1982, 1983c:Appendix D, 1985). These uncovered a cobblestone platform some 50 m long, constructed during the Bijac phase and subsequently covered in the first half of the fifth century A.D. by a courtyard group whose structures shared a common stucco floor (W. Fash 1991:88–93). The funerary offerings associated with the high-status Burial VIII-36, presumably the patriarch of this Acbi-phase courtyard, show that this individual had obtained luxury goods from distant regions. Among them were two Dos Arroyos

Polychrome vessels, more than one hundred large beads made from *Spondylus* shell hinges, and an heirloom Chicanel vessel from the central Petén. Other specialized craft goods were from closer at hand: the jade beads and pendants and locally made vessels fashioned in the international style of the day, including one imitation of a Teotihuacan cylindrical tripod vessel with modeled human faces on the sides.

The plan and the cross section of this burial are remarkably like those of the contemporary Burial A22 of Structure A-V at Uaxactun (Smith 1950:figure 121), again indicating that ideas, as well as goods and services (and, very likely, people [see Sharer et al., chapter 5 in this volume]), were traveling widely among the elites of the Copán Valley and their counterparts in other parts of the Maya world. The burial furniture of this grave has numerous elements identical to the offerings found with Copán Burial XXXVII-8, beneath the Motmot floor marker: white quartz divination stones, turtle shells, bones from cayman and deer (possibly his *wayob*, or guardians), eleven ceramic vessels, a bird carved in jade, and stingray spines. Barbara Fash's suggestion (chapter 4 in this volume) of water-management functions for this site's Late Classic lineage head leads me to wonder whether the crocodile necklace buried with this individual had something to do with reservoir management duties.

To these parallels we may add a structural feature of this patriarch's residential compound. On the plan map of this Acbi-phase courtyard in Group 9N-8 (figure 3.4), one can see the stones that formed the ground floor of a circular stone pavement on the central axis of the eastern structure (9N-sub-3). This circular feature is on the central axis of the building, in line with Burial VIII-36, which was placed east of the structure. The overall dimensions of Structure 9N-sub-3 and its placement on the east side of a plaza complex, with its stairs facing the west, constitute replications of Yax/Motmot Structures, the contemporaneous buildings associated with important rituals in the newly established regal-ritual center. This element on the central axis of Structure 9N-sub-3 originally functioned as the floor of a circular feature, reminiscent of the floor marker used by the founder of the new royal center and his son and successor in their Period Ending ceremony. Like the Motmot marker, the Structure 9N-sub-3 stone pavement was circular. The feature was slightly slumped in the middle, but excavations

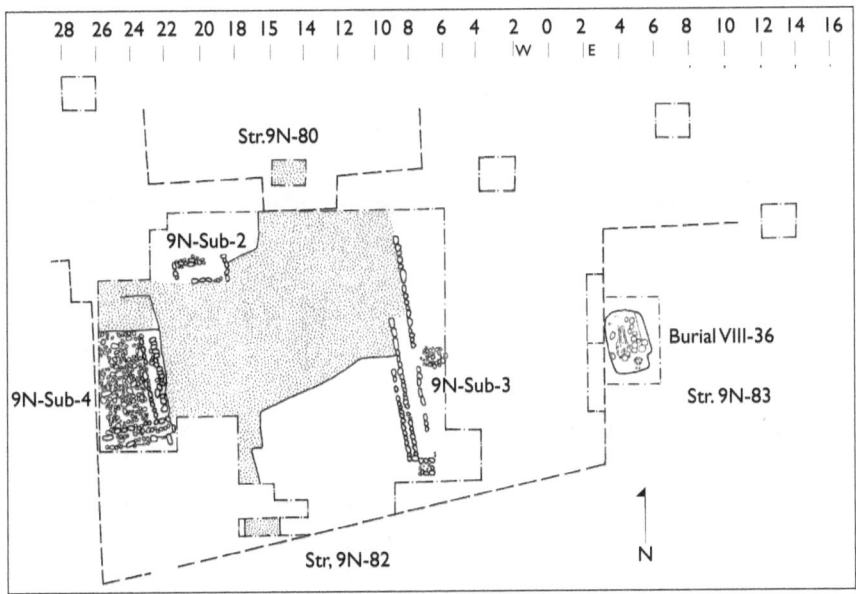

FIGURE 3.4

A plan map of the Acbi-phase courtyard in Group 9N-8, showing the location of features mentioned in the text. (Drawing by B. Fash)

beneath it encountered only sterile alluvial fill, showing that the stones did not function as a covering for any kind of offering or grave.

Just as the Late Classic Structure 9N-82 (the House of the Bacabs [Webster, ed., 1989]) was modeled after Acropolis Structure 10L-22 (W. Fash 1989; Sanders 1989), I believe that Structure 9N-sub-3 was designed to replicate Yax Structure on a smaller scale. The courtyard of Structure 9N-82 was built directly above the Acbi courtyard under discussion, showing that the replication occurred both at the beginning of the dynasty in the fifth century and during the reign of the last ruler in the late eighth century. Particularly important in this regard is Julia Hendon's (2000) work on storage in Group 9N-8 and its use in constructing collective memory, just as the public works in the Principal Group were designed for this purpose, albeit on a much larger scale. This kind of replication is precisely what Geertz documented for the Negara and what many scholars argue was the pattern for the Maya as well (Bricker 1981; Vogt 1969, 1983ax). The religious specialist laid to rest in Burial VIII-36 was sent to the afterlife with accoutrements in keeping with his profession, the most important of which are similar to those found in the Motmot cist. Likewise, his circular feature was found directly west of the building, mimicking that of the Motmot floor marker.

Given the replication of the compound, the circular ritual feature, the east-side ritual structure, and the funerary offerings of Burial VIII-36 from those of Motmot, the question arises whether the occupant was a secondary lord whose status derived from that of his own lineage (Sanders' [1989] and Webster's [chapter 2 in this volume] lineage model,) or "house," or was he a subject—even an offspring—of the royal line who was specifically assigned his status and duties in the eastern end of what was to become the kingdom's urban core (following Webster's Hawaiian model)? Of particular interest in this connection is the central pendant of Burial VIII-36's jade necklace, carved in the form of a bird with a three-pronged wing shaped like a *yax* sign. The bird's head bears the beak of a macaw carved on one side and that of a smaller-beaked bird (such as a quetzal) on the other. These features, taken together, can be read as *Yax K'uk' Mo'*, but whether this pendant is a family heirloom or merely a reminder of Copán's founder is a matter of conjecture.

Another large valley settlement where numerous monuments replicate those of the Principal Group is Morley's Group 9, the large settlement with at least one immense pyramid built on the alluvial spur where the modern town of Copán is situated (see figure 3.1). Altar T, with its crocodile and mythological figures, was discovered by Alfred Maudslay in the 1880s in the main square of the village Copán Ruinas, amidst numerous mounds. Nearby were other inscribed, freestanding monuments we can now assign to the reign of Ruler 16 (Stela 8, Altar U), as well as others commissioned by Rulers 13 (Altar S), 11 (Stela 7), and 9 (Stela 9), and even the battered remains of monuments that referred to rulers prior to K'inich Yax K'uk' Mo' (Stela 24; Stuart 1992). In analyzing the monuments from this area, Morley (1920) concluded that this locus was the first center of the Classic Maya tradition in the Copán Valley, predating the one established at the Principal Group (see also Stuart 1992, 1997, 2004).

Although it was once thought that the texts of Altars T and U might refer to brothers of the last Copán ruler, Yax Pasaj, Stuart (1997) now believes that those names are references to patron gods of the Copán polity. Thus, these late eighth-century monuments, as well as Stela 7 (bearing a portrait and history of Ruler 10), would seem to be monuments in honor of the ruling dynasty, not a rival, upstart lineage. Here it would appear that we are dealing not so much with replication by other noble households, but rather with a secondary regal-ritual center of the ruling lineage during the entire span of the dynasty of K'inich Yax K'uk' Mo'. That said, other large residential groups in this area of the town were likely those of other noble households.

In addition to these loci, there surely were others where offshoot members of the royal family, or of the noble households who may or may not have been related to the royal family by marriage, set up shop during the Early Classic period. Indeed, every Type 4 elite residential compound in the alluvial bottomlands of the eastern end of the Copán Valley has evidence for occupation, if not elaborate construction, during the Early Classic period (W. Fash 1983b, 1983c). As more investigations proceed in the foothills north of the alluvial bottomlands (Ashmore 1991; Maca 2002), we are coming to appreciate the time depth and complexity of the sites in that physiographic zone, which I have long argued (W. Fash 1983a) was an integral part of the urban core. Group 9 clearly has a long occupation sequence, certainly going back to Bijac times and likely earlier. Group 9J-5, located 1 km west-northwest of the Principal Group (see figure 3.1, #7), has Acbi-phase constructions (Maca 2002). Its hilltop neighbor, Group 9J-4, has earthen architecture that goes back to Bijac times (Carballo 1997). It seems to have been abandoned during the Early Classic Period and only sporadically visited (and not lived on) during the Late Classic period, perhaps owing in some manner to its associations with the political order displaced by K'inich Yax K'uk' Mo'.

But why did noble households in the Copán Valley emphasize Maya religious, artistic, and literary traditions? The essentially non-Maya nature of the domestic ceramic assemblage from the Classic-period Copán Valley has been commented on by scholars, beginning with John Longyear and continuing to the present (Bill 1997; Leventhal, Demarest, and Willey 1987; Longyear 1952; Urban and Schortman 1987; Viel 1983, 1993a, 1993b; Willey et al. 1994). In this connection,

WILLIAM L. FASH

Kathryn Josserand and Nicholas Hopkins (2002) have recently provided us with a very intriguing analogy to ponder. Medieval European royal courts in many countries that spoke decidedly different languages all adopted the French language, architectural tradition, and parlor styles to display their status and high culture. Josserand and Hopkins point out that many Classic Maya centers were situated in non-Maya enclaves (Quiriguá, in the decidedly non-Maya Lower Motagua Valley, immediately comes to mind) yet engaged in ostentatious displays of the court language, culture, and architecture that separated their occupants from the people surrounding them.

Approaching this same topic from a different vantage point, René Viel (1999b) has offered a provocative contribution to this discussion, based on the pectorals of the rulers and nobles portrayed on Altar Q and the Structure 10L-11 step. Viel hypothesizes that two competing political factions in the Copán Valley shared royal power, originally alternating on the throne in a hierarchical fashion but subsequently (beginning in the reign of Ruler 13) sharing power in a diarchy. He refers to these two groups as "a war faction" and "a fertility faction," and there is at least a suggestion that the two groups may be ethnically based. He further proposes concrete ways—including spatial analysis—in which this might be tested in the valley's residential groups and wards. Likewise, the toponyms on the proposed council house (B. Fash, chapter 4 in this volume) may also provide clues about the most important power players on the stage of Classic Copán. It is hoped that future investigations will reveal that these place names were recorded in stone inscriptions at their home base, as at Group 10L-2 on the south flank of the Acropolis (Andrews and Bill, chapter 7 in this volume; Andrews and Fash 1992).

Between the data sets that Viel (1999b) proposes and those that epigraphy and iconography can and will continue to provide, we may look forward to the day when more of the powerful nobility and their social context is illuminated and, equally important, the ethnicity of the valley occupants—both within and between the city's various wards—is clarified. The forms in which the valley elites replicated monuments and complexes within the Principal Group should also be of great interest, particularly if one can isolate non-Maya components in both the regal-ritual center and the valley, as Andrea Gerstle (1988) has suggested is possible in Patio D of Group 9N-8 in Las Sepulturas.

Cassandra Bill (1997) has provided the alternative view that the concentration of Ulua polychrome pottery in Patio D owes to chronological factors (that is, a very late occupation). If so, the differences that Gerstle (1988) noted in the architecture and burial patterns there may be attributable to late, evolving mortuary and architectural practices instead of ethnic differences.

After the establishment of the ball court, Yax/Motmot Structures, and the Mini-Acropolis of the South by K'inich Yax K'uk' Mo' and his illustrious successor Ruler 2, the regal-ritual center of Copán grew at a rapid clip. Sharer and his colleagues have demonstrated a tremendous burst of construction in the middle and latter half of the fifth century, including elaborate horizontal and vertical additions to the original nucleus. Indeed, it is beginning to appear as if nearly as much building took place during that relatively short span as did in the ensuing three centuries of dynastic rule in Copán. This is, of course, in keeping with comparative anthropological studies of preindustrial states. After the formation of the state, there is always a tremendous burst of monument construction and public works, as seen in Mesopotamia, Egypt, the Andes, and, of course, in Mesoamerica at the sites of Monte Albán and Teotihuacan (Feinman and Marcus, eds., 1998).

After its establishment around 9.0.0.0.0, the regal-ritual center of Copán seems to have prospered and grown through the sixth, seventh, and eighth centuries, to judge from archaeological and epigraphic data from both the site center and the residential areas of the supporting population. As the tunneling into the Acropolis has progressed, we have come to appreciate the vision and achievements of rulers who had heretofore been known only by an occasional reference in the Hieroglyphic Stairway and their portraits and name glyphs on Altar Q. The death heads that composed the centerpiece of the imposing roof crest of Rosalila seem to show some continuity with the theme of death and sacrifice that was carved on the final-phase Structure 10L-16-1st, with its skull stairway and numerous Tlaloc masks (B. Fash 1992a). This continuity in use of ritual space through time for Rosalila and Structure 10L-16 fits well with what we know of other parts of the Acropolis, where there were sequent constructions of the same type at the loci of the ball court and Structure 10L-22. Andrews and Bill (chapter 7 in this volume) make a similar case for buildings in the royal residential area on the south flank of the Acropolis. Table 3.1 presents a partial vista of the kinds of buildings and of activities that took place in the regal-ritual center at the end of the Late Classic period.

Both the PAC I and subsequent PAC II and Pennsylvania State University investigations in the Copán pocket recovered abundant evidence of a dramatic population increase during the seventh century (Webster, chapter 2 in this volume). As noted, a potentially illuminating research problem for the future is to test whether replication of the types posited here can be documented for other elite residences in the valley and to try to document their relations (biological and otherwise) with the contemporary rulers. Given the universal desire on the part of the Maya and other Mesoamerican nobility to mark their status and prestige through the acquisition and display of sumptuary goods and elaborate ceremonies—à la Negara—there was very likely trouble in this river city by the eighth century because of the relatively small confines and soil resources of the Copán Valley (Webster, chapter 2 in this volume). For all its enchanting aspects, inequality began to take its toll on the landscape and people of ancient Copán.

ELITE COMPETITION, EMULATION OF ROYALTY, AND POLITICAL DISINTEGRATION DURING THE LATE CLASSIC PERIOD

The model of elite competition leading to overexploitation of land resources and the downfall of divine kingship is one that the author has long sustained (W. Fash 1983b, 1983c, 1986, 1988, 1991). This model corresponds more clearly with the lineage model than the Hawaiian model in the useful comparisons presented in Webster's chapter 2 in this volume. In like fashion, the house model would also neatly explain increasing competition among the groups trying to build up patrimony for their particular house, as well as decreasing collaboration with the center. In earlier writings, I went so far as to suggest that the downfall of Copán was precipitated by a nobles' revolt rather than the peasant uprising envisioned by Eric Thompson (W. Fash 1983b, 1986). A number of Mayanists have considered and expanded on the theme of elite competition, which the discipline as a whole has generally accepted.

TABLE 3.1

Final-Phase Copán Acropolis Building Designations, Imagery, and Functions

Structure	Informal Designation	Imagery	Proposed Function
10L-9, 10L-10	Ball court	Solar, Hero Twins, maize	Ball games and feasts
10L-16	Temple 16	Founder, Tlaloc (central Storm god), skulls	Founder's temple
10L-18	Temple 18	Dance, war, underworld, maize	Funerary temple for final ruler
10L-20	Temple 20	Killer bats, blood scrolls	Jail for captives
10L-22	Temple 22	Mountain, maize, water, stone ruler portraits, cosmogram	"Temple of Meditation" *
10L-22A	Structure 22A	Mats, place names, "White-flower house," nonroyal figures, the ruler on a jaguar mat	Council house
10L-25	Platform	None	Dance platform for council house
10L-26	Hieroglyphic Stairway	Hieroglyphic steps and temple, Tlaloc, owls, shells flints, shields, rulers portrayed as warriors	Dynastic monument
10L-29	Structure 29	Celestial, sun disks, clouds	Ancestor shrine
10L-32	Structure 32	Chac masks, water lilies, portraits of ruler and nobles	Administrative/ water temple
10L-230	Temple 26 Annex	Skulls, fleshless long bones, *na* (house) signs	Charnel house

*Trik 1939; ruler's palace (Baudez 1989; Sanders 1989.)

The political instability resulting from status competition in the urban core and nearby Copán pocket elite-lineage compounds would have greatly exacerbated the problems presented by the breakaway of more distant satellite centers such as Quiriguá, Río Amarillo, and Los Higos, as postulated by Marcus (1976, 1992a, 1993). Robert Sharer and I (1991) therefore suggested that the Copán polity's collapse should be seen as a three-stage process: first, a decentralization of political authority; second, the breakdown of centralized (dynastic) rule; and finally, third, a depopulation of the Copán Valley in the ensuing decades.

Perhaps the single most useful and gratifying aspect of the Late Classic settlements preserved on the modern landscape of the Copán Valley is that the relative social status of a site's occupants can be perceived at a glance. The number and construction volume of the buildings that formed a particular residential group were seen from Willey and Leventhal's initial survey in 1975 to reflect the socioeconomic position of that site's residents. This observation led to the development of a typology of settlement and, through it, social ranking (Willey and Leventhal 1979). Subsequent broad horizontal excavations of residential sites by Willey's project (Willey, Leventhal, and Fash 1978) and Sanders' and Webster's (PAC II and subsequent Pennsylvania State University) projects (Sanders, ed., 1986; Webster, ed., 1989, 1992) have served to corroborate the typology. The quality of the architecture, graves and tombs, and associated domestic artifacts generally corresponds quite well with the typology-based assessments of a site before its excavation. Something of a surprise was the presence of inscriptions in the large, elite Type 3 and Type 4 sites in the urban ward of Las Sepulturas, which, of course, amply confirmed the social predictions of the initial settlement typology.

Indeed, the abundance of inscribed hieroglyphic thrones, altars, and facade sculptures containing both texts and pictorial imagery in the residential compounds of the Copán Valley nobility indicates that status competition was highly visible and very important business. Surveys, test probes, and broad horizontal excavations have shown that all of the Type 4 sites and probably at least half of the Type 3 sites in the Copán pocket were embellished with architectural sculpture, including, in many cases, elaborate full-figure hieroglyphic benches. Sanders (1989) pointed out the similarities of Structure 9N-82 to Structure 10L-

22 in the Acropolis in terms of overall layout and in the presence of an elaborate hieroglyphic bench with cosmological imagery. Using comparative anthropological evidence, he made a compelling case that Structure 9N-82 served as the palace of the head of household who was the patriarch of Group 9N-8, allowing him a backdrop suitable to the task of administering his lands and subjects.

The case for replication of functions between Patio A of Group 9N-8 and the East Court of the Acropolis is strengthened by the stairs that lined three of the four sides of Patio A, just as such steps lined three of the four sides of the final-phase East Court. Furthermore, the two jaguar heads found in Webster and Abrams' excavation of the west-side building of Patio A (Structure 9N-81 [Webster, Fash, and Abrams 1986]) have a larger and more imposing counterpart in the two jaguars that frame the stairs on the west side of the East Court of the Acropolis. Altar W' is now known to have been placed in the central part of Patio A (Webster 1989a), just as altars were set into the floor in front of the Jaguar Stairway in the East Court. John Stephens' (1841) interpretation of Copán's Great Plaza as a Circus Maximus was the first Western recognition that patios lined with steps, with sculptured icons in the plaza, were areas designed for public spectacles.

The theatre state model, of course, bolsters these interpretations and encourages us to imagine the kinds of pageantry that might have taken place in these settings (W. Fash 1998). That even some relatively small sites and patios have such stairways, such as Patio C of Group 9M-18, is particularly significant. Structure 9M-192 forms the north side of this patio. With its broad frontal stairway and perishable superstructure, this building is similar in form (and presumably function) to Structure 10L-30 of Patio A, Group 10L-2. Andrews and Bill (chapter 7 in this volume) see Courtyard A as the primary area for public ritual in Group 10L-2 and see Structure 10L-30 as a nonresidential building likely used as a dance platform. This is precisely the architecture we should expect to find if the same kind of public pageantry and ritual were taking place in Copán as that documented for competing elite lineages (or houses) of the theatre states of Indonesia and Southeast Asia.

Returning to our best-documented case for replication of functions between the uppermost (Type 4 group) nobility and the royal family in the regal-ritual center, in Group 9N-8 the central figure in the facade of Structure 9N-82 C 1st carries a central headdress motif similar to those seen on the most nearly contemporaneous ruler portrait in the Principal Group, Stela N (W. Fash 1986). Precisely the same headgear is worn by Yax Pasaj in his portrait on Structure 10L-32, in the building whose layout and functions most closely correspond with those of Structure 9N-82 (B. Fash, chapter 4, and Andrews and Bill, chapter 7, in this volume). For the noble compounds not immediately adjacent to the Principal Group, the importance of their palace/temple compound was no doubt enhanced if one of the two sacbeob led directly to it or passed next to it, as was the case for Groups 8N-11, 9M-16, 9J-4, and 10K-4. By these and other means, nobles could replicate the royal palace/temple compound and perquisites of rank and, via the roadway, demonstrate their interrelatedness (Kurjack 1974) and physical linkages to the members of the royal family.

Sarah Jackson and David Stuart (2001) have recently elucidated a pattern wherein individual rulers chose their own *aj k'uhun* (one who keeps things, one who venerates things), likely a keeper of records and, apparently, especially a recorder or keeper of tribute goods. They point out that in the inscriptions from Structures 9N-8 and 9M-146, different individuals are recognized as the aj k'uhun of Rulers 15 and 16. They believe that this marks that particular office as a highly personalized one—wherein the ruler chose the individual best suited to the task—instead of a post that was tied to a particular family or other corporate group. Even more intriguing is that Ruler 16 apparently practiced a Period Ending ritual at the home of the aj k'uhun of his predecessor, Ruler 15, at Structure 9M-146. How are we to interpret this visit and the consecration of a hieroglyphic bench in honor of the old keeper? As recognition for a job well done? Or as a measure of respect accorded someone who perhaps knew too much and needed to be appeased? In either case, these historical details give us much to ponder concerning the roles and aspirations of the literate nobility in Late Classic Copán.

Noble families residing outside the Copán pocket also signaled their importance by the use of hieroglyphic and pictorial sculptures. In two instances, these monuments included inscriptions in which the local lineage heads boast their own ajaw titles, to judge from Los Higos Stela 1 and Río Amarillo Altars 1 and 2. Marcus (1992a) read these lordly titles as emblem glyphs proper and used that interpretation to posit that all the satellite centers of Copán broke away during the eighth century. Again, the comparative anthropological data and evidence from other parts of Mesoamerica support the logic behind her conclusions. In the advanced seminar discussions, it was noted that neither of these sites' nobles used the *k'ul* (holy) title in these lordly appellatives, calling into question whether these glyphs, in and of themselves, signaled political independence from the old capital.

Unlike Quiriguá, which declared itself politically independent (Marcus 1976) and used its own true (*k'ul ajaw*) emblem glyph thereafter, the Río Amarillo and Los Higos lineage heads seem to have been more modest in their public pronouncements. The use of pictorial imagery on Structure 5 of Río Amarillo that is virtually identical to the imagery of Structures 10L-29 in Group 10L-2 and Structures 10L-16 and 10L-22 in the Principal Group (Barbara Fash, personal communications 1994; Saturno 2000), as well as the employment of the format and decorative elements of an older Copán monument (Stela 1) for the Los Higos stela, also stands in contrast to the post-independence Quiriguá stelae. The post–A.D. 738 Quiriguá stelae are designed to be different from those of Copán in their distinctive size, style, and costume elements, such as the use of the Manikin Scepter instead of the ceremonial bar.

Although their prestige and their programs of enchanting inequality shine through clearly, the degree to which Río Amarillo and Los Higos were politically and economically independent from Copán remains a question. More and better archaeological data are necessary to address this issue. Equally important questions are whether these centers were established in the fifth century or later and whether the lineages were set up there by the king (following the Hawaiian model) or established independently by aspiring lineage heads (following the lineage model). At Río Amarillo, William Saturno (2000) believes that the initial ties to the Copán dynasty were strong but that by the time Altar 2 was dedicated, Río Amarillo was making reference to a larger sphere of contact in its hieroglyphic texts.

The nine place-names on the facades of the council house of Structure 10L-22A give us a clue for discerning relative degrees of political authority among the kingdom's competing noble lineages. The identification of Group 10L-2 as one of the localities cited on the council house (Andrews and Fash 1992; Andrews and Bill, chapter 7, and B. Fash, chapter 4, in this volume) is encouraging in this regard. Barbara Fash believes that a number of other sites are the most likely candidates for such seats in the valley, particularly those carrying specific kinds of place-related niches, the T.600 (crossed-batons or founder [Schele 1992a]) sign, and Mexican year–sign imagery, such as Group 8N-11 (see figure 3.1, #8), Rastrojón (see figure 3.1, #9), Ostumán (see figure 3.1, #10), and Río Amarillo. It is equally encouraging that three other sites with sculpture monuments (Groups 9N-8, 9M-12, and 9M-18) provided no evidence of icons or glyphs that correspond with the toponyms and associated figural imagery from the council house. Were every site in the valley with sculpture to have something that tied it to Structure 10L-22A, we would have entirely too many councilors.

This leads us to the structural problem that the burgeoning elite lineages posed for the Copán kingdom. There were far too many eligible adult males for the available political offices, and the jockeying for position among the elite lineages that aspired to greater glory is thought by many of us to have been a major factor in the weakening of centralized authority in the kingdom. This situation served to undermine the authority and power—whether perceived or real—of the king himself. To recall a page from the Negara case, "in particular, the most immediate associates of the king, the other great *punggawas*—jealous kin, grudging lieutenants, near equals, and implicit rivals—were concerned to see that the king's ritual deactivation was literal as well, that he became so imprisoned in the ceremony of rule that his practical dependence on them was maximized and their own possibilities of display were enhanced" (Geertz 1980:123). The sculptures and public-seating accommodations in the residential compounds spanning the social spectrum from Types 2 to 4 in the Copán Valley show the importance that display and pageantry held in eighth-century Copán and likely elsewhere. This elite competition made for chronic instability throughout the Maya area during the closing century of the Classic era, as shown by the number of new regal-ritual centers formed by disgruntled members of the aristocracy in the old capitals and the frequency and intensity of the wars among all the major players and many minor ones (Martin and Grube 2000).

We must also address the issue of why the system failed to recover if we are to understand the Classic Maya collapse (Shimkin 1973). In the case of the Negara, the incursions of the Dutch and the larger world political economy were the main reasons cited by Geertz for its downfall. For the Maya area overall, Will Andrews (personal communications 1990; Andrews and Sabloff 1986) sees a similar role for the political economy of Terminal Classic Mesoamerica. Andrews posits that the more economically competitive and strategically agile elites of western Mesoamerica were clearly superior to the weakened and tradition-bound aristocracies of the southern Maya lowlands, whose economies and very cities were in decline and who could not agree on the rules of engagement in war (Demarest 1992b).

For an older kingdom like Copán, the chronic political instability of the competing elites within the valley was heightened by the manner in which Quiriguá won its independence. Doubtless, the famous feat of K'ak' Tiliw Chan Yopat gave encouragement to the other far-removed satellite centers with designs on secession, posing increasingly difficult challenges for a king whose authority rested primarily on pageantry and a fragile consensus. Given this political context, the ecological problems caused by a maladaptive settlement pattern, overexploitation of marginal soils, and a resident population too large for the available cultivable fields (Webster, chapter 2 in this volume), the situation became unmanageable even for a ruler who survived to a ripe old age, as did Yax Pasaj. The termination of the royal line that began with K'inich Yax K'uk' Mo' was a dramatic case of success breeding failure and of short-term goals and aspirations leading to long-term, insurmountable problems. The failure to recover from the succession crisis that followed the death of Yax Pasaj shows the degree to which the overall system had broken down in the Copán Valley by A.D. 822. The ceremonies and pageants launched by K'inich Yax K'uk' Mo' and Ruler 2 at the beginning of the ninth baktun proved increasingly difficult to sustain as the start of the next Great Cycle approached. Inequality could no longer enchant the people, and the Classic Maya political system in Copán came to an end.

4

Iconographic Evidence for Water Management and Social Organization at Copán

Barbara W. Fash

Many models seeking to define the parameters of Classic Maya society and the structure of its political organization have reconstructed patterns of subsistence and economics and have weighed the role of ideology in its rise and fall. This chapter examines the theme of water management in ancient Copán by combining components of ideology, cultural ecology, and materialism. Using a wide range of anthropological material, including reference to the natural environment, settlement studies, iconographic symbolism through the analysis of its sculptural facades, and sociopolitical and ethnographic research, I attempt to establish a link between these approaches to shed light on the role of water management in ancient Copán's political organization. Pertinent examples from across Mesoamerica are referenced and comparative material has been incorporated from Southeast Asia and South America to place interpretations of the Maya data into a wider cultural perspective.

The wealth of iconographic material available at Copán enables us to study the interplay between water symbolism and water management, a relationship not necessarily visually evident at other sites. A fundamental resource, water served as a link between the sacred realm of Maya cosmology and the functional domain of technology and politics. My studies of Copán sculpture lead me to believe that three iconographic motifs can be isolated to reveal the relationship of water symbolism to the political structure of water management systems in Mesoamerica: (1) the *cauac* or *tun* sign, as a drip-water stone, (2) the stepped niche or half-quatrefoil, a motif found throughout Mesoamerica and generally identified as a cave or mountain symbol, and (3) the water-lily headdress. Of the many sculptural themes available, I chose water symbolism as the focus for this contribution because I believe that its manipulation and management formed one of the basic structural relationships at the core of social organization in ancient Copán. The evidence from Copán's carved stone sculpture suggests that a complex organization of communal groups in the Copán Valley exercised a direct role in the central government of the polity in Classic times. Additionally, the public architectural contexts of these symbols were meant for general viewing in an effort to sanction the ruling elite and their system of governing (Hendon 1994; Schele and Miller 1986).

Early on, scholars noted that water resources and their manipulation were a conspicuous element of Maya settlement and subsistence (Flannery, ed., 1982; Hammond 1978; Harrison and Turner 1978; Matheny 1976; Puleston 1977; Puleston and Puleston 1971; Rands 1953, 1955; Sanders 1957; E. H. Thompson 1897; J. E. S. Thompson 1951; Turner 1974). Although early work touched on the need to explore ecological questions and community, as of 1956 the relationship between community and center had not yet been satisfactorily explained (Willey 1956:107). Significantly, Evon Vogt (1956:173–174) judged the concept of "settlement pattern" as a means for geographer, archaeologist, and ethnologist to discuss common problems concerning ecological determinants of human settlement patterns and the interrelationships between these patterns and other cultural features. Puleston and Puleston (1971:336) noted that "the necessity of organizing labor to carry out large public projects such as the construction of reservoirs may well have been a catalyst for the development of social stratification and the conceptualization of the state." Initially, agricultural hydraulic systems were a favored focus, but more recently emphasis has shifted to understanding the variety of human-engineered water systems designed and managed throughout the Maya area (Rice 1996;

Scarborough 1993, 2003; Scarborough, Connolly, and Ross 1994). The current study introduces iconographic evidence from Copán to examine the extent and implications of water management in ancient Maya societies, expanding on earlier iconographic studies by J. Eric, S. Thompson, Robert Rands, and Dennis and Olga Puleston.

Comparative studies demonstrate that when a society reaches certain levels of urbanization and sociopolitical complexity, it will have as part of its structure a system of management, either locally or state controlled, that coordinates and operates the mechanisms of subsistence (Geertz 1980; Harrison 1978; Palerm 1955; Sanders and Price 1968; Webster, Sanders, and van Rossum 1992). Whether the Classic Maya management systems were state controlled or locally controlled is still debated (see also Webster, chapter 2 in this volume). Yet, recent interest in water management studies is helping to unravel the complexities of the diverse systems at work in the Classic Maya landscape (Lucero 1999, 2002; Rice 1996; Scarborough and Isaac 1993; Scarborough, Schoenfelder, and Lansing 1999). Corporate systems functioning today among the living Maya show continuity since the time of the conquest, suggesting that these levels of managerial systems were well developed in Classic times (Farriss 1984; Vogt 1969, 1983b).

"Hydraulic" societies arise from successful technologies designed to control that most essential element of existence, water (Gelles 1990, 1996; Mabry, ed., 1996; Matheny 1978; Puleston 1976; Scarborough 1993; Wittfogel 1957, 1974). Although the Maya settled in a wide range of environments throughout eastern Mesoamerica and are not considered a hydraulic society in the traditional sense, their dependence on a reliable water source was as basic as any other culture's (Scarborough 1994, 2003). Depending on the different environmental conditions for water availability and population needs, they developed a variety of strategies that enabled them to achieve maximum utilization of their water resources in conjunction with agrarian systems (Ashmore 1984; Hammond 1978; Harrison and Turner 1978; Matheny 1978; Puleston 1977; Puleston and Puleston 1971; Scarborough 1993, 1994; Siemens and Puleston 1972; Turner 1978a, 1978b). Straightforward ecological and technological explanations for Maya water (and agrarian) management need to be complemented, however, by an awareness of the influential roles of ritual and ideology (Demarest 1992a). Matheny (1978:210) noted that "development of water systems was pragmatic but in some instances may have contained an element of the esoteric; this element may have been more important than is currently realized."

Research and in-depth analyses of the subsistence bases for the ancient Maya (Flannery, ed., 1982; Harrison and Turner 1978; Sanders 1973; Webster, chapter 2 in this volume) have, in many cases, been isolated from the ideological and ritual complexes that were manifested in a "hidden ecologically adaptive rationale" (Demarest 1992a:5). Although, as Robert Carneiro (1992:179) states, "what motivated people to act in new and different ways need not be symbolic," ideology and ritual validated the sociopolitical control and management of both land and water environs after these were established (Carneiro 1992:193). While concentrating on defining specific water configurations and their individual elements, studies of Maya art and architecture have also, to varying degrees, comprehensively addressed the subsistence systems they represented, rather than separate the two (Bassie-Sweet 1991; Coggins 1983; Hellmuth 1982, 1987b; Puleston 1977; Rands 1953, 1955; Reilly 1994; Schele 1979; Schele and Freidel 1990; Schele and Miller 1986; Taube 1992). These studies have succeeded in showing how the rulers' power was validated within a larger worldview defined, in part, by imagery. Disillusioned with what I viewed as an overly "cosmic" or "shaman-king" approach to many iconographic studies, I became intrigued when it appeared that symbol systems and ideology in the material record could inform us of the social processes at Copán. Rather than become caught up in the "chicken and egg" argument about whether ideology or ecological factors were the driving force in cultural behavior, I sought to reconstruct the activities and cultural developments brought about by the interplay between the two. Whether or not people accept my iconographic interpretations and social model, the mere existence of a wide variety of water-related visual representations in Copán tells us that water had more than just a functional role in this society. The symbols and the rituals performed to sustain these concepts in the Maya world relate to a system of political symbolism that can be documented for complex cultures globally (Cohen 1979).

Others have emphasized the crucial role of ideology in the rise and fall of the Classic Maya (Coe 1981; Demarest 1992a, 1992b; W. Fash 1983b, 1991, chapter 3 in this volume; Willey 1977), yet they call for

Iconographic Evidence for Water Management

more persuasive evidence to help explain how managerial systems functioned in conjunction with social, political, and economic adaptations among the ancient Maya (Demarest 1992a; Willey 1977). This chapter seeks to move beyond the focus on cosmic water ideology that the rulers embodied, to explore "ritualized ecological management," which, I hope, will broaden our views of Maya social institutions within this ideological framework.[1] Since the initial research and writing of this paper in 1994, other productive attention has been given to this topic (Beach and Dunning 1997; Dunning 1992; Dunning et al. 1999; Lucero 1999, 2002; Scarborough 1998), all of which enhances our understanding of the complexities of water management and brings us closer toward a consensus regarding the vital role it played in ancient Maya societies.

Water rituals in concert with hydraulic technology that began with the Olmec civilization on the Gulf Coast were further developed throughout Mesoamerica, with various systems remaining in continuous use until the Spanish Conquest (Angulo 1993; Carballal and Hernandez n.d.; Coe 1981; Cyphers 1999; Hansen 1991; Harrison 1993; Neely 2001; Ortiz and Rodríguez 1989, 1999; Reilly 1994; Rodríguez and Ortiz 1997). John L. Stephens (1841:404) noted during his journey that water was the most valuable possession in Yucatan. Landowners who invested much time and many resources in procuring water and maintaining tanks and reservoirs were in a position of power over the native population.

Ancient Mesoamerican cities and ceremonial complexes can be viewed as architectural replicas of the sacred natural landscape (Benson 1985; Broda, Carrasco, and Matos 1987; Schele and Freidel 1990; Vogt 1981a). The pyramids were mountains that provided an axis of communication with the gods and spirits; the courtyards surrounding them were the valleys and depressions that collected runoff, thereby creating shallow, watery ponds. In some cases, sites were surrounded by moats or built on islands to place temples in the center of this cosmovision, symbolically floating on the primeval waters of creation. Nahuatl terms recorded from the Aztec in the sixteenth-century chronicles reveal how the water-mountain concept remained central to the architectural program into the Postclassic; *altepetl*, a term for *village* or *community*, translates as "mountain of water" or "mountain filled with water" (Bierhorst 1985; Broda, Carrasco, and Matos 1987:93; López Austin 1978, 1997; Stark 1999).

Expanding on previous analyses of sculpture and architecture throughout the Copán Valley (Andrews and Fash 1992; Baudez 1983; B. Fash 1992a, 1992b; B. Fash et al. 1992; W. Fash 1989; Webster et al. 1998) and in an effort to "combine ideology with the study of ecology, economic, and political factors involved in culture change" (Demarest 1992a:7), the research presented here explores how water assumed political significance when, as a sacred cultural concept, it was augmented with technical hydraulic knowledge. The iconographic messages the ancient Maya displayed in their public and ritual spaces are still effective and explicit enough to transcend the centuries, helping "to demonstrate how ideology may be 'reconstructed' from the archaeological record" (Willey 1977). It is hoped that the Copán facade sculpture sample may prove significant and that its interpretation may eventually shed additional light on the meaning and use of these symbols at other sites in the Maya area and Mesoamerica.

WATER AND SETTLEMENTS

Located in the mountains of the Southeast Maya zone, the Copán Valley today has an abundance of water sources, unlike the karstic terrain of the southern lowlands and the semiarid landscapes of the northern lowlands, partially explaining why water management at water-rich sites such as Copán was overlooked until recently. Common sense and settlement studies tell us that people locate near a permanent water source. In addition to the natural springs, permanent water in Copán was available from stream and river sources, mountain drainages, and *aguadas* (natural depressions) dispersed along the floodplain (Turner et al. 1983). Water from these sources was potable during the dry season, but the river-dependent sources would have become murky and undrinkable at the height of the rainy season (Abrams 1994; B. Fash 1992a). Reservoir water sources would be less affected by this problem and could continue to supply drinking water and aquatic resources year-round. Reliance on springs and reservoirs is found in the water-rich environment of the Olmec for the same reasons (Cyphers 1999).

Consideration of water's importance for determining settlement in the Copán Valley was noted by William Fash in his proposal of the *sian*

ICONOGRAPHIC EVIDENCE FOR WATER MANAGEMENT

otot (equivalent to the Spanish *aldea*) as a social unit in the Copán polity (W. Fash 1983a). Ethnographer Charles Wisdom (1940:218) noted that aldeas are always located along streams, usually straddling them. If we look at the *sian otots* designated by Fash for Copán, their settlements generally cluster around major streams (Leventhal 1979, 1981; W. Fash 1983a). As is the case for Chorti clusters named for the stream they utilize (Wisdom 1940:217), in Copán most of the Type 4 groups (Willey and Leventhal 1979) outside the main center and the areas surrounding them are still known by the names of the main water sources running next to them: Comedero, Salamar, Petapilla, Titichón, and so on. Stuart and Houston (1994) find that Maya place names in the hieroglyphic texts frequently include a reference to water locales or "black holes." It is thought that during the Conquest, the Spanish confused names of rivers and mountains with towns (Chamberlain 1953:60), but ethnographic sources report that the natives made little distinction between the geographic features and place names (Vogt 1969; Wisdom 1940:217). From this we may infer that a sense of social distinctiveness developed among residential settlements situated nearby and using the same water sources.

ETHNOGRAPHIC EVIDENCE AND COMPARATIVE MATERIAL

Reviewing ethnographic data from the Maya area and comparative material from other regions has helped me to formulate a social model for water management in ancient Copán. It is evident from this investigation that water management has a major role in the social organization of cultures around the world. Evidence of the importance of water management in neighboring cultures encourages us not only to look for cosmological and functional equivalents among the ancient Maya, but also to ask why they would *not* be present. The following is a brief overview of the material I found most relevant to the Copán circumstances.

Zinacantan

The Zinacantan hamlet is a large settlement composed of *sna* (lineage-based) land holding groups and nonlineage-based water-hole groups (Vogt 1969). Several water-hole groups combine to form the hamlet, whose name is associated with a water feature. The water-hole group is a unified body comprising several smaller *sna* lineages sharing the same water source. Vogt (1969) postulates that water-hole groups have been an economic and social unit from at least Classic times. Two chosen representatives from the hamlet meet with the town president every week and perform administrative duties. The cooperative water-hole group mutually maintains its source; this includes annual cleaning and ritual offerings. The group elects a head with scribal skills to supervise construction work and maintenance, collect dues, and regulate the water-hole ceremonies performed twice a year. The water-hole ceremonies in Zinacantan villages are some of the numerous *k'in krus* ceremonies for the communities that involve shamans and male heads of households from several lineage groups (sna). In addition to cleaning rituals, offerings to the ancestors and "Earth Lord" are left along a circuit of mountainside cross shrines that includes the water source (Vogt 1969). Among the five classes of sacred natural features defined by Vogt, *vits* (mountain), *ch'en* (hole in the ground), and its subcategory *vo?* (active spring or water hole) figure most prominently (Vogt 1969:375,1981a).

The water-hole ceremonies in Zinacantan take place on May 1–3 and in October. A vestige of these rituals may still survive in Copán today. The Day of the Cross ceremony, now associated with the Catholic ritual calendar, is still celebrated on May 3rd in Copán and many places throughout Mesoamerica.[2] It also corresponds to the zenith passage of the sun for the first half of the year. The local padre in Copán heads a procession up the mountain to the large cross located on the top of Cerro de las Mesas, directly north and above the modern village. Women bring flowers to decorate the large cross (now of cement and painted green) and gourds of maize gruel to leave as offerings. People in town and in the surrounding hamlets erect small crosses in front of their homes and decorate them with flowers, following the Chorti custom (Wisdom 1940). They believe that if God is pleased by the offerings, he will send rain that afternoon.

In 1978 one of the Proyecto Arqueológico Copán Phase I (PAC I) randomly selected excavations in the valley was on the Cerro de las Mesas mountaintop. René Viel located artificial terraces and six depressions lined with stone, which he and geographers Billie Lee Turner and

William Johnson thought were for water use (Turner et al. 1983:115–116). Several depressions retained silt and water, and the geographers noted that these were near the *nacimientos de agua* and in humid contexts. A rough map of scattered mounds and one round "tower" are some of the unusual features found on the mountaintop (W. Fash 1983c:266–273). Instead of a defensive outpost, lookout, or residential settlement, I believe that the structures and features on the mountain were part of an ancient water shrine. This idea is strengthened by the existence of a modern cross at the summit, which overlooks the town, the valley proper, the Sesesmil basin, and the Ostuman pocket, and by the annual performance of a ceremony related to water, rain, and fertility at that spot.

Water-retention facilities and ritual shrines are found in neighboring culture areas within Honduras's modern borders. Reservoirs and ritual water features have been recorded from the Postclassic sites of Tenampua (Dixon 1987; Lunardi 1948:160; Popenoe 1936; Squier 1853, 1870) and Cerro Palenque (Joyce 1991). Joyce (1991:83) says that community development at Cerro Palenque, similar to Zinacantan, responded to economic factors such as exploitation of land and water, not solely along kinship lines.

Yucatan

Nancy Farriss's (1984) work in Yucatan offers further ethnographic support; she concludes that corporate Maya communities existed before the intervention of colonial rule. As the Maya adapted for survival under the Spanish, they drew up land deeds to protect their property. Colonial documents record that water holes (*hoyas, aguadas,* or *cenotes*) were particularly important features worth owning rights to (Farriss 1984:275). Some early land deeds also mention a section of territory, *chakan*, by the name of the cenote with which it was associated (Farriss 1984:276).

Like Zinacantan's water-hole rituals, Yucatecan ceremonies are tied to worship of Catholic saints and involve community groups that are "organized by territory, rather than lineage, occupation or some other principle" to support their specific saint cult collectively (Farriss 1984:330–331). A community is united by a shared interest in sustaining its saints. This common effort enables the community to maintain its identity while reinforcing the subjective alliance of territorial boundaries separating it from others. If, as noted above, these territories are defined primarily by their distance and association with a specific water source, then the water hole is essentially the base point for defining the geographic boundaries of a given community and the saints (in ancient times, "patron deities") associated with that water source.

Southeast Asia

Years ago, scholars began tapping the comparative resources of Southeast Asia and Indonesia, recognizing the numerous climatic and physical geographic traits they shared with Mesoamerica, as well as culture traits that gave rise to traditions with striking religious, architectural, and intellectual similarities (Bronson 1978; Coe 1957; Demarest 1992b; W. Fash, chapter 3 in this volume; Hall 1968; Willey and Shimkin 1974). In particular, the ancient Khmer city of Angkor in Southeast Asia provides comparative material in such architectural features as the catchment of sacred water from temple complexes into a vast reservoir system (Scarborough 2003). Natural water sources were imbued with sacred powers. Reservoirs, and the shrines and temples built near them, inherited this potency (Kramrisch 1946; Michell 1977; Stierlin 1970; Volwahsen 1969). Artificially constructed water sources had a variety of functions. They supplied clean water, served as fisheries and areas for garden cultivation, and were locales for ritual bathing. Without proper maintenance, such a system rapidly succumbs to the tropical environment. Today the unattended Khmer water system has created a considerable conservation problem (Hornik 1991).

At Copán, the occasional clogging of ancient drains causes water to back up into the plaza areas, not unlike the *thirtas* of Southeast Asia, demonstrating that with minimal effort, a courtyard could be blocked off and filled with water. George Byron Gordon (1893) recognized this curious aspect of the architectural layout in his first report on Copán: "All of the level places have regular and continuous slopes in some direction, generally towards the south, sufficient to throw off all the water, but in some cases it would be thrown into the very places where it would be least desirable to have it."

Others have looked at irrigation societies of Bali's *negaras* (classical theater-states) to help visualize the potential for water management among the Maya and ideology's role in its political development (Demarest 1992b; Lansing 1987, 1991; Scarborough 2003; Scarborough, Schoenfelder, and Lansing 1999). Fundamental to the organization of the negara is an elaborate public corporation called the *subak*, or "irrigation society" (Geertz 1980). Its members are the owners of terraces irrigated from a single watercourse. In addition to critical irrigation regulation, the subak conducts purification rituals, timed by the Balinese calendar and held at special rice fields and water-source temple shrines (Geertz 1980; Lansing 1987). A complex subak water-temple system to organize irrigation was necessary to ensure that planting and irrigation were rhythmically coordinated and produced optimum yield (Geertz 1980; Lansing 1991). Water-temple networks function as ecosystem regulators by "fulfilling a role in Balinese cosmology which places the instrumental logic of agricultural decisions in a wider religious context" (Lansing 1987:338).

South America
Physically closer to the Maya area than Southeast Asia, the ancient Andean cultures also shared a deeply rooted belief in the water source as a key element of their social systems. Irrigation and water management played a pivotal role in sociopolitical organization and cultural practices (Gelles 1990, 1996; Mitchell and Guillet, eds., 1994). Royal Inca estates had elaborate channels, reservoirs, and catchment basins (Hyslop 1990). In modern Andean communities, springs or other water sources are often considered to be places of the founding ancestors, and these tie families closely to their origins and ethnicity (Sherbondy 1982; Urton 1981). Water plays an important role in the quadripartite division of communities and is crucial to the definition of social versus nonsocial space (Urton 1981:45). The Inca of Cuzco established conceptual lines, or *ceques*, that functioned as "spatial reference points" for the royal divisions of their empire. Sherbondy (1994:74) found that the most important "water sources of the major irrigation canals in the Cuzco valley were *huacas* [shrines] located on the ceques assigned to the *panacas* or *ayllus* [local kinship groups] of royal descent, therefore entrusted with the care of the most critical water sources." A similar hierarchical order and management of vital water sources or reserves was likely at work in other New World cultures such as the Maya.

Barbara W. Fash

Origin myths of the ayllus point to the importance of ancestors for legitimizing the kinship group's rights to its land and waters (Sherbondy 1982:22–24). At the time of original settlement, ancestors emerged from water sources and claimed the site for their descendants. As in Zinacantan, ritual and labor projects unify people into a cohesive settlement, where ayllu groups form villages that are fundamental to Andean social and political organization (Sherbondy 1994:73).

WATER MOUNTAINS AND ARCHITECTURE

Throughout Mesoamerica, mountains and their caves are seen as the sources for the life-giving and powerfully sacred water the gods send to earth (López Austin 1978:62). For example, among the Lenca of western Honduras, the name *Celaque* for the highest sacred mountain in Honduras means "cradle of waters," being the source of eleven rivers. Maya architecture created an artificial landscape, with the pyramids representing mountains and the plazas representing valleys. One function of this artificial landscape was water catchment and retention (Beach and Dunning 1997; Harrison 1993; Scarborough 1993, 1996). At some sites, vast amounts of earth and clay were removed from large areas to form the fill for the pyramid-mountains; the resulting depressions gradually transformed into reservoirs or tanks (Harrison 1993; Scarborough 1993, 1996). Although excavations at virtually every major center in Mesoamerica have turned up evidence of drains, catchment features, or reservoirs, until recently "water management systems have been neglected in the Maya lowlands as an area of research interest" (Scarborough 1998). Previously, hydraulic studies in the Maya area focused on raised-field complexes and irrigation systems (Puleston 1976, 1977; Siemens and Puleston 1972; Turner 1978a, 1978b). If relics of irrigation technologies were not apparent, this was considered evidence that water management was not of consequence for that population. Yet it has been demonstrated that diverse systems of water management existed in the Maya area, making all regions of potential interest for their particular technological adaptations (Beach and Dunning 1997; Hansen 1991; Harrison 1993; Matheny 1978; Rice 1996; Scarborough 1993, 1996; Scarborough, Connolly, and Ross 1994; Scarborough et al. 1992). Recent studies have turned to look more intensely at still-water adaptations, particularly the carefully engineered reservoir/catchment-basin systems that relied on rainwater runoff from architectural constructions to replenish them with clear water. It is now recognized that during dry spells or periods of intensive rainfall in either water-poor or water-rich environments, silt-laden (rainy season) or dried-up (dry season) rivers and streams could become unreliable sources for drinking water. Reservoirs augmenting natural water sources improved this condition by ensuring a fresh water supply throughout the year.

PAC I investigations revealed numerous rectangular surface depressions suitable for water retention, making them excellent candidates for ancient reservoirs or well-managed lagoons (W. Fash 1983c:372; Turner et al. 1983:113–123). Karla Davis-Salazar (1994, 2001) later determined that ancient human modification to these lagoons and other natural features artificially altered them for use as water-retention facilities. Her extensive excavations found evidence indicating that ancient inhabitants increased the collection potential of these natural features without constructing stone-enclosed reservoirs. Although the lagoons did not contain a raised-field agricultural system, they could have constituted an aquatic habitat exploited by the ancient Copánecs for protein sources such as fish, snails, and freshwater shellfish and for cultivating edible and medicinal plants and supporting fruit trees year-round.

Davis-Salazar's study of the Copán water system also revealed a coexisting, dual set of adaptations:

1. The foothill villages and communities relied on specific water holes, mountain sources, or lagoons, accentuating the importance of shrines and ritual circuits.

2. The dense settlement around the floodplain *bajos* required organization and management revolving around reservoirs.

Carefully engineered water systems of catchment and runoff appear to have been in operation at Copán from the Early Classic period on, suggesting that they played an important role in cultural change over time. Drain channels within the Principal Group (Sharer, Miller, and Traxler 1992; Sharer et al., chapter 5 in this volume) and crisscrossing the landscape and residential units around it (Andrews and Fash 1992) can be dated in some instances to the Acbi phase (A.D.

400–600; Davis-Salazar 1994, 2001). The Acropolis contained three major catchment areas: the East Court, the West Court, and the Court of the Hieroglyphic Stairway.[3] The southerly flow of rainfall running off the smooth plaster surfaces into the plazas appears to have eventually emptied into a large reservoir in the El Bosque region. The West Court, marked by the presence of conch shells and Chak on the Reviewing Stand, has been interpreted as an underwater world (M. Miller 1986:83, 1988:161–162; Schele 1998). One might also consider that the enclosed plaza of the East Court with channels emptying east toward the river retained water, creating a shallow pond if the *ventanas* (corbeled drains) were sealed.[4]

Imagery on certain structures in the Principal Group suggests that the ancient Copánecs perceived the water that cascaded down the plastered roofs into internal pyramidal drains and out the mouths of sculptured earth and water deities as particularly sacred. This appears to be the case on Indigo Structure, a buried antecedent of Structure 10L-22, the fertility creation mountain (B. Fash 1992a, 1992b; Schele and Mathews 1998; Sharer, Miller, and Traxler 1992). The large masks spanning the lower registers of at least two sides of the structure have internal drains that empty through stone canals purposefully constructed to spew forth from the mouth region (figure 4.1).

WATER AND CAVE SYMBOLISM AND ITS ECOLOGICAL CONTEXT

An important symbol complex of water/cave/mountain imagery can be reconstructed from the material record, which, I believe, visually represented the Maya worldview of their sacred landscapes. This provides us with missing "representative evidence" in monumental art of the rulers' involvement with agriculture and hydraulics (Demarest 1992b:146). The symbol complex appears to be linked to a Maya deity described by J. Eric S. Thompson (1970:273–275): Tzultacah (Kekchi and Chol), Uitzailic (Chuh), and Itacai (Chorti), meaning "Mountain-Plain" or "Mountain-Valley." This deity is thought to inhabit or personify springs and rivers. It can be lord over particular mountains, where it dwells within caves, protecting maize and controlling thunder and lightning. "Thirteen Tzultacah" is a term sometimes used in prayers to embrace the whole body of Tzultacah as a single entity (J. Thompson

Iconographic Evidence for Water Management

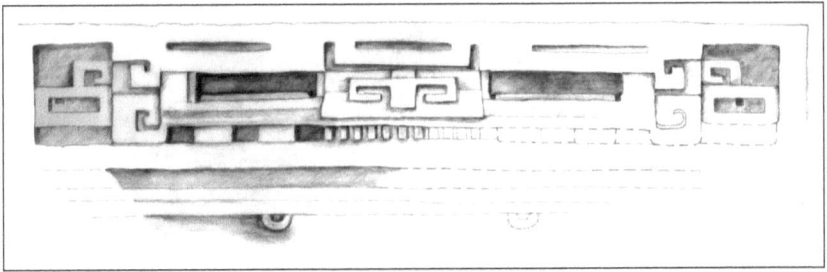

FIGURE 4.1
An Indigo Structure mask with drain canals emanating from the mouth.

1970). The number thirteen will figure into the picture again below.

Puleston (1976, 1977) called attention to flora and fauna iconography and water symbolism associated with sluggish streams, rivers, ponds, *aguadas*, swamps, and river floodplain environments. In the corpus of sculpture from Copán, these aquatic elements were portrayed repeatedly, suggesting that the ancient Maya cultivated, maintained, and worshiped the biodiversity of this environment. The combination of hydraulic sensibility and ritual formulas formed the basis of a regional "ethnohydrology" and ensured continuity of water maintenance over time.[5]

Water and cave imagery appears on many decorated structures and freestanding monuments in Copán. Structure 10L-22 is one of the best-known examples from the Acropolis. *Tun witz* monsters stacked on its four corners (figure 4.2a) label the structure as a sacred stone mountain (Freidel, Schele, and Parker 1993; M. Miller 1986, 1988; Stuart 1987, 1997).[6] In the Classic period, *tun* signs (a grapelike cluster of beads) denoted not only sacred stones (Morley 1915; J. Thompson 1951) but also a specific kind of sacred stone, such as the one that is depicted on the 10L-22 tun witz snouts and foreheads and represents cave formations dripping sacred virgin water (Bassie-Sweet 1996; B. Fash 1992a). Maize in many forms (personified and vegetal) sprouts from the Structure 10L-22 sacred mountain, perhaps indicating that it is symbolically the birthplace of maize, a place of creation, of life and fertility (B. Fash 1992b; Freidel, Schele, and Parker 1993).

I propose that three sculptural motifs in Copán relate to water and mountain caves and that these reveal an ideological base linking the

117

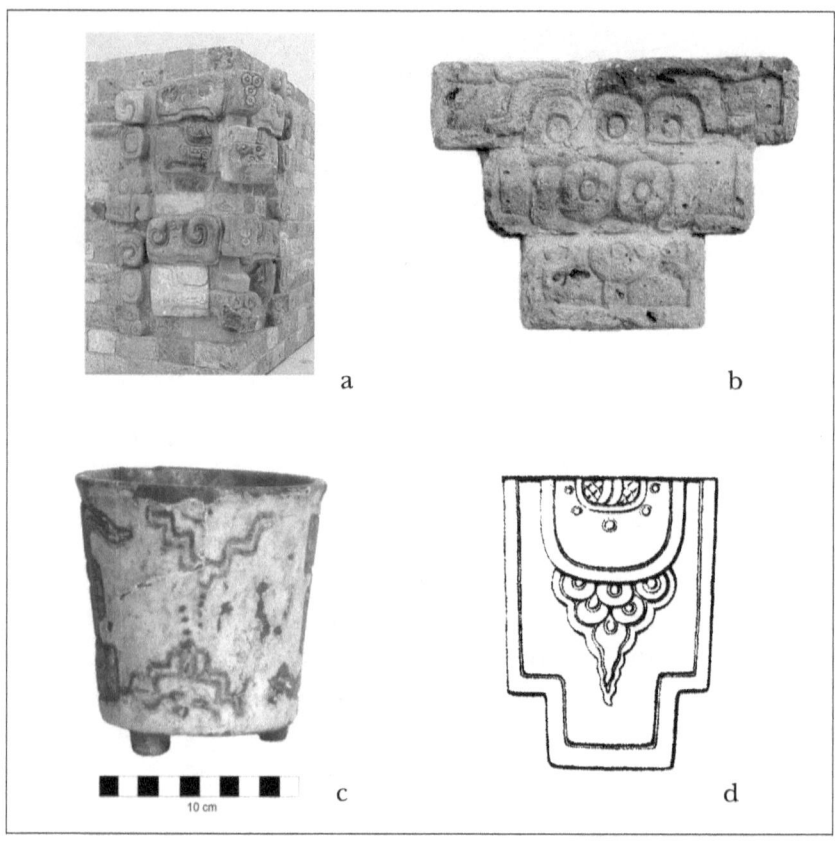

FIGURE 4.2

Tun *motifs from Copán: (a) Structure 10L-22, corner* witz *masks, (b) Structure 10L-41, stone facade sculpture, Group 10L-2, (c) vessel with painted stucco from the burial under Structure 10L-41, and (d) Stela J.*

ruler and nobles to water management. This symbol system, described below, may have been in much broader use throughout Mesoamerica.

The Tun Sign

Tun, a word that can mean *drum* or *stone* (Morley 1915; Vogt 1981b:165), is interpreted by Bassie-Sweet (1996) as referring to stalactites, the drums of Chak, the rain deity dwelling in the mountain caves.[7] Using different lines of reasoning, I independently came to the conclusion that the "grape" clusters in glyphs and iconography represent sacred, drip-water formations in caves (see figure 4.2). Supporting evidence is found on a carved modeled brownware vessel from Group 10L-2, 48/10/346 from Burial 3 of Structure 10L-41B (figure 4.4c; Bill 1997).[8] The vessel was stuccoed and painted with a design showing stepped motifs with infixed tun signs, placed one above another with droplets dripping between them (see figure 4.2c). The light blue/green yax color of the stucco suggests the color of water and may refer to the pristine primordial waters of creation.[9] It provides us with the clearest example I know to demonstrate that tun markings refer specifically to drip-water cave formations. The water-lily serpent (discussed below) can be understood to be a personification of tun.

The Quatrefoil and Half-Quatrefoil Motif

Although most specifically and widely accepted as related to caves, the quatrefoil motif (figure 4.3) is known to represent portals in general (Freidel, Schele, and Parker 1993), and in water-hole and cave imagery, it is the opening to these sources. It is also a symbol for flower, zero, centerpoint, navel, and completion or void (Schele and Freidel 1990; J. Thompson 1970). Caves and water holes and the portals leading to them shared similar iconographic depictions because they were understood to be aspects of the same natural phenomena and the abode of the earth deities (Bassie-Sweet 1996; Freidel, Schele, and Parker 1993; J. Thompson 1970; Vogt 1969, 1981a). The cave, often likened to the womb (Heyden 1981, 1991), and the water environment are focal points for Mesoamerican worldviews, namely, as sacred places of creation and fertility. They were physical features that provided a door or passage to the watery realm and abode of the ancestors (Bassie-Sweet 1991; Freidel, Schele, and Parker 1993; Stone 1995; J. Thompson 1970; Tozzer, ed. and trans., 1941). From the time of the Spanish conquest to the present, Maya groups have tenaciously held on to the cave and water ceremonies in an effort to sustain their beliefs, and water holes and caves continue to be places for communication with the ancestors (Vogt 1969; Wisdom 1940). The longevity and persistence in religious observance relating to the sacredness of the water hole/cave suggest that it was a powerful unification device rooted in the very beginnings of Mesoamerican culture and religion (Coe 1981; Heyden

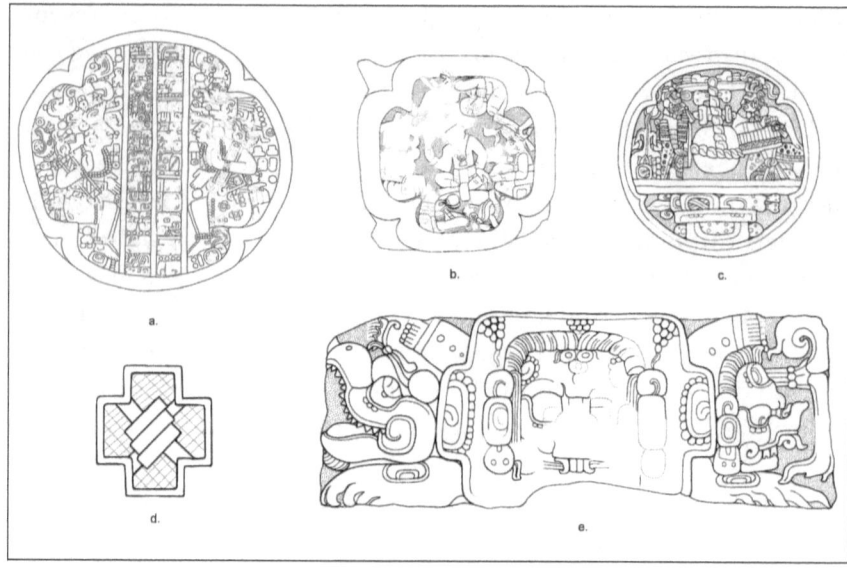

FIGURE 4.3

Quatrefoil motifs from Copán: (a) Motmot floor marker, (b) CPN 131, El Bosque plaza (after Baudez 1994:151, figure 72), (c) Ball Court IIb, playing alley floor marker, (d) Hieroglyphic Stairway, reclining figure's loincloth, and (e) Altar W', Group 9N-8 plaza, Las Sepulturas.

1981, 1991; Grove 1984, 1999). Caves, sites of ritual offerings and burial, must also be considered part of the settlement system (Pendergast 1971; Hammond 1981:177).

In Mesoamerican art, quatrefoils and the T-shaped stepped niche or half-quatrefoil with strings of beads around the border (see figures 4.3 and 4.4) have been interpreted as the earth or cave (Baudez 1988:140; Grove 1984), mountain place names (Caso 1928), the water-lily place (Schele and Grube 1990b), and water shrines (Bassie-Sweet 1996). Using quatrefoil examples with water lilies sprouting from their corners in the sculpture from Copán Structure 10L-18, Schele and Grube (1990b) argue that the plazas of the Principal Group's main courts are referred to in the hieroglyphs as the water-lily place, or *naab*, a portal to the supernatural world (figure 4.4f).[10] Depictions of solid beads clinging together have been identified as water or other sacred liquids, such as blood or maize gruel, called *atole* (Rands 1955;

ICONOGRAPHIC EVIDENCE FOR WATER MANAGEMENT

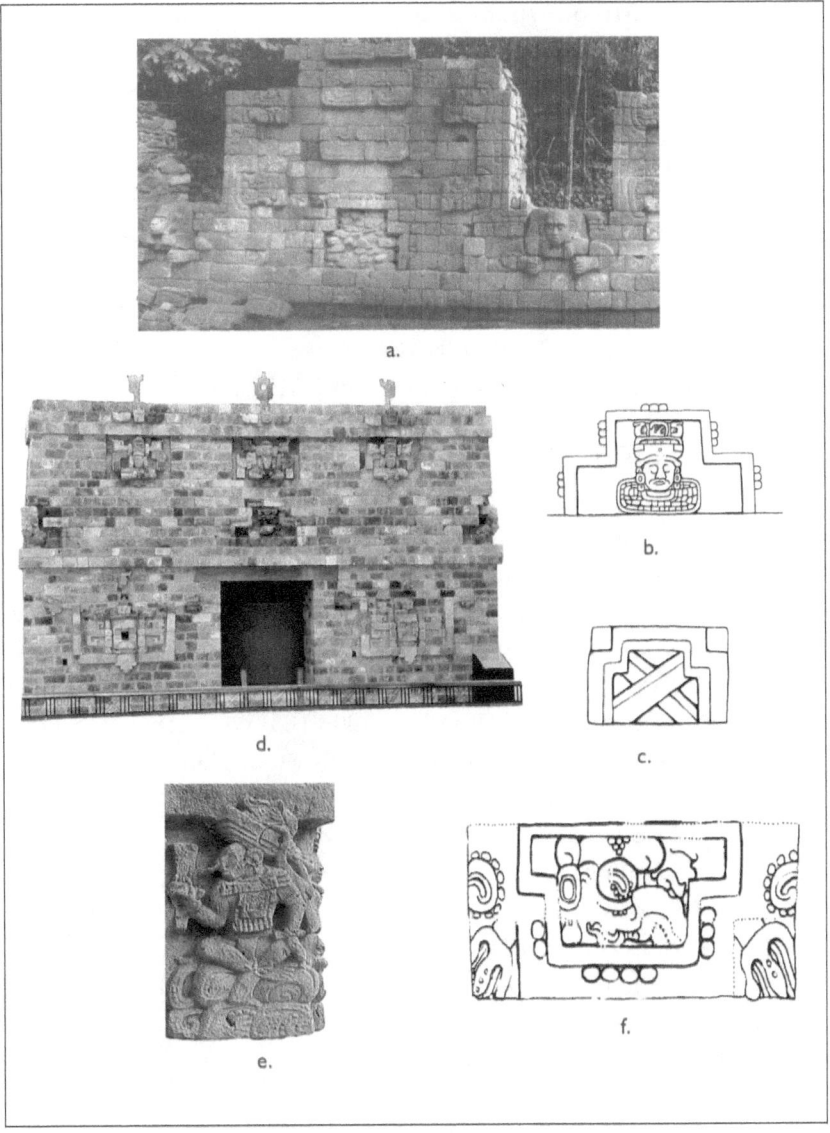

FIGURE 4.4

Half-quatrefoil motifs from Copán: (a) Structure 10L-29, the west façade, Group 10L-2, (b) Structure 8N-66S, detail of a niche with a katun *figure, Group 8N-11, Las Sepulturas, (c) Structure 10L-41, facade block, Group 10L-2, (d) Structure 8N-66S, full façade, (e) Altar Q, Ruler 15, pectoral, and (f) Structure 10L-18, southwest jamb, detail (after Baudez 1994:figure 96a).*

J. Thompson 1951; von Winning 1947). I suggest that full- and half-quatrefoils were understood as combined references to caves, holes, and depressions in the earth (portals) and to the water sources associated with them. The half-quatrefoil motif then encompasses the water hole, mountain/cave, and ancestor abode in one multivalent symbol. Stepped niches, reconstructed from facades at several residential sites in the Copán Valley (figure 4.4), may also have named sacred ponds or reservoirs and shrines on the ritual circuit (discussed further below).

The Water Lily and Water-Lily Headdress

A prominent aquatic motif in Copán is the water lily (Hellmuth 1987b; Maudslay 1889–1902; Rands 1953; Schele and Miller 1986; Spinden 1913:18–20; J. Thompson 1970), a symbol that Puleston (1976, 1977) demonstrated was connected with swampy environments such as raised fields and bajos and, by extension, with reservoirs and artificial ponds. He noted that the water lilies re-established themselves quickly in their experimental raised-field canals. Other important functions of the water lily include reducing evaporation, recycling organic waste, producing dissolved oxygen, and providing a microenvironment for numerous invertebrates (Harrison 1993:105; Wiseman 1983a:115). It was also possibly used as a medicinal and ritual plant because of its psychotropic properties (Dobkin de Rios 1974:150; Schultes and Hofmann 1992; Doris Stone, personal communication 1990). The hieroglyphic sign for the water lily, known as *Imix*, first of the twenty day names, is often paired with *kan* (maize) to symbolize fertility and abundance (J. Thompson 1970:72; Puleston 1977).[11] Puleston's ideological connection of the maize/water-lily symbol with the raised-field agricultural practices reflected the central importance of the system to the overall southern lowland Maya subsistence technology.

The water-lily headdress frequently worn by gods and monsters has been alternately described as the "Lily Pad" headdress (Hellmuth 1982:304; Schele 1979) or the "Water Lily Serpent" headdress of God H (Taube 1992:59; J. Thompson 1970:136). The Water Lily Serpent has been associated with the number thirteen, perhaps related to the Thirteen Tzultacah mentioned above. Naab is a term that refers to the water lily itself (J. Thompson 1970) and to standing bodies of water (Schele and Miller 1986:46). Depictions of the serpent deity wearing the water-lily headdress associate him not only with such a place but also with the spirit of the water (Bassie-Sweet 1996). The idea of water serpents emerging from the mountain, such as the Chorti belief in *chicchans* (J. Thompson 1970:136; Wisdom 1940), helps to explain the conflation of the serpent and water lily representing the water from caves or springs.

Here I suggest that when a water-lily headdress (Andrews and Fash 1992:figure 5), consisting of the long-nosed god, tied water lily, inverted beaded water lily, and crossed-bands and disk sash (figure 4.5), is worn by rulers or nobles in sculptural depictions at Copán, it relates to the explicit social structure of water-management duties and the wearer's divine ritual role of ensuring fertility and sustenance.[12] Rare in early monuments, water-lily symbolism appears to proliferate during the reigns of Ruler 15 and Ruler 16, appearing on such Late Classic monuments as Stela N and Structure 10L-11. Outside Copán's Principal Group, facade sculptures on Late Classic structures from Groups 9N-8, 8N-11, and 10L-2 show figures or masks with water lilies as a prominent part of their costume.

WATER MANAGEMENT AS A BASIS FOR SOCIAL ORGANIZATION: ICONOGRAPHIC EVIDENCE

As we have seen, recent research has broadened the definition of water management from the traditional irrigation focus to "the interruption and redirection of the natural movement or collection of water by society" (Scarborough 1993). This allows us to look for models that encompass wider ranges of water-related activities and to arrive at a comprehensive approach toward management and/or sociopolitical organization within a given region. My analysis of the iconography, coupled with ethnographic evidence and comparative material presented here, leads me to propose that the maize/water-lily patterns and the half-quatrefoil motif on Copán's sculpture facades reflect the ideology supporting a system of social organization based on water sources similar to that described for Zinacantan.

Structures 9N-82 and 8N-66S, Las Sepulturas

While surveying water-lily iconography among the stone sculptures of the Copán Valley, I identified a pattern on Structure 9N-82 at Group 9N-8, one of the largest residential units east of the Principal Group (W. Fash 1989; Webster 1989a). Of the six figures reconstructed from

FIGURE 4.5
Water-lily headdresses from Copán: (a) Ruler 15, Stela N, (b) Structure 9N-82, central figure, (c) Structure 10L-32, Group 10L-2, and (d) Structure 10L-11, Bacab head.

the excavated sculpture, the central figure above the doorway and its mirror image on the back side (see figure 4.5b) stand out as the only figures depicted wearing the water-lily headdress. Most likely, these central figures are repeating portraits of a high-status individual suggested to be the owner of the house (W. Fash 1989:67). The larger patron-deity figures in the frontal niches of the lower register wear beaded water lilies around their necks. W. Fash discussed in detail how these

ICONOGRAPHIC EVIDENCE FOR WATER MANAGEMENT

FIGURE 4.6
Structure 9N-82, Group 9N-8, Las Sepulturas, figure with maize headdress.

water-lily elements could be related to the patron of the scribes, linking components of the water-lily costume to this noble's scribal functions and his ties to the royal elites (W. Fash 1989). Jackson and Stuart (2001) have suggested a hieroglyphic decipherment of *aj k'uhun* for the God C title associated with this noble, inscribed on the interior bench. While including these scribal and courtly duties, I propose that the water-lily headdress may also be identifying this lord as a water manager for the sector.

I consider that the people depicted with maize headdress (figure 4.6) attire on Structure 9N-82 represent the individual snas (agriculturally based lineage groups; see Webster, chapter 2 in this volume) from the Las Sepulturas sector, similar to the Zinacantan lineage-based units. The central, more important figure wearing the water-lily headdress (see figure 4.5b) may be the head of the water-hole group, who carried out the supervisory role described by Vogt. Other titles and duties, such as war captain, could conceivably be subsumed by the head water-hole administrator.

At another residential group in the Sepulturas ward, Structure 8N-11, sculpture reconstructed from the excavations of the fallen facade of Structure 8N-66S revealed numerous water-lily motifs. They can be seen on the monster mask in the lower niche, the border of the niche, and the central roof ornaments of the east and west sides of the building (see figure 4.4d).[13] The other eight roof ornaments appear to be maize representations (Webster et al. 1998). Portrait-like figures wear beaded water-lily pendants and have maize vegetation in their headdresses, with the central figure singled out wearing more elaborate ear ornaments. Half-quatrefoil niches rest on the medial molding and repeat around the upper register (see figure 4.4b). Within their recesses are busts of an aged lord with a *katun* sign for a headdress, a possible toponymic reference to the group's ancestral water source. Katun cycles were important for prophecy and the transfer of offices in colonial times (Edmonson, ed. and trans., 1982; Jones 1992; Roys 1954, 1957) and were commemorated by ceremonies that included offerings and visits to shrines on a ritual circuit (Roys 1931; Tozzer, ed. and trans., 1941). The wide eastern sacbe with one terminus at the Principal Group and one at Group 8N-11 (figure 4.7) would have been ideal for such ritual processions and may have also functioned as a dam, as has been proposed for causeways at other Maya sites (Harrison 1993). The stepped half-quatrefoil niche on the medial molding of Structure 8N-66S can best be visualized as a full quatrefoil or cave on the horizon, with the lower half hidden from view. Because caves are sources of sacred water and abodes of the ancestors, the stepped niche is a logical symbol to designate water-hole groups and validate their common social identity.

Group 10L-2, El Cementerio, and the Fish

Group 10L-2, the elite residential group directly south of the Acropolis, often referred to as "El Cementerio," was governed by the royal family in the final three decades of the Copán dynasty (Andrews and Bill, chapter 7 in this volume). A telltale piece of iconographic evidence brought to light in the 1991 field season was the identification of the carved fish found inside the bench of the central room as a proba-

ICONOGRAPHIC EVIDENCE FOR WATER MANAGEMENT

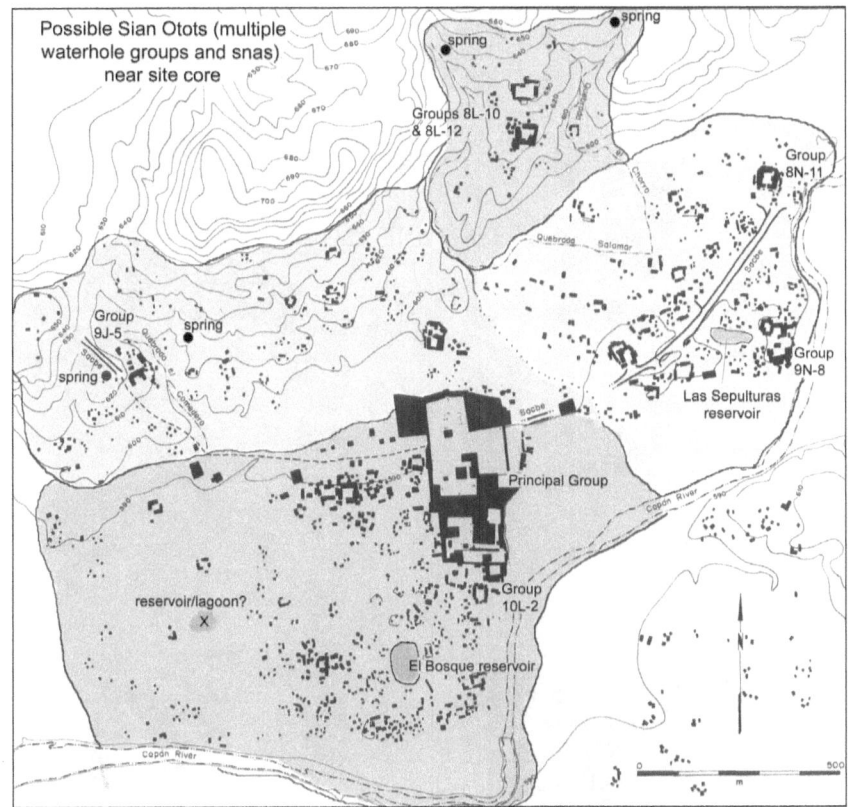

FIGURE 4.7
Four possible sian otots *near the site core, indicated by shading, composed of water-hole groups and* snas.

ble toponym for the group, translated as *canal*, or "place on high" (figure 4.8c). Other fish sculptures like it were associated with three other buildings in this group. The fish was linked with a fish toponym displayed on Acropolis Structure 10L-22A, inferred to be the council house, or *popol nah* (figure 4.8), suggesting to the author that a representative from Group 10L-2 was a member of the royal council (Andrews and Fash 1992; B. Fash and W. Fash 1991; B. Fash et al. 1992). Even today, raising fish continues to be a practice in landlocked Copán and neighboring Ocotepeque. I have witnessed people keeping in their homes anywhere from a few fish to masses of them in large water cisterns, or *pilas*.

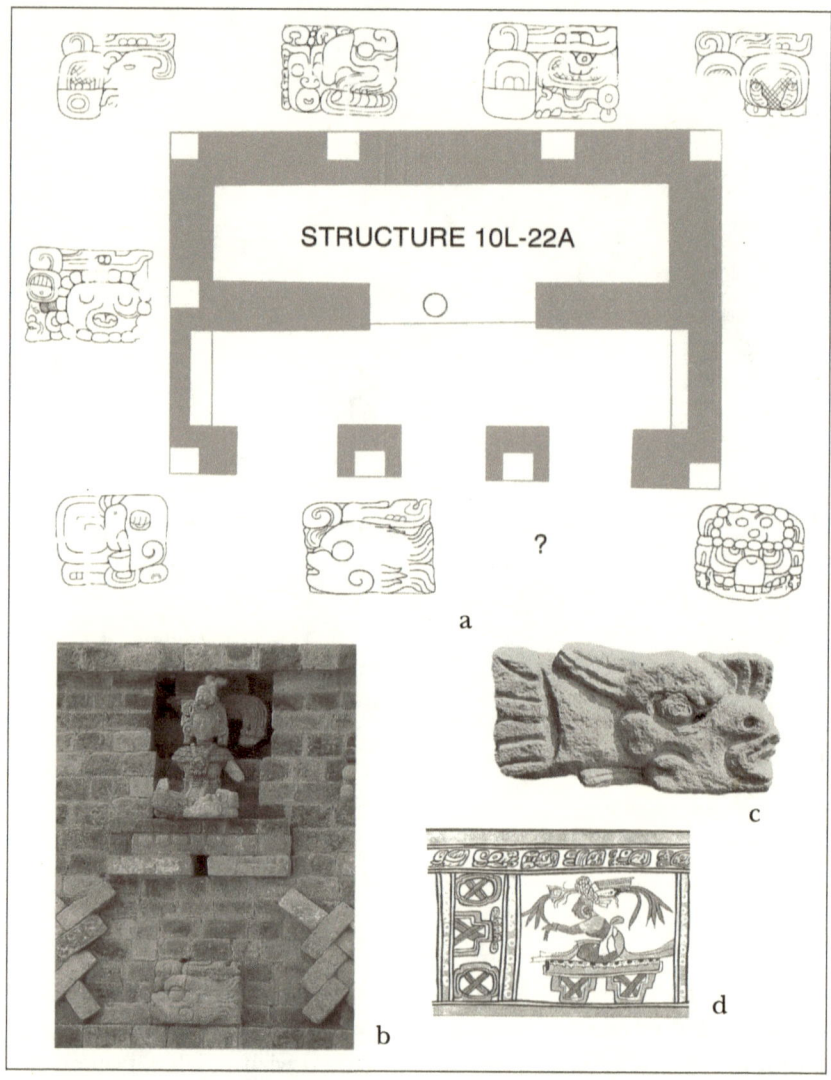

FIGURE 4.8

(a) Structure 10L-22A, plan and toponyms. (b) Structure 10L-22A, detail of figure over a fish glyph (note the crossed-bands and disk loincloth). (c) Fish from Structure 10L-32 cache, Group 10L-2. (d) Palmar Orange vessel from Tikal (P. Culbert 1993:figure 73).

On the upper facade of Structure 10L-32, the principal building of Courtyard A, all six of the human figures depicted wear a water-lily headdress (see figures 4.5c, 4.9a, and 4.9b). Water lilies also occur as follicles and plants sprouting from the foreheads of long-nosed Chak masks and as the structure's roof ornaments (Andrews and Fash 1992). The crossed-bands and disk sash in the headdress and loincloths is similar to the loincloths found on Structure 10L-22A (see figure 4.8b). Comparing the Structure 10L-32 sculpture themes with those of the Las Sepulturas Structure 9N-82 façade, one notes that, thematically, 10L-32 is predominantly about water and water lilies, whereas 9N-82 and 8N-66S combine a maize and water-lily focus. This leads me to interpret Structure 10L-32's six figures as the regional "water masters." Additionally, I have located a sculpture fragment in the Peabody Museum collection from Structure 10L-32 that may have been the scepter held by the central figure (figure 4.9d). Portions of another scepter in the collection may be from the mirror-image figure on the back of the structure. The scepter is a miniature version of the water-lily serpent, perhaps their ancestral patron deity (figure 4.9c), which I equate with the Tzultacah or Itacai deities described by Thompson (1970). The scepter was a symbol of the bearer's privileged connection with the earth deity's domain. As I see it, the scepter also explicitly denotes his hierarchical and ideological control over the social order of water management, including overseeing the associated rituals and engineering the technological layout of the main architectural center.

At Group 10L-2, long stone waterspouts channeled roof water off the back of several major structures into the catchment system that also drained the sunken plazas of the Acropolis and flowed south into the reservoir/bajo in the El Bosque region. The water-lily and fish iconographic evidence from Group 10L-2 suggests that this reservoir was under the management of the families residing there. *Canal*, perhaps a sacred name associated with this reservoir, may have metaphorically equated it with the primordial sea. The reservoir would have merited such a name because it was replenished by the rainfall runoff from the three sacred mountains–temple/plazas at the core of the civic-ceremonial center. *Canal* may have actually been *cainal*, place of the Itacai (Chorti earth deity), *ca* and *cai* being interchangeable words for *fish* (J. Thompson 1944). The group's water masters personifying the Itacai were ideologically linked to this realm closely associated with the primordial waters, caves, and earth deities. Not unlike the water sources of Southeast Asia, the Bosque reservoir would have been a principal water

Barbara W. Fash

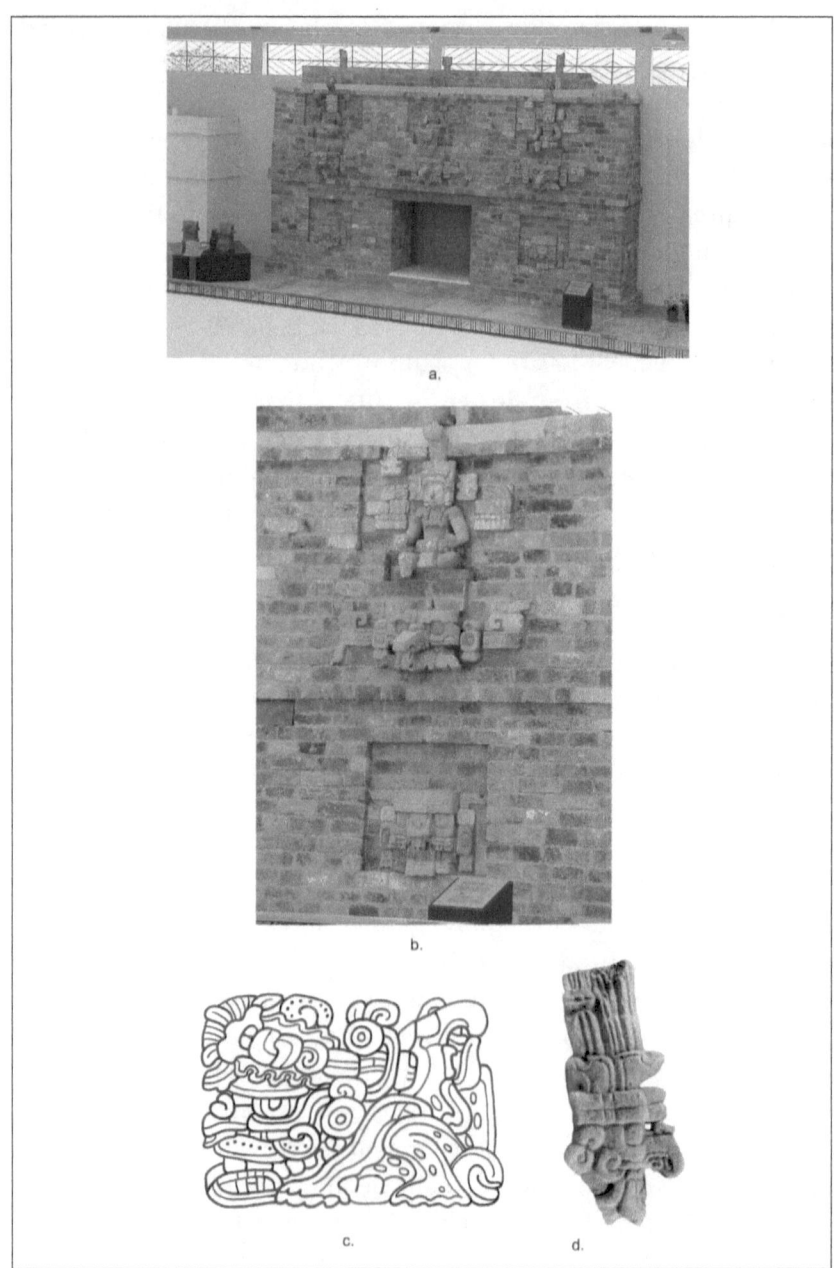

FIGURE 4.9
Water-lily serpents from Copán: (a) Structure 10L-32 facade, Group 10L-2, (b) Structure 10L-32, detail, (c) Stela 63, tun glyph, and (d) Structure 10L-32, scepter (courtesy Peabody Museum, Harvard University).

source imbued with sacred power under the supernatural control of the Tzultacah/Itacai.

The lineage shrine for Group 10L-2, Structure 10L-29 (see figure 4.4a) was decorated with celestial imagery, sun disks and cloud scrolls, but also had thirteen half-quatrefoil niches along the medial molding (Andrews and Fash 1992), which correspond to the number of levels in the Maya heavens, again recalling the thirteen Tzultacah/Itacai deities. Bassie-Sweet (1996) proposes that on the horizon are thirteen caves that are entrances to these celestial levels. I suspect that the thirteen Structure 10L-29 niches may represent the horizon entrance caves of the thirteen Tzultacah/Itacai earth deities. Rectangular pieces fallen from the niches' interior have been tentatively reconstructed to form a double-band or crossed-bands motif, possibly the same crossed bands in niches found in miniature at the nearby Structure 10L-41B (see figure 4.4c). Crossed-band motifs also mark the emanations falling from the mouths of the water-lily serpent on 10L-32 (see figure 4.9b), perhaps another visual reference to the Tzultacah/Itacai. The presence of thirteen niches on the Structure 10L-29 ancestor shrine can be seen as new support for suggestions by William Holland (1963) and Evon Vogt (1969, 1981a) that the modern belief that Maya ancestors are associated with the sky and traverse its thirteen levels had its roots in ancient times.

Other water motifs found on Structure 10L-41, a long residential building of the late Coner phase on the east side of Group 10L-2 Courtyard B, include multistepped configurations with tun signs (see figure 4.2b), maize sprouting as roof ornaments, and half-quatrefoil motifs on the lower register of Structures 10L-41C and 10L-41D (Johnson 1993). The multistepped configuration infixed with tun signs most likely represents drip-water formations or speleothems in caves, much the same as those described above on the earlier Acbi-phase vessel in the burial under Structure 10L-41Aa (48/10/346, see figure 4.2c, tun section) and Structure 10L-22 (see figure 4.2a; B. Fash 1992b). The stone-carved, stepped motifs on Structure 10L-41's façade may have been arranged above one another.

If the *canal* group was the largest corporate or communal group and was also at the city's center, it likely developed administrative duties reserved for elite families. I propose that this group administered the central repository for tribute and taxes coming in from its own urban sector, as well as the *sian otot* in the valley.

BARBARA W. FASH

The Role of the Popol Nah

Structure 10L-22A on the Acropolis has been proposed as the community/council house, or popol nah (*popol otot* in Chorti), of Copán (B. Fash et al. 1992; B. Fash and W. Fash 1991). Mat symbols surrounding the facade are interspersed with large glyphic toponyms, most likely referring to sociopolitical divisions in the Copán Valley (see figure 4.8a). This study proposes that the valley sociopolitical organization was centered around water-hole groups that sent a representative to the council house. Late Classic residential groups proposed as places or corporate groups represented at the central council house (B. Fash and W. Fash 1991) would have demonstrated evidence for this association by displaying half-quatrefoil niches on their structures.

Hamlet-scale residential settlements throughout the valley were potentially composed of several water-hole groups joined as aldeas or sian otots (see figure 4.7). These sectors may have elected a representative or governor (called *holpop* in Yucatan) to serve in the central council, or popol nah. The Copán council house appears to have displayed nine hieroglyphic toponyms of the settlement regions that were part of this proposed system. The toponym glyphs often contain a reference to a water source, cave, or black hole (B. Fash et al. 1992), three physical features named by the same term, *ch'en*, among modern Maya speakers (Vogt 1981a). Furthermore, a Maya village is often named after a distinctive feature or past event associated with the main body of water or water source within its territory (Vogt 1969; Wisdom 1940). Therefore, the nine Copán toponyms may combine references to both the names of the wards and the ancestral water features within their boundaries. Ancestral water sources in the Andes (see above) often carry names that refer to supernatural locations or replicate sacred locations from the important capital of Cuzco (Sherbondy 1992). This may explain why some of the toponyms in Copán are names that refer to supernatural locales in texts from other sites.

SUMMARY AND CONCLUSIONS

Based on the iconographic, ethnographic, comparative evidence discussed above, the sociopolitical model I have proposed for ancient Copán is as follows: At the simplest level, akin to the snas, were land-based, agrarian lineage groups, probably patrilineal, symbolized by maize icons. The snas, when united as larger water-hole groups, were represented by water-lily motifs. These were social units drawn together by their common use of a water source or management of an urban system such as a reservoir, perhaps coupled with agricultural complexes. The water-hole group reinforced territorial boundaries by participating in a belief system that required making ceremonial offerings to the water-hole spirits and ancestral patrons and maintaining water-hole and related shrines. A person at the *ah cul na* (Coe 1965:103) or *aj k'uhun* (Jackson and Stuart 2001; Stuart 1992, 1993) level in the hierarchy was elected head of the water-hole group. His responsibilities (both scribal and courtly) were to coordinate maintenance of the water source and the shrine, levy and collect taxes for ceremonial offerings, organize ritual meals, and keep track of the ceremonial schedule. If the water hole was a small spring system in the mountains, the water-hole maintenance duties were probably minimal. But if the water source was a large urban reservoir, the management duties were more demanding and likewise commanded more prestige. This is likely to be the level of organization represented on Las Sepulturas, Structure 9N-82, because it is near a large reservoir. Although the scale and complexity differ from that of Copán, the hierarchical nature of the water priests and temples in Southeast Asia is similar to the structure proposed for the sian otots and the popol nah. Several water-hole groups may have combined to form hamlets, which elected a representative (holpop level) to confer at the council house. Timing of water-hole rituals and disputes concerning water rights most likely fell to the holpop and aj k'uhun leaders to coordinate and settle within their individual ecological and ritual systems. With the existence of the popol nah, a meeting place for representatives with the ruling king, the regional water-based communities to some degree involved a centralized system. I suspect that this centralization served to synchronize the water and agricultural rituals, exact tribute, and settle disputes.

As population increased in the Late Classic reigns of Rulers 14–16 (W. Fash 1983b, 1991; Webster, chapter 2 in this volume), the influence and increase of subroyal elites in the valley and urban core were reflected in the iconographic programs at their residences, which flourished in ways not seen during earlier reigns. Half-quatrefoil niches and water-lily headdresses identified particular residences and nobles as key players in the water management hierarchy. Reservoirs provided the urban core population with a year-round source of potable water and aquatic resources, a compelling reason for people to settle there rather than on the hillsides, where seasonal springs were less reliable.

The royal family residing at Group 10L-2 may have traditionally presided over the principal water-management duties of the Copán center in a ritual-legal fashion, similar to those who coordinate water groups, settle disputes between subaks, and collect taxes to cover expenses for maintenance and ceremonies in the negara model (Lansing 1987, 1991; Geertz 1980). Close proximity to and ritual maintenance of the civic-ceremonial center's reservoir may explain how and why the Group 10L-2 elite evolved as the overall managers of the regional water systems and were able to garner sculptors to create lavish facades to heighten their status. When Yax Pasaj Chan Yopaat became the sixteenth ruler, the noble family's status was elevated, further bolstering their traditional water-management responsibility at the apex of the water system. Perhaps these water responsibilities, combined with the effective use of a visual symbol system, were the principal reasons Yax Pasaj Chan Yopaat was chosen to succeed Ruler 15. The management of the center's water system and overall coordination of the valley systems was a large responsibility requiring engineering skills and geomantic knowledge.[14] It no doubt required that these noble families devote concerted efforts to these ends. As members of the elite with access to specialized training and esoteric knowledge, they would have played a vital role in designing and engineering the sacred, urban architectural landscape whose runoff fed the principal, central reservoir in the Copán Valley. They became the ritual supervisors and tribute collectors for the center as other groups carried out the actual labor of cleaning, maintenance, and administrative functions at their local level.

Half-quatrefoil pectoral assemblages with cross-hatched interiors are worn by some of the rulers portrayed on Altar Q. These may refer to their common ancestral cave and water source (see figure 4.4e). Schele and Miller (1986) describe them as symbols for the mouth of the earth monster, synonymous with caves.[15] They serve as another example of the water-hole/cave imagery that lay at the core of the belief system in which the ruler was a pivotal figure. The council that met to regulate the social and political aspects of the valley communities composing the kingdom was fully visible in the architecture by Late Classic times. A simplified version of the system had possibly been in operation since K'inich Yax K'uk' Mo' centered the city proper and initiated the triadic plaza (naab) configuration.[16] Perhaps a similar organization was in operation at the site of Palenque, to judge from the half-quatrefoil cave niches with human personages on Pacal's sarcophagus lid. One reason we may not see water-management iconography at Copán before the Late Classic is that population growth did not put stress on the water system until that point.

Rulers see to it that political obligations, ideas of duty, and onerous tasks such as paying taxes are bearable by infusing them with religious meanings and sanctions, "and devotion to duty is conspicuously rewarded with honor, glory, wealth, and rank" (Carniero 1992:194). The present study argues that the construction of plazas, temples, and facades not only provided a stage for ritual pageantry and the making of "religion itself...the principal source" of a ruler's power (Demarest 1992b), but also creatively met functional needs.

I believe that the well-known quatrefoil with the *pop* (mat) sign across the opening (see figure 4.3d), found throughout Mesoamerica, symbolizes the ideological concepts and social structure of this overall water-management system, which brought together the components of societies into a unified whole. Leonardo López Luján has called my attention to the use of a similar motif at the site of Tajín, Mexico (Kampen 1972; see figures 4.7a, b). There, at a site where water symbolism and hydraulic architectural engineering are recurring features, the central role that water management played in its layout and political structure is useful for comparison (Cortés Hernández 1989; Koontz 1994). For Copán, the interwoven community aspect of the aldeas/villages was joined into one central organization, the proposed popol nah. This central governing structure existed for the welfare of the entire polity and was inextricably linked with its veneration of water and overall ecological management, including but not limited to agrarian management, as proposed by Webster (chapter 2 in this volume).[17]

Will Andrews noted, in his analysis of the excavations behind Structure 10L-32, that some late trash heaps were left around the plaza group. Although these were not substantial, they indicated to him that the status of the individuals living in that group declined (Andrews and Fash 1992). Refuse pileup, careless dumping, and improper disposal of human waste are modern-day problems that small villages like Copán Ruinas experience as a result of increasing population pressures and lack of community programs. Eventually, water sources become contaminated and lead to diseases. Other places in the third world are suffering from this plight with far graver consequences (Kaplan 1994; Parfit 1993).

Important as the water-management system in Copán may have been in the rise to statehood, its collapse, whether by force or by neglect, surely had grave consequences for any population that persisted in the valley after the abandonment of the ritual center and the elite compounds. Although a few individuals may have continued to conduct shrine ceremonies and ritual circuits, these could have had little effect on the silting up and contamination of the reservoirs. Instead of sacred water locales with reliable drinking water, they became stagnant pools and were used as dump sites (Davis-Salazar 1994, 2001). Within a short time, they became breeding grounds for diseases that may have brought death to major sections of the population or scared them away. The decline in the quality of drinking water and the reduction in aquatic resources may have begun earlier than abandonment of the site. Child mortality rates soared in the Late Classic (Storey 1992, chapter 8 in this volume) at the Las Sepulturas ward. If children were dying from dysentery-related sicknesses, their drinking and bathing water may have been contaminated.

Writing about the northern lowlands, albeit a considerably different landscape from Copán's, E. W. Andrews IV (1973:263) noted that "in ancient times the much greater population must have relied on the innumerable *chultuns*, which were the terminal storage points of water meticulously channeled from buildings and plaza areas in the ceremonial centers. A breakdown in maintenance and control of these water collection systems by elimination of the ruling groups could easily have led to abandonment of the centers themselves and major depopulation of the relatively rich sustaining areas surrounding them." As we see a similar scenario playing itself out on a global scale in the twenty-first century, we may yet be able to glean some information from the archaeological record that can be applied to our current ecological and population dilemmas.

Notes

In addition to the two anonymous reviewers, I would like to extend my thanks to Will Andrews, Karen Bassie-Sweet, Karla Davis-Salazar, Lisa Lucero, William Fash, Vernon Scarborough, and Evon Vogt for their discussions with me on the subject of water management, for their encouragement, and for their helpful comments on this chapter.

1. A term borrowed from J. Steven Lansing in his studies of water temples in Bali (Lansing 1991:14).

2. The last year I saw this procession in Copán was 1993, possibly because the padre was old.

3. The *ox witik* reference in the inscriptions might refer to the three plazas and the three "mountains" or pyramids.

4. This excessive eastwardly runoff to the floodplain along artificial surfaces may have eventually contributed to the destruction of the east side of the Acropolis (the corte) after the site was abandoned and the system neglected.

5. A term used in Andean studies (Sherbondy 1982).

6. A Middle Preclassic depiction of a water-lily headdress may be on Stela 2 at La Venta, which Benson contends had political implications (Benson 1971; Reilly 1994).

7. Evon Vogt (personal communication 2000) adds that the Ten-Ten drum played at the Fiesta of San Sebastian sounds like the dripping of water.

8. Bill's (1997) photograph shows only the carved side of this pot.

9. David Stuart (1987) first identified the mountain/*tun witz* aspects of these images. Previously, they were often referred to as Cauac monsters and thought to be associated with caves (Tate 1982; Taylor 1979).

10. Another example of this watery plaza place name may be depicted on Machaquila Stela 4, which mirrors the shape of the plaza outline, as noted by Ian Graham (1967:59; Stuart and Houston 1994:33).

11. The Imix sign is phonetically read as *ha*, or water (Fox and Justeson 1984; Stuart and Houston 1994:19). I interpret this as evidence that the water lily symbolized water locations in iconography and text.

12. Karl Lorenzen (n.d.) proposes that the iconography suggests that this vessel held *zuhuy ha*, the virgin water collected from a cave when it was interred, an idea I find compelling.

13. These same water-lily motifs are carried by Chak as he navigates watery locations depicted in the Dresden Codex (see pp. 65–69).

14. Carlson (1981) provides an exhaustive consideration of the geomantic model for the Maya.

15. Viel (1999b) argues for alternative interpretations of the Altar Q iconography.

16. Previously, it was proposed that the popol nah was instituted during Ruler 14's reign to draw the nobles in the valley into a central structure (B. Fash et al. 1992). With new evidence at hand, it can be hypothesized that the popol nah council had greater antiquity. We now view the explicit portrayal of the councilors and their toponyms on the facades of Ruler 14's council house as his statement of their increasing importance in the political life of Copán after the death of Ruler 13. This occurs at the same time Late Classic sculptural facades increase at residences throughout the valley.

17. The mat, crossed-bands, quatrefoil, and half-quatrefoil motifs found in a pattern on vessels from burial caches at Tikal (P. Culbert 1993:figures 73–75) may lend support to this iconographic interpretation (see figure 4.8d).

5

Early Classic Royal Power in Copan

The Origins and Development of the Acropolis (ca. A.D. *250–600)*

Robert J. Sharer, David W. Sedat, Loa P. Traxler, Julia C. Miller, and Ellen E. Bell

Most lowland Maya sites are dominated by Late Classic (ca. A.D. 600–850) architecture. It is not surprising, therefore, that archaeologists have acquired far more information about the Late Classic than about earlier eras, including the crucial Early Classic (ca. A.D. 250–600), when most of the characteristics of Lowland Maya civilization emerged (Grube, ed., 1995; Martin and Grube 2000; Sharer 1994; Willey and Mathews, eds., 1985). Important information about the Early Classic in the Maya lowlands has come from research at Calakmul (Folan 1988; Marcus 1987), Río Azul (Adams 1990, 1995), Tikal (Laporte 1989, 2003; Laporte and Vega de Zea 1988), Uaxactun (Valdés and Fahsen 1995), and other sites. To this expanding corpus of Early Classic data we offer the following synthesis, based on conjunctive research in the Acropolis of Copan, Honduras (Bell, Canuto, and Sharer, eds., 2004; W. Fash and Sharer 1991; W. Fash 1998; Sharer, Traxler, et al. 1999).

The purpose of this chapter is to combine archaeological and historical data to correlate the architectural growth of the Acropolis with the reigns of Copan's rulers during the Early Classic period. The archaeological information is based on sequences of architecture, artifacts, and associated features (caches, burials, and sculpture). The historical information is based on deciphered texts, many directly associated with archaeological remains (contemporaneous texts) and others with retrospective references to the Early Classic period.

ARCHAEOLOGY IN THE COPAN ACROPOLIS

From 1988 to 1996 the Copan Acropolis was investigated by excavations under the aegis of the Proyecto Arqueológico Acrópolis Copan (PAAC). Results from these research programs are well represented in this volume. One PAAC program used surface excavations to document the palace complex to the south of the Acropolis (Andrews and Bill, chapter 7 in this volume; Andrews and Fash 1992). Three programs within the Acropolis relied on tunneling, including the Early Copan Acropolis Program (ECAP), charged with excavating and integrating the overall sequence of Early Classic architecture. ECAP continued its investigations for seven field seasons (1997–2002) after the end of the PAAC. This chapter emphasizes the results of ECAP research and integrates findings from adjacent tunneling programs beneath Structure 10L-26 (W. Fash 1998, chapter 3 in this volume; Williamson 1997) and Structure 10L-16 (Agurcia Fasquelle 1996, 1997; Agurcia Fasquelle and B. Fash, chapter 6 in this volume).

MAYA ARCHITECTURE

The greatest investments in architecture were made for the use of the Maya rulers and their royal courts (Inomata and Houston, eds., 2001). Usually these royal buildings are centrally located within polity capitals, forming the longest sequences and densest concentrations of architecture (Sharer 1994:630–641). The term *acropolis* designates an architectural concentration that, over time, aggregated into a single, elevated, monumental complex (Andrews 1975:67). A prime example is the Copan Acropolis, the political and symbolic center of the Copan polity during the Classic period (figure 5.1). It comprises the succession of palaces, temples, and administrative buildings constructed for and used by Copan's rulers and their royal courts over a span of four centuries (Sharer, Fash, et al. 1999; Sharer, Miller, and Traxler 1992).

The Copan Acropolis, like many Maya monumental constructions, is an accumulation of many buildings, with newer structures superim-

EARLY CLASSIC ROYAL POWER IN COPAN

FIGURE 5.1
Perspective reconstruction of the Copan Acropolis: (1) Structure 10L-16, (2) Rosalila Structure, (3–9) sequence of early architecture, including the Cab, Hunal, Yehnal, and Margarita structures, the Hunal and Margarita tombs, (10) Altar Q (West Court), (11) Copan River cut (Corte), (12) Structure 10L-20 (destroyed by the Copan River) with Ante Structure beneath, (13) East Court, (14) Structure 10L-21 (mostly destroyed by the Copan River), (15) Sub-Jaguar Tomb, (16) Structure 10L-25 ("Dance Platform"), (17) Structure 10L-22, and (18) Structure 10L-22a ("Popol Nah"). (Painting by C. Klein, courtesy of the National Geographic Society)

posed over old. Tunnel excavations reveal this sequence of architecture and provide the framework for the archaeological and historical synthesis presented here. The sequence consists of platforms and substructures made of wet-laid earth or earth-and-rubble fill, with single- or multiple-terraced façades of adobe, cobbles, or masonry, used separately or together in a single construction (Sharer, Traxler, et al. 1999). The surfaces of earthen substructures were usually covered with durable clay coatings and were often painted red. Typically, the buildings on these earthen substructures were constructed of pole frameworks with wattle-and-daub or similar adobe-plastered walls. Terminated adobe buildings leave far less evidence in the Acropolis sequence, although remains of earthen floors, adobe wall stubs, and carbonized wooden roof beams have been recovered, along with more intact earthen substructures and stairways.

Over time, cut-stone masonry construction, used for platform and substructure façades and building walls, became increasingly common in the Acropolis (Sharer, Traxler, et al. 1999). Masonry façades and walls were covered with lime plaster, painted one or more colors, and often decorated with modeled stucco elements (replaced by plastered carved-stone elements by the Late Classic). Some building roofs were made with wooden beams and mortar; others had corbelled masonry vaults. Terminated masonry buildings typically leave far more durable remnants than do their adobe counterparts. Usually, terminated masonry buildings were partially demolished so that their upper portions could be used to fill interiors; they were then encased in fills of new and larger substructures surmounted by new buildings. Some masonry was salvaged for reuse in newer buildings. In rare cases, masonry buildings were carefully filled and preserved with minimal destruction, before being buried under new construction. Over time, these superimposed architectural successions produced a sequence in which each substructure preserves, within its core, remnants of its predecessors. Mixtures of wet-laid earth, cobbles, and demolition debris were utilized for most of the fills used to bury terminated construction.

The archaeology of the Acropolis documents each exposed building and its vertical and horizontal relationships to establish its age. Relative age assessments are based on stratigraphy, linking of floors, and architectural attributes. Dating of architecture is based on radiocarbon assessments (table 5.1), associated ceramics (Viel 1993b; Willey et al. 1994), and hieroglyphic texts.[1] A trial series of obsidian-hydration dates produced extremely aberrant results (table 5.2), so this dating method was abandoned.[2] Although age determinations derived from radiometric and artifact analyses provide time spans of a century or more, inscriptions often furnish far more precise dates.

The earliest constructions beneath the Acropolis date to the Terminal Preclassic/Early Classic transition (ca. A.D. 100–420), based on associated radiocarbon dates and ceramics (Bijac ceramic complex pottery, ca. A.D. 100–400). The first monumental constructions in the Acropolis architectural sequence were built over some of these initial small-scale constructions. Based on radiocarbon dates, calendrical

TABLE 5.1
Radiocarbon Dates from the Copan Acropolis

Time Span	Inferred Dates	Sample No.	Provenience	Conventional B.P. Date	Conventional 1 Sigma	Calibrated Intercept	Calibrated 1 Sigma	Calibrated 2 Sigma
2	A.D. 530–600	B 50885	Str. Ante C. 91-8	1490 ± 80	A.D. 380–540			A.D. 345–645
2	A.D. 530–600	B 50888	Str. Indigo (N)	1340 ± 80	A.D. 530–690			A.D. 565–880
2	A.D. 530–600	B 52193	Str. Indigo (S)	1480 ± 120	A.D. 350–590			A.D. 360–650
2	A.D. 530–600	B 56951	Sub-Jaguar Vessel 9	1320 ± 60	A.D. 570–690			A.D. 595–860
3	A.D. 510–530	B 57308	MAS Cache 92-4	1420 ± 50	A.D. 480–580			A.D. 470–650
5	A.D. 400–470	B 56949	Construction fill	1570 ± 70	A.D. 310–450			A.D. 255–595
5	A.D. 400–470	B 56950	Construction fill	2050 ± 110	210 B.C.–A.D. 10			385 B.C.–A.D. 210
5	A.D. 400–470	B 73460	Str. Cobalto	1570 ± 50	A.D. 330–430	A.D. 530	A.D. 430–560	A.D. 400–620
5	A.D. 400–470	B 73461	Str. Clavel C. 94-2	1590 ± 70	A.D. 290–430	A.D. 450	A.D. 410–560	A.D. 340–630
5	A.D. 400–470	B 73462	Str. Tartan	1900 ± 60	10 B.C.–A.D. 110	A.D. 110	A.D. 60–210	10 B.C.–A.D. 250
5	A.D. 400–470	B 73463	Sub Court 5C	1640 ± 70	A.D. 240–380	A.D. 420	A.D. 370–530	A.D. 250–590
5	A.D. 400–470	B 73467	Yune Floor C. 94-4	1720 ± 60	A.D. 170–290	A.D. 350	A.D. 250–410	A.D. 210–440
6	A.D. 250–400	B 73464	Sub Chinch Floor	1660 ± 70	A.D. 220–360	A.D. 410	A.D. 340–450	A.D. 240–560
6	A.D. 250–400	B 73465	Sub Chinch Floor	1600 ± 60	A.D. 290–410	A.D. 440	A.D. 410–550	A.D. 350–610
6	A.D. 250–400	B 73466	Sub Chinch Floor	1570 ± 80	A.D. 300–460	A.D. 530	A.D. 410–600	A.D. 340–650

All dates determined by Beta Analytic Laboratories.

TABLE 5.2
Obsidian-Hydration Dates from the Copan Acropolis

Time Span	Inferred Dates	Sample No.	Provenience	Internal Fissure Date	Exterior Rim Date
2	A.D. 530–600	49/3–5.1	Ante Str C. 91-4	**A.D. 573**	A.D. 1155
2	A.D. 530–600	49/4–10.1	Construction fill	A.D. 863	A.D. 1522
3	A.D. 510–530	1/6–56.1	Construction fill	**A.D. 310**	**A.D. 253**
3	A.D. 510–530	1/6–56.2	Construction fill	A.D. 834	A.D. 1169
3	A.D. 510–530	1/6–61.1	Construction fill	A.D. 676	A.D. 1034
3	A.D. 510–530	1/6–1.2	Construction fill	**A.D. 416**	A.D. 799
3	A.D. 510–530	1/6–1.3	Construction fill	A.D. 778	A.D. 1165
5	A.D. 400–470	1/20–328.1	Construction fill	A.D. 533	A.D. 1148
5	A.D. 400–470	1/28–3.2	Construction fill	A.D. 691	A.D. 1466

Boldface dates are considered reliable.
All dates determined by Christopher Stevenson of ASC Group, Inc.

inscriptions, and ceramics, the episodes of Acropolis construction span the remainder of the Early Classic and the Late Classic eras (generally corresponding to the Acbi ceramic complex, ca. A.D. 400–600, and Coner ceramic complex, ca. A.D. 600–800).

Each building within the sequence also preserves evidence of its uses in its size and form, as well as the presence or absence of specific features such as benches, associated artifacts or residues, decorative motifs, and hieroglyphic inscriptions. Associated texts sometimes record the names and titles of rulers known from other inscriptions and thus can link buildings to specific reigns. Caches—the residues of rituals conducted to dedicate, renew, or terminate important buildings—may indicate ceremonial functions. Elaborate interments, including royal tombs, may be associated with special-purpose buildings (shrines or funerary temples). The identity of some individuals buried in tombs can be proposed, based on associated hieroglyphic texts and other evidence. Overall, we follow the generic categories used in Maya archaeology to distinguish ceremonial ("temple") buildings from more secular ("palace") buildings with residential and administrative functions, while realizing that these are arbitrary labels describing overlapping functions. Nonmasonry construction and masonry construction were used for both types of structures. We refer to individual structures by our interim field designations.

The accumulation of Acropolis architecture is a reflection of Maya traditions, practices, and beliefs (Ashmore 1991; Sharer 1994:492–493). Each building and location had meaning for the people who created and used it. Ultimately, our study attempts to understand these ancient meanings. Architecture, like the rest of the Maya world, was charged with supernatural power. The activation and termination of that power was marked by important rituals (varying according to the building's function). The superimposition of architecture replicated the life cycle with the birth, life, death, burial, and rebirth of buildings (Schele and Freidel 1990). Superimposition also has the practical consequence of being the most efficient way to achieve higher and more elaborate constructions. Thus, both practical and ideological purposes were served by sequences of buildings that had the same functions and occupied the same location over time.

THE ACROPOLIS EXCAVATIONS

Investigating the sequence of architecture in the Copan Acropolis confronts a familiar problem in Maya archaeology—surface remains are only the latest versions of a series of stratified constructions. Trenching or clearing excavations are normally used to document underlying earlier buildings. Both methods are time-consuming and expensive; more important, both destroy overlying architecture and thereby raise justifiable ethical concerns. Trenching is more restrictive than clearing and thus less destructive, but it yields correspondingly less information about underlying architecture. In the 1930s, combined trenching and clearing excavations were used at Uaxactun to strip away successive layers of monumental construction in order to record underlying buildings, until all but the earliest stage had been removed (Ricketson and Ricketson 1937; Smith 1950). Thirty years later, a massive axial north-south trench, combined with secondary clearing and tunneling, was used to document the architectural sequence of Tikal's North Acropolis (W. Coe 1990). Even though the Uaxactun and Tikal results are impressive, the destruction of overlying buildings would be difficult to justify today.

The Copan Acropolis presents a unique opportunity for using tunnels to document its architectural sequence with minimal destruction. At most Maya sites, construction fills are dry-laid and loose, making tunneling dangerous if not impossible. But fills at Copan are wet-laid, producing an extremely dense and stable matrix that was safely tunneled without structural supports. In contrast to excavating from above, lateral tunneling does not disturb surface buildings, and the earliest stages of construction can be as fully documented as the later stages. By removing fill, each Acropolis tunnel followed and exposed architecture without destroying later superimposed construction; when walls or floors had to be penetrated, their components were recorded for future replacement. A final benefit was lower cost than that of conventional excavation, because tunneling requires far less matrix to be removed. Safety was increased by electric lights, ventilation fans, and multiple exits; excavators were supplied with hard hats and emergency flashlights.

The tunnels beneath Structures 10L-16 and 10L-26 sprang from the original shafts excavated by the Carnegie Institution of Washington in the 1930s. In 1975 it was proposed to use the stratigraphic exposure of the famous Corte, the eroded eastern flank of the Acropolis created by the Río Copan, as the starting point for tunnels to define the entire Acropolis architectural sequence (Willey, Coe, and Sharer 1976). The first *corte* tunnels were excavated in 1978 under the direction of George Guillemin (n.d.). After one season and the opening of 100 m of tunnels, this work was suspended following Guillemin's death. Thereafter, Becker (1983) and Murillo (n.d.) opened test excavations along the corte base. ECAP was created in 1988 to renew the corte tunneling excavations (Sharer, Miller, and Traxler 1992). Most ECAP tunnel network was excavated under PAAC auspices between 1989 and 1996, following all levels of superimposed architecture generally westward from the corte to reveal the sequence under the eastern Acropolis. The western portion has been left unexplored (except for the original Carnegie tunnel beneath Structure 10L-11). The extent of the sequence has been expanded by linking the ECAP network to the tunnels beneath Structures 10L-16 and 10L-26, producing 3 km of tunnels. These links, and the sharing of data among all three programs, enable us to reconstruct an overall architectural sequence for the Acropolis. Between

1997 and 2002, ECAP concentrated on stratigraphic and architectural probes and on the excavation, documentation, and conservation of two early royal tombs. The recording and preserving of exposed structures and the consolidation of all major tunnels for future access (some tunnels and all test pits have been back-filled) continued through 2003.

DOCUMENTING THE ACROPOLIS SEQUENCE

The extensive tunnel exposures of Acropolis architecture require a sophisticated recording system. In documenting the complexities of the architectural sequence, precise three-dimensional recording is critical to understanding both horizontal layouts and stratigraphic relationships. Tunneling excavation creates its own special problems, and these are especially difficult to overcome with traditional surveying methods. To solve these problems, ECAP used a computer-assisted mapping program developed at MASCA (Weiss and Traxler 1991). This is based on the COMPASS system, combining an electronic total station, data collectors, and Macintosh computers with computer-assisted drafting (CAD) software, to collect, analyze, and depict architectural data. The advantages of this system include increased speed in point recording and data transfer, increased accuracy in survey station setup, traverses, and recording, and increased flexibility in data manipulation.

The COMPASS system allows large-scale, two- and three-dimensional architectural recording. These are rendered into a series of computer-generated plans of Acropolis architecture at various stages in the construction sequence. Traditional section drawings also record the architectural sequences along several north-south and east-west lines of the Acropolis grid. Detailed architectural records (plans, elevations, and sections) were also made by traditional means, along with black-and-white, color, and digital photography. The full stratigraphic and architectural record is still being prepared, so the interpretations offered here must be considered provisional (Sharer, Traxler, et al. 1999).

THE HISTORICAL RECORD

Classic Maya written records pertain exclusively to the elite class, and the bulk of these (most of which are on freestanding monuments, buildings, and artifacts) refer to the concerns of Maya rulers and their immediate kin or clients (Stuart and Houston 1989). But even with a limited historical record, there are opportunities to check on reliability of accounts, such as comparing texts referring to the same events from two different sites (for comparison, see Houston 1988; Schele and Freidel 1990). Adding independent evidence obtained from archaeology, iconography, and other sources can further refine the process of crosschecking.

HISTORICAL SOURCES AT COPAN

Because Maya rulers recorded much information about their political successes (but seldom their failures), social relationships, and ideology, the combination of archaeological and historical information from the Acropolis provides several sets of conjunctive data. The inferences derived from one Acropolis data set can be used to check against and amplify another. This procedure goes beyond the Acropolis to include data sets from other areas of the Main Group and the Copan Valley (W. Fash and Sharer 1991). Overall, the data available for such conjunctive treatment at Copan are probably greater than those at any other Maya site, given Copan's long history of research and the multifaceted archaeological investigations that have been continuous since 1976.

At Copan, considerable historical information has been gleaned from carved texts on buildings and on the extensive corpus of carved monuments and from occasional inscribed artifacts (W. Fash and Stuart 1991; Stuart 2000, chapter 10 in this volume). Copan's famous freestanding monuments have been well documented (W. Fash 2001; W. Fash and Stuart 1991; Martin and Grube 2000; Morley 1920; Schele and Freidel 1990), although heavily weighted to the Late Classic period (Sharer 2004). The most notable architectural text is the Hieroglyphic Stairway of Structure 10L-26 (W. Fash and B. Fash 1990). Its final phase dates to the reign of the fifteenth ruler, and ongoing research by Stuart is reconstructing much of the retrospective historical information it contains—the most extensive inscription produced by the Maya (W. Fash 2001; Sharer 1994:652).

Other dynastic accounts exist at Copan, but the most famous retrospective record is provided by Copan Altar Q. It portrays a sequence of sixteen rulers around its four sides, beginning with the founder, K'inich Yax K'uk' Mo', and ending with the sponsor of the monument, Yax Pasah (W. Fash and Stuart 1991; Marcus 1976; Proskouriakoff 1993; Riese 1988; Schele 1986; Stuart 2004). The text on its upper surface provides three important historical references between September 6, 426, and February 9, 427 (Martin and Grube 2000; Schele 1989a; Stuart 2004; Stuart and Schele 1986), corresponding to the inauguration and arrival events that established K'inich Yax K'uk' Mo' as Copan's dynastic founder.

Dating and comparative evidence indicates that the architectural development of the Acropolis closely corresponds to the time span of Copan's dynastic period, defined by the reigns of sixteen rulers between ca. A.D. 426 and 820 (W. Fash 1991; W. Fash and Stuart 1991; Schele 1988, 1989a). There are retrospective accounts of possible rulers before this dynastic era (Schele 1987b; Stuart 1986, 1989b, 2000, 2004). Two Late Classic monuments, Stelae I and 4, mention events at 8.6.0.0.0 (159) and 8.6.0.10.8 (160) associated with a possible ruler, the Copan bat emblem, and an unidentified place name also appearing on Tikal Stela 31. These texts may refer to the beginning of the Copan polity (Schele 1987b; Stuart 1986, 2004) during the Terminal Preclassic period, and they suggest historical connections to the Petén 280 years before the dynastic founding by K'inich Yax K'uk' Mo' (Stuart 2004).

Archaeological evidence indicates that several areas in the Copan Valley were centers of activity at the time of the Terminal Preclassic events recorded on Stelae I and 4 (Canuto 2004; W. Fash 2001:88). To date, however, there is no clear evidence of activity in the Main Group or, more specifically, beneath the Acropolis that dates to this period. If the Copan polity was founded in the Terminal Preclassic (ca. A.D. 160), these events seem to have been situated in areas apart from the Acropolis. In addition, unlike the Early Classic dynastic founding era, there is little evidence in the Copan Valley of Preclassic ties to the Petén. Instead, the ceramic and architectural record of Late and Terminal Preclassic Copan suggests local cultural traditions closely allied to those of the surrounding Southeastern Maya area (Canuto 2004; Traxler 2004b).

Closer to the dynastic founding era, the famous Copan Tomb I carved peccary skull (W. Fash 2001:figure 24) has a retrospective date equivalent to A.D. 376 and depicts a ruler and a secondary figure that might represent a young Yax K'uk' Mo' (Stuart 2004). Also, a retrospective 8.19.0.0.0 (416) date on Stela 15 refers to Yax K'uk' Mo' ten years before his inauguration as ruler of Copan. Even though this passage is without reference to Copan or any other place, it does suggest that K'inich Yax K'uk' Mo' may have had ties to Copan before the 426 founding events (Stuart 2004).

Based on actual references to K'inich Yax K'uk' Mo', the dynastic founding era should extend over a period of at least a decade (416–427). If we include the possible depiction on the peccary skull, the founding era would be extended by some forty years (376–427). In any case, the dynastic founding era corresponds to the beginning of the Acbi ceramic complex, dated to ca. 400, signaled by the appearance of distinctive pottery such as thin orange ware and cylindrical tripod vessels (Viel 1993b; Willey et al. 1994). The Acropolis excavations generally equate the appearances of Acbi ceramics with initial monumental constructions, as elsewhere in the Main Group (Cheek 1983b; Traxler 2004b). For this reason, we have proposed that the origins of the Acropolis date to the dynastic founding era (Sharer 1996; Sharer, Fash, et al. 1999). Once established, these initial monumental constructions evolved into the regal center for Copan's rulers and their entourages, the structures of the Monument Plaza and Acropolis. The Acropolis was the major setting for the ritual and administrative affairs conducted by Copan's rulers (W. Fash and Stuart 1991; Sharer, Miller, and Traxler 1992). We also conclude that each Copan ruler had a royal residence on the Acropolis (Sharer, Fash, et al. 1999; Traxler 2001), although he probably also maintained a domestic residence in an adjacent complex (Andrews and Bill, chapter 7 in this volume).

NEW HISTORICAL TEXTS FROM THE ACROPOLIS

The Acropolis tunnels have uncovered a series of previously unknown Early Classic texts directly associated with architecture. These provide significant new information about Early Classic events and confirm the existence of Copan's Early Classic rulers. The full meaning of these texts derives from their decipherment, their archaeological contexts, and the interpretations based on these data. Although the information gained from these new Early Classic texts is greatly enhanced by their documented archaeological contexts, their full meaning remains unrealized because of incomplete decipherment.

Most of these inscriptions were revealed in their original contexts. Examples of such undisturbed contexts include the glyphs and iconographic motifs rendered in plaster on two substructures, Margarita (discussed below) and Motmot (W. Fash 1998, 2001). Evidence from four carved texts indicates that they remain in their original contexts. These are the texts carved on the Motmot marker and on the Papagayo, Ante, and Rosalila steps (all are discussed below). One monument, Stela 63, was broken, moved, and reset by the Maya, but there is secure evidence for its original location immediately adjacent to its final location (W. Fash 2001:85). Only one early Acropolis text was anciently moved without evidence for its original location. This is the text carved on the Xukpi Stone found reset on Margarita's summit (also discussed below). Fortunately, there is evidence that this text was not greatly displaced in time and space, and its deciphered message allows plausible choices for its original provenience.

THE ARCHITECTURAL SEQUENCE AND THE KINGS OF COPAN

We now turn to a conjunctive synthesis relating the Early Classic architectural development of the Copan Acropolis to Copan's dynastic history. A preliminary correlation of the Acropolis sequence with the historically recorded rulers of Classic-period Copan is outlined in table 5.3 (see also Stuart, chapter 10 in this volume). The earliest known architecture beneath the Acropolis comprises three foci of development (figure 5.2): the Early Acropolis (also known as "MAS"), the Northeast Court Group, and the Structure 10L-26 Group (Sharer, Fash, et al. 1999; Sharer, Traxler, et al. 1999).

As the name implies, the Early Acropolis represents the ancestor of the Late Classic Acropolis visible today (Sedat 1996; Sedat and Sharer 1997; Sharer, Traxler, et al. 1999). Because of its size and complexity and the practical limitations on the extent of tunneling, the various stages of the Early Acropolis could be only partially revealed by excavation. It began as a relatively small group of buildings situated about 100 m west of the Río Copan on a slightly elevated platform, directly beneath the central part of the Acropolis in its final form. Excavation

TABLE 5.3

Preliminary Correlation of the Copan Dynastic Sequence with Acropolis Architecture

Ruler	Dates	Time Span	Text/date	Acropolis Platforms	Acropolis Structures	NE Court Groups	NE Court Structures	Structure 26 Group	Tombs
16 Yax Pasaj Chan Yoaat	763-822	1			10L-16	10L-11	10L-21A		10L-18
15 K'ak Yipyaj Chan K'awiil	749-763	1					10L-21?	10L-26-1st	
14 K'ak' Joplaj Chan K'awil	738-749	1					10L-22A	Ball Ct. III	
13 Waxaklajun Ub'ah K'awil	695-738	1					10L-22	10L-26-2nd Ball Ct. IIB Esmeralda	
12 Smoke Imix	628-695	1					10L-20?		Scribe's
11 Butz Chan	578-628	1		Purpula?		1 (East Court)			Galindo?
10 Moon Jaguar	553-578	2					Red	Chorcha	
9 Sak Lu...?	551-553	2					Olive	Ball Ct. IIA	
8 Wil Ohl Kinich	532-551	2	Rosalila Step? Ante Step/540		Rosalila?	2A, B	Ante Indigo, Zopilote	Sub-Jaguar	
7 B'alam Nehn	524-532	3			Azul				
6 Muyal Jol?	c. 510-524	3		Purple	Celeste	3A, B	Aguila, etc.		
5 Yukuc?	c. 500-510	4		Limón Amarillo		Turquoise	Toucon, etc.		
4 Ku Ix	c. 480-500	4	Papagayo Step	Teal/Acatan		4A-C	Loro, etc.		
3 Ya...?	c. 470-480	4	Stela 63 Margarita Panel	Mitzil Tzapah Witik	Chilan	Marisla Maravilla	Caimito	Mascarones Papagayo	
2 K'inich Popol Hol	c. 437-470	5	Xucpi/437		Yehnal	Cobalto 5A-C		Tartan Cominos, etc.	Margarita
1 K'inich Yax K'uk' Mo'	426/27-437	5	Motmot/435	Yune	Hunal Cab	Uranio	Murillo	Motmot/Ball Ct. 1 Yax	Hunal
(Predynastic)		6			Chinchilla	Oregano			

Note: This table supersedes previous correlations (Sharer, Fash, et al 1999: Table 10.1). Ruler names are after Martin and Grube 2000 and Stuart personal communication, 2002.

was aimed at documenting the central core of this architectural development and, where possible, the spatial extent of each stage. This work has defined a sequence of monumental platforms, each higher and larger in extent than its predecessor. As it expanded, the Early Acropolis eventually joined and then buried the adjacent Northeast Court Group, forming the core of the final stage of the Acropolis.

The Northeast Court Group evolved along the west bank of the Río Copan. At the time of the earliest dynastic rulers, it was a series of courtyard groups situated beneath the East Court in the northeast quadrant of the later Acropolis. The first documented court group was constructed of adobe, succeeded by two stages constructed of masonry (Traxler 1996, 2001, 2004a). By the end of the Early Classic, the final stage of the Northeast Court Group was engulfed by the expanding Acropolis and disappeared.

The third foci, the 10L-26-Sub Group, comprises a sequence of temples and ball courts situated directly north of the Early Acropolis (B. Fash et al. 1992; W. Fash 1998; W. Fash and B. Fash 2000; Williamson 1997). Now mostly buried beneath Structure 10L-26, this group developed adjacent to the Early Classic platforms located under the Monument Plaza further to the north (Cheek 1983b). Through mutual expansion, the 10L-26-Sub Group was eventually connected and joined with the expanding Acropolis to the south.

Our discussion is organized by rather arbitrary time spans, numbered from earliest (Time Span 6) to latest (Time Span 1). These time spans were derived from the stratigraphic divisions visible in the Corte (Sharer, Miller, and Traxler 1992) and later extended by architectural linkages to other areas beneath the Acropolis. The dates for these spans are based on chronometric assessments, but they are preliminary estimates, subject to revision by further analyses. In fact, some aspects of the sequence presented here have been refined from previously published summaries (Sharer, Fash, et al. 1999:Table 10.1; Sharer, Traxler, et al. 1999) based on new findings.

As mentioned, we date the beginnings of monumental construction beneath the Acropolis at ca. A.D. 400. Soon thereafter, the three original centers of architectural development were connected by shared floors and platforms. In less than a century, all three had become integrated into a single, elevated architectural mass that we

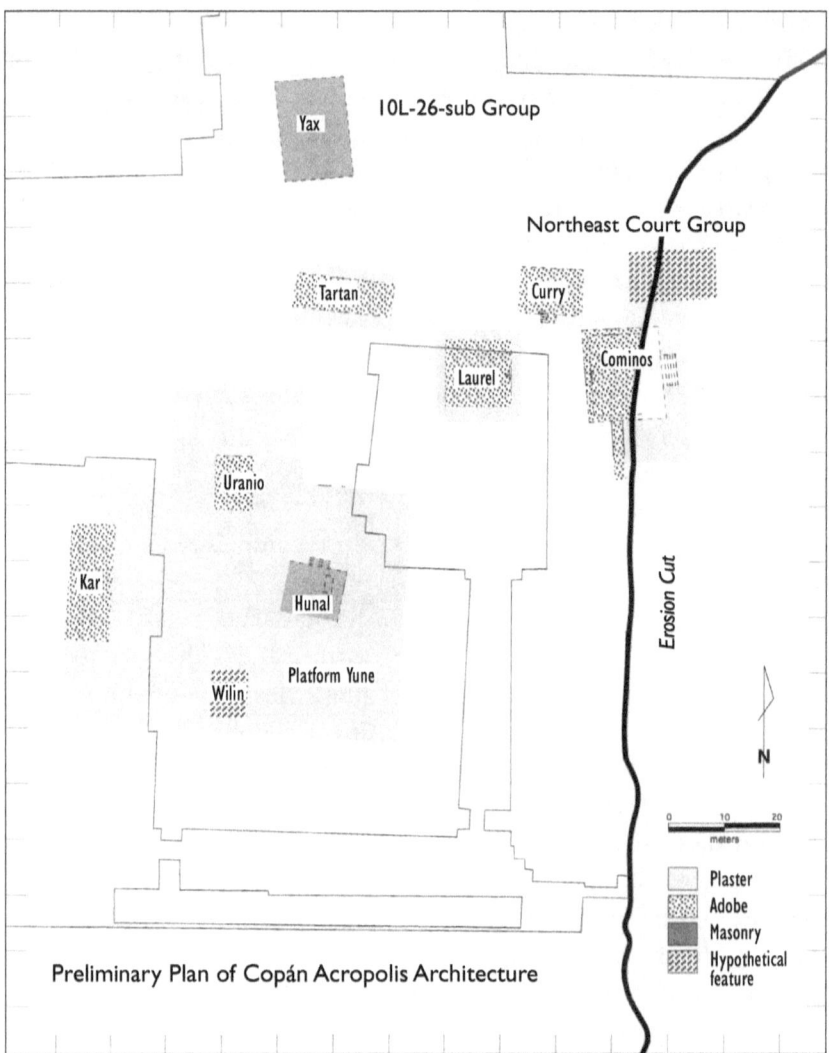

FIGURE 5.2

Preliminary plans of the Early Classic Acropolis, Time Span 5 (ca. A.D. 400–470): (above) Middle Stage of Yune Platform with Hunal and associated structures and (facing page) Witik Platform with Margarita and associated structures. (Prepared by L. P. Traxler)

define as the Acropolis. It took only a little more than one hundred years for the Early Classic Copan Acropolis to be expanded into a monumental elevated complex covering about the same north-south area as

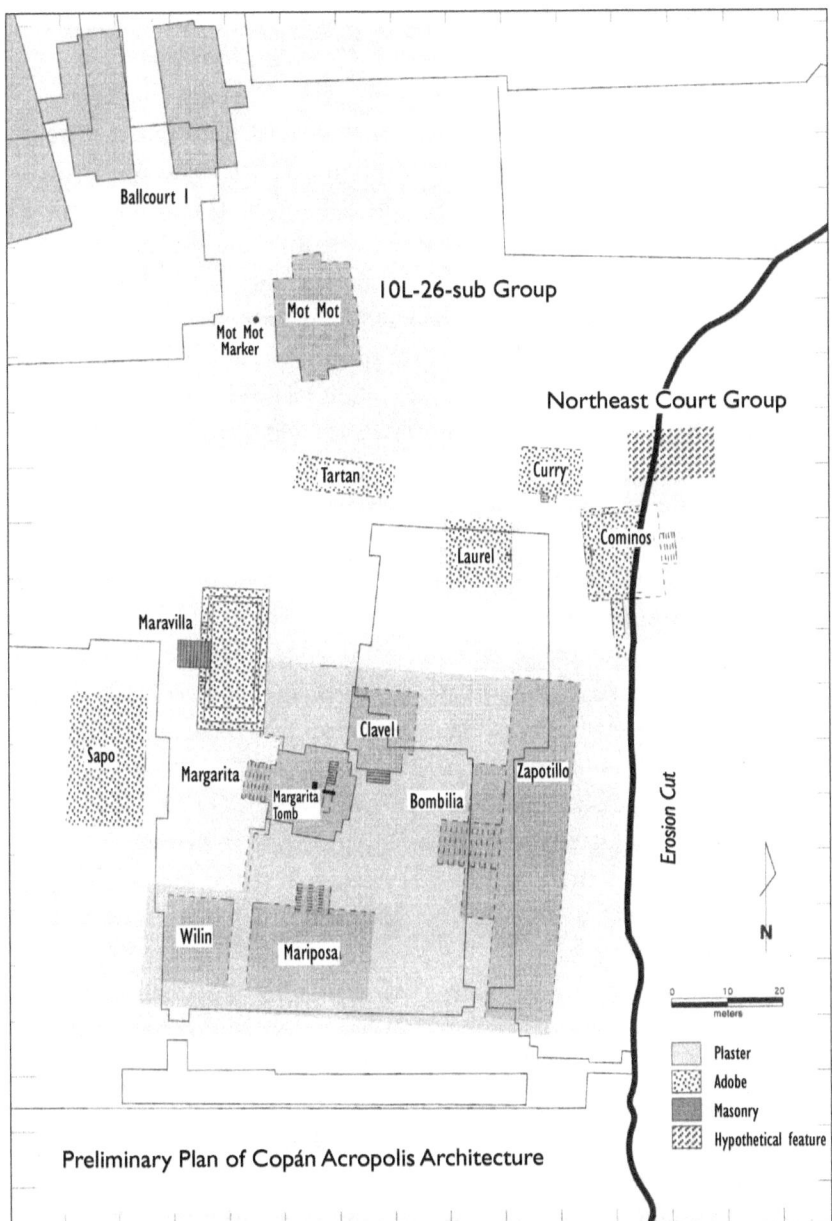

Preliminary Plan of Copán Acropolis Architecture

its final Late Classic form (refer to figure 6.1, in which Agurcia Fasquelle and B. Fash, this volume, present a stratigraphic section of the Early Acropolis).

THE PREDYNASTIC PERIOD (TIME SPAN 6, CA. A.D. 250–400)

The earliest and least known architecture beneath the Acropolis consists of several low, cobble-faced, earthen substructures constructed along the west bank of the Río Copan beneath the eastern margin of the Acropolis. Excavations in 1988 at the base of the Corte first exposed these cobble substructures, associated with human burials devoid of offerings (Murillo n.d.). The structures appear similar to a Bijac-period (100–400) substructure in the 9N-8 Group (Webster, Fash, and Abrams 1986). They also recall more extensive substructures beneath the Great Plaza to the north (Cheek 1983b; Traxler 2001, 2004b). Architecture of this kind is usually assigned residential or related functions. We assume that the earliest substructures beneath the Acropolis once supported nonelite residential buildings fashioned of perishable materials.

These cobble substructures are beneath an earth-and-plaster surface named *Chinchilla Floor* (average elevation 585.35 m). In 1994 an ECAP probe found the possible eastern edge of a cobble substructure associated with artifacts and carbon 0.60 m below this floor, and earlier cultural debris more than 1 m below this feature (elevation 583.45 m). This may correspond to an early occupational surface about a meter below Chinchilla, defined by Murillo (n.d.) in the southern corte. Chinchilla represents the initial platform along the west bank of the Río Copan, constructed over these remains of earlier occupation. An ECAP tunnel under the northeastern Acropolis found two larger Time Span 6 cobble constructions on Chinchilla Floor. One is a substructure that may be a precursor to the next construction stage (Cominos Substructure). The other appears to be a portion of a north-south wall (Oregano), several meters high, that paralleled the course of the Río Copan to its east. The wall's original extent and function remain conjectural because portions were destroyed by later construction and river erosion. Another segment may survive beneath the eastern edge of Yune Platform (see below).

The available dating evidence from pottery and radiocarbon samples (1-sigma ranges at A.D. 340–450, 410–550, and 410–600; see table 5.1) suggests that these Time Span 6 constructions are earlier than the historically dated dynastic founding events in A.D. 426 (late Bijac/early Acbi periods). Given the sparse exposures of Time Span 6 construction, this suggestion is more a hypothesis than a firm conclusion. But, given the characteristics of these structures, it may be that Copan's ruling center before A.D. 426 was located outside the site of the Acropolis (W. Fash and Sharer 1991:173).

THE DYNASTIC FOUNDING AND RULER 1 (EARLY TIME SPAN 5, CA. A.D. 400–437)

As mentioned, retrospective references to Copan's dynastic founder may begin as much as fifty years before the founding (Stuart 2000, 2004), although the earliest of these references (on the Copan peccary skull) appears to be unlikely (Sharer 2004). A more feasible reference on Stela 15 (416) is only ten years before the inauguration. There is also a mention of a K'uk' Mo' at Tikal on the Hombre de Tikal statue dated to A.D. 406 (Fahsen 1988; Martin and Grube 2000:33). These references may reflect events involving K'inich Yax K'uk' Mo' that culminated in his inauguration and arrival as Copan's ruler in 426/427. This span is reflected in the archaeological record by the appearance of new artifactual and architectural elements corresponding to the first part of the Acbi ceramic period (Sharer 2003a; Traxler 2004a). The dynastic founding events can also be correlated with the first major constructions underlying the later Main Group (Traxler 2004b), some of which were built over earlier earthen and cobble structures. In sum, data from archaeology, epigraphy, and allied sources are consistent with a hypothesis that K'inich Yax K'uk' Mo' founded a new royal capital on the west bank of the Río Copan, marked by events that might span one decade (416–426/427), two decades (406–426/427), or, less likely, half a century (376–426/427).

Beneath the Acropolis, this founding era is defined by the beginnings of the three separate groups that would eventually be integrated into a single Acropolis. In the Corte sequence, Time Span 5 corresponds to the construction of a new floor (average elevation 586.45 m) above the Chinchilla surface field-named *Murillo* (also called "Papo"). It capped a little more than a meter of fill forming a far larger platform along the west bank of the Río Copan. As with Chinchilla, we do not have evidence of its northern and southern limits, but Murillo Floor apparently abutted the higher ground level that supported the earliest stages of both the Early Acropolis and the 10L-26-Sub Group to the west.

The size and extent of the Time Span 5 constructions suggest that they were associated with elite activity and a shift in architectural concept and function from those of the earlier cobble substructures at this location. The construction of Murillo Floor (and Platform) and the first Time Span 5 buildings in all three groups began about the time Acbi ceramics were initiated (ca. A.D. 400), based on available ceramic associations and radiocarbon determinations (see table 5.1).

Time Span 5 substructures were constructed of adobe, cobbles, and cut-stone masonry. The adobe substructures supported perishable buildings, detected by the stubs of earthen walls, postholes, adobe masses, burned timbers, and other carbonized material. These adobe constructions were related to Preclassic architecture of the southeast Maya area and Maya highlands (Sharer, Traxler, et al. 1999). The apron-molding style of several of the earliest masonry constructions is nearly identical to Early Classic buildings in the central Petén. The *talud-tablero* style of one substructure could relate to Kaminaljuyu, to the Petén, or directly to central Mexico. Although these different construction methods and styles at Copan originated from distinct external regions, they coexisted in the earliest levels beneath the Copan Acropolis.

The Early Acropolis

The core sequence of the Early Acropolis has been worked out by Sedat and Lopez (2004; see also Sharer, Fash, et al. 1999; Sharer, Traxler, et al. 1999); its beginnings in Time Span 5 (ca. 400–470) are marked by substructures and buildings on an extensive low platform, Yune, that span an estimated fifty years (ca. 400–450). This initial platform was succeeded by a single-terraced platform stage, Witik (ca. 450–460), covered by an even larger single-terraced platform, Tzapah (ca. 460–470), each of which supported new substructures and buildings. By the end of Time Span 5, Tzapah Platform rose 5 m above the riverbank to its east.

In its earliest form, Yune was a ca. 70-by-70-m low, earthen platform constructed on the 0.6-m-higher ground west of Murillo Floor. The earliest Yune stage comprised an extensive paved space with a court group defined by three earthen structures on the northwest, south, and east. A burial with jade inlaid teeth was found under the northwest structure

FIGURE 5.3
Hunal Structure (Middle Stage of Yune Platform): talud-tablero style decoration on the northeastern substructure façade. (Photograph by D. W. Sedat)

(Uranio). A cache beneath the Yune Platform floor yielded a calibrated radiocarbon date of A.D. 250–410 (1-sigma range; see table 5.1), apparently from old wood. Postholes indicate that a perishable roof once protected a central earthen substructure, Cab, about 0.8 m high and 11 m north-south by 8.5 m east-west.

This basic layout was continued in the middle stage of Yune, with the addition of several larger constructions (see figure 5.2a). In the center, Cab was replaced by Hunal, a 1-m-high masonry substructure with a talud-tablero façade (figure 5.3). Hunal's size and form are unknown because all but its northeastern quarter was demolished before burial by later construction. The preserved portion includes remnants of a northern unbalustraded stairway and an eastern balustraded stairway, suggesting an eastern orientation and access. Hunal was refurbished several times with red-painted plaster and a terminal coat of coarse, cream-colored plaster.

Hunal's masonry summit building has traces of two rooms, one on the north with door jambs facing the northern stairway and one to the south that presumably faced the eastern stairway. If this building was symmetrical along its east-west axis, there was a third room on the south, presumably facing a vanished southern stairway. An earlier version of Hunal's summit building had walls ca. 1 m thick, indicating possible vaulted construction. The later version had thinner walls (0.6 m) closer to the substructure margins, increasing interior space and making a beam-and-mortar roof more likely. An interior, red-painted doorway (offset to the east) provided access between the northern and central rooms. Cord holders indicate that the central room could be closed off for privacy.

Fragments of painted plaster in demolition debris indicate that polychrome murals decorated the interior of one or both versions of Hunal's summit building. Among the scenes visible on these fragments are a seated figure gesturing toward a standing figure and painted footprints ascending a stairway, suggesting that the Hunal mural may have depicted an inauguration scene, perhaps that of K'inich Yax K'uk' Mo' (Bell n.d.).

The second version of Hunal's summit building provided space for a tomb intruded 2 m below the floor of its northern room. A 1.8-m-high, north-south-oriented, vaulted masonry chamber was constructed in this intrusion, measuring 2.7 m by 1.5 m. Before the vault was closed, a large stone slab was placed in the chamber, resting on four round, stone pedestals. The Hunal Tomb (Burial 95-2) contained the bones of a single individual placed supine (head to the south) on this stone bier, adorned by several large jade objects. The bones are of a robust male a little over 5'6" tall, between fifty-five and seventy years of age at death, with a series of healed bone traumas caused by combat-style injuries (Buikstra et al. 2004). Some bones were covered or painted with cinnabar, indicating, along with other evidence, that the tomb was re-entered at least once for secondary ritual activity. This activity or possibly seismic events displaced some bones and adornments to the tomb floor. Offerings on the floor included Early Classic pottery vessels and other objects (Bell et al. 2004).

The vault was capped by a masonry plinth that rose 30 cm above the north room floor. Tomb entry was likely by an unplastered, northern capstone twice the width of the others. The surface of the plinth was covered with at least two layers of plaster, the upper coat presumably applied following the final tomb re-entry. Although the evidence for multiple doorways and rooms suggests that Hunal's original function was residential, its use obviously changed with the death and burial of a prominent adult male in the Hunal Tomb. Following this interment and subsequent re-entry rituals, Hunal's summit building and much of its substructure were demolished to make way for a new masonry structure, which completely buried it and its tomb.

The Northeast Court Group

The Northeast Court Group sequence has been worked out by Traxler (1996, 2001, 2004a; see also Sharer, Fash, et al. 1999; Sharer, Traxler, et al. 1999). Acropolis Time Span 5 saw the earliest arrangements of palace-type buildings in the Northeast Court Group, comprising both substructures and buildings constructed of adobe enclosing relatively open central patios. Although these succeed earlier Time Span 6 structures on Chinchilla Floor, they depart from their predecessors in being far larger in extent and height, and in their formal arrangement around patios.

The initial architecture of Time Span 5 consists of simple, single-stage, earthen substructures about 1 m in height. These were modified and expanded over time. The best-known examples (see figure 5.2) form a three-sided patio group open to the south, designated Patio 5B (to allow for a probable Patio 5A to the east). The summit of the northern substructure (Curry) was reached by a southern outset adobe staircase. We assume that there were patio-facing staircases for the other substructures as well but that the eastern substructure (Cominos) might have faced east to Patio 5A, because no stairs have been found on its western side. A dull, earthen-based red paint covered both terrace and building surfaces.

The partially defined Patio 5C lies immediately west of structure Laurel on the west side of Patio 5B. A low adobe substructure (Tartan), constructed in several stages, defined the northern margin of Patio 5C, as well as the southern boundary for the 10L-26-Sub Group. A single, calibrated radiocarbon date from the burned timbers associated with Tartan (1-sigma range of A.D. 60–210; see table 5.1) apparently derives from wood of substantial age at the time of its use. A deposit of carbon from fill beneath Patio 5C yielded a calibrated radiocarbon date of A.D.

370–530 (1-sigma range; see table 5.1). A thin-plaster apron floor originally extended from the base of Tartan several meters to the south toward the Early Acropolis before merging with an earthen surface that formed the original floor of Patio 5C.

Lack of preservation inhibits descriptions of the adobe buildings that stood on the summits of these Time Span 5 substructures. But at least one, the building on the western Laurel Substructure of Patio 5B, had a tamped-earth interior floor covered with a series of very thin plaster surfaces. This building had thin, interior partitions (indicated by regular interruptions in its plaster floor), which define interior corners and lip-ups to the now-vanished walls of multiple rooms. Evidence for the roofs on these buildings comes from remnants of burned wooden supports and possible thatching.

The 10L-26-Sub Group

The sequence of the 10L-26-Sub Group has been worked out by Fash (1998, 2001; see also B. Fash et al. 1992; W. Fash and B. Fash 2000; Sharer, Fash, et al. 1999). The earliest known architecture in the 10L-26-Sub Group, Yax Substructure, is dated to Time Span 5 (see figure 5.2). Yax was built of masonry (no adobe construction has been defined in this group). Like Hunal to the south, Yax began a notable sequence of superimposed masonry architecture that spans Copan's dynastic period. In Yax's case, the sequence culminates in Structure 10L-26 and its famed Hieroglyphic Stairway, completed during the reign of Ruler 15 but in use to the end of dynastic rule (W. Fash 2001; Sharer, Fash, et al. 1999). Although little remains of Yax Substructure, it was apparently oriented to the west, because it had a west-facing stairway that may have led to an unpaved court beyond.

Yax was succeeded by a slightly larger masonry substructure, Motmot, which, in its creation, destroyed much of its predecessor. Motmot's façade has Petén-style apron moldings decorated by four modeled-stucco sky bands. Its western stairway was served by an extensive plaster floor (elevation 588.20 m) on its western and southern sides. To the west, the Motmot Floor is associated with Ball Court IA, the earliest at Copan. Immediately to the west of the Motmot stairway, a remarkable, early carved monument was set into the Motmot Floor (W. Fash and B. Fash 2000; Stuart 2000, 2004).

The Motmot marker is a disk-shaped limestone monument carved over Motmot's somewhat eroded upper surface (see figure 5.6), indicating that it was exposed for some time. It depicts two individuals identified as the dynastic founder, Yax K'uk' Mo' on the left side and his son, Ruler 2, on the right; a double-column hieroglyphic text separates the two. The text names Yax K'uk' Mo' of Copan (leaf-nosed bat emblem) and a dedication that took place at 9.0.0.0.0 (Stuart 2004). A second phrase refers to Copan Ruler 2 and a past date recorded by a distance number referring to the founder's Copan arrival in 427 (Stuart 2004). The scene appears to depict an important interaction, perhaps an heir designation from father to son. The figures' feet rest on symbols associated with sacred places (9 Imix and 7 Kan), and the Maya symbol for the entrance to the underworld frames the entire scene.

The Motmot marker covered a circular masonry chamber, linked by its form to Teotihuacan burial practices (W. Fash and B. Fash 2000; W. Fash 2001). The chamber contained the extremely well-preserved skeletal remains of a single adult female (Buikstra et al. 2004), as well as pottery, shell, jade, and organic offerings, and is associated with three presumed trophies (three male skulls). Evidence shows that the chamber was reopened at a later time, during which the incompletely decomposed remains of the principal interment were removed and subjected to smoking, then replaced. Additional offerings were placed at this time on the tomb capstone before being sealed by the setting of the Motmot marker (W. Fash 1998, 2001).

Discussion

The archaeological evidence indicates that at the beginning of Time Span 5, a new royal center was laid out and constructed on the east bank of the Copan River. This established a location that continued to develop as the Copan Acropolis for the remainder of the Classic period. From this point on, we can propose links between architectural stages and individual rulers. Some of these links are based on texts that were found associated with buildings and that provide dates and royal names; others are hypothetical, based on stratigraphic associations and chronological positions within the overall Acropolis sequence.

The combined historical and archaeological evidence indicates that the beginnings of Copan's new royal center were associated with three profound events that took place within a span of less than two decades. The first of these were the specific inauguration and arrival events associated with K'inich Yax K'uk' Mo' in A.D. 426 and 427, retrospectively recorded on Altar Q (Schele 1986; Stuart and Schele 1986) and referred to on the Motmot marker (Stuart 2004). The second event was the great calendrical Period Ending of 9.0.0.0.0, nine years later in A.D. 435, recorded by the Motmot marker. The third was the death of Yax K'uk' Mo', probably late in A.D. 437, a date recorded on the Xukpi Stone (discussed below). These three events continued to be fundamentally important to Copan's dynastic succession, and they were commemorated by Acropolis architecture long thereafter.

The basic template for the new royal center was established by the architectural plan of Time Span 5 and was followed (with one major modification) by all of Yax K'uk' Mo's descendants. In its original version, the new center followed a north-south axis, with a royal ritual and residential complex in the south (the Early Acropolis) and a temple and ballcourt complex (10L-26-Sub Group) to the north. Along the river to the east stood an allied royal palace (Northeast Court Group) (Sharer 1996; Traxler 2004b).

We link the initial stage of Yune Platform with the founding era events immediately before the actual inauguration of the founder (ca. 400–426). Expanded masonry construction of Yune Platform's middle stage can be linked with the beginning of K'inich Yax K'uk' Mo's reign. The focus of this complex was Hunal, a talud-tablero-style structure that we propose had a direct association with K'inich Yax K'uk' Mo', perhaps his royal residence. This original complex also included an expanded adobe substructure (Cobalto) that marked another important ritual focus, also probably associated with founding era events. This second significant locus was to be commemorated by two succeeding adobe structures for about a century.

Hunal anchored the southern end of the new center's axis, and its northern end was established by Yax, a new Maya-style masonry building dated to the beginning of the founder's reign. The other early component of this 10L-26-Sub Group was Copan's first-known masonry ball court. Both Yax's successor, Motmot Structure, and the Motmot marker apparently commemorate the 9.0.0.0.0 Period Ending ceremonies (W. Fash and B. Fash 2000). The new royal center also provided for future growth by creating an extensive platform along the west bank of the Río Copan (Murillo Floor). The first Northeast Court Group was built on this platform, comprising at least three large, multiroom adobe buildings on elevated earthen substructures (Patios 5A–C).

The death and burial of K'inich Yax K'uk' Mo' completed this intense period of construction activity at Copan. We correlate these events with the construction of a vaulted tomb beneath the floor of Hunal. Although the identity of Hunal Tomb's occupant may never be certain, consistent evidence indicates that this is the tomb of K'inich Yax K'uk' Mo' himself (Sharer, Traxler, et al. 1999; Sharer 2004).[3] Hunal and its tomb established the symbolic center for the Acropolis, which was maintained for the remainder of Copan's dynastic history by a succession of temples built over this locus. Several of these structures and at least one associated text (the Xukpi Stone, discussed below) refer to K'inich Yax K'uk' Mo'. Glyphic references to the founder and carved figures of Yax K'uk' Mo' adorned Structure 10L-16, the final temple built over this central location (Agurcia Fasquelle 1997; Taube 2004).

THE MAKING OF A DYNASTY: RULER 2 (LATE TIME SPAN 5, CA. A.D. 437–470)

The recovered archaeological and historical data summarized here have greatly amplified our knowledge of K'inich Yax K'uk' Mo's reign. First, there is evidence that he established a new royal center at Copan, placed in a location previously undeveloped by monumental construction. Although most of the new center's individual buildings were modest in scale, collectively they expressed a monumental design carried out over a large area with provision for future expansion (much of the Main Group) and included buildings of earth and masonry, rendered in new foreign-inspired styles. Second, he apparently reigned for a short period (ca. 426/427–437). Third, he reigned at an especially significant time, one that included the 9.0.0.0.0 Period Ending, allowing him to sponsor some long-remembered ceremonies around this auspicious date (W. Fash and B. Fash 2000; Sharer 2003c; Stuart 2004).

The status of K'inich Yax K'uk' Mo' as founder, like that of all dynastic founders, was a creation of his successors. In this case, the son who succeeded Yax K'uk' Mo' apparently honored his father and at the same time promoted his own interests. Of course, we can only speculate about Ruler 2's motives, but because success often breeds success, the son presumably strengthened his own position by boosting his father's prestige. Therefore, the status of K'inich Yax K'uk' Mo' as dynastic founder, embellished by his successors to increase their own power and prestige, probably originated with his son's promotional activities. This effort is most visible in the monumental expansions of the Acropolis begun during Ruler 2's reign.

The Early Acropolis

After his father's burial, Ruler 2's first major construction was dedicated to his father's commemoration as dynastic founder. We correlate this event in the Acropolis sequence with the construction of Yehnal, the structure that buried Hunal and its tomb. This was followed by expansions of structures on Yune's northern and western sides (see figure 5.2b). Together, these define the final version of Yune Platform (ca. 437–450). Yehnal's construction included provisions for a second vaulted chamber located adjacent to the Hunal Tomb. Although the Yehnal chamber remained unused for some time, its proximity to the Hunal Tomb indicates intent to share the same sacred space and probably reflects a close relationship between the individuals buried within each. This new Yehnal chamber was vaulted and, originally, almost 1 m higher than the adjacent Hunal Tomb. Several later modifications reduced its size. The Yehnal Chamber also had a staircase leading down from the new summit building to an entrance through its northern end-wall.

In contrast to its predecessor's talud-tablero façade, Yehnal was rendered in an apron-molded style (both were red-painted). Its substructure covered less area than Hunal, but Yehnal was almost twice as high (ca. 2 m). Whereas Hunal probably faced east, Yehnal's large outset stairway faced west, flanked by stucco-modeled panels painted in several colors. The excavated south panel (figure 5.4) is dominated by a central sun god mask, identified as *K'inich* (great sun) *Taj* (torch) *Wayib* (spirit companion), known from central Petén architecture (Martin and Grube 2000:195) and Tikal Stela 39 (LaPorte and Fialko 1990). A feline chinstrap is immediately below this mask. Across the top of the panel is a sky band, identified by a Lamat (great star) sign, and a

FIGURE 5.4
Yehnal Structure: modeled-stucco K'inich Ajaw mask on the western façade. (Photograph by D. W. Sedat)

Baktun Bird Deity. Pointing downward from this is a profile, square-nosed serpent head, possibly representing one of the Cosmic Monster's heads.

Yehnal had small auxiliary staircases on its northern and southern sides but, overall, established a west-facing orientation for a succession of temples that dominated the core of Copan's evolving Acropolis, culminating almost four centuries later with Structure 10L-16. Yehnal's decorated panels were preserved by careful burial, most likely because of their sacred importance. Its nearly unweathered, single-coated plastered surface indicates that Yehnal was used for only a short period.

Yehnal faced a courtyard to its west. Clavel Structure, with a south-facing staircase decorated on either side by modeled stucco panels, was constructed abutting Yehnal's northeast corner. A calibrated intercept radiocarbon date of A.D. 450 comes from a Clavel cache (see table 5.1). Elsewhere on Yune Platform, Uranio Structure was replaced by Cobalto, a larger earthen substructure more than 2 m high. A deposit of burned wood and broken jade, probably from a termination ritual, yielded a single, calibrated radiocarbon date of A.D. 430–560 (1-sigma range; see table 5.1).

All of Yune Platform's structures were buried under Witik Platform (ca. 450–460). At its center, a new and much larger structure, Margarita, replaced Yehnal. In the process, the vaulted Yehnal Chamber was modified and its staircase extended for continued access from Margarita's new summit building, Xukpi. A cache under its northeast corner contained a large amount of mercury. A small masonry crypt axially placed beneath the Xukpi floor (Cache 93-16) contained two heavily burned, lidded vessels. One held the burned bones of a turkey, and the other, an array of cut-shell and carved-jade pieces, including a large pyrite-mosaic mirror and mercury.

Like Yehnal, Margarita was painted red, with beautifully formed Petén-style apron moldings accented by cream-painted panels. It also continued a westward orientation with stucco-modeled panels (2.4 m high by 3.2 m long) on either side of its outset western staircase, facing an enlarged courtyard. The southern panel (figure 5.5) preserves much of its original polychrome paint (red, green, yellow, cream, and gray-blue, with fine-line detail in black). The central scene is a full-figure glyph reading *K'inich Yax K'uk' Mo'* composed of two full-figure, intertwined profile birds. The north bird is a quetzal (*k'uk'*) painted green with a red breast and a crest. The south bird is a Scarlet Macaw (*Mo'*) with a long red tail and body and bands of yellow and blue on its wing. On the heads of both birds are *yax* signs, and inside the beaks are profile heads of the Sun God (*K'inich*). Both birds stand on a large glyph group composed of a bar-and-dot number nine, an oval-shaped moon/Imix sign, and two human footprints (in relief). This composition is very similar to the glyph under the feet of the left-hand personage on the Motmot marker, identified as K'inich Yax K'uk' Mo' (figure 5.6; W. Fash and B. Fash 2000).

The northern stucco panel remains unexcavated, except for small portions cleared to verify its similarity in composition to the south side. An important difference is that the central glyphs beneath the two

FIGURE 5.5
Margarita Structure: modeled-stucco emblem of the founder's name, K'inich Yax K'uk' Mo', *on the western façade. (Photograph by D. W. Sedat)*

northern intertwined birds are composed of a scrolled motif, a Kan cross, and a bar-and-dot number seven. This glyph group is similar to the right-hand glyph under the feet of the right-hand personage on the Motmot marker identified as Ruler 2 (see figure 5.6). Margarita's position in the Acropolis architectural sequence indicates that it dates to the reign of the founder's son, Ruler 2.

To the northwest, a new and much larger adobe substructure, Maravilla, replaced Cobalto. Maravilla was maintained for a longer period than its predecessors, well beyond the use span of Witik Platform. It rose in three narrow terraces to a height of 5 m, its surface covered with red hematite paint. There are remnants of a red-painted adobe summit building, initially reached by narrow, inset adobe steps.

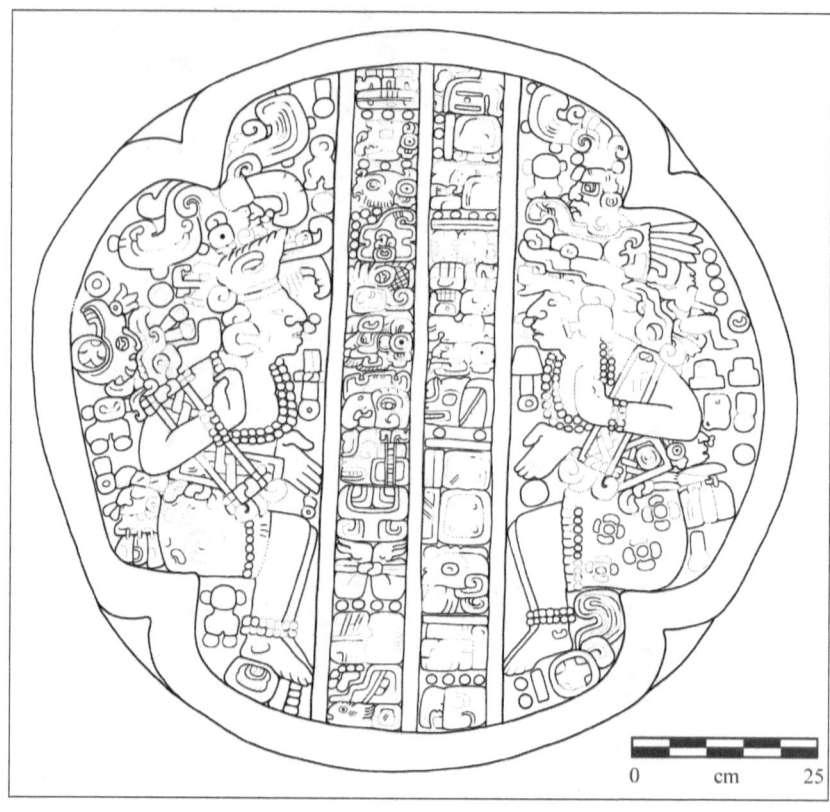

FIGURE 5.6

Motmot marker: preliminary drawing of the portraits of the founder (left) and Ruler 2 (right) and text. (Drawing by B. Fash)

A roof supported by four massive timber corner uprights (one timber remnant was recovered) protected both the substructure and the building. During its use span, a later outset west-facing staircase was constructed of adobe (in its upper extent) and masonry (in its lower extent beyond the roof drip line).

Witik was replaced by Tzapah Platform (ca. 460–470), which ultimately rose 5 m high and supported a new array of substructures. Margarita's western façade was unweathered and painted only once before being covered by an initial component of Tzapah Platform. This westward-projecting terrace buried not only Margarita's stairway but also the court to its front, leaving the Xukpi building on Margarita's summit accessible for an unknown interval. A north-facing stairway gave access to Tzapah Platform from a new elevated western court flanked by Maravilla on its east side.

Burial 95-1 was placed in Tzapah Platform on the axis of Margarita to the east. It consists of the bones of a single adult male extended supine, head to the west, wrapped in several reed mats. Accompanying the remains of this apparent dedicatory sacrifice were mosaic jade-and-hematite earflares, shells, and other jade mosaic jewelry, as well as several ceramic vessels and perishable materials painted with stucco. Cut-shell "goggles" on the cranium link this interment to central Mexico, reinforced by a bundle of atlatl darts found beside the skeleton (Bell et al. 2004).

Tzapah Platform buried almost all the previous architecture of Witik Platform. One important exception is Maravilla, which remained in use, although Tzapah encroached upon its southeast corner. Tzapah Platform provided open space around Xukpi building, which was flanked on its north side by a new substructure (Marisela). Soon thereafter, Xukpi was demolished and a new vaulted chamber was built over the stairway that led into the old Yehnal Chamber below (figure 5.7). Destined to be incorporated in the fill of a new substructure, Chilan, this upper chamber included a large and well-preserved stone with a carved text set (carved side up) as the base of its southern end-wall (figure 5.8).

The Xukpi Stone is named after the floor of Margarita's summit building, where it was reset. The text shares several characteristics with the Motmot text, including the use of unique or unusual glyphs that make decipherment difficult (Stuart 2004). As with the Motmot marker, the Xukpi text (Schele, Grube, and Fahsen 1994; Stuart 2004) does not begin with a date, but with an Introductory Glyph that may function as a verb glossed as "to venerate." The subject can be read as a death place (tomb or funerary shrine?). The protagonist is a Copan Ajaw, Ruler 2, followed by a possible reference to a dedication linked to an unusual date, "2 tuns 13 Ajaw," or 9.0.2.0.0 13 Ajaw 3 Keh (November 30, 437). The penultimate glyph pair names the dynastic founder, K'inich Yax K'uk' Mo'. The final two glyphs may refer to a title or relationship followed by the name of another individual (possibly read as *Siyaj K'ak'*).

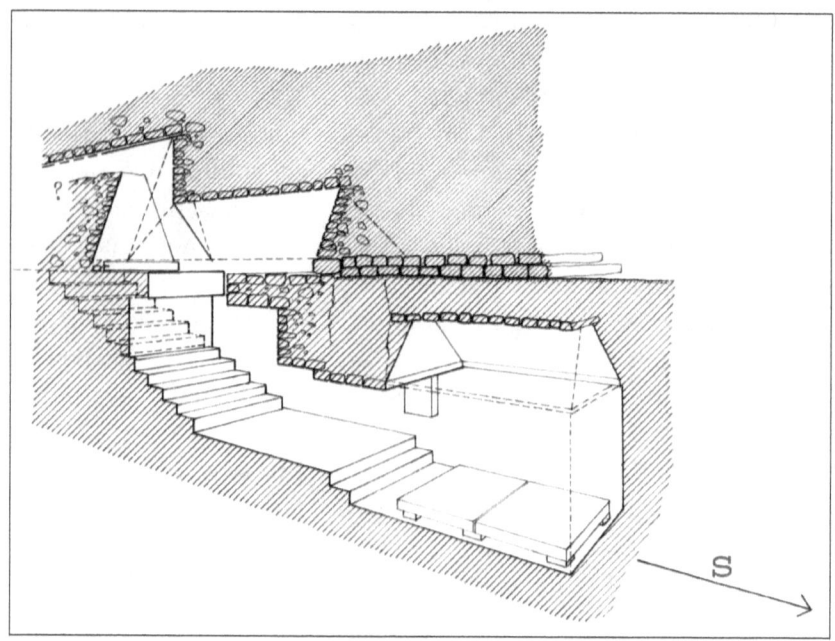

FIGURE 5.7

Margarita Tomb: a perspective view showing chambers 1 and 2. (Drawing by José Espinoza after an original drawing by R. Larios)

FIGURE 5.8

Xukpi Stone: preliminary drawing of the hieroglyphic text. (Drawing by L. Schele and F. López)

Its position and the traces of stucco, red paint, and burning indicate that the Xukpi Stone was a step or bench reset from a previous location. Thus, its 437 date, its references to both the dynastic founder, Yax K'uk' Mo', and his son, Ruler 2, and possible mention of a third individual were originally associated with a previous architectural setting (Sedat and Sharer 1994), mostly likely elsewhere on Margarita itself. The text probably refers to the Hunal Tomb, although this cannot be certain. What is certain is that the Hunal Tomb had been sealed and buried beneath both Yehnal and Margarita before the Xukpi Stone was reset. The date in the Xukpi text is consistent with the archaeological dating of both Yehnal and Margarita. Because the final modifications of the Margarita Tomb and construction of Chilan can be no earlier than the date in the Xukpi text, the 437 date provides support for the dating of both previous and subsequent activity.

The Margarita Tomb (Burial 93-2) was likely used for a royal interment about the time of the construction of the new burial-offering chamber (designated Chamber 2), along with further modifications in the old Yehnal chamber (Chamber 1) below (see figure 5.7). Chamber 2 held offerings of jade, pottery, and perishable materials (matting, textiles, or similar materials), including an extraordinary polychrome, stuccoed, cylindrical tripod (Vessel 1) rendered in a distinctive Early Classic fusion of central Mexican and Maya styles (Reents-Budet et al. 2004). This depicts a goggle-eyed Tlaloc figure peering out of the doorway of a temple set upon a talud-tablero substructure similar to the Hunal Substructure. Chamber 1 held the bones of an adult female in an extended supine position (head to the south) on a large stone slab, later broken by compression or tectonic activity, supported by four stone, drum-shaped supports. A stunning array of jade, shell, pottery, and other offerings adorned the remains. The buried individual was likely between fifty and seventy years old at death (Buikstra et al. 2004). The bones were painted with cinnabar (mercuric sulfide), and the chamber's interior is also stained with this red pigment. Early Classic pottery vessels, stuccoed mirrors, and other objects were placed on the floor beneath the slab. There is evidence for subsequent modifications and access to the tomb after the interment, indicating that for a number of years after burial, this lady continued to be venerated inside her tomb (Bell et al. 2004; Sharer, Traxler, et al. 1999).

Although Chilan buried Margarita, a new vaulted passageway allowed continued access from the north to the previously constructed tomb below. This new passageway was constructed in two stages, ultimately totaling 4 m in length. The access it provided from Chilan explains the evidence for continued activity in the Margarita tomb after the placement of the burial.

The Northeast Court and 10L-26-Sub Groups

Later expansions and refurbishments of the Northeast Court Group palaces can be assigned to the reign of Ruler 2. The eastern (Cominos) and northern (Curry) substructures of Patio 5B were expanded by the construction of second terraces on their summits, more than doubling their heights to 2.4 m and 2 m, respectively. A substantial plaster floor paved Patio 5C for the first time. This extended from the northern basal terrace of the Early Acropolis northward to its abutment with Tartan, where it overlies the earlier floor on the south side of this low substructure. A far more monumental undertaking saw Motmot Substructure, its associated floor, the Motmot marker, and Tartan Structure buried under the fill of an extensive new platform known as the "Gran Corniza." Much later, the southern façade of the Gran Corniza was almost completely demolished, but the location of its southern base was detected on the Patio 5C floor south of substructure Tartan.

In the 10L-26-Sub Group, the Gran Corniza Platform supported an extraordinary new building known as "Papagayo," which, in turn, fronted an elevated platform (Mascarones) to its east decorated by stucco masks. Inside the large room of Papagayo, located directly over the Motmot marker and its tomb, were found three fragments of a beautifully carved monument, Stela 63 (figure 5.9). Although two fragments had been reset at the time Papagayo was terminated and its room filled in, the base of the monument was still in situ on a low interior platform set against the rear (east) wall. This fact, its uneroded state and uncarved back, clearly indicates that Stela 63 was originally set against the wall inside Papagayo (W. Fash 2001:figure 38).

Stela 63 is a large rectangular stone carved with texts on three sides: two columns on the front and a row of cartouches on each side. Most of the inscription is on the largest (upper) fragment; the glyphs at its base were destroyed when the monument was broken. The text opens with a 9.0.0.0.0 Long Count date. The side texts refer to Ruler 2, named as child of K'inich Yax K'uk' Mo'. Unfortunately, the date of the dedication of Stela 63 (or Papagayo) is not given. It obviously must have been after the date of the Motmot marker and most likely within the reign of Ruler 2. W. Fash (personal communication 1993) suggests ca. 9.1.10.0.0 (A.D. 465) as the date for the dedication of both

Early Classic Royal Power in Copan

Papagayo and Stela 63, because Ruler 2 may have lived until about 472 (Schele and Grube 1994b) and an interval of ca. thirty years would be sufficient for the exposed Motmot Marker to erode before Papagayo buried it.

Discussion

Ruler 2's effort to promote his father as Copan's dynastic founder is reflected in the two texts he sponsored, recovered by the excavations beneath the Acropolis. Both of these refer to his father. With the Xukpi Stone, Ruler 2 apparently dedicated a mortuary temple or tomb in 9.0.2.0.0 (437). In the 10L-26-Sub Group, Stela 63 recalled the Period Ending events celebrated with his father, K'inich Yax K'uk' Mo'. Stela 63 was probably dedicated with the new shrine, Papagayo (which replaced Motmot), his father's temple, associated with Copan's first ball court.

Between the death of his father (probably in 437) and perhaps as late as the estimated end of Time Span 5 (ca. 470), Ruler 2 embarked on an unprecedented building program that we propose was designed to realize and expand his father's plans for Copan's new royal center. For this, we can now recognize him as Classic Copan's first great builder. The original earthen court structures of the Northeast Court Group were expanded. Ruler 2 must have sponsored the final phase of Yune Platform and its much larger Witik Platform, which replaced most of the buildings erected by his father,

Figure 5.9

Stela 63: preliminary drawing of the hieroglyphic text. (Drawing by B. Fash)

with the building of Yehnal over Hunal and its tomb, apparently as his father's first funerary temple. The sun deity masks and other motifs on Yehnal are evidence of its powerful cosmological associations and may refer to the founder's K'inich title. Yehnal was also provisioned with a tomb chamber adjacent to the Hunal Tomb, which was modified with the construction of the succeeding structure, Margarita, the new centerpiece of Witik Platform. Margarita was the second shrine over Hunal and its tomb, and the prominent display of the founder's name associated with supernatural locations on Margarita's façade is an obvious and explicit commemoration of Yax K'uk' Mo'. Either Yehnal or Margarita was the most likely structure originally associated with the Xukpi Stone, later reset as part of the Margarita Tomb's offering chamber just before the building of Chilan, the third temple directly over Hunal.

The original chamber inside both Yehnal and Margarita was again modified. Margarita's summit building was demolished and replaced by an offering chamber with the reset Xukpi Stone. Then the larger Chilan Structure, which provided a new northern entrance to the tomb, buried them all. Interred in this accessible tomb (ca. 465) was a royal woman, postulated as the founder's queen and Ruler 2's mother. This event marked the replacement of Witik Platform and its ritual buildings by the still larger Tzapah Platform and a new royal complex that expanded the template of its predecessors. There was a period of continued veneration inside the tomb, including the painting of the bones with cinnabar. We can only assume that Ruler 2 sponsored these rituals to venerate his mother, the matriarch of the new dynasty. It is reasonable to assume that Ruler 2 kept the Margarita Tomb open for veneration and that its final sealing took place after Ruler 2's death, probably during Ruler 3's reign.

DYNASTIC CONTINUITY: RULERS 3–5 (TIME SPAN 4, CA. A.D. 470–510)

Time Span 4 is marked by a new construction that greatly expanded the Acropolis and by the termination of the last Time Span 5 adobe architecture in the Northeast Court Group. On the wane by the end of Time Span 5, only a few adobe structures continued into Time Span 4. The most notable survivor was Maravilla, its summit building still so important as to be used and maintained while far more durable masonry architecture progressively covered its substructure. The continuous building program during this time span saw further integration of the Acropolis into a single complex, signaled by the junction of the Early Acropolis and the Northeast Court Group.

The Early Acropolis

During this span, a new Acropolis platform, Mitzil, ultimately covered Ruler 2's Acropolis and rose 10 m above the Río Copan. Mitzil Platform gave Copan's royal court a higher setting for the conduct of its ceremonial and civic duties. Mitzil also expanded the surface extent of the Acropolis. Beginning with the construction of a second terrace on top of Tzapah Platform, Mitzil Platform produced an Acropolis twice as high as its predecessor, and one that endured for a far longer time. In its final form, Mitzil was a monumental two-tiered platform that buried all the previous Tzapah substructures. In the center of the Acropolis, Chilan Structure was buried beneath Celeste but was almost totally demolished by later construction (Agurcia Fasquelle 1997; Agurcia Fasquelle and B. Fash, chapter 6 in this volume).

A northward outset and a new westward-projecting terrace later expanded Mitzil Platform. Although the central axis shifted to the south, access to Mitzil's summit remained on the west side by a new inset staircase with decorated panels on either side. To the northeast, Mitzil encroached around the adobe substructure of Maravilla, but the venerable summit building and western stairway (and the court at its base) remained open and in use throughout this period (figure 5.10). Ultimately, an expanded two-tiered façade (Teal/Acatan) was added to the east and north sides of Mitzil. At this time, a new outset western staircase was built over the previous stage's decorated panels. The expansion of Mitzil's north side buried a succession of earlier northern façades.

A final series of major modifications were made to Mitzil Platform at the end of Time Span 4. Twin inset stairways (Chirmol) were constructed on its east side, giving direct access to the Río Copan from the summit of the Acropolis. An expanded northern lower terrace (Amarillo) was built against Gordon Platform (Court 4B, below) and abutted the second terrace of the Mitzil Acropolis. Amarillo was, in

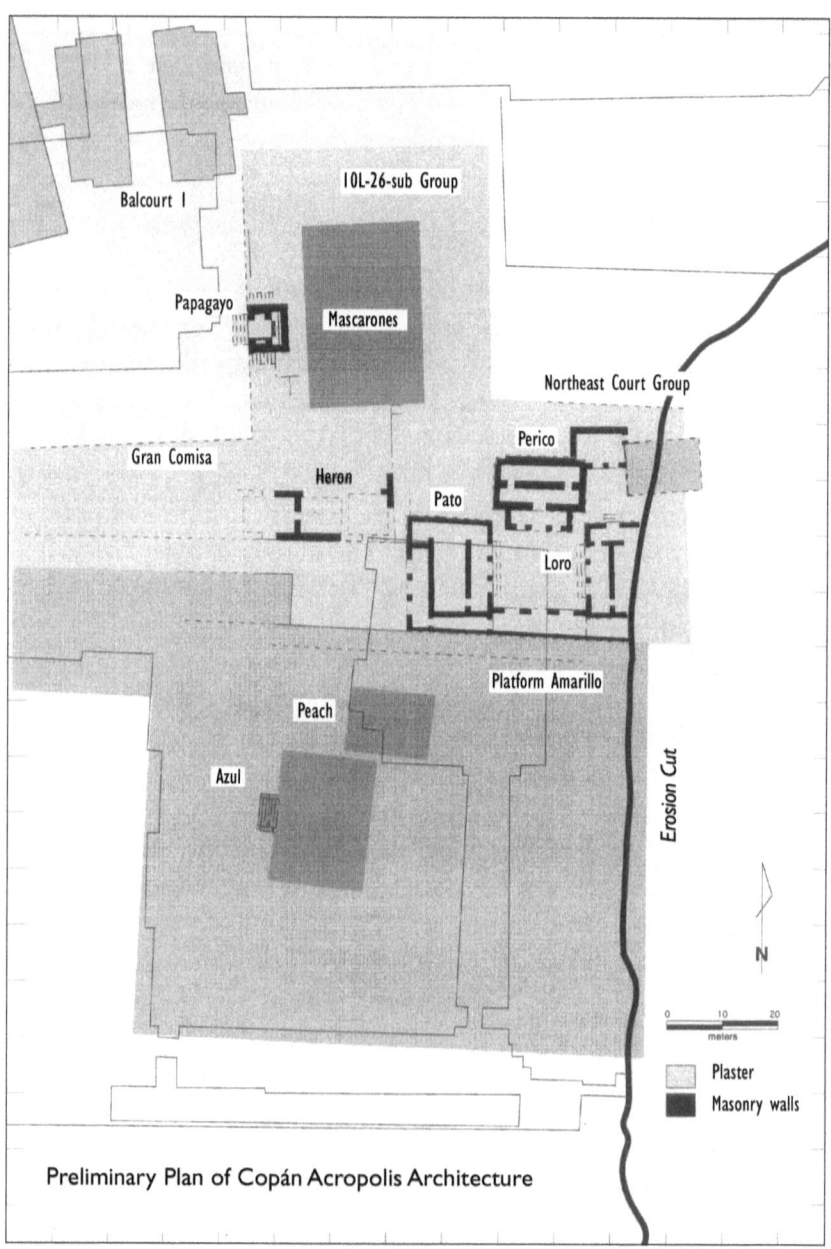

FIGURE 5.10
Preliminary plan of the Early Classic Acropolis, Time Span 4 (ca. A.D. 470–510). (Prepared by L. P. Traxler)

turn, abutted by one of the later additions to Court 4B, Toucan building. This same Amarillo terrace continued westward as the southern limit of Court 4C, and further west it encased the lower portions of the adobe Maravilla Substructure, transforming this important ancient temple into an outset from the northwest corner of the early Acropolis.

A new façade (Limón) represents a later expansion of Mitzil's second terrace along its northern side. This construction finally terminated Maravilla, demolishing the adobe building on this ancient substructure's summit and bringing an end to almost a century of use for this important earthen temple.

The Northeast Court Group

Patios 5B and 5A were terminated by Gordon, a monumental masonry platform constructed against the northeast corner of the lower terrace of Mitzil Platform. Gordon Platform was the first step in integrating the Early Acropolis with the Northeast Court Group, a process that culminated in the engulfing of this palace complex by the continuous northward expansions of the Early Acropolis. Gordon Platform extended 40 m to the north of the Early Acropolis and for an unknown distance to the east (later destroyed by the Río Copan). The western terrace of Gordon apparently stepped down to join Patio 5C's plaster floor, but excavation shows that this union was anciently demolished.

For a short time after the construction of Gordon, two adobe buildings of Patio 5B continued to be used, even though their adobe substructures were buried. This is indicated by the abutment of Gordon's plastered floor against the walls of the adobe buildings on the eastern and northern Patio 5B substructures. In contrast, the western building was completely demolished and buried by Gordon Platform. Sometime after Gordon was built, the surviving adobe buildings of Patio 5B were also demolished. These were replaced by relatively low masonry substructures, averaging about 1 m in height. Each of these supported a large, multidoorway, multiroom masonry building, Loro on the east and Perico, the most elaborately decorated building, on the north, forming Court 4B (see figure 5.10), the direct successor of the underlying Patio 5B. Later, Gordon Platform was extended to the west to support another large, multiroom building, Pato, and the space on the south side of Court 4B was filled by a fourth masonry building (Toucan), its back wall abutting the north terrace of a later façade of Mitzil (Amarillo). Also at a later time, Gordon Platform was extended to the north to support two additional buildings, Cockatoo and Sparret.

Even though all but the lower walls of these courtyard buildings was demolished when Court 4B was terminated, evidence of their elite palace functions survives from the arrangement, size, and number of rooms, as well as other details (Traxler 1996, 2001, 2004a). The great quantities of painted and modeled stucco found in demolition layers indicate that colorful and elaborate modeled motifs adorned the upper zones of these structures. The northern Perico's distinctive attributes indicate that it may have been a ritual focus. Its two northern rooms were probably vaulted and are set on a higher substructure than its front room. The lower wall on the west side was also decorated by modeled stucco. The interior medial wall of Loro building was decorated by two columns of glyphs rendered in orange and red paint, largely destroyed when the building was demolished.

The construction of Pato on the west side of Court 4B also saw the burial of Patio 5C to the west. The result was Court 4C, at the level of Gordon Platform and paved with a new plaster floor. This construction also covered the Gran Corniza Platform to the north, raising the extended Court 4C floor about 50 cm higher than the Gran Corniza's original surface.

The Court 4C floor abuts a low masonry substructure supporting a very large, multiroom masonry building on the north side of the court (Heron), which, in turn, merged further north with the terraces around Papagayo Structure in the 10L-26-Sub Group. Court 4C was bounded on the south by the Early Acropolis and on the east by Court 4B. Court 4B, in turn, was flanked on its east by Court 4A, closest to the river. Although Court 4A was later all but destroyed by the Río Copan, its western building (Loro) likely accessed this courtyard via doorways on its east side.

In its final Time Span 4 form, the Northeast Court Group was an arrangement of large, multiroom, multidoorway palace buildings arranged around three east-west-aligned courtyards, bounded on the south by progressively larger and higher monumental platforms of the Early Acropolis. Overall, the evidence suggests that these northeast courts served as a palace complex, probably providing for the residential and administrative needs of the immediate kin and most powerful clients of Copan's rulers.

The 10L-26-Sub Group

As with other pivotally important buildings, Papagayo was destined to survive longer than most Acropolis structures. Early in Time Span 4, there was an important rededication of Papagayo, commemorated by a new text carved on an altar or step within its room. Unfortunately, much of the text was deliberately erased later.

This carved text is in front of Stela 63 on the east side of the room inside Papagayo building (W. Fash 2001:figure 38). The surviving portion of the text refers to a rededication of the building by the fourth ruler, K'altuun Hix (Stuart 2004). The rededication date has not survived, but W. Fash (personal communication 1993) suggests ca. 9.2.10.0.0 (A.D. 485). The reference to Ruler 4 as the protagonist on the carved step is evidence that Papagayo remained in use during the reigns of at least three Copan kings (Rulers 2–4). In fact, Fash (2001) concludes that Papagayo (and its companion, Mascarones) remained in use far beyond the reign of Ruler 4.

Discussion

All of Ruler 2's efforts would have been in vain if the royal succession had not been assured. That this was so is made clear by later events, although no contemporaneous texts dealing with his immediate successor, Ruler 3, have been found. Ruler 3's reign is estimated at ca. 470–480, a period that saw the further expansion of the Acropolis with the initial construction stage of Mitzil Platform. Ruler 4 (ca. 480–500) rededicated Papagayo, as recorded on the carved step inside the building. This era also coincides with further expansion of the Mitzil Platform in the Acropolis and a major change in the Northeast Court Group involving the termination of the old adobe platforms, replaced by a new monumental masonry platform. Soon thereafter, a far larger complex of masonry buildings arranged around three courtyards (Courts 4A–C) succeeded the old adobe buildings.

The new palace buildings may have continued to be used during the reign of little-known Ruler 5. No texts are known from this reign (the all-but-destroyed painted text in Loro building on the east side of Court 4B might be a candidate). In any case, although Ruler 5's reign was seemingly short-lived (ca. A.D. 500–510), further Acropolis constructions appear to have continued unabated during this interval.

ACROPOLIS EXPANSION: RULERS 6 AND 7 (TIME SPAN 3, CA. A.D. 510–532)

A major northward expansion of the Acropolis marked this interval, terminating Courts 4A-C of the Northeast Court Group. Overall, if viewed from the Río Copan during Time Span 3, Copan's royal center formed a three-level profile against the western sky. The highest portion remained the summit of Mitzil Platform, crowned by the elaborate temples and palaces of Copan's rulers. At the base of its 5-m-high upper terrace was a broad platform that ran 40 m to the north, ending with two terraces on its northern margin. This northern extension of the Acropolis was elevated more than 5 m above the river and likely supported new temple and palace buildings (later destruction removed most traces of these structures). Furthest to the north was the lowest complex, composed of a new courtyard group that replaced and continued the functions of its Time Span 4 and 5 predecessors.

The Early Acropolis

Time Span 3 saw the construction of the final stage of the Early Acropolis, a massive expansion (Purple Platform) that extended the first terrace of the elevated royal complex 40 m northward, burying the palaces of Courts 4A-C that formerly lay at its base (figure 5.11). This span also saw the east side of the Acropolis modified by cancellation of the twin stairways leading to the Río Copan. A single radiocarbon date from a cache on the south side of the Time Span 3 Early Acropolis has a calibrated 2-sigma date of A.D. 470–650 (see table 5.1).

The Northeast Court Group

The construction of Purple Platform included a new low platform that extended 30 m northward from its northern base. This undoubtedly supported the same residential and administrative functions as its buried predecessors of Time Spans 5 and 4. The new Time Span 3 palace complex was composed of an upper group of buildings on

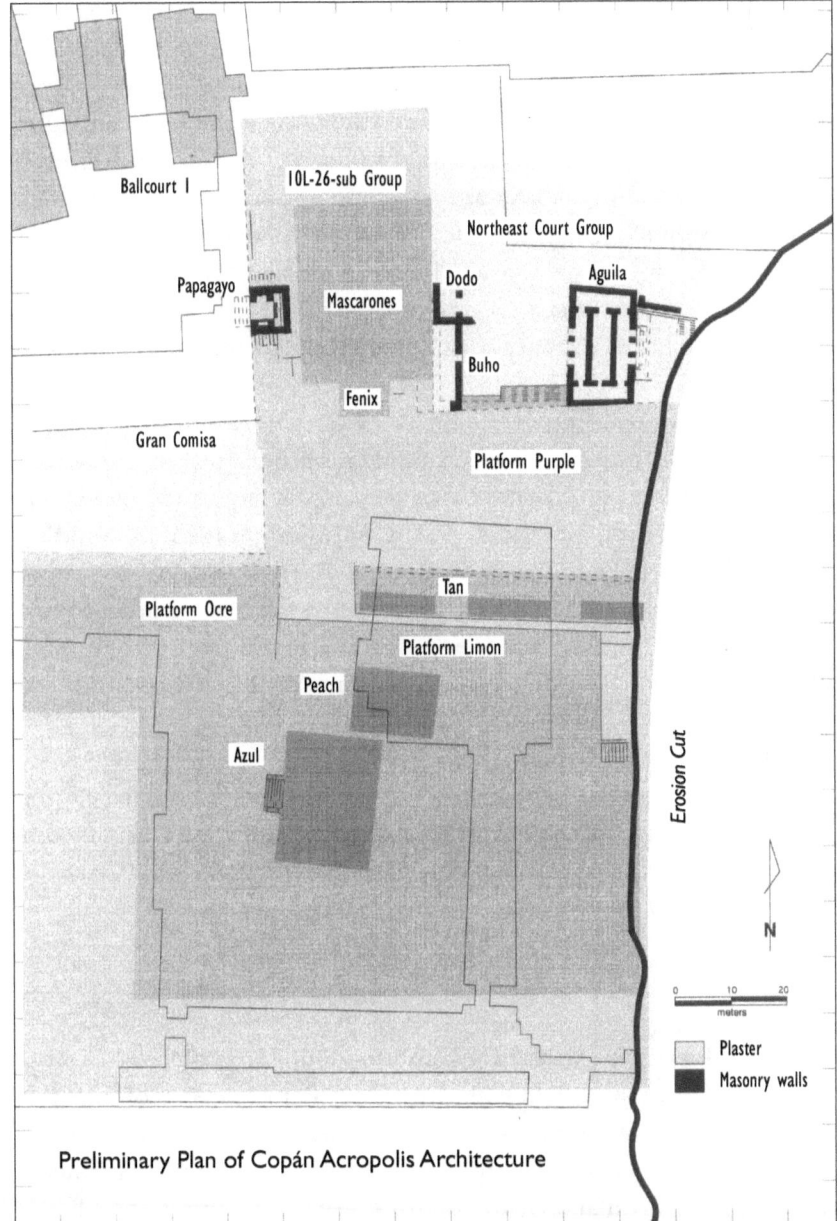

FIGURE 5.11
Preliminary plan of the Early Classic Acropolis, Time Span 3 (ca. A.D. 510–530). (Prepared by L. P. Traxler)

Purple Platform and a lower group immediately to the north (see figure 5.11). The buildings on Purple Platform have not been excavated in any detail. The lower buildings are better documented and comprise two east-west–aligned groups arranged around central courts (Miller and Morales 1997). On the east stood Court 3A, now mostly destroyed by the Río Copan. Court 3A was flanked on its north side by a building (Gavilan) supported by a substructure nearly 2 m high, now bisected by the Corte. A large three-doorway building (Aguila) on a slightly lower substructure formed the west side of Court 3A. Both had outset staircases. Little is known about the building (Halcon) on the south side of this court.

On its west side, Aguila also had a set of three doorways leading to Court 3B. This western court was flanked on the north by an almost totally demolished substructure that presumably supported a now vanished building and on the west, by another multiroom building (Buho). The terraces of Purple Platform defined the south side of both courts. Later renovations and additions to these courts included an outset stairway and new terrace facings leading to the platform's summit and to at least one later demolished building from Court 3B.

The 10L-26-Sub Group

Papagayo and Mascarones structures continued to be in use during Time Span 3. With its northward displacement, the new Court 3B complex was now situated immediately east of the 10L-26-Sub Group; in fact, its western margin abutted the eastern terraces of Mascarones structure.

Discussion

While Papagayo, Mascarones, and the founder's ball court continued to be used in the 10L-26-Sub Group, a major expansion of the Early Acropolis to the south can be dated to about the time of the sixth and seventh rulers, Muyal Jol? and Balam Nehn (or "Waterlily Jaguar"), respectively (Martin and Grube 2000:196–197). The tradition of building ever-larger Acropolis stages following the basic template established by the founder culminated in this expansion. The result was the termination and burial of the Time Span 4 Northeast Court Group beneath a major northern expansion of the Acropolis that supported a new bilevel complex of royal palace buildings replacing the vanished earlier palace structures.

THE GREAT BUILDER: RULER 8 (TIME SPAN 2, CA. A.D. 532–551)

The penultimate stage in the Acropolis sequence marks the final constructions of the Early Classic period. The Time Span 2 Acropolis represents an architectural transition between the template followed in the first century of Acropolis growth and that followed during the subsequent Late Classic era (Time Span 1, ca. A.D. 600–800). The Time Span 2 Acropolis was based on a new and larger terraced northern platform that canceled Purple Platform and buried it, along with the final version of the Northeast Court Complex, under 5 m of fill. With this expansion, the Acropolis summit covered an area equivalent in its north-south axis to its Late Classic final stage, ending the career of the entity defined here as the Early Acropolis.

The new Time Span 2 Acropolis produced a reversal of the fundamental architectural pattern seen in its previous stages and terminated the sequence of three successive courtyard-palace complexes located on its northern flank. It is assumed that a new Time Span 2 palace complex was relocated elsewhere, most likely to the southern side of the Acropolis. Excavations there directed by E. Wyllys Andrews (Andrews and Bill, chapter 7 in this volume) point to a surge of new buildings at the beginning of the Late Classic that converted and expanded what had formerly been a small group into a new elite palace complex. From this time onward, the core of Copan was composed of an Acropolis with a royal palace group on its southern flank, a 180-degree reversal of the original pattern followed during its first century of development (Sharer, Miller, and Traxler 1992:154).

The 10L-26-Sub Group

The termination of Ball Court IA and its replacement by the larger Ball Court IIA (Strömsvik 1952) can be placed within Time Span 2. But the nearby Papagayo continued to be used throughout the rest of the Early Classic era. Its eventual termination was marked by the breakup of Stela 63 and the deposition of its two upper fragments in two places within the room, along with sculptured Macaw heads from the destruction of

Ball Court IA (W. Fash 2001:89). Part of Ruler 4's text on Papagayo's interior step may have been erased at this time as well (see also Sharer 2003a). Early in the reign of Ruler 13, Papagayo was partially demolished and buried, to be succeeded by a larger temple known as "Esmeralda," which also buried the larger Mascarones Substructure east of Papagayo (W. Fash 2001:139).

The Successors of the Northeast Court Group

Although the old palace complex was presumably relocated to the south, the new Time Span 2 Acropolis supported at least two new courts, designated Courts 2A and 2B, built on the new northern platform (figure 5.12). These new courts probably represent a shift in functions from their predecessors, for they apparently served both royal residential and ceremonial purposes. The Río Copan has destroyed nearly all of the eastern Court 2A, surviving only from the remains of one elevated temple on its northern side (Zopilote). The northern Time Span 3 staircase initially continued to provide access to Court 2A (east of Zopilote) but was blocked further west by a succession of new buildings on the north side of Court 2B (Miller and Morales 1997).

Court 2B developed into an important component of the Time Span 2 Acropolis, constructed directly over the earlier courtyard groups. The elaborately decorated buildings around Court 2B's flanks reflect its importance. One of the earliest substructures on its north side (Indigo) was decorated by mosaic masks and surmounted by a building with mosaic corner masks (Chachalaca), apparently the earliest version of a succession of corner-masked buildings beneath Late Classic Structure 10L-22. Indigo provides two calibrated 2-sigma radiocarbon dates (see table 5.1). On its east side, Court 2B was defined by the elaborately decorated Ante Substructure (figure 5.13). Ante's location was consecrated by a basal cache symbolizing the three layers of Maya cosmos—the sky, the earth, and the watery underworld—represented by three layers of bird bones, jade artifacts, and seashells, arranged inside a large, sealed, stone vessel. Before Ante's stairway was built, six offerings were placed on its axis extending to the west, containing *Spondylus* shells and jade artifacts (no caches are known from the preceding Northeast Court Group buildings). Radiocarbon dates obtained from several of these caches produced inconsistent results (table 5.1 gives one such date).

EARLY CLASSIC ROYAL POWER IN COPAN

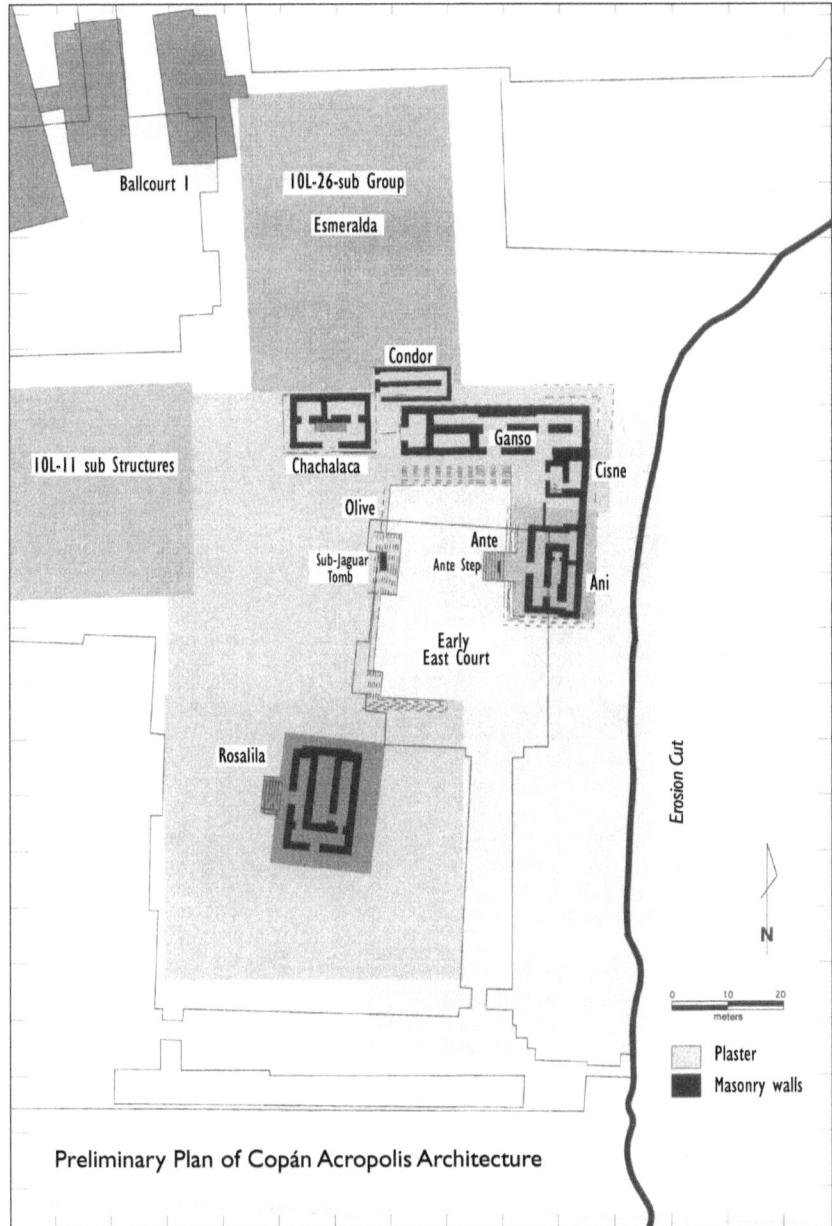

FIGURE 5.12
Preliminary plan of the Early Classic Acropolis, Time Span 2 (ca. A.D. 530–600). (Prepared by L. P. Traxler)

FIGURE 5.13

Ante Structure: western façade, stairway, and superstructure exposed by excavation in the Acropolis East Court. (Photograph by R. J. Sharer)

FIGURE 5.14

Ante Step: preliminary drawing of the hieroglyphic text. (Drawing by L. Schele and A. Morales)

On the central step of Ante's west-facing stairway is a carved hieroglyphic text (figure 5.14). Initial readings indicated associations with Ruler 7 and possibly Ruler 10 (Morales, Miller, and Schele 1990). The recent identification of Ruler 8's name on the Hieroglyphic Stairway has enabled Stuart (personal communication 2001) to recognize this ruler's name on the Ante Step. The Ante Step text begins with a somewhat problematic Long Count of 9.5.7.?.2, corresponding to ca. 540, followed by a reference to the eighth ruler, Wil-Ohl K'inich. This dates the dedication of Ante Structure to the reign of Ruler 8. The Ante text closes with a date corresponding to 9.4.18.6.12 (532), Ruler 8's accession date.

Ante's substructure rises in two terraces, the lower being elaborately decorated with stucco macaw masks once brightly painted in red, green, and other colors. Ante supported a multiroom building (Ani), also decorated by elaborate stucco masks and other motifs. Although its front was demolished before the construction of the Time Span 1 East Court stairs, Ani's eastern (back) wall was preserved nearly to its full height, revealing an elaborated decorated façade that may have once been dramatically visible, rising more than 25 m above the Río Copan (if buildings in the now destroyed Court 2A to the east did not block the view). Ani is situated beneath and 10 m west of its successor, the now vanished Structure 10L-20 constructed in Time Span 1.

During the use of Court 2B, a variety of masonry and vaulted buildings were constructed on the northern, eastern, and western sides of its central courtyard—an earlier version of today's East Court. On the west, a succession of substructures and buildings culminated in a monumental terrace with an outset staircase (Olive), which the Time Span 1 Jaguar Stairway later covered. On the north, Court 2B was bounded by a broad stairway leading to another succession of important structures, the antecedents of the famous Late Classic buildings of the East Court, Structures 10L-21, 10L-21A, 10L-22, and 10L-22A (Miller and Morales 1997).

Under the western Olive stairway, excavations uncovered an intact masonry tomb chamber, sealed by eight large capstones (see figure 5.1). Named for its location as the *Sub-Jaguar Tomb*, it contained the skeletal remains of a male extended supine, head to the north, on a bier made from two stone slabs. Carved-shell and other adornments covered the remains. On the floor beneath the slab were pottery vessels and other offerings (Traxler 1994). The tomb vessels date to ca. A.D. 550, based on form and typological affiliations (René Viel, personal communication 1992). A carbon sample taken from inside one tomb vessel provides a somewhat later date with a 2-sigma range of A.D. 595–860 (see table 5.1), probably contaminated by observed tree-root intrusions into the tomb. The architectural stratigraphy indicates that the tomb dates later than the construction of Ante Platform (ca. 540) but before the final paving of Court 2B. This and other evidence point to the tomb as being that of Ruler 8 (532–551), named on the Ante Step. His successor, the short-reigned Ruler 9 (551–553), cannot be ruled out, however.

One of the last Early Classic Acropolis buildings, Rosalila, was the successor of Celeste Structure during Time Span 2, immediately south of Court 2B (see figure 5.12). This truly extraordinary building, exposed in tunnel excavations directed by Ricardo Agurcia Fasquelle (1996), defined the center of the Acropolis. Covered by elaborately modeled and painted stucco masks and other motifs, Rosalila was the final Early Classic temple in the sequence of buildings dedicated to the dynastic founder that began with Yehnal 150 years before. Its elaborate façade motifs confirm that Rosalila was dedicated to K'inich Yax K'uk' Mo' (Agurcia Fasquelle and B. Fash, chapter 6 in this volume; Martin and Grube 2000:198; Taube 2004). Unlike its predecessors, though, Rosalila was maintained and used for an extensive period of time, indicated by the many coats of plaster and paint on its exterior and the evidence of repairs and modifications to its masonry.

On the west-facing staircase of Rosalila's substructure is a badly eroded text consisting of two rows of glyphs, much like the Ante text. Stuart (2004) noted similarities to the Ante text in one portion of Ruler 8's name on the Rosalila text, originally linked to Ruler 10. From the eroded status of the text and from other evidence documented by Agurcia's excavations, it is clear that Rosalila continued to be used well into Time Span 1. When Rosalila was finally terminated, the method reflected its sacred status. The building was carefully preserved intact, its rooms filled up to their vault stones (Agurcia Fasquelle 1996). Rosalila was succeeded by a little-known temple (Purpula) that was later almost completely demolished by the construction of the final structure in this ancient and important central Acropolis location. This final temple was built during the reign of Copan's last-known ruler, Yax Pasah, and is now Structure 10L-16.

Discussion

The expansion of the Acropolis during Time Span 2 modified the basic template established by the founder more than a century earlier. This final Early Classic stage produced a higher and larger Acropolis that extended all the way to the 10L-26-Sub Group, burying the Court 3 complex and canceling forever the existence of the Northeast Court Group palaces. It appears that Copan's royal palace complex was then reestablished on the southern flank of the Acropolis, where it was to expand and prosper throughout the Late Classic period.

The modified template of the Time Span 2 Acropolis set the stage for this royal complex over the final 250 years of Copan's history. The sponsor of this transformation can be now identified as Copan's eighth king, Wil Ohl K'inich, based on the reading of this ruler's name on two texts from Time Span 2 buildings. As a result, we conclude that Wil Ohl K'inich, or a nameless architect working for him, must have been one of Copan's greatest planners and builders.

The northern portion of the newly expanded Acropolis supported a new architectural complex comprising a series of elaborately decorated masonry and vaulted buildings constructed over the succession of old palaces and their courtyards buried below. These new buildings were arranged around Court 2B, which shared the same elevated and terraced platform as the remainder of the Acropolis. One of these, Ante Structure, was built on the east side of Court 2B, where it was later succeeded by Structure 10L-20. The Ante stairway text furnishes the historical evidence for this episode, including a dedication date (ca. 540) and Ruler 8's name and accession date (532). Ruler 8 is the most likely candidate for the burial recovered from the Sub-Jaguar Tomb located on the west side of Court 2B.

To the south, Stuart (2004) has identified the traces of Ruler 8's name on the stairway text of Rosalila. The obvious centerpiece of Copan during the later portion of the Early Classic era, Rosalila was a new and elaborately decorated temple situated in the heart of the Acropolis directly over Margarita and its tomb. The highest temple for its time at Copan, Rosalila's location was certainly no accident, for it represented continuity with the original sacred core of the Acropolis established by Hunal and its associations with the dynastic founder, the pair of royal tombs, and the royal succession.

THE FINAL EARLY CLASSIC KINGS: RULERS 9 AND 10 (TIME SPAN 2, A.D. 551–578)

This interval corresponds to the reigns of Rulers 9 and 10. We know very little about Ruler 9, except that his reign was a scant two years. We presume that he oversaw the burial of his predecessor, who was likely interred in the Sub-Jaguar Tomb. The monument breakage pattern suggests that a major disruption may have occurred at Copan during this era, dated at ca. 554–564 (Sharer 2004). If so, it may be that this event is related to the premature death of Ruler 9. His successor, "Moon Jaguar" (Ruler 10), reigned for about twenty-five years (553–578) and is known from two monuments, Stela 9 and Stela 17 (Martin and Grube 2000:198). One or more of the later buildings around Court 2B were probably dedicated by this ruler.

THE TRANSITIONAL KING: RULER 11 (TIME SPAN 2, CA. A.D. 579–628)

The architectural stratigraphy indicates that Court 2B was filled in during the reign of Butz Chan, the eleventh ruler. His reign (579–628) marked the transition between the Early and Late Classic Acropolis. A new plaza surface capped the filling of Court 2B, burying all the substructures and staircases of its flanking buildings. As with courtyard filling operations seen previously in the Acropolis sequence, the summit buildings around Court 2B were left open and functioning for a time before finally being terminated and replaced by the Late Classic buildings of Time Span 1.

A final feature of the Court 2B termination was the construction of a vaulted tomb set against Ante's southern façade. Excavated in the early nineteenth century by Juan Galindo (W. Fash 2001:48), the "Galindo Tomb" may have been the burial place of Ruler 10, who was interred at the beginning of Ruler 11's reign. The filling of Court 2B signaled the beginning of the last major renovation of the Acropolis, corresponding to the beginning of Coner ceramics (ca. A.D. 600). The ensuing construction of the new Time Span 1 buildings created the Acropolis East Court visible today.

THE LATE CLASSIC KINGS: RULERS 12–16 (TIME SPAN 1, CA. A.D. 628–822)

Although the Time Span 1 Acropolis is beyond the limits of our research, we can outline the remainder of the eastern Acropolis's history based on our colleagues' work. One significant conclusion seems clear from this research: Compared with the first two hundred years of its Early Classic history, the pace and volume of Acropolis construction *decreased* significantly during its final two hundred years of development.

We propose that the twelfth successor, Smoke Imix (A.D. 628–695), was the architect of the new Time Span 1 Acropolis. As with its predecessors, this final version of the Acropolis was constructed in several stages, and, given his very long reign, Ruler 12 may have been responsible for sponsoring a number of its buildings. During his reign, the construction of Chorcha in the 10L-26-Sub Group engulfed much of the ancient Papagayo temple and buried Mascarones, its eastern companion. Smoke Imix is identified as the ruler buried in the Scribe's Tomb intruded into Chorcha (W. Fash 2001:111). Esmeralda Structure succeeded Chorcha and its tomb and finally terminated and buried Papagayo. Both Esmeralda and the penultimate Structure 10L-26-2nd belong to the reign of the thirteenth ruler, Waxaklajun Ub'ah K'awil (W. Fash 2001:139), who also sponsored the initial version of the Hieroglyphic Stairway (W. Fash 1998). After a lull following the demise of Waxaklajun Ub'ah K'awil in 738, the final version of the Hieroglyphic Stairway and its crowning temple, Structure 10L-26, were completed during the reign of Ruler 15 (W. Fash 1998, 2001; W. Fash and Stuart 1991).

One by one, the old Court 2B buildings were buried by new monumental stairways and a series of new buildings erected around the Time Span 1 East Court. The largest of these, Structure 10L-22, was the culmination of a series of palace-like buildings occupying the East Court's northern side. Carved texts on the building record that Structure 10L-22 was built early in the reign of the thirteenth ruler, Waxaklajun Ub'ah K'awil (Stuart 1989a). To its east stood Structure 10L-21, probably built late in the reign of Ruler 13 or immediately after his capture and sacrifice (Miller 1991). To the west, Structure 10L-22A, proposed as the *popol nah*, or ruling council house (B. Fash et al. 1992), was built during the reign of the fourteenth ruler, K'ak' Joplaj Chan K'awil (Martin and Grube 2000:206).

A later building, Structure 10L-21A, wedged between Structures 10L-21 and 10L-22, has an inscribed date that places it in the reign of the sixteenth ruler, Yax Pasah (W. Fash 2001:168). The sixteenth ruler also built the final temple constructed above Margarita and its tomb,

Structure 10L-16, and Structure 10L-11 at the north end of the West Court (W. Fash and Stuart 1991). Of the buildings along the east side of the East Court, Structures 10L-19, 10L-20, and 10L-20A stood until about a century ago, when the Río Copan swept them away. The southernmost of these, Structure 10L-18, survives and has been identified as the funerary shrine for Yax Pasah (Becker and Cheek 1983).

CONCLUDING THOUGHTS

Our research interprets the meaning of architecture gleaned from a combined archaeological and historical perspective—how remnants of the built environment reflect Copan's Early Classic development as a polity capital. Data from the time of Copan's dynastic founding and the first two centuries thereafter provide unprecedented information about the scale and characteristics of Acropolis architecture during the critical Early Classic era. This allows inferences about Copan's sociopolitical organization at the crucial time of the founding of the ruling dynasty, as well as during its initial era of development (W. Fash 1988).

The theoretical basis for such research is grounded in the proposition that the construction, use, and demolition of architecture reflect the characteristics of the society that creates it (de Montmollin 1989). We can derive many potential meanings from such architectural expressions (Lawrence and Low 1990), and these are subject to different interpretations (Ashmore 1991). At the same time, our Acropolis research is but one means to reconstruct the origins and growth of the Copan polity during the Early Classic period. The fullest picture of this development can be achieved only by combining our results with those obtained by the other research programs at Copan and its environs (Baudez, ed., 1983; Canuto 2004; Sanders, ed., 1986, 1990; Webster, Freter, and Gonlin 2000). Therefore, what we offer here is not only preliminary and subject to modification by ongoing research, but also merely one part of a picture that will be complete when all relevant research at Copan is synthesized (W. Fash and Sharer 1991).

We begin with the critical issue of whether Maya dynastic history is based on actual persons and events or is the creation of later rulers to increase the prestige and authority of their position as heads of state (Webster and Freter 1990b). The results from archaeological excavation beneath the Acropolis provide explicit evidence that the Early

Classic kings of Copan were real individuals who, by their actions, directed the founding and development of the Copan polity. This evidence has implications for discussions about the meanings derived from Maya historical texts, but at a more specific level, it makes clear that Copan's Early Classic rulers were responsible for establishing the Acropolis as Copan's royal center and for setting the basic pattern of its architectural development.

The beginnings of this Classic-period royal center are deeply buried beneath the heart of the Acropolis, but we now trace its growth from its origins as a relatively small group of buildings on the west bank of the Río Copan. In its initial stage, this royal center comprised three architectural complexes, each likely with different albeit overlapping functions, which established a pattern followed throughout the history of the Acropolis. We have proposed that the southernmost of these three groups was the original royal center, the ritual and residential buildings for K'inich Yax K'uk' Mo', who established this new complex to assert his claims to power as Copan's ruler. Several fragmentary earlier texts (Stuart 1989a) suggest that he did so at the expense of an already established authority. As to who Yax K'uk' Mo' was and where he came from, several options will surely be debated for years to come. The current evidence suggests that he was an outsider with wide-ranging contacts who came to Copan and established a new political order (Sharer 2003a, 2003b; Sharer, Fash, et al. 1999; Stuart 2000).

The apparent external connections for Yax K'uk' Mo' invite further study. The first is the central Mexican connection seen in some of the earliest architecture and ceramics associated with the first royal complex beneath the Acropolis (Sharer 2003a; Stuart 2000, 2004). Hunal, a small masonry substructure with talud-tablero façade (perhaps recalled by the painted scene on Vessel 1 from the Margarita Tomb), marked the sacred center of the Acropolis for four hundred years. Both the Hunal and Margarita tombs contain a number of offering vessels from central Mexico (Reents-Budet et al. 2004). Burial 95-1, an apparent dedicatory sacrifice made during a later expansion of this central complex, is that of a warrior with several central Mexican items placed west of Margarita Structure (Bell et al. 2004). The burial chamber beneath the Motmot marker is circular, the only known example of this mortuary form at Copan, recalling similar interments at Teotihuacan in central Mexico (W. Fash 1998). Obviously, the important associations made by later Copan rulers between the founder and central Mexican motifs (Agurcia Fasquelle and B. Fash, chapter 6, and Stuart, chapter 10, in this volume) were rooted in historical fact. We now need further research to clarify the meaning of these connections between the founder and central Mexico.

The earliest levels beneath the Acropolis have revealed evidence of other connections beyond Copan. One of these, possibly related to the first, is with Kaminaljuyu and the Maya highlands (Valdés and Wright 2004). The earliest elite residential structures and several of the earliest temple platforms were constructed of adobe, reminiscent of Kaminaljuyu and other Maya highland sites. This connection appears at the time of the founder and continues during the reign of his son, Ruler 2. Some of the pottery vessels of this time period are imports from Kaminaljuyu or local imitations of Maya highland types (Reents-Budet et al. 2004).

Another crucial external link is to the central Petén, more specifically to Tikal. Some of the earliest retrospective dates referring to the predynastic era have Tikal links (Stuart 2004). Several lines of evidence associate K'inich Yax K'uk' Mo' with Tikal (Sharer 2004; Sharer, Fash, et al. 1999). Several decades before Copan's A.D. 426 founding, a K'uk' Mo' is mentioned at Tikal (Martin and Grube 2000:33). Of course, Tikal's architecture and artifacts reflect its long-standing associations with Teotihuacan (LaPorte and Fialko 1990). Either Tikal or Kaminaljuyu could have been the inspiration for the talud-tablero style of Hunal Structure, as could Teotihuacan itself. If the remains in the Hunal Tomb belong to K'inich Yax K'uk' Mo', as the evidence suggests, isotopic analysis of the bones reveals that he was originally from the Tikal region (Buikstra et al. 2004). The second earliest structure beneath Structure 10L-26, Motmot, and the first two temples that replaced Hunal—Yehnal and Margarita—feature the apron-molding style of Tikal and the central Petén. Derivatives of this style remained in use at Copan during the Early Classic, as seen on the façades of Ante Substructure, constructed a century later. The suggestion that elite colonists from Tikal founded Copan's subordinate center, Quiriguá (Jones and Sharer 1980; Sharer 1988), takes on new meaning with epigraphic evidence that Quiriguá was founded in tandem with Copan (Looper 1999; Martin and Grube 2000:216).

A substantial effort to construct a new royal center featuring a variety of architectural styles marks the beginnings of the Classic Copan polity. The events of the dynastic founding were kept alive by historical records and commemorated by buildings, monuments, and even pottery vessels over a span of four hundred years. Beyond pointing to the specific origins of K'inich Yax K'uk' Mo', the external connections associated with the new royal center show that the Early Classic Copan polity did not evolve in isolation, but fully within a Mesoamerican cultural context.

Traxler (2004b) has shown that the initial constructions beneath the Monument Plaza also date to the founding era. This indicates that Yax K'uk' Mo's new capital was constructed along a north-south axis that extended 400 m in length. This new royal center underwent an almost continuous series of major expansions during the first century following the dynastic founding. From the original royal buildings on Yune Platform, which covered an area of ca. 4,200 m^2 during the founding era, an Acropolis covering an estimated minimum of 24,000 m^2 was achieved by ca. A.D. 530.[4] This represents an area six times greater than the original Yune Platform and almost as large as the area covered by the Acropolis in its final Late Classic stage. The amount of labor invested over this span exceeds that at any later time in the Copan Acropolis (Carrelli 1997, 2004). Together, these findings fit the pattern of other newly established state systems, based on their initial investments in monumental constructions (Marcus 2004; Trigger 1974). Thus, the scale, pace, and functions of architecture in the earliest levels of the Main Group lead us to conclude that K'inich Yax K'uk' Mo' established Copan as the capital of a preindustrial state (Marcus 2004; Traxler 2004a) and his immediate successors maintained and expanded this state organization (Marcus 1992b).

The documented construction and use of a sequence of Early Classic palaces beginning in the founding era (Traxler 1996, 2001, 2004a), often diagnostic of state systems (Flannery 1998), further supports this proposition. In addition to the considerable time and energy expenditures for the initial stages of the Acropolis (Carrelli 1997, 2004; for comparison, see Abrams 1987), concurrent settlement and organization changes within the domain of the newly established Copan polity (Canuto 2004) also reflect a state-level organization with Copan as its capital.

After a century of growth, the Early Classic Acropolis reached a culmination in Time Span 2 (ca. A.D. 530). This stage was apparently planned and carried out during the reign of the eighth ruler, Wil Ohl K'inich, who, alongside Ruler 2, can now be recognized as one of Copan's great builders. The form of the Time Span 2 Acropolis changed one component of the original three-group pattern established by the founder. The old northeast location of the adjacent royal palace complex was terminated for good and may have been transferred to a new location south of the Acropolis (where it is known today as the Cemetery Group). The complex sequence of buildings of Time Span 2 probably extended to the reign of Ruler 11, Butz Chan, by which time the Acropolis had essentially reached its maximum area. By the standard Maya archaeological chronology, this reign also marked the transition between the Early and Late Classic periods. The reign of Copan's twelfth king, Smoke Imix, opens the final version of the Acropolis, corresponding to Time Span 1 and the Late Classic era, when this royal complex, founded by K'inich Yax K'uk' Mo', reached its ultimate architectural expression.

The unprecedented extent of archaeological tunneling beneath the Acropolis has documented the complex building sequence that reflects the Classic-period history of Copan. As a result, we are now able to understand to a far greater degree than ever before the origins and evolution of royal architecture and how it reflects actual events and the careers of the rulers who shaped Copan's Early Classic history.

Notes

The research and consolidation programs beneath the Copan Acropolis were conducted under the auspices of the Instituto Hondureño de Antropología e Historia, with support from the University of Pennsylvania Museum (Francis Boyer and Shoemaker Research Funds), the Asociación Copan, the USAID mission in Honduras, the National Geographic Society Committee for Research and Exploration, the National Science Foundation, the Selz Foundation, the Foundation for the Advancement of Mesoamerican Studies, the Maya Workshop Foundation, the Holt Family Foundation, the Kislak Foundation, the University of Pennsylvania Foundation, and a number of private donors. We are grateful to all these institutions for their vital support; we also wish to thank all the many people who have worked with us at Copan and who made our research possible.

1. Thirty-one samples excavated by ECAP were submitted to Beta Analytic for determining calibrated radiocarbon dates. Fifteen samples yielded 1-sigma and intercept dates, but sixteen yielded only 2-sigma-range dates because of small sample size. A number of samples yielded aberrant dates, apparently because of the presence of old carbon or subsequent contamination. Table 5.1 presents fifteen dates obtained from the most secure proveniences, although several of these appear to contain old carbon.

2. Christopher Stevenson of ASC Group, Inc., determined the age of nine obsidian artifacts excavated by ECAP from a range of secure Acropolis contexts, using both interior fissure and exterior rim measurements. Even though exterior rim measurements are used for most obsidian-hydration dates, all but one of the Acropolis dates determined by this method were extremely aberrant, yielding dates averaging 649 years younger than the deposit age (range 269–966). Only one exterior rim date could be reliable, given that it is 277 years older than the deposit age, consistent with its secondary context (construction fill). Three of the internal fissure dates are considered reliable—one date from a primary context is within the deposit age range, and two dates from secondary contexts are slightly older than the deposit age. The other six interior-fissure dates are aberrant because they average 207 years (range 63–304) later than the deposit age, although by far less than the exterior rim dates (see table 5.2). These findings raise doubts as to the reliability of exterior-rim obsidian dates used to propose a revised chronology for the end of Pre-Columbian occupation in the Copan Valley (Webster and Freter 1990b; Webster, Freter, and Gonlin 2000).

3. The evidence suggesting that the Hunal Tomb is the burial place of the Copan dynastic founder includes its stratigraphic position and tomb vessels dating to the founding era. Several tomb offerings have links to the founder, including a large, jade bar pectoral very similar to the single bar pectoral on the Altar Q portrait of K'inich Yax K'uk' Mo'. A shell pectoral from the tomb is "name-tagged" with a title used exclusively for the founder, Wi Te (Stuart 2004). Excavation reveals that a succession of funerary temples overlay Hunal and its tomb; several of the better-documented examples explicitly refer to K'inich Yax K'uk' Mo' as royal ancestor.

4. Both are based on projections from known extents of architecture revealed by ECAP's tunnels. The original Yune Platform covered an area estimated at 70 by 70 m. The Time Span 2 Acropolis (ca. A.D. 530) covered an estimated area of 150 by 160 m (not including an unknown additional area swept away by the Río Copan).

6

The Evolution of Structure 10L-16, Heart of the Copán Acropolis

Ricardo Agurcia Fasquelle and Barbara W. Fash

Structure 10L-16 is at the center of the Copán Acropolis, which was the center of the ancient kingdom of Copán and the seat of its social, political, economic, and religious power (Agurcia Fasquelle and Valdés 1994; Demarest 1992b; W. Fash 1998, 2001; Freidel 1992; Freidel, Schele, and Parker 1993; M. Miller 1986, 1988; Schele and Freidel 1990; Sharer 1994; Sharer, Fash, et al. 1999; Sharer, Miller, and Traxler 1992; Sharer, Traxler, et al. 1999). Because this geographic focal point for the city is also a physical manifestation of its rulers' primary cosmological concern, its architectural and iconographic evolution should reflect the changing nature of this concern through time.

The Acropolis consists of two enclosed plazas—the West and East Courts— surrounded by buildings. Structure 10L-16 sits between the two of these, with its main staircase facing the West Court. At the base of the stairway rests the most famous historical monolith of Copán, Altar Q, which portrays all the dynastic rulers of the city in chronological order. Structure 10L-16 is the highest construction in the Copán Main Group, reaching a height of more than 20 m above the West Court and 30 m above the Great Plaza (to an absolute height of 620 m above sea level).

Ricardo Agurcia Fasquelle and Barbara W. Fash

The East and West Courts, as well as the buildings surrounding them, have been treated in many recent publications (Agurcia Fasquelle and Valdés 1994; B. Fash 1992a; W. Fash 1991, 1998, 2001; Freidel, Schele, and Parker 1993; M. Miller 1986, 1988; Schele and Freidel 1990; Sharer, Miller, and Traxler 1992; Sharer, Traxler, et al. 1999), which point out that their art and architecture are laden with religious symbolism that marks them as an animated landscape. The Copán rulers developed this center for veneration and sacrifice in honor of supernatural forces and deceased ancestors. It is in this context that the evolution of the central building of the Copán Acropolis, Structure 10L-16, is presented here.

Most of the research summarized here has been carried out since 1988 as part of the Proyecto Arqueológico Acrópolis de Copán (PAAC) and its antecedent, the Copán Mosaics Project.

THE EVOLUTION OF THE 10L-16 SITE

Structure 10L-16-1st was the last of a long series of mostly west-facing structures at the heart of the Copán Acropolis. These sequential building stages go back to the very beginning of the Acropolis as subsequent edifices were constructed one over another (figure 6.1). At Copán, the customary pattern of construction was to build up pyramids in stages or layers, usually partially demolishing the previous building and using it as fill for the next phase. Structure 10L-16-1st became the tallest structure on the Acropolis as a result of this process. Studying the façade sculpture and stucco decoration of this building series, we have come to understand that all phases commemorated the entombment of the first dynastic ruler, K'inich Yax K'uk' Mo', buried 30 m below the floor of the final structure, within the earliest structure at this sacred spot. The history of the dynasty we see played out on Altar Q at its base is forever enshrined in this sequence of superimposed buildings.

Earliest Constructions

The earliest structure identified so far by ECAP (the Early Copán Acropolis Program, directed by Robert Sharer) on this central axis of the Acropolis is the substructure given the field name *Hunal*. Hunal is a small masonry construction with *talud-tablero* architecture. The researchers believe that it once supported the residence of Copán's

The Evolution of Structure 10L-16

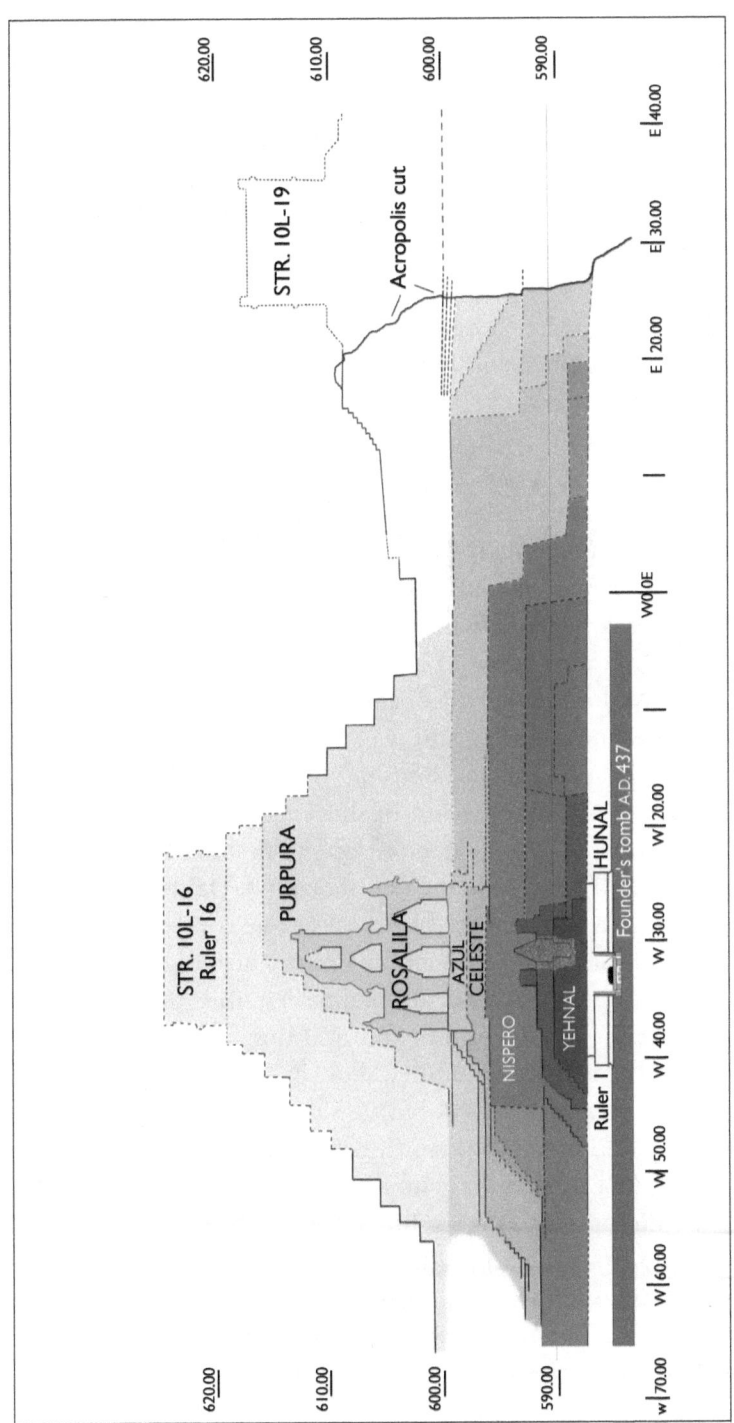

Figure 6.1
Cross section of the Copán Acropolis on the central axis of Structure 10L-16. (Reconstruction drawing by B. Fash after R. Larios and F. López)

first ruler, whose remains they believe they have recently found buried inside (Sharer 2003a, 2003b, 2004; Sharer et al., chapter 5 in this volume).

A 2-m-tall substructure named Yehnal overlies this earliest construction. In 1995 one of Hunal's west-facing stuccoed panels was uncovered next to a demolished stairway. It consists primarily of a large and beautifully conserved red portrait of the Sun God, Ahau Kin or K'inich Ahau, patron deity of Copán's royal lineage (Sharer et al., chapter 5 in this volume; refer to figure 5.4). Yehnal has been tentatively dated to the very beginning of the fifth century A.D. and the reigns of Copán's earliest dynastic rulers (Sharer, Fash, et al. 1999; Sharer et al., chapter 5 in this volume), whose primary concern, as reflected in this building's iconography, was cosmological.

The building and the substructure that covered Yehnal are nicknamed *Xukpi* and *Margarita*, respectively. Nothing remains of Xukpi except the floor scars of its walls. The substructure, Margarita, is well preserved and has large modeled stucco panels flanking its stairs on the west side (Sharer et al., chapter 5 in this volume; refer to figure 5.5). These panels are dominated by a beautifully executed polychrome scene of a quetzal and a macaw with necks intertwined and a *yax* glyph attached to their heads. From the birds' mouths emerge small portraits of K'inich Ahau. The combination of these iconographic elements allows us to read them as the name of Copán's first ruler, K'inich Yax K'uk' Mo' (Sun-Eyed Resplendent Quetzal Macaw). On its upper edge, a sky band frames the scene, whereas the lower one consists of an earth band. Margarita is dated to the beginning of the fifth century and the earliest rulers of Copán (Sharer et al., chapter 5 in this volume).

After numerous modifications and additions buried Margarita first, Xukpi was eventually demolished and covered by a massive platform on whose summit the Maya built a substructure named *Celeste* (10L-16-4th). This edifice is known only from a series of small test excavations showing that its superstructure was completely destroyed during the next building stage, that of Rosalila and its substructure, Azul. At least on its north, east, and south sides, Celeste had the exact same floor plan and dimensions as the Azul Substructure. This leads us to believe that their iconography was also the same, perhaps similar to that of their predecessors. The stratigraphy developed by ECAP

The Evolution of Structure 10L-16

FIGURE 6.2
Rosalila Structure, buried inside Structure 10L-16. (Reconstruction painting by C. Klein, National Geographic Society)

below this structure and our own excavations above it indicate that this building was in use from about A.D. 470 to 571 (Robert Sharer, personal communication 1996).

Rosalila

Built less than 2 m above Celeste, Rosalila (10L-16-3rd) is the first example of a completely preserved superstructure at Copán; its architecture and sculpture are, for the most part, just as they were when Rosalila was in use by the ancient Maya (figure 6.2). Besides being spared the ritual destruction that all other Acropolis structures underwent before others were built over them, this structure was buried with great care. Its moldings and recesses were carefully filled with mud and smaller rocks, as were its large, stuccoed, decorative panels, which still retain their original multicolored paint.

While Rosalila was in use, the sculpture was repeatedly plastered

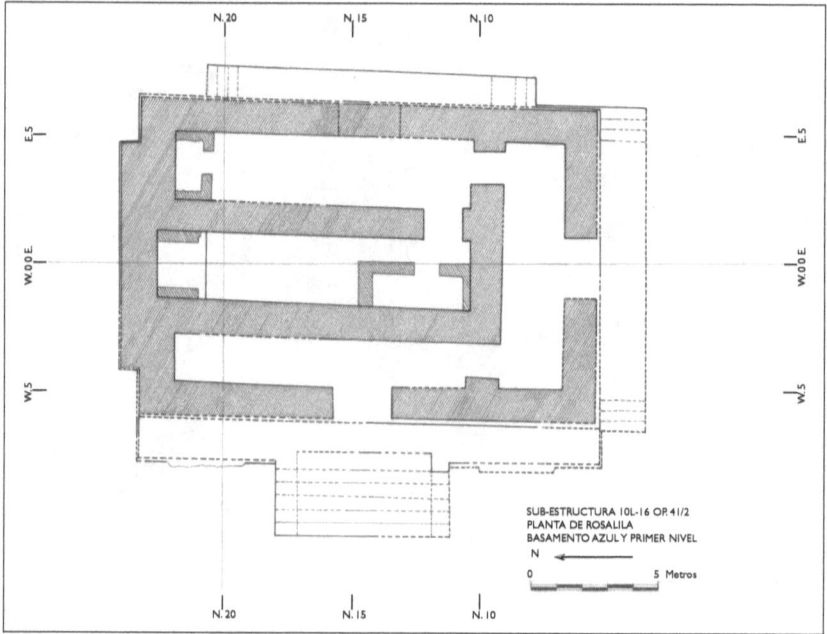

FIGURE 6.3

Floor plan of Rosalila's lower level. (Drawing by R. Larios, F. López, and J. Ramos)

and painted; some sections show as many as seven layers of refurbishing. The last layer is different from the rest. It is coarser and thicker, and it covered the entire building in white. We suspect that the white coat was part of an elaborate burial scheme for Rosalila, perhaps a symbolic killing of the color and the building before interment, signaling its revered position as a sacred center or axis mundi.

Because of its complexity, the cosmic iconography of Rosalila and Azul is discussed in a separate section below. We believe that they shared the same tradition as the earlier constructions.

Rosalila consists of three main levels mounted one above the other and rising 12.9 m. The lowermost has a floor plan of 18.5 by 12.5 m, with its main axis running from north to south. It is 5.7 m tall and has a medial molding at 2.6 m that marks the upper edge of the doorways and divides the facade of this lowest level into two decorative fields.

This lowest section of the building has four rooms, with an average size of 11.2 by 2.4 m (figure 6.3). The west and south rooms have doorways to the outside and are internally connected by narrow passageways. These chambers had corbeled vaults and were stuccoed. Red-painted bands appeared on the walls below the vault spring, and remains of wooden beams that once spanned and supported the vaults' sides were above.

Above the vault spring, the stucco was discolored gray and black by soot from incense burners and braziers, several of which were found in situ (figure 6.4). The use of torches to light these dark precincts probably contributed to the soot that tarnished the stuccoed floors of Rosalila's rooms.

The second level rises 3.7 m over the first and is 11 m long by 5 m wide, leaving a 3-m corridor on its exterior that is bounded by a 40-cm-high parapet over the edge of the lowest level. A medial molding runs around this section of the building at the height of its single doorway on the north side. The floor plan of the second level consists of a single room, 8.6 by 2.4 m. There is no access from the first level of Rosalila to the second because the second and third stories' primary role was that of a decorative roof-comb.

The third level is the most poorly preserved of the three, with a total height of 3.5 m and a floor plan of 4.3 by 8.2 m. Inside were three small cubicles separated by two roofed, narrow corridors that show up as slot windows on the building's eastern and western facades. The northern cubicle was mostly destroyed during the construction of 10L-16-1st, but its layout can be easily reconstructed.

Rosalila rests on a 3-m-tall substructure named Azul. Like its predecessors, Azul's principal stairway is on the west side, consisting of seven steps. The fifth step has a carved hieroglyphic text with a Long Count date that Linda Schele and Nikolai Grube originally reconstructed as 9.6.17.3.2 (A.D. 571), toward the end of the reign of Ruler 10, whose name Schele and Grube constructed as part of the text (figure 6.5). A reanalysis of the text by David Stuart suggests that it commemorates a dedication date in the reign of Ruler 7 (Sharer et al., chapter 5 in this volume).

The style of the facade adornments and their execution in thick stucco suggest an Early Classic date for Azul, similar to finds at Maya sites such as Tikal and Kohunlich (Segovia Pinto 1969, 1981; Valdés 1991). The ceramics from the fill of Azul belong to the Acbi phase (A.D. 400–625). The close proximity of Rosalila to Stela P, erected by Ruler 11 in A.D. 623, and their artistic similarities have led Agurcia Fasquelle

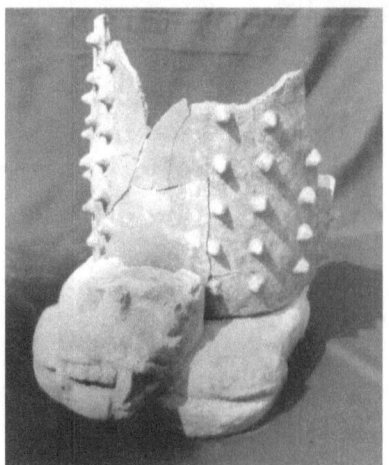

FIGURE 6.4

Incense burners found on the backbench of Rosalila's central room. (Photos by R. Agurcia Fasquelle and J. Ramos)

The Evolution of Structure 10L-16

Figure 6.5
Hieroglyphic step of the Azul Substructure. (Drawing by B. Fash)

to conclude that the stela was once placed in front of the Rosalila/Azul structure.

For close to a century, Rosalila was the principal ancestor shrine as other constructions went up around it. The repeated refurbishing of its stuccoed surfaces and the ceramics in the fills covering it attest to this. Its main staircase was not buried until after the appearance of Coner-phase ceramics (ca. A.D. 625) at the end of Ruler 11's reign. After that time, the building still continued to be used.

When Rosalila was finally buried, its termination rituals were elaborate, including exotic offerings of eccentric flints, chert knives, carved jade, stingray spines, spiny oyster shells, baby shark vertebrae, jaguar claws, and several ceramic incensarios, two of which rested on carved stone bases portraying snarling felines (figures 6.5 and 6.6). Perhaps the costliest part of terminating Rosalila was its embalmment in a thick coat of white stucco followed by covering it with a fill of stones and mud without destroying its fragile, modeled stucco reliefs.

Probably at the end of the seventh century or the beginning of the eighth, Rosalila was covered by a large terraced substructure, 10L-16-2nd, named *Purpura*. Its best-preserved section is the southwest corner, where we were able to trace its profile for 14 m in six terraces (figure 6.7). The terraces above these, if there were any, and the superstructure were systematically destroyed and used as fill during the construction of the final version of Structure 10L-16 (10L-16-1st). Purpura's masonry of neatly cut tuff blocks, as well as its fill of reddish clay and river cobbles, is among the best built by the Maya at Copán. Preliminary estimates indicate that this earlier substructure formed about 70 percent of the bulk of 10L-16-1st, making the final stage of construction practically a veneer.

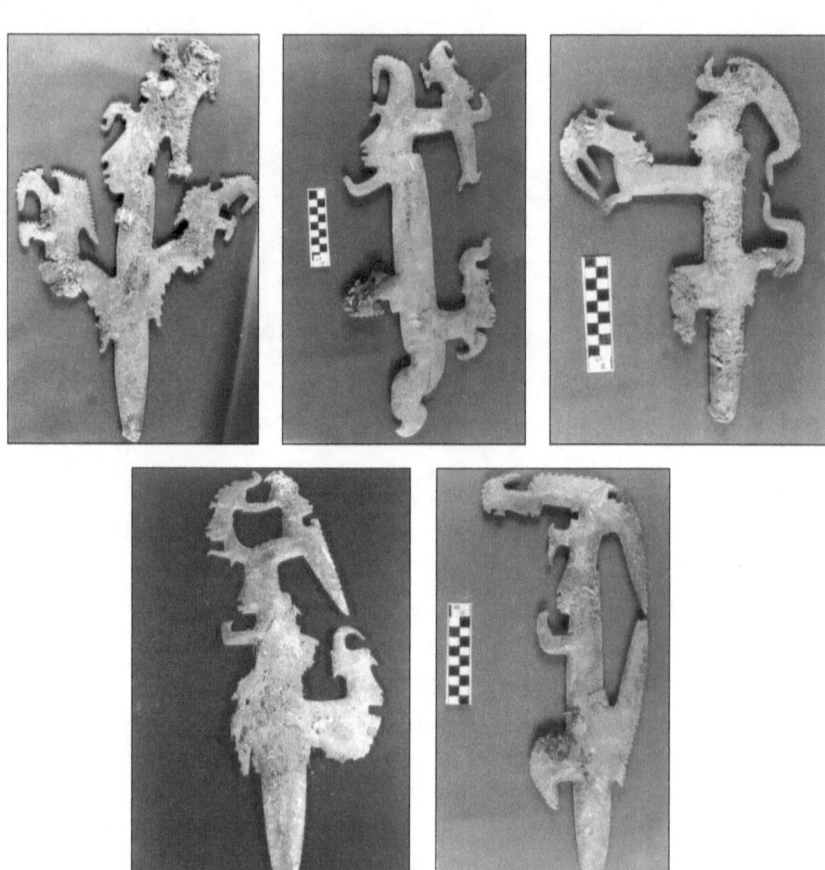

FIGURE 6.6
Termination offering of eccentric flints inside Rosalila. (Photos by R. Flores)

Coner-phase ceramic samples from the fill of Purpura indicate a Late Classic date. Carved stone sculpture instead of modeled stucco like Rosalila's decorated Purpura's facade. The high relief of this sculpture indicates that it was well past the early transitional stage of this change (represented at Copán by structures such as Indigo and Oropéndola) and well into its florescence during Ruler 13's reign (B. Fash and Taube 1996).

Structure 10L-16-1st

Structure 10L-16-1st, the last monumental construction at this

The Evolution of Structure 10L-16

FIGURE 6.7
Buried terraces of Purpura. (Photo by R. Agurcia Fasquelle)

FIGURE 6.8
West side of Structure 10L-16. (Photo by R. Agurcia Fasquelle)

central locus, rises 20 m over the West Court, making it the tallest building of the Copán Acropolis. At its base, it is more than 40 m on a side. It is freestanding on all sides except the north. There, it is attached to a lower platform, on which sit several smaller structures, including Structure 10L-25. B. Fash (1992a, 1992b) has suggested that Structure 10L-25 was a stage for ceremonial dances. In the process of building 10L-16-1st, in what appears to be an unprecedented move at this site, the Maya shifted the central axis of construction 13 m to the south of that of Rosalila/Azul, Celeste, Margarita, Yehnal, and Hunal.

The west side of Structure 10L-16 is dominated by a 19-m-high central staircase, 16.2 m wide at its base, that rises in forty-six steps divided into two sections (figure 6.8). The lower part is composed of nineteen steps that retain much of their thick stucco cover. The upper portion has twenty-seven larger steps and is narrower (10.6 m wide), giving the staircase the appearance of an inverted T. On each side of the staircase are ten stepped terraces with an average height of 1.9 m. These were constructed with uniform, volcanic tuff blocks measuring about 20 by 26 cm. A thin coat of stucco covered the terraces' vertical surfaces. A thick layer of gravel laid in mortar and finished with finely polished

The Evolution of Structure 10L-16

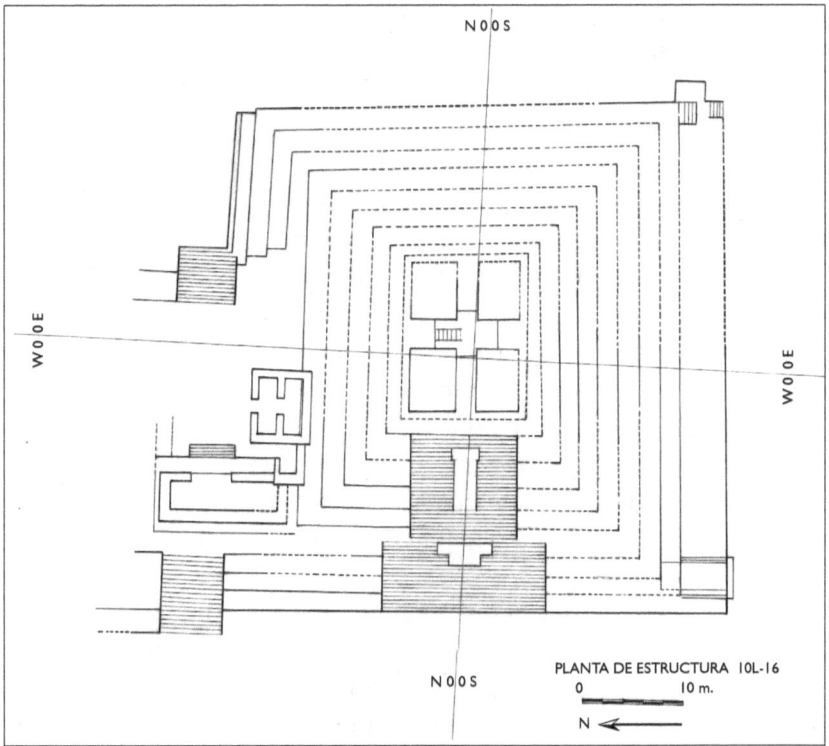

FIGURE 6.9
Plan of Structure 10L-16. (Reconstruction drawing by R. Larios and F. López)

stucco sealed the tops. Unfortunately, the attractive exterior veneer of these terraces covered a poor yellowish fill of loose, sandy soil and blocks of tuff (from Purpura's facades), which led to the collapse of the majority of its substructure's upper five terraces and most of the superstructure.

The first investigations of Structure 10L-16 were conducted by Alfred P. Maudslay in the 1880s. At that time, the substructure foundation was a mass of rubble held together by tree roots. He discovered the lower inner chamber of the temple on top, which had walls standing to 6 feet in height and an inner stairway, from which he surmised there must have been an upper story (Maudslay 1889–1902:25). The pyramidal substructure is a square building with doorways on all four sides facing the cardinal directions (figure 6.9). To begin construction, four large blocks of masonry, each approximately 6 by 4 m, were placed on the stuccoed surface of the tenth terrace. These occupy practically all the space on the summit, leaving only two narrow, intersecting corridors about 2.5 m wide to form the rooms. A narrow walkway was also left around the outside.

The next construction episode in the building closed the intersecting corridors, creating four independent rooms. The west room, with its door on the stairway's central axis, was the principal one and was sealed with a bench bearing an elegantly sculpted mosaic representing a split serpent head (figure 6.10). Today, the walls stand less than 4 feet tall, and the sculptures and niche decoration that Maudslay discovered have been displaced and dispersed over time.

The north room was closed with a staircase leading to a second story of the building. No vestiges were left of this upper level, but there is no doubt that it was a planned part of the building. The huge blocks of fill that form the walls of the first floor were designed to support its load.

Walls sealed the rooms on the south and east sides at their inner ends. Evidently, the Maya had structural problems with this two-story tower design, for the next construction phase removed the earlier inner walls and placed them closer to the entrances, creating a larger nucleus of fill at the building's center. This same problem has been documented on Structure 10L-11, which has the same floor plan and is contemporaneous with Structure 10L-16 (Ruler 16 commissioned them both).

At the base of the Structure 10L-16 stair sits the renowned Altar Q. Between the two, Jeffrey Stomper in 1988 found a rectangular cyst containing the skeletal remains of fifteen jaguars (W. Fash 1991:169). Just east of the cyst were two small shafts, each containing the remains of a macaw (figure 6.11).

Agurcia Fasquelle's stratigraphic excavations in 1990, approaching Altar Q from the north, confirmed that it had been erected at the same time as the final stage of Structure 10L-16. Four carved, cylindrical pedestals were found supporting the altar's corners. At some point, smaller carved blocks had been placed between the pedestals and sculpted with the names of several rulers (figure 6.12).

The ceramics from the fill of the final construction stage of Structure 10L-16 place it in the Coner phase, between A.D. 625 and 850.

FIGURE 6.10

The west room of Structure 10L-16 (after A. P. Maudslay 1889–1902).

This ceramic evidence, the sculpture style, and the epigraphic data confirm that it was built during the reign of Copán's sixteenth ruler, Yax Pasaj. The stratigraphic association with Altar Q implies a date close to the dedication of Altar Q in A.D. 776.

FIGURE 6.11
Jaguar cyst behind Altar Q. (Photo by B. Fash)

FIGURE 6.12
Pedestals and sculpture found under Altar Q. (Photo by R. Agurcia Fasquelle)

THE ICONOGRAPHY OF THE 10L-16 SITE

To gain a better understanding of the evolution of the cosmological message encapsulated in the series of buildings erected over this central axis of the Copán Acropolis—and, as of now, documented in only a very fragmentary way for the earliest structures (Yehnal, Margarita, and Celeste)—it is necessary to take a closer look at the iconography of Rosalila/Azul and Structure 10L-16-1st.

The Iconography of Rosalila

Rosalila has been the senior author's major focus of research since its discovery in 1989 (Agurcia Fasquelle and Fash 1991, 1992; Agurcia Fasquelle and Valdés 1994; Agurcia Fasquelle, Stone, and Ramos 1996), and work here is still in progress. The result of the restrictions imposed by our tunneling methodology, our concern for the long-range conservation of the archaeological remains we uncover, and our desire to preserve research areas for future generations is that a great deal of Rosalila remains buried, in spite of our carefully structured program for obtaining systematic and representative samples of its art and architecture. Consequently, although a large and complete corpus of data exists and its primary register is complete, future research will unquestionably disclose new information that could lead to the refinement and revision of the analysis presented here.

Rosalila continues to surprise us. An example of this occurred in 1994 when B. Fash, aided by Fidencio Rivera, began a microstratigraphic study of the colored stucco layers of Rosalila's panels to provide a master plan for a full-scale replica of this building, which is the centerpiece of the new sculpture museum at Copán (figure 6.13). Besides confirming that the panels did not always retain the same color compositions during their frequent repainting, the clearing away of some later stucco coats revealed an enormous amount of incised iconographic detail that was an important part of the original panels but had been lost as coat after coat of stucco was added. To leave most of this final stage of the building intact, only selected areas were chosen for removal of the termination stucco layer. The essential information for reconstruction has been recovered, but one can only speculate about how much more carved detail remains hidden just below the surface.

The intricate stuccoed artwork of Rosalila's facades speaks of a

FIGURE 6.13
Full-scale replica of Rosalila in the sculpture museum at Copán. (Photo by R. Agurcia)

complex cosmological message. For the purpose of this chapter, we have divided its composition into a series of smaller components, as defined by the architecture of the building and its substructure. This segmentation facilitates the presentation of the data, but we must not forget that it is meant to be seen as an integrated whole (figure 6.14).

Rosalila's substructure, Azul, has been exposed almost completely on its east (or back) side, half on its west (or front) side, and for only 1 m on its south side. Although there are minute traces of modeled stucco motifs on the east side, these are not sufficient to permit any significant interpretations. On the west, the section north of the central stair has been almost completely exposed. Here we have uncovered a well-preserved mask of the Sun God (God G of the Schellhas system) with his head mounted on a rectangular shield with feathered edges (figure 6.15). The portrait is almost entirely painted in red, with well-preserved traces of jade-green paint on the earflares. As currently exposed, it is 3.1 m wide by 2.2 m high.

The eyes on this anthropomorphic visage are large and have the

The Evolution of Structure 10L-16

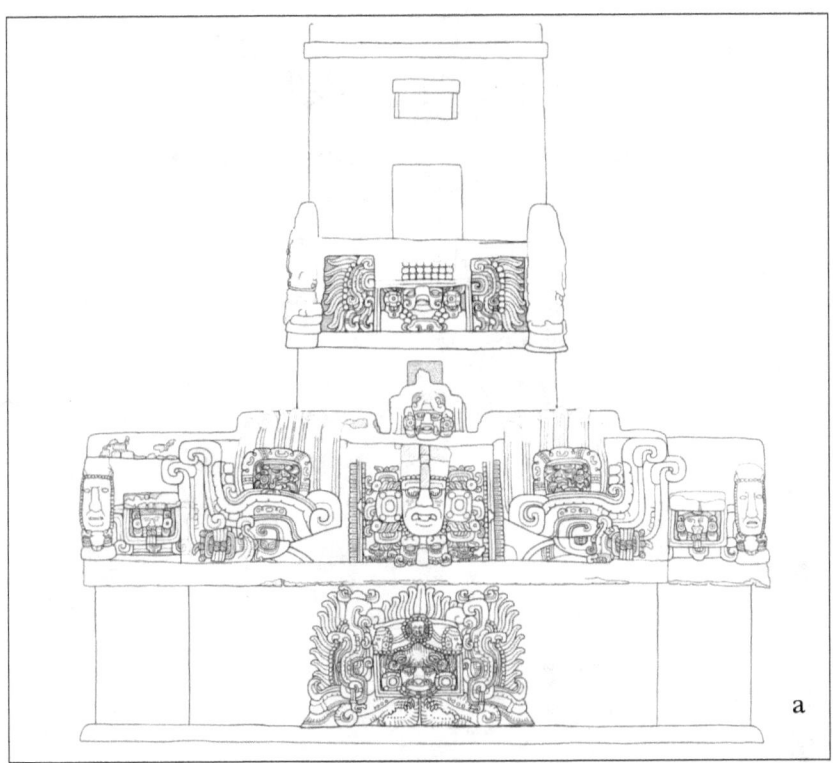

Figure 6.14
Reconstruction drawings of Rosalila: (a) west side and (b) north side. (Drawings by B. Fash)

FIGURE 6.15
Mask of the Sun God on the Azul Substructure. (Photo by R. Agurcia Fasquelle)

squint-eye markings typical of the Sun God, making him appear cross-eyed. On his cheeks, three circles form a triangle that may represent jaguar spots, a symbol of the Sun God's nocturnal aspect. Unfortunately, the nose and mouth in this example are damaged, so the typical Roman nose is missing, as are the T-filed incisors that should protrude from the mouth. On the edges of the mouth are moustache-like curls.

The face is outlined in beads and bordered by conventional Early Classic earflare assemblages. These consist of large, square, jade flares with four studs on their corners, bound above and below with twisted strands and tassels. The snout-and-nostril motif is appended to the central disk (Freidel and Schele 1988:78). At the base of, and probably above, each assemblage is a serpent-like personification head. Excavation restrictions prevented the upper personification heads and the Sun God headdress from being fully exposed. Enough can be seen to recognize a jawless, fanged, zoomorph head with square earflares. Below the squarish jaw of the K'inich Ahau is a badly eroded chin mask still recognizable as a stylized animal head with squint-eye markings. Like similar masks on Yehnal at Copán and at Tikal (A. Miller 1986:figure 9; Valdés 1991:figures 4, 5) and Kohunlich (Segovia Pinto 1981:figures 152–160), this chin mask may have been a representation of a jaguar.

This K'inich Ahau mask is similar to Early Classic stucco-modeled panels placed next to the main staircase of substructures at other lowland Maya sites. Its similarity to those at Kohunlich is remarkable (Segovia Pinto 1969, 1981). Hellmuth (1987a) has illustrated Tzakol-phase modeled incensarios with similar representations of this deity.

The representation of this same deity on Yehnal and Margarita asserts geographic and historical continuity at Copán. This is further reinforced by the iconography of Rosalila, the building atop Azul, where the Sun God reigns supreme.

On Azul's south side, directly below Rosalila's south door, a 1-m-wide trench gave us a limited view of the substructure on this flank. Visible here, on the upper edge, is a large scroll reminiscent of the elbow on the leg of the bird on Rosalila's first level and on the leg of the serpent from the second level (discussed below). On the lower edge of the substructure appears to be a repeating *tun* sign, like that of the monster mask mandible on Rosalila's second level. The glyph band is like one found in a comparable location on the west side of the Margarita Substructure.

The systematic excavations we have undertaken show that the

iconography on Rosalila is similar on all four sides, particularly in its lowermost and principal section. Exceptions, particularly on the two upper levels that form the roof-comb, will be noted as we describe them.

The lower level of Rosalila, the only part of the building easily accessible, is divided horizontally by the medial molding running around it at the height of the doorways and vertically by the doorways themselves. Below the molding and at the sides of the doors were seven panels that, by all indications, were the same. One has been fully excavated (south of the main doorway on the west side), and two more have been partially excavated (one west of the doorway on the south side and another at the center of the north side, which lacked a door).

These panels had been previously interpreted as representations of the Principal Bird Deity/Celestial Bird/ Monster Bird/Vucub Caquix in the process of regurgitating an Old God, tentatively identified as God D or Itzamná (Agurcia Fasquelle and Valdés 1994; W. Fash 1991:100). Our excavations of the north side panel in 1995 require a re-evaluation of this identification. The Maya buried this panel before any of the others as part of a remodeling that annexed Rosalila to a structure north of it. The panel is the best preserved of all, retaining incised details and coloring that are unparalleled on this building (figure 6.16).

The scene consists of a large avian effigy, with squint-eye serpent wings on the sides and large talons below. At the center of it is a bright red portrait of the Sun God, K'inich Ahau. He has squint eyes, and three dimples on his cheeks form a triangle. His nose and upper lip are destroyed, but curling fangs and moustache-like curls are still visible at the corners of the mouth. The simple earflares are squared beads with buttons on their corners. His headdress consists of a green-colored quetzal, *k'uk'*, with the eyes of a macaw, *mo'*. Although his beak is broken off, the identification of the quetzal is straightforward because of its coloration and diagnostic feathered crest. The identification of the eyes is more difficult but is aided by the representation of both the quetzal and the macaw, with their corresponding eyes, on the Margarita Panel (Sharer et al., chapter 5 in this volume; refer to figure 5.5). The Rosalila bird has many traits of the Early Classic macaw, for example, a heavy-lidded eye with yellow coloring and a pupil outlined by a semicircular incision.

This is not the Principal Bird Deity, as the weathered panel on the

The Evolution of Structure 10L-16

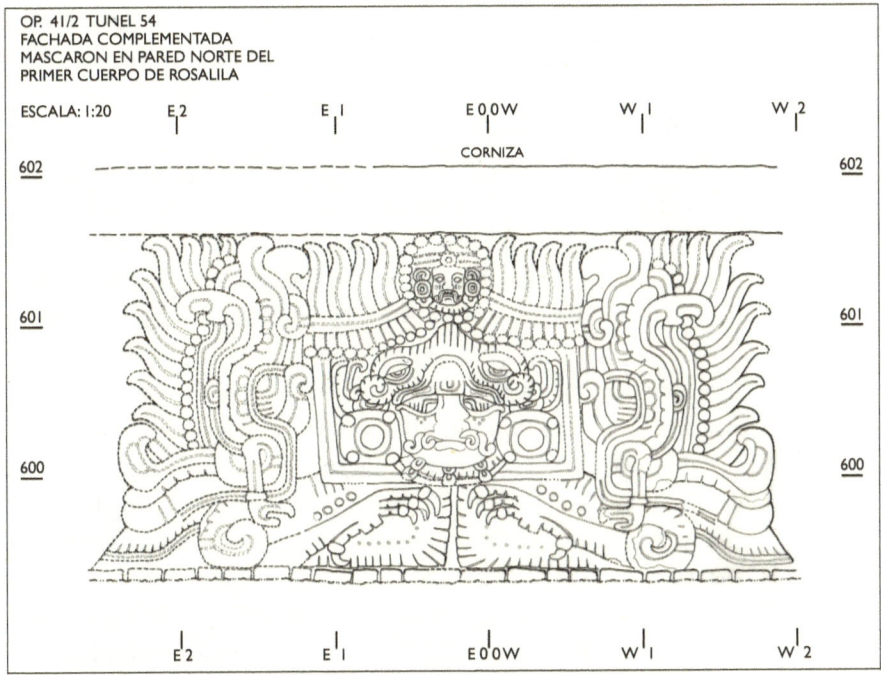

FIGURE 6.16

Sun God and Bird on Rosalila's north side. (Drawing by J. Espinoza and J. Ramos)

west side had led us to believe, but an iconographic personification of the founder's name, *K'inich Yax K'uk' Mo'*. The same combination of symbols (the *k'inich* prefix followed by the headdress of the quetzal with the eye of a macaw) was used in many hieroglyphic expressions for this ruler's name, particularly those on top of Altar Q.

The serpent wings on the sides echo the message of the main visage. The eye markings are the same as the Sun God's. Karl Taube (personal communication 1996) also noted that the serpents' upper fangs are portrayed as macaw beaks, and he suggested that they, too, implied the founder's name. It is also probable that they refer, redundantly, to avian representations of the sun at Copán, which, as Claude Baudez (1994:265) has illustrated, use the macaw as a favorite form.

Above the medial molding, the iconography of Rosalila becomes more complicated. At present, the west side is completely exposed, as is most of the north side. The other two sides are known almost exclusively from their upper edges. The central motifs of all four sides seem to be the same. Toward the corners, only the opposite sides of the building are symmetrical—north and south are identical, as are east and west.

At the center of the building is a large anthropomorphic face that is preserved only on the north side in a somewhat damaged state (figure 6.17). This appears to be the same deity as on the Azul Substructure and also seems closely related to the one below Rosalila's medial molding. The head emerges from the center of a feathered, rectangular shield and has squint eyes, three circle marks on its cheeks, and a single T-shaped, filed tooth. Although the nose is now battered, it was large. Around the face are slight indications of a band of beads, but the earflare assemblages were completely washed away by two rainspouts that drained the roof. Agurcia believes that this main mask of the building also had a K'inich Yax K'uk' Mo' headdress that would have allowed the composition as a whole to be read as the founder's name. Evidence for this is missing, with the exception of a down-curving stone hook that probably served as the mount for the quetzal's beak. The chin mask is equally destroyed, except for two down-curved, stone hooks that were its armature.

Above where the headdress would have been, on a small column that projects above the parapet of the first level of this building, are two stacked faces. The lower is easily identified as a K'inich Ahau portrait. The upper one is more eroded but could be a quetzal. Further microstratigraphic cleaning of these masks could provide more detailed insights into their iconography.

The central Sun God head, which visually dominates the iconography of Rosalila's main body is avian in nature. To each side of its head are outstretched wings in the form of upside-down serpents from whose maw surges a small cartouche with a Sun God at its center. These solar cartouches or sun disks have a detailed representation of the god's head in profile and are framed by a scalloped cartouche, not unlike the yaxkin calendar sign. It was one of these that B. Fash cleaned, revealing a vast array of incised details not apparent with the stucco termination layer in place. These included all the typical Sun God characteristics: a forward-projected, bound hank of hair, a large Roman nose, a clearly marked, square squint eye, three circles on the cheek, a large protruding tooth, a moustache-like emanation from the mouth, and a kin sign

The Evolution of Structure 10L-16

Figure 6.17

Central Sun God mask on Rosalila's north side. (Photo by R. Agurcia)

on the back of his cheek. The combination of elements on these cartouches allows the clearest identification of any deity on Rosalila. Because these wings belong to the central mask, they confirm his identity as K'inich Ahau (figure 6.18).

The serpent wings on the north side of Rosalila have a series of elements that are not present on those of the west side. The principal one is a personified perforation bundle (or Perforator God) that doubles as K'inich Ahau's forearms and the serpent's eyebrow. Another significant alteration is that the bundle on the wing/arm at the east side of the central panel is marked with an *akbal* (darkness) sign, whereas that on the west side is marked with a mirror (brightness) sign. Beyond these bundles, the Sun God's hands are missing, perhaps indicating that they had been sacrificially cut off or that the Sun is a sacrificer.

Beyond the serpent wings, forming the corners of the building on the west side, are large serpent heads with mouths wide open and an anthropomorphic head sprouting from them. The only well-preserved head is on the northeast corner of the building. It has beads around it, a large nose, and a single tooth in its mouth, but no other markings are visible (although later stucco coats could have covered some). Its identification is problematic. It could be another portrait of the Sun God, a youthful maize god, or a young ruler, as seen in other Early Classic manifestations (for example, Hellmuth 1987b:figures 48 and 639; Franco Torrijos et al. 1981:figure 214). The serpent heads from which he comes are similar to those on the double-headed serpent bar (and vision serpent) commonly held by Copán kings on stelae (for example, Stela A).

On the north side, beyond the serpent wings, human faces emanate from inset niches. Each has a red turban headdress and a bow tie, with a triangular nose plaque over the mouth. On the nose plaque are three circles forming a triangle, not unlike the god markings on the Sun God masks. Baudez (1994:278) has pointed out that in Copán sculpture, the turban is worn by the king and, more frequently, by his ancestors. He considers it to be an emblem of the city. These personages are almost certainly the portraits of ancestral rulers (possibly K'inich Yax K'uk' Mo') being called forth from the underworld (figure 6.19).

This interpretation is reinforced by the location of these portraits between sacrifice bundles (toward the center of the building) and vision serpents (on the corners). The niches from which they emerge

The Evolution of Structure 10L-16

FIGURE 6.18
Solar cartouche on the south side of Rosalila: (top) before cleaning and (bottom) after cleaning. (Photos by B. Fash)

are framed by curls and dangles that could be fangs of the vision serpent or foliage. One of the niche's sides is a slot window that goes

FIGURE 6.19
Turbaned niche figure from Rosalila's north side. (Photo by R. Agurcia Fasquelle)

through to the upper, vaulted area of the temple's rooms. Inside the rooms, excavations revealed an accumulation of soot from incensario smoke. On the exterior, this would have made for a dramatic re-enactment of the blood-sacrifice rite calling forth the ancestors. Whereas the turban marks this figure as a royal ancestor, like the figures on Altar Q, the nose plaque has been associated by Hellmuth (1987b:353) with blood sacrifice.

The second level of Rosalila—which, with the third, forms the temple's roof-comb—is dominated by a central *cauac* or Witz Monster mask that marks the building as a sacred mountain just like Structure 10L-22 (B. Fash 1992a, 1992b; W. Fash 1991; M. Miller 1986; Schele and Freidel 1990). This element has been exposed mostly on the building's east side, but its presence has been confirmed on the west side. It has no counterpart on the other two sides of the building. On the east and west sides, this mask crosses the medial molding and occupies the full height of the second level.

In view of the fact that in its heyday Rosalila crowned the Acropolis, flanked by two other magnificent structures (Oropéndola on the south and Peach/Colorado on the north), and that it is clearly marked as a mountain, the glyphic reference to Ox Witik, or three mountains (Stuart 1992:171), found in various texts referring to a location in Copán, is likely a reference to the Acropolis and these three buildings.

Most of the eastern Witz Monster mask is well preserved. The exceptions to this are the upper part of its forehead, which is partially eroded, and its large, downward-turned nose, which is broken off on the east side but complete on the west. It has large squint eyes and a stepped cleft forehead; on its cheeks, as well as forehead, are mirror markings. At the mask's edges, blending into these cheek markings are akbal symbols that belong to a profile portrait of this same creature, extending to the north and south of the main mask. B. Fash interprets these markings as designating the mountain deity's dualistic nature and notes that the dark profile head is hidden but the light frontal head is fully visible. These have teeth represented by tun glyphs and profuse tun signs on their forehead and snout. This same version may be repeated on the Azul Substructure's south side. The stepped cleft markings on the forehead end in spirals encasing corn kernels. These probably exalt the fertility aspects of the sacred mountain.

The next iconographic elements of this section of the building, the bodies of snakes, partially cover the profile-head Witz Monster masks. In each case, the snake's head forms the corner of the building, as it does on the upper register of the lower level. From its open mouth emanates another mask, whose identity cannot be determined because it is almost completely eroded on all exposed sides.

The snake's body, with large trapezoidal markings and smaller crosshatched ones, undulates down from the head and then rises straight, continuing on to the third level of the building. Below the body is a reptilian, three-toed arm that seems to mark the snake as a saurian creature and therefore as the Celestial Monster. Freidel and Schele (1988:78) have suggested that the snake in the Preclassic period transforms to a caiman in the Classic period. Possibly, this is a transitional representation. In conjunction with this cosmic interpretation, Rudy Larios believes that the snake's body arches over Rosalila's third level, forming an arch of the heavens like that found on the interior doorway of Structure 10L-22. The stucco decoration on both sides of the building is eroded in its uppermost sections, so this reconstruction cannot be confirmed.

On the north and south sides of the second story, a central panel was placed over the medial molding. Below the molding, we found only red-painted stucco with no modeled motifs. The north side was badly damaged during the construction of 10L-16-1st, but telltale markings of the decoration remain in situ. The south side is well preserved and consists of a central zoomorphic creature with serpent wings. We believe the zoomorph to be a bird (perhaps a quetzal), but the details of its nose and mouth are gone. It wears a beaded necklace that ends in an inverted trifoil element found frequently on scribes at Copán. Its headdress consists of a rectangular, beaded band. The serpent wing's snout is aimed down, an uncommon posture elsewhere on this building.

The third level of Rosalila is the least well preserved of the three, primarily because the construction of 10L-16-1st destroyed its north side and roof. When the axis of Structure 10L-16-1st was shifted 13 m to the south, its terraces cut into the earlier construction. In this process, the whole northern cubicle of the third level disappeared, and the central section was cut off diagonally, losing about one-third of its upper edge. On the western side of Rosalila, the central mask is sufficiently well preserved to be identified. It consists of a death head with spiral eyes and a fleshless lower mandible. It wears beaded, squared earflare assemblages. Next to these are narrow slot windows, followed by the trapezoidal-marked serpent bodies that rise from the lower section of the roof-comb. Next to these and continuing to the corners are elongated serpent wings with plumage.

Karl Taube (personal communication 1996) has suggested that the death head may represent an incensario and the serpents symbolize the smoke issuing from it. The numerous incensarios found inside, as well as the thick deposits of soot on its interior floors and walls, lend credibility to this interpretation. Miniature temple models found at Copán, such as those from Group 10L-2 (Andrews and Fash 1992:figure 17), show such a scene on their roofs. Rituals involving fire and smoke, such as those for the conjuring of ancestors, were important in Rosalila as in earlier and later buildings at this spot.

Rosalila was the major religious sanctuary of Copán at the end of the sixth century A.D. Such was its importance that even when it was buried, it was spared destruction and instead was embalmed and covered with such extraordinary care that its soft stucco artwork was con-

The Evolution of Structure 10L-16

FIGURE 6.20

The west side of Structure 10L-16. (Drawing by B. Fash after H. Hohmann)

served. It was probably one of the last in its genre of stucco-decorated buildings, for the next ones to be commissioned began the tradition of mosaic stone sculpture at Copán. The external facades of Rosalila were profusely adorned with a complex cosmological message whose full meaning we are only beginning to understand.

In line with a rich Preclassic and Early Classic tradition of the Lowland Maya (Freidel and Schele 1988; A. Miller 1986; Segovia Pinto 1969; Valdés 1991) and with their immediate architectural ancestors of the Copán Acropolis (Yehnal and Margarita), Rosalila and Azul portray a gigantic cosmogram whose principal deity is the Sun God, K'inich Ahau. This patron deity of the rulers is incorporated, at least in Rosalila's lower masks, into the founder's name. The cosmogram may also reinforce the idea that the deceased ancestors are transformed into the sun after death. Around this stellar god are scenes of creation, the heavens, the sacred mountain, and death, intertwined with the instruments that royal mortals used to try to control these forces—sacrificial bundles, incense burners, vision serpents, and bicephalic serpent bars. The powerful message carried by this ancient building is a forerunner of that manifested by later kings on Structures 10L-11, 10L-16, and 10L-22 of the Acropolis, which made the Sun Kings of Copán the central players of the Maya cosmos (Baudez 1985, 1994).

The Iconography of Structure 10L-16 and Altar Q

A 19-m-tall central stairway that rises in two sections (figure 6.20) dominates the west side of Structure 10L-16. The upper portion is narrower than the lower, giving the stairway the appearance of an inverted T. Both sections of the stairway are interrupted by sculpted panels that have been reconstructed by B. Fash and K. Taube in the sculpture museum at Copán. The lower panel has the remains of a T-shaped outset with thirty large, sculpted skulls resembling a *tzompantli* (Aztec-period skull rack) surrounding a huge goggle-eyed Tlaloc (figure 6.21).

The second panel consists of a rectangular cartouche framed by a rope with a spine-like decoration. At each corner is a cut-away crescent shape with a skeletal serpent's head emerging in profile. The large rectangle forms an enormous ancestor cartouche or sun shield with a portrait of K'inich Yax K'uk' Mo' in the guise of the warrior Sun God at its center. The third panel is an open monster mouth with a *pu* mountain sign beneath the lower jaw and serpent markings flanking the sides. Repeating scrolls surround the gum line; a bound figure found in situ on the stairway appears to have been seated in the open mouth.

The west room, with its door over the stairway's central axis, was decorated with a narrow bench bearing an elegantly sculpted mosaic representing a split serpent head that is interpreted as a vision serpent. We believe that a seated portrait of the founder, K'inich Yax K'uk' Mo', was located within the serpent's mouth and, therefore, that he was the main ancestor called forth from the Underworld at this location (figure 6.22).

Our excavations produced more than 1,400 sculpture fragments, most of which came from the mosaic panels decorating the building's facade. The central iconographic motif of Structure 10L-16 is a goggle-eyed supernatural, best described as Tlaloc. There are six different rep-

FIGURE 6.21
Skull rack (tzompantli) *from the stairway of Structure 10L-16, as reconstructed by B. Fash and K. Taube. (Photo by Ricardo Agurcia Fasquelle)*

resentations of it, the most prominent being large mosaic masks mounted on the superstructure's outer walls at each side of the doorways and in the corners (figure 6.23). Other representations include shields, heads, incensarios, and rectangular blocks.

Another major motif of this building is an elaborate, interlocking eye motif made up of kan crosses and lidded goggle eyes. The fall pattern of these pieces indicates that they were originally set over the doorways on the north and south sides. Other loose motifs include feathers, fans, ropes, dangles, shells, *petates* (mats), year signs, and anthropomorphic figures.

The sculpture found on Structure 10L-16 depicts themes of warfare, death, and sacrifice (Stone, Morales, and Williamson 1996). This is attested by the frequency of the goggled-eyed Tlaloc, who is associated with war (Pasztory 1974) and with warriors who procured victims for sacrifice (Schele 1984). The Mexican year sign has been shown to

FIGURE 6.22
Reconstruction of the vision serpent bench on Structure 10L-16. (Drawing by B. Fash)

symbolize the same theme (Proskouriakoff 1973). Ropes were important in war-captive imagery (Baudez and Mathews 1979), and the skulls often portrayed on Maya and Aztec *tzompantli* came from the sacrifice of these victims.

These themes of warfare, death, and sacrifice provide a link between Altar Q and Structure 10L-16, reinforcing their stratigraphic association. Altar Q, commissioned by Yax Pasaj, portrays the sixteen rulers of the K'inich Yax K'uk' Mo' dynasty seated on their name glyphs. It shows Yax Pasaj receiving the baton of office from the founder and, in so doing, proclaims Yax Pasaj as the descendant of all

THE EVOLUTION OF STRUCTURE 10L-16

FIGURE 6.23
Sculpture motifs from Structure 10L-16: (a) interlocking eye and Kan cross, (b) Tlaloc with year sign, (c) small Tlaloc effigy head, (d) Kan cross, (e) Tlaloc shield, (f) Yax K'uk' Mo' glyphs (K'uk' portion missing), (g) full-figure Tlaloc warrior with shield, and (h) large mosaic Tlaloc with year signs. (Drawings by B. Fash)

the great rulers of Copán (figure 6.24). Schele (Schele and Freidel 1990:311) has suggested that on the text on the altar's upper surface, Yax Pasaj calls Altar Q the *Altar of Yax K'uk' Mo'*. Yax Pasaj hoped to legit-

235

FIGURE 6.24
Altar Q in the sculpture museum. (Photo by R. Agurcia Fasquelle)

imize his power through this artistic confirmation of his divine relationship with the ancestral rulers, especially the founder, K'inich Yax K'uk' Mo'.

Structure 10L-16 also seems to emphasize Yax Pasaj's relationship with the founder. Yax Pasaj's repeated use of the goggle-eyed Tlaloc motif on the building echoed K'inich Yax K'uk' Mo's goggle-eyed portrayal on Altar Q. Here the founder holds the same type of serpent shield in his hand as two found in our excavations, which Taube (1992:61–63) has shown represents a war serpent closely tied to Teotihuacán. This close association between the two rulers is also echoed on the structure by (1) glyphs that phonetically spell *yax* and *mo'* and were also found in our excavations (we lack only the K'uk' element to complete his name), (2) the sculpted outset panels on the stairway, with representations of both the founder and Tlaloc, and (3) the vision serpent's representation in the central room, with the founder coming out of its mouth.

The Evolution of Structure 10L-16

The cache of fifteen jaguars found between Altar Q and Structure 10L-16 may have been an offering to the ancestors, one for each ruler who preceded Yax Pasaj (W. Fash 1991:169). The macaws in the associated shafts could also symbolize the lineage founder, K'inich Yax K'uk' Mo' (Sun-Eyed Resplendent Quetzal Macaw).

The bellicose nature of the iconography on Structure 10L-16 closely ties it to that of Structure 10L-26 and the Hieroglyphic Stairway (B. Fash 1992a; W. Fash 1991; W. Fash et al. 1992). Both are monuments for ancestor worship in the context of warfare and sacrifice. No ancestors were portrayed on the facade of the temple on top of Structure 10L-16, as is the case on Structure 10L-26. But Altar Q, a synthesis of dynastic rulership, has them all.

CONCLUSIONS

The central message carried by the iconography of this sequence of constructions—from Yehnal, to Margarita, to Rosalila, to Structure 10L-16-1st, from the second ruler to the sixteenth, and from about A.D. 400 to 776—remained constant: a world cosmogram creating a stage on which the Sun Kings of Copán played their sacred role as the central figure of world order. In this cast of superstars, one stood out above all others—K'inich Yax K'uk' Mo', founder of the Copán dynasty, greatest Sun King of all, and source of divine sanction for all later kings. At the base of this sequence probably lie his remains and those of the house that founded Copán as a sacred, royal Maya center.

Acknowledgments

The ideas presented here are the result of numerous consultations with a wide range of scholars and friends over a number of years. Principal among these are William Fash, Nikolai Grube, Justin Kerr, Rudy Larios, Julie Miller, Alfonso Morales, Lee Parsons, Linda Schele, Donna Stone, David Stuart, and Karl Taube. The present synthesis is our own.

7

A Late Classic Royal Residence at Copán

E. Wyllys Andrews and Cassandra R. Bill

One of the largest and most elaborate residential complexes at Copán during the Late Classic lay at the south end of the Acropolis. The size of many structures in Group 10L-2, the quantity of architectural and other sculpture, the presence of rich tombs discovered in the 1890s, and its location at the edge of the Acropolis suggest that the occupants were of high status, perhaps members of the ruling dynasty.

Several seasons of investigations in Group 10L-2 have enabled us to combine into one rich panoply the stratigraphic and artifact data from extensive excavations in buildings situated around two large courtyards, the architectural and sculptural information from this neighborhood, and what the Maya wrote on monuments found in and near these buildings. We have been able to apply both the methods and interests of household archaeology and the tools and data appropriate for illuminating the developing political form of a Maya court. The opportunity to expose and examine in detail these aspects of a royal domestic compound, aspects that often are not brought together into one coherent view in Maya archaeology, makes this project highly unusual.

We will use the remains of Group 10L-2 to address several issues and follow several strands that are sometimes interwoven in the following pages. First, this residential compound includes a range of building types. This variety is surely related to the high social and economic status of some of its occupants in the Late Classic and to the labor and artisans they could command. Few excavated Maya residential complexes have presented such functional diversity.

We can show a continuity of structure form through multiple episodes of construction in some buildings, and we believe that this indicates a continuity of function. Once a building had a function, that use and that location were maintained during modifications. The size and number of buildings increased during the Late Classic, probably reflecting the occupants' wealth and power, and access to the group became increasingly limited as entryways were eliminated.

We believe that we can link some members of Group 10L-2 to a corporate descent group, probably an extended lineage, through inscribed monuments, sculptural decoration on the buildings, and other archaeological evidence. From the great variation in size and elaboration among houses and even among rooms in the same house, we infer that a range of social and economic statuses existed within one co-resident group. Members of the same lineage possessed different status and wealth, and some residents of Group 10L-2 were likely unrelated retainers or servants.

An examination of the ceramics and artifacts from buried middens in different parts of the royal residential compound suggests that certain activities were carried out more frequently in some areas than in others and that these areas also have different architecture.

The last head of this group was Yax Pasaj Chan Yopat, the sixteenth ruler. The opportunity to link a noble Maya residential complex to a specific group and to specific individuals is rare. In this part of Copán, it allows us to document the range of architectural subgroups that formed part of one extensive, noble, residential compound.

Today Group 10L-2 includes a central courtyard bordered by large buildings (Courtyard A), at least two smaller, adjacent courtyards ringed by residential and other structures (Courtyards B and C), and several other buildings and open spaces (figure 7.1; the unexcavated Courtyard C to the west is not included).

LATE CLASSIC ROYAL RESIDENCE

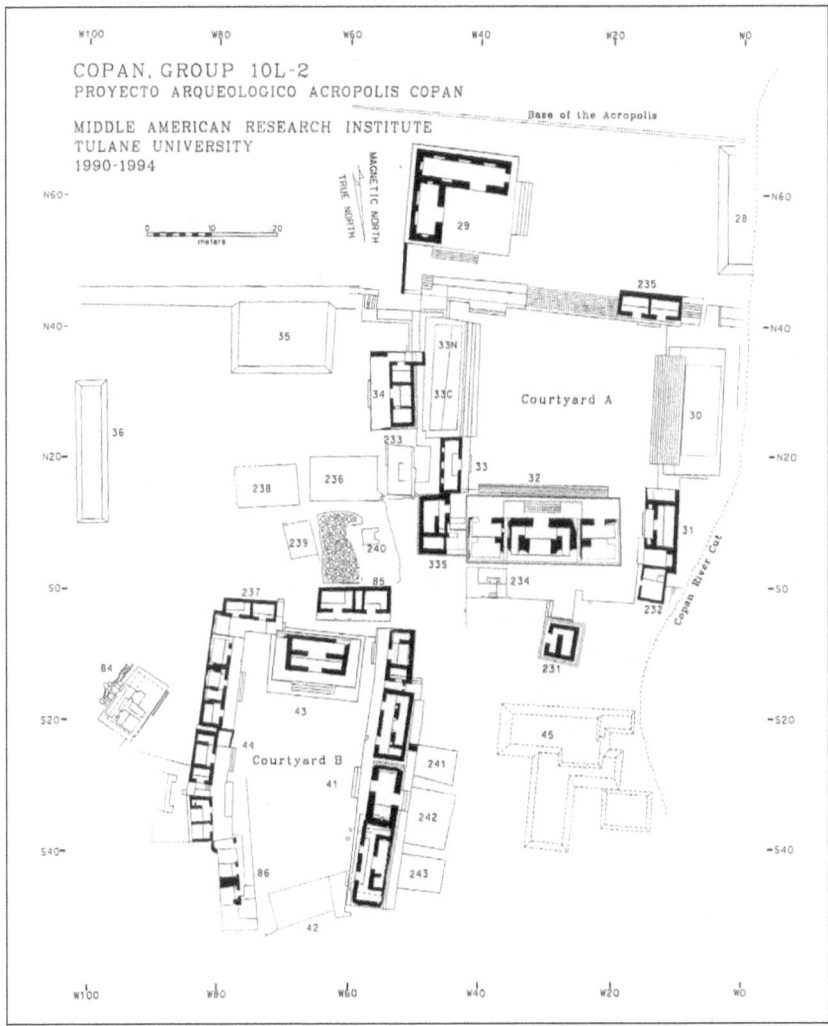

FIGURE 7.1

Plan of Group 10L-2 at the end of the Late Classic period (late Coner phase).

As one of the participating institutions in the Copán Acropolis Archaeological Project from 1990 to 1994, Tulane University excavated all the buildings around Courtyards A and B and several platforms west of Courtyard A. Excavations showed that all the visible structures in Group 10L-2 date to the Late Classic (Bill 1997). We found few architectural remains of the Early Classic period, and those were deeply buried, but privileged families occupied Group 10L-2 well before the end of the Early Classic. The first buildings on Courtyards A and B date to about A.D. 650. Most of these were modified, expanded, or completely replaced in the following century and a half, so Group 10L-2 was far more impressive in A.D. 800, even though the basic plan was still in place.

The earliest-known constructions around both courtyards date to the reign of Ruler 12 (A.D. 628–695), probably early in his term. Ruler 16 (Yax Pasaj Chan Yopat), who ruled from A.D. 763 until about 820, built three of the large final buildings and probably other, smaller ones. A substantial part of the architecture, some of it now buried, dates to the reigns of Ruler 13 (Waxaklajun Ub'ah K'awil, A.D. 695–738), Ruler 14 (K'ak' Joplaj Chan K'awil, A.D. 738–749), and Ruler 15 (K'ak' Yipyaj Chan K'awil, A.D. 749–?) (W. Fash 2001:79–80; Martin and Grube 2000:190–213), but we are not yet able to attribute individual buildings to each ruler. Some excavated buildings show three major periods of construction. We suspect that much of the construction between Rulers 12 and 16 dates to the time of Ruler 13, perhaps because of the length of his rule and the extent of what he built on the Acropolis.

As buildings were enlarged, and as rooms and platforms were added to the original structures, the open spaces between them disappeared, and both courtyards became more enclosed and private, with fewer entrances (Andrews and Fash 1992).[1] From more limited beginnings at the end of the Early Classic, Group 10L-2 grew to be the most architecturally varied, Late Classic residential complex yet investigated at Copán. It is by no means the only dense concentration of ruined structures near the Acropolis, however, and likely not the largest. Group 10L-18, centered about 200 m west of the Court of the Hieroglyphic Stairway, is a massive concentration of ruins, at least as impressive as Group 10L-2. It, too, was probably a royal residence.

Although the spatial organization, architecture, and artifact remains within Group 10L-2 show variation, this complex of buildings appears distinguishable from surrounding constructions. Its more tightly enclosed spaces, with buildings facing inward, resulted in reduced accessibility and greater privacy. Often set on high platforms and vaulted, the buildings were generally larger than those to the south and west, in the zone known as *El Bosque*, and many facades bore stone

Late Classic Royal Residence

sculpture. The three known courtyards, especially Courtyards A and B, were carefully planned and tightly enclosed. They are separated spatially from the less symmetrical building groups to the south and west. The east-west terraces of the Acropolis form the north edge of the group, and the Copán River cut delineates the current east edge.

Group 10L-2 today is the west and central part of what was most likely a more extensive complex of buildings. The Copán River in the late nineteenth and early twentieth centuries washed away the east side of the Acropolis and part of our group. Courtyard A, due south of the East Court, would most likely have been on the centerline of the group. If Group 10L-2 was originally symmetrical, the river has carried off a courtyard at the southeast corner of Courtyard A—corresponding in position to our excavated Courtyard B—and conceivably one in about the same relative position as the unexcavated Courtyard C, just west of A and B. We know that it washed away the east side of the sprawling Structure 10L-45, south of Courtyard A, and nearly all of two structures (10L-28 and 10L-97) at the east edge of Courtyard A, because parts of these three still remain. Our sample is therefore incomplete, in part because not all the extant ruins in the group have been investigated (Courtyard C and Structure 10L-45, most importantly) and in part because we do not know how large the complex was.

The excavated portion of Group 10L-2 includes three groups of structures, and these adjacent building complexes appear to have been used for different purposes throughout the Late Classic period. Courtyard A is the most extensive, with some of the largest buildings. It was the focus of the royal residential complex in Group 10L-2 during the final decades of the Late Classic. Its dominant structure was the house of Yax Pasaj, the sixteenth ruler in the Copán dynasty and the head of an extended lineage that may have included the residents of a large area south of the Acropolis beyond Group 10L-2. Courtyard A, however, was only partly domestic. Other buildings around the courtyard were used by the residents of Group 10L-2 for public rituals or were not lived in. Courtyard B, immediately southwest of Courtyard A, has two large buildings that also seem to have been for lineage or communal activities, although perhaps for less public rituals than those conducted around Courtyard A. The rest of the structures around Courtyard B, of variable size and quality, were domestic. The third area, which we call "El Cementerio" (the traditional name for the entire Group 10L-2), is a large rectangular space just west of Courtyard A and north of Courtyard B. Low platforms here originally supported noble residences and tombs. During the Late Classic, this area appears to have been filled in for work space and perishable dwellings or outbuildings, perhaps used by lower-ranking residents of the surrounding courtyards or by servants.

In brief, although this area was dominated by individuals whose inscriptions and architectural sculpture proclaimed their ties to the royal line, the individual buildings within the group vary in architectural form, size, and quality. Also, the groups to which these buildings belong contrast sharply with one another. These differences reflect buildings with distinct functions and individuals or families of status ranging from royalty to commoner.

GROUP 10L-2 BEFORE THE LATE CLASSIC PERIOD

Middle Preclassic ceramics of the Uir phase were found directly above river sands in excavations about 100 m south of Courtyard B (Viel 1983:479–481, 1993b:42–50). Both Viel (1983:498–499, 1993b: 50–66) and Longyear (1952:23–25) describe greater amounts of Late Preclassic pottery from excavations in the same area (table 7.1). In none of our seven deepest excavations in Courtyards A and B did we find material this old. In Courtyard A, the earliest pottery in the lowest levels of our two deep test excavations, just above sterile river gravels, belonged to the Protoclassic and Early Classic Bijac complex (ca. A.D. 1–400). In both excavations, however, this earliest material was mixed with Early Classic Acbi sherds. Bijac pottery was also the earliest material above sterile sand under Courtyard B, again, usually mixed with Acbi sherds.

Deep strata in Group 10L-2 were undulating, following the early river and flood deposits on the valley floor. In Courtyard A, our test units encountered river gravels at depths varying by more than a meter. In Courtyard B, the most productive Early Protoclassic Bijac (ca. A.D. 1–100) deposit was a deep pit filled with a great variety of stone objects and broken ceramic vessels. This pit lay not far below the surface, just south of Structure 10L-43. About 25 m to the northeast, a deep excavation showed that a small Acbi platform had been built deeper than this

TABLE 7.1
Chronology of Group 10L-2, Copán

Period	Date	Phase
Early Postclassic	1100	Group 10L-2 abandoned
	1000	Ejar
Terminal Classic	900	Group 10L-2 abandoned
		Terminal Coner
Late Classic	800	Late Coner
	700	Early Coner
	600	Acbi-Coner Transition
		Late Acbi
Early Classic	500	Early Acbi
	400	
	300	Late Bijac
Protoclassic	200	
	100	Early Bijac
	0	
Late Preclassic	100	Chabij

Note: The period designations follow the traditional divisions used in the Maya area. Phase divisions for the Late Preclassic and Protoclassic follow Viel (1999a) and W. Fash (2001), with slight changes resulting from our radiocarbon dates for Early Bijac. The earliest-known cultural deposits in Group 10L-2 date to the early Protoclassic. The Terminal Coner phase dates from about A.D. 820 (the end of the Copán dynasty) until A.D. 850 or 900 and is shown ending at A.D. 875 in this chart. Manahan proposed the dates for the small Early Postclassic settlement about 100 m south of Group 10L-2, reporting nine radiocarbon dates from the house platforms he excavated (W. Fash, Andrews, and Manahan 2004; Manahan 2000). Forty-two obsidian-hydration dates determined by AnnCorinne Freter from the 1990 Tulane excavations in Courtyard A were reported by Andrews and B. Fash (1992:table 2).

trash pit, just above sterile sand. Other low Acbi platforms appeared at similar levels in other excavations in Courtyard B. Group 10L-2 was, therefore, occupied in the Bijac phase, but the earliest recovered traces here of platforms faced with uncut stone, badly eroded and then covered by red alluvial loam, date to early Acbi.

This homogeneous, featureless, red alluvial silt appeared in Courtyard B just below the earliest courtyard surface and continued down with few visible changes, grading into sterile, red, river sand and gravel. The silt attests to the continuing deposition of river sediments in Group 10L-2 long after the Preclassic period. In Courtyard B, not until almost the beginning of the Late Classic do red silt deposits seem to stop. This implies that until this time, the Copán River was not sufficiently controlled to prevent at least occasional flooding of the area around Courtyard B. Our observations are in accord with those of geomorphologist William Johnson, who concluded that the river continued to erode parts of the floodplain and deposit layers of sand, mud, or clay on this low terrace until nearly the beginning of the Late Classic period (W. Fash 2001:43; Turner et al. 1983:86–87). The area just to the north, including Courtyard A and the zone west of it, was built up earlier, and the deposits of red loam are absent except just above sterile river sands. In Courtyard A, abutting the Acropolis, well-preserved masonry platforms and buildings lie below the Late Classic surface. This higher area may have been less prone to annual flooding and may also have been protected before the Late Classic, perhaps by walls or man-made levees.

The only substantial late Acbi building partially exposed during our excavations, 10L-34-2nd, had high room walls of mud and rough stones covered by mud plaster. It had been buried under Structure 10L-34, which formed the southern side of a small, west-facing courtyard of three vaulted buildings at the beginning of the Late Classic period. Structure 10L-34 was the only one of the three not buried by later structures.

A few Acbi platforms and burials were found in excavations below the extensive Late Classic constructions. A deep Acbi midden lay under a more extensive Coner midden northwest of Courtyard B. Some of it was deposited by occupants of an early residential platform that was near or under the Late Classic Structure 10L-36, a long residential structure on the east side of Courtyard C. A late Acbi burial of an adult, probably a male, under 10L-41A, at the northeast corner of Courtyard B, contained three elaborate, locally produced Sovedeso Negative–painted vases with *tun/cauac* motifs (Bill 1997:382–383, figure 4.4b). These may be the finest vessels known from Group 10L-2 and are technically the most difficult to produce. The house of this individual has not been identified, but the huge, unexcavated Structure 10L-45, just east of 10L-41, may contain late Acbi buildings. We encountered an Acbi midden along its west side, and no other origin of this trash seems as likely.

THE EARLIEST VAULTED BUILDINGS, ELITE TOMBS, AND MORTUARY REMAINS OF THE LATE CLASSIC PERIOD

El Cementerio is the name used by Copanecos for all of Group 10L-2, the area south of the Acropolis protected since the late nineteenth century by a high fence (Longyear 1952:16). The rich burials to which the name refers were found a century ago in low platforms west of Courtyard A. We use the name El Cementerio when referring to this limited area.

Architecture and several elaborate burials indicate that high-status individuals in late Acbi and early Coner occupied this area, but its nature and function later changed. After the removal of its masonry building, at least one platform was resurfaced, perhaps for perishable structures or work and service areas. Thick layers of soil washed in around the platforms, eventually creating living surfaces as elevated as the earlier platforms. The new deposits are rich in trash, consisting mostly of utilitarian pottery, tools, and animal bones (see below).

Three small, vaulted buildings are situated on the north, east, and south sides of a tiny courtyard near the northwest corner of what would later be Courtyard A. These date to the Acbi-Coner ceramic transition, about A.D. 600–650. The northern structure, 10L-Sub 14 and 14 East, consisted of three small, vaulted rooms, all with benches; one bench had a wall niche above it. The east building, 10L-Sub 10, faced west. It had one large room with a high central bench and flanking chambers. High bench sidescreens separated the bench from the raised side chambers. The southern member is 10L-34, a larger, four-room building

FIGURE 7.2

Structure 10L-34 after consolidation, from the northwest. This building and two others north of it, just west of Courtyard A, formed a small, three-sided arrangement of vaulted structures that faced west toward 10L-36. Occupants of these earliest vaulted structures in Group 10L-2 may have been interred in Copán Tombs 1 and 2 and Burials 2 and 3 in 10L-238, which lie southeast of 10L-34.

on a wide 1.5-m-high platform (figure 7.2). Its fourth room, an addition, opened north onto the courtyard. The north and south buildings look like domestic structures, but the dominant 10L-Sub 10, with its high bench centered in the only room, was a more formal space for audiences or ceremonies. Later architecture buried the northern and western structures but not 10L-34.

Just south of 10L-34, two slightly lower, rectangular platforms faced with roughly cut stones (10L-236 and 10L-238) contain the rich, vaulted Copán Tombs 1 and 2, excavated by the first Peabody Museum expedition in 1892 (Gordon 1896:29–31; Longyear 1952:40–42). These interments, like an important burial in 10L-34, date to the Acbi-Coner transition. Structure 10L-236 supported a north-facing superstructure of which nothing is left except the plaster floor and the basal course of the surrounding walls. Immediately behind the superstructure, though, and aligned with it, in the fill of the platform was Copán

Tomb 1. Structure 10L-238, slightly later, contained one large, vaulted tomb (Copán Tomb 2) and two smaller, vaulted crypts excavated in 1994, all luxuriously furnished with early Coner polychromes. No evidence of a superstructure remained on 10L-238, which may have been constructed solely as a burial platform. A third platform immediately south of 10L-238 (10L-239), faced with well-cut stones, was contemporaneous. Loose capstones we found beside it suggest that a vaulted tomb in its fill or nearby had been looted.

The two small, vaulted crypts in 10L-238 excavated in 1993 and 1994 contained bones partially covered with red ochre, indicating that the crypts had been reopened or that the bodies were deposited after partial decomposition (figure 7.3). One crypt contained an adult; the other held a small child. Rebecca Storey (chapter 8 in this volume) notes that several high-status burials from the Acropolis were accorded this treatment. These probably include the skeletons of K'inich Yax K'uk' Mo', the founder of the dynasty, and his wife (Sharer, Traxler, et al. 1999:7, 11; Sharer et al., chapter 5 in this volume). No other known interments in Group 10L-2 show evidence of this rare postmortem ritual, nor is there evidence of revisitation and painting of skeletons in Group 9N-8 in Las Sepulturas (Storey, chapter 8 in this volume). This contrast indicates that the four burials in 10L-236 and 10L-238 in El Cementerio claimed the highest status at Copán. Gordon (1896:29–31) did not say whether George Owens and Marshall Saville noticed red ochre on the bones in Copán Tombs 1 and 2.

Further evidence of early, high-status occupation appeared in a stone-lined, slab-roofed crypt placed below the spot where the northeast corner of 10L-86 would later be, near the south end of Courtyard B. Under the adult male's head was placed an exquisitely carved, miniature, double-headed jaguar throne, originally painted red (figure 7.4). Although it is just large enough to sit on, its primary purpose was to symbolize royalty and rulership.

Jaguar thrones are associated exclusively with Maya rulers. Representations of one-headed or bicephalic jaguar thrones on stelae, architectural sculpture, stucco reliefs, and murals have been found at Late Classic Palenque, Piedras Negras, Tikal, Uxmal, and Chichén Itzá and on painted and modeled ceramic vessels from the southern and northern Maya lowlands (Kowalski 1987:229–236; Proskouriakoff

FIGURE 7.3

Small vaulted crypts in Structure 10L-238, El Cementerio, dating to the Acbi-Coner transition, ca. A.D. 600–650. These were placed beside and just south of Copán Tomb 2, excavated by Harvard University in 1892. The famous Copán Tomb 1, which contained the carved peccary skull, was placed in Structure 10L-236, a few meters to the east. (a) Burial 2. (b) Burial 3. Scale 1:20.

LATE CLASSIC ROYAL RESIDENCE

FIGURE 7.4
Miniature double-headed jaguar throne, 47 cm long and 16 cm high, from an Acbi-Coner transition burial just east of Structure 10L-86, near the southwest corner of Courtyard B, Group 10L-2.

1950:figure 54b; Robertson 1985:28, figures 91, 92). On the stelae and reliefs, rulers with known names and life spans sit or stand on the thrones; the murals and vessels depict seated rulers and gods. One- and two-headed jaguars or similar creatures were carved at Copán, sometimes on altars (Agurcia Fasquelle 1994:70, 81; Baudez 1994:141, 147, figures 67, 68; Robicsek 1972:figure 96, plate 182), but the early Courtyard B miniature is the first jaguar throne from the Copán Valley. This unique sculpture indicates that the family of the individual buried below 10L-86 was entitled to own and bury a royal object.

The famous incised peccary skull from Copán Tomb 1, the most elaborate early tomb in Group 10L-2, has been suggested by Linda Schele, Nikolai Grube, and Federico Fahsen (1995:1–2) to portray K'inich Yax K'uk' Mo' (W. Fash 2001:52, 88, figure 24; Robicsek 1972:plates 290, 291; Sharer et al., chapter 5 in this volume). It appears to refer to an event (perhaps at Tikal?) in A.D. 376, fifty years before K'inich Yax K'uk' Mo's inauguration as king of Copán, suggesting that the skull bore a retrospective inscription and was an heirloom. Its owner, perhaps the head of the family that lived in Structures 10L-34, 10L-Sub 10, and 10L-Sub 14, likely traced his line back to the founder.

The individuals who moved into Group 10L-2 near the end of the Early Classic must have been members of the royal family. Robert Sharer and his colleagues' extensive excavations in the east side of the Acropolis encountered Early Classic residential buildings (probably the royal family's domestic structures) around courtyards northeast of the earliest ceremonial structures at the base of the Acropolis. Sharer and his colleagues believe that Ruler 8, who reigned from A.D. 532 to 551, buried these residential courtyards when he enlarged the Acropolis. They suggest that the royal domestic complex was moved south to Group 10L-2 in this span (Sharer, Fash, et al. 1999:234–236; Sharer et al., chapter 5 in this volume; Traxler 2001:68). This postulated movement would have been slightly earlier than the formal arrangement of three buildings on platforms around a small courtyard in Group 10L-2 (Structures 10L-Sub 10, 10L-Sub 14 and 14 East, and 10L-34, dating to ca. A.D. 600–650). Group 10L-2 did host, however, a high-status Acbi occupation from A.D. 500 to 600 that included at least one building, several platforms, a rich burial, and extensive middens, as described above.

COURTYARD A IN THE LATE CLASSIC PERIOD

Courtyard A, closest to the base of the Acropolis, has the largest structures in Group 10L-2, including the house of Ruler 16. It was the ritual, administrative, and elite residential focus of the complex of buildings and courtyards south of the Acropolis. This rectangular space shares a striking feature with at least two other important Late Classic Copán courts. Both the East Court of the Acropolis and Courtyard A of Group 9N-8 have platforms on three sides, with wide stairs and wide steps that could have served as seats for large numbers of spectators at public rituals, ceremonies, processions, and dances (W. Fash 1998, chapter 3 in this volume). Courtyard A of Group 10L-2 has similar stairs with wide steps appropriate for sitting or standing, but these were constructed along all four sides of the courtyard. On three sides, these wide stairs provide access to long, relatively high platforms or terraces without superstructures, probably used for public events. This repeated pattern supports the idea that the stairs were built so that viewers would congregate on them.

Access from Group 10L-2 to the Acropolis was provided by a narrow stair that rose from what is now the east limit of the terrace on which Structure 10L-29 rested (at the current edge of the Copán River cut, just north of Structure 10L-28) to the south side of Structure 10L-18, Yax Pasaj's tomb at the southeast corner of the Acropolis. The last ruler of the dynasty built his own memorial twenty years before his death, at precisely the spot where the stairs from his familial residence below reached the great structures of the realm in which he conducted the affairs of the Copán state.

THE BUILDINGS OF YAX PASAJ ON COURTYARD A (STRUCTURES 10L-32 AND 10L-30)

Structure 10L-32-1st is the commanding structure on Courtyard A, occupying the south side of the courtyard and facing north to the broad stair that leads up to the lowest terrace of the Acropolis (Gordon 1896:25–26; Hohmann and Vogrin 1982:56, figures 213–217). Because the Peabody Museum cleared it in 1892 and left it to collapse further, much less of the building remained intact than would have been the case had it not been investigated. All interior floors and most exterior surfaces were cleared in 1892, and almost the only remaining cultural deposits—and sculpture unmoved since its fall—lay east of and behind 10L-32, with a 30-cm layer in front of the structure that was missed in 1892. Structure 10L-32 consists of a large, vaulted central building on a 3.5-m-high platform and two contiguous, smaller, vaulted side buildings at a lower level. All are in a line so as to resemble a single structure, fronted by a wide lower stair and a narrower upper stair leading to the center building (figures 7.5 and 7.6). The central building contains one room that has a large bench with sloping side walls, flanked by narrow, raised lateral chambers. The entire bench, upon which rested two altars with hieroglyphic inscriptions, is visible from the room's doorway. Its visibility from outside distinguishes it from many benches more hidden from external view in residential structures in Group 10L-2 and elsewhere at Copán.

The lower buildings to the east and west of the main structure have front rooms level with the terrace outside and large, raised rear chambers entered through wide openings flanked by thick, weight-bearing walls. This is more like the room arrangements in shrines or temples than the floor plan of typical high-status residential buildings, such as 10L-34, 10L-41A, and 10L-44B on Courtyard B (see below). Although Structure 10L-32 is identified as Yax Pasaj's house, he and members of his immediate family may not have slept in it or used it for domestic purposes. The side buildings, at least one of which contained a large

FIGURE 7.5
Structure 10L-32, the house of Yax Pasaj on Courtyard A, Group 10L-2. (Reconstruction drawing by B. Fash)

niche in the center wall of its front room, may have been used for the corporate group's activities or rituals and for storage.

The masonry of Structure 10L-32-1st (and of 10L-30-1st and 10L-41A-1st, Yax Pasaj's other buildings in 10L-2) is well squared, with facing stones of more standardized dimensions than those used in earlier buildings in Group 10L-2. This uniformity in size resulted in courses that are, for this group, unusually even. Most facing stones were newly quarried, reflecting the labor available to the individual who commissioned 10L-32.

The upper facade of Structure 10L-32 bore extensive sculptured motifs. The dominant image, reconstructed by Barbara W. Fash and others working with her since 1987 (Andrews and Fash 1992:67–70; B. Fash, chapter 4 in this volume), was a larger-than-life human figure, repeated six times around the front and back of the building near the cornice (refer to figure 4.2c; see figures 7.5 and 7.7a). Only one head has been found, that of a young man. His headdress is a knotted water-lily assemblage surrounded by feathers and serpent elements. The figures appear to have sat, with one leg folded under the other, on long-nosed water-lily monsters, of which there were also six (refer to figure 4.3, a and b; see figure 7.7b). The roof ornaments of 10L-32, rising above the seated figure, were also water lilies. The front of 10L-32 carried four different short-nosed masks framed by earflares and vegeta-

FIGURE 7.6
Structure 10L-32: (top) north side after consolidation (photograph by W. Fash) and (bottom) wide lower stair and narrower upper stair of large blocks.

tion elements (see figure 7.7c). These were possibly mounted beside the central doorway and on the upper platform beside the stair.

The Group 10L-2 inscriptions are discussed below in the section "The Personal Hieroglyphic Monuments of Yax Pasaj." They show

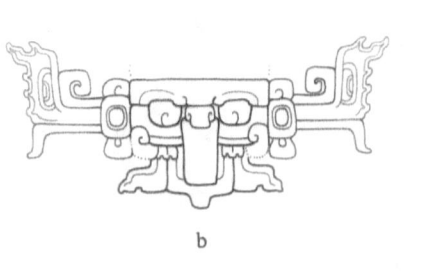
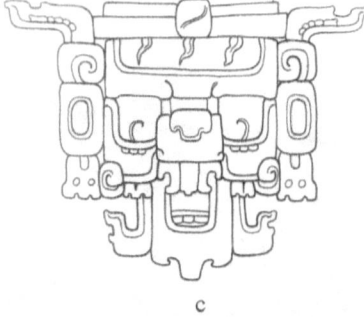

FIGURE 7.7

The sculpture of Structure 10L-32, the house of Yax Pasaj on Courtyard A, Group 10L-2: (a) young lord, possibly Yax Pasaj, with water-lily headdress, (b) long-nosed water-lily monster, over which the young lord probably sat, (c) masks with leafy elements, centrally located on the front of 10L-32, and (d) bench in center room of Structure 10L-32. (a, b, and c reconstructed by B. Fash) without ambiguity that Yax Pasaj, the sixteenth and final ruler in the Copán dynasty, lived in this group and that Structures 10L-32 and 10L-30 were his buildings. His three most important monuments in Group 10L-2 mention a ceramic statue, a "gift of Chak," that was the companion of his reign (Schele 1995; Stuart, personal communication to SAR advanced seminar participants 1994). Yax Pasaj's supernatural companion and patron was the god of rain, thunder, and lightning. We think that the young man portrayed on the facade of 10L-32 may be Yax Pasaj and, following Barbara Fash (Andrews and Fash 1992:67), the deity on whom he sits is Chak, replete with water-lily imagery. Barbara Fash (chapter 4 in this volume) thinks that these six figures may be "water masters," who controlled water management at Copán.

Structure 10L-32-1st is far smaller than Structure 10L-11, dedicated in A.D. 773, and Structure 10L-16, finished by A.D. 775. The latter are Yax Pasaj's main buildings on the Acropolis, probably his royal public residence and his temple. But those were the great structures of his realm, the supreme architectural attestation of the Copán dynasty's might, as had been the buildings of earlier rulers at these spots. They were public statements of Yax Pasaj's rule, whereas 10L-32 was his personal house, inherited through his family.

We have no dedication date for 10L-32-1st. Except for Structure 10L-18 (Yax Pasaj's tomb), all his major constructions date to the first dozen years of his reign. It seems likely, therefore, that he would have also built his own house before A.D. 775.

Structure 10L-32 is strikingly similar to Structure 8N-66 in Group 8N-11 (the so-called "Skyband Group"), excavated in 1990 by Pennsylvania State University (Bricker and Bricker 1999; Webster, Fash, et al. 1998). Structure 8N-66 was probably built during Yax Pasaj's reign by the head of the group living in 8N-11, who, Barbara Fash thinks, may have been a representative to the council house on the Acropolis (W. Fash, chapter 3 in this volume; Webster, Fash, et al. 1998:332). Structure 8N-66 is also a three-building complex with a wide stair and a central building with a long bench and side chambers that, unlike those of 10L-32, appear to be domestic. On its upper and lower facades, it also bore sculpture that is remarkably like that of 10L-32 in placement, style, and content (refer to figure 4.6d).

Under Structure 10L-32 are two earlier structures, their remains consisting of platform fill with a few platform facing walls, floor fragments, and building wall stubs. No effort was made to preserve the earlier structures, from which most shaped and carved stones were removed during the enlargements. Both bore a single superstructure, instead of three, as in 10L-32-1st, and both had wide stairs facing north onto Courtyard A. Like 10L-32-1st, they may have been residences of the extended corporate group's head. The earlier of the two interior constructions, 10L-32-3rd, contains ceramics of the Acbi-Coner transition and may therefore date between A.D. 600 and 650. It is the earliest-known structure on Courtyard A, perhaps as early as the small, three-sided Acbi-Coner group just to the northwest.

Structure 10L-32-2nd contained a deep, vaulted tomb below its front terrace, with steep steps leading down into it. This indicates that it had been constructed in anticipation of the owner's death (figure 7.8). The tomb was broken into and looted in the Postclassic, after the building above it had collapsed, and we found none of its original contents. The tomb must have been built by and for Yax Pasaj's predecessor—his father, older brother, father's brother, or even mother's brother, an unnamed noble who was not the preceding king of Copán, Ruler 15 (see below; Schele and Grube 1987; Stuart 2001).

Yax Pasaj placed a remarkable cache below the center of his throne in the main building of 10L-32-1st—a large stone fish, tenoned for insertion into the facade of a building (refer to figure 4.7c). Several other fish fragments appeared in the fill of 10L-32-1st, but no other fish we found had been carved from a single block, and none had been placed in an axial position. These fish had presumably been set into the facade of 10L-32-2nd, which Yax Pasaj completely dismantled, except for the tomb. A sufficient number of fragments have been found to make us think that the fish was a common element on the building.

The 10L-32 fish are similar to a carved fish from the front facade of Structure 10L-22A, a mat house (*popol nah*), or council house, above the East Court of the Acropolis (refer to figure 4.7, a and b; B. Fash 1992a:figures 9, 10c; B. Fash et al. 1992:figures 12, 13). The popol nah fish is one of nine different hieroglyphs that rested on the medial molding, each below a seated noble and between sculptured mats (symbols of political authority) at regular intervals around the building. The prominent 10L-22A fish faces south toward Group 10L-2. These glyphs probably refer to the names of places within the Copán realm, and the

LATE CLASSIC ROYAL RESIDENCE

FIGURE 7.8
Vaulted tomb in Structure 10L-32-2nd, looted in antiquity. This may have contained the remains of Yax Pasaj's father. (a) South wall of tomb, with capstones removed during consolidation, steps on left. (b) East-west section, with steps on left, showing stones surrounding niche in south wall. The tomb is 200 cm long.

lords seated above them may be local chiefs or corporate group heads (*holpopob*) who represented these places when visiting the popol nah (B. Fash et al. 1992:432–435). Some of the glyphs may refer to places with mythical names (Stuart and Houston 1994:26, 72).

Courtyard A was the center of the "fish" place (*canal*, or *cainal*) mentioned on the council house (B. Fash, chapter 4 in this volume; B. Fash et al. 1992:429). It was the first place on the council house to be tentatively identified. This proposed link strengthens the argument that the nine lords on the council house and the places they represent were real. As William Fash (2001:135) points out, the existence of such a geographic council as part of the governing structure indicates the extent to which Copán relied on administrative institutions no longer based solely on kinship.

Group 10L-2 would have been thought of as the fish place from at least the end of the seventh century or the beginning of the Late Classic. Combined epigraphic, sculptural, and stratigraphic evidence places the construction of the council house, and therefore the importance of the fish place, during the reign of Ruler 14 (A.D. 738–749), possibly in A.D. 746 (B. Fash et al. 1992:435–436). If so, Group 10L-2 was the fish place by at least the reign of the fourteenth ruler, and indications from Group 10L-2 are that it was so known even earlier. The sculpture on 10L-32-3rd, the earliest predecessor inside Yax Pasaj's house, is unknown, but a contemporaneous vaulted building beside it, 10L-31, bore a carved fish on its upper facade. Because the earliest buildings around Courtyard A go back to the reign of Ruler 12 (A.D. 628–695), the identification of this area with the fish must be at least this early. The fifteen fish glyphs (T738) recorded by J. E. S. Thompson (1962: 316–318) at Copán are Late Classic. Of these, the earliest may be the glyph on Ruler 11's Stela P at A.D. 623. By this time, Group 10L-2 was the seat of a royal family, although Courtyards A and B had not taken their final form. The council itself may have been a development relatively late in Copán's history, an effort by Ruler 14 after the capture and death of Ruler 13 to strengthen the Copán polity by decentralizing and sharing power (W. Fash 2001:134). It could have been present from the beginning of the dynasty, however, integral to noble governance throughout the history of the realm (B. Fash, chapter 4 in this volume).

Structure 10L-30 was Yax Pasaj's other building on Courtyard A,

FIGURE 7.9
Structure 10L-30 from the southwest, after consolidation. This large platform, with a wide stairway similar to that of 10L-32, never supported a building. Its masonry is identical to that of 10L-32. Yax Pasaj likely built it for ceremonies about the same time he built his house. A similar platform, 10L-30-2nd, is inside the final structure.

forming its east side (figure 7.9). The masonry of 10L-30 is so similar in appearance to that of 10L-32, we believe that they were constructed at the same time. Also built over an earlier platform that was parallel and similar in plan to the final one, 10L-30 is a 4-m-high, two-tiered substructure with a summit platform a few centimeters high. It has a wide stair built with the same long, massive blocks used in the upper stair of 10L-32. The steps in the center, not far above the base of the stair, were missing. Sculpture was possibly robbed from this part of the stair in the Postclassic, as it had been from Temples 16 and 26. Little if any sculpture was found in the collapse debris.

Structure 10L-30-1st never supported a building. The broad summit platform and wide stair would have served admirably for dances and rituals Yax Pasaj chose to have performed in his large residential courtyard.

A round altar was found partly buried in a midden near the northwest corner of 10L-30, probably pushed from the platform's summit

FIGURE 7.10

Structure 10L-33: (a) 10L-33 after consolidation. (b) 10L-33 South after consolidation. (c) Reconstruction of upper facade in the Copán Sculpture Museum, showing founder's glyphs on the cornice and a motif with a Mexican year sign over the doorway. (Museum reconstruction by B. Fash) sometime before the north-facing wall of the platform collapsed over it. The monument commemorates the erection of a stone at the completion of Yax Pasaj's second katun in office in A.D. 783.

EARLY BUILDINGS AROUND COURTYARD A

Structures 10L-33 and 10L-31 flank Yax Pasaj's house. They were built about the same time as 10L-32-3rd, ca. A.D. 650–700. Although new structures were built against each one, the original buildings were not covered or enlarged, in contrast to 10L-32-3rd and most of the buildings around Courtyard B.

Structure 10L-33 is a one-room, vaulted building with a single, large, C-shaped bench (figure 7.10a). Despite the bench, which covers most of the interior space of 10L-33, this building was probably intended for ritual or administrative purposes. The three large niches in the rear wall over the bench, the absence of burials in or beside the structure, the lack of domestic debris, the dissimilarity to typical residential buildings, and the architectural sculpture suggest that this was not merely a residence.

The upper facade bore, above a medial molding of one or two beveled stones, repeated variants of the "founder's glyph," with crossed (torch?) bundles below an *ajaw* head (T600). The founder's glyph at Copán is associated with the first ruler of the dynasty and with later kings, linking this building and the group that commissioned it to K'inich Yax K'uk' Mo' (see figure 7.10c). The crossed bundles in the founder's glyph are usually combined on Structure 10L-33 with goggle (Tlaloc) eyes bordered by a line of tight little scrolls, a glyph Linda Schele read as *ch'ok* (sprout). She read the glyph as "Sprout-Tree-House" (*ch'ok-te-nah*) and argued that the group in Group 10L-2 was thus a sprout, or lineage, from the founder (Schele 1986, 1992a). A further sculptural motif, possibly set over the doorway, contained a Mexican "year glyph."

David Stuart (2000:492–493; chapter 10, this volume) has recently offered a different interpretation of the founder's glyph. Because the last element of the founder's glyph is always -*naah*, he points out, it must refer to a building. He reads the glyph at Copán and other sites as *wi-te-naah* (origin house). As on Structure 10L-33 and other buildings at Copán, the glyph is often associated with Teotihuacan symbolism at lowland Maya sites. Stuart (2000:492–493, 509) thinks that it "might be the name for an important type of ancestral shrine found at many sites," a building that was "a place of ritual fire and burning," perhaps originally a "ritual locale at Teotihuacan." Structure 10L-33, with its three niches above a full-length bench and its repeated founder's glyphs with the goggle eyes and scroll motifs, may have been a shrine to the ancestors or patron deities.

An L-shaped, vaulted addition of two sets of rooms (10L-33-South), each with front and raised rear chambers, was constructed at the south end of Structure 10L-33, closing the southwest corner of Courtyard A (see figure 7.10b). This addition, in contrast to the original structure, appears to have been domestic. The new facades carried sculptural motifs that included the founder's glyph and Mexican year glyphs; the latter were much like those that appeared on 10L-33 itself, although without the goggle-eyed variant of the founder's glyph. The prominent and repeated use of the central Mexican year glyph on 10L-33 (and on 10L-29, discussed below) recalls the strong Teotihuacan connections that appeared at Copán with K'inich Yax K'uk' Mo'.

A raised masonry walkway ran from the east side of 10L-33-South to the west side of 10L-32-3rd, showing that these two buildings were contemporary. A large, rectangular drain pierced this walkway to drain Courtyard A at its southwest corner. Although later expansions of 10L-32 covered both these buildings and the walkway, the drain remained, growing longer as it passed through more massive platforms.

The construction of Yax Pasaj's 10L-32-1st covered much of 10L-33-South and caused part of its vault to be torn down, turning it into a cul-de-sac that was partially hidden but never properly repaired. The late occupants eventually allowed a midden to accumulate in the remaining paved patio outside the room doors, but not inside the rooms. Like other middens around the base of 10L-32, it grew until it was sealed by the collapse of the walls and vaults of both 10L-32 and 10L-33-South. The ceramics in this midden suggest that it is the latest assemblage we encountered in Group 10L-2, almost certainly postdating the dynastic collapse. Its position immediately outside the doorway of a residence, in a patio-like area that may have been covered by a thatch roof, is unique in Group 10L-2.

Earlier low Acbi-Coner platforms to the north of 10L-33 were covered in two stages by a long platform attached to the north end of 10L-

33. Its wide stair, starting at the level of the courtyard, led to a low summit platform that never supported a masonry superstructure. The final platform (10L-33-Center and 10L-33-North) is similar in form to the larger and later ceremonial structure (10L-30) that Yax Pasaj built facing it across Courtyard A and was probably an even closer match to 10L-30-2nd.

Structure 10L-31, a one-room vaulted building about the size of 10L-33, sits at the southeast corner of Courtyard A, facing west toward 10L-32 (figure 7.11). Occupying most of the room, a large bench runs the full length of the rear wall and contained the burial of an infant in its fill. Two large, deep niches face each other outside the front doorway across a raised but unroofed antechamber to the vaulted room. Its unusual form suggests that it was not primarily a residential building.

Structure 10L-31 was roughly contemporaneous with 10L-30-2nd. A carved fish fallen from the upper facade near its southwest corner is similar to those found in the fill of 10L-32-1st and to the one on the council house. Like the fish that presumably came from the adjacent 10L-32-2nd, it identified the building as belonging to the dominant group in the "fish" neighborhood.

THE ANCESTRAL SHRINE OF THE FOUNDER'S DESCENDANTS (STRUCTURE 10L-29)

The south side of the Acropolis has a 20-m-wide terrace at its base, about 4 m high, forming its first stage and burying the remains of Early Classic structures. A wide stair leads from this terrace down to Courtyard A, and a narrow stair at its current east edge (the Copán River cut) provides access to the top of the Acropolis beside 10L-18, Yax Pasaj's tomb.

Structure 10L-29, on this terrace at the northwest corner of Courtyard A, is a large, two-room, L-shaped, vaulted building on a platform about 1.5 m high, probably dating to A.D. 700–750 (figure 7.12). The doorways and stairs face east and south onto Courtyard A. The long, wide rooms have no benches; the only remaining features inside were nine large niches (figure 7.13b), one of which contained an intact *Spondylus* bivalve pair offering when the vault collapsed. One niche in the west room had the form of a half-quatrefoil, a niche shape sometimes found in Copán tombs. The floor of the north room showed a

FIGURE 7.11

Structure 10L-31, a vaulted building with a porch just east of 10L-32. (top) After consolidation, from Structure 10L-32, with north side of 10L-232 and single-room shrine between 10L-31 and 10L-232. (bottom) After consolidation, showing one of the two niches flanking the center doorway.

pattern of ritual censer use in the corners and in the centers of the two doorways.

The upper facade of 10L-29 bore sculpture on all sides (refer to figure 4.6a; see figures 7.12 and 7.13a). The largest motif, repeated ten

LATE CLASSIC ROYAL RESIDENCE

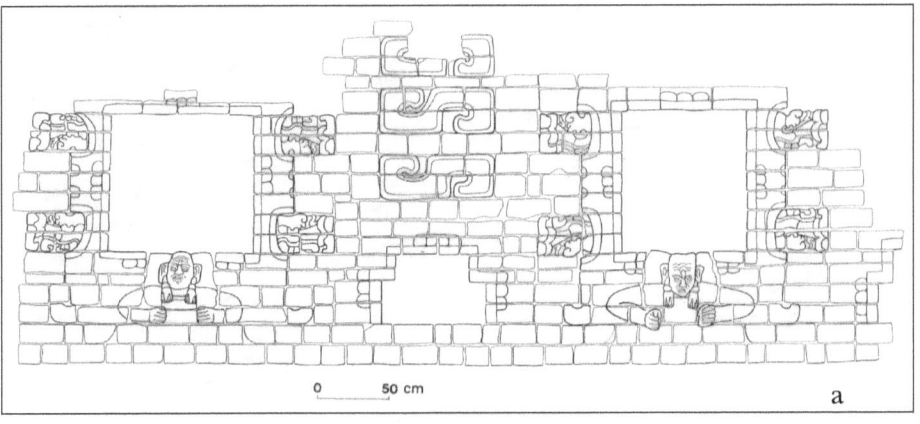

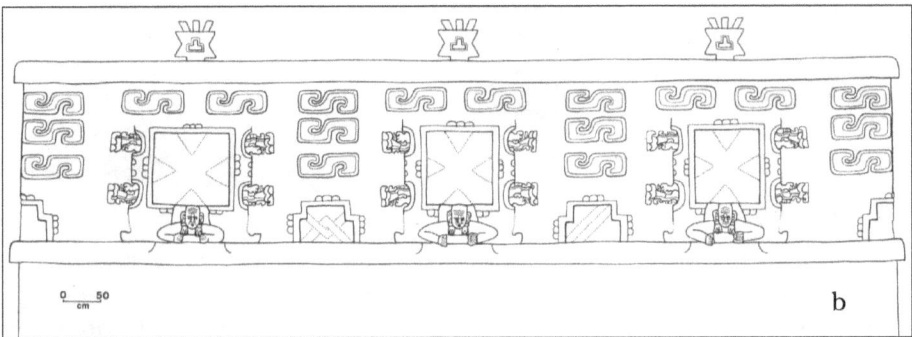

FIGURE 7.12

Structure 10L-29, the ancestral shrine of the founder's lineage, partial reconstructions of the upper, west facade: (a) stone-by-stone reconstruction, showing only those sculptured stones the position of which is reasonably certain, and (b) hypothetical reconstruction of the west facade, in which dotted motifs indicate alternative arrangements of the pieces that fell from the niches. (Drawings by J. Johnson and B. Fash, based on analysis with R. Larios)

times, is a rectangular panel with stylized serpent heads emanating from the four corners. Roughly similar configurations at Palenque and Yaxchilán have been called "ancestor cartouches" because they contain figures of ancestors (McAnany 1995:43). Barbara Fash believes that the panels contained a *kin* (sun) sign (Andrews and Fash 1992:71–74, figures 9, 10; B. Fash, chapter 4 in this volume).

Just below each serpent panel protruded the larger-than-life head, shoulders, and arms of a male, resting on the medial molding

FIGURE 7.13

Structure 10L-29: (a) reconstruction of a section of the south facade in the Copán Sculpture Museum, showing a lower facade with founder's glyphs and Mexican year signs and an upper facade with scrolls and a rectangular panel with a kin *sign inside, serpent heads emanating from each corner, and a male supernatural being below it (the roof ornaments show upside-down* T, *or* ik, *perforations), and (b) niche in north wall of north room after restoration. (Museum reconstruction by B. Fash)*

(Maudslay 1889–1902:1:9; Stephens 1841:1:139). The heads look alike and have comparable ear pendants, but they are not identical. The 10L-29 figures are deities, not men, marked as such by their facial features, including a high forehead with three deep wrinkles, a prognathous, monkey-like lower face, and large ears and pendants. They resemble the monkey-men gods kneeling on the Reviewing Stand of 10L-11 in the West Court, perhaps the deity Chak (B. Fash, chapter 4 in this volume; M. Miller 1988:160) and, more generally, the monkey-faced patron deity of scribes and artists (Coe 1977). These features suggest that they are the supernatural patrons of individuals who have the right to possess and manipulate esoteric knowledge. Their position under the serpent panels, or ancestor cartouches, further intimates that they are associated with the ancestors of the group that built this temple.

Half-quatrefoil niches with crossed-band motifs inside them alternate with the sun/serpent/ancestor panels, and stacked S-shaped cloud or smoke scrolls occupy virtually all the remaining space. The roof ornaments likewise have upside-down T-perforations (see figure 7.13a), possibly representing simplified half-quatrefoils. Barbara Fash (chapter 4 in this volume) believes that the facade of 10L-29 bore thirteen of these half-quatrefoil niches, representing caves that were entrances to the thirteen levels of the heavens (Bassie-Sweet 1991). By entering these caves, the ancestors gained access to these levels.

The sun/serpent/ancestor panels, monkey-man deities, half-quatrefoil cave entrances, many large niches for offerings, censer traces on the floor, and absence of benches, domestic remains, and subfloor tombs denote 10L-29 as a shrine dedicated to worshiping, making offerings to, and communicating with family ancestors and other gods. Linda Schele and Nikolai Grube argued that lineage shrines of this kind, called *waybil* (sleeping or dreaming places of god), existed at many Maya sites (Freidel, Schele, and Parker 1993:188–190; Grube and Schele 1990).

The lower facade, in an area visible from Courtyard A below, bore repeated founder's glyphs with Mexican year glyphs above and below each one (see figure 7.13a). These link 10L-29 with K'inich Yax K'uk' Mo', emphasizing his connection with Teotihuacan, and suggest that this building was an important ancestral shrine, an origin house, or *wi-te-nah* (Stuart 2000:492–493). The burn marks in the doorways and corners of 10L-29 demonstrate that it was a building where offerings were regularly burned.

COURTYARD B

The northern entrance to Courtyard B was a few meters from the southwest corner of Courtyard A. Some of the people whose regular activities took them to Courtyard A and the Acropolis must have lived in buildings around Courtyard B. We excavated Courtyard B after Courtyard A, and we thought that Courtyard B would be the domestic compound Courtyard A had turned out not to be. Although this

FIGURE 7.14
Structure 10L-41 after consolidation: (a) 10L-41A, (b) 10L-41B, (c) 10L-41C, (d) 10L-41D, and (e) beveled platform cornice in front of 10L-41B, C, and D, after consolidation.

proved to be true in part, one building at the north end of the courtyard, 10L-43, was a shrine, and 10L-41, on its east side, was a long structure that may have combined religious, semipublic uses with limited residential functions. Like the buildings and platforms around Courtyard A, many (but not all) of the structures around B contained earlier versions under them. Usually, the process of renovation destroyed most of the existing building or platform.

c

d

e

Partway through the Courtyard B construction sequence, a flagstone floor was laid over the entire area. Toward the end of the sequence, the level of the courtyard was raised again, and the new surface was plastered. These two building levels helped tie together construction events in separate buildings.

Courtyard B drained toward its southeast corner, as did Courtyard A, downstream and away from the river. Between the southwest corner of 10L-42 and the southeast corner of 10L-86 is a drain, lined and covered with stone slabs.

STRUCTURE 10L-41: A MULTIPURPOSE BUILDING

The platform of Structure 10L-41 supports four vaulted buildings that differ from one another in their internal arrangements but not as much in external appearance (figure 7.14). All went through two or three episodes of rebuilding. The northern building is the smallest and the latest, separated from the next by a passage. The southern three, originally without the north structure, started as separate buildings but later formed a nearly continuous facade on a single platform that probably postdates A.D. 700. This building and its possible use have been discussed in greater detail elsewhere (Andrews et al. 2003).

In late 1892 and early 1893, the Peabody Museum partially cleared Structure 10L-41 (Hohmann and Vogrin 1982:57–58, figures 228–242; Shorkley 1892–1893). Few trash deposits remained to help us infer activities, and most architectural sculpture had been moved from where it fell.

The final platform, about 1 m high and 34 m long, forms a terrace in front of the four buildings. Its upper edge on the courtyard side of Structures 10L-41B, C, and D (but not A) consisted of two beveled and tenoned stones set one above the other to create a recessed, angular molding (see figure 7.14e). These beveled stones are similar to those used in the medial molding of 10L-33 in Courtyard A and in the medial or superior molding of Structure 10L-44B, across Courtyard B.

The northern building, 10L-41A, was a domestic structure (see figure 7.14a). It has a main room with a bench along the back wall and a smaller north chamber with a raised floor, entered from the main room. The builders of 10L-41A placed a modeled cachepot deep in the fill below the central bench and, inside it, arranged jades, *Spondylus* and oyster shells, and fire-blackened chert (figure 7.15). The south room

LATE CLASSIC ROYAL RESIDENCE

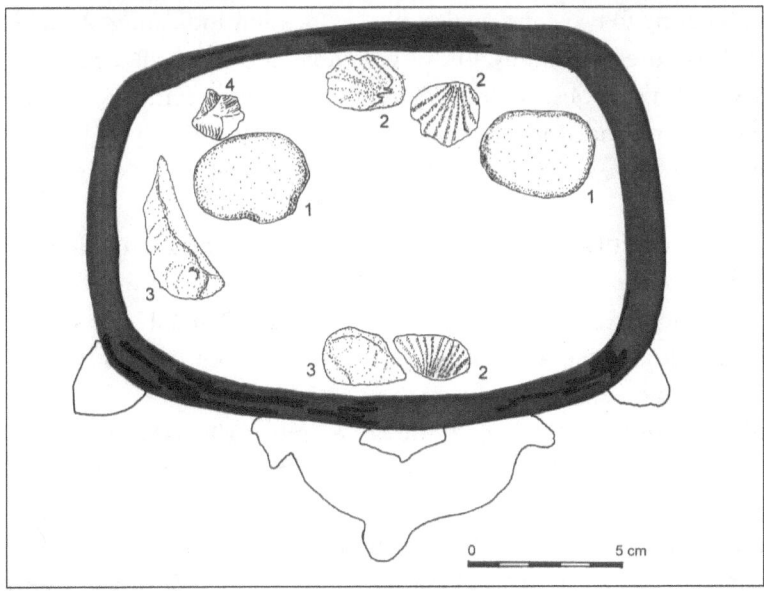

FIGURE 7.15
Structure 10L-41A, Cache 1, placed in the fill of 10L-41A-1st, a meter under the surface of the bench along the back wall of the central room. The vessel has appliqué cacao pods and a human face painted yellow, with red eyes. Beside it rested a small cave formation. (top) Sepultura Unslipped cache pot. (bottom) Diagram of the offerings inside the cache pot: (1) jades, (2) Spondylus shells, (3) oyster shells, and (4) fire-blackened chert.

has a low, full-length bench and its own doorway on the south side. Because 10L-41A shares architectural design and masonry features with Yax Pasaj's two late buildings on Courtyard A (10L-30 and 10L-32), we think that he commissioned it early in his reign. Because 10L-32 does not look like a domestic structure and 10L-41A does, we think that Yax Pasaj may have had 10L-41A built as his personal living and sleeping quarters.

Structures 10L-41B, 10L-41C, and 10L-41D formed a unit, probably with one sculptural program. Each is about the same size, but most formal similarities end there. Structure 10L-41B is a long room with two wide doorways facing the courtyard, a wide front part of the room for activities at floor level, and a wide, high bench running the length of the rear wall (see figure 7.14b). Two massive piers rise from the front of the bench along the room centerline, supporting a long vault on each side. The outer doorways face these piers, which are blank except for a niche in the bench face below each. 10L-41B contained three juvenile burials dating to two construction phases, possibly indicating occupation or, at least, use by a family. On its bench lay several small ceramic cups and grinding stones, sealed below wall collapse, evidence of either domestic or ritual food preparation or consumption just before its destruction. The ceramic cups are Surlo Orange-brown, of the Coner phase.

Structure 10L-41C, the central building of the original unit, is a single large room without a bench (see figure 7.14c). It has one off-center doorway facing the courtyard and one leading to a small back stair. The south inside wall has a niche, with a low rise in floor level in front of it. A low plinth or seat is set against the north inside wall.

Structure 10L-41D, built at the same time as 10L-41C, has two doorways facing Courtyard B. They lead to a narrow interior space with a low step up after one enters the room. A huge central bench is flanked by two side chambers with niches (see figure 7.14d). The plan of 10L-41D is comparable to that of Yax Pasaj's 10L-32 on Courtyard A and to that of 8N-66, with the Skyband Bench (Webster, Fash, et al. 1998), but the doorways, like those of 10L-41B, open onto high masonry screen walls. In most domestic rooms at Copán, the doorway opens directly onto the bench, as it does in throne or audience rooms. In 10L-41D (as in 10L-41B), the bench was not visible from outside, and the partial front screen walls coming out from its side screens provided additional privacy. Two round pedestals for stone incense burners lay just in front of the platform, indicating that rituals had been conducted in front of 10L-41D.

The remains of earlier constructions are buried under each building of 10L-41 (figure 7.16). The original platforms and superstructures were built between A.D. 650 and 700, judging from the ceramics, and the entire complex was rebuilt two times before Yax Pasaj constructed 10L-41A-1st. The two earlier superstructures partially preserved inside 10L-41B are strikingly like the final building. Although the penultimate building in 10L-41D had been almost totally dismantled, the earliest shows similarities to the final one. 10L-41C-1st, the central construction, contained one and probably two earlier platforms, but all traces of their superstructures had been removed. 10L-41A-1st also contained one earlier platform without other remaining features, but it was built after the southern three were essentially completed. Each time the complex was enlarged, the architects appear to have repeated the original building forms. The continuity in form argues for continuity of function from one phase to the next. Structure 10L-41 is therefore not a fortuitous assortment of superstructures, but a planned set of three contiguous buildings forming a coherent complex of different floor plans, maintained through time. Yax Pasaj added a small house to the north end of this complex.

Three platforms at least a meter high were constructed behind 10L-41 against the low terrace running along its east side (Structures 10L-241, 10L-242, and 10L-243). Excavations in 1893 (Shorkley 1892–1893) removed the fill of all three, leaving only the exterior, well-dressed, squared-block platform facing. Each probably supported an unvaulted building. These may have been used for storage or as attached residences. At least one platform contained an earlier, smaller structure.

Most of the recovered sculpture of 10L-41-1st, because of the excavations a century earlier, was found in piles near the building, not where the stones fell. Many carved stones were surely missing by 1993. The reconstruction of the facade has far less direct evidence to support it than do the reconstructions of 10L-32 and 10L-29 (figure 7.17).

The facades of 10L-41B, C, and D bore thirteen small, half-quatrefoil niches, possibly with human heads attached to their bottom margins. Barbara Fash (chapter 4 in this volume; refer to figure 4.6c)

FIGURE 7.16
Structure 10L-41, construction phases I–V, all Coner phase: (a) phase I, (b) phase II, (c) phase III, (d) phase IV, and (e) phase V.

LATE CLASSIC ROYAL RESIDENCE

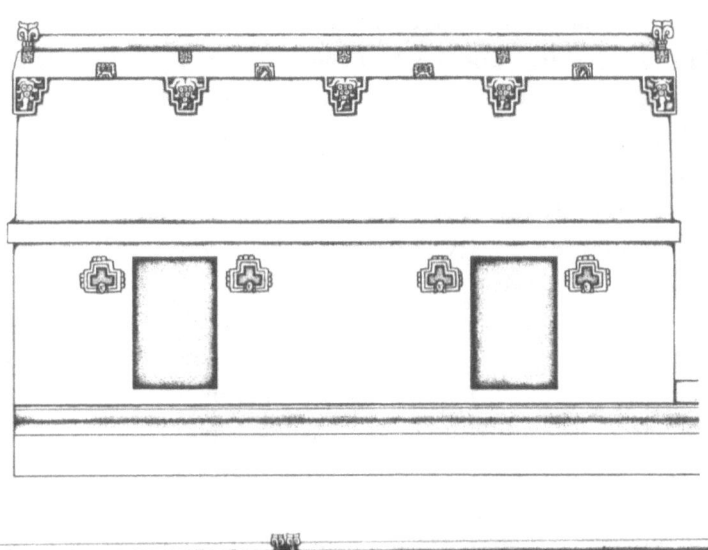

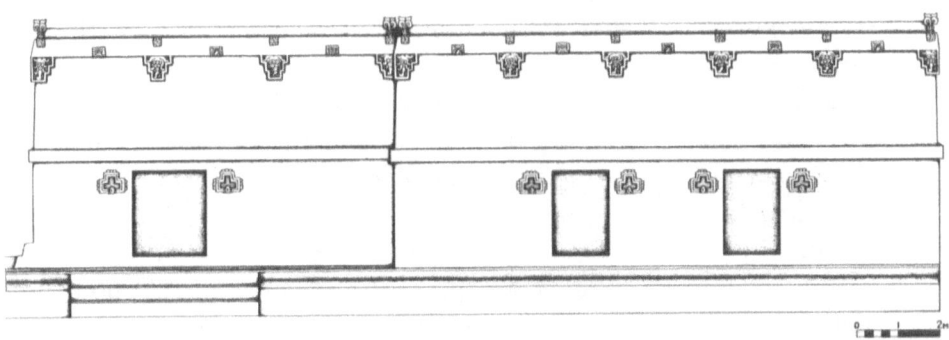

FIGURE 7.17
Hypothetical reconstruction of the sculpture placement on the west facade of Structures 10L-41B, C, and D, facing Courtyard B: (top) Structure 10L-41B and (bottom) Structures 10L-41C and D. Drawings join at the break. (Drawing by J. Johnson)

identifies these as caves, as on Structure 10L-29. Another frequent motif on 10L-41 was a stepped enclosure with *cauac* signs inside, which Barbara Fash interprets as a drip-water cave formation. The roof ornaments were maize plants. These iconographic elements suggest that this complex had to do with water and fertility.

Several other repeated motifs are Venus glyphs, set near the top of the cornice, skybands (crossed bands), and goggle-eyed Tlalocs bordered by little scrolls, possibly set at the bottom of the cornice. The last of these may refer, as on 10L-33, to the descent group that owned this set of three buildings. Linda Schele and Nikolai Grube speculated that the iconography of 10L-41 referred to Tlaloc-Venus warfare, and they suggested that the buildings housed young noblemen in training for warfare or ritual. This idea need not be incompatible with Barbara Fash's preceding suggestion.

Communal houses are known for several modern Maya groups, and Landa (Tozzer, ed. and trans., 1941:124) wrote about young men's houses, but structures of this kind have been difficult to identify in the archaeological record. At Late Postclassic Mayapán, Tatiana Proskouriakoff (1962:89) wrote that the twenty-one colonnaded halls in the Main Group "probably served as living quarters for unmarried boys being trained in the arts of war and ritual." Robert Carmack (1981:287–290, 385) argued, however, that the colonnaded halls at Mayapán were "probably lineage houses," equivalent to the Quiché "big houses" with many entrances and columns at Utatlán that he thought were "primarily administrative centers for the major lineages." At Copán, Charles Cheek and Mary Spink (1986:89–92) concluded that a four-room building near the northeast corner of the Great Plaza was a communal house that combined several functions.

Structure 10L-41 must have provided some combination of communal, administrative, ritual, and perhaps residential use, but it was built, enlarged, and used by only one segment of Copán noble society, the corporate group of Yax Pasaj.

HOUSES ON THE WEST, NORTH, AND SOUTH SIDES OF COURTYARD B

Structures 10L-44 and 10L-86 form a nearly continuous line of four multiroom buildings, set on two platforms about a meter high, that extend almost 50 m, the full length of the west side of Courtyard B. Structure 10L-44, to the north, consists of three buildings, A, B, and C, from north to south. Its two stairways are centered in front of 10L-44A and 10L-44B. The buildings contain a dozen rooms of varying masonry quality and size, but all the rooms have large benches covering all or most of the rear wall. We think that all these rooms were domestic—used for sleeping, eating, and other household activities—but were occupied by individuals or small families of differing statuses.

The northern building contains three large rooms with stone walls of squared blocks rising to at least the top of the doorway, roofed with perishable materials. The central building, 10L-44B, was the only one that carried a vault. It contained a central room with a large bench and a niche between the bench and the doorway. A smaller side room had a south doorway, an overall arrangement that is almost the mirror image of the later 10L-41A across the courtyard. Two additional rooms were added on to the east and south sides of this core. Structure 10L-44B bore no sculpture, but its medial or superior molding was of beveled stones similar to those used in the two-part, beveled platform molding of Structures 10L-41B, C, and D across the courtyard. The south building, 10L-44C, contained two rooms with benches, like 10L-44A. Although it was built at the same time, the entire structure is faced by unshaped river cobbles and roughly shaped stones, as are the facing walls of the platform section on which it rests.

Structure 10L-86, at the south end of 10L-44, is a low platform that in its final stage supported four small rooms with benches. The masonry is of river cobbles and unshaped stones, with roughly squared stones in benches and jambs. Despite its small size and crude construction, 10L-86 was enlarged, rearranged, and subdivided several times. Its development, masonry quality, and room sizes give the impression of an expanding family of low status and limited resources. Behind 10L-44C is a large, low platform with a C-shaped bench (10L-44 West). This probably housed individuals of lower status, who could enter 10L-44 by steps just in front of the bench.

Like 10L-41, 10L-44 contains at least two earlier construction stages, but neither was found consistently throughout 10L-44. A continuous courtyard floor linked the third and final construction phase to other late structures around Courtyard B, including the penultimate stage of 10L-41 across the courtyard. The latest platform additions to 10L-41 rest atop these flagstones, indicating that this building complex was the last in Courtyard B to see major alterations.

The pattern of renovation revealed by excavations in 10L-44 appears to have been less planned and coordinated than in 10L-41B, C, and D, which look as if they were rebuilt and enlarged all at the same time, according to a master plan. This difference reflects less overall control and greater initiative at the family or individual level in 10L-44.

We know less about the early buildings in 10L-44 than in 10L-41, but they do not appear to have been smaller versions of the final ones. The careful rebuilding of special-purpose structures documented in 10L-41 did not happen in 10L-44.

Each of the two small, unvaulted buildings on 1-m-high platforms on the north side of Courtyard B (10L-237 and 10L-85) contained two rooms, and each room contained a large bench. Together, these buildings formed the original north end of the courtyard, predating the vaulted shrine, 10L-43. Neither of the two unvaulted structures bore sculpture or other features to indicate that they were anything besides dwellings.

Structure 10L-237, at the courtyard's northwest corner, is the smaller and earlier of the two, as early as any building investigated on Courtyards A and B, built with cobbles and roughly shaped stones but enlarged with shaped stones. Structure 10L-85, to the east of 10L-237, is larger and later, with masonry of well-squared blocks.

Structure 10L-42 is a low platform with an unvaulted building on the south side of Courtyard B. For most of its history, it was a domestic structure, with the number of rooms increasing over time, all with benches. The final modifications, at about the same time as the latest major constructions in Courtyard B, turned 10L-42 into a platform lacking a masonry building.

A SHRINE AT THE NORTH END OF COURTYARD B (STRUCTURE 10L-43)

Centered at the north end of Courtyard B is a two-room, vaulted building on a 140-cm-high platform (figure 7.18). Structure 10L-43 seems to have been built in front of Structures 10L-85 and 10L-237 about halfway through the Courtyard B sequence, during its most intensive construction episode. Until this time, 10L-85 and 10L-237 formed the northern edge of the courtyard. The stair and the only doorway of 10L-43 face south onto the courtyard. Its facades bore no sculpture. The doorways to the front and rear room are wide and centrally placed, and the floor of the rear room steps up about 20 cm. Neither room contained a bench, and none of the remaining walls included a niche, although the collapsed side and rear walls of the back room could have. A drip-water cave formation and a fragment of an

FIGURE 7.18

Structure 10L-43, a late temple lacking sculptural decoration, at the north end of Courtyard B: (top) from the south after clearing and (bottom) the east side after consolidation.

obsidian blade showing little evidence of use were cached just under the floor of the outer (south) room. A headless deer had been placed as an offering at the base of the rear platform facing, near the central north-south axis.

The position of 10L-43, the height of its platform relative to others around Courtyard B, the absence of benches, the raised rear room, and the two caches identify it as a shrine, not a domestic structure. Altar I″, a small round stone found near the southwest corner of 10L-43, had been broken in half, presumably when the building was destroyed. It carries the Calendar Round date 11 Ahau 18 Mac (9.18.0.0.0, A.D. 790), one of the latest dates at Copán.

STRUCTURE 10L-36 IN EL CEMENTERIO (HARVARD UNIVERSITY 1892 EXCAVATIONS)

The 1990–1994 Tulane University project excavated several structures in Group 10L-2 that were investigated by Harvard University in 1891–1895. The only major excavated building we did not reexamine was Structure 10L-36, a multiroom, 5-m-by-22-m structure about 50 m west of Courtyard A. John G. Owens' 1892 notes (Gordon 1896:26–28; Owens 1891–1892) mention pieces of plaster floors, low walls, the absence of roof (vault) stones, and much trash, some of which lay beside the meter-high platform. Owens excavated thirty-seven skeletons in and near 10L-36, a number that is astonishingly large when compared to the forty-five or so we found in four seasons in all of Group 10L-2. None of the burials were in a crypt of cut stones, but some included polychrome vessels of the Coner phase and the preceding Acbi-Coner transition.

Structure 10L-36 forms the west side of an open area bordered on the east by the three Acbi-Coner transition vaulted structures mentioned above. To the south, it is delimited by low platforms (10L-236 and 10L-238) that contained Acbi-Coner burials of high-ranking individuals. This long building also forms the northeast side of Courtyard C, which, except for 10L-36, remains unexcavated.

Its abundant refuse, many burials, remains of low walls on the summit, and length tell us that 10L-36 was a residence for many individuals. The quality of masonry and burial furnishings suggest that they were not of the highest rank. Structure 10L-36 may have been the largest residence of the group living in this area just before Courtyards A and B were laid out, with higher-status members of a royal family living in 10L-34, 10L-Sub 10, and 10L-Sub 14.

LATE CLASSIC ROYAL RESIDENCE

CHANGING PATTERNS OF DOMESTIC USE AND DRAINAGE WEST OF COURTYARD A IN THE EIGHTH CENTURY

Sometime between A.D. 650 and 700, as the focus of ritual activities, administration, and residence in Group 10L-2 moved to Courtyards A and B (and perhaps to Courtyard C and to other courtyard groups to the east washed away by the river), the privileged status of El Cementerio (the area west of Courtyard A) appears to have declined. Instead of a noble residence, it was a work area, perhaps including perishable dwellings, of which no traces remain today (Starratt 2001). Instead of new platforms faced with cut blocks, much construction seems to have taken the form of raised areas without dressed facing stones. Trash was allowed to accumulate nearly everywhere. Small, simple structures were built beside the rear walls of 10L-33 (10L-233) and 10L-32 (10L-234) at the southeast corner of Courtyard A.

Structure 10L-233 is a single-room domestic building with a C-shaped bench on a platform facing the rear wall of 10L-33. Three burials had been placed around the base of the platform, and a thin sheet midden had accumulated between the front of 10L-233 and the back of 10L-33. The building's position and crude masonry demonstrate that the occupants of 10L-233 were both connected to and of lower status than those who controlled 10L-33 and other structures in Courtyard A.

Structure 10L-234, an even smaller room with a C-shaped bench on a platform, was built up against the rear platform face of 10L-32. Perhaps the dwelling of servants, it was in use at the time of the ruler's house.

One other new structure was built behind 10L-33-South. Structure 10L-240 is a C-shaped platform two courses high and barely more than 2 m on a side. A perishable superstructure must have risen from it, facing the back wall of 10L-33-South. The open part of the C was entirely filled with a thick deposit of mostly utilitarian pottery. Too small to have been a residence, bedroom, or workroom, it may have been used for storing perishable materials in ceramic vessels.

Structure 10L-236, the large platform that at the beginning of the Coner phase supported a substantial superstructure and contained Copán Tomb 1, was rebuilt. The original platform walls were removed, and the platform was reoriented almost 10 degrees east to correspond to the alignment of Courtyard A. The superstructure was torn down, and the platform surface was raised about 30 cm. Any new enclosed or open structure on 10L-236 was entirely perishable. This may have become a work, craft, or food-preparation area; the deep deposits of trash around this platform attest to such activities. Food preparation is demonstrated by the large amount of animal bone in this area, compared to the smaller amounts encountered in and around Courtyards A and B (Starratt 2001).

Structure 10L-238, which contained Copán Tomb 2 and two other, smaller, vaulted crypts, may also have been resurfaced, but it was in such bad shape that we could not tell. Little can be said about the late use of 10L-238, which had much less trash around its base than did 10L-236.

The large, low, open area south of 10L-236 and north of Courtyard B seems to have experienced drainage problems early on. Sometime after the reorientation of 10L-236, the addition of irregular layers and pockets of earth and rock elevated most of this area as much as a meter (Starratt 2001). This would have raised the area above potential rainy-season flooding and channeled runoff to the east and west. Lenses of trash in the fill show that this was an intermittent process, not one concentrated effort.

Ending in a rough line of irregular boulders, the raised area (its west side is shown with cobbles in figure 7.1) extended north to 10L-36 and south almost to 10L-85. On the east, a battered line of rough facing stones runs south-southeast from a bridged drain between 10L-236 and 10L-233 to almost the northeast corner of Courtyard B. This sloping face of large stones diverted water to the east, away from the raised work area and Courtyard B and into a low area behind Yax Pasaj's house. From here, rain water drained around the south side of 10L-231 and then east toward the river and south along the back side of 10L-41.

The raised area may have supported perishable dwellings or ramadas covering work or storage areas, but much of it may also have been covered simply to prevent erosion. Rough retaining walls held back the earth fill of the "platform" as long as Group 10L-2 was maintained, but afterward the crude structure disintegrated.

THE PERSONAL HIEROGLYPHIC MONUMENTS OF YAX PASAJ

About a dozen hieroglyphic monuments have been found in

Group 10L-2 (Andrews and Fash 1992:74–81). Although some of these may have originally come from atop or near the Acropolis, six or seven were associated with buildings in Group 10L-2. At least three of these refer to events in the life of Yax Pasaj.

In 1892, Peabody Museum archaeologists found Altar F' (figure 7.19) in the collapsed masonry and building fill behind the central building of 10L-32. It originally rested on the bench, the rear part of which slid down the back of the building. We can be sure of this because a small fragment of the Altar F' inscription that spalled off when 10L-32 collapsed was found in this debris in 1990 and refitted by Barbara Fash (Andrews and Fash 1992:figure 13; Gordon 1896:25–26, 1902:figure 26).

The inscription of Altar F' (Schele 1995) names Yax Pasaj. It says that a clay statue named *U Yak' Chak* (gift of Chak) was modeled on 9.17.4.1.12 2 Chuen 4 Pop (3 February 775) and that the statue "died" on 9.17.17.12.1 4 Imix 9 Mol (24 June A.D. 788).[2] It continues with a distance number leading back to an action by Yax Pasaj on 9.16.13.11.1 9 Imix 9 K'ank'in (28 October A.D. 764, sixteen months after his accession), when "he came out in holiness." The date on which the statue died is repeated, with the statement that David Stuart and Linda Schele (Schele 1995:3) translated as "it went in the company of (*yichnal*) Yax Pasaj," implying "a procession in which the deity was carried in the company of the king" and which "may have ended in the death of the statue."

Altar G' is a small, partly eroded, circular table altar with four wide legs found in an open area about half a kilometer south-southwest of the Acropolis, not far south of Group 10L-2 (Morley 1920:374–375, figure 54, plate 24d). Its remaining glyphs refer to Yax Pasaj's ceramic statue, U Yak' Chak, and its death or termination on the date in A.D. 788 that was inscribed on Altar F' (Schele 1990a, 1995).

Late in the history of Group 10L-2, trash accumulated along the north side of Structure 10L-30, and a round altar was pushed off the top of Yax Pasaj's ceremonial platform, coming to rest nearly undamaged in the midden at its northwest corner. The growing pile of garbage eventually hid the desecrated monument. Finally, the platform's north face collapsed and buried the altar, which we uncovered in 1990. The Structure 10L-30 altar commemorates the celebration of

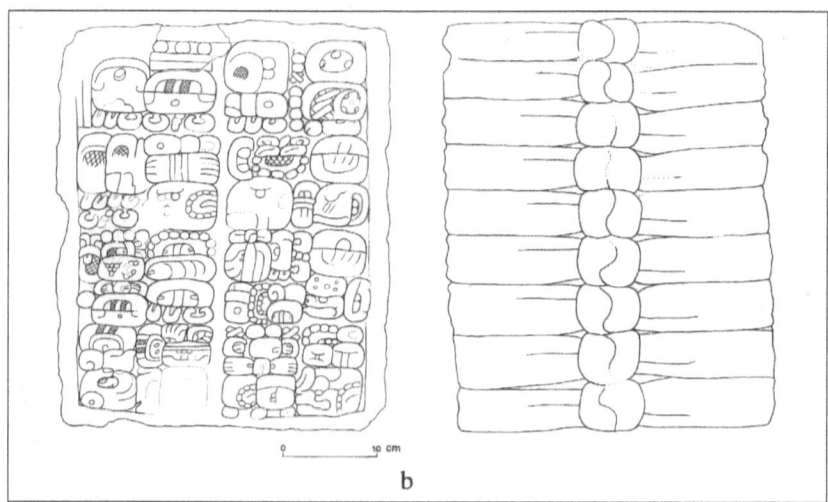

FIGURE 7.19

Altar F', recovered by the Peabody Museum behind Structure 10L-32 in 1892, is 46 cm high, 36 cm wide, and 33 cm deep. It stood on the throne in Yax Pasaj's house until the building collapsed. The inscription names Yax Pasaj and says that his companion, a ceramic effigy called "gift of Chak," was modeled in 775 and "died" in 788. It also refers to an action by Yax Pasaj in 764, sixteen months after his accession, when "he came out in holiness." (a) Photograph by William Fash and Barbara Fash and (b) drawing by Barbara W. Fash.

FIGURE 7.20

The round altar found at the base of the northwest corner of Structure 10L-30, excavated in 1990 (CPN 19469), probably was cast off the summit of 10L-30, falling into a Terminal Coner midden that was forming at the base of the building and that continued to accumulate over the altar. It is 30 cm in diameter and 8 cm thick. The altar commemorates the erection of a katun *stone, possibly in 783. It also states that the ceramic effigy mentioned on Altar F', Yax Pasaj's companion, was brought out at this celebration. (a) Photograph and (b) drawing by Barbara Fash.*

the placement of a *katun* stone (figure 7.20; Copán sculpture catalog number [CPN] 19469; Schele 1990c, 1995:3). The occasion is believed to have been the end of Yax Pasaj's first katun in office on 9.17.12.5.17 4 Kaban 10 Zip (19 March 783). The altar states that U Yak' Chak was brought out or manifested at the celebration of Yax Pasaj's first katun of rule, and the ceramic effigy is referred to as the *yitah yahawil* (the companion of the lord or his office).

Two other monuments are closely associated with 10L-32. One is a shattered rectangular altar that, like Altar F', rested on the bench of the central building in 10L-32 (figure 7.21; CPN 19222; Andrews and Fash 1992:figure 14). A piece of this altar (CPN 2834) somehow found its way to the West Court of the Acropolis and was identified by Barbara Fash. The second, Morley's Altar G", was found in Courtyard A in front of Structure 10L-32 by Gustav Strömsvik in 1936 (Morley 1939:288). It is an eroded, circular table with short, squat legs. Morley saw parallels between this undated monument and Yax Pasaj's Altar GN, found a short distance south-southwest of Group 10L-2. Given Altar G"'s similarity to Morley's Altar G' and position in front of 10L-32, it was probably Yax Pasaj's monument as well. Two fragments of another round altar were found a few meters east of Structure 10L-29, but over the years, a number of pieces of sculpture had been collected here, and its origin is uncertain (Andrews and Fash 1992:figure 19).

The Group 10L-2 monuments include three small, round altars. Half of one (CPN 23748) was excavated in 1991 beside Structure 10L-29 above Courtyard A (figure 7.22; Andrews and Fash 1992:figure 18a). A similar altar, broken in half, Morley's Altar I" (1939:278, 291–292, plate XXVIIIb) was found by Edwin Shook in 1937 at the southwest corner of 10L-43 in Courtyard B. The third, Altar W (CPN 19119), was found by the Peabody Museum expedition in 1892, possibly in Group 10L-2 (Andrews and Fash 1992:figure 18b; Gordon 1902:figure 14; Morley 1920:364–365, plate 24c). Altars I" and W, as well as two additional, very similar altars found south of Structure 10L-26 in 1987, bear the Calendar Round date 11 Ahau 18 Mac (9.18.0.0.0, A.D. 790). The Structure 10L-29 fragment found in 1991 bore the *tzolkin* date 11 Ahau, but the presumed 18 Mac *haab* date is missing.

Another group of inscribed monuments consists of three miniature shrines or houses found near Structures 10L-29 and 10L-33 (Andrews and Fash 1992:figures 16, 17). Several of these four-sided houses have been found in residential groups around the Acropolis (Grube and Schele 1990; Hohmann 1995:243–249). Toward its base, the stone usually projects slightly on all sides to display a platform on which the house sat. Roofs shaped like those of thatched houses were carved separately and sometimes bear inscriptions. The front of the house has a recessed door in which a god is depicted. The two-glyph

LATE CLASSIC ROYAL RESIDENCE

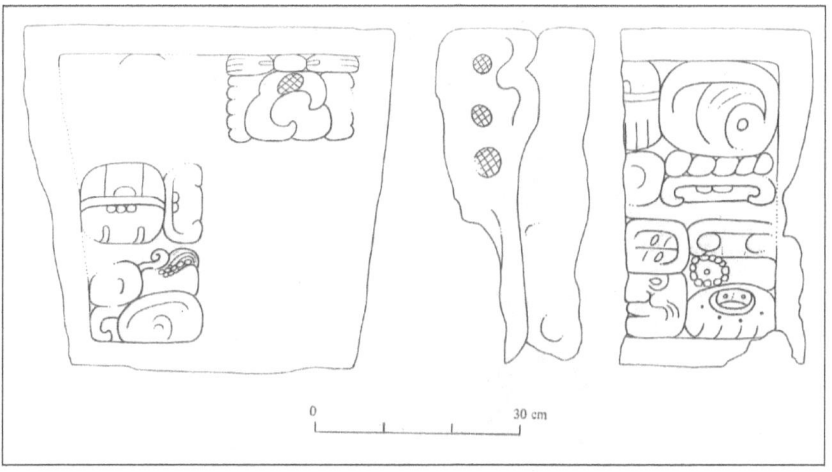

FIGURE 7.21
Fragment of a broken rectangular altar (CPN 19222) excavated from high in the superstructure collapse debris just behind the central room of Structure 10L-32 in 1990. It probably rested next to Altar F' on Yax Pasaj's throne. Part of this still incomplete altar was found in the West Court (CPN 2834). (Drawing by B. Fash)

inscriptions on one side have been read as *u waybil ch'ul* (the sleeping place of god, or of holiness), and the inscription on the other side has been suggested to be a name (Freidel, Schele, and Parker 1993:188–190; Grube and Schele 1990:3).

One house found near Structure 10L-29 names Yax Kamlay, who is named on other late monuments and who once was considered to be Yax Pasaj's brother and an important official in his court (CPN 21141; Andrews and Fash 1992:figure 16, a–c; Schele and Freidel 1990:333–334; Schele et al. 1989). A second Group 10L-2 house, nearly identical to the first, was found by the 1891–1895 Peabody Museum expedition west of Courtyard A, south of 10L-29 (CPN 19075, 19094; Andrews and Fash 1992:figure 17). David Stuart (personal communication 1997) reads the name on this shrine also as *Yax Kamlay*. A third miniature shrine found just east of Structure 10L-29 bears the name of an individual not previously recognized in the inscriptions of Copán (Andrews and Fash 1992:figure 16d). Nikolai Grube and Linda Schele (1990:5) read his name as *Ahau Butz'*, and they guessed that he, like Yax Kamlay, was a close relative of Yax Pasaj.

FIGURE 7.22

Half of a round altar found in 1991 on the plaster floor at the base of the northeast corner of the Structure 10L-29 platform (CPN 23748, 42 cm across and 17 cm thick). The altar bears the tzolkin *date 11 Ahau. Four very similar round altars, including one found in 1937 at the southwest corner of Structure 10L-43 on Courtyard B, bear the Calendar Round date 11 Ahau 18 Mac (A.D. 790). This altar from 10L-29 likely did also.*

Late Classic Royal Residence

David Stuart (personal communication 1997) believes that, just as U Yak' Chak was an image of a god, not of a person, the names on these small shrines, including Yax Kamlay and Yahaw Chan Ahbak, belong to gods and not to humans. The little houses are, as their inscriptions say, the sleeping place of gods. The shrines, as Joyce Marcus (personal communication 1998) has noted, might also refer to clay statues (like U Yak' Chak), the images of the supernatural patrons or patron deities of Yax Pasaj and other rulers.

One implication of Stuart's interpretation is that a rank of named individuals—brothers or other close relatives of the king, individuals who in the initial project readings were thought to hold important positions in the ruler's court—is eliminated from the inscriptions at Copán. Instead, these inscriptions name deities or companions who provide support of a different kind. References to other office holders remain, including holpopob, the lineage heads seated around the upper facade of the popol nah, and the noble owners of the houses who were allowed to erect hieroglyphic benches during the reign of Yax Pasaj, perhaps his relatives. These two categories of nobles, as well as those who carried the aj k'uhun title (Jackson and Stuart 2001), perhaps meaning "one who venerates, obeys" (David Stuart, personal communication 2003), probably constituted a single nobility that possessed and exhibited varying degrees of privilege and power. These noble office holders represented several corporate groups, probably extended lineages, but all may have been linked by marriage alliances.

The inscriptions and architecture of Group 10L-2 help us to understand Yax Pasaj's origin, identity, and spheres of activity, his residential neighborhood and its relationship to the Copán dynasty, and his use of supernatural imagery to reinforce his claim to authority. This information enables us to consider several questions. The first concerns the ruler and his antecedents. The monuments in Group 10L-2 mention only one ruler—Yax Pasaj. They identify Group 10L-2 as his residence and Structures 10L-30 and 10L-32 as his buildings. No monuments of earlier rulers have been found in Group 10L-2, and there is no evidence that earlier kings lived here. The elite group that moved here toward the end of the Early Classic had royal ties, and those who came after them called themselves descendants of the founder of the dynasty, but no later kings are named here. If our investigations had been superficial, it could be argued that monuments of previous rulers were buried inside later constructions or had been removed. Excavations in and around Courtyards A and B have been extensive and deep enough, however, to reveal that earlier monuments are rare or absent. Yax Pasaj did not destroy, bury, or remove freestanding monuments of earlier rulers on the Acropolis, and we would not expect him to have done so in Group 10L-2.

Yax Pasaj's actions and his inscribed monuments mark him as coming from Group 10L-2. Previous Late Classic rulers did not come from Group 10L-2, and Yax Pasaj was not descended from them. Yax Pasaj largely dismantled and buried Structure 10L-32-2nd under his own house, honoring the carved fish on its facade by placing a complete specimen in a cache under his throne. The placing of the cache implies that Yax Pasaj was from here and that he considered himself a member of the group symbolized by the fish. 10L-32-2nd contained a large vaulted tomb built in anticipation of the death of the house's owner, and Yax Pasaj sealed and covered this tomb. The tomb's owner and occupant was presumably Yax Pasaj's father—the husband of the "woman from Palenque" he claimed as his mother on Stela 8 (Grube, Schele, and Fahsen 1995; Marcus 1992b:256–257, 1995:13; Schele and Freidel 1990:330–331; Schele and Grube 1987)—or possibly some other close relative. This person would have been an important noble, but he was not the preceding ruler.

The identification of Group 10L-2 as Yax Pasaj's residence may help explain the absence of hieroglyphic benches here. Carved benches have been excavated in three large buildings in Las Sepulturas, including the House of the Bacabs (Schele and Freidel 1990:329–331; Webster, ed., 1989), Structure 9M-146 (Schele and Freidel 1990:328–329; Willey, Leventhal, and Fash 1978), and Structure 8N-11 (Webster, B. Fash, et al. 1998). Another dating to Yax Pasaj's reign was found in Group 10K-4 near the entrance to the archaeological park (Baudez 1994:235, figure 112b). The benches are interpreted as instruments of political patronage, showing Yax Pasaj's attempt to enlist the support of other heads of noble families in the Copán realm by appointing them to political offices and sharing status symbols. This political system may have deep roots in the Maya area, as Bardsley (1996) has suggested, but the ruler's dependence on his supporting lords is argued to have gained force during Yax Pasaj's reign (W. Fash 1983b:310–314, 2001:160–165; B. Fash et al. 1992). If so, no inscribed bench would be necessary in the king's own residential group. Even if the carved benches simply document the growing independence of the lords, we still might not expect such a monument in the king's own house.

A second matter is Yax Pasaj's companion, U Yak' Chak. The ceramic image of the god Chak is mentioned prominently on all three of Yax Pasaj's monuments in Group 10L-2 that have long, legible inscriptions. U Yak' Chak was important enough for the king to record his "birth" and "death" and the ritual occasions on which the image accompanied the king. Two of these monuments were carved, surprisingly, after the statue's "death."

Why was this image so important? Early in his reign or before, Yax Pasaj appears to have taken Chak as his supernatural patron and ritual companion. A modeled ceramic figure was imbued with the vital force of the deity and a life of its own. In telling us its birth and death dates, the inscriptions give us more information than we have for many rulers of Copán. For thirteen years, a portable image of this god was his companion. At the time of its "death," we do not know whether Chak was ritually interred or smashed. From Chak, Yax Pasaj received supernatural power (Marcus 1992b:262, 301). Yax Pasaj's right to rule may have been strengthened by or, in part, derived from his companion, for he did not inherit the throne from his father.

On 10L-32, Yax Pasaj was depicted as a young man sitting above the head of a long-nosed monster who may be Chak (Andrews and Fash 1992:67). If so, the identification of the ceramic image of the god Chak with the supernatural being on which Yax Pasaj sits, on the house he built, provides a rare link between one individual's inscribed monuments, his architectural sculpture motifs, and his supernatural patron.

Despite the importance of U Yak' Chak in Yax Pasaj's Group 10L-2 monuments, this ceramic image is not mentioned in other inscriptions at Copán. Nor is Yax Pasaj's relationship with Chak, so prominently portrayed on 10L-32, referred to elsewhere. His relationship with this deity was personal, probably involving private and semiprivate rituals. It was not recorded on his monuments erected in the public context of the Acropolis, but only in and near his palace and lineage shrines.

Finally, in considering as a whole the message Yax Pasaj intended to convey through the sculpture he placed on his buildings in Group 10L-2, we should notice what he chose not to portray. The final ruler did not use the founder's glyph, with or without the goggle-eye and scroll addition. Nor did he employ the Mexican year sign, despite the likelihood of his belonging to the group that claimed descent from K'inich Yax K'uk' Mo' and carved Mexican year signs on 10L-33, 10L-33-South, 10L-29, and 10L-41. Structure 10L-32 bears no Tlaloc or war imagery, so striking on his Temple 16 and present earlier in Group 10L-2 on 10L-33 and 10L-41. Images of war and Teotihuacán may have been more fitting for his public buildings than for his residential compound.

HUMAN BURIALS

In four years, we excavated the remains of fifty-two skeletons in forty-eight burials. To these can be added thirty-seven burials with forty skeletons excavated by the Peabody Museum in 1892 (Gordon 1896:26–31). Except for three individuals in two masonry tombs (Copán Tombs 1 and 2 in El Cementerio), all the 1892 Harvard burials were found in or near Structure 10L-36. The Carnegie excavations in 1938 and 1939 (Longyear 1940, 1952:35–50) yielded two masonry tombs and three simple graves.[3]

Most of the burials, including those recorded by Harvard and Carnegie, date to the Late Classic, as do nearly all the constructions and ceramics from Group 10L-2. The burial ages have been determined from accompanying ceramic vessels or estimated from architectural stratigraphy. Eight individuals were Early Classic (two late Bijac [A.D. 250–400] and six Acbi [A.D. 400–600]), and eighty-five dated to the Late Classic (four Acbi-Coner transition [A.D. 600–650] and eighty-one Coner [A.D. 650–850]).

The graves range from shallow, cramped cavities in trash dumps, soil, or platform fill to elaborate masonry vaults stocked with polychrome vessels, jewelry, and other artifacts of exquisite craftsmanship. The former far outnumbered the latter. Most of the graves show no preparation beyond digging a hole large enough for the body, often flexed. In contrast, the furniture associated with burials shows a more even gradation from lavish to nonexistent.

Five of the eight masonry crypts date to the Acbi-Coner transition (A.D. 600–650) and apparently were occupied by members of some of the first noble or royal families to move south of the Acropolis into Group 10L-2. These have been discussed in an earlier section.

The other three crypts date later in the Late Classic. One of them is the vaulted burial chamber in Structure 10L-32-2nd, 2.0 m long, 0.65 m wide, and 2.0 m high, with one inverted T-shaped niche, three high steps, and a mostly missing antechamber. Plundered and partially destroyed in antiquity, possibly by the small Early Postclassic group living 100 m south of Group 10L-2, this tomb probably contained the remains of Yax Pasaj's father or another close relative.

CERAMICS AND OBSIDIAN AS INDICATORS OF ACTIVITIES IN GROUP 10L-2

Architecture, sculpture, inscriptions, and arrangement of structures point to Courtyard A as the center of Group 10L-2, with the most important structures. Courtyard B, with two religious and administrative buildings, was a mixed elite and not-so-elite residential area. The late El Cementerio appears to have been an area devoted to support activities, with or without permanent residents. Harold E. Starratt and William F. Doonan's analyses of ceramics and obsidian from middens in Group 10L-2 also indicate that these areas differed.

Nearly one hundred middens of different kinds were excavated, most of which dated to the Coner phase, ca. A.D. 650–850. Few of these could be associated exclusively with one building, but many sealed trash deposits almost certainly came from several contemporaneous, adjacent structures. The items discarded in these middens should reflect the activities of those who used the nearby buildings.

Starratt's analysis of vessel forms in a large number of these middens—which, together, included more than 100,000 sherds from Courtyards A and B and El Cementerio—shows that storage vessels (jars and other vessels with restricted orifices, including those probably used for liquids) were more common in Courtyard A than would have been expected by chance (Starratt 2001; Starratt and Doonan 2001). In El Cementerio, storage vessels were relatively less common. We interpret this to indicate that the elite owners of Courtyard A buildings stored food, liquids, and other substances in their buildings, that they may have done so with greater frequency than did the occupants of Courtyard B, and that El Cementerio saw less storage. Vessels used for serving and eating (bowls, ollas, platters, and cylinders) showed the opposite, being less common in Courtyard A and more common in El Cementerio than expected. Although it seems likely that the occupants of Courtyard A (and probably B) ate in or near their own houses, the higher frequency of serving and eating dishes in El Cementerio than in Courtyard A suggests that food was prepared there and carried to Courtyard A. As eating and serving dishes seem to have broken more often in El Cementerio than in Courtyard A, they may have been cleaned and stored in the food-preparation area between meals.

Doonan's microscopic use-wear analysis of obsidian prismatic blades from Group 10L-2 suggested differences between the use of these cutting and scraping tools in Courtyard A and in El Cementerio (Doonan 1996; Starratt and Doonan 2001). Courtyard A middens contained more unused blades and blades used on relatively soft materials, such as meat and vegetable fibers, than would have been expected. This suggests that individuals in Courtyard A stored unused blades and that they used obsidian blades for eating and possibly making clothing or adornments. Blades used on relatively hard materials, such as bone, were less common in Courtyard A middens. In El Cementerio, the pattern was reversed. Blades used on bone were more common, and blades used on soft materials were less frequent than expected. This suggests that El Cementerio was an area where meat was butchered and prepared, indicated by an unusually large number of animal bone fragments in middens and general excavations there.

The Late Classic deposits in El Cementerio also contained more ground and chipped stone tools and more trash than nonmidden deposits elsewhere in Group 10L-2. Although we did not recognize workshops or localized evidence for craftsmanship of specialized items or activities such as spinning or stone masonry anywhere in Group 10L-2, the overall frequency of discarded and broken artifacts indicates that El Cementerio was a work zone for nearly the last two centuries of the Late Classic.

THE SIZE AND DEMOGRAPHIC COMPOSITION OF GROUP 10L-2

In drawing together the archaeological and epigraphic evidence from Yax Pasaj's residential group, we focus now on issues of spatial organization, demography, and social differentiation. One question is, what part of the site did Yax Pasaj control or represent as a corporate group head, in contrast to his administration of the entire realm as ruler? His neighborhood must have extended beyond what we identify as Group 10L-2. A second question concerns the demographic composition of the compound—who lived in Group 10L-2?

One problem is that we can never know the full extent of the group because some of it has washed away. The group must have included Courtyard C, still unexcavated, but should it also be expanded to include nearby courtyard groups and isolated structures? If so, how many and how far? One of Yax Pasaj's personal monuments, Altar G', was found on the surface, about 500 m southwest of the Acropolis, but we do not know how it got there. If the distribution of his most personal monuments—those referring to his supernatural companion, U Yak' Chak—mark the extent of the area occupied by the group of which he and his ancestors were head, then his family's domain included parts of the densely occupied zone just west and south of Group 10L-2, known as "El Bosque." The range in quality of habitations in the excavated portions of Group 10L-2 enables us to identify these few courtyards as a tightly delimited, high-status residence. The inclusion of some or much of El Bosque in Yax Pasaj's group would add greatly to its size, population, and socioeconomic diversity. The extension would also provide Yax Pasaj's lineage with a power base in keeping with its growing importance during the Late Classic period. A wider definition of Yax Pasaj's group to include some of the surrounding settlement raises the question of where its limits were. In the absence of clear architectural or geographic divisions, however, we will not be able to define these limits. As population grew, so did the royal compound, and its borders in A.D. 650 would not have been those of 800.

The issue of the demographic composition of large Maya residential groups with expensive architecture has been discussed in many studies of Copán (Andrews and Fash 1992; Diamanti 1991; B. Fash et al. 1992; W. Fash, 1983b, 1998, 2001; Gillespie 2000; Harrison and Andrews n.d.; Hendon 1991, 1992; Sanders 1989, 1992; Webster 1989a, 1992) and other sites (Harrison 1970, 1999; Haviland 1981, 1992; Haviland and Moholy-Nagy 1992; Inomata and Houston 2001; McAnany 1995; Webster 1998a, 2001). Archaeologists often ask how individuals in a large residential group were related, how much social and economic differentiation existed within a residential kinship group, and how material, especially architectural, differentiation in a residential group should be interpreted. For example, were small, simple, inexpensive dwellings in a group containing high-status houses occupied by unrelated servants or retainers, or did they house younger and less privileged members of the same kin group, or both? Most would agree that the answers will vary from area to area within the Maya lowlands, from large site to small site, and from one period to another. Many would also agree that precision in defining the composition of residential groups will remain difficult to achieve.

In Group 10L-2, is it reasonable to think that all the residents were related to Yax Pasaj, even distantly? We have investigated approximately twenty-five structures in Group 10L-2 that, together, contained about fifty rooms. Many of these, although not the largest ones, appear to have been domestic. A population well beyond one hundred individuals in Courtyards A and B and El Cementerio is likely. The residents of Structure 10L-45, of buildings on Courtyard C (including Structure 10L-36), and around probable courtyards southeast of Courtyard A washed away by the river might more than double this figure.

For the reasons summarized below, we think that many, perhaps most, individuals in Late Classic Group 10L-2 were related. Servants, certain individuals who performed specific functions, various other individuals, and perhaps families were not. David Webster (1989a:12–14), William Sanders (1992), Julia Hendon (1992), and other members of the Pennsylvania State University Copán Project (PAC II) have reached similar conclusions about the social groups living in the nearby Las Sepulturas residential area. At other large sites, such as Tikal, noble residential groups are thought to have contained high-ranking families and unrelated servants (Haviland 1981, 1992).

Yax Pasaj's compound includes buildings of different sizes and purposes and greatly varying quality of construction. Few, if any, buildings around Courtyard A were purely domestic. Most were for administration, audiences, public enactment of rituals, dances, offerings to ancestors and deities, and other elite activities. Courtyard B came closer to being a residential courtyard, but even here, two of the most prominent structures were a shrine and a range of four buildings, only one of which was domestic.

Domestic buildings vary from sumptuous to simple. Rooms requiring great investment in labor may be adjacent to simple ones. Structures 10L-41A and 10L-44B are large, made of well-cut blocks, vaulted, and conspicuously located. The rooms of 10L-42, 10L-44C, and 10L-86, also facing Courtyard B, had crudely faced walls and benches, and the upper walls and roofs were perishable. Structure 10L-44 West, behind 10L-44C, is large, but its floor was laid barely above ground level, and its walls were entirely perishable. Despite its simplicity, we should not forget that the individuals who lived in 10L-44 West had direct access by an inset masonry stair to the two best sets of rooms on 10L-44. In contrast, Structures 10L-241, 10L-242, and 10L-243, in a comparable position behind 10L-41, were several courses high and of stones identical in quality to those of 10L-41 itself.

Houses of presumedly lower-status individuals around Courtyard A include 10L-233, facing the rear wall of 10L-33, which is marked as a house of the founder's lineage; 10L-234, a tiny building nestled against the back of Yax Pasaj's house; and possibly part of 10L-33-South at the very end of the Classic period, originally a noble residence but later badly damaged and hidden by the expansion of Yax Pasaj's house. These are roughly comparable in the quality of their construction to the least impressive structures around Courtyard B. The poorest buildings around Courtyard A are situated in secondary or dependent positions, however. Some structures of equal size and construction quality are situated immediately on Courtyard B.

Building quality—and surely status—varies substantially, then, within this noble residential complex. The individuals in one building or in adjacent buildings, if their locations were of equivalent prominence and visibility, shared a close relationship, most likely family ties. Extended families with some familial connection to Yax Pasaj can therefore be argued to have been externally and internally ranked, by age, by distance to the ruler, and by inherited titles, roles, and economic advantage. The status of individuals and their families may have fluctuated within their lifetimes as a result of changing relationships with the head of the residential group.

Some individuals in the least pretentious dwellings in Group 10L-2 may have been resident retainers, unrelated to the noble lineage. The residents of the least imposing structures around Courtyard A may have held this status, but the evidence from architecture and artifacts is not conclusive. El Cementerio in the middle and late Coner phase became an extensive, raised work area, with greater quantities of domestic ceramics, tools, and animal bones than around Courtyards A and B. We found no remains of houses of this time in El Cementerio. The walls of any late dwellings here were perishable, and the area was so disturbed that no masonry foundations were discerned. The area may have served as either a work area or both a work and dwelling space for individuals of low status.

The evidence for internal social and economic differentiation within Group 10L-2 is compelling. We are unwilling to attribute the visible architectural differences to the existence of a single, high-status, royal or noble lineage and a separate servant underclass. The archaeological record at most sites reflects social inequality within residential compounds. Also, as at Copán, the architectural remains usually show that Maya domestic groups were hierarchical, with families ranging from high to low status (McAnany 1995:116, 119–123, 147, 158–159; Roys 1943:35–36).

This conclusion renders it unlikely that all families in Group 10L-2 belonged to one extended lineage or one kinship group of any kind, although membership in such a kinship group may have been an important organizing and unifying fiction. There can be little doubt, however, that individuals in Group 10L-2 constituted a corporate group, each family with varying stakes in its maintenance through time. The term house, which places primary emphasis on the maintenance of an estate through time (Gillespie 2000), may be an appropriate way to characterize this self-perpetuating social unit. MacAnany's (1995) study of the Classic Maya lineage, however, shows that it, too, is a useful analytical device.

THE DECLINE OF COPÁN AND THE ABANDONMENT OF GROUP 10L-2

The archaeological and epigraphic evidence from Yax Pasaj's residential compound provides information about the dynastic collapse and subsequent abandonment of Copán in the ninth century. From the perspective of Group 10L-2, the demise of this Classic site appears to have occurred in stages. The last thirty years of Yax Pasaj's reign may have been a period of decline for the Copán dynasty, as William Fash (2001:171–175) has argued.

Yax Pasaj commissioned his buildings on the Acropolis and in his residential neighborhood at the beginning of his reign. His first temple, Structure 10L-21A, may have marked his accession in A.D. 763, and his two greatest monuments, Temples 11 and 16, were apparently dedicated in A.D. 773 and 775, respectively (Schele and Looper 1996:133, 141). Nothing new was built on the Acropolis during the final forty-five years of his rule except Temple 18. Thought to be his funerary temple, it was dedicated in A.D. 801 (Becker and Cheek 1983; Schele and Grube 1995:171). Compared to the massive, earlier Temples 11 and 16, Temple 18 is modest. As a tomb, however, it is truly impressive, even by Copán royal standards.

Yax Pasaj's three buildings in Group 10L-2—Structures 10L-30, 10L-32, and 10L-41A—were almost certainly built within a few years of one another; their masonry styles and construction techniques are the same. Although they are not directly dated, they, too, were most likely built when he was a young man.

His inscribed monuments were also more frequent in his early years. Not one in Group 10L-2 postdates A.D. 790. On the Acropolis, none of his inscriptions were carved after A.D. 800. The last two or three decades of his life are nearly bereft of monuments. If it were not for two late monuments announcing his death, the demise of the dynasty, and a successor's short-lived effort to found a new dynasty or political order (W. Fash 2001:177–179; Stuart 1993:344–346), we would have little indication from the archaeological record that central political authority at Copán lasted beyond the final decades of the eighth century. This decline in construction and in inscribed monuments might be taken to indicate a decline in the fortunes and resources of the central political authority. We have tended to regard it that way. The early date of his buildings and monuments may, however, reflect no more than a decision by an aging Yax Pasaj not to undertake massive new projects on the Acropolis or in Group 10L-2, except for his own tomb.

Near the end of the Late Classic, middens began to accumulate in several parts of Group 10L-2, as they did around some buildings on the Acropolis proper. The buildings themselves were kept clean and in good repair for a time. The trash, however, may reflect a deterioration of the urban infrastructure, an inability to control a large labor force, and a decline in the power and status of the occupants of the royal residence. These late middens in Group 10L-2 may predate the death of

Yax Pasaj, which would suggest that his rule was weakening, or they may have accumulated after his death and the collapse of central rule at Copán, or both. The stratigraphic position of most accumulations, however, is clear. Their fresh surfaces were covered by the collapsed wall and vault debris that marked the general destruction of the center of Copán, discussed below.

The ceramics from these middens are late in the Coner phase, showing declining frequencies of decorated types such as polychrome vessels and other special wares. The assemblage associated with the midden found on the patio of Structure 10L-33-South, in particular, represents a later facet of the Coner phase (Terminal Coner) than that associated with the late surface middens around the exterior of other structures in Group 10L-2, including the middens behind 10L-32 that were covered when it fell. The fresh 10L-33-South patio midden, however, like the others, was sealed by the collapse of 10L-32 and 10L-33-South. The accumulation of trash over the chipped, round altar found to the north of Structure 10L-30, a monument probably thrown off this high platform at the time nearby buildings were destroyed, similarly suggests the continuation of some occupation in Group 10L-2 after the end of the dynastic period, as does a late occupation in Group 9J-5, west of the Main Group (Maca 2001). Two radiocarbon dates from late middens sealed by collapsed building masonry in Courtyard A, cal A.D. 810 (870) 930 and cal A.D. 810 (910) 970, both 1-sigma, are consistent with an occupation that lasted toward the end of the ninth century, but they do not rule out an earlier or later abandonment.[4]

Two of the vaulted buildings we excavated on Courtyard A (Structures 10L-29 and 10L-33) had been brought down by burning the lintels over doorways and niches. Structure 10L-41B, on Courtyard B, also appears to have been burned. Two small, round altars dating to A.D. 790 on 10L-29 and 10L-43 were broken in half during this destruction, as were the carved altars inside 10L-32 (Andrews and Fash 1992:79).

This devastation is likely to have included the entire center of Copán, not just Group 10L-2. Burned lintels were found on the clean floors of Structure 10L-22A, the popol nah (B. Fash et al. 1992:427), one of the few major untouched structures on the Acropolis to have been excavated in recent years. Pieces of charred wood were found in 1936 on the terrace in front of Waxaklajun Ub'ah K'awil's Temple 22 next door, but the significance of these is unknown (Trik 1939:103).

Yax Pasaj's tomb in 10L-18 was looted, and the remains of the body and burial artifacts were removed shortly before the vaults collapsed. The burial chamber contained a layer of earth and ash above broken stucco, and the excavators noted traces of fire in the tomb and the burned surfaces of many remaining artifacts (Baudez 1983:413; Becker and Cheek 1983:412). Whether the burning and the removal of the burial and tomb furnishings were part of an intentional pillage that culminated in the destruction of the building or were part of a ritual movement of the burial is not certain. Earlier Copán rulers, however, do not appear to have been removed from their tombs.

The facade of Structure 9N-82, the House of the Scribe in the Las Sepulturas group, a few hundred meters from the Acropolis, was burned before the walls fell (W. Fash 1989:52–54). This was ritual destruction of prominent family symbols, the full-size figures of scribes flanking the doorways. The House of the Scribes did not, however, collapse because the lintel burned. Structure 9N-81, an adjacent special-purpose building, had burned while still in good condition, but this may have been accidental (Webster 1989a:21).

The destruction of or damage to these buildings in the East Court and in Group 9N-8 is not as securely placed as the burning and collapse in Group 10L-2, but it also occurred at the end of the Late Classic. None of the structures was rebuilt. Late middens had accumulated around the base of Temple 22 and the popol nah before their vaults collapsed, as they had in the royal residence. This suggests the same sequence of trash accumulation and destruction in the East Court that we are able to document in Group 10L-2.

Two inscriptions from the Acropolis provide a date for the collapse of the dynasty and a possible date for the destruction of some of its buildings. Stela 11, found near Yax Pasaj's tomb and dated to A.D. 820, shows what is thought to be a deceased Yax Pasaj. It has been interpreted as referring to the decline of the Copán dynasty (W. Fash 2001:177–179; Grube and Schele 1992; Stuart 1993:344–346). Readings of Stela 11 by Nikolai Grube and Linda Schele (1992:3) and by Elisabeth Wagner (1995) indicate that this collapse may have been accompanied by the "arrival of the torch and the war serpent," a symbolic representation of warfare or internal strife and destruction by burning. This reading of Stela 11 could be consistent with the collapse of the Copán dynasty, Yax Pasaj's death, and the burning of the site, all before A.D. 820, but it does not preclude a destruction of Copán after the king's death. The latest known date at Copán is A.D. 822, on the unfinished Altar L, which shows the seating of U Cit Tok' and a failed attempt to establish a new dynasty under the aegis of Yax Pasaj, who faces U Cit Tok' (W. Fash 2001:177–179).

We see two possible ways to date and interpret this evidence of possible royal decline, the death of the king and the failed attempt to create a new dynasty, trash accumulation, and eventual destruction of at least part of the royal compound. The first is that the process unfolded during the late years of Yax Pasaj's rule, indicating a gradual erosion of the fortunes of the realm and its leaders, and ended shortly after his death. This argument would be consistent with Kazuo Aoyama's (2001:356) documentation of reduced obsidian exchange at Copán in the latter half of the Late Classic period, indicating "great internal instability" and a gradual decline of political authority. The second is that the process of decline in his later years may be exaggerated and the buildup of garbage and destruction of the royal buildings happened relatively quickly after his death and the political collapse. The violence that may be indicated on Stela 11 suggests violence in the royal compound by A.D. 820. Bill's (1997, 2003) isolation of a Terminal Classic facet of the Coner phase in the late middens, though, would support a short postdynastic occupation in Group 10L-2 before the buildings came down. We lean toward this latter interpretation.

The available evidence could, therefore, be taken to support destruction of the royal residence and its surviving inhabitants—and the entire central precinct—after the dynastic collapse. This occupation did not last much past the destruction of the buildings. Current ceramic evidence does not indicate a long Terminal Classic, that is, "postmonumental" (Bey, Hanson, and Ringle 1997), occupation of other parts of the Copán area. A small and unrelated Early Postclassic settlement approximately 100 m south of Group 10L-2 is now known to have been in existence by about A.D. 950 or 1000 (see below). If we allow fifty years between the final disappearance of the Copán Maya and the arrival of this new group, the Terminal Classic postdynastic occupation must have ended before A.D. 900.

Until recently, the only ceramic evidence for later activity at the site consisted of a few Plumbate vessels and contemporary Early Postclassic types found in a few burials excavated near the Acropolis in the late nineteenth century, as well as a few sherds of the same types scattered around the Acropolis. Partly because these Early Postclassic imported fine wares were rare and were found only in ceremonial contexts, it has been argued (Webster 1999, 2002; Webster and Freter 1990b:81; Webster, Freter, and Gonlin 2000:204–205; Webster, Freter, and Rue 1993) that the domestic types in use at Copán in the Postclassic must have remained essentially similar to those of the Late Classic Coner assemblage. The contexts of these Coner-like domestic types beyond the Main Group, throughout the Copán Valley, are suggested by the same authors to date well into the twelfth century A.D. by obsidian-hydration dates. This means a duration of more than five hundred years for the Coner ceramic complex, the origins of which can now be traced back to A.D. 600. The reliability and interpretation of the Copán obsidian-hydration dates have been questioned (Anovitz et al.1999; Braswell 1992, 1997; Canuto 2002; W. Fash and Sharer 1991; Riciputi et al. 2002). We believe that the obsidian-hydration sequence is not supported by direct evidence from any other source.

Kam Manahan's excavations of a small Early Postclassic group of houses located about 100 m south of Group 10L-2 (Braswell and Manahan 2001; Manahan 2000, 2002a, 2002b, 2003) have produced for the Early Postclassic period (called the "Ejar phase" by Viel [1983, 1993b]) a well-defined ceramic assemblage that differs dramatically in content from the Late Classic Coner-phase assemblage. As now understood, the Early Postclassic Ejar assemblage includes the fine wares (for example, Plumbate and Las Vegas Polychrome) previously assigned to that phase (Viel 1993b) and long recognized as marking activity at the site during this period (Longyear 1952). In Manahan's excavations, these types were found directly associated in tombs and middens with domestic wares that appear to be technologically and stylistically unrelated to earlier Coner-phase types. Little about the Ejar-phase domestic wares suggests the kinds of gradual developments and changes in ceramic production that are seen, for example, between the closely related pottery types of the Early Classic Acbi and Late Classic Coner phases. Instead, these wares show an abrupt break with previous Copán ceramic traditions. They are much cruder and less technologically standardized, for example, than the earlier, well-made pottery of the Late Classic period.

The origin and identity of these Early Postclassic immigrants to Copán are unknown. They may have been part of a non-Maya population that surrounded Copán in Classic times and appears to have occupied the Copán Valley in the Preclassic. The Las Vegas Polychrome in their ceramic assemblage suggests ties to the east. Two intact pedestal censers found by Alfred Maudslay (1889–1902, vol. 1, plate 22, a and b) in Structure 10L-16 are identical to Terminal Classic incense burners used in termination rituals at Quelepa in eastern El Salvador (Andrews 1976, figure 129). If Manahan's Ejar settlers placed these vessels, the late arrivals may have been Lenca.

The complete Early Postclassic ceramic assemblage that has now been defined for Copán provides a means to evaluate the nature and extent of postdynastic occupation in the surrounding region. A test-pitting program by Manahan (1999) at various locations in the Copán pocket did not find other samples of these types of pottery. The Río Amarillo subregion, in contrast, saw a small rural population during the Ejar phase (Canuto 2002:217). Like the Ejar artifacts near the Acropolis, those of the Río Amarillo region are utterly different from those of the final Late Classic Coner inhabitants of Río Amarillo sites, showing no signs of relationship to them. Canuto's Ejar sites never overlie Coner sites—they are either in previously uninhabited places or at sites that had been unoccupied since the Protoclassic.

The destruction of the site center and some surrounding groups, whether it happened about A.D. 820 or slightly later, was followed by rapid population decline and abandonment of the Copán pocket. The small Early Postclassic occupation, which has been dated to about A.D. 950 or 975 to 1050 or 1075 (Canuto 2002:217; W. Fash, Andrews, and Manahan 2004; Manahan 2000, 2002a, 2000b), was characterized not only by a unique ceramic assemblage but also by a lithic industry, as well as platform construction, that differed entirely from that of the late Coner phase (Braswell and Manahan 2001). This suggests that a hiatus of anywhere from fifty to one hundred years may have separated a final, brief postdynastic phase of occupation at Copán and the resettlement of small areas afterward.

LESSONS FROM A ROYAL RESIDENTIAL COMPOUND

In this final section, we comment on the growth and changes that can be documented in Group 10L-2. We also return to the issues raised at the beginning of this chapter. These include the range of building types found in a royal residence, their functions, and the meaning of these differences in terms of status and wealth; continuity of architectural function contrasting with and accompanying nearly constant growth and renovation; increasing restriction of access as a means of reinforcing status and privilege; and the linkage of Group 10L-2 with a corporate descent group, in contrast to the more public role of the Acropolis.

Preceding sections of this chapter, relying on the chronological sequence derived from radiocarbon dates and from the ceramic stratigraphy (Bill 1997), have summarized architectural evidence that Group 10L-2 possessed high-status occupants in the Early Classic period but that until perhaps as late as A.D. 600, there is no certain evidence of an occupation by families related to Copán royalty. At about this time, vaulted tombs and crypts were constructed in Group 10L-2 to contain individuals with whom their families interred magnificent objects that could have belonged only to members of a royal line. Shortly afterward, Courtyards A and B were defined, and some of the first buildings around Courtyard A bore sculpture stating that the inhabitants were descendants of K'inich Yax K'uk' Mo', the founder of the Copán dynasty. These facades were also adorned with central Mexican year signs, which Maya royalty increasingly adopted during the Late Classic to proclaim their real or imagined Teotihuacan or highland Mexican heritage. The royal and noble families that moved into Group 10L-2 toward the beginning of the Late Classic may have moved from the northeast residential patio groups of the early Acropolis. The northward expansion of the Acropolis buried these groups by about A.D. 550 (Sharer et al., chapter 5 in this volume; Traxler 2001).

After this initial construction phase during Ruler 12's reign (A.D. 628–695), there seem to have been two major enlargements of buildings around both courtyards, culminating in Yax Pasaj's own buildings shortly after he came to the throne. In large part because Group 10L-2 does not have inscribed monuments predating Yax Pasaj's reign, we are unable to link specific constructions to individual rulers. Because we see no evidence that Rulers 12 through 15 came from or lived in this group, it is unlikely that these rulers commissioned new structures here. Yax Pasaj's accession in A.D. 763 presumably took place shortly after the death of the fifteenth ruler and after an unknown but longer interval following his own father's death. This individual, the head of Group 10L-2, was probably buried in the tomb in 10L-32-2nd that was looted in antiquity.

The buildings of Group 10L-2 attest to the increasing power and prestige of this compound's inhabitants during the Late Classic period, a process that culminated in a head of the compound acceding to the throne as the last king of Copán. Thus, we can follow an architectural group as its leader changed from being the head of an important part of a Maya city to being the ruler of the entire city and as Group 10L-2 became, maybe for the first time, the residence of a king.

Yax Pasaj's new constructions in Group 10L-2, as on the Acropolis, appear to have been finished during his first decade in office. The last forty-five or so years before his death saw no significant new architecture and few carved monuments here. This leads us to wonder whether he was able to draw on fewer resources as time passed or whether the flurry of construction after his inauguration followed a time-honored pattern for Maya rulers. He died shortly before A.D. 820, probably in his seventies, and was buried in the tomb he had built years before. The dynasty ended, for reasons discussed in the concluding chapter to this volume. The continued accumulation of trash around the important buildings of Courtyard A reflected the failing infrastructure of Copán. Some families continued to live around Courtyards A and B after the political collapse, but this occupation ended soon with the burning and destruction of buildings at the site's center.

Our excavations of all the structures around Courtyards A and B and the investigation of earlier constructions inside them, to the extent that it was feasible to do so without destroying the final buildings, allow us to describe patterns of activity, growth, and change in this royal residential group. These general observations are discussed in the preceding pages.

Although the addition of new structures and the renovation of existing buildings ensured a constantly changing residential landscape, tradition weighed heavily on each generation of architects. Some buildings that appear to have had important functions for the corporate group, such as Structure 10L-31 and the original 10L-33, on Courtyard A, remained unaltered from their construction near the beginning of the Late Classic period until the abandonment of the site. Other structures—such as 10L-32, the house of the head of the group, and the long, multiroom 10L-41 on Courtyard B—were renovated twice. Each time, the form of the buildings remained similar, implying the maintenance of the same functions from one rebuilding to the next.

The growth of Group 10L-2 over two centuries increasingly restricted access to the courtyards and the buildings facing onto them. At the beginning of the Late Classic, both courtyards were open, with no physical restriction of access. By A.D. 800, new structures or expansions of existing buildings filled in the space between buildings, greatly limiting access. Courtyard A could be entered only by a narrow stair leading down from Temple 18, Yax Pasaj's tomb at the southwest corner of the Acropolis, or by a passage along the east side of 10L-32 that then turned behind 10L-32 and led to the only entrance to Courtyard B, an L-shaped passage at its northeast corner. This privacy was intentional and desired. To achieve this, the builders closed off a few possible entrances where no buildings existed. The restriction of access accompanied the residential complex's increasing wealth and size, a process that has been documented at other Classic Maya royal architectural groups, including Tikal and Uaxactún.

The three areas of Group 10L-2 that we investigated were home to different activities. Courtyard A, with the largest structures, was largely nonresidential. Most structures were for religious, ceremonial, and administrative activities. We think that even the house of Yax Pasaj, identified as his by an altar that rested on its throne, was not where he slept or where his immediate family resided. Courtyard B, in contrast, includes many buildings with room, doorway, and bench arrangements typical of Copán residences. One of these, 10L-41A, was possibly Yax Pasaj's personal residence. Even in this courtyard, however, the largest structure, 10L-41, was designed for group ritual and administrative purposes, as well as perhaps special residential functions. A small temple dominated the north end of the courtyard. El Cementerio, west of Courtyard A, with rich tombs, was the seat of the first Classic noble residence south of the Acropolis about A.D. 600. Later, it appears to have become a work area, filling in with trash. Any late houses or shelters in this area were perishable and left no trace. These three areas are distinguished most readily by their architecture. This conclusion is also supported by differing frequencies of ceramic vessel forms, obsidian blade use-wear patterns, and animal bones and other trash in Courtyards A and B and El Cementerio.

If the great Late Classic buildings on the Acropolis were the focus of public activities, the places where the Copán realm was administered and where ceremonies took place that were attended by and benefited the largest number of citizens, then Group 10L-2 should be understood as the place of secular and sacred activities that were more limited in their impact and number of participants, more the private concern of the corporate descent group that had lived there since the end of the Early Classic. If each Copán ruler maintained a royal residence on the Acropolis, as Sharer and others have argued (Sharer et al., chapter 5 in this volume; Sharer, Fash, et al. 1999; Traxler 2001), some, including Yax Pasaj, whose Acropolis residence was surely Structure 10L-11, also had residences in nearby compounds.

Courtyards A and B in Group 10L-2 were surrounded by the residences of many of the most powerful members of this group. Although very close to one another, these were of widely differing size and quality of construction. The differences suggest that this noble residence, like comparable residential complexes several hundred meters to the northeast in Las Sepulturas, included individuals of varying status and wealth (Sanders 1992; Webster 1989a). Most inhabitants of these courtyards probably were related, but some of the smallest and least costly structures may have housed unrelated clients or retainers. Much of the labor for the daily support of Yax Pasaj's residential complex, however, must have come from areas of less impressive domestic housing surrounding the formal courtyards.

The richness of the data from Group 10L-2 results from the integration of careful studies of fallen sculpture and architecture, deep stratigraphic excavations of buildings and platforms, complete recovery of many middens and burials of different kinds, detailed analysis of ceramics and artifacts, and continuing studies of hieroglyphic inscriptions that link buildings, events, deities, and one ruler in this residential compound. The written record in Group 10L-2 describes events and supernatural patrons not mentioned elsewhere in the hieroglyphic record at Copán, thereby giving us an idea of what was considered appropriate to record in the more private confines of Yax Pasaj's residential court. The absence of any one of these lines of evidence would have left the archaeological record far less complete—together, they allow us to create an image of an elite neighborhood developing, through historical events we will never fully know, into one part of a complex Maya royal court. The archaeology of Yax Pasaj's residential compound shows how, in several ways, a powerful elite group at a Maya site manifested its growing status and influence until, finally, its head acceded to the throne of the realm about half a century before the site collapsed.

Many related problems remain to be studied. The limitation of our investigations in Group 10L-2 to two courtyards and their immediate surroundings means that we were unable to address the question of how extensive an area Yax Pasaj controlled as head of his corporate group. It is possible that much of the El Bosque zone to the south and west was part of the "fish" group. Even with extensive excavations in this broad area, however, it would be difficult to resolve the identity of its occupants and their relations to the inhabitants of Group 10L-2.

Another issue that Maya archaeologists have not been able to address directly is the relationship between noble groups and the agricultural land they owned or over which they held certain rights (see Webster, chapter 2 in this volume). Our investigations have not illuminated the matter.

Through much of the Late Classic, Group 10L-2 was not the home of those who ruled. Another goal of future archaeologists at Copán should be the identification of the architectural groups of other noble families whose head became ruler. One complex to investigate is Group 10L-18, including more than fifty structures about 200 m west of the Plaza of the Hieroglyphic Stairway. The ways in which this and other nearby groups differ from and resemble Yax Pasaj's neighborhood will tell us much about the fortunes of noble families at Copán.

Notes

The excavations in Group 10L-2 by the Middle American Research Institute of Tulane University were directed by E. Wyllys Andrews and were carried out from 1990 through 1994 as part of the Copán Acropolis Archaeological Project (PAAC), directed by William L. Fash. Support for the Tulane excavations and subsequent consolidation of the buildings, analysis, and writing has been provided by the Instituto Hondureño de Antropología e Historia, with funds from the United States Agency for International Development, the Middle American Research Institute and Tulane University, the National Geographic Society (1993 and 1994), a National Science Foundation Fellowship to Cassandra R. Bill, a Fulbright Fellowship to Harold E. Starratt, and a Dumbarton Oaks Summer Fellowship to William F. Doonan.

The Copán project has been a cooperative effort of many individuals. We are grateful for years of friendship with our many colleagues in the field and for their support. Among them are Bill Fash, director of the PAAC; Barbara Fash, sculpture coordinator of the PAAC, in charge of the analysis of Group 10L-2 architectural sculpture; Bob Sharer and Ricardo Agurcia Fasquelle, co-directors of the PAAC; the late Linda Schele, Dave Stuart, and Nikolai Grube, the Copán project epigraphers; Carlos Rudy Larios, who directed all architectural consolidation for PAAC; Fernando López, who supervised the mapping of Group 10L-2 and some excavations after we left; Oscar Cruz, regional chief of the IHAH in Copán Ruinas, unfailingly helpful in professional and personal matters; Bill Sanders and Dave Webster, directors of the previous archaeological project (PAC II) at Copán and at Group 8N-11 in 1990; our friend Juan Ramón (Moncho) Guerra, PAAC foreman; and all the highly skilled and meticulous excavators from Copán Ruinas, many of whom had amassed almost twenty years of archaeological experience by 1995. At Tulane, Kathe Lawton and Jim Aimers turned our field maps and building plans into AutoCAD and MicroStation maps. Graduate students from Tulane University and other institutions served as field supervisors, and their field reports are filed at Tulane and at the IHAH Centro in Copán.

1. Andrews and B. Fash (1992) published a summary of the results of the 1990 and 1991 seasons in Group 10L-2. This report included the buildings around Courtyard A and Structure 10L-29. Some of our interpretations, based on readings of epigraphers, have changed since then, but the earlier article presents information and illustrations of the buildings around Courtyard A that are not repeated in detail here. The excavations in Courtyard B and in El Cementerio are reported comprehensively here for the first time.

2. The historical inscriptions of Group 10L-2 have been the subject of differing interpretations (MacLeod 1989; Schele 1988, 1990a, 1990c, 1993, 1995). The difficulty with the three most important monuments discussed in this chapter has stemmed mostly from uncertainty about what U Yak' Chak was—a person, a deity, or a ceramic effigy of the god Chak. An article written after the 1990 and 1991 excavations in Group 10L-2 (Andrews and Fash 1992) reflected the consensus of

project epigraphers then that U Yak' Chak, or Yak'u Chac, was a person—a close associate and possibly a relative or brother of Yax Pasaj.

The comments in this chapter follow an interpretation by David Stuart at the 1994 School of American Research advanced seminar on Copán, which Linda Schele (1995) summarized and expanded. U Yak' Chak is now thought to have been a ceramic statue of the god Chak, which was a gift of Chak and a divine companion to Yax Pasaj. Both Schele (1988) and Barbara MacLeod (1989) raised this possibility in their first considerations of Altar F'. Stuart's 1994 reading provided confirmation that Yax Pasaj Chan Yopat, not an individual named Chak, was the occupant of Structure 10L-32 and Group 10L-2.

3. (The following note on the human skeletal remains was written by Jennifer C. Piehl, who is preparing the report on human skeletal remains from Group 10L-2.)

Although the study of the Harvard and Carnegie materials was rudimentary, analysis of the human remains recovered by Tulane in 1990–1994 provides us with information on mortality and paleopathology from a sample of fifty-two individuals interred in Group 10L-2. The total number of burials found in this group by all projects was ninety-eight, seventy-six of which have been aged either in the field or in the laboratory. Thirty-nine of these individuals died as adults, and thirty-seven died younger. Of the twenty-nine subadults whose age has been estimated in the laboratory, twenty-five (86 percent) died by age five. The 49 percent of our sample who died before reaching adulthood is remarkably close to Storey's (1992:164, 1997:119) 46 percent subadult figure from a sample of 264 skeletons from Group 9N-8 in Las Sepulturas. The high mortality rate in Group 10L-2 corresponds to that in Group 9N-8. The incidences of infection and iron deficiency anemia are high in this sample, as in Group 9N-8, indicating similar stresses of poor nutrition and disease. One potential difference between the two groups lies in the frequencies of slight and systemic infections. Group 10L-2 adults have a higher incidence of systemic infections than slight infections, the reverse of what is found in Group 9N-8. This, combined with correspondingly lower rates of linear enamel hypoplasia, may mean that the Group 10L-2 population may have had a slightly better ability to buffer itself against nutritional, parasitic, and disease stresses, possibly because of its higher elite status (Piehl 2001). Regardless of this possible buffering ability, the population of Group 10L-2, like all populations at Copán, clearly relied heavily on maize as a dietary staple. This situation, combined with the stresses of parasitism and infectious disease, created an environment in which health status was low even among the elite ranks.

4. We dated eleven radiocarbon samples from Courtyard A (nine of which

were reported in Andrews and Fash 1992), seven from Courtyard B, and four from El Cementerio. The two dates reported here are from sheet middens that accumulated during the final occupation of Courtyard A. One Late Coner sample came from a 3-cm midden on the plaster floor 50–100 cm from the base of the south platform face of Yax Pasaj's house, 10L-32, immediately below collapsed platform and building masonry. The charcoal was mixed with burned red earth, indicating a fire on the floor at the base of 10L-32 just before the building fell (Beta-40306, 1180 ± 50 BP, cal A.D. 810 [870] 930, 1-sigma). The second Late Coner sample is from a 5–10-cm-deep midden on the plaster floor in front of 10L-233, extending between the rear platform faces of 10L-33 and 10L-34, whose collapsed masonry buried it (Beta-64091, 1160 ± 80 BP, cal A.D. 810 [910] 970, 1-sigma). Two other radiocarbon samples from similar sealed contexts behind Structure 10L-32 produced much earlier dates (Beta-40305, 1470 ± 100 BP, cal A.D. 500 [600] 650 and Beta-40307, 1370 ± 80 BP, cal A.D. 620 [650] 720, both 1-sigma).

8

Health and Lifestyle (before and after Death) among the Copán Elite

Rebecca Storey

Rulership is the central political and religious institution of the Classic Maya. The personal characteristics and lifestyle of a ruler and his immediate family should therefore help us to understand how this institution was integrated into Maya daily life. That is, how did the life led by the very top of the social hierarchy differ from that of other segments of the society? The iconographic evidence left by the Maya documents much pomp and circumstance surrounding the rulers and some of their immediate family, at least on certain occasions (Inomata and Houston 2001; Schele and Freidel 1990). Did this translate into a privileged lifestyle with comforts not available to other members of the society and a daily experience distinct from that of other individuals of noble status? If so, how many people led this special lifestyle? These questions go to the heart of what kind of hierarchical society Classic-period Copán was. How stratified was it?

Social organization, in this case, is a window into the extent of potential political and economic power available to the rulers and into the nature of interaction among various components of the society. If rulership was an institution defining a ritual, political, and economic separateness from all other segments of the society, then finding some indication of this privileged lifestyle in the physical remains of rulers and their immediate family should be possible. This chapter explores evidence for the similarities and discontinuities between the highest stratum and other elite individuals in Early and Late Classic Copán society.

Certainly, since the Middle Preclassic, mortuary patterns have indicated probable status levels in Copán society (W. Fash 2001:67–71), with some individuals entitled to rich offerings of jade and fine ceramics. Exactly when the society differentiated into nobles and commoners, however, is unclear. In A.D. 426 a charismatic individual founded a long-lived dynasty, and his family had enough power and prestige to erect stelae and sponsor construction in the Acropolis (W. Fash 2001:81, chapters 1 and 3 in this volume). Inscriptions document fifteen successors to this first ruler into the ninth century, after which evidence of rulership in the form of monumental construction and sculpture disappeared. Despite the decline of central authority, noble houses—such as the 9N-8 compound, the House of the Bacabs (Webster, ed., 1989)—maintained prominence in the society for more than a century, until final abandonment of the area.

During the time of rulership, the iconographic images seem to separate the ruler and his family from the rest of society, but the extent of the social gulf between rulers and their noble courtiers is unclear.

EVIDENCE FROM BURIAL RITUAL

This chapter examines both treatment at death and skeletal evidence of health and habitual activity to investigate possible differences in rank and privilege between rulers and nobles. Mortuary treatments indicate the degree of corporate involvement in funerary rites, the resources available to the living to lavish upon their dead, and the status of the deceased, as well as of the mourners (Binford 1971; Brown 1995). By documenting the qualitative differences in graves, the age and sex pattern of the richest ones, and the varying degrees of energy invested on graves, mortuary analysis reveals the complexities of social positions in past societies (Binford 1971). Richer graves for infants, children, and young adults than for many older adults may indicate that certain aspects of status were likely ascribed. If only older individuals merited rich graves, then status probably had to be achieved.

Greater energy expended on the grave, protracted ritual surrounding the death, special treatment of the corpse, and the quantity and quality of offerings demonstrate a higher social position held in life and commemorated in death, as well as the higher rank of those involved in the mortuary rituals for the deceased.

Skeletal evidence provides clues through comparison of episodes of stress, quality of nutrition, and indicators of lifestyle recorded in the bone. If rulers lived with fewer stresses and enjoyed an easier lifestyle than nobles, then this would support a model of a ruling dynasty with a particularly buffered existence. If not, then the ruling dynasty was just an elite group with special functions and was otherwise very much like other noble families in its daily routine.

The Acropolis Skeletal Sample

The overall Copán skeletal sample is large but has several biases. It is made up of individuals from the Late Classic, with a few from earlier periods, and is mostly from elite Type 4 compounds in or near the urban core. These residences contain individuals holding elite or noble status within the Copán polity, as well as retainers and lesser relatives who would have benefited from living in an elite compound. Few skeletons represent either rural and urban commoners or, conversely, the top of the society from the Acropolis/Principal Group.

The Acropolis sample is small but has the advantage of including both Early and Late Classic interments, so some chronological comparisons can be made. Twenty-seven burials have been recovered from the Acropolis/Principal Group by the PAAC and PAC Phase I projects. Several burials from the ECAP, as well as some from the PAC Phase I project, are not included here (see W. Fash and Agurcia Fasquelle, chapter 1 in this volume, for a discussion of these projects). This chapter discusses a total of seventeen individuals. This number—too small and, as will be seen, too biased to be treated as a real biological population—includes a few individuals from the 10L-2 compound just to the south of the Acropolis.

The 10L-2 compound has been identified as the personal domestic residence of the ruler and his family during part of the Late Classic (Andrews and Bill, chapter 7 in this volume) and therefore belongs to the apex as well. The 10L-2 sample is more representative in age and sex than the Acropolis sample but also contains individuals who probably were not members of the ruler's immediate family (the people of interest here), judging by variations in living conditions and mortuary treatment. The individuals with the most elaborate tombs in the main buildings should represent the highest strata; four are included in the sample of seventeen. The information from this small sample concerns the personal characteristics of individuals who merited interment in these locations. The biological and mortuary indicators of this sample are compared with those of the larger sample of 244 individuals from the 9N-8 compound. This compound, the House of the Bacabs, is one of the elite compounds in the urban core and can provide a base for comparisons of both mortuary treatment and biological indicators of stress typical of elite individuals and privileged nonelite individuals during the Late Classic.

The seventeen individuals exhibit two mortuary treatments. Eleven, the honored dead, are the obvious focus of burial ritual and include three of the elaborate tombs inside the Acropolis and other interments from the Acropolis and Group 10L-2. The others likely represent sacrificed individuals. The latter include the three crania with Burial XXXVII-8, two individuals (Burial XXXVII-3) in the royal tomb inside 10L-26, and Burial XXXVII-6. These individuals may or may not be from the Copán polity, but they could be elites. High-ranking captives that could be sacrificed were an important trophy of Maya warfare (Schele and Freidel 1990). Their personal characteristics are also of interest.

The Honored Dead

The skeletons of probable rulers are Burial XXXVII-4 and Burial I-5 of the Sub-Jaguar Tomb. Close family members or high-ranking officeholders interred inside the Acropolis include Burials XXXVII-1, XXXVII-2, XXXVII-5, and V-4. (The prefixes refer to the excavation operations that recovered these individuals: Operation XXXVII, the investigation under Structure 10L-26, the Hieroglyphic Stairway; Operation V, excavations in the Principal Plaza; and Operation I, excavations in the main Acropolis.) All are adults, mature individuals over thirty-five years of age at death, and probably males.

Three individuals are Early Classic in date, from the first few generations after the founding of the Copán dynasty. Burial XXXVII-1 was an extended interment placed in a stone cist in an important location, "directly beneath the large plaster sculpture on the east side of a large platform located due east of Papagayo structure, and pre-dating the latter by one construction phase" (W. Fash 2001:94). These earlier structures are now buried deep under Structure 10L-26, but this was long an important location in the Copán Acropolis (Sharer et al., chapter 5 in this volume). This individual was accompanied by a nice set of offerings, including three ceramic vessels, four pieces of shell, and two large pieces of jade, as well as two obsidian blades and two bone needles (W. Fash 2001:94). The individual was in his early fifties at death, although his teeth are not very worn. The lack of arthritis and of marked muscle crests seems to indicate a life without great physical exertion. The individual has no evidence of any cranial or tooth modifications, common among Late Classic elites. These practices appear to be rarer during the Early Classic, although both individuals in Hunal and Margarita tombs (Sharer et al., chapter 5 in this volume) have cranial modification (Buikstra, personal communication 1994). This individual is accompanied by a vessel that names Ruler 1, probably indicating a close connection with the royal family.

Burial XXXVII-2 was an extended interment, also in a stone cist, next to Burial XXXVII-1. This individual is accompanied by one ceramic vessel but has one carved jade bead identifying him as a lord (W. Fash 2001:95). He was older, around sixty years of age at death. Although the arthritic changes present are not much for an individual of his age, the bones are probably the most robust of any in the Copán skeletal sample and show definite development of the muscle crests. This individual was active as an adult. There is no evidence of tooth modification. The cranium is mostly missing, so modification there cannot be judged.

Notably, both these individuals show evidence of revisitation and treatment of the body after death. Although the cists and offerings are of the type found in other elite burials at Copán, their location in the Acropolis is obviously a special one. The body of XXXVII-1 was covered with red ochre and appears to have been painted several times after it was skeletonized. Individual XXXVII-2 was also painted with red ochre (but less so than XXXVII-1), again, when skeletonized. In fact, this individual was probably painted only once, compared with the layers that were applied to XXXVII-1, especially his skull. The bodies were extended and in anatomical position, so painting involved picking up individual bones, covering them with ochre, and replacing them. Both these bodies have some parts of the skeleton missing. It could be just the vagaries of preservation, but both are missing the left arm and the hands. Burial XXXVII-1 is missing the right forearm as well, and Burial XXXVII-2, the feet and most of the skull. Possibly, some bones were removed for a purpose, but these skeletons could also have been elsewhere and deposited in their cists only when skeletonized and painted. The missing bones were just attrition that often happens in processing and moving bodies. Putting remains in anatomical position would not be difficult for people accustomed to dealing with skeletons and skeletal elements.

These burials do suggest that among the highest levels of Maya society, the period between death and final interment might have been protracted. The burial cists of these individuals would have been accessible behind the platform until deeply buried by the construction of the Mascarones terraced pyramid. Thus, the cists might be the original burial place, where the skeletons were tended until their final interment. This would account for the careful anatomical position. On the other hand, the location of Burial XXXVII-1 directly below a plaster decoration on the platform might indicate that the cists were constructed just before final interment and the bodies were moved from another location. Both scenarios are possible. Such protracted burial ritual was not uncommon cross-culturally, nor was the practice of depositing skeletons in a temporary place or grave and then moving skeletonized elements to a final resting place, accompanied, of course, by mortuary ritual. As Hertz (1960) notes, this treatment underscores the importance of the individuals being buried or the occasion of their interment.

Burial V-4 was buried just east of the first ball court and near the early buildings now under Structure 10L-26. The tomb is square, with stone walls and floor, and probably had a wooden roof. Notable about this burial are the offerings and seated burial position, which are similar to Esperanza Phase burials at Kaminaljuyu. This individual might have been from that center and allied to the Copán rulers in a way that merited this interment. The offerings are very rich, including nine ceramic vessels, a shell necklace, jade earspools, a shell headdress, and

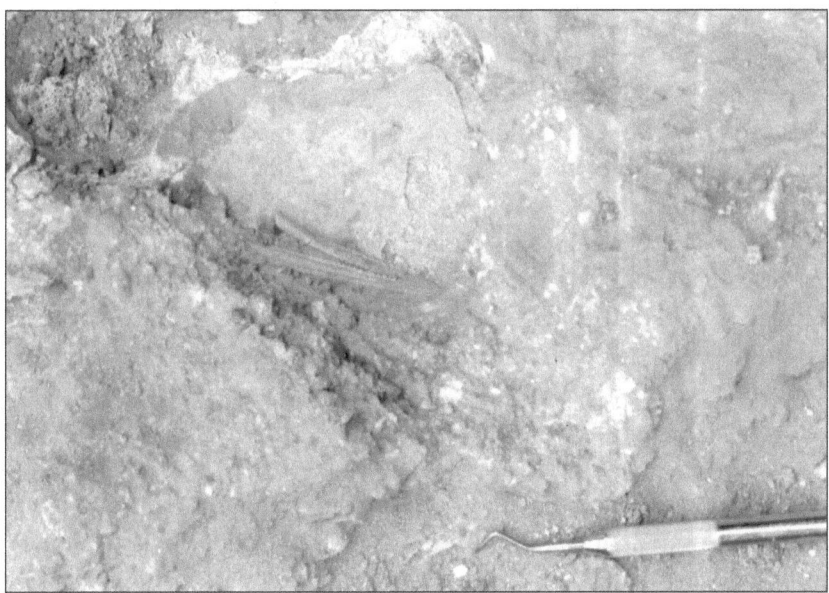

FIGURE 8.1
Stingray spines resting on the ilium of Burial XXXVII-5.

shell bracelets, pendents, and disks (Viel and Cheek 1983). There are also jade beads and a pyrite mirror. This male, about thirty-five to forty-five years old at death, has definite cranial deformation but no tooth modification. He, also, was a gracile person without very developed muscle markings. The skeleton does not appear to have been disturbed after placement, nor is there any evidence that it was painted with ochre when skeletonized. The lack of revisitation or further treatment of the corpse is in contrast to others buried in the Acropolis area and may indicate that this was a foreigner, because burial did not involve protracted ritual.

From a later time during the transition from Early to Late Classic, Burial XXXVII-5 is another individual who probably represents a member of the royal family, buried in the residential structures forming part of the Northeast Group (Sharer et al., chapter 5 in this volume). These structures are believed to have been the royal palace at the time of this individual's interment. This is a male, about forty-five, with two jade pieces on his person (one in the mouth) and a bag of stingray spines in the pelvic area (figure 8.1). This individual has very pronounced, developed crests on the arms, especially the right arm. A distinctive bone spur, which could also be from use, is on the right hip socket. The cause of these changes has not yet been determined, but the crests on the forearms associated with heavy lifting are not the ones developed here. The leg crests are developed but do not show the exaggerated changes of the arms.

Burial XXXVII-5 had no evidence of cranial deformation, but two grooves incised in upper central incisors indicate that his teeth had been modified artificially. After being skeletonized, the body had been covered with red ochre, seemingly several times, on the superior surfaces that would have been exposed. The body was not moved after interment, and all parts of the skeleton are present. Burial treatment was similar to that of Burials XXXVII-1 and XXXVII-2.

Group 10L-2, located at the south end of the Acropolis, includes the royal residential complex or family compound of the last rulers of Copán during the Late Classic. The group also includes far more than that (Andrews and Bill, chapter 7 in this volume). Four individuals in tombs, representing the highest status, have been analyzed and compared with the Acropolis sample. In Group 10L-2 appear to be one female and three males: one male was over fifty at death, and the others were between thirty and forty-five. Two interesting similarities to the burials in the Acropolis are present in Group 10L-2. One probable male, Burial 48-13-8, has great calculus build-up on lower anterior teeth, like the individual in the Sub-Jaguar Tomb (discussed below). Burial 48-11-3, a probable male, appears to have been painted with ochre only on the exposed bones when skeletonized, like XXXVII-5. This individual has modified teeth, but not enough cranium was preserved to check for modification. He is the only one out of the four with clear evidence of muscle markings. Burial 48-11-2 also has dental modification. Burial 48-15-1 has cradleboard flattening only on the cranium, but no teeth available to score for modification.

The Skeletons of Probable Rulers

Of the probable rulers in elaborate, dressed-stone tombs, Sub-Jaguar Tomb (I-5) is Early Classic in date and Burial XXXVII-4 is Late Classic. Elaborate grave offerings and evidence of complicated, protracted ritual accompany both. As would be expected for individuals at the very pinnacle of a society, these interments involved far more wealth and ritual, with the succeeding ruler probably presiding over rites, than any other burial described here and any presently known outside the Acropolis.

The individual in the Sub-Jaguar Tomb is fragmentary, but much of the skeleton is at least represented (see Sharer et al., chapter 5 in this volume, for a description of the tomb and its contents). This individual is male, based on cranial morphology, and was most likely in his sixties at death, based on arthritic changes in the thorax and evidence of vertebral arthritis and disk degeneration, although the teeth are not very worn. He also has tremendous dental calculus or tartar build-up on the lingual side of his anterior teeth, an indication of poor oral hygiene and diet. Interestingly, one type of diet that has been linked to calculus build-up is a protein-rich one (Hillson 1979), which might indicate the special lifestyle enjoyed by the individual in the last years of his life. This individual does have some ridge development on the phalanges of the hands, indicative of habitual gripping during life, but less than Burial XXXVII-4. There are definite muscle markings and very developed crests on the forearms, indicating an active lifestyle and habitual use. The arthritis of the shoulder and spine, as well as arm development, probably indicate that this individual was doing something with his upper torso, perhaps related to weapons or the ball game.

The skeleton did, however, receive distinctive treatment after death. As this is now believed to be Ruler 8 (Sharer et al., chapter 5 in this volume), the elaborate treatment is not surprising. The body was covered in several layers of ochre when skeletonized. It was not cremated, because none of the bone is calcined, but there appears to be scorching on some bones, including the skull, and the left ulna has the warping and cracks seen in bone exposed to fire while it still has flesh. It may have been by a fire during funeral rituals, for example. Obviously, the burial was an extended interment, but there are hints that parts may have been removed and returned. Some of the skeleton's right side seems to have fallen on the floor around the slab it was lying on and perhaps into vessels placed there. A piece of the distal right femur was by the right humerus, which should not happen with an extended burial. One of the tarsals of the feet was in a vessel containing pieces of the right hand. One vessel held the right radius, right ulna, and right humerus head. The rest of the right humerus was on the floor, which should not happen if the arm just fell off the slab. It is almost as if parts of the right side were moved; some pieces may have been deliberately stored in the vessels. More strangely, the right radius has an area of the crest that is definitely polished, as if the bone was rubbed. Even though the body is essentially in its articulated position, it is possible that parts were removed periodically and returned. Evidence of water damage exists in the tomb and on the bones, so natural processes might have caused all the "movements" and polishing. The bones are, nevertheless, thoroughly covered with ochre, which means that they were picked up and painted once or several times. Only some time after death was the skeleton no longer revisited and the tomb finally closed.

Burial XXXVII-4 was in a large stone tomb within an earlier structure inside Structure 10L-26. The size of the tomb and the accompanying burial offerings are spectacular, but not surprisingly, for this has been identified as the tomb of Ruler 12 (W. Fash 2001:106–113). There were 113 ceramic vessels, a jade necklace and earspools, and twelve effigy censers. The body was lying on reed mats and jaguar pelts. The tomb contained numerous marine shells and microscopic fragments of sea fans and other marine species (W. Fash 2001:112). Two other individuals (discussed below) accompanied Ruler 12.

The skeleton of Ruler 12 is difficult to age because poor skeletal preservation has left us only a thin shell of bone and two teeth. The unusual decay resulted from the body's being encased in a cocoon of unfired clay (W. Fash 2001:112). On the basis of tooth wear and the lack of arthritic involvement on the articular surfaces of the distal humerus and right patella, the individual appears to have been youthful at death (figure 8.2), in his early forties to early sixties. This ruler was one of the more important of the Copán polity and had a very long reign of sixty-seven years, according to dates on monuments (W. Fash 2001:101–113, chapter 3 in this volume). This suggests that the individual was elderly—a "four katun" lord, or about eighty years of age at death—but because of the fragmentary preservation, age at death does not provide one of the better means of identifying him.

Because the skeleton appears to be younger than his dates imply, literalness about these dates may not be warranted. Anthropologists

HEALTH AND LIFESTYLE

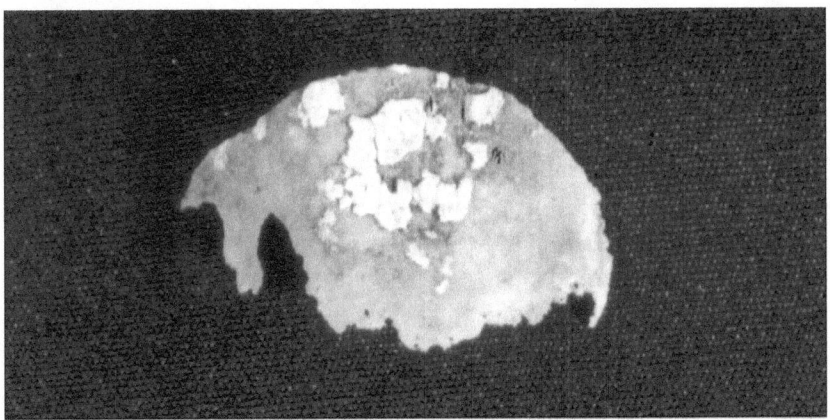

FIGURE 8.2
Patellar surface of Burial XXXVII-4. Although bits of the shroud adhere to the surface, this kneecap illustrates the generally poor preservation of skeletal elements. The smooth articular surface shows no arthritic involvement.

have repeatedly demonstrated that for many societies, age in relative terms was more important than chronological age. It is possible that "four katun" could mean nothing more than living into the fourth katun, past sixty years, much as people today in their third decade can be only twenty-one years old. Alternatively, this could be a general honorific given to individuals perceived as long-lived or in the relative position of elder in their society, loosely correlated with chronological age. It is also possible that all such life-event dates commemorated the ritual involved, which would have a variable relation with actual chronological age. Ritual death and burial may be the final markers, when succession passed to the next individual (see Hertz 1960 for ethnographic examples), not the day of physical death. A delay may have occurred if special treatment and burial of a corpse was involved. Tomb-building programs and auspicious ritual dates may have affected when the final interment occured. The evidence of postmortem treatment of corpses, especially the royal ones, as well as the fact that these tombs were built with access for probable postmortem rituals, argues for a prolonged mortuary ritual. In this case, stairs into the tomb chamber were not sealed until the end. The effigy censors were fired and smashed at some point, and the last one was not placed and fired until the final capstone of the tomb chamber had been placed (W. Fash 2001:112). After death, there may have been several years before final interment. The successor was in place but perhaps not yet in control until the preceding ruler had completed a passage from bodily death, to revered skeleton, to final interment, paralleling the journey from life through the Underworld to Revered Ancestor. All this is speculative, and the skeleton may be an individual near eighty years of age. An individual perhaps sixty to sixty-five would be expected if Ruler 12 ascended as a small child, received an honorific age, and several years elapsed before his tomb and final ceremony were completed.

The presence of muscle markings on pieces of long bones and the robustness of the ulna fragment point to a male. Interestingly, the few articular surfaces present on the legs, arms, and feet present no arthritic changes, but there are some moderate ones of the hands. The wrist and phalanges of both hands have changes on the third to fifth digits, not the thumb or second digit. Changes such as marked ridges along the edges of the phalanges should be due to use and may result from gripping. In ancient Egypt, such changes were found on the right hand of an individual identified as a scribe (Kennedy, Plummer, and Chiment 1986). This individual had both hands involved, although larger size indicates that the individual was right-handed. The gripping was probably a habitual activity, maybe the result of scribal activity. For Ruler 12, then, both war-related and writing gripping may have been part of his daily routine. The presence of many paint pots and the image of a scribe on one ceramic vessel (W. Fash 2001:111) do indicate that this ruler valued scribes. The body was probably painted with red ochre when skeletonized and was wrapped in some type of cloth. The interment does not appear to have been disturbed much after placement, but preservation is such that it is impossible to tell whether any skeletal elements were removed or replaced incorrectly. There is no evidence of the skull or mandible, for example, but the two teeth and jade earspools seem to indicate that these elements were present originally.

PROBABLE SACRIFICED INDIVIDUALS

Of the probable sacrificed individuals from Operation XXXVII, two apparently accompanied a ruler, and four were probably sacrificed

HEALTH AND LIFESTYLE

in connection with some other ritual. Burial XXXVII-3 was in the Late Classic tomb of XXXVII-4. This individual was probably around twelve years old at death, according to tooth eruption standards. Judging by pelvic criteria and the lack of epiphyseal fusion (which would normally have started in a female), this is probably a male, but children are less accurately sexed on skeletal criteria alone than adults. The thickness of the bone cortex on the femur is distinctive and probably indicates that the individual had good nutrition for the last few years of his life. There is no evidence of cranial deformation or tooth modification. The body was not painted in red ochre, had no obvious offerings, and was placed on the floor at the head of the slab containing the main interment. In the summer of 2001, more of this tomb was excavated, and another skeleton about the same age was found nearby. Although not yet studied in any depth, it is interesting how similar the two individuals are. Differences in the morphology of teeth indicate that these are probably not identical twins, but fraternal twins may be possible. These individuals were either retainers or captives sent off with the royal lord, but it is not possible to be sure which. Placing other individuals within a royal tomb was apparently common among the Late Classic Maya, but others this young are not mentioned. Ritual and appropriate human sacrifice in Pre-Columbian Mesoamerica called for the sacrifice of individuals of all ages and both sexes, so finding children/boys in this situation is not surprising.

Burial XXXVII-6 is a headless skeleton interred—without lavishing any particular care on the grave, except for the placement of the body—inside an earlier building under Structure 10L-26. This is a robust male who was in his early forties at time of death. He was placed on his back in a flexed position, but there is absolutely no sign of the cranium. The burial position is consistent with both his wrists and ankles being tied, but they could also just be crossed (no rope would remain preserved). There is no evidence of any cutmarks or painting with red ochre, at least after it was skeletonized. The individual has strong muscle markings on the long bones. The interment was not disturbed after placement.

Burials XXXVII-7, XXXVII-9, and XXXVII-10 are three crania associated with the tomb of XXXVII-8, the Motmot individual discussed below. Two of these had been decapitated only shortly before their placement; they still have some cervical vertebrae present (although with absolutely no cutmarks, unfortunately). The XXXVII-7 did not and may have been a curated skull. All three were thoroughly smoked, like the main interment, but otherwise had no special treatment except for their placement. Burial XXXVII-10 was inside the tomb, and the other two were on top of the tomb. The two with vertebrae may, in fact, have been sacrificed only when the tomb was about to be sealed, probably some time after the death of Burial XXXVII-8.

Burial XXXVII-7 is a male who was in his forties at death. He had two active abscesses in the mandible and several caries. Most interestingly, this individual has a traumatic depression and three probable cutting wounds on the cranium. All were healed, so they happened some time before death. This individual could very well have been a warrior, possibly elite in rank. Because there are no vertebrae, this could very well have been a curated trophy skull for some time before its placement.

Burial XXXVII-9 is a male who was in his early fifties at death, definitely not young or even in his prime, but robust. The teeth also had one carie and four abscesses on both the maxilla and mandible. This individual also has a lot of calculus on the back of the anterior teeth, which could indicate a good diet. There is no evidence of any trauma on this cranium.

The male of Burial XXXVII-10 is the oldest of the three crania, probably more than sixty years old at time of death. There were caries and several active abscesses on the maxilla and mandible (figure 8.3). There is no evidence of any trauma, but the individual did have serious arthritis on the vertebrae. This is partly the result of age but may also indicate use of the neck and head for some weight-bearing activity. As with the other crania, it is possible, but not provable, that this is from an elite individual. None of the three had any cranial or dental modification. The ages of these crania are interesting, though, in that all are older individuals. Perhaps risk of being captured and sacrificed in war increased with age among the Maya elite!

A Most Unusual Tomb and Individual

The burial not yet discussed is that of Burial XXXVII-8 in the elaborate Motmot tomb now inside 10L-26 (W. Fash 2001:81–83), but this is probably the best-preserved skeleton in the Copán skeletal collection.

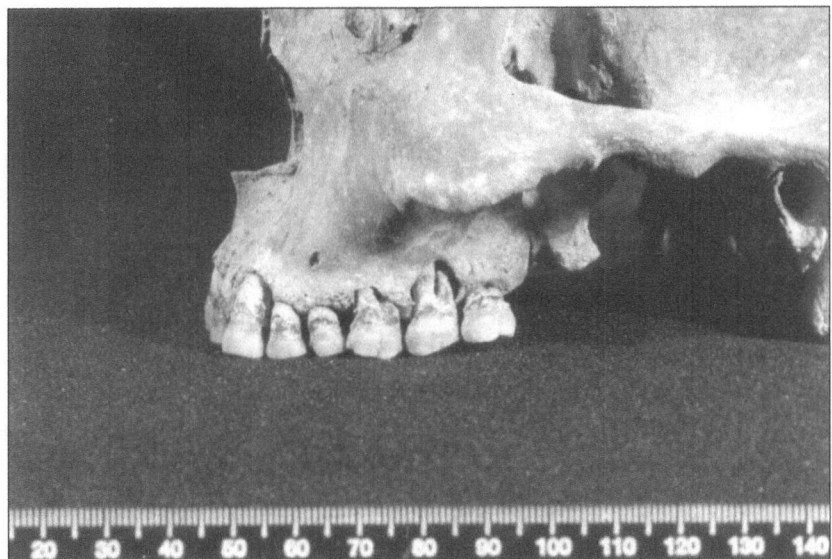

FIGURE 8.3

The maxilla of Burial XXXVII-10, showing the abscesses and the smoking of the skull, especially visible in the dark smudges on tooth roots and the cheek area.

This individual is also very early in relation to the sample, probably dating to the time of Ruler 1. This burial was in a cylindrical cist, in itself a distinctive form and perhaps copied from Teotihuacan (W. Fash and B. Fash 2000), underneath the Motmot floor marker set in the plaza floor near the earliest ball court. The marker seems to refer to at least some aspects associated with this burial but also commemorates an important calendar ending. It mainly depicts Ruler 1 and Ruler 2, neither of whom is likely to be this individual. An almost complete but headless deer, two human skulls (XXXVII-7 and 9), and still-liquid mercury were found on the capstones. The deer sacrifice appears to be mentioned on the marker. Inside the cist with the body was another skull (Burial XXXVII-10). The marker also refers to "smoke-entering" (W. Fash 2001:83), which may mean the involved treatment of this corpse. There is no evidence that the body was exposed to fire sufficient to cause warping or cracking, but it was quite smoked or smudged, thoroughly to the inside of the cranium and the roots of the teeth. Probably skeletonized, or nearly so, when this was done, the body still maintained some articulation, indicating that this was carefully done. When excavated, most of the body had been placed back in somewhat of a jumble, but the lower legs were still in their articulated position and likely had not been moved since the original interment. The original position was probably seated. As with the Sub-Jaguar Tomb, if bones were moved, care was taken in putting them all back; only a few hand bones were missing from this burial. As in the Sub-Jaguar Tomb, possibly some of the skeleton was removed from the burial for some time for a purpose but finally returned and eventually sealed in the tomb. As mentioned above, the accompanying skulls had also been smoked.

Who was this individual? The distinctive corpse treatment, the accompanying objects, and the burial location seem to signify an important individual. The sex of this individual is problematic. The pelvis is morphologically female, especially using Phenice's (1969) characteristics of the pubis (although it appears to lack at least one of the most characteristic female traits, the ventral arc). The skull, however, has more masculine morphology. Jane Buikstra (personal communication 1994), who has also looked at the skeleton, decided that it is a female, but several features about this burial make a female sex problematic. The individual is about 157 ± 2.5 cm in stature (estimation from standard osteological formulae), which would be short for the male average but tall for females, compared with the 9N-8 sample. The femur circumference and some other measures, however, are in the male range for the Copán elite sample, indicating robustness. The individual has a healed parry fracture on the right ulna with also a healed periosteal reaction. The bone healed with good alignment, so this should not have hindered movement. Such fractures often result from warding off a blow with the arm and usually not from an accidental fall. That this might be a war wound or an injury suffered in a ball game cannot be discounted, and such an injury is much more likely in the life of an elite male than a female. Also, this individual was accompanied by three trophy skulls, another situation linked with violence and warfare. The individual is not very old, most probably between thirty and thirty-five years of age at death.

Thus, this mortuary context would indicate a male but contains a skeleton with mixed male and female characteristics. There are several possibilities. This could be a female, even with the indications of male lifestyle. The individual could be one of those uncommon males likely to be mistaken for female. Male pelvic morphology is more variable because selection for childbirth does not constrain it. Therefore, males can have a female pelvis (Meindl et al. 1985). This individual's pelvis certainly has no indicators of childbirth. I believe that the individual was more likely what is called an "intersexed" or "transgendered" person, an individual with both male and female characteristics. Such individuals, called *berdache* (Roscoe 1994), were found among many groups of Native Americans in North and Central America and were often associated with ritual and supernatural power. They could be shamans and could be of either sex, taking on characteristics of the opposite. Roscoe (1994:370) states that such individuals form a "distinct and autonomous social status on par with the status of men and women," constituting third and fourth genders. It is possible that this is a female who dressed and acted as a male, which is known to have occurred in at least one instance among the Maya (Sigal 2000).

The Maya depict cross-dressing in sculptural iconography, including Stela H at Copán, and the power of ritual encompassing both male and female procreative powers in the bloodletting of the penis, combining blood and semen (see Sigal 2000 for a recent discussion). In addition, Maya deities seem to have the dualistic aspects of both male and female (Edmonson 1993), so gender crossing was not a foreign idea to the Maya at Copán. Many reseachers on transgendered individuals seem to assume that the individuals were biologically male or female but that they chose to live as a different gender (for example, Roscoe 1994 and references therein). Although most individuals are clearly sexually dimorphic as male or female, several chromosomal and hormonal syndromes result in individuals with genitalia of both sexes, intersexed individuals, such as Klinefelter's (XXY) individuals and individuals with androgen insensitivity syndrome. Survey of existing medical literature indicates that these can occur in 0.2 percent to 2.0 percent of all births (Blackless et al. 2000). The potential ritual importance of this condition suggests that such an individual may have received special treatment (and several were likely born to the Maya in Copán over the Classic period). If this individual was born elsewhere, as bone chemical analysis seems to indicate (Buikstra 1997), this condition could have added to the individual's "aura." Whereas such people are stigmatized in modern Western societies and often surgically altered to become either male or female (Blackless et al. 2000), clear third or fourth gender types among the Maya were probably treated as quite special, born with unique ritual powers, an aspect of the divine made visible. If this individual was a powerful shaman or close associate of Ruler 1, given the circumstances of the mortuary treatment, then such an intersexed person would have been a very good candidate for special commemoration, for being the centerpiece of the ritual indicated by the Motmot marker. Unfortunately, there is no clinical information on how the skeletons of such individuals might appear. True hermaphrodites with aspects of both genitalia do exist but can often appear like other males (Blackless et al. 2000). Perhaps only DNA testing in the future will allow resolution of this individual's sex.

The individual also had caries and several active abesses in the mouth. The only indication of some arthritic changes is that the sacroiliac joint is surrounded by bone projections or spurs. This could have been caused by extra weight on the joint and might indicate obesity, but not all skeletal biologists are agreed on this interpretation. There is no evidence of any cranial deformation or dental mutilation. In fact, the skeleton does not look at all like that of a particularly imposing person, which might lend credence that this was an individual with spiritual powers. All in all, it appears to have belonged to a medium height, possibly plump individual with female hips, with no great evidence of any particular muscular strength but the general robusticity of a male. Of course, bones do not tell the whole story, but the presence of intersexed individuals in the past should be expected. In my opinion, this is the best interpretation. Who this individual was in the history of the early Copán kingdom is unknown.

EVIDENCE FROM HEALTH AND LIFESTYLE

Many studies in biological anthropology have found that the better the socioeconomic status, the better the lifestyle and health of the individual in a stratified society. This circumstance is due to the better nutrition and generally better hygiene, medical care, and protection afforded wealthier individuals in such a society, compared with their poorer counterparts (for example, Millard 1994). Because status is usually ascribed from birth in stratified societies, this advantage is enjoyed throughout the life span. In societies where status may be largely achieved, advantages tend to accrue to individuals only as adults. As children, they may not have been buffered from the usual stresses suffered by children in that society.

Skeletons are relatively poor records of an individual's health because only chronic or severe physiological stresses affect bone and the individual must survive for at least some time after the stress. Acute stresses that cause death are usually not visible on the skeleton, but the skeleton does provide a series of indicators for morbidity and lifestyle. The ones used here are dental hypoplasias, porotic hyperostosis, and stature. These indicators reveal childhood stresses, as well as periosteal reactions, arthritis, and muscle markings indicative of adult lifestyle and health conditions.

During childhood, stresses severe enough to interfere with normal growth processes can be preserved on the skeleton, if the child survives. These stresses reveal how healthy children were during the crucial first five years. In preindustrial societies, mortality was high. Dental enamel hypoplasias are a good example of this kind of stress indicator. A *hypoplasia* is a dent or pit in the tooth indicating that the enamel is thinner than normal because of physiological stress interfering with the normal enamel formation (Skinner and Goodman 1992). Because a wide variety of stresses can cause hypoplasia, it is a nonspecific indicator. Studies on contemporary children have revealed, however, that this indicator is sensitive to moderate malnutrition (May, Goodman, and Meindl 1993). That is, malnutrition makes children susceptible to the formation of a hypoplasia resulting from a disease episode. The number of hypoplasias present on susceptible teeth indicates how many stress episodes an individual had to survive during the first six years, but controversy exists over whether individuals with more hypoplasias are frailer and more subject to early mortality as adults than individuals who have one or none (Goodman and Armelagos 1988; Wood et al. 1992). Be that as it may, only the number of hypoplasias present in an adult are compared here. No matter what the implications for adult longevity, an individual with no hypoplasia went through childhood more easily than an individual with one or more, because the former did not have to survive a severe stress episode. The former individual probably had a more protected childhood, with better nutrition than the latter, and ought to be typical of very high-ranking individuals.

Porotic hyperostosis is a lesion of the skull that is indicative of iron-deficiency anemia during childhood (Stuart-Macadam 1985). The anemia is likely the result of an interaction of disease with a lack of iron in the diet. Thus, again, nutrition can be a factor, although parasites and gastrointestinal diseases can also bring on such anemia even when dietary iron is sufficient. These latter causes of porotic hyperostosis mean that the indicator can be one of hygiene and general quality of living conditions. Although the presence of skeletal lesions indicates that the anemia was severe and chronic, it is not necessarily a life-threatening condition. In fact, the ability of most individuals in the population to survive the episode could be seen as evidence of the society's adaptive capacity (Martin et al. 1991). If the individual survives the stress of which the anemia was part, the lesion heals and remains scorable in adults as an indicator of stress during childhood. Here, the interpretetation of the presence of a porotic lesion in an adult skull is that nutrition and disease conditions and/or hygiene environment were poor enough to subject the individual to the debilitating effects of anemia.

Adult stature can also be used as an indicator of childhood environment. Complex interactions of genetics and environment affect stature (Tanner 1978), but chronic malnutrition and ill health cause children to grow up shorter than they should. There is evidence that individuals with stunted growth are more subject to adult ill health and earlier death than individuals not so affected by their childhood environment (Elo and Preston 1992). This particular indicator has already been used for the Classic Maya. Haviland (1967) found that individuals at Tikal buried in tombs were significantly taller than those who were not, indicating better lifelong nutrition for the elite than for commoners, as well as probable genetic differences from status endogamy. At Altar de Sacrificios, Saul (1972) also found that the two individuals from tombs in his sample were taller than average, although such a small sample can only be suggestive. As Haviland (1967) hypothesized for Tikal, stature can be used to indicate the quality of childhood environment because even though genetic endowment may have made the elite taller than commoners, the environment of their childhood allowed them to reach their genetic potential.

Just as enamel hypoplasias, porotic hyperostosis, and stature indicate the quality of an individual's childhood, other indicators are affected by the quality of life during adulthood. Several arthritic syndromes exist, but the one of interest, osteoarthritis, is usually degenerative and results from both age and wear and tear on a joint (Ortner and Putschar 1981). Arthritic changes can indicate individuals' habitual activities (Bridges 1994; Merbs 1983); genetic factors can account for variations in how quickly such changes become evident on the bone. Bones also contain crests where ligaments and tendons attach; these can be developed by biomechanical activity as well (Merbs 1983). Thus, from arthritic and crest information we can glean some indication of the physical labor performed during the adult years. Gracile individuals with little crest development or arthritis probably did not do much physical labor and may be typical of a society's upper strata. On the other hand, Maya rulers were to be proficient in warfare and probably also the ball game (Schele and Freidel 1990), so perhaps good fitness and training in physical arts were prerequisites of rulership. Such individuals might have skeletal indicators of considerable physical activity, and as already detailed, most of the individuals in the sample do have clear evidence of muscle markings and an active lifestyle.

Periosteal reactions are also indicators of an individual's health environment and are nonspecific because a wide variety of pathological conditions can cause them. These reactions take the form of new bone laid down in response to a bacterial infection from trauma (from localized overlying muscle and tendon) or to a systemic infection that ultimately affects several bones. The infectious agent is usually *Staphylococcus* or *Streptococcus* bacteria (Ortner and Putschar 1981). The infections are chronic and not usually life-threatening but are transmissible between individuals, so they do indicate something about hygiene, the frequency of interindividual contact, and the level of host resistance (Martin et al. 1991). Quality of nutrition and the disease load present in the environment, especially for systemic infections, affect host resistance to disease. Although children may be more susceptible to the infectious agents that cause periosteal reactions, these agents are also present in adults. On bone, the reaction can be active, partially healed at the time of death, or completely healed. If the bone reveals only a healed periosteal reaction, one cannot tell how far in the past an adult suffered the infection. Nevertheless, this indicates an episode of morbidity. The proportion of adults affected also indicates the health and hygiene environment of the society.

Studying biological indicators like these on skeletons reveals only chronic conditions. But these indicators are directly informative about sufficiency of nutrition and buffering from disease during childhood, disease load and host resistance during adulthood, and physical activity and labor. A privileged lifestyle feeds and protects children well and also cushions adults. All these indicators result from some sort of stress, and less stress in an individual's environment suggests a better, more protected lifestyle.

Table 8.1, which lists the various health and lifestyle indicators, shows that most individuals, whether honored dead or sacrificial victims, have at least some signs of stress suffered during childhood and varying indicators of stress during adulthood. Those individuals with no evidence of either hypoplasias or porotic hyperostosis are fragmentary and cannot be scored for the evidence of stress. Most adults do appear to have been somewhat active during life, although two were gracile and apparently not active. Arthritis is generally slight for individuals who are at least middle-aged at death, so the actual wear and tear of their activities was probably moderate. Porotic hyperostosis is present in six individuals from childhood, but infection is uncommon and rarely systemic, which could indicate good nutrition and perhaps buffering of contact with other people. Some of these individuals, however, did have calculus, caries, and abscesses, the results of generally poor diet and dental hygiene. Thus, even though these individuals do not appear to have been completely safe from stress during childhood, the adult years were good in terms of lifestyle. This is particularly true for the honored dead. The Early Classic individuals are no better or worse than those of the Late Classic.

Comparison with the nonruling elite at 9N-8 provides perspective on the biological indicators of lifestyle for rulers or other honored dead (the sacrificed are not counted here). Because all but one of the individuals in the Acropolis sample are adult males, only adult males are used for the comparison. In the 9N-8 skeletal sample, there were fourteen adult males in formal stone tombs, the highest status present.

HEALTH AND LIFESTYLE

TABLE 8.1
Skeletal Indicators of Stress in Elite Burials at Copán

Burial	Number of Hypoplasias	Porotic Hyperostosis	Stature	Arthritis	Infectious Reactions
Honored Dead					
XXXVII-1	1	None	166 cm	None	None
XXXVII-2	1	Cannot score	173 cm	Slight	Yes, localized
XXXVII-5	1	Slight	162 cm	Slight	Yes, systemic
XXXVII-4	None	Cannot score		Slight	Cannot score
XXXVII-8	2	Moderate	157 cm	Slight	Yes, localized
I-5	2	None		Severe	None
V-4	1	Moderate		Slight	Yes, systemic
48-15-1	Cannot score	None	152 cm	None	None
48-13-8	2	None	158 cm	Slight	None
48-11-2	None	Cannot score		Cannot score	None
48-11-3	1	Cannot score	159 cm	Slight	Yes, localized
Sacrificed Individuals					
XXXVII-3	2	None	Too young	None	None
XXXVII-6	Cannot score	Cannot score	166 cm	Slight	None
XXXVII-7	2	Moderate		Cannot score	Cannot score
XXXVII-9	2	Moderate		Slight	Cannot score
XXXVII-10	1	Slight		Serious	Cannot score

(Seven females also had such tombs, evidence that this most elaborate of mortuary treatments was available to both sexes, although males were obviously favored.) In the 9N-8 sample, half were over age fifty at death, and half were between the ages of twenty-five and fifty, so ages are roughly similar. The 9N-8 average stature was 163 cm, and that of the Acropolis was 163 cm (from Early to Late Classic), so these are the same. For the other indicators of childhood stress, only 10 percent of the scorable 9N-8 males had no evidence of a hypoplasia; only two (20 percent) of the honored dead lacked it. Hypoplasias were a ubiquitous stress, but slightly less in the highest elites. For porotic hyperostosis, three out of seven had it (50 percent could not be scored for this indicator), the same proportion for the Acropolis. In infection, 79 percent had periosteal reactions, whereas the proportion for the ruling Acropolis was 50 percent. In arthritis, 36 percent of the 9N-8 sample had arthritic changes of the shoulder, and 64 percent had these in the knee as well, whereas the Acropolis sample had mostly slight changes, and rarely were both joints involved. Basically, the 9N-8 and Acropolis samples are very similar in the childhood indicators, and the Acropolis sample is better in infections and arthritis for the adult lifestyle indicators. The Sub-Jaguar individual did have caries in the teeth and an active abscess on the mandible, which could have been a dangerous source of acute infection. The sample sizes and differences are too small for any statistical significance.

The information presently available from elite individuals in the Copán skeletal sample indicates that the majority had one or more indicators of severe stress during childhood in both the Early and Late Classic. Thus, they do not appear to have been particularly protected from problems with malnutrition or disease during the crucial growing years. As adults, the adult males from the ruling family seem to have had less infection and less arthritic involvement of working joints, such as the shoulder and knee, than the nonruling elite. Some individuals were involved in some physical activity, but the labor was probably not hard. They were apparently living in such a way as to benefit from both good nutrition and more careful contact with other individuals.

The main distinction between the Acropolis and Group 10L-2 tomb sample and the other elites is the elaborateness of the burials in mortuary ritual. The 9N-8 tombs contained a variety of grave goods, but there does not appear to have been quite the ceremony that attends most individuals in the Acropolis. In terms of materials and workmanship, most of the Acropolis honored dead had very expensive grave offerings. Even sacrifices were placed in very important ritual locations. The painting of bodies after they are skeletonized, however, has no counterpart in 9N-8. A few of the latter do have some paint, but this appears to be lucky preservation from what was on the body when it was placed. There is no real evidence of revisitation of bodies after interment in 9N-8, unlike the Acropolis sample, where honored dead were often revisited and sometimes partly removed and returned. At least for certain adult males, the rulers and families could provide more elaborate interments and more protracted mortuary rituals. After death, the "lifestyle" of the corpse in the Acropolis does appear to have been better than that of the nonruling elite.

Other Classic Maya sites provide information that the elaborate treatment postulated here for some individuals was not uncommon. Most dramatic is the evidence of revisiting, painting, and moving skeletal parts at Caracol, especially in the Central Acropolis tomb burials. As Chase and Chase (1996:77) put it:

> Some were buried immediately following death; others were buried and completely moved;...some were only partially disturbed—perhaps in search of relics....The presence of multiple individuals inside a tomb, the evidence for multiple entries, and the fact that individuals might be wholly or partly moved following death reveals [sic] a pattern not typical in the Maya lowlands, but one that may offer insights into Maya beliefs with regard to death.

They go on to postulate that the elaborate, prolonged burial ritual discussed by Hertz (1960) was present at Caracol. The evidence from Copán indicates that, far from being an atypical pattern, it may indeed be the usual one for burials of the highest rank.

Distinctive treatment at Copán indicates that an extended burial position was maintained for several bodies. This would require elaborate wrapping and bundling, but there is certainly evidence that the Maya could do this. In the recent discovery of the tomb of Jaguar Paw of Calakmul, the body, in an extended anatomical position, appears to have been wrapped with cloth completely impregnated with a latex-like substance and then sealed with a resin layer, all this in direct contact with the bones (Carrasco Vargas et al. 1999:53). This wrapping, although the researchers do not indicate this, would have been best and stablest when the corpse already was largely reduced to a skeleton. Such a wrapping certainly would preserve the anatomical position of the skeleton and probably would be strong enough to allow the skeleton to be moved. Cinnabar pigment partially covered this Calakmul individual, and the two main tombs discovered by the ECAP project had individuals painted with cinnabar (Sharer, Traxler, et al. 1999). This is equivalent to the ochre painting that is commonest here. Thus, evidence exists that important corpses were subject to elaborate treatment of the bones and probably prepared for protracted visition of the body and/or removal of all or parts of the skeleton for various rituals. This treatment, to echo Chase and Chase (1996), would have been reserved for very few individuals and probably indicates very high office in the Copán polity. As in 9N-8, most individuals were buried soon after death and not moved or revisited.

Distinguishing ruling families from other elites on archaeological grounds (Haviland and Moholy-Nagy 1992) is easy. What we do not know is how much the lifestyles of the two groups differed. The evidence of childhood stress indicators suggests that neither group buffered its children. Undoubtedly born to elite rank, their status was ascribed, but they do not appear to have been pampered or well-fed. They had to survive stress episodes severe enough to be recorded in their teeth and, very often, also in their cranium in the form of porotic hyperostosis. Elite males at Copán were not particularly tall at 163 cm, and how much childhood environment might have stunted the adult statures in this population is unknown. With the evidence of common problems in hypoplasias and the development of porotic hyperostosis, it is probably fair to say that the childhood environment affected the adult stature of many elite individuals at Copán. A comparison of the individuals, especially the males, from 9N-8 with those of smaller rural groups, however, indicates that significant differences by status exist in health and stress indicators (noble versus commoner) during the Late Classic (Storey 1998, 1999). Most dramatic is a significant difference in male stature between the highest-status individuals of 9N-8 and the rural commoners, indicating that the highest levels were tall for their society. The elite, as might be expected, were better off than the lowest-status individuals.

In the iconography involving ruling families, all the pomp and circumstance usually surround adults, except for probable designated heir apparents (Schele and Freidel 1990), suggesting that elite status, although ascribed, may not have been translated into real privilege until achievement of some adult status within the family. This was true of the elite of 9N-8, where generally only adults merited tombs and elaborate grave offerings, as it was of the Acropolis sample. Thus, probably on a daily basis, most of the elite led much the same kind of life, with privileges as adults but no particular care when they were children. When an individual became a ruler or gained high office within the ruling family, he or she did enjoy a very different life and treatment after death, but ceremony, care, and special treatment were reserved for very few individuals.

Except for the inability of even the highest statuses to protect children from severe chronic stresses, the evidence presented here cannot totally prove the preceding reconstruction. Possible chronological differences also cannot be determined because of very small sample size. Classic Maya society has been seen as a two-status society of elites and commoners that may have had a more complex organization (Chase and Chase 1992). The nature of these other levels is not yet understood. On the other hand, a basic redundancy in the layout and functions of households varies only by size and expense of construction at Copán. This might be a clue that daily life for all segments of the society was similar, with the only differences being that elites had varying access to rare and valued foods on certain occasions and the use of some expensive items. The hygiene conditions and buffering were not well controlled for children. Some elite adults were able to command much more care and privilege than others, but otherwise there is no evidence that the social gulf between rulers and the other elite went beyond a pampered lifestyle for the very top few, and only after they became rulers, high officeholders, and perhaps heirs apparent. Pending further evidence, there is no reason to conclude that elites were stratified at Copán. Some members of the highest-ranking family could command quite a bit of ritual and a lot of ceremony, but only for themselves, not for their family and certainly not for most of their children. Real privilege came with the achievement of ritual and political position, not ascription of being born to a particular elite lineage.

The poorer nutrition and hygiene suggested by biological indicators on all elites studied, both Early and Late Classic, seem to indicate that the Copán kingdom always faced some basic problems. Living conditions of elites throughout the rise and fall of the kingdom were not good, although adequate to keep the polity going for several hundred years. Elaborate houses, fancy material items, pomp and ceremony, and certain good foods were available to elites (Lentz 1991), especially to the ruling family.

The fall of the Copán kingdom may have occurred because elites were never able to command the resources to improve their lot significantly over that of commoners. All elites in hierarchical societies distinguish themselves from lower-status individuals, but the important question is, how much are they able to control, exploit, and coerce others to provide the necessities of life? The evidence of stress indicators supports the interpretation that elites were less impacted than most rural commoners but still affected. What if elite were distinguished mostly by their larger labor pool and the productivity generated just because they had larger households, not by their ability to coerce the rural commoners for food and labor at will? What if rural commoners only had to provide corvee labor during quiet agricultural periods and the nobles had to feed them during this time, usually from their own accumulated surplus, even though the commoners had provided some of that surplus?

Elite life might have been punctuated by times of feasts and rituals, but otherwise, daily life, with its risks, was very similar everywhere in the Copán polity. This pattern would be expected in a society in which lineages compose the underlying residential group (Webster, chapter 2 in this volume). In such a situation, individuals could be of varying status and have varying workloads, but each residential compound could be self-sufficient and have very similar daily environments. This might suggest that the stratification indicated at Copán by various types of archaeological evidence was tenuous, more show than through real, sustainable differences. If life became tough during the Terminal Late Classic and the general pattern was loss of population, the elite were just as subject to problems, because their own household production was impacted by any agricultural problems or the breakdown of trade relations with other polities. Moreover, they might not have been able to counteract what had been the prevailing pattern of largely self-sufficient, elite households. Trying to extract more from the peasants might have caused those who remained to move farther away, as the pattern of rural settlement indicates from the Terminal Classic to Postclassic (Webster, chapter 2 in this volume). For hundreds of years, the elite households had provided a focus of ritual and social organization, a centralizing core for the Maya. The dissolution of elite households would also dissolve the focus that held the culture together for so long. The whole fabric of society crumbled, the population continued to decline and move away, and ultimately, the Copán kingdom was no more.

9

Seats of Power at Copán

Linda Schele and Matthew G. Looper

This chapter proposes interpretations of Maya hieroglyphic collocations that include the "impinged-bone" glyph (T571/598/599) at Copán. The impinged-bone occurs frequently in ancient Maya inscriptions. Its decipherment began with David Stuart's work on the toponyms in Copán's inscriptions, which led eventually to Stuart and Houston's (1994) study of Classic Maya place names. They, and many who were following their early work, identified a specific phrase that often accompanies toponyms consisting of a sky sign (T561) followed by the glyph nicknamed the "impinged-bone" by J. E. S. Thompson (1962:223). Comparative studies of these phrases, especially those included in the Texas Workbooks beginning in 1987, identified a number of allographs of the impinged-bone, including a bird with a trefoil shape in its eye (figure 9.1; Schele 1987a). Stuart had earlier identified a similar bird as a **kV** [*k* plus vowel] syllable in the *ux witik* collocation at Copán (figure 9.2). It was also observed that the impinged-bone is commonly complemented by T23 **na**. Using these clues, Barbara MacLeod (letter dated February 8, 1993, distributed to epigraphers) suggested that the bird is an owl, *kuh* or *kuy* in many Mayan languages, and that **ku** combined with **na** yields a reading of *kun*.[1] Grube and Schele (1994) confirmed her proposed value of **ku** for the bird by showing the phonetic spelling of this owl as *kuy* in both monumental and codical texts. MacLeod gave a primary translation of *kun* as "seat," based on the modern Ch'ol entry of *kunil* as "platform for corn" (*cunil* ["plataforma para maíz"], Aulie and Aulie 1998:20). According to MacLeod, the glyph also references "residence," "place," or "origin" in Maya texts (in Schele 1992c:232–235).

Initially, many epigraphers accepted this decipherment, but others have questioned it for a number of reasons. For one, there is no clear substitution of the impinged-bone by a syllabic spelling that employs the common "kawak" **ku** (T528). Second, in both its substitution contexts at Copán and Caracol, the bird with a trefoil eye replaces a **ki** syllable, not **ku** (see figure 9.2). Finally, there may be subtle graphic distinctions between the bird with the trefoil eye and the bird that substitutes for the impinged-bone. For example, the impinged-bone bird (see figure 9.1f, g) usually has a prominent nasal emanation that is absent in the **ki** allographs (see figure 9.2). An alternative interpretation of the impinged-bone glyph as **CH'EEN** (cave, cliff) has been suggested by Stuart, Houston, and Robertson (1999:15), although a full argument was not published.[2]

Linda Schele (1987a) identified other glyphic references to *kun* in an analysis of the Group of the Cross texts at Palenque, in which the word is spelled syllabically. Schele and David Stuart independently observed that the small shrines inside the temples of the Cross Group are called *pib' nah* in the texts. Schele showed that a collocation reading **ku-nu**, or *kun*, replaces *pib' nah* in some examples (figure 9.3) and that *pib' nah* is a word for "oven," "underground house," or "sweatbath." Developing these ideas further, Houston (1996) identified the shrines of the Cross Group as symbolic sweatbaths in which gods were ritually "born" and purified, and he discussed the relationship between sweatbaths and birth lore throughout Mesoamerica.

In their discussions of the term *kun*, both MacLeod (in Schele 1992c:232–235) and Houston (1996) cited Yucatec entries for *kun* as "oven," and Houston noted the semantic overlap between this term and *pib' nah*. But there is another meaning of *kun* that enriches our understanding of these structures' function. In Yucatec, *kun* is glossed

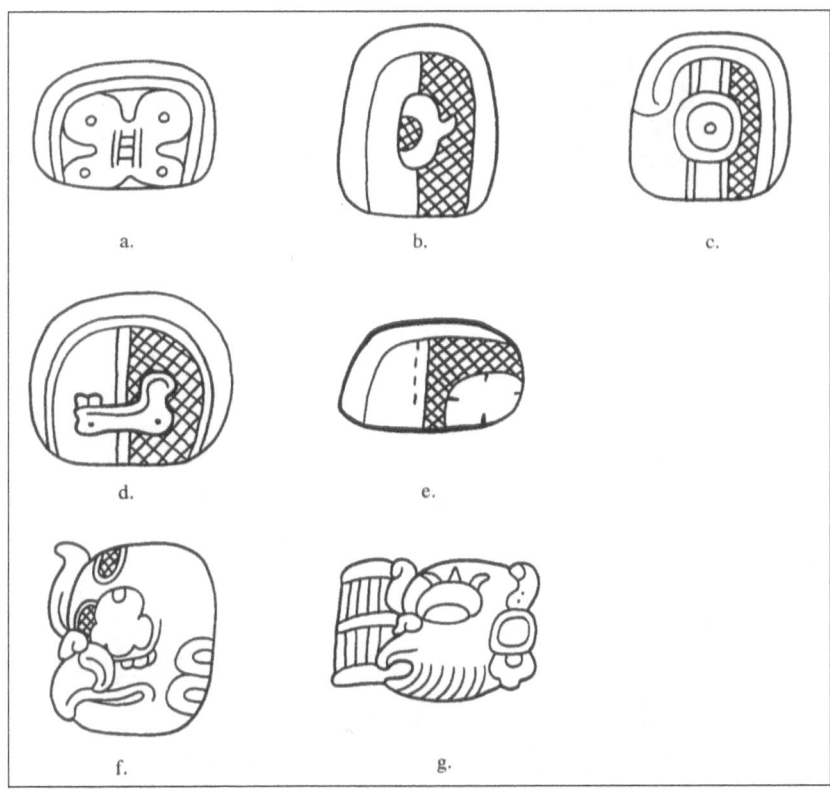

FIGURE 9.1

Impinged-bone allographs: (a) Tikal Stela 31, F27, (b) Palenque Temple of the Cross, jamb, B2, (c) Dos Pilas Stela 8, F22, (d) Copán Stela I, D9, (e) Codex style plate, (f) Copán Stela 10, B10, and (g) Tikal "Marcador," C6. (Drawings by M. Looper)

"enchantment, magic, conjuration" ("encanto, hechizo, conjuro," Barrera Vásquez et al., eds., 1980:352). Thus, as a location, *kun* may signify a site for magical conjuration (Schele 1987a). The presence of portraits of Itzamnah Mut (the Principal Bird Deity) on the frontal entablature of the Cross Group shrines reinforces this meaning. *Itz* is another word for "wizard," "witchcraft," and "enchantment," and in Maya art, Itzamnah Mut identifies places of conjuration (Freidel, Schele, and Parker 1993:410–412).

Since the initial decipherments were made, the concept of the places named with the impinged-bone glyph has become increasingly

FIGURE 9.2

/ki/ allographs: (a) **UX-wi-ti-ki**, Copán Altar Q, D5, and (b) **CH'UHUL-K'AN-tu-ma-ki**, Caracol Structure B19 Stucco, **Glyph** 30–31. (Drawings by M. Looper)

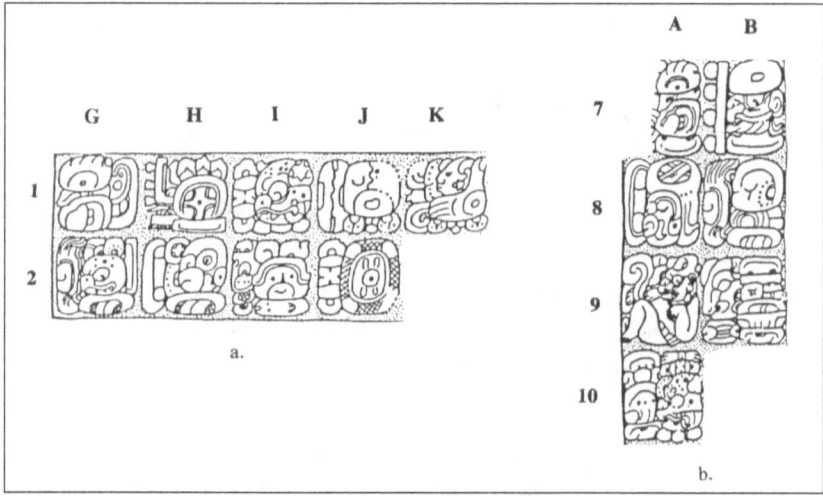

FIGURE 9.3

Contexts of pib'il nah and kunil from Palenque, Temple of the Foliated Cross: (a) Alfarda, G1-K1, and (b) jamb panel, A7–A10. (Drawings by Linda Schele, © David Schele, courtesy Foundation for the Advancement of Mesoamerican Studies, Inc., www.famsi.org)

important to the understanding of Classic-period religion and politics. Schele and Grube (1994a) discussed these roles in the politics and sacred geography of the Maya Classic period. In the summer of 1994,

Matthew Looper and Linda Schele surveyed all the examples of the impinged-bone in the hieroglyphic corpus to determine the range of contexts in which it appears. Later discussions with Nikolai Grube further enriched these interpretations. This chapter presents a summary of the contexts in which the impinged-bone appears in Classic Maya texts, before addressing examples at Copán, especially those from the outlying stela program of Ruler 12. We suggest that, like the kun mentioned at Palenque, the objects and places identified by the impinged-bone glyph are seats or platforms connected to rituals of spirit conjuration, usually in the form of deity images. Presumably because they were made of perishable materials such as wood, these images left little trace in the archaeological record. Therefore, hieroglyphic texts and associated iconography provide a unique source of information relating to the use and significance of these objects.

CONTEXTS OF KUN AND THE IMPINGED-BONE

At Palenque, the principal action recorded for the 5 Eb' 5 K'ayab' date associated with the pib' nah/kun structures is *och nah* (the structure is entered) (see figure 9.3a, b; Stuart 1998). Each of these texts names the actor as the patron god of the temple—in each case, the Triad god whose birth is recorded in associated texts. The gods are named *uch'uhil* or *ujuntan*, respectively, the god of or the cherished one of K'inich Kan B'alam II, the Palenque ruler. This "house entering" is the final event mentioned in the Group of the Cross texts and thus represents the culminating action in the dedication of the buildings. It occurred on the eighth tropical-year anniversary of K'inich Kan B'alam's accession and represents the moment he brought the patron gods of Palenque to reside in the temples he had built for them. This may have been conceived as a purely spiritual act, but we consider that it also probably involved the installation of statues in these temples. Nikolai Grube (personal communication with Schele, 1994) suggested that the gods installed in each city's kun were local patron deities.

Two other texts from Palenque use both *kun* and the impinged-bone (henceforth in transcriptions, *[IB]*) in the context of references to patron gods (figure 9.4). A phrase from the main tablet of the Temple of the Foliated Cross (figure 9.4a) relates the location of an important event in the following manner: *uti lakam ha' chan [IB] tu-[IB]*

LINDA SCHELE AND MATTHEW G. LOOPER

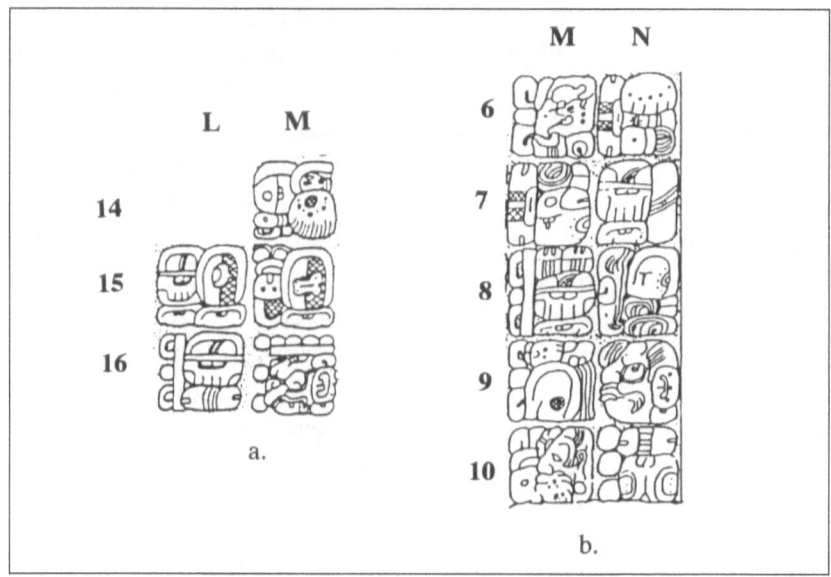

FIGURE 9.4

References to seats/platforms and kunil *at Palenque: (a) Temple of the Foliated Cross, main panel, M14–M16, and (b) Temple of Inscriptions, middle panel, M6-N10. (Drawings by Linda Schele, © David Schele, courtesy Foundation for the Advancement of Mesoamerican Studies, Inc., www.famsi.org)*

wak chan chak ux b'olon chahk (It happened at Lakam Ha' sky seat/platform, in the seat/platform of six/stood-up? sky red Ux B'olon Chahk). Here, the text designates the seat of Lakam Ha', a toponym for the city center of Palenque, as pertaining to a lightning deity, Ux B'olon Chahk. In this case, the impinged-bone may refer to the large central platform or cliff upon which the center of Palenque was built. The Temple of Inscriptions middle panel (figure 9.4b) names a supernatural location as *jun ajaw chak yotot chak nukul chan ?? wak chan-?? ukunil jun nal ye* (One Ajaw Red House, Red Grand? Sky ??, the Stood-up? Sky [is] the seat of Jun Nal Ye [First Father]). These passages suggest that Palenque was considered to be the seat of one of the Chahks and that a celestial location was revered as the seat or conjuring place of First Father.

The impinged-bone refers to a special residence for gods in two inscriptions from Tikal. Stela 5 (figure 9.5a) records the placement of a

SEATS OF POWER AT COPÁN

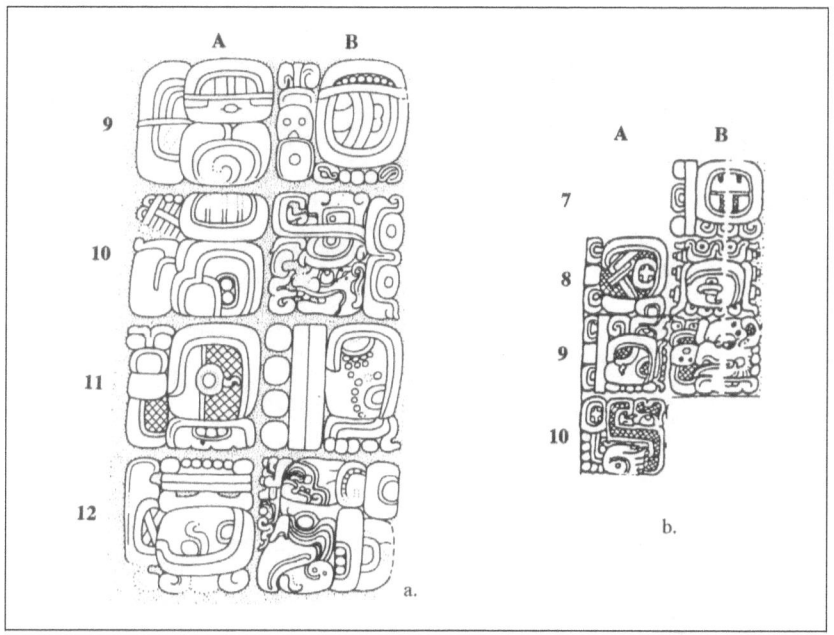

FIGURE 9.5

Contexts of the impinged-bone at Tikal: (a) Tikal Stela 5, A9-B12; (b) Tikal Temple IV, Lintel 2, B7-A10. (University Museum Tikal Project, 69-5-52 and 69-5-98)

sak ?? lak ta yotot, "cache plate in the house of" one of the patron gods of Tikal.[3] The deity name is followed by *tu-[IB] chanlajun tun* (in the seat/platform of the fourteen stones). This passage suggests the identification of the impinged-bone with the low platform in front of the North Acropolis where most of Tikal's stelae were erected. Simon Martin (1996) first presented a convincing interpretation of a passage from Tikal Temple 4 Lintel 2 (figure 9.5b). As he noted, the event is a war event against "Wak Kab'nal," a toponym referring to Naranjo. The rest of the passage indicates that this location is the seat/platform of the "Square-Nosed Beastie." Grube (1988) and Schele (1986) independently identified this being as a supernatural patron of Naranjo from whom a numbered succession was counted. The war took place at the seat/platform of this patron deity.

The impinged-bone glyph also appears in association with the Holmul dancer, a form of the Maize God. On a polychrome vessel

FIGURE 9.6

Polychrome ceramic vessel (Kerr #3400): (a) column A and (b) column B. (Drawing by M. Looper)

(Kerr File #3400), the dancers are pictured with the following names (figure 9.6): (a) *wak chanal nal kalomte' tan [IB] kan ajaw b'akab'* (Six Sky Place Maize warrior, in the middle of the seat/platform of the Calakmul ajaw, b'akab') and (b) *wak hixnal nal kalomte' tan [IB] ch'uhul*

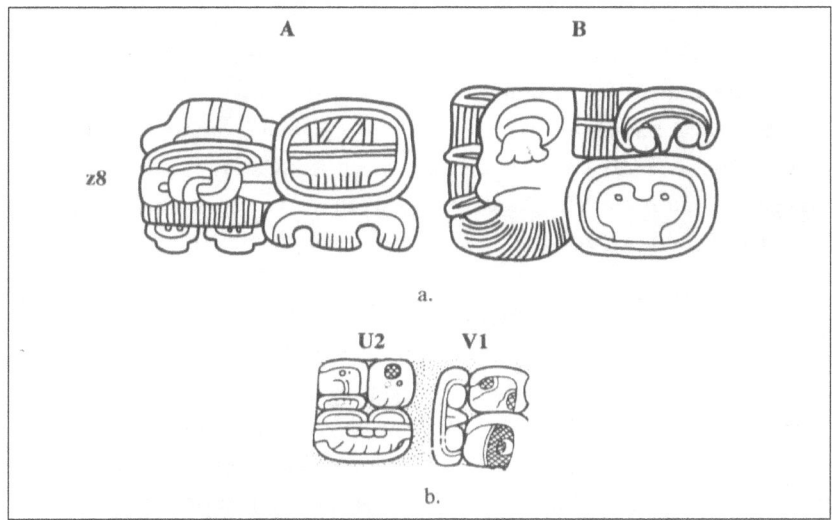

FIGURE 9.7
Sky– and earth–impinged-bone collocations: (a) Tikal Stela 39, Az8–Bz8, and (b) Yaxchilán Lintel 25, U2–V1. (Drawings by M. Looper)

mutal ajaw (Six Jaguar Place Maize warrior, in the middle of the seat/platform of the holy Tikal ajaw). On the Buenavista Vase (Reents-Budet 1994:figure 7.4), either the name glyph of Tikal, *mutal*, or a moon sign adorns the personified thrones borne in the backrack of the Maize God. These seats usually consist of a *witz* (mountain, hill) monster framed with a sky band. The Principal Bird Deity (Itzamnah Mut) perches on the sky band, and the animals sitting inside these backracks are a serpent-dragon, a jaguar, and sometimes a monkey. Werner Nahm and Nikolai Grube (in Freidel, Schele, and Parker 1993:276) pointed out that these animals correspond to the three thrones of Creation, cited in texts and images from Quiriguá and Palenque. The texts of Kerr 3400, then, suggest that these three thrones are the referent of the impinged-bone collocation. The vessel provides strong evidence that the impinged-bone refers specifically to a seat for supernatural beings.

The impinged-bone commonly appears in toponyms in formulaic phrases (figure 9.7). It is often paired with a sky glyph, **CHAN**, or the earth glyph, **CHAB'/KAB'**. In the first case, the sky–impinged-bone may originally have referred to places where the sky met the earth at the horizon. In Classic texts, it is used as a general term for the most sacred parts of cities, perhaps the shrines where the gods were kept or where the king was enthroned (figure 9.7a). However, *chan* or *ká'an* (Yucatec) also has meanings of "high" or "elevated," suggesting that the combination of **CHAN** with the impinged-bone may specifically refer to a raised platform.[4] In the example from Tikal (figure 9.7a), the reference may be to the original platform on which the North Acropolis is built.

In contrast, the combination of **CHAB'/KAB'** and the impinged-bone may indicate a low or subterranean platform or plaza, because *kab'* in Yucatec may mean "low" or "below," in addition to "earth" or "territory."[5] An example of this usage appears on Yaxchilán Lintel 25, in which events are recorded as having taken place *tan ha' siyan chan* (in front of the water of Siyan Chan), a reference to the principal plaza of Yaxchilán located at the river's edge (see figure 9.7b). Moreover, on Lintel 25, *uchab'/ukab'* precedes the impinged-bone glyph. This information may suggest either the possession of these structures and territories by the ruler Itzamnah B'alam II or the plaza's relatively low position. In some examples, the impinged-bone directly follows the **TAN** glyph, to indicate that an action takes place "in the middle of the seat/platform [city]" (for example, Caracol Stela 3, A15–B15; Beetz and Satterthwaite 1981:figure 4).

The identification of the sky- and earth-impinged-bone collocations as references to platforms or courts is assured by the iconography of several monuments. On Uxbenka Stela 11, for example, the bird allograph of the impinged-bone adorns the lower register on which the ruler stands (Wanyerka 1996:figure 4). The text of Quiriguá Stela D includes a reference to a royal ceremony at a location named with a dotted skull glyph followed by **NAL** and the bird allograph of the impinged-bone (figure 9.8a). On the south face of the stela, the king is shown standing on a basal register composed of the same dotted skull compound (figure 9.8b). The association of impinged-bone locations with supernatural conjuration probably relates to the supernatural context of the event depicted on this monument (see Looper 2003: 140–143).

Many texts record warlike actions against impinged-bone places (Schele and Grube 1994a). The earliest example occurs on the Early

FIGURE 9.8

Reference to a seat/platform in the text and image of Quiriguá Stela D: (a) D21 and (b) south basal register. (Drawings by M. Looper)

Classic Marcador from Tikal, on the side that records the 8.17.1.4.12 war against Uaxactún (see figure 9.9a; Schele and Freidel 1990). The verb (C6) consists of the bird variant of the impinged-bone, with a rattlesnake tail emerging from the eye. The tail reads **OCH** (enter) (Stuart 1998); thus, the phrase indicates that a seat/platform is entered. This place is followed by a shell glyph (D6) that Fahsen (1992) associated with the sculptural decorations on Uaxactún Structure A-V. He proposed that this seat/platform was located within this structure. The following glyphs read *siyan chan ch'uh ochk'in waxaklajun ub'ah chan* (Uaxactún god, west eighteen ?? serpent), identifying Structure A-V as the place entered by a war serpent (Freidel, Schele, and Parker 1993:299). This text suggests that a war deity was conjured into the seat/platform at Uaxactún during the conquest of the site.

Naranjo Stela 23 records another violent action against the seat of a defeated enemy (Schele and Freidel 1990:191, figure 5:16). The text indicates that on the date 9.13.19.4.18, the seat/platform of the contemporary lord of Yaxha was burned (Schele and Grube 1994a:148). The Hieroglyphic Stairway at Naranjo also records that a seat/platform was attacked, in this case, at Naranjo (see figure 9.9b). The text begins with the "star war" verb over the main sign of the Naranjo emblem glyph (N1). The following impinged-bone glyph (preceded by the third-person possessive pronoun *u*-) specifies that the royal or holy

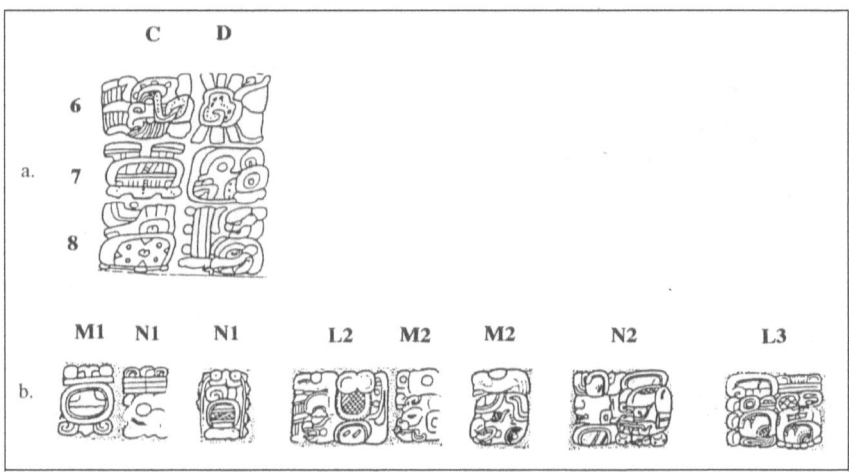

FIGURE 9.9

The impinged-bone in references to warfare: (a) Tikal "Ballcourt Marker," C6–D8 (drawing by Linda Schele, © David Schele, courtesy Foundation for the Advancement of Mesoamerican Studies, Inc., www.famsi.org), and (b) Naranjo Hieroglyphic Stairway, Step VI, M1–L3, (from Corpus of Maya Hieroglyphic Inscriptions, *vol. 2, part 2,* Naranjo, Chunhuitz, Xunantunich, *reproduced courtesy of the President and Fellows of Harvard College).*

seat/platform of Naranjo was the specific victim. The clause continues with the account of the torture of the Naranjo king Sak Chuwen, under the authority of the Calakmul ruler. A similar text on Toniná Monument 122 (figure 9.10) is coupled with an image of the defeated Palenque king K'inich K'an Hoy Chitam II. Beginning with the right column, the date is followed by the "star war" verb placed directly over the possessed impinged-bone (A3). The text then continues onto the thigh of the captive, where the owner is named. The results of this action are represented by the bound and supine image of the defeated king.

The final example is perhaps the most telling. On Tamarindito Hieroglyphic Stairway 2, Step 3, the date 9.16.9.15.10 is associated with an "axe event" that records the destruction of Tamarindito (M1; figure 9.11; see Martin and Grube 2000:63). The next glyph (N1) is the possessed sky–impinged-bone combination. Next, at O1–M2 is a rephrasing of this defeat as the lowering of the war emblems of the *(i)tz'at winik* (wise person). Finally, these actions are attributed to the agency of the

Seats of Power at Copán

Figure 9.10

Toniná Monument 122. (Drawing by Linda Schele, © David Schele, courtesy Foundation for the Advancement of Mesoamerican Studies, Inc., www.famsi.org)

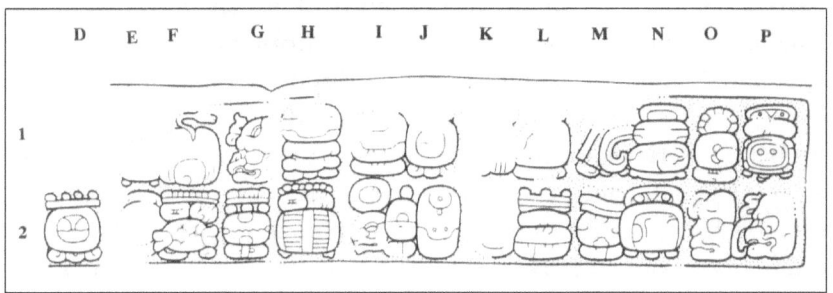

Figure 9.11

Tamarindito Hieroglyphic Stairway 2, step 3, D2–P2. (Drawing by S. Houston)

patron deities of the Petexbatun polity. The text suggests the close connection between sky–impinged-bone locations and patron deities.

A final important context of the impinged-bone glyph is in a name attributed to rulers of the Calakmul polity. MacLeod (letter dated February 8, 1993, distributed to epigraphers) suggested that the title reads *yuk(n)om kun* (one who forms alliances between seats/stations [polity centers]) and refers to the role of the rulers of Calakmul as important alliance-makers in the Maya world. If correct, this reading suggests that the concept of seats or platforms referenced by the impinged-bone played a central role in the way war was waged, victory assessed, and alliance maintained.

SACRED SEATS AND PLATFORMS AT COPÁN

The impinged-bone appears frequently in the inscriptions of Copán (Schele and Grube 1990a). This chapter does not comment on every example but instead focuses on those that inform the history of the city and its political structure or further enrich our understanding of the relationships between seats/platforms and supernatural power. At Copán, the sky–impinged-bone combination occurs only with Xukpi, the main sign of the Copán emblem glyph, or with Ux Witik, the toponym identified by Stuart and Houston (1994). Although these authors maintain that Ux Witik named the Copán locality itself, we suggest that it originally referred to a specific structure in the early Copán Acropolis. The *xukpi chan [IB]* (Copán-sky-seat/platform) is mentioned in the context of one of the earliest recorded events in Copán's history (8.6.0.10.8, July 14, 160) on Stela I (figure 9.12a; Schele 1987b). A tantalizing reference to the *witik* sky–seat/platform appears in an Early Classic stela fragment, following an expression reading *upatb'u(il)* (its construction) (figure 9.12b). The text of Altar A' contains another probable reference to the early constructions of the Acropolis (figure 9.12c). Unfortunately, the upper row of glyphs was cut off, but enough remains to reconstruct the original content of the text. The second clause begins with *ipatlaj k'inich yax k'uk' mo' nal...ch'uhul witik chan [IB]*, (and then it is built, the Ruler 1 place...holy Witik sky seat/platform). This reference suggests the identification of the Ux Witik sky–seat/platform as one of the early Acropolis structures built in the times of Ruler 1, such as Hunal or possibly Margarita, which bore this ruler's name as a stucco decoration.

Texts at Copán also employ the impinged-bone with reference to seats for spirits. An important example is seen on Altar T, originally erected by Ruler 16 in the village area to celebrate the first *k'atun* anniversary of his accession (figure 9.13). The image of a caiman is

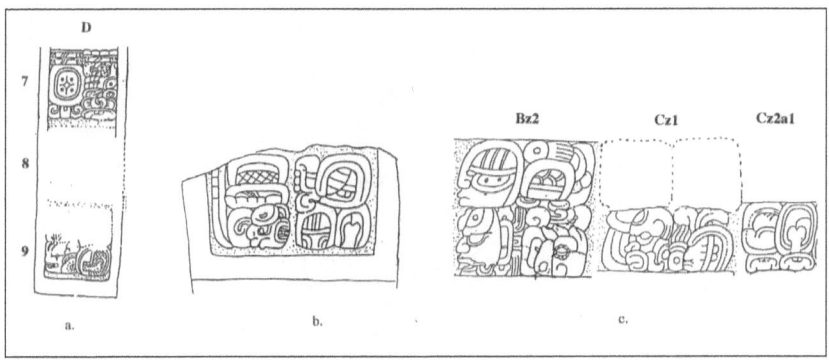

FIGURE 9.12

References to early seats/platforms at Copán: (a) Stela I, D7–D9, (b) Early Classic stela fragment, and (c) Altar A', Bz2, Cz1, Cz2a1. (Drawings by Linda Schele, © David Schele, courtesy Foundation for the Advancement of Mesoamerican Studies, Inc., www.famsi.org)

FIGURE 9.13

Copán Altar T, detail. (Drawing by Linda Schele, © David Schele, courtesy Foundation for the Advancement of Mesoamerican Studies, Inc., www.famsi.org)

shown draped across the altar top. On all four sides of the monument and on the altar top, seated on the creature's legs, are portraits of twenty spirit beings, many with mixed human and animal features. On the front side, flanking a central text, two pairs of these figures are seated on toponymic glyphs. The leftmost toponymic sign is unreadable, but the adjacent glyph consists of a serpent head with the impinged-bone glyph in its eye. The first toponym on the right side is Huk Ik' K'anal (Seven Black Yellow Place), a commonly cited supernatural location.

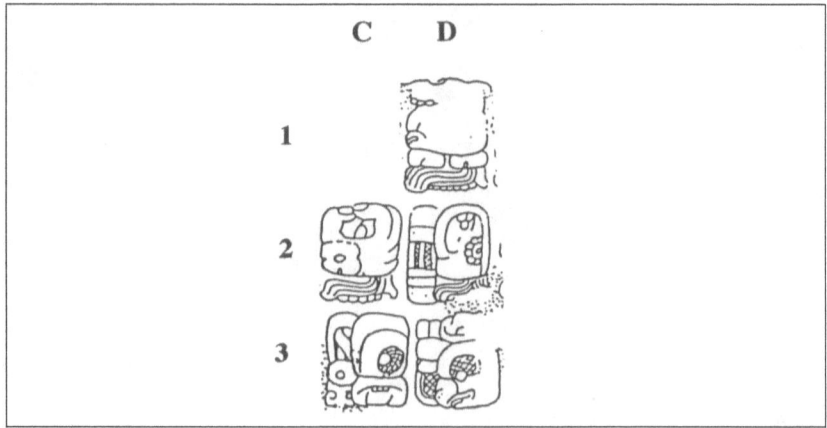

FIGURE 9.14
Copán Altar U, D1–D3. (Drawing by Linda Schele, © David Schele, courtesy Foundation for the Advancement of Mesoamerican Studies, Inc., www.famsi.org)

Next to the corner, the collocation consists of *yax* (first) and the impinged-bone infixed into the bent kawak sign that also occurs in references to early events in the history of Copán as recorded on Stelae I and 4. On Altar T, the impinged-bone glyphs are incorporated into supernatural locations that support spirit beings.

Other squat, boulder-like sculptures at Copán are, themselves, identified as seats/platforms through the impinged-bone glyph. Altar U, like Altar T, pertained to the village area. The dedication text of this monument reads *patwan k'inich ?? tun nuk [IB] tunah? ok?* (It is built, the sun-faced throne stone, the grand? seat/platform at its structure? base?) (figure 9.14). Because archaeological data concerning the architecture with which the altar was associated are lacking, we cannot confirm that the monument was originally erected adjacent to a building. Nevertheless, the reference to this monument by the impinged-bone glyph, as well as the T150b/c sign, suggests its function as a ceremonial seat or throne. This role would be consistent with interpretations of the zoomorphs of Quiriguá, which represent mythological thrones established by the gods during cosmogenesis (Looper 2002, 2003).

A number of texts at Copán describe rituals and other kinds of actions conducted at critical moments in the city's history in association with seats/platforms named with the impinged-bone. As we shall see,

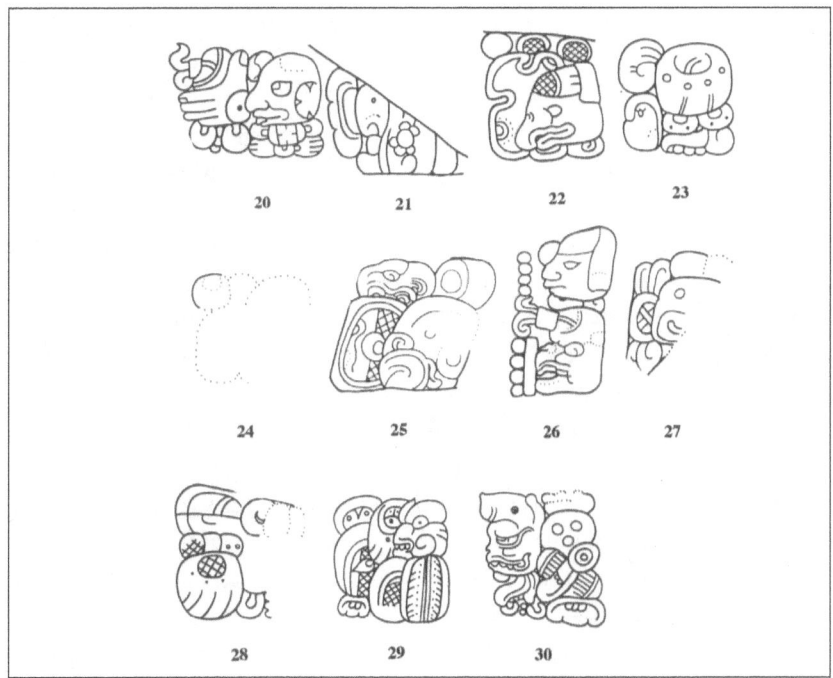

FIGURE 9.15

Copán Stela J, east text, 20–30. (Drawing by Linda Schele and M. Looper, © David Schele, courtesy Foundation for the Advancement of Mesoamerican Studies, Inc., www.famsi.org)

most of these events involve patron deities of Copán. The most detailed ritual text occurs on the east (mat) face of Stela J in the phrase recording the actions of Ruler 1 on the 9.0.0.0.0 Period Ending (figure 9.15). The passage begins on the first strand after the initial series date and a distance number of 13.10.0.0 that leads back to the 9.0.0.0.0 date. The first section of the passage (20–22) reads *ch'amay k'awil k'inich yax k'uk' mo' ux witz ajaw* (Ruler 1, three hills/mountains ajaw, takes K'awil). The reading of the next glyph (23) is unknown, and the last glyph on the first strand (24) is damaged. The text continues on the second strand, beginning in the upper-left corner. The first glyph (25) is preceded by the pronoun *u-*, a conflated earth sign **CHAB'/KAB'**, and the impinged-bone. The next glyph is *ch'uh* (god[s]). The events of the 9.0.0.0.0 Period Ending, then, take place at the "low seat/platform of the gods." Nikolai Grube and Simon Martin (personal communication with

361

Schele, 1994) suggested that the next block (26), *chan [te] ajaw, b'olon k'awil*, gives the names of patron gods of Copán, analogous to the Triad gods of Palenque (see also Houston and Stuart 1996). The next glyph (27) is the name of another Copán deity, K'uy ?? Ajaw.

The text disappears under a crossing strand and continues with another verb, which is also partly eroded (28). The next glyph (29) begins with the possessed impinged-bone, followed by *mak pas* (close, open). This peculiar phrase is related to the expression on Copán Stela A, where it is recorded that the cruciform vault under the stela was opened, then closed (Schele and Grube 1990a; Schele and Mathews 1998:160–161). The Stela J text suggests that a similar, low chamber or seat was closed and then opened. The final legible glyph in the passage (30) consists of a head of unknown value, the syllabic signs **wi** and **ya**, and then the *wi' te' nah* collocation that seems to refer to a lineage house or dynastic shrine (Schele and Grube 1992a; see also Stuart 2004).

A similar event may be recorded on the floor marker near the Motmot structure, which caps an offering-laden burial deep under Structure 10L-26 (figure 9.16; W. Fash, chapter 3 in this volume). There are two dates in this text, but various researchers in the Copán project disagree as to how they should be read (for comparison, see Stuart 2004). We shall present our preferred solution here while acknowledging that there are alternative interpretations. One date is the same 9.0.0.0.0 date seen on Stela J, although on the Motmot marker, the calendar round was erroneously recorded as 8 Ajaw 14 Keh. The syntax of the text is sufficiently difficult to make it unclear which event series occurred on this date. Linda Schele, Federico Fahsen, and Nikolai Grube (1994) suggested that the reading order for this text, as well as for the near contemporary Xukpi text, is verb[s]-subject[s]-date. The actions performed are the giving of offerings, and the actor is named at A6–A7 as Ruler 1. This information complements that given on Stela J for the same date.

The second date and its events, beginning at B5, are associated with Ruler 2, the successor of Ruler 1. The verb at B5 begins with the conjunction *i-* in the upper left, indicating that the chronological frame moves forward at this point. A distance number of 7.10.5 or 10.7.5 is written at B8–B9; however, because the calendar round of the second date is not recorded, the date of this second action cannot be

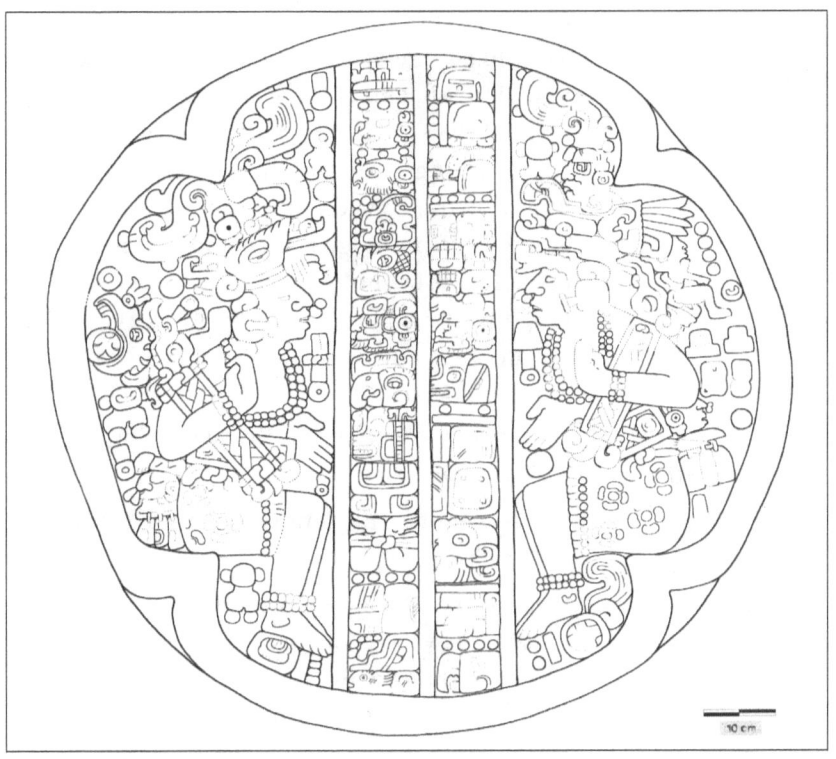

FIGURE 9.16

Copán Motmot marker. (Drawing by B. Fash, with modifications by Linda Schele)

determined with certainty. In addition to the conjunction, the block at B5 contains flames in the upper right corner, while the sign in the lower left is an Early Classic variant of the impinged-bone. In short, although eroded, the text may indicate that several years after the 9.0.0.0.0 Period Ending ceremony, on 9.0.7.10.5 or 9.0.10.7.5, a seat/platform was burned. It is probable that the impinged-bone refers to either the stone marker itself or the pit below it. Further, this event may have been the referent of the Stela J inscription, which records the closing and opening of a seat/platform in association with a 9.0.0.0.0 date.

The identification of this location as a special seat apparently continued after the floor marker was put in place and dedicated. Ruler 2 commissioned the Papagayo Structure, which covered Motmot and the marker. In the first manifestation of this building, Stela 63 stood against

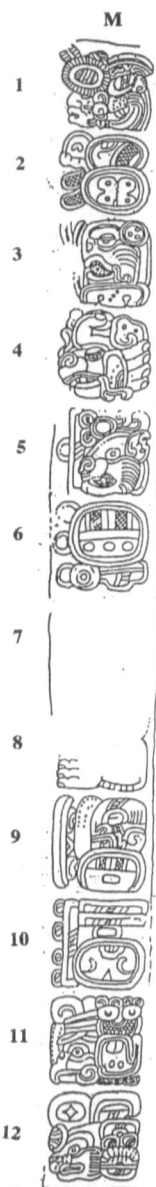

FIGURE 9.17

Copán Papagayo Step, side. (Drawing by Linda Schele, © David Schele, courtesy Foundation for the Advancement of Mesoamerican Studies, Inc., www.famsi.org)

the back wall. At some later date, Ruler 4 placed a steplike stone or "altar" in front of the stela (W. Fash, B. Fash, and Davis-Salazar 2004; Grube and Schele 1988). Although the fires laid on the stone during its termination rituals destroyed much of the text on the upper side, the text along the front edge remains mostly intact (figure 9.17). It begins with an *ub'ah* expression, followed by the collocation **a-CHAB'/KAB'-[IB]**. In Yukatek, *ah-* and *ak-* mean "settle" or "seat" and are used to form diverse expressions:

- '*ahkuuns*—Seat firmly (Bricker, Po'ot, and Dzul 1998:2)

- *ak*—Asentar (Barrera Vásquez et al., eds., 1980:5)

- *aktal*—Fundarse y estar fundada alguna cosa o asentada y fija en alguna parte; asentarse, fundarse y ponerse fija alguna cosa (Barrera Vásquez et al., eds., 1980:6)

- *ak-kabtah*—Poner o asentar de puesto en el suelo o sobre otra cosa, alguna vasija o cosas así, para que queden fijas (Barrera Vásquez et al., eds., 1980:6)

The senior author suggested that these meanings apply to the example on the Papagayo step and that the reference is to a firmly placed low seat/platform.[6] The presence of the impinged-bone suggests that the step may have been the functional replacement for the earlier Motmot marker. Indeed, its companion monument, Stela 63, deliberately echoes the text on the Motmot marker in that it cites the 9.0.0.0.0 Period Ending with the same "error" in the calendar round as its predecessor. Statues of the patron deities of Copán may have been placed on top of the step while the building was in use.

THE 9.11.0.0.0 STELA PROGRAM OF RULER 12

Although it encompasses the entire valley, the program of stelae dedicated by Ruler 12 on 9.11.0.0.0 seems to refer to important seats of deities in the city center. This set of monuments includes Stelae 2, 3, 10, 12, 13, and 19. The dates in the group commemorate Ruler 12's accession and the stations of Venus, beginning with a maximum elongation of the Morning Star and culminating in the heliacal rising of the Evening Star on the 9.11.0.0.0 *k'atun* ending. In turn, the accession date and its twenty-fourth anniversary on Stela 3 are connected through their association with Venus to the founding events recorded on Altar Q (Grube, Schele, and Fahsen 1991; Schele 1989a, 1991; Schele and Grube 1992a, 1992b; Schele and Mathews 1998).

Interpretations of Classic-period astronomy by Freidel, Schele, and Parker (1993) have enriched our understanding of the context of these events and their relationships to Maya Creation narratives. For example, the founding events that took place on September 6 and 9, 426, occurred when the Gemini-Orion nexus stood at zenith at dawn. The Maya interpreted this astronomical event as the same as the appearance of the sky on the day of Creation, August 13, 3114 B.C. On the accession of Ruler 12 and its twenty-fourth anniversary (February 5, 628, and February 7, 652), the sky was in its reciprocal Creation pattern with the Milky Way in the form understood as the World Tree at dawn. Venus was located in Sagittarius on both nights. It seems clear that these astronomical cycles structured the interpretation of dynastic founding and subsequent political events in terms of cosmogenesis. In other words, this set of monuments functioned as a great cosmic clock of Venus that integrated dynastic history, the Period Ending, and Creation.

Seats and platforms of gods, referenced by the impinged-bone, play an important part of this stela program. Stela 2 (figure 9.18), the monument erected on the north platform of the ball court, has the earliest date in the sequence: 9.10.15.0.0 (November 7, 647) (Schele 1992b). This date is only fifteen days after the *one-k'atun* anniversary of Ruler 12's accession, which is referenced through the distance number that ends the reverse text (B11). The accession itself is recorded at the top of the right (west) side of the stela at C1. The next date recorded is 9.11.0.0.0 12 Ajaw 8 Keh, the featured date in the stelae program (C5–C6). The principal event of the Period Ending, written at C7b–C8a, reads *ilahi*

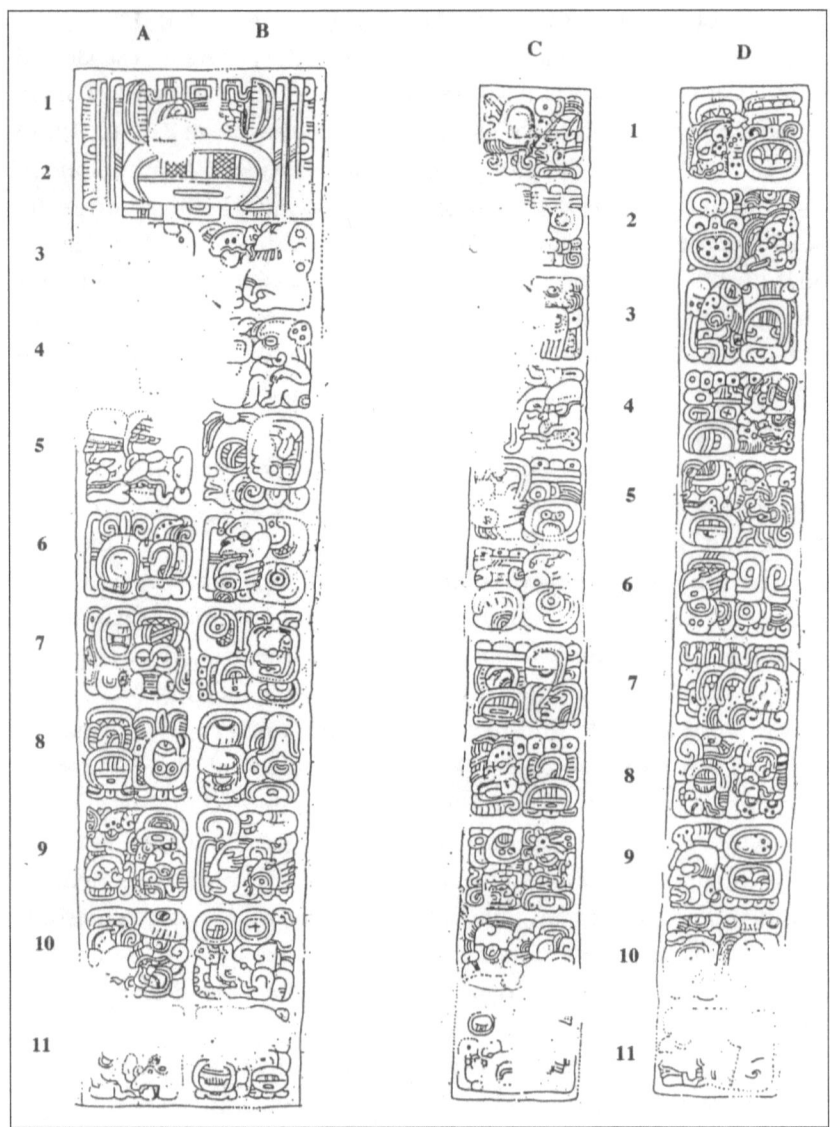

FIGURE 9.18

Copán Stela 2. (Drawing by B. Fash)

nah [lB] (the first seat/platform was witnessed). Names and titles of Ruler 12 follow at C8b–C11. On the opposite side of the monument are references to various gods, including the proper names of Copán's patron deities, Chante Ajaw and B'olon K'awil (D4). This information suggests that the seat observed during the Period Ending, like that mentioned on Stela J, pertained to the patron gods of the city. The location of these two monuments near the ball court and Structure 10L-26 suggests that this particular seat was located in the vicinity.

The remaining text on the east side of Stela 2 refers to the ritual performed and is important in interpreting other outlying stelae. The passage, introduced by a glyph (D5) that may read *ha'i*, seems to function as a focus marker or demonstrative (Werner Nahm and Nikolai Grube, personal communication with Schele, 1994). The verbs that follow read *utzutzlaj* (he finished it) and *yatij?* (they belonged to?). The reading for the second verb derives from sixteenth-century Tzotzil gloss of at as "count," "belong to," "be in partnership with" (Laughlin 1988:137; Barbara MacLeod and Nikolai Grube, personal communication with Schele, 1994). The name of the object that was finished (D7a) begins with a superfix that appears to read logographically as **TZIK** and syllabically as **tzi** (Schele, Fahsen, and Grube 1994). The double kawak **PIH/pi** is a glyph used to mark bundles in pottery scenes (Schele and Grube 1993). Thus, the name of the object might be *tzik yax pi[h]* (venerated first bundle). Although the context is different on Stela 2, this particular bundle is regularly associated with Period Endings of three tuns. The next glyph (D7b) is *uchab'ji* (under the authority of), followed by a couplet often associated with this bundle and with Period Endings: *chanal ch'uh chab'al ch'uh* (celestial god, earthly god) (D8). This is followed by *utz'akaj* (its ordering) (D9) and two eroded blocks (D10–D11).

The second stela in the series, Stela 12, is located on a hill east of the acropolis and has an initial series date (9.10.15.13.0) that is 260 days after the Stela 2 date. The inscription on the right side continues with a complex passage that is not at present interpretable, although the actor is clearly named as Ruler 12 (C8–D8). An *uchab'ji* agency expression at C10 links him to Ruler 1, thereby implying that the living king acted under the authority of the deceased. The last four glyphs (C13–D14; figure 9.19) record the "scattering" verb twice, followed by two terms that may refer to bundles. The text continues on the left side, with the bird variant of the impinged-bone at E1 followed by an eroded section that seems to record Ruler 12's name. The rest of the text is

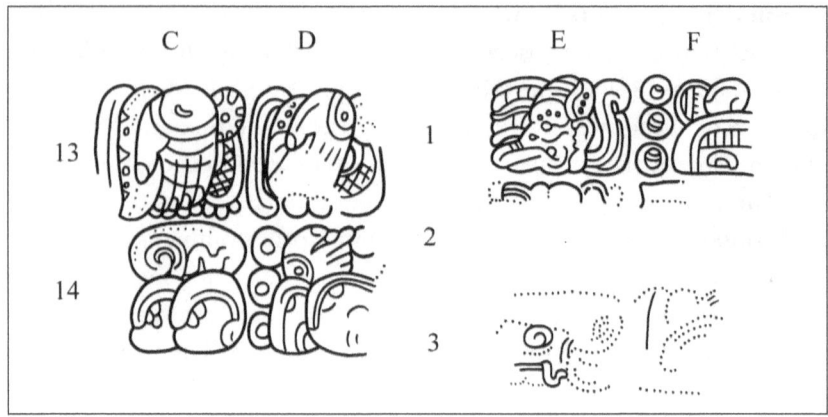

FIGURE 9.19
Copán Stela 12, C13–D14, E1–F3. (Drawing by D. Stuart and B. Fash)

damaged but can be reconstructed by comparing it with Stela 2, to which it is closely parallel. It includes the references to the images of Copán's patron gods (E5–E8), followed by the bundle ritual, beginning at F8. If these readings are correct, then this text records that the king scattered incense before bundles that were placed on a seat or platform. These bundles were associated with images of the patron gods of Copán and with the celestial and earthly gods invoked during the scattering ceremony.

The alignment of Stela 12 with Stela 10, its complement on the opposite side of the valley, has long been thought to be significant. Viewed from Stela 12, the sun sets over Stela 10 on April 12 and September 1 (Gregorian).[7] The initial date on Stela 10 is 9.10.19.13.0 (July 3, 652)—exactly four tuns after the date on Stela 12 (July 24, 648). Due to erosion, the contents of this text are less clear than Stelae 2 and 12. However, columns B and C prominently mention the Copán sky/high seat/platform and Ux Witik (figure 9.20a), and column D makes reference to *tzik pi[h] chanal ch'uh tzik pi[h] chab'al ch'uh* (venerated bundle celestial god, venerated bundle earthly god) (D5–D6; figure 9.20b). Besides repeating expressions on Stelae 2 and 12, these references introduce a series of sacred locations, including *?? way ?? nahb' nal xukpi chan* [IB], (?? transform? ?? lake place, Copán sky/high seat/platform) (D8–D9; figure 9.20b). The **WAY** glyph may indicate a cave or underworld portal, and the **NAHB'** may refer to the artificial water holes that

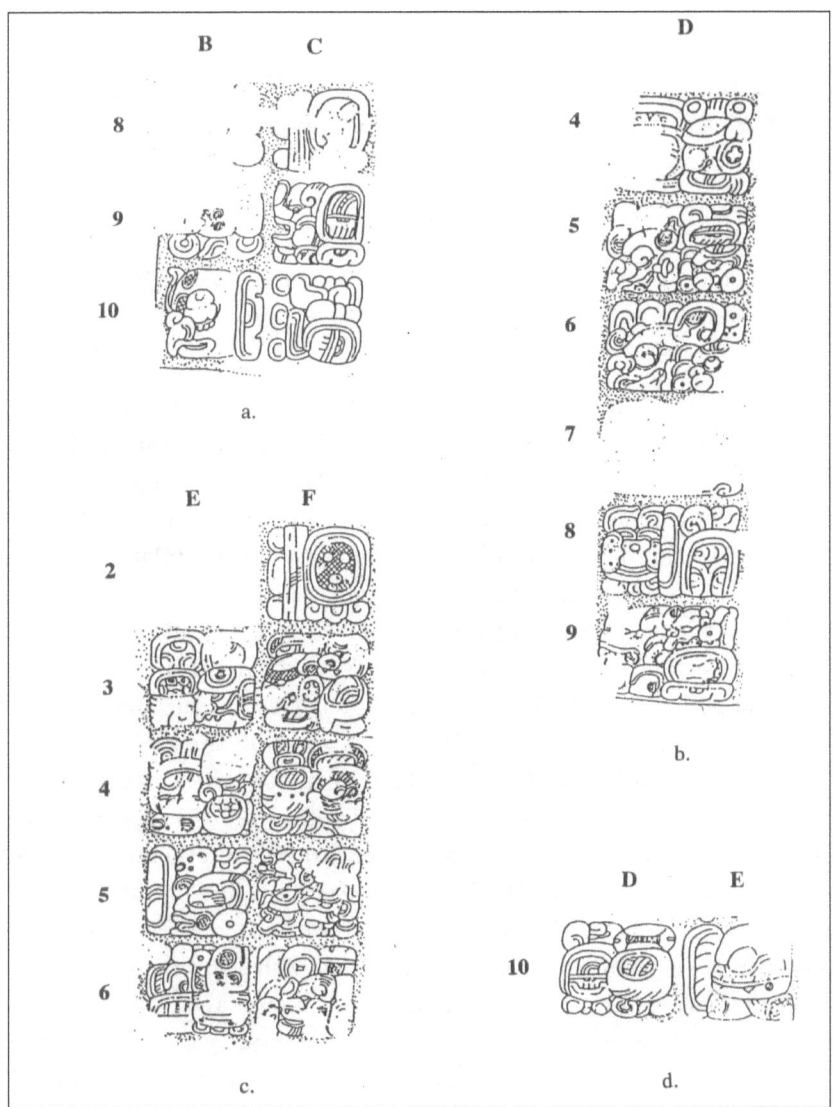

Figure 9.20

(a) Copán Stela 10, B8–C10, (b) Copán Stela 10, D4–D9, (c) Copán Stela 10, F2–F6, and (d) Copán Stela 13, D10–E10. (Drawings by Linda Schele, © David Schele, courtesy Foundation for the Advancement of Mesoamerican Studies, Inc., www.famsi.org)

lay to the east and west of the acropolis. The stela closes with a record of the 9.11.0.0.0 Period Ending and the conjuration of a vision serpent by the king (F2–F6; figure 9.20c).

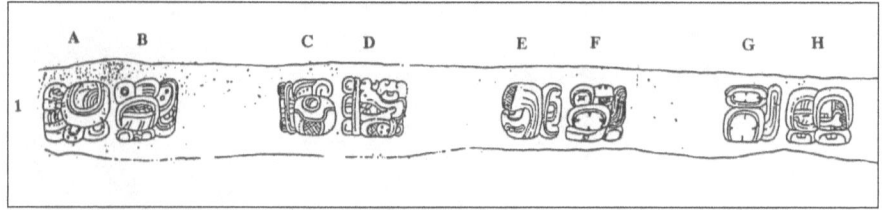

FIGURE 9.21

Copán Stela 13 Altar. (Drawing by Linda Schele, © David Schele, courtesy Foundation for the Advancement of Mesoamerican Studies, Inc., www.famsi.org)

Stela 13, located at the opposite, east entrance to the valley, also celebrates the 9.11.0.0.0 date and records that Ruler 12 called out the vision serpent named Chanal Chak B'ay (D10–E10; see figure 9.20d). The inscription also includes a reference to Chante Ajaw and B'olon K'awil (D1–E1), but the remaining text is more closely related to Stela 7, a Ruler 11 monument, than to the other outlying stelae of Ruler 12. The same cannot be said of the Stela 13 altar, which also refers to a seat/platform in a particularly revealing way (figure 9.21). Eight glyphs are arranged in horizontal pairs around the altar so that a pair of glyphs marks each cardinal direction. The text begins with the PSS initial sign (A1) and *patlaj* (it is made) (B1). The object created is named at C1 with a possessed **OHL** portal glyph, modified by a T128 superfix. This structure parallels the expression on Stela 10 (D8) that names a portal with the T128 followed by **WAY** (see figure 9.20b). The portal is further referenced at D1–E1 with *huk chapaht* (seven centipede), followed by *k'in ajaw lak'in chan [IB]*, (sun ajaw, east sky/high seat/platform). This reference suggests that the dedication of monuments by Ruler 12 established directional seats or platforms around the valley perimeter at the same time he renewed the seats of the patron gods in the city center.

In summary, sacred seats and platforms, referenced in the inscriptions of Copán by the impinged-bone glyph and its allographs, were important throughout the city's history. Such structures are mentioned in association with dates as early as A.D. 160, but without precise identification. One of the most sacred deity seats may have first been set in place by the founder himself on the occasion of the end of the ninth *b'ak'tun* (A.D. 436) and was probably located in the vicinity of the Structure 10L-26–ball court nexus. This epigraphic evidence complements the extensive archaeological evidence of ritual, building, and the deposition of sacra such as offerings and human remains within this zone (W. Fash, B. Fash, and Davis-Salazar 2004; W. Fash, chapter 3, and Sharer et al., chapter 5, in this volume).

Despite the obliteration of this nexus under tons of later construction, its politico-religious significance endured into the Late Classic period. It is particularly celebrated on the most elaborate program of monuments ever erected at Copán—the 9.11.0.0.0 Period Ending stelae cycle of Ruler 12. By highlighting ceremonies involving deity bundles at an impinged-bone place on several monuments, the texts create a web of meaning that focuses on the central stela in the program, Stela 2. Associated with the zone of Structure 10L-26 and the ball court, this monument renews emphasis on the area as a key seat of royal power at Copán.

Notes

The senior author, Linda Schele, originally conceived and presented the paper at the School of American Research advanced seminar in 1994 and submitted a copy for publication in 1995. The junior author, Matthew Looper, began to revise and update the paper in 1999, attempting to reflect the senior author's interpretations throughout. In this chapter, boldface indicates readings of glyphs, with logographs rendered in capital letters. Mayan words are italic.

1. For example, Yucatec: *ku* (la lechuza agorera), *ah kuy* (especie de lechuza) (Barrera Vásquez et al. 1980:342); Ch'ol: *xcu* (lechuza [tipo de tecolote, ave]) (Aulie and Aulie 1998:146).

2. Proto-Ch'olan: **ch'en* (cave) (Kaufman and Norman 1984:119). Yucatec: *ch'é'en* (well) (Bricker, Po'ot, and Dzul 1998:82).

3. Nikolai Grube (in Houston 1993:101) noted that the same deity appears with a 4 Ajaw 8 Kumk'u (13.0.0.0.0) date on Dos Pilas Panel 18, A3.

4. Ch'ol: *chan* (alto) (Aulie and Aulie 1998:29). Yucatec: *ká'an* (sky, height) (Bricker, Po'ot, and Dzul 1998:123); *ká'anhá'an* (haughty) (Bricker, Po'ot, and Dzul 1998:123); *ka'an* (cielo) (Barrera Vásquez et al. 1980:291); *ka'anal* (cosa alta) (Barrera Vásquez et al. 1980:292).

5. *kab* (bajo o abajo) (Barrera Vásquez et al. 1980:277).

6. An alternative interpretation of the a preceding the earth–impinged-bone would identify it as a second-person pronoun. The junior author notes the

compound **a-CH'UH-IL/li**, *ach'uhil* (your gods), at E2 on the same step.

7. Morley (1920:133; 1926) first discussed this alignment. Aveni (1977) checked it with modern instrumentation and suggested that 10L-22 and other buildings on the south end of the Acropolis addressed this axis. Morley suggested that the earlier of the two days would serve as a good marker for the beginning of the planting season, although the ancient agricultural season likely began in early February, as it does today.

10

A Foreign Past

*The Writing and Representation
of History on a Royal Ancestral Shrine
at Copan*

David Stuart

After four decades, Mayanists are now accustomed to the idea that ancient Maya artisans and scribes, when composing and carving monumental inscriptions, were principally concerned with the commemoration of historical events surrounding kings, their families, and their courts. Yet, despite our long acceptance of this historical paradigm in Maya research, it is surprising how little attention has been paid to ancient Maya concepts of history—one might call these "historical ideologies"—and how these gave shape to the written records now left to be studied. As Sahlins (1995) and numerous others have shown, ideas of what constitutes "history" may vary considerably from culture to culture, where they may be shaped by fundamental differences in temporal structures, language, and cosmology. In this perspective, history is interwoven with innumerable other factors that define the way a particular culture views itself and its proper place in the surrounding world. Maya notions of history, not surprisingly, are bound to differ from our own ideas of what constitutes "the past" (Lowenthal 1985). Even so, we still lack much understanding of how Maya culture in the Classic period framed its textual representations of earlier people, events, and social relations. This chapter is hardly so ambitious, for it focuses only on a few important inscriptions at one of many Maya sites with a vibrant tradition of written history. Yet, through these, we can approach general questions of how Maya notions of the past were culturally construed. Such a detailed treatment of a single tradition will, we hope, illuminate some general issues concerning the ways Maya dynasts of the Classic period chose (or chose not) to represent themselves and their forebears.

This chapter focuses on one temple at Copan where the inscriptions and ornate decoration embody and convey history as no other Maya monument does. This is Structure 10L-26, the temple of the Hieroglyphic Stairway, a pyramid once dominating the north side of the main Acropolis (figure 10.1). As is well known, Structure 10L-26's stairway bears the longest extant Maya inscription and presents a remarkable overview of local dynastic history. The dates and events recorded on this massive document were not randomly constructed, of course, but rather served as background for a single event that, as we shall see, motivated the dedication of the stairway itself—the burial of Ruler 12 within its substructure. Another key inscription from Structure 10L-26 is the so-called "Temple Inscription" from the building's upper temple, recently reconstructed in an almost complete form from its earlier jumbled state. This text is also unique in many ways and offers a strange twist on the historical themes presented in the stairway.

Before delving into these monuments, however, it is first necessary to present the fundamentals of Copan's dynastic history as presently known, updating some earlier discussions by me and by others (W. Fash 1991; Martin and Grube 2000; Stuart 1992). The issues raised touch on historiography, archaeology, and iconography, but at the center of this treatment is Copan's idiosyncratic documentary record. Copan's local style of monumental writing emphasizes or ignores certain topics and themes that are treated differently elsewhere. These patterns offer a unique means to explore the concerns and activities of royal court society in the Classic period. Specifically, while historical information is of supreme intrinsic interest, the ancient textual and symbolic patterning of that history illuminates how Copan positioned itself and its own identity in the Maya and Mesoamerican world. Structure 10L-26's display of names and events is obviously anchored in Copan's own histori-

A FOREIGN PAST

FIGURE 10.1
Structure 10L-26 in 1987. (Photograph by the author)

cal circumstances, but the ordering and visual presentation of such written information reveal much about Maya notions of the past and ancestral remembrance.

Historical events are obviously a major emphasis in Mesoamerican texts, yet some Maya sites emphasize historical subjects and narratives more than others. As it happens, Copan generally seems "ahistorical" when compared with Palenque or Yaxchilan, for example (Stuart 1992). The stelae and altars of the Acropolis seem little more than ritual markers bearing the names of various kings, and the details of Copan's political history are frustratingly absent for the most part. The Hieroglyphic Stairway, by contrast, is not only immensely long, but also vast in its narrative scope, encompassing mythological events and centuries of royal history. It must have been remarkably novel in its time, even from the perspective of kingdoms where records of historical details were more firmly rooted as textual genres. Few, if any, other Maya inscriptions even attempted to present their contents on a comparable public scale.[1]

David Stuart

HISTORICAL BACKGROUND TO THE HIEROGLYPHIC STAIRWAY

Copan's Classic-period dynasty of sixteen rulers spanned a period of nearly four centuries, and the basic outline of the royal history is today well understood (Martin and Grube 2000; Newsome 2001; Schele and Freidel 1990:306–345; Stuart 1992, 1997, 2004). As background, here I offer the barest sketch of the dynastic history relevant to the interpretations of the stairway, focusing mainly on four kings: K'inich Yax K'uk' Mo' (Ruler 1), Ruler 12, Waxaklajun Ub'aah K'awil (Ruler 13), and K'ahk' Yipyaj Chan K'awil (Ruler 15).[2]

Copan's so-called founder was the now famous K'inich Yax K'uk' Mo', first identified as an Early Classic ruler by the author in 1984. He is, of course, the first of the seated figures depicted in the sequence of sixteen kings on the periphery of Altar Q. According to the text on the upper face of the stone, he "arrived" at Copan from some foreign locale in the year A.D. 427, approximately five months after receiving the charter of royal office at his point of origin. His outsider status seems to be emphasized by the Teotihuacan-style elements that are routinely part of his costume in Late Classic depictions. For this reason, he is often assumed to be a native of highland Mexico or perhaps Kaminaljuyu (Coggins 1988). Despite the suggestive evidence, there is probably no need to go so far to explain his origins. The name *K'inich Yax K'uk' Mo'* is decidedly Mayan (Great Sun Green Quetzal Macaw), and his nearest contemporary portrait shows the early king in pure Maya regalia; only in his later portraits is this ethnic difference emphasized. The evidence suggests that he was ethnically Maya, and the study of his likely remains in the Hunal tomb further suggests that he spent most of his early years in the central lowlands (Sharer et al., chapter 5 in this volume). No textual data resolve the issue, but there is good reason to believe that his connections to Teotihuacan were real and lasting enough to be remembered by later dynasts at Copan. I believe that the main political event commemorated in Altar Q's text could have involved a visit to the highland city by the Maya nobleman then named K'uk' Mo' Ajaw, who three days later departed for the lowlands with his newfound emblems of royal office (Stuart 2004). This scenario necessitates a view of Teotihuacan as a pancultural pilgrimage center associated with the sacred charter of rulership, much as it remained throughout later stages of Mesoamerican history. As we will see, the preoccupation with a Teotihuacan "heritage" would dominate the symbolism of Copan's Late Classic political art.

K'inich Yax K'uk' Mo' is intimately tied to the so-called "founder's glyph" first discussed by Schele (1992a). This distinctive-looking sign combination always ends in the sign -NAAH (house), suggesting that it is the name of a particular type of house or structure. As I have discussed elsewhere (Stuart 2000, 2004), the full reading is perhaps *wite'-naah* (origin house), which, in its many examples, seems strongly linked to Teotihuacan symbolism. The same building term is cited in several inscriptions at other sites (Yaxchilan and Machaquila, among others) and may refer to a ritual locale at Teotihuacan. Its prominence in the inscription atop Altar Q suggests that nearby Structure 10L-16, with its clear Teotihuacan symbolism, may have been a local Copan version of an origin house.

K'inich Yax K'uk' Mo's establishment of a new dynastic order at Copan represented the foundation of the community as a major Classic center, although there are clear indications that Copan already had a long political history before this time (Stuart 2004). His arrival probably was timed to coincide roughly with the change of the *b'ak'tun* in A.D. 435 (9.0.0.0.0), recorded in several later Copan texts as being of profound historical importance. His son was a significant participant in the rituals centered on this calendrical station, and the double portrait of father and son on the circular Motmot marker may indicate that both were living witnesses to the event. The b'ak'tun ending was the probable date for the major construction of the early Motmot phase of Structure 10L-26, which we will prove significant to the interpretation of the texts and array of iconography in the building's final phase.

Here, we will not discuss most of the early rulers who succeeded Ruler 2, because the history surrounding them is so poorly known, except for a few dates and architectural developments around the site core. Ruler 8 seems to have been a major figure responsible for the construction of the magnificent Rosalila structure, probably around A.D. 540. This temple, at the core of the Acropolis, was clearly designed as the ritual center for the ancestral cult of the initial dynast, K'inich Yax K'uk' Mo', whose name is emblematically repeated on its outer walls. It is interesting to see that this temple, devoted to the founder, contains none of the visual allusions to central Mexico that became important much later in Copan's artistic history.

The next ruler who plays a significant role in the architectural history of Structure 10L-26 is the twelfth of the sequence, sometimes known in the literature as "Smoke Imix" (an unfortunate nickname that has no relationship to the king's true name). In many ways, he was the most powerful and influential of Copan's sixteen kings. He assumed the throne on February 8, 628, either as a child or a very young man, and reigned sixty-seven years. Interestingly, during the early seventh century, several long-lived and important rulers held sway over other Maya kingdoms, among them K'inich Janahb' Pakal of Palenque and Itzamnah B'ahlam I of Yaxchilan. Together, these and other lords gave shape to the political landscape that would dominate Classic Maya history for the next two centuries, before the collapse. At Copan, Ruler 12 appears to have consolidated political control and wielded it over a considerable distance from the Copan Valley. One of the more distinctive features of his rule was the erection of several inscribed monuments around the perimeter of the valley itself, on mountainsides away from standing architecture. These monuments likely held cosmological significance associated with the world directions and possibly commemorated royal rituals held near important mountain-top shrines that have long since vanished. Nonetheless, they reveal that Ruler 12 constructed monuments beyond Copan's Acropolis and its immediate area. Within the Acropolis area itself, Ruler 12 constructed several more stelae and altars and, no doubt, helped to give shape to much of the Acropolis architecture as we know it. At about this time, as well, we find an inscription naming Ruler 12 at Quiriguá, perhaps suggesting that Copan in these years was politically dominant over its much smaller neighbor. This possibility will emerge as very significant in the consideration of the next king. After nearly seventy years on the throne, Ruler 12 died on July 2, 695, and was buried in a large tomb discovered in 1988 deep within Structure 10L-26 (W. Fash, Beaubien, et al. 2001; W. Fash, Williamson, et al. 1992). The presence of the royal tomb at this location led directly to the conception and design of the Hieroglyphic Stairway and all subsequent modifications of the pyramid.

FIGURE 10.2
Photograph of 1895 excavations at Structure 10L-26, showing the upper slumped steps above the section discovered in situ. (Photograph courtesy the Peabody Museum of Archaeology and Ethnology, Harvard University)

LOOKING AT TWO PHASES OF THE HIEROGLYPHIC STAIRWAY

The probable son of the long-lived Ruler 12 was the thirteenth ruler, Waxaklajun Ub'aah K'awil. His ample modifications to the Great Plaza, with the dedications of the principal stelae (Newsome 2001), gave the northern area of the Acropolis much of its current form. One of his principal architectural accomplishments was the amplification of the Structure 10L-26 pyramid above the tomb of his father, corresponding to what has come to be known as the "Esmeralda" phase of the building (W. Fash 2002). The Hieroglyphic Stairway now seems to have been a part of this refurbishment, but the construction history of the building and its inscribed steps is exceedingly complex. To untangle the evidence, we must rely on a mutually informed consideration of both the textual and stratigraphic records.

The stairway is badly weathered in many areas, and only about one-third was found in its original place, the upper two-thirds having tumbled from place at some point in antiquity. When excavated by Owens and Gordon (Gordon 1902), a large section from the upper stairway was discovered to have slumped down the pyramid, luckily retaining much of its original order (figure 10.2). Nonetheless, a complete restoration of the stairway has proved impossible because of many very eroded blocks. What remains are several historical dates relating the accession and death of various rulers, as well as a few obscure yet tantalizing "floating" sections that are out of context and thus defy any meaningful translation.

Archaeologists at Copan have long assumed that the stairway was a single-phase enterprise conceived and produced under the reign of Ruler 15. There is now good reason to revise this view, at least somewhat. As seen in its present reconstructed form (dating to 1939), the inscription on the stairway appears to be one long text without breaks or interruptions. The carving styles of the glyphs and the information contained within the hieroglyphs suggest, however, that the stairway was constructed in two parts and at two different times, with the final monument consisting of separate but thematically linked inscriptions. The best evidence for this is the presence of two dedication events in the stairway inscription, one associated with the date 9.13.18.17.9 (A.D. 710) recorded on Step 1 and another with 9.16.4.1.0 (A.D. 755).[3] Significantly, both dedicatory passages (figure 10.3a, b) make use of the verb *pat-wan* (to build, shape, form) (Stuart 1998), clearly indicating that two stairways were built over a five-decade period.

These two parts of the stairway can be easily recognized by looking at the carving styles of the glyphs. The lowermost section, fourteen steps of which were discovered by Owens and Gordon in situ, is carved with relatively small glyphs in an ornate style, using sharp contours and fine, incised lines. These are similar to the glyphs found on the sides of Stela C in the main plaza, dating to 9.14.0.0.0 6 Ajaw 13 Muwan.[4] Some fallen glyphs from the stairway display the same size and carving style and, presumably, were set originally near the lower part that is still in place. A very different treatment of carving is visible on the numerous

A Foreign Past

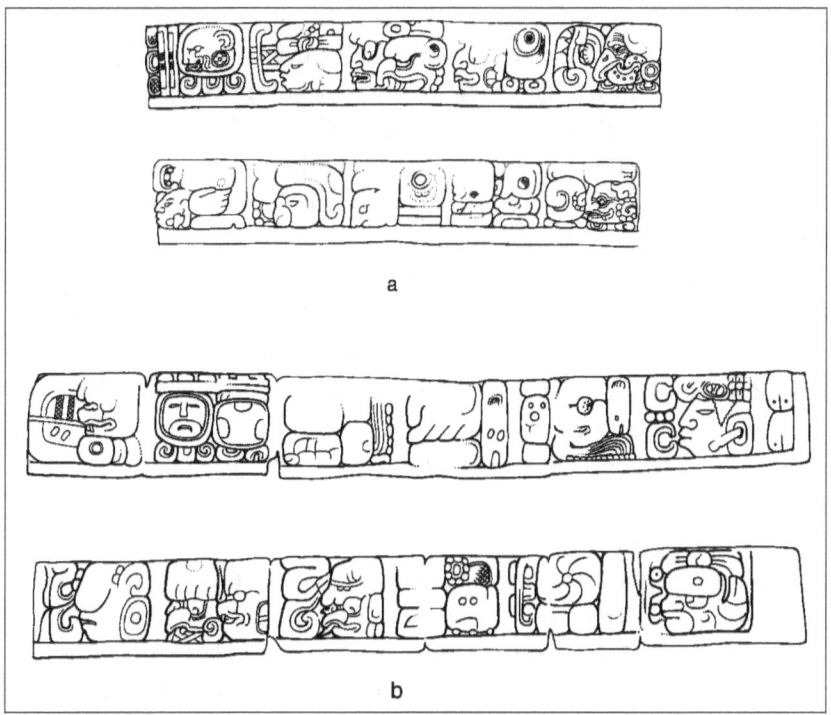

Figure 10.3
Dedicatory statements from the Hieroglyphic Stairway: (a) Step 1 and (b) Step 38. (Drawings by the author, based on preliminary drawings by B. Fash)

remaining blocks from the upper stairway. The glyphs are larger in size and show much rounder, balloon-like contours that are most similar to the glyphs on Stela M, placed directly in front of the stairway and dating to 9.16.5.0.0. The similar styles of Stelae C and M correspond very well to the two dedicatory dates of the inscription.[5]

The Hieroglyphic Stairway, I therefore posit, is really composed of two distinct stairways: the original, in the reign of Waxaklajun Ub'aah K'awil, and the later, upper section, added by Ruler 15 well into his own reign. If the stairway in its present form (more or less) was the result of a modification by Ruler 15, what would the original setting of the earlier stairway have been? Armed with this epigraphic evidence, W. Fash (2002) suggests, based on the architectural investigations of Rudy Larios and Fernando López, that the earliest version was originally placed on the eastern side of the pyramid, above where Larios has found indications of a stairway destroyed during the building's final-phase construction. This stairway was associated with the Esmeralda phase of construction, otherwise known as 10L-26-3rd. According to Larios and Fash, the western side of the building did not have a stairway at all and represented a significant, though temporary, reorientation of the building away from the main plaza. The assignment of the initial stairway to the temple's Esmeralda phase agrees with the hieroglyphic dating of the steps to the early reign of Waxaklajun Ub'aah K'awil.

Returning to the stairway itself, some glyphs from the upper section of the stairway (found, by Gordon, slumped down above the lower portion) exhibit both carving styles.[6] Some of the lowermost steps within the fallen section may actually be part of the first stairway, suggesting that the beginning of the earlier inscription survives in its original position relative to the later glyphs. Unfortunately, most of these glyphs are badly weathered, so it is impossible to be certain where on the complete stairway this transition took place. On the basis of several large iconographic sculptures recovered in the Owen and Gordon excavations, Barbara Fash (personal communication 1987) speculates that a decorated outset platform similar to that on Structure 10L-11 may have been built in the upper or middle reaches of the entire stairway. Such a platform would have had the practical function of allowing Ruler 15's section of the stairway to be read easily; from the plaza floor, this would surely have been impossible.

The narrative structure of the stairway's two inscriptions is now easier to comprehend, for we are no longer forced to explain why the dedication of another, earlier stairway would be the final climactic event of one very long inscription. In its original form, this first stairway contained a record of the early kings of Copan, listing their accession and death dates. This is indicated by the bottom-most steps discovered in place by Gordon and inscribed with the following dates:

9.5.19.3.0	8 Ajaw 3 Sotz'	Accession of Ruler 10
9.7.4.17.4	10 K'an 2 Keh	Death of Ruler 10
9.7.5.0.8	Lamat 6 Mak	Accession of Ruler 11

9.9.14.16.9	2 Muluk 2 K'ayab'	Death of Ruler 11
9.9.14.17.5	6 Chikchan 18 K'ayab'	Accession of Ruler 12

Between the list-like presentation of these royal inaugurations and the final dedication phrase is a lengthy, though badly damaged, passage on Steps 4, 5, and 6 that records the death and burial of Ruler 12. After this comes an eroded passage of noncalendrical glyphs, followed finally by the record of 9.13.18.17.9 12 Muluk 7 Muwan, the dedication date on Step 1 (see figure 10.3a). This final date on the bottommost step is more specifically a stairway dedication, for the glyph ye-b'u-li, for *y-ehb'-il* (his steps), is clearly discernible in the penultimate block. The full dedication passage in the last two glyphs of the bottom step can be read *pat-wan y-ehb'-il u-muk-il 'Copan'-ajaw* (built are the steps of the burial of the Copan lord), this surely being a reference to Ruler 12. The final steps of the Hieroglyphic Stairway thus connect the monument directly and explicitly to the deceased Ruler 12, stating that it is a monument "of his burial."

Ruler 10 is the earliest ruler mentioned in the section remaining in situ, but blocks of other, earlier Initial Series dates clearly show that the timeline of the dynastic narrative extended much further back in time. From the various scattered fragments, it is now possible to reconstruct a selection of dates, including the accessions of Rulers 8 (9.4.18.6.12) and 9 (9.5.17.13.7), although their original placement above Step 14 is impossible to determine. A long section of text runs along several steps above the accession record of Ruler 10, and we can only presume that this pertained to some historical events from Ruler 9's reign.

One newly reconstructed step commemorates the accession of K'inich Yax K'uk' Mo', recording the 8.19.10.10.17 date famous from Altar Q, but in Initial Series form (figure 10.4). A number of blocks from this vitally important inscription have yet to be joined, but the surviving portions suggest that they relate significantly more information on Copan's dynastic founding than Altar Q. Presumably, this accession date for the first king came near the beginning of the stairway's earliest phase, wherever that originally was.

The slumped portion of the stairway excavated by Gordon and kept in its original order includes the possible transition point between

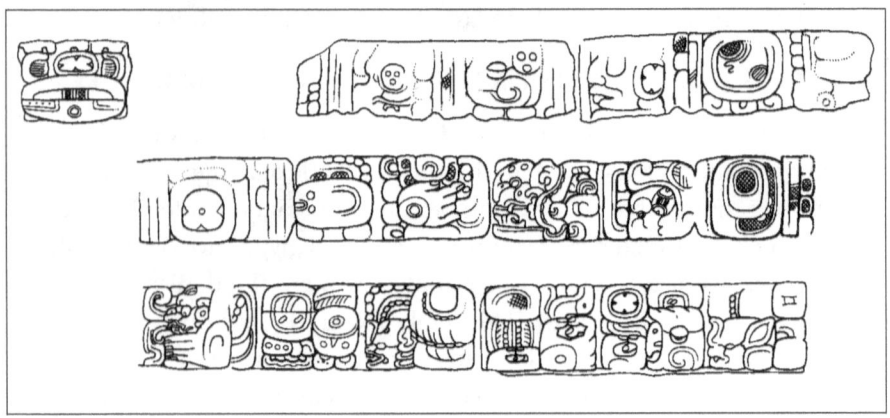

FIGURE 10.4
The accession record of K'inich Yax K'uk' Mo', assembled from various loose blocks of the Hieroglyphic Stairway. (Drawing by the author, based on preliminary drawings by B. Fash)

the smaller, finely carved glyphs of the lower steps and the larger, balloon glyphs of the upper portion. This "seam" comes between what are now Steps 33 and 34, where the transition is visible not only in the sculptural style of glyphs, but also in the size of the stone construction blocks, as already noted. In this section, then, we may have the initial steps of the lower section in order, in a section that preceded the accession reference to K'inich Yax K'uk Mo'. Sadly, most of this is eroded beyond hope of legibility, but one intriguing passage includes a lengthy Long Count date using periods far higher than the b'ak'tun, rather like other "Grand Long Counts" at Coba and Yaxchilan. This mythical date, far in the past, seems to be connected with temple dedications overseen by certain gods. At least five such "god houses" are named in this enigmatic section, and I believe that they pertain to a previously unknown aspect of Classic Maya creation mythology.

Great pains were evidently taken by Ruler 15 to ensure that the second stage of the Hieroglyphic Stairway, with its associated decorative and iconographic sculpture, would conform to the earlier steps. In the forty-seven years after the first steps were dedicated, Copan experienced severe political and military misfortunes as a result of Waxaklajun Ub'aah K'awil's capture and defeat by Quiriguá in A.D. 738. By appending his own staircase to the earlier monument, Ruler 15 seems to have been motivated, in part, by a need to update the extensive and important information on Copan's dynastic history. In so doing, he drew his own connections to Ruler 12, his distant predecessor. It is significant that Ruler 15 also makes note of the fact that the modified stairway is still "of" Ruler 12 (see figure 10.3b).

Ruler 15's stairway follows much the same structure as the earlier section. Numerous unarticulated blocks bearing the name of Waxaklajun Ub'aah K'awil suggest that he, too, was a major protagonist of that narrative. Large sections of the later stairway are largely out of order, but we do read several dates with assurance. Important among these is 11 Ajaw 18 Zak, or 9.14.15.0.0 (on what is now Step 67), another date in the reign of this important ruler. A featured event recorded soon afterward is the death of Waxaklajun Ub'aah K'awil in connection with the Quiriguá conflict of 9.15.6.14.6 6 Kimi 4 Tzek, followed, in turn, by a long passage explaining its significance from the Copan viewpoint (figure 10.5). The initial statement on the Quiriguá-Copan war is surprisingly nonbellicose: *siyaj Yaxhaal Chaak* (Yaxhaal Chaak was born). Yaxhaal Chaak is an important aspect of the Maya storm god whose name literally means "First-Rain Chaak," and he is occasionally depicted on painted vessels from the central Petén region. The 6 Kimi 4 Tzek date of the war corresponds to May 3, A.D. 738, the very day that is widely celebrated throughout the Maya area as the Day of the Cross and is heralded as the official start of the rainy season. This passage clearly is used to establish the timing for the important episode, and one wonders whether the timing of the conflict was directly related to this day of profound agricultural and ritual importance. Later in the same section of the stairway, we read *k'a'ay u-?-sak-ik'-il tu-tok' tu-pakal* (his [?] breath expired in war). This casts the defeat in a somewhat nobler light than the texts of Quiriguá, which state that the Copan ruler "was chopped," or beheaded (Stuart 1992).[7] I suspect that many of the loose blocks in a similar carving style went with this passage, discussing in some detail that fateful event. The upper-stairway inscription goes on to record the accession date of Ruler 14, his death nine years later, and then the accession of Ruler 15. Significantly, the last readable date of this upper portion of the stairway commemorates the making of "Ruler 12's" stairway on 9.16.4.1.0, the last date of the entire Hieroglyphic Stairway inscription. Although the beginning of

David Stuart

Figure 10.5

Sections of the Hieroglyphic Stairway recording the war with Quiriguá. (Drawings by the author, based on preliminary drawings by B. Fash)

this later section of the stairway text is missing, one can see that its internal structure is very much the same: a series of historical records featuring royal accession and death dates, culminating in a highlighted statement of a stairway being built and dedicated.

Both texts on the stairway seem self-contained and essentially conceived as two separate, though complementary, inscriptions. Their respective historical contents do not overlap, yet they conform to a similar discursive pattern. Moreover, the chronology of the upper section begins, as far as one can tell, within the reign of Waxaklajun Ub'aah K'awil, who, presumably, presided over the stairway dedication mentioned at the end of the lower section. The stylistic differences between the two text fragments, as I have described them, co-vary with the content: the sharper, more deeply carved glyphs of the bottom steps discuss the earliest kings, and the rounder carving of the other section seems restricted completely to a discussion of the history between the time of Waxaklajun Ub'aah K'awil and the second recorded dedication under Ruler 15.

The later king's modification of the original stairway confirms the powerful significance of the original stairway inscription, implying that the latter must have been considered, in some manner, the "official history" of the site and its long-lived dynasty. His refurbishment of Structure 10L-26 may even reveal Ruler 15's desire to best his predecessor, for in his text, he summarizes forty years of history in the same amount of space Waxaklajun Ub'aah K'awil used to recount the preceding three centuries. Then again, we must remember that the point of these texts is not necessarily self-aggrandizement. The focal point of the narrative, when all is said and done, is Ruler 12, arguably the greatest king in Copan's history.

THE TEMPLE INSCRIPTION

The vaulted temple atop Structure 10L-26, associated with the final phase of the pyramid, was largely gone when first investigated by Maudslay. A large array of sculptured stone from its outer façade (B. Fash 1992a:figure 16) and interior is the only indication of its former grandeur, and determining even its precise dimensions is difficult today. The temple's outer decoration emphasized an explicitly militaristic, Teotihuacan-like iconography, whereas the interior design was confined to an ornate, full-figure inscription adorning one of the long interior walls. This "Temple Inscription," as it is generally called, is surprisingly complete, given the temple's complete collapse. In 1996 Barbara Fash and I oversaw its reconstruction in Copan's Museo de Escultura, where it is now on display. The long, horizontal band of glyphs is partly carved on beveled stones, indicating that it decorated the vault spring of the temple interior. Curtain holes are evenly spaced among these glyphs, indicating that it was placed above very large and shallow "niches" that probably held some sort of image. The remaining sections form two well-finished, vertical edges of what was in all likelihood the same niche or door.

The text is one of the finest examples of scribal art from Mesoamerica and perhaps one of the most intriguing inscriptions yet discovered in the Maya area. Close inspection of the glyphs reveals that many are adorned with "Teotihuacan" visual elements, as if they were designed to conform to the temple's overall concern with central Mexico and the messages conveyed by its visual style. Some of the signs are, indeed, completely unrecognizable as Maya glyphs proper, but

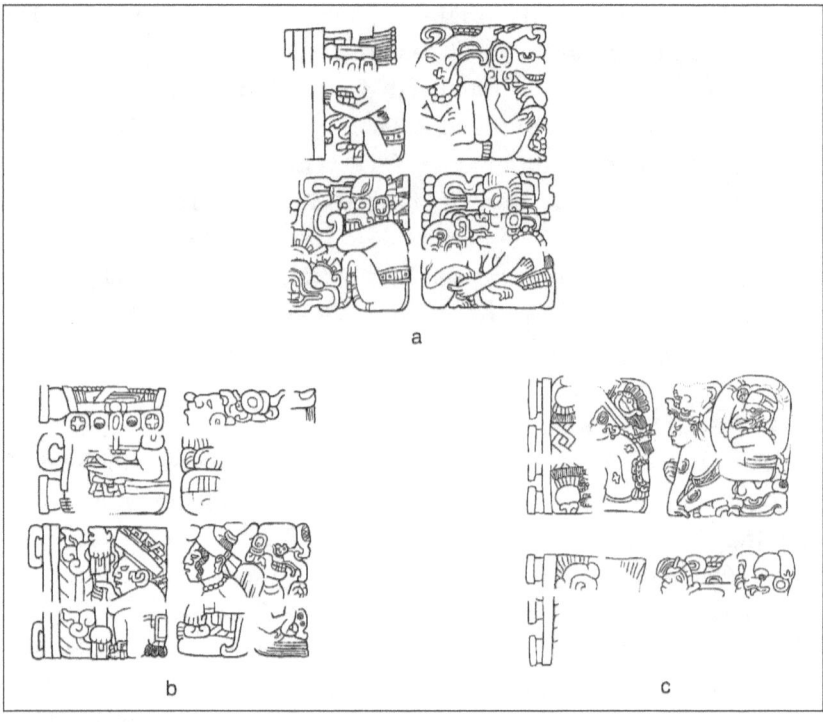

FIGURE 10.6

Three parallel passages in the Temple Inscription of Structure 10L-26. (Drawings by the author)

others are clearly Maya signs with Teotihuacan-style elements attached. In all respects, these hybrid glyphs are unique in the corpus of Maya inscriptions.

The Teotihuacan-style glyphs and those of a more conventional Maya form are of equal number and were placed in alternating columns. On the two flanking sections that bear double columns, the leftmost column only was composed of the odd Teotihuacan-style elements; those to the right were conventional-looking, albeit elaborate, Maya glyphs. At first glance, it would seem that the text is composed in a conventional format of double columns, reading two glyphs across, then down, and so on, but this is not the case. Instead, the inscription is read in vertical columns and has two parallel components, one "Teotihuacan" and one Maya. That is, like the Rosetta Stone, the inscription presents a single text written in two very different-looking scripts.

Comparisons of paired glyphs within the inscription show this remarkable format (figure 10.6a–c). Column pE in the horizontal band shows two "Teotihuacan" glyphs, the first composed of the number *18* and a small Tlaloc and the second showing hybrid figure-combining features of Tlaloc and K'awil (God K). Column pF, immediately to the right, displays two standard Maya glyphs: a full-figure number "18" (showing the personified variants of *8* and *10*) and, below, a **B'AAH** gopher with **K'AWIL**. Obviously, the two glyphs of column pF render the name of Waxaklajun Ub'aah K'awil. In another comparison (figure 10.6b), column pI shows a frontal-view Tlaloc with a numerical coefficient of 2 above a second glyph representing a seated man with a staff and a coefficient of 11. The column to the right, pJ, displays the Maya head variant of 2 above a "K'atun" glyph, and below, a clearly recognizable, full-figure version **11-HAAB'** ("11 Tuns"). Evidently, the frontal-view Tlaloc functions as an equivalent to "K'atun," and the seated person with the staff serves as a parallel to "Tun." In column pK (figure 10.6c), the combination of the full-figure "8" and a goggled-eyed character seems to be a rendering of the "8 Ajaw" day sign in pL. Similarly, in pM, an "8" attached to some odd-looking creature appears to parallel "8 Sotz'" in the neighboring column to its right.

A similar pattern holds for most of the glyphs in the Temple Inscription, although perhaps not so obviously in all cases. In column pG, for example, two "Teotihuacan" glyphs seem to have no clear relationship to the name of Ruler 14 that appears at their side in column pH. Despite some ambiguous pairings, however, there can be little doubt that the Temple Inscription employs two parallel texts, one in a Teotihuacan style, apparently to be read first, and a "translation" in standard Maya. Despite some initial hopes, the odd glyphs do not reproduce any true writing system from highland Mexico, and they now seem quite different from the elements of writing now known from the Teotihuacan tradition (Taube 2000). Because of the text's overall affinities to Maya conventions, one might consider the "Teotihuacan" glyphs as no more than an elaborate typeface or "font" that was deemed visually and thematically appropriate to the temple and its Teotihuacan flavor.

David Stuart

The content of the Temple Inscription is difficult to discern. The vertical section that was positioned originally to the left of the niche or door of the temple has a date of 5 ? 4 K'ayab', followed by the verb *patwan* (it is built). This date is almost certainly 9.13.14.0.1 5 Imix 4 K'ayab', which falls in the reign of Waxaklajun Ub'aah K'awil and, oddly enough, predates the dedication date of the earlier Hieroglyphic Stairway. Presumably, this refers to the construction of an earlier phase of Structure 10L-26, possibly an earlier ancestral shrine built above Ruler 12's tomb. The last glyph of these columns is *u-kab'-j-iiy* (he oversaw it), suggesting that the text continues up to the horizontal band, but which glyph comes next is, again, hard to determine. The long, horizontal sequence of reconstructable glyphs includes the names of Waxaklajun Ub'aah K'awil and Ruler 14, as well as a distance number (2.11.0.0) that connects to the Period Ending 9.16.5.0.0. The event associated with this Period Ending is written *och-k'ahk'* (fire-entering), a standard architectural dedicatory rite that surely corresponds to the construction and ritual activation of Structure 10L-26's upper temple. The text continues down the right-hand vertical columns with the name of Ruler 12, probably naming him as the "owner" of the ancestral shrine.

As noted, the "Teotihuacan" glyphs of the Temple Inscription do not represent any true script tradition from Mesoamerica but instead appear to have been invented by a remarkably creative local scribe for this one text and temple. Their appearance is strange to us, no doubt, and I think that a similar response was probably the intended effect on ancient audiences allowed into the temple. But why construct a "false" text here within the temple and not in the outer inscriptions of the Hieroglyphic Stairway, which are all presented in standard legible format? This is a difficult question to answer, but I suspect that the highly restricted use of the interior temple space might go a little toward explaining the esoteric and purposefully obscure style. Perhaps a conventional Maya inscription would have seemed out of place within the confines of a small temple so heavily adorned with the visual elements of Teotihuacan. By contrast, the Hieroglyphic Stairway, in its earlier and later phases, presented a legible history designed to be read and absorbed within a public setting. Inside the upper temple, the written message was obscured by an overarching concern with a style that evoked another place and time.

TEOTIHUACAN AND THE IDEA OF THE PAST

The question now to be asked is, Why would a funerary monument devoted to a recently deceased king—the father of the first builder, in fact—call on the symbols of a distant and probably "dead" Mesoamerican culture? For the Maya of Copan, what profound meanings surrounding Teotihuacan called for its symbolism to dominate some of the kingdom's most imposing architectural monuments? An obvious comparison is to be drawn between the similar decorative schemes of Structures 10L-26 and 10L-16. Structure 10L-16 is the tallest building of the Main Group and is centrally located over the probable tomb of K'inich Yax K'uk' Mo'. It was evidently a dynastic shrine devoted to the founder, and his name glyph and image are continuously cited in the architectural decor. The complex iconographic program of that temple's final phase was perhaps even more explicitly evocative of Teotihuacan symbolism than Structure 10L-26 (W. Fash and B. Fash 2000:figure 14.7). Given the placement of Altar Q at the base of its stairway, there also exists the intriguing possibility that Structure 10L-16 was a local Maya model of the *wite'naah* (origin house) cited so prominently in the altar's text as the place of K'inich Yax K'uk' Mo's accession. Structure 10L-16 is unquestionably the founder's personal shrine, and the strong Teotihuacan imagery seems perfectly in keeping with the wider pattern we find in Copan's Late Classic iconography and writing.

The similarities to Structure 10L-26 are obvious in many ways, but there is one key and revealing difference between the buildings. Structure 10L-26 does not feature K'inich Yax K'uk' Mo' in any special way; he is simply one of the many dynasts recorded in the history of the steps. Rather, it is Ruler 12 who is the personal focus of the written history of both the stairway and the Temple Inscription. He remains the protagonist of the temple through two major renovations over a period of five decades. The two pyramids can be seen as different ancestral shrines focused on the most notable and prominent kings of Copan history. Yet, it is curious that both temples should so strongly evoke a distant time and place. The particularly strong Teotihuacan associations of K'inich Yax K'uk' Mo' in Copan's art have already been noted by many writers (Coggins 1988; W. Fash and B. Fash 2000; Stuart 2000), but Ruler 12 is seldom, if ever, shown in such obviously foreign clothing

(Stela 6 may be an exception). Yet, it seems quite evident that the founder was not the sole possessor of a highland style in Copan's art.

The explanation of highland iconography on Ruler 12's great temple lies, I believe, in Maya concepts of time's passage, particularly through representations of dynastic origins that are distantly removed from the viewer in both space and time. By the seventh century, Teotihuacan's style was the visual code of a deceased culture, but its powerful message of political authority seems to have remained strong in Mesoamerica for centuries to come (Carrasco, Jones, and Sessions 2000). Even beyond Copan, artists used elements of Teotihuacan costume and ritual to provide the sense of a remote past to their own political history. Retrospective scenes of Early Classic kings at Piedras Negras and Palenque, for example, depict them as warriors in Teotihuacan costume (Stuart 2000), but it is difficult to draw direct connections between highland Mexico and those particular historical figures. In addition to age, the foreign insignia at these other sites also conveyed a sense of ethnic and social distance, as Stone (1989) has noted in a key study of Teotihuacan symbolism in Classic Maya art. As I have argued elsewhere (Stuart 2000), the significance of central Mexican imagery in the Maya area foreshadows the meanings surrounding Tollan, the "Place of Cattails," so often cited as a mythic place of political and ethnic origin among Mesoamerican elites during the post-Classic.

We might draw upon powerful parallels within European history, wherein Classical centers of ancient political and cultural authority were used since the Renaissance as sources for the basic symbolic vocabulary of law, politics, and civilization (Lowenthal 1985). Teotihuacan seems a place with similar "Classical" presence among the later Maya, who chose to adopt elements of its iconography for use in certain settings, and only on the heels of Teotihuacan's own demise during the sixth century. This was no late and desperate attempt to construct a "false" political heritage, however. Many years of Copan archaeology make it abundantly clear that the evocation of Teotihuacan on Structure 10L-26 was grounded in historical reality, specifically, in K'inich Yax K'uk' Mo's own intimate and direct connection with Teotihuacan in the fifth century. Although the founder is not featured heavily in the texts and symbolism of Structure 10L-26, his mark on the temple's design is present, providing the underlying connection to the political and religious symbols of central Mexico.

Structure 10L-26 signals a profound change in Copan's royal ancestral cult, which had for so long focused (it seems) on K'inich Yax K'uk' Mo'. The founder's own major shrine was the Rosalila structure (and later phases of Structure 10L-16), probably dedicated by Ruler 8 around A.D. 540 and long the dominating temple of Copan's Acropolis. After a long series of relatively short-lived kings during the sixth and seventh century, Ruler 12's lengthy reign of sixty-seven years must have been a transforming experience for both the fortunes of the polity and the local institutions of rulership. The king's long-felt impact may be signaled on the side of Altar Q, where his portrait is shown sitting, rather than sitting atop the glyph for "5 K'atuns." All the other kings are on their personal name glyphs (with the significant exception of the founder—again, the two kings are treated similarly). Arguably, Copan's "Classic" period began with Ruler 12. With the building of Structure 10L-26 by Rulers 13 and 15, we see him celebrated in an elaborate and permanent expansion of the royal ancestral cult. It seems appropriate, therefore, that the visual cues of royal ancestry and authority—the foreign iconography—might have carried over from earlier traditions that focused exclusively on the founding king. Ruler 12 became a new and probably refreshing focus of Copan's state religion, and his veneration may have served to dust off an aging local ideology. As Lowenthal notes (1985:373), the "empathetic identification with great precursors, like idealization and imitation, derived from the urge to reanimate the past in the present."

Notes

An initial draft of this paper was written in 1994 for the Copan advanced seminar at the School of American Research, Santa Fe, New Mexico. Throughout the lengthy time of this paper's evolution, I have benefited greatly from comments and feedback from all of the seminar's participants. Some of the more novel ideas put on paper in 1994, including my overview of Teotihuacan's role in Maya history at Tikal and Copan (Stuart 2000), have naturally made their way into other publications. I would particularly like to thank Barbara Fash for her unfailing energy in documenting and preserving the Hieroglyphic Stairway and for our many years of productive collaboration on studying Copan's art and writing.

1. Other very long historical texts include the Temple of the Inscriptions at Palenque and the Temple of the Inscriptions at Tikal. The latter's roof-comb text perhaps offers the best comparison to the sheer physical scale of Copan's stairway. All these inscriptions are likewise large in their narrative scope.

2. These are, I think, reasonably accurate transliterations, but a simple number designation is provided when no complete reading of a name glyph is possible.

3. The first dedication date falls about five years into the reign of Waxaklajun Ub'aah K'awil. Until recently, it was presumed, by me and others (Schele and Larios 1991), to record the dedication of yet another stairway on an earlier, buried phase of 10L-26 (W. Fash, Williamson, et al. 1992). As later discussions will show, the two construction phases of the stairway are probably visible on the pyramid's exterior.

4. Gordon (1902:37) noted the chronological connection to Stela C a century ago: "It is not unlikely that when the dates of Stela C are understood, this monument will be found to belong to the same period as the Hieroglyphic Stairway. The two monuments have certain technical affinities in the carving, as though they might have been the work of the same master."

5. The stairway's earlier glyphs also correspond closely in style to several inscribed stone vessels (so-called *incensarios*) discovered in the outer fill of Structure 10L-26-1st and dated to the thirteenth *haab'* anniversary of Waxaklajun Ub'aah K'awil's inauguration, or 9.13.16.6.8.

6. Here, I refer to the two overall styles that correspond to the different construction episodes. Within these two phases, the stairway blocks were carved in several styles that are presently being studied in some detail with the hope that they will aid in the further refitting of the steps.

7. It is significant that the defeat is recorded so prominently at Copan twenty years after the fact, when there are no longer any indications that it was Quiriguá's political subordinate. The lengthy notation of the Quiriguá war on the Hieroglyphic Stairway contradicts Marcus's (1992b:360) assessment that military defeats were selectively omitted from Mesoamerican native histories (see Nicholson [1971] for an opposing view from Aztec sources).

11

Issues in Copán Archaeology

E. Wyllys Andrews and William L. Fash

In this concluding chapter, we review some of the issues, conclusions, and problems considered in more detail in the preceding pages, dwelling longer on some than others. We also discuss matters of importance in Copán archaeology that are not dealt with directly in this volume. Pointing out uncertainties and disagreements, we show that there is not always consensus among the scores of archaeologists who have worked in the Copán Valley.

THE PRECLASSIC AND PROTOCLASSIC COPÁN VALLEY

The Copán Valley was occupied during the Early Preclassic at least as early as 1400 B.C. Rich burials show that by about 1000 B.C., some individuals had amassed or inherited considerable wealth, possessed precious exotic commodities such as jade, and had access to ceramics that shared stylistic motifs (as well as, perhaps, complex supernatural references) with areas as far away as the Basin of Mexico.

The Middle Preclassic is not well known, although it is found at a number of locations around the valley. No evidence yet exists for the tall pyramidal platforms and large settlements characteristic of the years between 800 and 400 B.C. on the Gulf Coast, Chiapas, the Pacific Piedmont of Guatemala, the Valley of Guatemala, and western El Salvador. Our knowledge of the Late Preclassic is equally patchy, in part because the meanders and floods of the Copán River have washed away many remains of this period from the valley floor. Artifacts of this period, however, are scattered around the Main Group at Copán and the valley. This modest recorded occupation contrasts with almost all other regions of the Maya lowlands, where the Late Preclassic was a time of extraordinary population growth and increased social complexity (most strikingly in the Mirador Basin of northern Guatemala). It is possible that the Late Preclassic at Copán was, indeed, a time of vibrant growth and that archaeologists simply have not recovered its remains.

During the Protoclassic and Early Classic Bijac phase, from A.D. 1 to 400, Copán began to grow, with buildings concentrated in the vicinity of what would later become the Acropolis. Several earthen platforms with roughly dressed masonry were constructed below the ballcourt area of the Great Plaza, cobble-faced public platforms appeared between A.D. 250 and 400 at the base of the East Court of the Acropolis, and a large Bijac cobble-faced, earthen platform was exposed in Group 9N-8. The massive Northwest Platform, west of the Great Plaza, dates to the Acbi phase, but underneath it lie Preclassic constructions. A large, potbelly boulder sculpture, similar to one found long ago in the Great Plaza, was found on the surface of this platform during the 2000 field season. Architectural and sculptural remains therefore attest to a community of some stature centuries before the Classic dynasty of kings.

Were the early inhabitants of the Copán Valley ethnic Maya? In the absence of written records, inferring linguistic affiliation (or lack thereof) from similarities in material remains becomes increasingly dubious as the archaeological remains increase in age. Copán, however, because it lies at the southeast edge of the Maya area, surrounded by groups long seen as non-Maya, has a long history of such speculation. Full-fledged Classic Maya architecture, pottery, and inscriptions did not appear until after A.D. 400, and Late Preclassic and Protoclassic pottery at Copán was more like that of central Honduras and eastern El Salvador than that of the Guatemala highlands or lowlands (Andrews

1976). Archaeologists, beginning with Sylvanus Morley, have therefore considered it likely that the early inhabitants of the valley were not ethnically Maya (Demarest 1988, 1996; Longyear 1952:79–82; Schortman 1986).

E. W. Andrews (1976:143, 180–181) included Longyear's Archaic ceramic complex at Copán in the Uapala ceramic sphere, which spread over eastern and central El Salvador and parts of central and western Honduras. Primarily because the Lenca, with strikingly similar ceramics, occupied this area in early historic times, scholars speculated that they were the people living in this region, including Copán, as far back as the Late Preclassic (Andrews 1976; Braswell, Andrews, and Glascock 1994:174). In a complementary argument, Robert Sharer and Marcello Canuto (2002)—utilizing survey and excavation data collected in recent years by William Fash and his students and by Jay Hall, René Viel, Allan Maca, Marcello Canuto, Ellen Bell, and Jorge Ramos at Copán, Cerro Chino, Los Achiotes, and El Guayabal—have hypothesized that the Copán drainage during the Late Preclassic, but not the Classic, was characterized by certain consistent features of site location, spatial organization, and architectural design found elsewhere in central Honduras (the Uapala region) in later periods. They draw the conclusion that one ethnic group occupied this entire area in Pre-Maya times and that the Lenca are the logical candidate.

René Viel (1999a) suggests that Chol or Chorti Maya first moved gradually into the Copán Valley during the Protoclassic, probably from the area around Kaminaljuyu in the Guatemala highlands, and that the Chol or Chorti brought with them water-management skills that enabled them to drain, raise, and plant the low, swampy terrain on the valley bottom for the first time. Robert Sharer and Marcello Canuto (2002) likewise point to the scale and design of the earliest earthen structures at the base of the Acropolis to argue that during the Protoclassic, the closest architectural ties of the Copán Valley were west to Kaminaljuyu and south toward Chalchuapa, rather than east to the Lenca.

Several lines of archaeological evidence from the base of the Acropolis, summarized below, suggest that centuries later, a group from the Petén brought the trappings of Maya classicism to the site. Close contacts with highland Guatemala in the Protoclassic, including population movements, are not incompatible with an Early Classic intrusion by an elite group into the Copán Valley from the Petén.

If the early inhabitants of the Copán Valley were not Maya, by about A.D. 400 they were being ruled by elite individuals who were culturally Maya and spoke a Mayan language. The Copán Valley may therefore have been bilingual. Kathryn Josserand and Nicholas Hopkins (2002) have suggested that Classic-period spoken and written Maya was Cholan, a "standard language" spoken by Maya elites everywhere, and that non-elite Maya spoke Yucatecan, Cholan, or other vernaculars. They suggest that the elite spoke, in addition to Cholan, the vernacular of their community. In a widespread spoken and written tradition of the kind suggested by Josserand and Hopkins, elite Maya colonizers of new lands would often have been raised in a bilingual society. They and their children would not be adrift in a community where most members spoke a different tongue, be it Lenca or some highland Maya language, and the probable situation at Copán becomes less anomalous.

THE BIRTH OF THE CLASSIC DYNASTY

A vast network of tunnels excavated into the east side of the Acropolis by Robert Sharer, Ricardo Agurcia Fasquelle, William Fash, and their collaborators has enabled them to reconstruct in detail the growth of much of this grand structure from its beginnings through the end of the dynasty at about A.D. 820. All combined, the excellent condition of many early architectural remains below later platforms, the intact tombs with good preservation of human bones, and the nearly contemporaneous and retrospective historical inscriptions provide information about the founding of a Classic Maya dynasty that is probably unequaled today in its detail by that from any other known Maya site.

The founder, K'inich Yax K'uk' Mo', a foreigner, inaugurated the dynasty at Copán in A.D. 426, although he is named on a Period Ending stela here ten years earlier. Welcome or not, he was able to establish a new group of residential, religious, and administrative buildings at what thereafter became the center of Copán, and he was able to assume rulership of the site and valley (W. Fash, chapter 3 in this volume; W. Fash and B. Fash 2000; Proskouriakoff 1993:4–10; Sharer et al., chapter 5 in this volume; Stuart 2000). An inscription with a date of A.D. 437, when he was fifty-five to seventy years old, probably marked his death and tomb. The same text associates him with Siyah K'ak', a personage in the inscriptions of Tikal and several other sites who arrived at Tikal in A.D. 378 from the west as an emissary of Spear-Thrower Owl, possibly the ruler of Teotihuacan, according to David Stuart. An individual named K'uk' Mo' Ahaw is mentioned in Tikal texts about a generation before K'inich Yax K'uk' Mo' arrived at Copán, and the two are likely to have been the same individual. Siyah K'ak', who apparently placed a son of the Teotihuacan ruler on the Tikal throne within a year of his arrival, may have established the precedent for a similar intrusion at Copán and simultaneously at Quirigua nearly fifty years later. By that time, K'inich Yax K'uk' Mo' had established himself as a lord and warrior. K'inich Yax K'uk' Mo' was born about the time Siyah K'ak' arrived at Tikal, and it would be interesting to know their relationship.

K'inich Yax K'uk' Mo's masonry house at the base of the Acropolis was built with a highland Mexican or Teotihuacan *talud-tablero* and murals, in contrast to most other early platforms at Copán, which were made of earth or adobes with cobble or stucco facing. Teotihuacan vessels were placed as offerings in his vaulted tomb and his wife's. The burial of an unidentified woman in front of one of K'inich Yax K'uk' Mo's platforms, under a floor marker that shows the founder and his son, Ruler 2, is a cylindrical, stone-lined crypt of a kind typical of Teotihuacan but unknown in the Copán Valley and rare elsewhere in the Maya lowlands. Another burial near the tomb of K'inich Yax K'uk' Mo' contained a warrior with Teotihuacan goggle eyes and other markers. The importance of Teotihuacan to the founder of the dynasty and to those who accompanied him is intriguing, especially because bone strontium analysis of remains in what is thought to be his tomb indicates that he grew up in the central Petén (Buikstra et al. 2004). Perhaps he was a descendant of Teotihuacan royalty, the son of a man who arrived at Tikal in A.D. 378. If so, we should not forget that central Mexican stylistic traits associated with the founder are accompanied and, in fact, outweighed by Petén Maya features, such as the style of the floor marker over the round tomb containing the unidentified woman, the Petén-style vaulted tomb, and the imported lowland Maya vessels accompanying the deceased. Just as possible, K'inich Yax K'uk' Mo' was a Tikal noble who was not in the direct line of succession at that site but who claimed, or whose son emulated, the foreign style that was the mark of royalty at Tikal during these years (Coggins 1975).

Shortly after K'inich Yax K'uk' Mo's death, two new buildings covered the house and tomb identified as his. These contained the rich tomb of a high-status woman, most plausibly his wife, who may have belonged to the ruling Copán family. She was about his age at her death, which suggests that she married him in middle age, probably when he arrived at Copán. These new structures were built with apron moldings, in Petén style. Her grave furnishings, in a typical Petén-style vaulted tomb like that of her presumed spouse, were an eclectic mix of lowland Maya, Teotihuacan, and highland Guatemalan goods. This points either to the cosmopolitan tastes and background of the ruling family, much like those of the probable relatives of K'inich Yax K'uk' Mo' at Tikal, or to the diverse source of gifts left by those who attended her funeral.

THE ORIGIN OF THE STATE AT COPÁN

Sharer et al. (chapter 5 in this volume) call Ruler 2 the first great builder of Copán. They are impressed with the massive construction in the decades after the founding of the dynasty. With one continuous platform, Ruler 2 linked three groups of buildings created by his father, thereby forming the initial Acropolis. We know little about the next four rulers, beyond their depictions on Altar Q, but they continued the rapid pace of construction set by Rulers 1 and 2. William Fash and Sharer agree that the greatest rate and volume of building on the Acropolis occurred in the Early Classic and that the final two centuries of the Classic period showed a decline in both. Looking also at the very early constructions under the modern village, Fash (chapter 3 in this volume) suggests that "nearly as much building took place during that relatively short span [A.D. 426 to ca. 500] as did in the ensuing three centuries of dynastic rule in Copán."

If the volume and rate of construction at the center of the site in the Early Classic exceeded that of the Late Classic, what does this indicate about growth in social complexity and the origin of the Copán state? Opinions vary. William Fash and Robert Sharer (1991; chapters 3 and 5, respectively, in this volume) observed firsthand the early architectural remains under the Acropolis, including large residential buildings that, like the more public structures, must have required significant labor input from the community. They were impressed with the amount of effort expended at the beginning of the dynasty and in the immediately ensuing years. In accord with Joyce Marcus's (1992a, 1998) argument that the maximal sizes of territorial states were often reached early in their history, Fash and Sharer conclude that a preindustrial state existed at Copán during the reign of K'inich Yax K'uk' Mo' and that the greatest expansion of the Copán polity was at the start of the dynasty, when it held hegemony over the newly founded center of Quiriguá.

Another important variable an archaeologist must take into account in gauging social and political complexity is population, and it is here that the greatest disagreement arises. David Webster (1999; Webster and Freter 1990a, 1990b) believes that the Early Classic population of the Copán Valley was about four to five thousand, in contrast to a peak Late Classic population estimated to have been in the range of twenty to twenty-eight thousand. A population this small probably had not developed a state-level political organization. Webster thinks that the state level of complexity was reached about 150 or 200 years later, early in the Late Classic period. His estimate relies on settlement surveys of the valley, primarily those undertaken by Pennsylvania State University during the Proyecto Arqueológico Copán II. William Fash and Robert Sharer believe that the Penn State survey data are biased, because the principal goal of that survey was the definition of the Coner-phase settlement of the valley, beginning about A.D. 650. That project, which included excavations of surface structures and associated stratigraphic test pits, concentrated on visible surface (Late Classic) ruins. Because Late Classic sites are more monumental and more extensive and were often built above buried Early Classic sites, the PAC II settlement survey was more likely to find Late Classic sites. The survey was not designed to find pre-Coner occupations, and when it did, these were only a small part of those earlier sites. The result is that the low, pre-Coner population estimates of PAC II are considered to be too low and not reliable. We believe that many unrecorded Early Classic remains lie buried throughout the Copán Valley.

An additional problem with pre-Coner demographic estimates is that the farther back in time one goes, the greater the likelihood that the river washed away settlements both large and small on the valley floor. If Karla Davis-Salazar (2001, 2003), Barbara Fash (chapter 4 in this volume), and René Viel (1999a) are correct in interpreting water management as a central focus of administration during the Classic period, fewer Late Classic sites would have been destroyed than earlier ones.

ROSALILA, AN EARLY CLASSIC SHRINE TO THE FOUNDER OF THE DYNASTY

The most magnificently preserved Maya temple ever uncovered is Rosalila, a blood-red, three-story shrine dedicated to both the sun god, K'inich Ahaw, and to K'inich Yax K'uk' Mo', the dynastic founder and first of the Copán Sun Kings (Agurcia and B. Fash, chapter 6 in this volume). Rosalila is the fifth in a series of seven superimposed constructions in the same spot, beginning with the house of K'inich Yax K'uk' Mo' and ending with Temple 16. The temple was at first thought to date late in the reign of Ruler 10 (A.D. 553–578), but David Stuart has recently recognized a portion of Ruler 8's name on the Rosalila platform step inscription. He now dates the inscription to the reign of that king (ca. A.D. 532–551) (Stuart 2004; Sharer et al., chapter 5 in this volume). Ruler 11 placed his Stela P (A.D. 623) directly in front of Rosalila, and the temple was not covered until about A.D. 700, during the reign of Ruler 12 or 13. This shrine to the ruling dynasty was a strikingly beautiful and powerful building, with polychrome stucco, full-figure representations of K'inich Yax K'uk' Mo' below the medial molding, and avian representations of K'inich Ahaw with yax signs on the upper facade, along with witz monster masks, celestial monsters, macaw heads, snakes, and death's heads. Perhaps in part because of this beauty, the shrine was carefully preserved intact and not demolished to be used as fill, the usual fate of buried buildings. Reconstructed by Barbara Fash and others as the centerpiece of the Copán Sculpture Museum, Rosalila creates for the spectator what no other exhibit has or ever will—the experience of standing before an Early Classic Maya temple that comes alive as one watches supernatural creatures writhe across and up its surfaces from one story to the next.

MODELS OF POLITICAL AND SOCIAL ORGANIZATION AT COPÁN

Archaeologists have increasingly investigated water conservation, drainage, channeling, and irrigation at Maya sites in recent years. The model proposed here by Barbara Fash is a comprehensive synthesis of the relationships of water management, social organization, political structure, sculptural iconography, and ideology for the ancient Maya (Davis-Salazar 2001, 2003; Scarborough 1994, 1996). Barbara Fash argues that water management was an important political activity from the beginning of the Copán dynasty and that the iconography of sculptured building facades documents this concern with water, especially during the Late Classic. She believes that Copán Valley settlement clusters, which generally contain or lie near a stream, mountain source, lagoon, or reservoir, are comparable to the water-hole groups (snas, or "agriculturally based lineage groups") described by Vogt (1969, 1981a) in Zinacantan and to the *sian otot* of the Chorti reported by Wisdom (1940) and suggested by William Fash (1983a) to be socially and geographically akin to Copán architectural compounds. Her comparisons of water-management systems at Angkor, in Bali, and in the Andes make the argument for a hydraulic society at Copán more understandable and convincing.

Copán rulers and nobles used water imagery to identify themselves as heads of water-hole groups. This includes water-lily headdresses, water-lily monsters, stepped motifs with tun/cauac signs that represent drip-water cave formations with drops of water falling from or on them, fish (in one instance), and half-quatrefoils. The last of these have been identified as caves, which are linked with mountains and water sources and were thought to be the abode of the ancestors. Fash argues that this motif became the symbol of water-hole groups at Copán and elsewhere. Water imagery abounds, but the best examples are late, on three buildings in Group 10L-2 and on two structures in separate compounds in Las Sepulturas.

The council house at Copán (10L-22A) united the heads of nine geographic units at Copán into one administrative or advisory body (B. Fash et al. 1992; W. Fash and B. Fash 2002). It was built during the reign of the fifteenth ruler and was used thereafter. Although no precursor of this building has been identified, Barbara Fash argues that a popol nah would have been necessary by the time of K'inich Yax K'uk' Mo' to bring together the heads of the separate water-hole groups that formed the Copán polity. This interpretation is a departure from earlier publications that viewed the council house as a late innovation designed to reintegrate polities wanting to secede or become self-administered, by increasing political participation of subsidiary lords in the affairs of state. The creation of the council house late in Copán's history is one of several pieces of evidence used to advance the hypothesis that for the last hundred or so years of the Late Classic, the fortunes of Copán and its kings declined. Although we believe that the polity was increasingly stressed, some of the evidence for its gradual decline before the collapse of the dynasty about A.D. 820 remains equivocal. The existence of an advisory council as early as the beginning of the Copán dynasty would potentially eliminate one line of reasoning supporting the argument for a long and gradual decline of the Copán polity. On the other hand, we note that Structure 10L-22A is our first *material* evidence of such a council.

In a valley where water was abundant year-round, why would water management have been an issue of the greatest importance? Barbara Fash points out that river water becomes undrinkable at the height of the rainy season, making maintenance of large, artificial reservoirs and care of hillside springs crucial for the welfare of a large population. René Viel's (1999a) deep excavations in the vicinity of the Acropolis have suggested that during the Formative period, the low terrace on which the Classic site rests was a swamp. He thinks, as noted above, that the Protoclassic and Classic population came from the Guatemala highlands, where extensive irrigation and drainage canals had been dug at Kaminaljuyu, and that the primary administrative task of early heads of the polity was water management and increased agricultural production on newly raised and drained terraces on the old floodplain. His new data buttress Barbara Fash's earlier interpretations of Copán Late Classic iconography.

Several excavated residential groups in Las Sepulturas, such as Groups 9N-8 and 8N-11, have large buildings with extensive sculpture on their facades and long hieroglyphic benches that may name the ruler, Yax Pasaj, and also the building's owner, the head of the local group. These individuals were nobles of high standing and considerable wealth and power. In contrast to some other areas of the Maya lowlands, however, the titles of subroyal Copán Valley lords have remained undeciphered. The title of sajal, for example, is unknown at Copán. Following a number of other efforts to identify subordinate lords and their titles at Copán, Sarah Jackson and David Stuart (2001; Stuart, personal communication 2003) suggested that the *God C* title, generally considered by epigraphers to be a term of rank, might be read *aj k'uhun* (one who keeps things, one who venerates, obeys, or one of the holy paper). The title, appearing on hieroglyphic benches away from the center of Copán, refers to the owners of the buildings and is not used with names of rulers. The aj k'uhun was closely associated with royalty, sometimes with a previous ruler.

Although the Copán dynasty is given as an unbroken succession from A.D. 426 to 820, the relationship of each ruler to his predecessor is often unknown. Some are sons of the preceding ruler, and some, like the last king, Yax Pasaj, are not. The common lack of parentage statements makes it likely that, as at other lowland Maya sites where the hieroglyphic record allows investigation of this issue, more than one lineage or other corporate group was able to install a ranking member as ruler of the realm. The inscriptions have not yet provided direct evidence of such groups, but distinct residential complexes around the center of the site and in more distant parts of the valley are obvious candidates. René Viel (1999b) has recently speculated that rulership at Copán did rotate in a complex fashion among several corporate groups. Their identity, he suggests, is indicated by the attributes of the pectorals worn by the sixteen rulers depicted on the famous Altar Q.

Copán rulers—from the founder, K'inich Yax K'uk' Mo', to Ruler 12, to Yax Pasaj—created holy "seats of power," which were platforms, altars, or other sculptures where gods or spirits were conjured. These are referred to in the Copán inscriptions by the impinged-bone glyph and are probably read as kun (Schele and Looper, chapter 9 in this volume). These sacred places were the visible foci of royal power and where the living ruler gave evidence of his unique ability to draw upon the supernatural forces of the gods and of nature. Linda Schele and Matthew Looper show how these physical elements of royal legitimacy remained central to the dynasty and to the Copán realm throughout the life of the city. They suggest that the original ux witik seat of Copán power was a structure of the early Acropolis, perhaps Hunal or Margarita, during the reign of K'inich Yax K'uk' Mo'. The "three mountains," a toponym identified with the site of Copán, are similarly linked to the Early Classic temple Rosalila and the large structures

Oropéndola to its south and Peach/Colorado to its north by Agurcia and Barbara Fash (chapter 6 in this volume) and with Temples 16, 22, and 26 by William Fash (chapter 3 in this volume). The conception of Copán as a "three-mountain" site appears to have lasted throughout the life of the Acropolis and the Classic dynasty.

David Webster's review of social and agricultural development in the Copán Valley compares and evaluates two models. The settlement model is derived from years of excavation and survey, and the soil model and computer simulation, elaborated by John Wingard (1996), is based on a soil and agricultural survey of the valley and on two hundred soil samples. Webster finds that the two models fit remarkably well with patterns of land use, population growth, and population decline (but see our comments below concerning the Copán collapse and the rapidity of population decline).

Wingard's soil model reconstructs a relatively gradual population growth in the Copán pocket and in the valley generally, at least until about A.D. 650 or 700, with 3,000 inhabitants by A.D. 400, 6,000 by A.D. 650, and perhaps 6,400 by A.D. 675. The reconstructions of Copán history by William Fash and by Robert Sharer et al. in this volume probably imply greater populations at an earlier time than Wingard suggests. The rapid, subsequent increase to a maximum population in excess of 20,000, when hillside soils were brought under cultivation and then heavily eroded, would not appear to conflict with other reconstructions. The slow decline in population levels after A.D. 900, however, although consistent with Webster's interpretation, conflict with what most other authors in this volume see as a much more rapid collapse.

Webster provides a useful discussion of two possible models of social integration in the Copán Valley. One consisted of "large, internally ranked kinship groups." The other was a more stratified system similar to that of Hawaii, in which a far wider gulf separated ruling families from commoners and the nonroyal elite segments of society derived authority not from their own lineage but by delegation from the ruler. He finds that the first of these fits better with what we know of Maya social organization. We think that most Mayanists would agree.

Webster makes a strong case that as population in the Copán Valley grew and productive and relatively level fields became ever more valuable, the elite were increasingly forced to manage the agricultural economy to preserve social stability and maintain elite prerogatives and the flow of tribute and labor. Eventually, the eroded landscape and unsustainable population levels constrained effective management of resources by the nobility, and the polity began an irreversible decline.

As the architecture, inscriptions, and artifacts of Classic Copán testify, this city on the southeast periphery of the Maya area was never isolated from powerful population centers to the north and west. The founding of the dynasty in a region that was probably not ethnically Maya seems to have involved direct stimulus from Tikal. Ties to Palenque are suggested by the early two-headed jaguar miniature throne in Group 10L-2; the similarity between the first Hieroglyphic Stairway at Copán and the Temple of the Inscriptions at Palenque, both built by sons to house their fathers' tombs; and the fact that the mother of the final ruler, Yax Pasaj, came from Palenque, perhaps adding the distinction and status that propelled him to the throne. Copán Early Classic building styles and construction techniques, as well as imported and foreign-inspired ceramics, attest to direct or indirect ties with Kaminaljuyú and Teotihuacán.

Hieroglyphic inscriptions at Copán and especially Quirigua, 50 km to the north, tell of the changing relationship between these two sites from the founding of the Copán dynasty until the collapse of both sites early in the ninth century (W. Fash, chapter 3 in this volume; Looper 1999; Marcus 1976:130–149; Schele 1989b, 1990b). The intrusive Quiriguá dynasty appears to have been established in A.D. 436 by Copán (under the aegis of Tikal?). For centuries afterward, Quiriguá appears to have been subservient to its larger neighbor—remaining a part of the Copán state. Quiriguá later rebelled, killing Waxaklajun Ub'ah K'awil and achieving independence in A.D. 738 after a long struggle. Matthew Looper (1999) believes that Quiriguá enlisted Calakmul, far to the north, as an ally in this struggle. Copán likely remained closely associated with Tikal, the probable source of its founding dynasty (and that of Quiriguá as well), so an alliance of Quiriguá with Tikal's great rival would have been a logical move in its bid for independence or supremacy in the south. Waxaklajun Ub'ah K'awil's Stela A in A.D. 731 states that Copán, Tikal, Calakmul, and Palenque were the cities at the four corners of the world (Marcus 1976:145). Perhaps at this date, shortly before Quiriguá joined with Calakmul, Copán was still on good terms with all three powerful and distant Maya states. The successful Quiriguá rebellion, upsetting the balance of power in the south, may have initiated a gradual decline in Copán's fortunes that continued through the reigns of the last three kings of the dynasty. Just before the collapse of both sites, a close relationship was reestablished, but this time it may have been more as equals.

Although we learn about Copán's ties to other powerful cities in the Maya area and beyond through imported elite goods, shared architectural styles, and especially hieroglyphic inscriptions, what evidence exists that will help us understand the relationships between the city and its hinterland and the surrounding communities, some of which, to the east, may not have been Maya? Kazuo Aoyama (2001) has studied the chipped-stone artifacts of many sites in the Copán Valley and the surrounding region to determine the role of obsidian exchange in the local political economy. His analysis of more than ninety thousand artifacts shows that, beginning with Yax K'uk' Mo', Copán controlled (or, at least, was a prime participant in) the procurement and distribution of obsidian blade cores from the major source of Ixtepeque, about 80 km to the southwest. The central groups at Copán had access to more obsidian than did elite households nearby in the valley, and comparable households of neighboring regions had still less. Aoyama concludes that Copán rulers imported cores and then distributed them to the heads of local groups and also to rulers of neighboring polities. He suggests that food, perhaps in short supply for residents of the Copán pocket toward the end of the Classic period, may have been exchanged for obsidian.

Such evidence of economic interaction with surrounding areas leads Aoyama to argue that large-scale exploitation of obsidian was important in the Classic Copán political economy. He thinks that administration of this procurement and exchange network was a key responsibility of the state, helping to foster a centralized and socioeconomically heterogeneous city comparable to other urban centers in Mesoamerica in the managerial functions it served. This view of Copán stands in marked contrast to the characterization by William Sanders and David Webster (1988) of this city and most other Maya cities as "regal-ritual" centers with limited administrative roles and sociopolitical structures closely tied to kinship.

Do the sweeping models of political evolution put forth by Joyce Marcus (1992a, 1993, 1998) and Arthur Demarest (1992b) adequately describe the trajectory of the Copán polity? Both Marcus's dynamic model and Demarest's galactic polity model attempt to explain the cyclical rise and decline of early states. Marcus's data are drawn from the late Maya themselves, whereas Demarest's theory draws on Southeast Asian comparisons. William Fash believes that the rapid rise of the Copán state at the beginning of the dynasty does fit these models. External evidence from neighboring sites such as Quiriguá and internal evidence from the Copán Valley suggest that the Copán polity weakened during the Classic period as noble families living at nearby and distant sites in the Copán Valley attempted to increase their power and independence. The current investigation of large sites in various areas of the Copán Valley should give us a far more detailed picture than we now have of Copán's relations with its close neighbors through time.

THE HIEROGLYPHIC STAIRWAY AND THE TEMPLE 26 INSCRIPTION: THE CONSTRUCTION OF HISTORY

Rosalila and Structure 10L-16, the structure that Yax Pasaj eventually built above it, were monuments to K'inich Yax K'uk' Mo'. In contrast, Temple 26 (10L-26) and its Hieroglyphic Stairway, the longest inscription the Maya ever carved, was an ancestral shrine dedicated primarily to the entire Copán dynasty and especially to the greatest king in the dynasty, Ruler 12, whose reign spanned nearly seventy years at the beginning of the Late Classic period (W. Fash 2001:139–150; Stuart 2000, chapter 10 in this volume). Ruler 13, Waxaklajun Ub'ah K'awil, buried his father in an enormous tomb set into a predecessor of Structure 10L-26 and then, fifteen years later, dedicated the first part of the hieroglyphic stair, which chronicled the Copán dynasty through his father's rule. William Fash (2002) has presented architectural evidence that this original stairway was placed on the east side of Structure 10L-26-3rd (Esmeralda), perhaps in emulation of Palenque's Temple of the Inscriptions. After the death of Ruler 13, the stairway on the east side was removed and then placed on the west side of the final phase, Structure 10L-26-1st, by Ruler 15, who also added a whole new section of stairway blocks, the elaborate balustrades, and possibly the human figures (W. Fash 2002). The two sections of stairway blocks are distinguished by different glyph styles that are also characteristic of dated monuments of Ruler 13 (Stela C) and Ruler 15 (Stela M). William Fash (2001:139) believes that Ruler 13's early inscription originally formed the upper part of the east stairway to a building later covered by 10L-26 and that it was moved at that time to the final west stairway.

The building commissioned by Ruler 15 atop Structure 10L-26 had collapsed, but much of a long inscription has been reconstructed from glyph blocks found during excavation. Stuart (2000, chapter 10 in this volume) describes this text as consisting of alternating columns, the first containing standard, Maya full-figure glyphs and the next column consisting of "hybrid glyphs" that include "Teotihuacan visual elements." Some of the latter are unrecognizable as Maya glyphs, and some are identifiable Maya glyphs with Teotihuacan-style elements adorning them. Stuart notes that they do not resemble elements of a Teotihuacan graphic system that has recently been identified (Taube 2000), suggesting instead that the alternating columns are more like a "font" that utilized central Mexican characters. Some of the Mexican elements appear to correspond to Maya words; the meaning of others is unclear. The content of the text, however, relates chiefly to the history of Copán.

The significance of this unique text is murky. Did the Maya scribe know a central Mexican writing system that has not been discovered? Did he record a lingua franca, complex or attenuated, that educated Late Classic Mesoamericans from many regions could be expected to know? Maya royalty during the Late Classic period, as Stuart and others argue (Demarest and Foias 1993; B. Fash 1992a; W. Fash and B. Fash 2000; Stone 1989), associated their own images with symbols of Teotihuacan, especially those with connotations of war and Teotihuacan military might, documenting their political and cultural ties with the greatest city of Mesoamerica, now well past its flower. Nowhere was this attempt to harness the glory of the Teotihuacan heritage more visible in the sculptural record than at Copán, where, as at Tikal, the founding of the dynasty was symbolically tied to this western city. The Temple 26 inscription is the most intriguing of these links and symbolic associations.

A LATE CLASSIC ROYAL RESIDENCE

Toward the end of the Early Classic period, according to Robert Sharer (chapter 5 in this volume), an expanding mass of ceremonial structures engulfed the traditional Early Classic royal residence on the northern and eastern flanks of the Acropolis. The residence of the ruling family thereafter ceased to form part of the Acropolis proper. Shortly after the Early Classic royal residence was buried, a family whose possessions and burial practices identify them as descendants of royalty built a group of three small, vaulted houses in Group 10L-2, just south of the Acropolis. Within a generation or two, very likely before A.D. 650, they had erected new residential, religious, and administrative buildings around Courtyards A and B and in adjacent (but unexcavated) complexes. The excavation of Courtyards A and B revealed a succession of platforms and buildings of differing form and function (Andrews and Bill, chapter 7 in this volume). The earliest constructions around the courtyards comprised elite residences, a dance platform, a large royal family shrine (a *waybil*) for conjuring deities and ancestors, and other ritual and administrative buildings. Sculptured facades display the founder's glyph and the Mexican year sign, which are interpreted as proclaiming the relationship of the builders to K'inich Yax K'uk' Mo'.

Most buildings in Group 10L-2 were enlarged or entirely replaced by larger ones more than once, indicating the growing importance of this residential compound. Nothing, however, indicates that any of the Late Classic rulers before Yax Pasaj Chan Yopat lived here or came from here. Not a single hieroglyphic monument from this group is thought to predate the sixteenth ruler. Altars with hieroglyphic inscriptions indicate that Structure 10L-32-1st was the house of Yax Pasaj and that 10L-30 was his ceremonial platform, both probably built about the time he took the throne. Carved fish on the facade of the penultimate building inside Yax Pasaj's house, probably his father's residence, are identical to the fish place name on the council house. Thus, this residential group must have been one of the eight or nine represented in the king's *popol nah*.

Group 10L-2 illustrates several processes that have been documented elsewhere in the royal compound at Copán, in the Copán

Valley, and at other Late Classic Maya sites. The population in Group 10L-2 grew between A.D. 600 and 820. The number and size of residential and nonresidential structures multiplied, and some residential buildings were both enlarged and subdivided to augment the number of rooms. As the extent of architecture around Courtyards A and B increased, the space between structures disappeared and access was severely limited. The only direct entrances to Courtyard A were eventually a narrow stair from the southwest corner of the Acropolis and a passage out to the south that led in a roundabout way to Courtyard B; the only way into Courtyard B became a narrow, L-shaped passage at its northeast corner. These had become some of the most private and least accessible living areas at Copán.

A major theme in the archaeology of the Acropolis is continuity of building function at one spot. A prime example is the series of buildings that commemorated K'inich Yax K'uk' Mo', beginning with his house, continuing with the structures his son built over it, culminating in the Early Classic with Rosalila, which was, in effect, buried alive long afterward, and ending with Yax Pasaj's 10L-16-1st. A further illustration is the long sequence of constructions under the Temple of the Hieroglyphic Stairway; the primary purpose of these, like the stairway itself, appears to have been the glorification of the dynasty. The clearest instances of such continuity of form and purpose in Group 10L-2 are seen in the three building periods of Structure 10L-41, each of which produced three buildings in a line, with sufficient continuity of form to suggest a plan that was followed for about a century and a half. A further example is 10L-32-1st, 2nd, and 3rd, probably the residence of the ranking member of the residential group for nearly two centuries.

Now that we have a reasonably clear picture of Yax Pasaj's residential compound, we should reconsider the nature of the royal palace and the royal court at Copán. Because the ruler divided his hours and his responsibilities between two distinct, if adjacent, places, the palace can be understood to have two components, one public and one more private, together forming what William Sanders and David Webster (1988) called the royal compound. Yax Pasaj's buildings and carved monuments on the Acropolis and the plazas to the north, with those of his predecessors, were political, religious, and aesthetic statements directed toward a large audience—the people of Copán, the valley, and the realm and foreigners. The buildings and monuments in Group 10L-2 seem oriented primarily toward a smaller constituency that centered on Yax Pasaj's own corporate group. Broad stairways with wide treads for standing or sitting and two large, flat-topped platforms on Courtyard A, one enlarged by Yax Pasaj, make it clear that public ceremony and dance were among the most important activities in Group 10L-2 throughout the Late Classic.

Although Structure 10L-11 may have been Yax Pasaj's official royal residence on the Acropolis, his home was in Group 10L-2, and he fulfilled different roles in this area. Much of the domestic side of his halfcentury reign no doubt transpired in Group 10L-2, possibly in 10L-41A at Courtyard B, as well as in 10L-32. Is this pattern new with Yax Pasaj, or can it be traced back in Copán history?

Recent excavations in the early Acropolis hint that this division within the royal court may extend back to the beginning of the dynasty (Sharer et al., chapter 5 in this volume). Loa Traxler (2001) has described an arrangement of buildings at the base of the Acropolis at the time of K'inich Yax K'uk' Mo' that suggests a distinction within the royal court between public and less public locales. The royal palace compound—that is, the royal court—of the founder and at least his first three successors included a "primary group" of structures that formed the royal household, containing at least three residential structures, and a nearby complex of at least four courtyard groups to the northeast thought to have been mostly residences of other members of the court of K'inich Yax K'uk' Mo', with one or more specialized structures. The existence of a divided royal compound, perhaps comparable to Yax Pasaj's public/private areas, from the earliest days of the dynasty suggests that this was a permanent feature of Copán royal life and that we might expect to find separate residential compounds for the Late Classic rulers (and their relatives) who preceded Yax Pasaj. Group 10L-18, west of the Court of the Hieroglyphic Stairway, is a dense concentration of large buildings that may have served as the residence of earlier rulers during the Late Classic period. This pattern likely indicates that rulers' strongest ties were to local corporate residential and landholding groups, what Gillespie (2000) and others describe as a "house," rather than to a single royal lineage.

Succession to the Copán throne did not always follow a straight line from father to son, passing, at least twice in the Late Classic period, to individuals whose relationship to their predecessors is unclear. These epigraphic conclusions, taken with the evidence that Ruler 16 came from a residential compound with great power and time depth, show that there were multiple competing noble lines, or houses, at Copán instead of one royal family.

Recent interpretations of certain hieroglyphic inscriptions in Group 10L-2 provide crucial negative evidence concerning the nobility and the political offices they held at Copán. An individual named U Yak' Chak on Altar F', from Structure 10L-32, was thought to have been the owner of this house and a close associate of Yax Pasaj. Also, two names, *Yax Kamlay* and *Yahaw Chan Ahbak*, inscribed on small, house-shaped shrines in Group 10L-2 were considered to have been those of close relatives or brothers of the last king, important members of Yax Pasaj's court. David Stuart now believes that all three were deities, supernatural patrons of Yax Pasaj, thus eliminating individuals and the poorly defined ranks they were thought to occupy and placing Yax Pasaj himself as the head of Group 10L-2. In their place, we have Jackson and Stuart's office of aj k'uhun, mentioned above. Some of them were the heads of groups seated around the upper register of the popol nah, and some were other noblemen who carved hieroglyphic benches for their houses during the reign of Yax Pasaj. All these office-holders formed part of a single Copán nobility whose power, privilege, and influence on the ruler varied with the fortunes of the corporate group from which it ultimately drew its strength. As Barbara Fash (chapter 4 in this volume) argues, management of the water supplies for the city may have been a primary responsibility and right of the families that lived in Group 10L-2.

THE COLLAPSE OF COPÁN

Has a quarter-century of survey and excavation at Copán, in the site center and throughout the valley, revealed what caused the collapse of Classic Maya society at Copán? In general, yes. But the specific causes, their relative importance, and the order of events, no. As we try to see past the broad ecological, demographic, political, and social patterns that preceded the failure (which most scholars accept to some degree), the specific sequence of events is still unknown, and so are the effects and relative importance of these processes and trends. Epigraphers are able to suggest readings for a few inscriptions that date from the end of the dynasty and perhaps immediately afterward (in itself, a remarkable situation that has no parallel), but this information is limited and unclear.

What were these long-term processes? Most striking was a great increase in population during the Classic period, from a few thousand before K'inich Yax K'uk' Mo' founded the dynasty, to a peak of twenty to twenty-eight thousand about four hundred years later. As the numbers grew, settlement covered more of the best land on the valley bottom, likely reducing yields or increasing competition for diminishing yields. The settlement survey shows an expansion up the hillsides onto less fertile soils, eventually causing deforestation, soil depletion, and extensive erosion on some slopes. Despite increasing pressure on the land, the population appears not to have expanded significantly outside the Copán Valley in quest of good agricultural land. Perhaps these people were prevented from doing so by groups already living in those valleys. Perhaps they were constrained by rulers and the elite, who wanted labor close at hand.

Analysis of Copán skeletal remains indicates that the entire Late Classic population—especially children of all ranks, nearly half of whom died before reaching adult age—suffered from nutritional stress and infections (Piehl 2001, 2002, note 3 to chapter 7 in this volume; Storey 1992, 1999, chapter 8 in this volume; Whittington 1999; Whittington and Reed 1997). Rebecca Storey (chapter 8 in this volume) reports that this was also true for the children of the nobility and that only a few pampered, high-ranking adults show some buffering from stress. These results have usually been taken to show that health was declining as the Copán population outstripped its resources (for example, Webster, Freter, and Gonlin 2000).

Jennifer Piehl (2001), however, argues that the nutritional stress and disease found in the Late Classic Group 10L-2 skeletal sample does not indicate deteriorating health leading to a crisis that helped precipitate the dynastic collapse. She thinks that the skeletal data show what could be expected "from a maize-reliant urban population with limited dietary diversity...." The small Early Classic sample of skeletons from Group 10L-2 shows a level of nutritional stress and disease equal to that found later, suggesting to Piehl (2001) that this pattern of environmental stress was long-standing and established well before the Late Classic and its population peak. The high levels of severe infection (which had healed in many cases) seen in the skeletons from Group 10L-2 indicate to Piehl (2001, 2002) that the occupants of Copán, like those of most lowland sites, lived in an area of endemic disease. The high levels also demonstrate that individuals were sufficiently buffered against this stress, so they could survive for a long time with infections, rather than succumb to them in short order. This does not present a picture of excellent health, but the buffering effect does reflect an elite population that, subsisting on a maize-reliant, urban Maya diet, had enough health reserves to live a longer life upon reaching adulthood than those at many other sites in the lowlands in the Late and Terminal Classic. This Late Classic population from Group 10L-2 also shows relatively infrequent and less severe signs of stress in childhood among individuals who reached adult age (Piehl 2002), confirming that in spite of increasing population and decreasing agricultural resources, an immediate crisis of survival was not imminent during the Late Classic at Copán.

Population in the Copán Valley increased greatly in the Late Classic, and the consequent ecological stress seems certain. Together, these could have endangered the food supply for nearly all the inhabitants of the valley, especially in times of drought. What we do not know for certain, though, is whether the situation was so much worse toward A.D. 800 that it became the prime factor in causing the collapse of Copán society. The physical remains of the Copán inhabitants themselves do not demand this explanation.

Population increase and environmental stress also created social and political changes at Copán that could have resulted in a loss of stability and conflict within the valley and throughout the Copán realm. William Fash (1983b, 2001, chapter 3 in this volume) believes that as the overall population increased, so did the elite sector of society. Eventually, land and tribute labor became insufficient, and, most important, there were not enough political offices to satisfy the growing number of noble families. The result, Fash argues, was too many elite males and finally "a nobles' revolt" against the central political authority, the ruler and his administration and family. The council house, by bringing together and assigning authority to a number of these potentially dissident heads of local corporate groups, may have mitigated this divisiveness.

Evidence for conflict about the time of the collapse of the dynasty has recently been uncovered in Group 10L-2 (Andrews and Bill, chapter 7 in this volume). Several buildings appear to have been burned and destroyed at the time of Yax Pasaj's death or, more likely, a short time later. On the Acropolis, the council house and possibly Yax Pasaj's tomb were also burned. Most buildings on the Acropolis and some in Group 10L-2 were excavated before such details were expected and noticed. For that reason, the number of known desecrated structures may be small.

Who tore down the buildings in the royal compound? Several possibilities exist, but we have no good way of choosing one over another. Disaffected nobles living in or near the Copán Valley, peasant farmers throwing off an increasingly burdensome yoke, an organized force from Quiriguá or from a far more distant city, such as Calakmul or Seibal, are all potential sources of attack. So, too, is violence directed at this southeastern Maya site by non-Maya sites or coalitions to the east who may have seen that Copán, like many Maya centers around this time, was vulnerable. Arguments can be adduced for and against these suggestions and others.

Today we have a far better understanding of the society that collapsed at Copán and of the forces, external and internal, with which it had to contend. All or most of the factors indicated above were probably involved; it was a complex process of interrelated developments, not an event that can be explained by a single cause. To comprehend the decline or collapse of the Classic Maya, one must look, as archaeologists have often said, at each region and each site, for the configuration of factors and events were different everywhere. Years of research at and around Copán have given us a clearer view of this area than we have of most.

At the same time, we must not lose sight of the Maya lowlands as a whole, because the collapse occurred throughout this large and ecologically diverse area between about A.D. 800 and 925, with a few exceptions, such as Chichén Itzá, sites on the east coast of the Yucatán Peninsula, and some riverine sites in northern Belize. One feature that all regions of the Maya lowlands shared in the Late Classic was population growth. Peak population figures were reached about A.D. 800 or a little later in nearly every region—except for a few areas (such as the El Mirador Basin) that may have been able to sustain fewer inhabitants than before because of major ecological changes (drying and silting in of permanent lakes or wetlands, in this instance). Population densities and totals varied dramatically from one area and one site to another, from perhaps twenty-five thousand in the Copán Valley to several times that at larger sites such as Tikal, Calakmul, Caracol, and Cobá. The social and political organizations of communities of greatly varying sizes must have differed as well. Some of the driest land with the thinnest soil, for example, around Chunchucmil in northwest Yucatán seems to have borne some of the highest population densities. Reasons remain unclear. Why, given this enormous demographic and resource diversity, did sites throughout the Maya lowlands decline to nearly the point of abandonment within about a century?

Could there have been one additional provocation, one overriding circumstance that affected nearly all areas and all sites, making it virtually impossible for sites everywhere to maintain previous population densities and causing disruption of political and social systems that depended on relatively stable populations? If so, a long period of drought is the most likely candidate. Recent evidence from cores suggests that the years from A.D. 800 to 1000 may have seen the worst drought since the beginning of the Holocene (deMenocal 2001; Haug et al. 2003; Hodell, Curtis, and Brenner 1995; Hodell et al. 2001; see Gill 2000 for a general overview of this question, Dunning and Beach 2000:197 and Demarest 2001 for cautionary responses, and P. Culbert 1988 and Lucero 2002 for differing, if not incompatible, points of view). Rainfall can fluctuate greatly during a lengthy drought, and some areas receive far more rain than others in a given year. Droughts, despite this variation, can affect large areas for a long time.

Major droughts are recorded during the Colonial period in the Maya area, but they are well nigh impossible to detect archaeologically. The effect of a long and severe drought would have been the key element leading to the social and political disruption and depopulation that archaeologists attribute to the series of complex, interrelated processes noted above. Most Maya archaeologists today are not inclined to accept a long drought beginning about A.D. 800 as the proximate cause of the Classic collapse. Nonetheless, it now appears that this drought did occur, and we believe that it should be included as one critical factor in the complex forces that irreversibly changed Classic Maya society.

THE DURATION AND DEMOGRAPHY OF THE COPÁN COLLAPSE

Although the authors in this volume differ in opinion about the ultimate causes of the collapse at Copán, the differences seem to us to be more a matter of emphasis than serious disagreement. Of greater concern are the rate and timing of depopulation. The traditional view is that the Coner phase lasted less than a century beyond the collapse of the dynasty in A.D. 820 and that the disappearance of Coner ceramics by A.D. 900 or shortly afterward marked the abandonment of Classic Copán. Most of the participants in the SAR advanced seminar generally took this position, including Ricardo Agurcia, Will Andrews, Barbara Fash, Bill Fash, and Bob Sharer. This view is also shared by Kazuo Aoyama (2001), Cassandra Bill (1997), Geoffrey Braswell (1992), Marcello Canuto (2002), Kam Manahan (2002a, 2002b), and René Viel (1993a, 1993b). David Webster and other Pennsylvania State University anthropologists associated with the Proyecto Arqueológico Copán II and subsequent investigations in the valley have advanced another interpretation of the late chronology of the Copán Valley (Webster 1999, 2002, chapter 2 in this volume; Webster and Freter 1990a, 1990b; Webster, Freter, and Gonlin 2000; Webster, Freter, and Rue 1993). In their view, the dynastic collapse at about A.D. 820, when the population of the Copán Valley was approximately twenty-five thousand, was followed by a protracted demographic decline outside the royal compound that left nearly half this number of inhabitants at A.D. 1000 and nearly four thousand farmers in the valley at A.D. 1100 (Webster 2002: figure 52).

The argument for a slow population decline is supported by several computer simulations, but especially by more than two thousand obsidian-hydration dates calculated by AnnCorinne Freter (1988) from 239 sites in the valley. A huge number of these dates from many sites are later than A.D. 900, suggesting that these sites were occupied late. Some of the obsidian-hydration dates fall as late as A.D. 1250, indicating a small population still present at this time. The ceramics associated with the late obsidian-hydration dates were of the Coner complex, implying a duration of about 550–600 years for this Late Classic complex.

We believe that the demographic decline in the Copán Valley followed rapidly on the heels of the dynastic collapse and did not drag out over two or three or four hundred years. The obsidian-hydration chronology for Copán, we think, is unreliable (Braswell 1992; Canuto 2002). The relationship of hydration-rind thickness to temperature, relative humidity, soil pH, exposure time, and other factors is not fully understood. Because slight variations in some of these factors can result in hydration-rind thickness differences that indicate dates centuries apart, no consensus exists that obsidian-hydration dating, at this stage in its development and as it has generally been employed, can be considered a reliable chronometric technique (Anovitz et al. 1999; Riciputi et al. 2002)

Robert Sharer et al. (chapter 5 in this volume) report dates calculated by Christopher Stevenson of ASC Group, Inc., from nine obsidian-hydration rinds from Copán tunnel excavations. All except one of these dates from exterior-rim measurements are far too late, averaging 649 years younger than the age of the Classic-period deposit that contained them. Six of nine interior-fissure dates are also too young for their context.

Michael D. Glascock of the Missouri University Research Reactor (MURR) ran another test of the obsidian-hydration dating method at Copán for the Tulane Group 10L-2 project. In this test, 346 surface-rind measurements and 497 internal-fissure measurements were made, using slides from forty artifacts from well-dated contexts (Braswell 1997, 2003, personal communication 2003). Applying the same technique employed by the PAC II, Glascock found that 11 of 75 (14.7 percent) surface-rind slides yielded dates consistent with their contexts. The internal fissure method produced somewhat more encouraging results, but only 63 percent of the dates fell within their expected range. Two independent labs have therefore been unable to reproduce the results, accuracy, or precision reported by the PAC II hydration program.

In Group 10L-2 at Copán, by contrast, thirty-six of forty-two obsidian-hydration dates from known Late Classic contexts excavated in 1990 fell within or near their estimated spans (Andrews and Fash 1992:table 2, dates calculated by AnnCorinne Freter). Of fourteen obsidian-hydration dates reported recently from Late Classic contexts at Xunantunich, Belize, only one is considered reliable. The authors say that "obsidian dates are generally 150 to 200 years too young when compared with contexts dated by radiocarbon. More important, they did not consistently cluster according to their associated ceramic dates" (LeCount et al. 2002:58–59, table 6, dates calculated by UCLA Obsidian Hydration Laboratory). This last finding raises doubts about the current utility of obsidian hydration even as a relative dating technique.

As we noted above, a protracted demographic collapse at Copán would mean that the Coner ceramic complex continued with little change in the Copán Valley from about A.D. 650 until 1200, because Coner ceramics are invariably associated with the late obsidian-hydration dates. Ceramic assemblages were changing rapidly in adjacent areas of Mesoamerica and northern central America from A.D. 800 to 1200, and there is no reason to think Copán would have been sheltered from normal contacts and exchange during this time. The persistence of a Classic-period ceramic complex with little change for five or six centuries would be highly unusual, even unique, in Mesoamerica.

Webster (chapter 2 in this volume; Webster, Freter, and Gonlin 2000:150–151) notes that some radiocarbon dates, as well as many obsidian-hydration dates, indicate occupation of sites throughout the Copán Valley long after the collapse of the dynasty. He describes the best example, a "well-excavated rural site" (99A-18-2) that produced five AMS dates on bone collagen from burials associated with Coner or Coner-like ceramics (Webster, chapter 2 in this volume). The one-sigma ranges are A.D. 646–768, 687–873, 883–997, 985–1029, and 1278–1411. The first two are within the Coner phase, as traditionally defined by ceramicists. The last three, however, could be interpreted as merely unreliable rather than as evidence of a protracted population decline, especially because the latest one, if correct, would require an extension of the Coner ceramic complex into the fourteenth century and the Protohistoric period.

A far more compelling reason has surfaced to dispute the argument that the Coner ceramic complex persisted for several centuries in the Copán Valley. A small settlement dating to the Early Postclassic Ejar phase has been found only a couple hundred meters south of the Acropolis. There, Kam Manahan has reported a dispersed group of about eight simple residential platforms that housed a small population whose material culture suggests that they were not descended from the Late Classic Coner-phase inhabitants of Copán (Andrews and Bill, chapter 7 in this volume; W. Fash, Andrews, and Manahan 2004; Manahan 2000, 2002b, 2003).

Ejar platform masonry was scavenged from nearby mounds, including sculpture looted from royal buildings of Group 10L-2 and the Acropolis. The platforms are not oriented to one another and do not form courtyards. The crude utilitarian pottery is of coarser pastes and less standardized forms than in Coner. Coner types and forms do not continue into the Ejar phase, nor does there appear to be any evolution of forms or decorative motifs from Coner to Ejar. Tohil Plumbate, Las Vegas Polychrome, and Fine Orange ware, long identified as hallmarks of the Ejar phase, appeared in small quantities alongside utilitarian wares in burials, middens, fill, and surface deposits. The Ejar chipped-stone assemblage also seems unrelated to Coner. Obsidian blades either were reused Coner fragments or were imported with typical Early Postclassic ground striking platforms, often from central Mexico or other distant sources. Small, crude projectile points, a rarity in the Classic period, became common. Manahan's survey of the Copán pocket in quest of other concentrations of Ejar remains was unsuccessful, but Marcello Canuto (2002) has reported small, post-abandonment, Ejar-phase sites in the Río Amarillo subregion of the Copán Valley. All these sites, Canuto notes, are newly founded or were abandoned in the Protoclassic; no Ejar materials occur at abandoned Coner-phase sites. We see a clear disjunction between the locations occupied by people using Coner ceramics and later people using Ejar ceramics.

Manahan's nine radiocarbon dates from Ejar residential contexts place this final Copán occupation at about A.D. 950 to 1050, with the intercepts of most dates falling near the center of this range. If we allow fifty to one hundred years between the end of the Coner occupation and the arrival of Ejar immigrants, the end of Coner would fall between A.D. 850 and 900. It is unlikely that a small group of Ejar settlers with a different material culture and possibly a different language would have been able to move into downtown Copán, build houses, loot the central structures, and begin farming if they had to contend with five to twelve thousand Copánecos already growing crops on all the best land.

After this relatively short Early Postclassic occupation, Copán was again abandoned. Copán was visited during the Colonial period, but not until the nineteenth century do permanent farmers seem to have moved back into the Copán pocket from Guatemala.

COPÁN RULERS AND THEIR PUBLIC MONUMENTS

Most of the investigations presented in this book focus on the ruling elite of Classic Copán, on plazas and patios, buildings, sculptural programs, inscriptions, and their successes and failures to integrate the realm. With a few exceptions, authors relegate the bulk of the population—the farmers, laborers, and craftsmen—to the subordinate rank they held in life. Most of the chapters investigate how kings and their supporters used their power to strengthen and legitimize their privileged positions. Generation after generation, their status was maintained and enhanced by their ability to commission massive structures that buried the accomplishments of their forebears and by iconography and written text that glorified their importance in Copán society, in not only the wider Maya and Mesoamerican world but also the universe of ancestors and supernatural beings. The power of the Copán state may have waxed and waned in the Classic period as surrounding polities fell under and slipped out of its control, but the Acropolis, with its surrounding plazas and nearby noble residential compounds, continued to grow, an ever more impressive testament to stability, temporal power, and the divine authority of the Copán king.

The building programs undertaken by kings when they came to power provide the clearest indications of how ideological strategies persisted and changed. We emphasize here some of the long-term decisions of Copán rulers to reinforce their authority through architecture and sculpture. Early Classic kings built ever larger structures over the original buildings of K'inich Yax K'uk' Mo', investing in these structures great sanctity and dynastic authority. Rosalila, the huge shrine of Ruler 11, was the climax of this early tradition, although later structures continued to rise on this spot.

Ruler 12, whose reign began in A.D. 628, launched a new tradition by erecting stelae, some around the edges of the Copán pocket and a number in the central plazas. Ruler 13 followed his lead, perfecting the three-dimensional sculptural style and placing eight massive stelae in the Great Plaza. Ruler 13 also started the Hieroglyphic Stairway, completed by Ruler 15, which told the history of the dynasty that would culminate in his rule.

If the buildings and iconography of the Early Classic dynasty emphasized the founder and his family, Late Classic rulers, especially Rulers 12 and 13, focused on their own images on stelae and on their position in the historical sequence to justify their rule. It is tempting to link this change in the way the dynasty presented itself to a break in the dynastic sequence following Ruler 11's death.

Finally, after Ruler 15 completed the Hieroglyphic Stairway, Yax Pasaj abandoned the policy of commissioning stelae, turning his efforts to enlarging 10L-11 and 10L-16, the second of which is the final structure covering the buildings of K'inich Yax K'uk' Mo' and Rosalila, and enlarging buildings in his own residential compound. He chose to deny the "cult of personality" embraced by his four Late Classic predecessors. Instead, Yax Pasaj stressed his allegiance to and direct descent from the founder's line on Altar Q, at the base of 10L-16. His decisions concerning how to represent himself are consistent with what we know of him from inscriptions and the sculptural iconography of Group 10L-2: he was not the son of Ruler 15, yet his local group had always proclaimed their descent from the founder.

This summary of how four centuries of Copán kings portrayed themselves to justify their accession to the ultimate position of power oversimplifies complex events and choices. The patterns of what the rulers did, however, stand starkly before us. Whether they all understood and intended the ideological messages they were sending through architecture, iconography, and texts is uncertain. At least twice in the history of this Maya city, however, a new royal actor consciously decided to use his control over public monuments to portray himself and his authority in a vastly different light.

Nearly three decades of continuous archaeological and epigraphic research in the Copán Valley have facilitated the reconstruction of an ancient Maya city and its hinterland to a degree unparalleled elsewhere in Mesoamerica, but the task is hardly begun. The lessons learned so far suggest directions and caveats for future research and are, in fact, guiding some current investigations.

First, one of the most profitable ways to study the rise and fall of Copán is to excavate a wide range of secondary and tertiary sites throughout the valley. The emphasis of the Copán Mosaics Project and the Copán Acropolis Archaeological Project, which inform most of the chapters in this volume, has been on the large structures at the center of the site and their royal and noble patrons, but research during the preceding decade focused to a great extent on the study of ancient remains scattered throughout the Copán Valley. Investigations since 1995 have likewise concentrated on smaller sites at a distance from Copán in an effort to better understand the city and the state centered there.

Next, we still do not have a good handle on population size and fluctuation in the valley, because remains of many periods, perhaps especially the Late Preclassic and Early Classic, may be buried under alluvium or Late Classic overburden. Also, political complexity and control of manpower cannot easily be inferred from survey and documentation of population growth. Knowledge of this kind must be based, in large measure, on the excavation of the full range of public buildings in an effort to reconstruct sociopolitical institutions and thereby the range of personnel using those buildings.

Finally, excavations in recent years have shown that we should continue to document and interpret the variable and dynamic roles of both nearby and distant regions of Mesoamerica in shaping the growth and fortunes of the Copán Valley.

References

Abrams, E. M.
1987 Economic Specialization and Construction Personnel in Classic Period Copán, Honduras. *American Antiquity* 52:485–499.
1994 *How the Maya Built Their World: Energetics and Ancient Architecture.* Austin: University of Texas Press.

Abrams, E. M., and D. Rue
1988 The Causes and Consequences of Deforestation Among the Prehistoric Maya. *Human Ecology* 16(4):377–395.

Adams, R. E. W.
1977 *The Origins of Maya Civilization.* School of American Research Advanced Seminar Series. Albuquerque: University of New Mexico Press.
1990 Archaeological Research at the Lowland Maya Site of Río Azul. *Latin American Antiquity* 1:23–41.
1995 Early Classic Maya Civilization: A View from Río Azul. In *The Emergence of Lowland Maya Civilization, The Transition from the Preclassic to the Early Classic*, edited by N. Grube, pp. 35–48. Acta Mesoamerica 8. Möckmühl, Germany: Verlag Anton Saurwein.

Agurcia Fasquelle, R.
1994 Copán. Atenas del nuevo mundo/Athens of the New World. In *Secretos de dos cuidades mayas/Secrets of Two Maya Cities: Copán y/and Tikal*, by R. Agurcia Fasquelle and J. A. Valdés, pp. 16–90. San Pedro Sula, Honduras: Credomatic.
1996 Rosalila, el corazón de la Acrópolis: el templo del rey-sol. *Yaxkin* 14:5–18. Tegucigalpa.
1997 Rosalila, An Early Classic Maya Cosmogram from Copán. *Symbols*:32–37. Cambridge, MA: Peabody Museum of Archaeology and Ethnology and Department of Anthropology, Harvard University.

Agurcia Fasquelle, R., and W. L. Fash
1991 Maya Artistry Unearthed. *National Geographic Magazine* 180(3):94–105.
1992 *Historia escrita en piedra: guia al parque arqueológico de las ruinas de Copán.* Tegucigalpa, Honduras: Asociación Copán e Instituto Hondureño de Antropología e Historia.

References

Agurcia Fasquelle, R., D. K. Stone, and J. Ramos
1996   Tierra, tiestos, piedras, estratigrafía y escultura: investigaciones en la estructura 10L-16 de Copán. In *Visión del pasado maya: Proyecto Arqueológico Acrópolis de Copán*, edited by W. L. Fash and R. Agurcia Fasquelle, pp. 185–201. San Pedro Sula, Honduras: Credomatic.

Agurcia Fasquelle, R., and J. A. Valdés
1994   *Secretos de dos cuidades mayas/Secrets of Two Maya Cities: Copán y/and Tikal.* San Pedro Sula, Honduras: Credomatic.

Andrews, E. W. IV
1973   The Development of Maya Civilization after Abandonment of the Southern Cities. In *The Classic Maya Collapse*, edited by T. P. Culbert, pp. 243–265. School of American Research Advanced Seminar Series. Albuquerque: University of New Mexico Press.

1976   *The Archaeology of Quelepa, El Salvador.* Publication 42. New Orleans: Middle American Research Institute, Tulane University.

1990   Early Ceramic History of the Lowland Maya. In *Vision and Revision in Maya Studies*, edited by F. S. Clancy and P. D. Harrison, pp. 1–19. Albuquerque: University of New Mexico Press.

Andrews, E. W., and B. W. Fash
1992   Continuity and Change in a Royal Maya Residential Complex at Copán. *Ancient Mesoamerica* 3:63–88.

Andrews, E. W., J. L. Johnson, W. F. Doonan, G. E. Everson, K. E. Sampeck, and H. E. Starratt
2003   A Multipurpose Structure in the Late Classic Palace at Copán. In *Maya Palaces and Elite Residences: An Interdisciplinary Approach*, edited by J. J. Christie, pp. 69–97. Austin: University of Texas Press.

Andrews, E. W., and J. A. Sabloff
1986   Classic to Postclassic: A Summary Discussion. In *Late Lowland Maya Civilization: From Classic to Postclassic*, edited by J. A. Sabloff and E. W. Andrews, pp. 433–456. School of American Research Advanced Seminar Series. Albuquerque: University of New Mexico Press.

Andrews, G. F.
1975   *Maya Cities: Placemaking and Urbanization.* Norman: University of Oklahoma Press.

Angulo, V. J.
1993   Water Control and Communal Labor during the Formative and Classic Periods in Central Mexico (ca. 1000 B.C.–A.D. 650). In *Economic Aspects of Water Management in the Prehispanic New World*, edited by V. L. Scarborough and B. L. Isaac, pp. 151–220. Greenwich, CT: JAI Press.

References

Anovitz, L. M., J. M. Elam, L. R. Riciputi, and D. R. Cole
1999   The Failure of Obsidian Hydration Dating: Sources, Implications, and New Directions. *Journal of Archaeological Science* 26:735–752.

Aoyama, K.
1999   *Ancient Maya State, Urbanism, Exchange, and Craft Specialization: Chipped Stone Evidence from the Copán Valley and the La Entrada Region, Honduras (Estado, Urbanismo, Intercambio, y Especialización Artesanal entre los Mayas Antiguos: Evidencia de Litíca menor del Valle de Copán y la Región de la Entrada, Honduras)*. Spanish translation by R. Gassón. University of Pittsburgh Memoirs in Latin American Archaeology, no. 12. Pittsburgh, PA: University of Pittsburgh, Department of Anthropology.

2001   Classic Maya State, Urbanism, and Exchange: Chipped Stone Evidence of the Copán Valley and Its Hinterland. *American Anthropologist* 103:346–360.

Ashmore, W.
1981   Some Issues of Method and Theory in Lowland Maya Settlement Archaeology. In *Lowland Maya Settlement Patterns*, edited by W. Ashmore, pp. 37–69. School of American Research Advanced Seminar Series. Albuquerque: University of New Mexico Press.

1984   Classic Maya Wells at Quiriguá, Guatemala: Household Facilities in a Water-Rich Setting. *American Antiquity* 49:147–153.

1991   Site-Planning Principles and Concepts of Directionality among the Ancient Maya. *Latin American Antiquity* 2:199–226.

Aulie, H. W., and E. W. de Aulie
1998   *Diccionario ch'ol de Tumbalá, Chiapas, con variaciones dialectales de Tila y Sabanilla*. Serie de Vocabularios y Diccionarios Indígenas "Mariano Silva y Aceves," no. 121. Coyoacán, Mexico: Instituto Lingüístico de Verano.

Aveni, A. F.
1977   Concepts of Positional Astronomy Employed in Ancient Mesoamerican Architecture. In *Native American Astronomy*, edited by A. F. Aveni, pp. 3–19. Austin: University of Texas Press.

Bardsley, S.
1996   Benches, Brothers, and Lineage Lords of Copán. In *Eighth Palenque Round Table, 1993*, edited by M. G. Robertson, M. J. Macri, and J. McHargue, pp. 195–201. San Francisco: Pre-Columbian Art Research Institute.

Barrera Vásquez, A., J. R. Bastarrachea Manzano, W. Brito Sansores, R. Vermont Salas, D. Dzul Góngora, and D. Poot Tzul, eds.
1980   *Diccionario maya Cordemex: maya-español, español-maya*. Mérida: Ediciones Cordemex.

Bassie-Sweet, K.
1991   *From the Mouth of the Dark Cave: Commemorative Sculpture of the Late Classic Maya*. Norman: University of Oklahoma Press.

References

1996   *At the Edge of the World: Caves and Late Classic Maya World View*. Norman: University of Oklahoma Press.

Baudez, C.

1983   Artefactos de la tumba. In *Introducción a la arqueología de Copán, Honduras, tomo II*, edited by C. Baudez, pp. 413–420. Tegucigalpa: Secretaría de Estado en el Despacho de Cultura y Turismo.

1985   The Sun Kings at Copan and Quirigua. In *Fifth Palenque Round Table, 1983*, edited by M. G. Robertson and V. M. Fields, pp. 29–38. San Francisco: Pre-Columbian Art Research Institute.

1988   Solar Cycle and Dynastic Succession in the Southeast Maya Zone. In *The Southeast Classic Maya Zone*, edited by E. H. Boone and G. R. Willey, pp. 125–148. Washington, DC: Dumbarton Oaks.

1989   House of the Bacabs: An Iconographic Analysis. In *House of the Bacabs, Copan, Honduras*, edited by D. L. Webster, pp. 73–81. Studies in Pre-Columbian Art and Archaeology, no. 29. Washington, DC: Dumbarton Oaks.

1994   *Maya Sculpture of Copán: The Iconography*. Norman and London: University of Oklahoma Press.

Baudez, C., ed.

1983   *Introducción a la arqueología de Copán, Honduras*. 3 vols. Proyecto Arqueológico Copán. Tegucigalpa: Secretaría de Estado en el Despacho de Cultura y Turismo.

Baudez, C., and P. Mathews

1979   Capture and Sacrifice at Palenque. In *Tercera Mesa Redonda de Palenque, Vol. IV*, edited by M. G. Robertson and D. C. Jeffers, pp. 31–40. Palenque, Chiapas, and Monterey, CA: Pre-Columbian Art Research.

Beach, T., and N. Dunning

1997   An Ancient Maya Reservoir and Dam at Tamarindito, El Petén, Guatemala. *Latin American Antiquity* 8:20–29.

Becker, M. J.

1983   Excavaciones en el corte de la Acrópolis. In *Introducción a la arqueología de Copán, Honduras, tomo II*, edited by C. Baudez, pp. 349–379. Tegucigalpa: Secretaría de Estado en el Despacho de Cultura y Turismo.

Becker, M. J., and C. D. Cheek

1983   La Estructura 10L-18. With contributions by C. Baudez, B. Riese, and A. S. Dowd. In *Introducción a la arqueología de Copán, Honduras, tomo II*, edited by C. Baudez, pp. 381–500. Tegucigalpa: Secretaría de Estado en el Despacho de Cultura y Turismo.

Beetz, C. P., and L. Satterthwaite

1981   *The Monuments and Inscriptions of Caracol, Belize*. University Museum Monograph 45. Philadelphia: University of Pennsylvania Museum.

References

Bell, E. E.
n.d.   Early Classic Ritual Deposits within the Copán Acropolis: The Material Foundations of Political Power at a Classic Period Maya Center. Ph.D. diss., Department of Anthropology, University of Pennsylvania, Philadelphia.

Bell, E. E., M. A. Canuto, and R. J. Sharer, eds.
2004   *Understanding Early Classic Copan.* Philadelphia: University of Pennsylvania Museum.

Bell, E. E., R. J. Sharer, L. P. Traxler, D. W. Sedat, and C. W. Carrelli
2004   Tombs and Burials in the Early Classic Acropolis at Copan. In *Understanding Early Classic Copan,* edited by E. E. Bell, M. A. Canuto, and R. J. Sharer, pp. 131–157. Philadelphia: University of Pennsylvania Museum.

Benson, E. P.
1971   *An Olmec Figure at Dumbarton Oaks.* Studies in Pre-Columbian Art and Archaeology, no. 8. Washington, DC: Dumbarton Oaks.
1985   Architecture as Metaphor. In *Fifth Palenque Round Table, 1983,* edited by M. G. Robertson and V. M. Fields, pp. 183–192. San Francisco: Pre-Columbian Art Research Institute.

Bey, G. J. III, C. A. Hanson, and W. M. Ringle
1997   Classic to Postclassic at Ek Balam, Yucatán: Architectural and Ceramic Evidence for Defining the Transition. *Latin American Antiquity* 8:237–254.

Bierhorst, J.
1985   *A Nahuatl-English Dictionary and Concordance to the Cantares Mexicanos, with an Analytic Transcription and Grammatical Notes.* Stanford, CA: Stanford University Press.

Bill, C. R.
1997   Patterns of Variation and Change in Dynastic-Period Ceramics and Ceramic Production at Copán, Honduras. Ph.D. diss., Department of Anthropology, Tulane University, New Orleans.
2003   A Ceramic Perspective on the Classic Maya Collapse at Copán. Paper presented at the 102nd Annual Meeting of the American Anthropological Association, Chicago.

Binford, L. R.
1971   Mortuary Practices: Their Study and Their Potential. In *Approaches to the Social Dimensions of Mortuary Practices,* edited by J. A. Brown, pp. 6–29. Memoirs of the Society for American Archaeology, no. 25. Washington, DC: Society for American Archaeology.

Blackless, M., A. Charuvastra, A. Derryck, A. Fausto-Sterling, K. Lauzanne, and E. Lee
2000   How Sexually Dimorphic Are We? Review and Synthesis. *American Journal of Human Biology* 12:151–166.

References

Braswell, G. E.
1992 Obsidian-Hydration Dating, the Coner Phase, and Revisionist Chronology at Copán, Honduras. *Latin American Antiquity* 3:130–147.
1997 La cronología y la estructura del colapso en Copán, Honduras. *Los investigadores de la cultura maya* 5:263–273. Campeche, Mexico: Universidad Autónoma de Campeche.
2003 Obsidian Hydration Dating and the Chronology of the Collapse at Copán: New Approaches and New Data. Paper presented at the 102nd Annual Meeting of the American Anthropological Association, Chicago.

Braswell, G. E., E. W. Andrews V, and M. D. Glascock
1994 The Obsidian Artifacts of Quelepa, El Salvador. *Ancient Mesoamerica* 5:173–192.

Braswell, G. E., and T. K. Manahan
2001 After the Collapse: Obsidian Production and Exchange at Terminal Classic and Early Postclassic Copán. Paper presented at the 66th Annual Meeting of the Society for American Archaeology, New Orleans.

Bricker, H. M., and V. R. Bricker
1999 Astronomical Orientation of the Skyband Bench at Copán. *Journal of Field Archaeology* 26:435–442.

Bricker, V. R.
1981 *The Indian Christ, the Indian King: The Historical Substrate of Maya Myth and Ritual.* Austin: University of Texas Press.

Bricker, V. R., E. Po'ot Yah, and O. Dzul de Po'ot
1998 *A Dictionary of the Maya Language as Spoken in Hocabá, Yucatán.* Salt Lake City: University of Utah Press.

Bridges, P. S.
1994 Vertebral Arthritis and Physical Activities in the Prehistoric Southeastern United States. *American Journal of Physical Anthropology* 93:83–93.

Broda, J., D. Carrasco, and E. Matos Moctezuma
1987 *The Great Temple of Tenochitlan: Center and Periphery in the Aztec World.* Berkeley: University of California Press.

Bronson, B.
1978 Angkor, Anuradhapura, Prambanan, Tikal: Maya Subsistence in an Asian Perspective. In *Pre-Hispanic Maya Agriculture*, edited by P. D. Harrison and B. L. Turner II, pp. 255–300, Albuquerque: University of New Mexico Press.

Brown, J.
1995 On Mortuary Analysis with Special Reference to the Saxe-Binford Research Program. In *Regional Approaches to Mortuary Analysis*, edited by L. A. Beck, pp. 3–26. New York: Plenum Press.

References

Buikstra, J.
1997   The Bones Speak: High-Tech Approaches to the Study of Our Ancestors. Paper presented to the Loren Eiseley Associates, University of Pennsylvania Museum, Philadelphia.

Buikstra, J., D. Price, J. Burton, and L. Wright
2004   Tombs from the Copan Acropolis: A Life History Approach. In *Understanding Early Classic Copan*, edited by E. E. Bell, M. A. Canuto, and R. J. Sharer, pp. 191–212. Philadelphia: University of Pennsylvania Museum.

Canuto, M. A.
2002   A Tale of Two Communities: Social and Political Transformation in the Hinterlands of the Maya Polity of Copán. Ph.D. diss., Department of Anthropology, University of Pennsylvania, Philadelphia.
2004   The Rural Settlement of Copan: Changes through the Early Classic. In *Understanding Early Classic Copan*, edited by E. E. Bell, M. A. Canuto, and R. J. Sharer, pp. 29–50. Philadelphia: University of Pennsylvania Museum.

Canuto, M. A, and W. J. McFarlane
1999   Una comunidad rural en los alrededores de Copán: un desarrollo precoz. In *XIII Simposio de investigaciones arqueológicas en Guatemala, 1999*, edited by J. P. Laporte, H. Escobedo, A. C. de Suasnávar, and B. Arroyo, pp. 1129–1148. Guatemala: Museo Nacional de Arqueología y Etnología.

Carballal Staedtler, M., and M. Flores Hernández
n.d.   Water Control Technology in the Basin of Mexico during the Postclassic Period. In *Precolumbian Water Management: Ideology, Ritual, and Power*, edited by L. J. Lucero and B. W. Fash. Tucson: University of Arizona Press. In press.

Carballo, D. M.
1997   Investigaciones arqueológicas en Cerro Chino, Honduras. Field report on file at the Centro de Investigaciones, Instituto Hondureño de Antropología e Historia, Copan, Honduras.

Carlson, J.
1981   A Geomantic Model for the Interpretation of Mesoamerican Sites: An Essay in Cross-Cultural Comparison. In *Mesoamerican Sites and World-Views*, edited by E. P. Benson, pp.143–215. Washington, DC: Dumbarton Oaks.

Carmack, R. M.
1981   *The Quiché Mayas of Utatlán: The Evolution of a Highland Guatemala Kingdom*. Norman: University of Oklahoma Press.

Carneiro, R. L.
1992   Point Counterpoint: Ecology and Ideology in the Development of New World Civilizations. In *Ideology and Pre-Columbian Civilizations*, edited by A. A. Demarest and G. W. Conrad, pp. 175–203. Santa Fe, NM: SAR Press.

References

Carrasco, D., L. Jones, and S. Sessions
2000 *Mesoamerica's Classic Heritage: From Teotihuacan to the Aztecs.* Boulder: University Press of Colorado.

Carrasco Vargas, R., S. Boucher, P. Alvarez González, V. Tiesler Blos, V. García Vierna, R. García Moreno, and J. Vásquez Negrete
1999 A Dynastic Tomb from Campeche, Mexico: New Evidence on Jaguar Paw, a Ruler of Calakmul. *Latin American Antiquity* 10:47–58.

Carrelli, C. W.
1997 Análisis preliminar de la construcción de la acrópolis de Copán en el clásico temprano: un estudio de energética. *Yaxkin* 16:16–23. Tegucigalpa.
2004 Measures of Power: The Energetics of Royal Construction at Early Classic Copan. In *Understanding Early Classic Copan,* edited by E. E. Bell, M. A. Canuto, and R. J. Sharer, pp. 113–127. Philadelphia: University of Pennsylvania Museum.

Carsten, J., and S. Hugh-Jones, eds.
1995 *About the House: Lévi-Strauss and Beyond.* Cambridge: Cambridge University Press.

Caso, A.
1928 *Las estelas zapotecas.* Monografías del Museo Nacional de Arqueología, Historia y Etnografía. Mexico City.

Chamberlain, R. S.
1953 *The Conquest and Colonization of Honduras, 1502–1550.* Publication 598. Washington, DC: Carnegie Institution of Washington.

Chase, A. F., and D. Z. Chase
1992 Mesoamerican Elites: Assumptions, Definitions, and Models. In *Mesoamerican Elites: An Archaeological Assessment,* edited by D. Z. Chase and A. F. Chase, pp. 3–17. Norman: University of Oklahoma Press.
1996 Maya Multiples: Individuals, Entries, and Tombs in Structure A34 of Caracol, Belize. *Latin American Antiquity* 7:61–79.

Cheek, C. D.
1983a Excavaciones en la Plaza Principal. In *Introducción a la arqueología de Copán, Honduras, tomo II,* edited by C. Baudez, pp. 191–289. Tegucigalpa: Secretaría de Estado en el Despacho de Cultura y Turismo.
1983b Las excavaciones en la Plaza Principal, resumen y conclusions. In *Introducción a la arqueología de Copán, Honduras, tomo II,* edited by C. Baudez, pp. 319–348. Tegucigalpa: Proyecto Arqueológico Copán, Secretaria de Estado en el Despacho de Cultura y Turismo.

Cheek, C. D., and M. L. Spink
1986 Excavaciones en el Groupo 3, Estructura 223 (Operación VII). In *Excavaciones en el área urbana de Copán, tomo 1,* edited by W. T. Sanders, pp. 27–154. Tegucigalpa: Instituto Hondureño de Antropología e Historia.

Coe, M. D.
1957 The Khmer Settlement Pattern: A Possible Analogy with That of the Maya. *American Antiquity* 22:409–410.
1965 A Model of Ancient Community Structure. *Southwestern Journal of Anthropology* 21:97–114.
1977 Supernatural Patrons of Maya Scribes and Artists. In *Social Process in Maya Prehistory: Studies in Honour of Sir Eric Thompson*, edited by N. Hammond, pp. 327–347. London: Academic Press.
1981 Religion and the Rise of Mesoamerican States. In *The Transition to Statehood in the New World*, edited by G. D. Jones and R. R. Kautz, pp. 157–171. Cambridge: Cambridge University Press.

Coe, W. R.
1990 *Excavations in the Great Plaza, North Terrace, and North Acropolis of Tikal.* Tikal Report No. 14. 6 vols. Philadelphia: University of Pennsylvania Museum.

Coggins, C. C.
1975 Painting and Drawing Styles at Tikal: An Historical and Iconographic Reconstruction. Ph.D. diss., Department of Fine Arts, Harvard University, Cambridge, MA.
1983 *The Stucco Decoration and Architectural Assemblage of Structure 1-Sub, Dzibilchaltun, Yucatan, Mexico.* Publication 49. New Orleans: Middle American Research Institute, Tulane University.
1988 On the Historical Significance of Decorated Ceramics at Copan and Quirigua and Related Classic Maya Sites. In *The Southeast Classic Maya Zone*, edited by E. H. Boone and G. R. Willey, pp. 95–124. Washington, DC: Dumbarton Oaks.

Cohen, A.
1979 Political Symbolism. *Annual Review of Anthropology* 8:87–113.

Cortés Hernández, J.
1989 Elementos para un intento de interpretación de desarrollo hidráulico del Tajín. *Arqueología* 5:175–190.

Cueva, J. A.
1996 Entrevista, en Prefacio. In *Visión del pasado maya: Proyecto Arqueológico Acrópolis Copán*, edited by W. L. Fash and R. Agurcia Fasquelle, pp. 11–28. San Pedro Sula: Asociación Copán and Centro Editorial SRL.

Culbert, T. P.
1988 The Collapse of Classic Maya Civilization. In *The Collapse of Ancient States and Civilizations*, edited by N. Yoffee and G. L. Cowgill, pp. 69–101. Tucson: University of Arizona Press.
1991 Polities in the Northeast Peten, Guatemala. In *Classic Maya Political History: Hieroglyphic and Archaeological Evidence*, edited by T. P. Culbert, pp.128–146. School of American Research Advanced Seminar Series. Cambridge: Cambridge University Press.

References

1993   *The Ceramics of Tikal: Vessels from the Burials, Caches, and Problematic Deposits.* Tikal Report No. 25, Part A. University Museum Monograph No. 81. Philadelphia: University of Pennsylvania Museum.

Culbert, T. P., ed.
1973   *The Classic Maya Collapse.* Albuquerque: University of New Mexico Press.

Culbert, T. P., L. J. Kosakowsky, R. E. Fry, and W. A. Haviland
1990   The Population of Tikal, Guatemala. In *Precolumbian Population History in the Maya Lowlands,* edited by T. P. Culbert and D. S. Rice, pp. 103–121. Albuquerque: University of New Mexico Press.

Cyphers, A.
1999   From Stone to Symbols: Olmec Art in Social Context at San Lorenzo Tenochtitlán. In *Social Patterns in Pre-Classic Mesoamerica,* edited by D. C. Grove and R. A. Joyce, pp. 155–181. Washington, DC: Dumbarton Oaks.

Davis-Salazar, K. L.
1994   Preliminary Field Report, Proyecto Arqueológico Acrópolis Copán. Field report on file at the Centro de Investigaciones, Instituto Hondureño de Antropología e Historia, Copán, Honduras.
2001   Late Classic Maya Water Management at Copán, Honduras. Ph.D. diss., Department of Anthropology, Harvard University, Cambridge, MA.
2003   Late Classic Maya Water Management and Community Organization at Copán, Honduras. *Latin American Antiquity* 14:275–299.

de Montmollin, O.
1989   *The Archaeology of Political Structure: Settlement Analysis in a Classic Maya Polity.* Cambridge: Cambridge University Press.

Demarest, A. A.
1986   *The Archaeology of Santa Leticia and the Rise of Maya Civilization.* Publication 52. New Orleans: Middle American Research Institute, Tulane University.
1988   Political Evolution in the Maya Borderlands: The Salvadoran Frontier. In *The Southeast Classic Maya Zone,* edited by E. H. Boone and G. R. Willey, pp. 335–394. Washington, DC: Dumbarton Oaks.
1992a   Archaeology, Ideology, and Pre-Columbian Cultural Evolution: The Search for an Approach. In *Ideology and Pre-Columbian Civilizations,* edited by A. A. Demarest and G. W. Conrad, pp. 1–13. Santa Fe, NM: SAR Press.
1992b   Ideology in Ancient Maya Cultural Evolution: The Dynamics of Galactic Polities. In *Ideology and Pre-Columbian Civilizations,* edited by A. A. Demarest and G. W. Conrad, pp. 135–157. Santa Fe, NM: SAR Press.
1996   Closing Comment. In *The Maya State: Centralized or Segmentary,* by J. W. Fox, G. W. Cook, A. F. Chase, and D. Z. Chase. *Current Anthropology* 37:822.
2001   Climatic Change and the Classic Maya Collapse: The Return of

Catastrophism. Review of *The Great Maya Droughts: Water, Life, and Death*, by R. B. Gill. *Latin American Antiquity* 12:105–107.

Demarest, A. A., and A. E. Foias
1993   Mesoamerican Horizons and the Cultural Transformations of Maya Civilization. In *Latin American Horizons*, edited by D. S. Rice, pp. 147–191. Washington, DC: Dumbarton Oaks.

Demarest, A., P. Rice, and D. S. Rice, eds.
2004   *The Terminal Classic in the Maya Lowlands*. Boulder: University of Colorado Press.

deMenocal, P. B.
2001   Cultural Responses to Climate Change during the Late Holocene. *Science* 292:667–672.

Diamanti, M.
1991   Domestic Organization at Copan: Reconstruction of Elite Maya Households through Ethnographic Models. Ph.D. diss., Department of Anthropology, Pennsylvania State University, University Park.

Diamond, J.
2002   Life with the Artificial Anasazi. *Nature* 419:567–569.

Dixon, B. M.
1987   Conflict along the Southeast Mesoamerican Periphery: A Defensive Wall System at the Site of Tenampua. In *Interaction on the Southeast Mesoamerican Frontier: Prehistoric and Historic Honduras and El Salvador*, edited by E. J. Robinson. BAR International Series 327(i):142–153. Oxford.

Dobkin de Rios, M.
1974   The Influence of Psychotropic Flora and Fauna on Maya Religion. *Current Anthropology* 15:147–164.

Doonan, W. F.
1996   The Artifacts of Group 10L-2, Copán, Honduras: Variation in Material Culture and Behavior in a Royal Residential Compound. Ph.D. diss., Department of Anthropology, Tulane University, New Orleans.

Dunning, N. P.
1992   *Lords of the Hills: Ancient Maya Settlement in the Puuc Region, Yucatán, Mexico*. Monographs in World Archaeology, no. 15. Madison, WI: Prehistory Press.

Dunning, N. P., and T. Beach
2000   Stability and Instability in Prehispanic Maya Landscapes. In *Imperfect Balance: Landscape Transformations in the Precolumbian Americas*, edited by D. L. Lentz, pp. 179–202. New York: Columbia University Press.

Dunning, N. P., V. L. Scarborough, F. Valdez Jr., S. Luzzadder-Beach, T. Beach, and J. G. Jones
1999   Temple Mountains, Sacred Lakes, and Fertile Fields: Ancient Maya Landscapes in Northwestern Belize. *Antiquity* 73:650–660.

References

Earle, T. K.
1978 *Economic and Social Organization of a Complex Chiefdom: The Halelea District, Kaua'i, Hawai'i.* Anthropological Papers, no. 63. Ann Arbor: Museum of Anthropology, University of Michigan.

Edmonson, M. S., ed. and trans.
1982 *The Ancient Future of the Itza: The Book of Chilam Balam of Tizimin.* Austin: University of Texas Press.
1993 The Mayan Faith. In *South and Meso-American Native Spirituality: From the Cult of the Feathered Serpent to the Theology of Liberation*, edited by G. H. Gossen in collaboration with M. León-Portilla, pp. 65–85. New York: Crossroads Press.

Elo, I. T., and S. H. Preston
1992 Effects of Early-Life Conditions on Adult Mortality: A Review. *Population Index* 58:186–212.

Fahsen, F.
1988 *A New Early Classic Text from Tikal.* Research Reports on Ancient Maya Writing, no. 17. Washington, DC: Center for Maya Research.
1992 A Toponym in Waxaktun. *Texas Notes on Precolumbian Art, Writing, and Culture*, no. 35. Austin: Center of the History and Art of Ancient American Culture, Art Department, University of Texas.

Farriss, N. M.
1984 *Maya Society under Colonial Rule: The Collective Enterprise of Survival.* Princeton, NJ: Princeton University Press.

Fash, B. W.
1992a Late Classic Architectural Sculpture Themes in Copán. *Ancient Mesoamerica* 3:89–104.
1992b Copán Mosaic Sculpture: Puzzles within Puzzles. Paper presented at the 10th Annual Maya Weekend, University Museum, University of Pennsylvania, Philadelphia.

Fash, B. W., and W. L. Fash
1991 "He at the Head of the Mat": Archaeological Evidence for a Classic Maya Council House from Copán. Paper presented at the 90th Annual Meeting of the American Anthropological Association, Chicago.

Fash, B. W., W. L. Fash, S. Lane, C. R. Larios, L. Schele, J. Stomper, and D. Stuart
1992 Investigations of a Classic Maya Council House at Copán, Honduras. *Journal of Field Archaeology* 19:419–442.

Fash, B. W., and K. A. Taube
1996 The Evolution of Dynastic Architectural Sculpture at Copán. Paper presented at the 61st Annual Meeting of the Society for American Archaeology, New Orleans.

References

Fash, W. L.
1982 A Middle Formative Cemetery from Copan, Honduras. Paper presented at the 81st Annual Meeting of the American Anthropological Association, Washington, DC.
1983a Deducing Social Organization from Classic Maya Settlement Patterns: A Case Study from the Copán Valley. In *Civilization in the Ancient Americas: Essays in Honor of Gordon R. Willey*, edited by R. M. Leventhal and A. L. Kolata, pp. 261–288. Albuquerque: University of New Mexico Press; Cambridge, MA: Peabody Museum of Archaeology and Ethnology, Harvard University.
1983b Maya State Formation: A Case Study and Its Implications. Ph.D. diss., Department of Anthropology, Harvard University, Cambridge, MA.
1983c Reconocimiento y excavaciones en el valle. In *Introducción a la arqueología de Copán, Honduras, tomo I*, edited by C. Baudez, pp. 229–469. Tegucigalpa: Secretaría de Estado en el Despacho de Cultura y Turismo.
1985 La secuencia de ocupación del Grupo 9N-8, Las Sepulturas, Copán, y sus implicaciones teóricas. *Yaxkin* 8:135–149. Tegucigalpa.
1986 La fachada esculpida de la Estructura 9N-82: composición, forma e iconografía. In *Excavaciones en el área urbana de Copán, tomo I*, edited by W. T. Sanders, pp. 319–382. Tegucigalpa: Instituto Hondureño de Antropología e Historia.
1988 A New Look at Maya Statecraft from Copan, Honduras. *Antiquity* 62:157–169.
1989 The Sculptural Facade of Structure 9N-82: Content, Form, and Significance. In *The House of the Bacabs, Copan, Honduras*, edited by D. Webster, pp. 41–72. Studies in Pre-Columbian Art and Archaeology, no. 29. Washington, DC: Dumbarton Oaks.
1991 *Scribes, Warriors, and Kings: The City of Copán and the Ancient Maya*. London: Thames and Hudson.
1998 Dynastic Architectural Programs: Intention and Design in Classic Maya Buildings at Copan and Other Sites. In *Function and Meaning in Classic Maya Architecture*, edited by S. D. Houston, pp. 223–270. Washington, DC: Dumbarton Oaks.
2001 *Scribes, Warriors, and Kings: The City of Copán and the Ancient Maya*. Rev. ed. London: Thames and Hudson.
2002 Religion and Human Agency in Ancient Maya History: Tales from the Hieroglyphic Stairway. *Cambridge Archaeological Journal* 12(1):5–19.

Fash, W. L., and R. Agurcia Fasquelle, eds.
1996 *Visión del pasado maya: Proyecto Arqueológico Acrópolis Copán*. San Pedro Sula: Asociación Copán and Centro Editorial SRL.

Fash, W. L., R. Agurcia Fasquelle, and E. Abrams
1981 Excavaciones en el sitio CV 36, 1980–1981. *Yaxkin* 4:111–132. Tegucigalpa.

References

Fash, W. L., R. Agurcia Fasquelle, B. W. Fash, and C. R. Larios Villalta
1996   Future of the Maya Past: The Convergence of Conservation and Restoration. In *Eighth Palenque Round Table, 1993*, Palenque Round Table Series, no. 10, pp. 203–211. San Francisco: Precolumbian Art Research Institute.

Fash, W. L., E. W. Andrews, and T. K. Manahan
2004   Political Decentralization, Dynastic Collapse, and the Early Postclassic in the Urban Center of Copán, Honduras. In *The Terminal Classic in the Maya Lowlands: Collapse, Transition, and Transformation*, edited by A. A. Demarest, P. M. Rice, and D. S. Rice, pp. 260–287. Boulder: University Press of Colorado.

Fash, W. L., H. F. Beaubien, C. E. Magee, B. Fash, and R. V. Williamson
2001   The Trappings of Kingship among the Classic Maya: Ritual and Identity in a Royal Tomb from Copán. In *Fleeting Identities: Perishable Material Culture in Archaeological Research*, edited by P. B. Drooker, pp. 152–169. Center for Archaeological Investigations, Occasional Paper No. 28. Carbondale: Southern Illinois University Press.

Fash, W. L., and B. W. Fash
1990   Scribes, Warriors, and Kings: The Lives of the Copan Maya. *Archaeology* 43(3):26–35.
1996   Building a World-View: Visual Communication in Classic Maya Architecture. *RES* 29/30:127–147. Peabody Museum of Archaeology and Ethnology, Harvard University, Cambridge, MA.
2000   Teotihuacan and the Maya: A Classic Heritage. In *Mesoamerica's Classic Heritage: From Teotihuacan to the Aztecs*, edited by D. Carrasco, L. Jones, and S. Sessions, pp. 433–463. Boulder: University Press of Colorado.

Fash, W. L., B. W. Fash, and K. L. Davis-Salazar
2004   Setting the Stage: Origins of the Hieroglyphic Stairway Plaza in the Great Period Ending. In *Understanding Early Classic Copan*, edited by E. E. Bell, M. A. Canuto, and R. J. Sharer, pp. 65–83. Philadelphia: University of Pennsylvania Museum of Archaeology and Anthropology.

Fash, W. L., and K. Z. Long
1983   Mapa arqueológico del valle de Copán. In *Introduccíon a la arqueología de Copán, Honduras, tomo III*, edited by C. Baudez, pp. 1–48. Tegucigalpa: Secretaría de Estado en el Despacho de Cultura y Turismo.

Fash, W. L., and R. J. Sharer
1991   Sociopolitical Developments and Methodological Issues at Copán, Honduras: A Conjunctive Perspective. *Latin American Antiquity* 2:166–187.

Fash, W. L., and D. S. Stuart
1991   Dynastic History and Cultural Evolution at Copán, Honduras. In *Classic Maya Political History: Hieroglyphic and Archaeological Evidence*, edited by

T. P. Culbert, pp. 147–179. School of American Research Advanced Seminar Series. Cambridge: Cambridge University Press.

Fash, W. L., R. V. Williamson, C. R. Larios, and J. Palka
1992 The Hieroglyphic Stairway and Its Ancestors: Investigations of Copan Structure 10L-26. *Ancient Mesoamerica* 3:105–115.

Fedick, S. L.
1996 *The Managed Mosaic: Ancient Maya Agriculture and Resource Use.* Salt Lake City: University of Utah Press.

Feinman, G., and J. Marcus, eds.
1998 *Archaic States.* Santa Fe, NM: SAR Press.

Flannery, K. V.
1998 The Ground Plans of Archaic States. In *Archaic States*, edited by G. Feinman and J. Marcus, pp. 15–57. Santa Fe, NM: SAR Press.
1999 Process and Agency in Early State Formation. *Cambridge Archaeological Journal* 9(1):3–21.

Flannery, K. V., ed.
1982 *Maya Subsistence: Studies in Memory of Dennis E. Puleston.* New York: Academic Press.

Flannery, K. V., and J. Marcus
1994 *Early Formative Pottery of the Valley of Oaxaca,* with technical ceramic analysis by W. O. Payne. Memoirs of the Museum of Anthropology, no. 27; Prehistory and Human Ecology of the Valley of Oaxaca, vol. 10. Ann Arbor: Museum of Anthropology, University of Michigan.

Flinn, M. W.
1981 *The European Demographic System, 1500–1820.* Baltimore, MD: Johns Hopkins University Press.

Folan, W. J.
1988 Calakmul, Campeche: el nacimiento de la tradición clásica en la gran mesoamerica. *Información* 13:122–190.

Fox, J. A., and J. S. Justeson
1984 Polyvalence in Mayan Hieroglyphic Writing. In *Phoneticism in Mayan Hieroglyphic Writing*, edited by J. S. Justeson and L. Campbell, pp. 17–76. Publication 9. Albany: Institute for Mesoamerican Studies, State University of New York.

Fox, R. G.
1977 *Urban Anthropology: Cities in Their Cultural Settings.* Englewood Cliffs, NJ: Prentice Hall.

Franco Torrijos, E., A. Romano Pacheco, C. Navarrete, and V. Segovia Pinto
1981 *Kohunlich: una ciudad maya del clásico temprano.* Mexico, D.F.: San Angel Ediciones.

References

Freidel, D.
1981 Continuity and Disjunction: Late Postclassic Settlement Patterns in Northern Yucatan. In *Lowland Maya Settlement Patterns*, edited by W. Ashmore, pp. 311–332. School of American Research Advanced Seminar Series. Albuquerque: University of New Mexico Press.

1992 The Trees of Life: Ahau as Idea and Artifact in Classic Lowland Maya Civilization. In *Ideology and Pre-Columbian Civilizations*, edited by A. A. Demarest and G. W. Conrad, pp. 115–133. Santa Fe, NM: SAR Press.

Freidel, D., and L. Schele
1988 Symbol and Power: A History of the Lowland Maya Cosmogram. In *Maya Iconography*, edited by E. P. Benson and G. G. Griffin, pp. 44–93. Princeton, NJ: Princeton University Press.

Freidel, D., L. Schele, and J. Parker
1993 *Maya Cosmos: Three Thousand Years on the Shaman's Path*. New York: William Morrow.

Freter, A.
1988 The Classic Maya Collapse at Copan, Honduras: A Regional Settlement Perspective. Ph.D. diss., Department of Anthropology, Pennsylvania State University, University Park.

1992 Chronological Research at Copan: Methods and Implications. *Ancient Mesoamerica* 3:117–133.

1994 The Classic Maya Collapse at Copan, Honduras: An Analysis of Maya Rural Settlement Trends. In *Archaeological Views from the Countryside: Village Communities in Early Complex Societies*, edited by G. M. Schwartz and S. E. Falconer, pp. 160–176. Washington, DC: Smithsonian Institution Press.

Galloy, J.
1993 Early Copan Settlements at the Locus of the Modern Town. M.A. thesis, Department of Anthropology, Northern Illinois University, DeKalb.

Geertz, C.
1980 *Negara: The Theatre State in Nineteenth-Century Bali*. Princeton, NJ: Princeton University Press.

Gelles, P. H.
1990 Channels of Power, Fields of Contention: The Politics and Ideology of Irrigation in an Andean Peasant Community. Ph.D. diss., Department of Anthropology, Harvard University, Cambridge, MA.

1996 The Political Ecology of Irrigation in an Andean Peasant Community. In *Canals and Communities: Small-Scale Irrigation Systems*, edited by J. B. Mabry, pp. 88–138. Tucson: University of Arizona Press.

Gerry, J. P.
1993 Diet and Status among the Classic Maya: An Isotopic Perspective. Ph.D. diss., Department of Anthropology, Harvard University, Cambridge, MA.

References

Gerry, J. P., and H. W. Krueger
1994   Regional Diversity in Classic Maya Diets. Paper presented at the 59th Annual Meeting of the Society for American Archaeology, Anaheim, CA.

Gerstle, A. I.
1988   Maya-Lenca Ethnic Relations in Late Classic Period Copan, Honduras. Ph.D. diss., Department of Anthropology, University of California, Santa Barbara.

Gill, R. B.
2000   *The Great Maya Droughts: Water, Life, and Death.* Albuquerque: University of New Mexico Press.

Gillespie, S. D.
1989   *The Aztec Kings.* Tucson: University of Arizona Press.
2000   Rethinking Ancient Maya Social Organization: Replacing "Lineage" with "House." *American Anthropologist* 102:467–484.

Gonlin, N.
1993   Rural Household Archaeology at Copan, Honduras. Ph.D. diss., Department of Anthropology, Pennsylvania State University, University Park.

Goodman, A. H., and G. J. Armelagos
1988   Childhood Stress and Decreased Longevity in a Prehistoric Population. *American Anthropologist* 90:936–944.

Gordon, G. B.
1893   Report on the Work of the Peabody Museum Expedition at the Ruins of Copan during the Season of 1892–1893. Peabody Museum Archives, Central American Expedition (93-27/2.3), Cambridge, MA.
1896   *Prehistoric Ruins of Copan, Honduras. A Preliminary Report of the Explorations by the Museum, 1891–1895.* Memoirs of the Peabody Museum of American Archaeology and Ethnology, vol. 1, no. 1. Cambridge, MA: Harvard University.
1898   *Caverns of Copan, Honduras: Report on Explorations by the Museum, 1896–1897.* Memoirs of the Peabody Museum of American Archaeology and Ethnology, vol. 1, no. 5. Cambridge, MA: Harvard University.
1902   *The Hieroglyphic Stairway, Ruins of Copan: Report on Explorations by the Museum.* Memoirs of the Peabody Museum of American Archaeology and Ethnology, vol. 1, no. 6. Cambridge, MA: Harvard University.

Graham, I.
1967   *Archaeological Explorations in El Peten, Guatemala.* Publication 33. New Orleans: Middle American Research Institute, Tulane University.

Graham, I., and E. Von Euw
1978   *Corpus of Maya Hieroglyphic Inscriptions: Naranjo, Chunhuitz, Xunantunich.* Vol. 2, pt. 2. Cambridge, MA: Peabody Museum of Archaeology and Ethnology, Harvard University.

REFERENCES

Grove, D. C.
1984   *Chalcatzingo, Excavations on the Olmec Frontier.* New York: Thames and Hudson.
1999   Public Monuments and Sacred Mountains: Observations on Three Formative Period Sacred Landscapes. In *Social Patterns in Pre-Classic Mesoamerica*, edited by D. C. Grove and R. A. Joyce, pp. 255–299. Washington, DC: Dumbarton Oaks.

Grube, N.
1988   Städtegründer und "Erste Herrscher" in Hieroglyphentexten der klassischen Mayakultur. *Archiv für Völkerkunde* 42:69–90. Museum für Völkerkunde, Vienna.

Grube, N., ed.
1995   *The Emergence of Lowland Maya Civilization: The Transition from the Preclassic to the Early Classic.* Acta Mesoamericana 8. Möckmühl, Germany: Verlag Anton Saurwein.

Grube, N., and L. Schele
1988   Cu-Ix, the Fourth Ruler of Copán and His Monuments. *Copán Note 40.* Copán, Honduras: Copán Mosaics Project and the Instituto Hondureño de Antropología e Historia.
1990   Royal Gifts to Subordinate Lords. *Copán Note 87.* Copán, Honduras: Copán Mosaics Project and the Instituto Hondureño de Antropología e Historia.
1992   Yet Another Look at Stela 11. *Copán Note 106.* Copán, Honduras: Copán Acropolis Archaeological Project and the Instituto Hondureño de Antropología e Historia.
1994   Kuy, the Owl of Omen and War. *Mexicon* 16(1):10–16.

Grube, N., L. Schele, and F. Fahsen
1991   Odds and Ends from the Inscriptions of Quirigua. *Mexicon* 13(6):106–112.
1995   The Tikal-Copan Connection: Evidence from External Relations. Version 2. *Copán Note 121.* Copán, Honduras: Copán Acropolis Archaeological Project and the Instituto Hondureño de Antropología e Historia.

Guillemin, G. F.
n.d.   Estudio y sondeo del flanco oriental de la Acrópolis, Copán temporada 1978. Field report on file at the Centro de Investigaciones, Instituto Hondureño de Antropología e Historia, Copán, Honduras.

Hall, D. G. E.
1968   A History of South-east Asia. 3d ed. London: Palgrave MacMillan.

Hall, J., and R. Viel
1994   In Search of the Preclassic at Copán, Honduras: Results of the 1993 University of Queensland Field Season. In *Archaeology in the North*, edited by M. Sullivan, S. Brockwell, A. Webb, and F. D. McCarthy, pp. 381–393. Darwin: North Australia Research Unit, Australian National University.

1998 The Formative of Copán. Paper presented at the 63rd Annual Meeting of the Society for American Archaeology, Seattle.
2004 The Early Classic Copan Landscape: A View from the Preclassic. In *Understanding Early Classic Copan*, edited by E. E. Bell, M. A. Canuto, and R. J. Sharer, pp. 17–28. Philadelphia: University of Pennsylvania Museum.

Hammond, N.
1978 The Myth of the Milpa: Agricultural Expansion in the Maya Lowlands. In *Pre-Hispanic Maya Agriculture*, edited by P. D. Harrison and B. L. Turner II, pp. 23–34. Albuquerque: University of New Mexico Press.
1981 Settlement Patterns in Belize. In *Lowland Maya Settlement Patterns*, edited by W. Ashmore, pp. 157–186. School of American Research Advanced Seminar Series. Albuquerque: University of New Mexico Press.

Hansen, R. D.
1991 The Maya Rediscovered: The Road to Nakbe. *Natural History* (May):8–14.

Harrison, P. D.
1970 The Central Acropolis, Tikal, Guatemala: A Preliminary Study of the Functions of Its Structural Components during the Late Classic Period. Ph.D. diss., Department of Anthropology, University of Pennsylvania, Philadelphia.
1978 Bajos Revisited: Visual Evidence for One System of Agriculture. In *Pre-Hispanic Maya Agriculture*, edited by P. D. Harrison and B. L. Turner II, pp. 247–253. Albuquerque: University of New Mexico Press.
1993 Aspects of Water Management in the Southern Lowlands. In *Economic Aspects of Water Management in the Prehispanic New World*, edited by V. L. Scarborough and B. L. Isaac, pp. 70–119. Greenwich, CT: JAI Press.
1999 *The Lords of Tikal: Rulers of an Ancient Maya City*. London: Thames and Hudson.

Harrison, P. D., and E. W. Andrews
n.d. The Palaces of Tikal and Copán. In *Palaces of the New World*, edited by S. T. Evans and J. Pillsbury. Washington, DC: Dumbarton Oaks. In press.

Harrison, P. D., and B. L. Turner II
1978 *Pre-Hispanic Maya Agriculture*. Albuquerque: University of New Mexico Press.

Haug, G. H., D. Günther, L. C. Peterson, D. M. Sigman, K. A. Hughen, and B. Aeschlimann
2003 Climate and the Collapse of Maya Civilization. *Science* 299:1731–1734.

Haviland, W. A.
1967 Stature at Tikal, Guatemala: Implications for Ancient Maya Demography and Social Organization. *American Antiquity* 32:316–325.

References

1981   Dower Houses and Minor Centers at Tikal, Guatemala: An Investigation into the Identification of Valid Units in Settlement Hierarchies. In *Lowland Maya Settlement Patterns*, edited by W. Ashmore, pp. 89–117. School of American Research Advanced Seminar Series. Albuquerque: University of New Mexico Press.

1992   Status and Power in Classic Maya Society: A View from Tikal. *American Anthropologist* 94:937–940.

Haviland, W. A., and H. Moholy-Nagy

1992   Distinguishing the High and Mighty from the Hoi Polloi at Tikal, Guatemala. In *Mesoamerican Elites: An Archaeological Assessment*, edited by D. Z. Chase and A. F. Chase, pp. 50–60. Norman: University of Oklahoma Press.

Hellmuth, N. M.

1982   Classification and Iconography of Tzakol (Early Classic) Maya Ceramics, Guatemala, Belize, and Mexico. Report to the Foundation for Latin American Research, Los Angeles.

1987a   *Monster und Menschen in der Maya-Kunst: Eine Ikonographie der altern Religionen Mexikos und Guatemalas.* Graz, Austria: Akademische Druck-u. Verlagsanstalt.

1987b   The Surface of the Underworld: Iconography of the Gods of Early Classic Maya Art in Peten, Guatemala. Ph.D. diss., Foundation for Latin American Anthropological Research, Culver City, CA.

Helms, M. W.

2000   *The Curassow's Crest: Myth and Symbols in the Ceramics of Ancient Panama.* Gainesville: University Press of Florida.

Hendon, J. A.

1991   Status and Power in Classic Maya Society: An Archaeological Study. *American Anthropologist* 93:894–918.

1992   Variation in Classic Maya Sociopolitical Organization. *American Anthropologist* 94:940–941.

1994   Architectural Symbols of the Maya Social Order: Residential Construction and Decoration in the Copán Valley, Honduras. In *Ancient Images, Ancient Thought: The Archaeology of Ideology*, edited by A. S. Goldsmith, S. Garrie, D. Selin, and J. Smith, pp. 481–495. Proceedings of the 23rd annual Chaacmol Conference. Calgary, Alta., Canada: University of Calgary Archaeological Association.

2000   Having and Holding: Storage, Memory, Knowledge, and Social Relations. *American Anthropologist* 102:42–53.

Hertz, R.

1960   *Death and the Right Hand.* Translated by R. Needham and C. Needham. Glencoe, IL: The Free Press.

Heyden, D.
1981 Caves, Gods, and Myths: World-View and Planning in Teotihuacan. In *Mesoamerican Sites and World Views*, edited by E. P. Benson, pp. 1–39. Washington, DC: Dumbarton Oaks.
1991 La matriz de la tierra. In *Arqueoastronomía y etnoastronomía en Mesoamérica*, edited by J. Broda, S. Iwaniszewski, and L. Maupomé, pp. 501–515. Mexico: Instituto de Investigaciones Históricas, Universidad Autonoma de Mexico.

Hillson, S. W.
1979 Diet and Dental Disease. *World Archaeology* 11:147–162.

Hodell, D. A., M. Brenner, J. H. Curtis, and T. Guilderson
2001 Solar Forcing of Drought Frequency in the Maya Lowlands. *Science* 292:1367–1370.

Hodell, D. A., J. H. Curtis, and M. Brenner
1995 Possible Role of Climate in the Collapse of Classic Maya Civilization. *Nature* 375:790–793.

Hohmann, H.
1995 *Die Architektur der Sepulturas-Region von Copán in Honduras*. 2 vols. Graz, Austria: Academic Publishers.

Hohmann, H., and A. Vogrin
1982 *Die Architektur von Copán (Honduras)*. 2 vols. Graz, Austria: Akademische Druck-u. Verlagsanstalt.

Holland, W. R.
1963 *Relationships Between Contemporary Tzotzil and Ancient Maya Religion*. Manuscript at Tozzer Library, Harvard University, Cambridge, MA.

Hornik, R.
1991 The Battle of Angkor. *Time*, 6 April, pp. 70–72.

Houston, S. D.
1988 Political History and the Decipherment of Maya Glyphs. *Antiquity* 62:135–152.
1993 *Hieroglyphs and History at Dos Pilas: Dynastic Politics of the Classic Maya*. Austin: University of Texas Press.
1996 Symbolic Sweatbaths of the Maya: Architectural Meaning in the Cross Group at Palenque, Mexico. *Latin American Antiquity* 7:132–151.

Houston, S. D., and D. S. Stuart
1996 Of Gods, Glyphs and Kings: Divinity and Rulership among the Classic Maya. *Antiquity* 70:289–312.

Hyslop, J.
1990 *Inka Settlement Planning*. Austin: University of Texas Press.

References

Inomata, T., and S. D. Houston, eds.
2001   *Royal Courts of the Ancient Maya.* 2 vols. Boulder, CO: Westview Press.

Jackson, S., and D. S. Stuart
2001   The *Aj K'uhun* Title: Deciphering a Classic Maya Term of Rank. *Ancient Mesoamerica* 12:217–228.

Johnson, J. L.
1993   The Sculpture of Structure 10L-41, Group 10L-2, Copán, 1993 (Operation 48/11). Field report on file at the Middle American Research Institute, Tulane University, New Orleans, and the Centro de Investigaciones, Instituto Hondureño de Antropología e Historia, Copán, Honduras.

Jones, C., and L. Satterthwaite
1982   *The Monuments and Inscriptions of Tikal.* Philadelphia: University Museum, University of Pennsylvania.

Jones, C., and R. J. Sharer
1980   Archaeological Investigations in the Site-Core of Quiriguá. *Expedition* 23(1):1–19.

Jones, G. D.
1992   Rebellious Prophets. In *New Theories on the Ancient Maya*, edited by E. C. Danien and R. J. Sharer, pp. 197–204. Museum Monograph No. 77. Philadelphia: University Museum, University of Pennsylvania.

Josserand, J. K., and N. A. Hopkins
2002   Classic Maya Social Interaction and Linguistic Practice: Evidence from Hieroglyphic Inscriptions and Mayan Languages. In *La organización social entre los mayas. Memoria de la Tercera Mesa Redonda de Palenque, II,* edited by V. Tiesler Blos, R. Cobos and M. G. Robertson, pp. 354–372. Mexico City: Instituto Nacional de Antropología e Historia; Mérida: Universidad Autónoma de Yucatán.

Joyce, R. A.
1991   *Cerro Palenque: Power and Identity on the Maya Periphery.* Austin: University of Texas Press.

Joyce, R., and S. D. Gillespie, eds.
2000   *Beyond Kinship: Social and Material Reproduction in House Societies.* Philadelphia: University of Pennsylvania Press.

Kampen, M. E.
1972   *The Sculptures of El Tajín, Veracruz, Mexico.* Gainesville: University of Florida Press.

Kaplan, R. D.
1994   The Coming Anarchy. *Atlantic Monthly* 273(2):44–76.

Kaufman, T. S., and W. M. Norman
1984   An Outline of Proto-Cholan Phonology, Morphology, and Vocabulary. In *Phoneticism in Mayan Hieroglyphic Writing,* edited by J. S. Justeson and L.

Campbell, pp. 77–166. Publication 9. Albany: Institute for Mesoamerican Studies, State University of New York.

Kennedy, K. A. R., T. Plummer, and J. Chiment
1986   Identification of the Eminent Dead: Penpi, A Scribe of Ancient Egypt. In *Forensic Osteology: Advances in the Identification of Human Remains*, edited by K. J. Reichs, pp. 290–307. Springfield, IL: Charles C. Thomas.

Kidder, A. V.
1950   Introduction to *Uaxactun, Guatemala: Excavations of 1931–1937*, by A. Ledyard Smith, pp. 1–12. Publication 588. Washington, DC: Carnegie Institution of Washington.

Kirch, P. V.
1984   *The Evolution of the Polynesian Chiefdoms*. Cambridge: Cambridge University Press.

Koontz, R. A.
1994   The Iconography of El Tajín, Veracruz, Mexico. Ph.D. diss., Department of Art, University of Texas, Austin.

Kowalski, J. K.
1987   *The House of the Governor: A Maya Palace at Uxmal, Yucatan, Mexico*. Norman: University of Oklahoma Press.

Kramrisch, S.
1946   *The Hindu Temple*. Calcutta: University of Calcutta.

Kurjack, E. B.
1974   *Prehistoric Lowland Maya Community and Social Organization: A Case Study at Dzibilchaltun, Yucatan, Mexico*. Publication 38. New Orleans: Middle American Research Institute, Tulane University.

Lansing, J. S.
1987   Balinese "Water Temples" and the Management of Irrigation. *American Anthropologist* 89:326–341.
1991   *Priests and Programmers: Technologies of Power in the Engineered Landscape of Bali*. Princeton, NJ: Princeton University Press.

Laporte, J. P.
1989   Alternativas del clásico temprano en la relación Tikal-Teotihuacan: el Grupo 6C-XVI, Tikal, Petén. Ph.D. diss., Universidad Nacional Autónoma de México, Mexico, D.F.
2003   Thirty Years Later: Some Results of Recent Excavations in Tikal. In *Tikal: Dynasties, Foreigners, and Affairs of State*, edited by J. A. Sabloff, pp. 281–318. Santa Fe, NM: SAR Press.

Laporte, J. P., and L. Vega de Zea
1988   Aspectos dinásticos para el clásico temprano de Mundo Perdido, Tikal. In *Primer Simposio Mundial sobre epigrafía Maya*, pp. 127–140. Guatemala: Asociación Tikal.

References

Laporte, J. P., and C. Vilma Fialko
1990 New Perspectives on Old Problems: Dynastic References for the Early Classic at Tikal. In *Vision and Revision in Maya Studies*, edited by F. S. Clancy and P. D. Harrison, pp. 33–66. Albuquerque: University of New Mexico Press.

Larios, C. R., and W. L. Fash
1985 Excavación y Restauración de un Palacio de la Nobleza Maya de Copán. *Yaxkin* 8(1–2):111–134. Tegucigalpa.

Laughlin, R. M.
1988 *The Great Tzotzil Dictionary of Santo Domingo Zinacantán, with Grammatical Analysis and Historical Commentary.* 3 vols. Smithsonian Contributions to Anthropology, no. 31. Washington, DC: Smithsonian Institution Press.

Lawrence, D. L., and S. M. Low
1990 The Built Environment and Spatial Form. *Annual Review of Anthropology* 19:453–505.

LeCount, L. J., J. Yaeger, R. M. Leventhal, and W. Ashmore
2002 Dating the Rise and Fall of Xunantunich, Belize. *Ancient Mesoamerica* 13:41–63.

Lentz, D.
1991 Maya Diets of the Rich and Poor: Paleoethnobotanical Evidence from Copán. *Latin American Antiquity* 2:269–287.

Leventhal, R. M.
1979 Settlement Patterns at Copan, Honduras. Ph.D. diss., Department of Anthropology, Harvard University, Cambridge, MA.
1981 Settlement Patterns in the Southeast Maya Area. In *Lowland Maya Settlement Patterns*, edited by W. Ashmore, pp. 187–209. School of American Research Advanced Seminar Series. Albuquerque: University of New Mexico Press.

Leventhal, R. M., A. A. Demarest, and G. R. Willey
1987 The Cultural and Social Components of Copan. In *Polities and Partitions: Human Boundaries and the Growth of Complex Societies*, edited by K. Maurer Trinkaus and W. Ashmore, pp. 179–205. Anthropological Research Papers, no. 37. Tempe: Arizona State University.

Livi-Bacci, M.
1997 *A Concise History of World Population.* Translated by C. Ipsen. Malden, MA: Blackwell.

Longyear, J. M. III
1940 A Maya Old Empire Skeleton from Copan, Honduras. *American Journal of Physical Anthropology* 27:151–154.
1952 *Copan Ceramics: A Study of Southeastern Maya Pottery.* Publication 597. Washington, DC: Carnegie Institution of Washington.

Looper, M. G.

1999 New Perspectives on the Late Classic Political History of Quirigua, Guatemala. *Ancient Mesoamerica* 10:263–280.

2002 Quiriguá Zoomorph P: A Water-Throne and Mountain of Creation. In *Heart of Creation: The Mesoamerican World and the Legacy of Linda Schele*, edited by A. Stone, pp. 185–200. Tuscaloosa: University of Alabama.

2003 *Lightning Warrior: Maya Art and Kingship at Quirigua.* Austin: University of Texas Press.

López Austin, A.

1978 La cruz y el petate en la simbologia mesoamericana y la relación entre un dios patrono y el oficio de su pueblo. *Notas antropologicas* 1(2):7–9. Instituto de Investigaciones Antropológicas, Universidad Autónoma de México, Mexico, D.F.

1997 *Tamoanchan, Tlalocan: Places of Mist.* Translated by B. R. Ortiz de Montellano and T. Ortiz de Montellano. Niwot: University Press of Colorado.

Lorenzen, K. J.

n.d. Community Shrines and Family Oratories: The Differentiation of Public versus Private Ritual in Late Postclassic Maya Religion. In *Ancient Mesoamerica*. Cambridge: Cambridge University Press. In press.

Lowenthal, D.

1985 *The Past Is a Foreign Country.* Cambridge: Cambridge University Press.

Lucero, L. J.

1999 Water Control and Maya Politics in the Southern Maya Lowlands. In *Complex Polities in the Ancient Tropical World*, edited by E. A. Bacus and L. J. Lucero, pp. 35–49. Archaeological Papers, no. 9. Arlington, VA: American Anthropological Association.

2002 The Collapse of the Classic Maya: A Case for the Role of Water Control. *American Anthropologist* 104:814–826.

Lunardi, M. F.

1948 *Honduras maya: ethnología y arqueología de Honduras.* Tegucigalpa: Sociedad de Antropología y Arqueología de Honduras y el Centro de Estudios Mayas.

Mabry, J. B., ed.

1996 *Canals and Communities: Small-Scale Irrigation Systems.* Tucson: University of Arizona Press.

Maca, A. L.

2000 Spatio-Temporal Boundaries in Classic Maya Settlement Systems: Copan's Urban Foothills and the Excavations at Group 9J-5. Ph.D. thesis, Department of Anthropology, Harvard University, Cambridge, MA.

REFERENCES

2001 Valley Bottom, Meet the Foothills: Socio-Spatial Conjunction and the Legacy of W. W. Taylor in the Archaeology of Copán. Paper presented at the 66th Annual Meeting of the Society for American Archaeology, New Orleans.

MacLeod, B.
1989 The Text of Altar F': Further Considerations. *Copán Note* 52. Copán, Honduras: Copán Mosaics Project and the Instituto Hondureño de Antropología e Historia.

Manahan, T. K.
1995 The Nature of the Classic Maya Collapse at Copan, Honduras. M.A. thesis, Department of Anthropology, Northern Illinois University, DeKalb.
1999 Excavation Report of the 1999 Field Season Copán Postclassic Archaeological Project: Operation 58/4. Field report on file at the Centro de Investigaciones, Instituto Hondureño de Antropología e Historia, Copán, Honduras.
2000 Reexaminando los días finales de Copán: nuevos datos de la fase Ejar. In *XIII Simposio de investigaciones arqueológicas en Guatemala, 1999*, edited by J. P. Laporte, H. Escobedo, A. C. de Suasnávar, and B. Arroyo, vol. 2, pp. 1149–1155. Guatemala: Museo Nacional de Arqueología y Etnología.
2002a La fase Ejar de Copan, Honduras, y el fin de la dinastía clásica maya. In *XV Simposio de investigaciones arqueológicas en Guatemala, 2001*, edited by J. P. Laporte, H. Escobedo, and B. Arroyo, pp. 33–40. Guatemala: Museo Nacional de Arqueología y Etnología.
2002b Reevaluating the Classic Maya Collapse at Copán: New Data and New Socioeconomic Implications. In *La organización social entre los mayas prehispánicos, coloniales y modernos. Memoria de la Tercera Mesa Redonda de Palenque I*, edited by V. Tiesler Blos, R. Cobos, and M. G. Robertson, pp. 329–337. Mexico: Instituto Nacional de Antropología e Historia; Mérida: Universidad Autónoma de Yucatán.
2003 The Collapse of Complex Society and Its Aftermath: A Case Study from the Classic Maya Site of Copán, Honduras. Ph.D. diss., Department of Anthropology, Vanderbilt University, Nashville.
2004 The Way Things Fall Apart: Social Organization and the Classic Maya Collapse of Copan. *Ancient Mesoamerica* 14(1):121–139.

Manzanilla, L.
1993 Daily Life in the Teotihuacan Apartment Compounds. In *Teotihuacan: Art from the City of the Gods*, edited by K. Berrin and E. Pasztory, pp. 90–99. New York: Thames and Hudson.

Marcus, J.
1974 The Iconography of Power among the Classic Maya. *World Archaeology* 6(1):83–94.

1976   *Emblem and State in the Classic Maya Lowlands: An Epigraphic Approach to Territorial Organization.* Washington, DC: Dumbarton Oaks.

1987   *The Inscriptions of Calakmul: Royal Marriage at a Maya City in Campeche, Mexico.* Technical Report 21. Ann Arbor: Museum of Anthropology, University of Michigan.

1992a   Dynamic Cycles of Mesoamerican States. *Research and Exploration* 8:392–411.

1992b   *Mesoamerican Writing Systems: Propaganda, Myth, and History in Four Ancient Civilizations.* Princeton, NJ: Princeton University Press.

1993   Ancient Maya Political Organization. In *Lowland Maya Civilization in the Eighth Century A.D.*, edited by J. A. Sabloff and J. S. Henderson, pp. 111–183. Washington, DC: Dumbarton Oaks.

1995   Maya Hieroglyphs: History or Propaganda? In *Research Frontiers in Anthropology*, edited by C. R. Ember, M. Ember, and P. Peregrine, pp. 2–24. Englewood Cliffs, NJ: Prentice Hall.

1998   The Peaks and Valleys of Ancient States: An Extension of the Dynamic Model. In *Archaic States*, edited by G. M. Feinman and J. Marcus, pp. 59–94. Santa Fe, NM: SAR Press.

2003a   Monumentality in Archaic States: Lessons Learned from Large-Scale Excavations of the Past. In *Theory and Practice in Mediterranean Archaeology: Old World and New World Perspectives*, edited by J. K. Papadopoulos and R. M. Leventhal, pp. 115–134. Los Angeles: Cotsen Institute of Archaeology, University of California.

2003b   Recent Advances in Maya Archaeology. *Journal of Archaeological Research* 11:71–148.

2004   Primary and Secondary State Formation in Southern Mesoamerica. In *Understanding Early Classic Copan*, edited by E. E. Bell, M. A. Canuto, and R. J. Sharer, pp. 357–373. Philadelphia: University of Pennsylvania Museum.

Martin, D. L., A. H. Goodman, G. J. Armelagos, and A. L. Magennis

1991   *Black Mesa Anasazi Health: Reconstructing Life from Patterns of Death and Disease.* Occasional Paper No. 14. Carbondale: Center for Archaeological Investigations, Southern Illinois University.

Martin, S.

1996   Tikal's "Star War" against Naranjo. In *Eighth Palenque Round Table, 1993*, edited by M. G. Robertson, M. J. Macri, and J. McHargue, pp. 223–236. San Francisco: Pre-Columbian Art Research Institute.

Martin, S., and N. Grube

2000   *Chronicle of the Maya Kings and Queens: Deciphering the Dynasties of the Ancient Maya.* London: Thames and Hudson.

Matheny, R. T.
1976 Maya Lowland Hydraulic Systems. *Science* 193:639–646.
1978 Northern Maya Lowland Water-Control Systems. In *Pre-Hispanic Maya Agriculture*, edited by P. D. Harrison and B. L. Turner II, pp. 185–210. Albuquerque: University of New Mexico Press.

Maudslay, A. P.
1889– *Biologia Centrali-Americana: Archaeology.* Vol. 1. London: R. H. Porter
1902 and Dulau.

May, R. L., A. H. Goodman, and R. S. Meindl
1993 Response of Bone and Enamel Formation to Nutritional Supplementation and Morbidity among Malnourished Guatemalan Children. *American Journal of Physical Anthropology* 92:37–51.

McAnany, P. A.
1995 *Living with the Ancestors: Kinship and Kingship in Ancient Maya Society.* Austin: University of Texas Press.

Meindl, R. S., C. O. Lovejoy, R. P. Mensforth, and L. Don Carlos
1985 Accuracy and Direction of Error in the Sexing of the Skeleton: Implications for Paleodemography. *American Journal of Physical Anthropology* 68:79–85.

Merbs, C. F.
1983 *Pattern of Activity-Induced Pathology in a Canadian Inuit Population.* Archaeological Survey of Canada No. 119. Ottawa: National Museums of Canada.

Michell, G.
1977 *The Hindu Temple: An Introduction to Its Meaning and Forms.* New York: Harper & Row.

Millard, A. V.
1994 A Causal Model of High Rates of Child Mortality. *Social Science and Medicine* 28:253–268.

Miller, A. G.
1986 *Maya Rulers of Time/Los soberanos mayas del tiempo: A Study of Architectural Sculpture at Tikal, Guatemala/un estudio de la escultura arquitectónica de Tikal, Guatemala.* Philadelphia: University of Pennsylvania Museum.

Miller, J. C.
1991 Investigations of Temple 21, Copán. Paper presented at the 47th International Congress of Americanists, New Orleans.

Miller, J. C., and A. Morales
1997 Espacios variables: el desarrollo de la Acrópolis al fin del clásico temprano de Copán, Honduras. *Yaxkin* 16:24–48. Tegucigalpa.

Miller, M. E.
1986   Copan, Honduras: Conference with a Perished City. In *City-States of the Maya: Art and Architecture*, edited by E. P. Benson, pp. 72–108. Denver: Rocky Mountain Institute for Pre-Columbian Studies.
1988   The Meaning and Function of the Main Acropolis, Copan. In *The Southeast Classic Maya Zone*, edited by E. H. Boone and G. R. Willey, pp. 149–194. Washington, DC: Dumbarton Oaks.

Millon, R.
1981   Teotihuacan: City, State, and Civilization. In *Archaeology*, edited by J. A. Sabloff, pp. 198–243. Supplement to the *Handbook of Middle American Indians*, vol. 1, V. R. Bricker, general editor. Austin: University of Texas Press.

Mitchell, W. P., and D. Guillet, eds.
1994   *Irrigation at High Altitudes: The Social Organization of Water Control Systems in the Andes*. Publication 12. Washington, DC: Society for Latin American Anthropology, American Anthropological Association.

Morales, A., J. C. Miller, and L. Schele
1990   The Dedication Stair of "Ante" Temple. *Copán Note* 76. Copán, Honduras: Copán Acropolis Archaeological Project and the Instituto Hondureño de Antropología e Historia.

Morley, S. G.
1915   *An Introduction to the Study of Maya Hieroglyphs*. Bureau of American Ethnology, bulletin 57. Washington, DC: Smithsonian Institution.
1920   *The Inscriptions at Copan*. Publication 219. Washington, DC: Carnegie Institution of Washington.
1926   The Copan Expedition. In *Research in Middle American Archaeology*, by S. G. Morley, pp. 277–282. Year Book No. 25. Washington, DC: Carnegie Institution of Washington.
1939   Recent Epigraphic Discoveries at the Ruins of Copan, Honduras. In *So Live the Works of Men*, pp. 277–293. Hewett Seventieth Anniversary Volume. Albuquerque: University of New Mexico Press.

Murdy, C.
1991   Investigaciones arqueológicas en el valle del Río Camotán, Departamento de Chiquimula, Guatemala, 1989–1990. Report on file at the Instituto de Antropología e Historia, Guatemala.

Murillo, S.
n.d.   *Investigaciones del corte arqueológico, Ruinas de Copán*. Report on file at the Centro de Investigaciones, Instituto Hondureño de Antropología e Historia, Copán, Honduras.

References

Murtha, T.
2002   Land and Labor: Classic Maya Terraced Agriculture at Caracol, Belize. Ph.D. diss., Department of Anthropology, Pennsylvania State University, University Park.

Neely, J. A.
2001   A Contextual Study of the "Fossilized" Prehispanic Canal Systems of the Tehuacan Valley, Puebla, Mexico. *Antiquity* 75:505–506.

Newsome, E. A.
2001   *Trees of Paradise and Pillars of the World: The Serial Stela Cycle of "18-Rabbit-God K," King of Copan.* Austin: University of Texas Press.

Nicholson, H. B.
1971   Pre-Hispanic Central Mexican Historiography. In *Investigaciones contemporáneas sobre la historia de México: memorias de la Tercera Reunión de Historiadores Mexicanos y Norteamericanos, Oaxtepec, Morelos, 4–7 de noviembre de 1969*, pp. 38–81. Mexico: Universidad Nacional Autónoma de México and El Colegio de México; Austin: University of Texas Press.

Nuñez Chinchilla, J.
1966   Una cueva vitiva en la zona arqueológica de las ruinas de Copán. *Revista de la Sociedad de Geografía e Historia de Honduras* 18:43–48.

Ortiz, P. C., and M. del Carmen Rodríguez
1989   Proyecto Manatí 1989. *Arqueología* 1:23–52.
1999   Olmec Ritual Behavior at El Manatí: A Sacred Space. In *Social Patterns in Pre-Classic Mesoamerica*, edited by D. C. Grove and R. A. Joyce, pp. 225–254. Washington, DC: Dumbarton Oaks.

Ortner, D. J., and W. G. J. Putschar
1981   *Identification of Pathological Conditions in Human Skeletal Remains.* Smithsonian Contributions to Anthropology, no. 28. Washington, DC: Smithsonian Institution Press.

Owens, J. G.
1891–   Peabody Museum Honduras Expedition, Copan 1891–92. Field Notes
1902   on Excavation of "Mound 36," including a Specimen Catalog. Cambridge, MA: Central American Expedition Records, 92-49, Peabody Museum, Harvard University.

Pahl, G. W.
1977   The Inscriptions of Río Amarillo and Los Higos: Secondary Centers of the Southeastern Maya Frontier. *Journal of Latin American Lore* 3(1):133–154.
1987   The Survey and Excavation of La Canteada, Copán, Honduras: Preliminary Report, 1975 Season. In *The Periphery of the Southeastern Classic Maya Realm*, edited by G. W. Pahl, pp. 227–261. UCLA Latin American Studies, vol. 61. Los Angeles: UCLA Latin American Center, University of California.

References

Paine, R. R.
1996   Model Life Table Fitting by Maximal Likelihood Estimation: A Procedure to Reconstruct Paleodemographic Characteristics in Archaeological Demography. Ph.D. diss., Department of Anthropology, Pennsylvania State University, University Park.

Paine, R. R., and A. Freter
1996   Environmental Degradation and the Classic Maya Collapse at Copan, Honduras (A.D. 600–1250). *Ancient Mesoamerica* 7:37–47.

Paine, R. R., A. Freter, and D. L. Webster
1996   A Mathematical Projection of Population Growth in the Copan Valley, Honduras, A.D. 400–800. *Latin American Antiquity* 7:51–60.

Palerm, A.
1955   The Agricultural Base of Urban Civilization in Mesoamerica. In *Irrigation Civilizations: A Comparative Study*, edited by J. H. Steward, pp. 28–42. Social Science Monographs 1. Washington, DC: Pan American Union.

Parfit, M.
1993   New Ideas, New Understanding, New Hope. *National Geographic Magazine*. Special ed.: Water.

Parsons, L. A.
1986   *The Origins of Maya Art: Monumental Stone Sculpture of Kaminaljuyu, Guatemala, and the Southern Pacific Coast*. Studies in Pre-Columbian Art and Archaeology, no. 28. Washington, DC: Dumbarton Oaks.

Pasztory, E.
1974   *The Iconography of the Teotihuacan Tlaloc*. Studies in Pre-Columbian Art and Archaeology, no. 15. Washington, DC: Dumbarton Oaks.

Pendergast, D. M.
1971   *Excavations at Eduardo Quiroz Cave, British Honduras (Belize)*. Occasional Paper No. 21. Toronto: Art and Archaeology, Royal Ontario Museum.

Phenice, T. W.
1969   A Newly Developed Visual Method of Sexing the Os Pubis. *American Journal of Physical Anthropology* 30:297–301.

Piehl, J. C.
2001   Status, Diet, and Nutrition: An Analysis of Human Remains from Group 10L-2, Copán, Honduras. Paper presented at the 66th Annual Meeting of the Society for American Archaeology, New Orleans.
2002   Paleopathological Indicators of Buffering Abilities and Cultural Behavior at Group 10L-2, Copán, Honduras. Paper presented at the 67th Annual Meeting of the Society for American Archaeology, Denver.

Pohl, M. D., ed.
1990   *Ancient Maya Wetland Agriculture: Excavations on Albion Island, Northern Belize*. Boulder, CO: Westview Press.

References

1994 Late Classic Maya Fauna from Settlement in the Copan Valley, Honduras: Assertion of Social Status through Animal Consumption. In appendix D of *Ceramics and Artifacts from Excavations in the Copan Residential Zone*, by G. R. Willey, R. M. Leventhal, A. A. Demarest, and W. L. Fash, Jr., pp. 459–476. Papers of the Peabody Museum of Archaeology and Ethnology, vol. 80. Cambridge, MA: Harvard University.

Popenoe, D. H.
1936 The Ruins of Tenampua, Honduras. *Annual Report for 1935*, pp. 559–572. Washington, DC: Smithsonian Institution.

Proskouriakoff, T.
1946 *An Album of Maya Architecture*. Publication 558. Washington, DC: Carnegie Institution of Washington.

1950 *A Study of Classic Maya Sculpture*. Publication 593. Washington, DC: Carnegie Institution of Washington.

1962 Civic and Religious Structures of Mayapan. In *Mayapan, Yucatan, Mexico*, by H. E. D. Pollock, R. L. Roys, T. Proskouriakoff, and A. Ledyard Smith, pp. 86–169. Publication 619. Washington, DC: Carnegie Institution of Washington.

1973 The *Hand-Grasping-Fish* and Associated Glyphs on Classic Maya Monuments. In *Mesoamerican Writing Systems*, edited by E. P. Benson, pp. 165–178. Washington, DC: Dumbarton Oaks.

1993 *Maya History*, edited by R. A. Joyce. Austin: University of Texas Press.

Puleston, D. E.
1976 The People of the Cayman/Crocodile: Riparian Agriculture and the Origins of Aquatic Motifs in Ancient Maya Iconography. In *Maya Symposium of North America: An Interdisciplinary Conference on the Art and Civilization of the Ancient Maya: Aspects of Ancient Maya Civilization*. St. Paul, MN: Hamline University.

1977 Art and Archaeology of Hydraulic Agriculture in the Maya Lowlands. *Social Process in Maya Prehistory; Studies in Honour of Sir Eric Thompson*, edited by N. Hammond, pp. 449–467. London: Academic Press.

Puleston, D. E., and O. S. Puleston
1971 An Ecological Approach to the Origins of Maya Civilization. *Archaeology* 24(4):330–337.

Rands, R. L.
1953 *The Water Lily in Maya Art: A Complex of Alleged Asiatic Origin*. Anthropological Papers, no. 34. Bureau of American Ethnology, bulletin 151, pp. 75–153. Washington, DC: Smithsonian Institution.

1955 *Some Manifestations of Water in Mesoamerican Art*. Anthropological Papers, no. 48. Bureau of American Ethnology, bulletin 157, pp. 265–393. Washington, DC: Smithsonian Institution.

Reed, D. M.
1994 Ancient Maya Diet at Copán, Honduras, as Determined through the Analysis of Stable Carbon and Nitrogen Isotopes. In *Paleonutrition: The Diet and Health of Prehistoric Americans*, edited by K. D. Sobolik, pp. 210–221. Occasional Paper No. 22. Carbondale: Center for Archaeological Investigations, Southern Illinois University.
1997 Ancient Maya Diet at Copán: Insights from Stable Isotopes and Porotic Hyperostosis. In *Bones of the Maya*, edited by S. L. Whittington and D. M. Reed, pp. 157–170. Washington, DC: Smithsonian Institution Press.
1998 Ancient Maya Diet at Copan, Honduras. Ph.D. diss., Department of Anthropology, Pennsylvania State University, University Park.

Reents-Budet, D.
1994 *Painting the Maya Universe: Royal Ceramics of the Classic Period*. Durham, NC: Duke University Press.

Reents-Budet, D., E. E. Bell, R. L. Bishop, and L. P. Traxler
2004 Early Classic Ceramic Offerings at Copan: A Comparison of the Hunal, Margarita, and Sub-Jaguar Tombs. In *Understanding Early Classic Copan*, edited by E. E. Bell, M. A. Canuto, and R. J. Sharer, 159–190. Philadelphia: University of Pennsylvania Museum.

Reilly, F. K. III
1994 Enclosed Ritual Spaces and the Watery Underworld in Formative Period Architecture: New Observations on the Function of La Venta Complex A. In *Seventh Palenque Round Table, 1989*, edited by M. G. Robertson and V. M. Fields, pp. 125–135. San Francisco: Pre-Columbian Art Research Institute.

Rice, D. S.
1996 Hydraulic Engineering in Central Peten, Guatemala: Ports and Inter-Lacustrine Canals. In *Arqueología mesoamericana: homenaje a William T. Sanders*, coordinated by A. G. Mastache, vol. 2, pp.109–122. Mexico, D.F.: Instituto Nacional de Antropología e Historia, Arqueología Mexicana.

Riciputi, L. R., J. M. Elam, L. M. Anovitz, and D. R. Cole
2002 Obsidian Diffusion Dating by Secondary Ion Mass Spectrometry: A Test Using Results from Mound 65, Chalco, Mexico. *Journal of Archaeological Science* 29:1055–1075.

Ricketson, O. G., and E. B. Ricketson
1937 *Uaxactun, Guatemala. Group E<M>1926–1931*. Publication 477. Washington, DC: Carnegie Institution of Washington.

Riese, B.
1986 Late Classic Relationship between Copan and Quirigua: Some Epigraphic Evidence. In *The Southeast Maya Periphery*, edited by P. A. Urban and E. M. Schortman, pp. 94–101. Austin: University of Texas Press.

REFERENCES

1988 Epigraphy of the Southeast Zone in Relation to Other Parts of the Maya Realm. In *The Southeast Classic Maya Zone*, edited by E. H. Boone and G. R. Willey, pp. 67–94. Washington, DC: Dumbarton Oaks.

Robertson, M. G.
1985 *The Sculpture of Palenque. Volume III. The Late Buildings of the Palace.* Princeton, NJ: Princeton University Press.

Robicsek, F.
1972 *Copan: Home of the Mayan Gods.* New York: Museum of the American Indian, Heye Foundation.

Rodriguez, M. del Carmen, and P. Ortiz
1997 Olmec Ritual and Sacred Geography at Manatí. In *Olmec to Aztec: Settlement Patterns in the Ancient Gulf Lowlands*, edited by B. Stark and P. Arnold III, pp. 68–95. Tucson: University of Arizona.

Roscoe, W.
1994 How to Become a Berdache: Toward a Unified Analysis of Gender Diversity. In *Third Sex, Third Gender: Beyond Sexual Dimorphism in Culture and History*, edited by G. Herdt, pp. 329–372. New York: Zone Books.

Roys, R. L.
1931 *The Ethno-botany of the Maya.* Publication 2. New Orleans: Middle American Research Institute, Tulane University.

1943 *The Indian Background of Colonial Yucatan.* Publication 548. Washington, DC: Carnegie Institution of Washington.

1954 The Maya Katun Prophecies of the Books of Chilam Balam, Series I to American Anthropology and History, vol. 12, no. 57, pp. 1–60. Publication 606. Washington, DC: Carnegie Institution of Washington.

1957 *The Political Geography of the Yucatan Maya.* Publication 613. Washington, DC: Carnegie Institution of Washington.

Rue, D. J.
1987 Early Agriculture and Early Postclassic Maya Occupation in Western Honduras. *Nature* 326:285–286.

Sahlins, M.
1995 *How "Natives" Think: About Captain Cook, for Example.* Chicago: University of Chicago Press.

Sanders, W. T.
1956 The Central Mexican Symbiotic Region: A Study in Prehistoric Settlement Patterns. In *Prehistoric Settlement Patterns in the New World*, edited by G. R. Willey, pp. 115–127. Viking Fund Publications in Anthropology, no. 23. New York: Wenner-Gren Foundation for Anthropological Research.

1957 "Tierra y agua" (Soil and Water): A Study of Ecological Factors in the Development of Meso-American Civilizations. Ph.D. diss., Department of Anthropology, Harvard University, Cambridge, MA.

1972 Population, Agricultural History, and Societal Evolution in Mesoamerica. In *Population Growth: Anthropological Implications*, edited by B. Spooner, pp. 101–153. Cambridge, MA: MIT Press.

1973 The Cultural Ecology of the Lowland Maya: A Reevaluation. In T*he Classic Maya Collapse*, edited by T. P. Culbert, pp. 325–365. School of American Research Advanced Seminar Series. Albuquerque: University of New Mexico Press.

1989 Household, Lineage, and State at Eighth-Century Copan, Honduras. In *The House of the Bacabs, Copan, Honduras*, edited by D. L. Webster, pp. 89–105. Studies in Pre-columbian Art and Archaeology, no. 29. Washington, DC: Dumbarton Oaks.

1992 Ranking and Stratification in Prehispanic Mesoamerica. In *Mesoamerican Elites: An Archaeological Assessment*, edited by D. Z. Chase and A. F. Chase, pp. 278–291. Norman: University of Oklahoma Press.

Sanders, W. T., ed.

1986 *Excavaciones en el área urbana de Copán, tomo I.* Tegucigalpa: Instituto Hondureño de Antropología e Historia.

1990 *Excavaciones en el área urbana de Copán, tomos II y III.* Tegucigalpa: Instituto Hondureño de Antropología e Historia.

Sanders, W. T., and J. W. Michaels, eds.

1977 *Teotihuacan and Kaminaljuyu: A Study in Prehistoric Culture Contact.* University Park: Pennsylvania State University Press.

Sanders, W. T., J. R. Parsons, and R. S. Santley

1979 *The Basin of Mexico: Ecological Processes in the Evolution of a Civilization.* New York: Academic Press.

Sanders, W. T., and B. J. Price

1968 *Mesoamerica: The Evolution of a Civilization.* New York: Random House.

Sanders, W. T., and D. L. Webster

1988 The Mesoamerican Urban Tradition. *American Anthropologist* 90:521–546.

Saturno, W. A.

2000 In the Shadow of the Acropolis: Río Amarillo and Its Role in the Copán Polity. Ph.D. diss., Department of Anthropology, Harvard University, Cambridge, MA.

Saul, F. P.

1972 *The Human Skeletal Remains of Altar de Sacrificios: An Osteobiographic Analysis.* Papers of the Peabody Museum of Archaeology and Ethnology, vol. 63, no. 2. Cambridge, MA: Harvard University.

Scarborough, V. L.

1993 Water Management in the Southern Maya Lowlands: An Accretive Model for the Engineered Landscape. In *Economic Aspects of Water Management in the Prehispanic New World*, edited by V. L Scarborough and B. L. Isaac, pp. 17–69. Greenwich, CT: JAI Press.

References

1994   Ancient Water Management in the Southern Maya Lowlands. *Research & Exploration* 10:184–199.

1996   Reservoirs and Watersheds in the Central Maya Lowlands. In *The Managed Mosaic: Ancient Maya Agriculture and Resource Use*, edited by S. L. Fedick, pp. 304–314. Salt Lake City: University of Utah Press.

1998   Ecology and Ritual: Water Management and the Maya. *Latin American Antiquity* 9:135–159.

2003   *The Flow of Power: Ancient Water Systems and Landscapes.* Santa Fe, NM: SAR Press.

Scarborough, V. L., M. Becher, J. L. Baker, J. D. Hensz, and G. Harris

1992   Water Management Studies at La Milpa, Belize. Washington DC: National Geographic Society Report.

Scarborough, V. L., R. P. Connolly, and S. P. Ross

1994   The Pre-Hispanic Maya Reservoir System at Kinal, Peten, Guatemala. *Ancient Mesoamerica* 5:97–106.

Scarborough, V. L., and B. L. Isaac, eds.

1993   *Economic Aspects of Water Management in the Prehispanic New World.* Greenwich, CT.: JAI Press.

Scarborough, V. L., J. W. Schoenfelder, and J. S. Lansing

1999   Early Statecraft on Bali: The Water Temple Complex and the Decentralization of the Political Economy. *Research in Economic Anthropology* 20:299–330.

Schele, L.

1979   Genealogical Documentation on the Tri-Figure Panels at Palenque. In *Tercera Mesa Redonda de Palenque, Vol. IV*, edited by M. G. Robertson and D. C. Jeffers, pp. 41–70. Palenque, Chiapas, and Monterey, CA: Pre-Columbian Art Research.

1984   Human Sacrifice among the Classic Maya. In *Ritual Human Sacrifice in Mesoamerica*, edited by E. H. Boone, pp. 7–48. Washington, DC: Dumbarton Oaks.

1986   The Founders of Lineages at Copán and Other Maya Sites. *Copán Note* 8. Copán, Honduras: Copán Mosaics Project and the Instituto Hondureño de Antropología e Historia.

1987a   *Notebook for the Maya Hieroglyphic Workshop at Texas, with Commentaries on the Group of the Cross at Palenque.* Austin: Institute of Latin American Studies, University of Texas.

1987b   Stela I and the Founding of the City of Copán. *Copán Note* 30. Copán, Honduras: Copán Mosaics Project and the Instituto Hondureño de Antropología e Historia.

1988   Altar F' and the Structure 32. *Copán Note* 46. Copán, Honduras: Copán Mosaics Project and the Instituto Hondureño de Antropología e Historia.

1989a The Inscription on Altar Q. *Copán Note* 66. Copán, Honduras: Copán Mosaics Project and the Instituto Hondureño de Antropología e Historia.

1989b Some Further Thoughts on the Quirigua-Copán Connection. *Copán Note* 67. Copán, Honduras: Copán Acropolis Archaeology Project and the Instituto Hondureño de Antropología e Historia.

1990a Commentary on Altar G. *Copán Note* 89. Copán, Honduras: Copán Acropolis Archaeology Project and the Instituto Hondureño de Antropología e Historia.

1990b Early Quiriguá and the Kings of Copán. *Copán Note* 75. Copán, Honduras: Copán Acropolis Archaeology Project and the Instituto Hondureño de Antropología e Historia.

1990c Preliminary Commentary on a New Altar from Structure 30. *Copán Note* 72. Copán, Honduras: Copán Acropolis Archaeology Project and the Instituto Hondureño de Antropología e Historia.

1991 Venus and the Monuments of Smoke-Imix-God K and Others in the Great Plaza. *Copán Note* 101. Copán, Honduras: Copán Acropolis Archaeology Project and the Instituto Hondureño de Antropología e Historia.

1992a The Founders of Lineages at Copán and Other Maya Sites. *Ancient Mesoamerica* 3:135–144.

1992b The Initial Series Dates on Stelae 2 and 12. *Copán Note* 104. Copán, Honduras: Copán Acropolis Archaeology Project and the Instituto Hondureño de Antropología e Historia.

1992c *Notebook for the 16th Maya Hieroglyphic Workshop at Texas.* Austin: Institute of Latin American Studies and the Department of Art, University of Texas.

1993 A Reexamination of U-Yak'-Chak. *Copán Note* 111. Copán, Honduras: Copán Acropolis Archaeological Project and the Instituto Hondureño de Antropología e Historia.

1995 The Texts of Group 10L-2: A New Interpretation. *Copán Note* 118. Copán, Honduras: Copán Acropolis Archaeological Project and the Instituto Hondureño de Antropología e Historia.

1998 The Iconography of Maya Architectural Façades During the Late Classic Period. In *Function and Meaning in Classic Maya Architecture,* edited by S. D. Houston, pp. 479–517. Washington, DC: Dumbarton Oaks.

Schele, L., F. Fahsen, and N. Grube
1994 The Floor Marker from Motmot. *Copán Note* 117. Copán, Honduras: Copán Acropolis Archaeology Project and the Instituto Hondureño de Antropología e Historia.

Schele, L., and D. A. Freidel
1990 *A Forest of Kings: The Untold Story of the Ancient Maya.* New York: William Morrow.

References

Schele, L., and N. Grube

1987 The Brother of Yax-Pac. *Copán Note* 20. Copán, Honduras: Copán Mosaics Project and the Instituto Hondureño de Antropología e Historia.

1990a A Preliminary Inventory of Place Names in the Copán Inscriptions. *Copán Note* 93. Copán, Honduras: Copán Acropolis Archaeology Project and the Instituto Hondureño de Antropología e Historia.

1990b The Glyph for Plaza or Court. *Copán Note* 86. Copán, Honduras: Copán Acropolis Archaeological Project and the Instituto Hondureño de Antropología e Historia.

1992a The Founding Events at Copán. *Copán Note* 107. Copán, Honduras: Copán Acropolis Archaeology Project and the Instituto Hondureño de Antropología e Historia.

1992b Venus, the Great Plaza, and Recalling the Dead. *Copán Note* 108. Copán, Honduras: Copán Acropolis Archaeology Project and the Instituto Hondureño de Antropología e Historia.

1993 *Pi* as "Bundle." *Texas Notes on Precolumbian Art, Writing, and Culture*, no. 56. Austin: Center for the History and Art of Ancient American Culture, Art Department, University of Texas.

1994a *Notebook for the XVIIIth Maya Hieroglyphic Workshop at Texas.* Austin: Institute of Latin American Studies and the Department of Art, University of Texas.

1994b Who Was Popol-K'inich? A Re-evaluation of the Second Successor in the Line of Yax-K'uk'-Mo' in Light of New Archaeological Evidence. *Copán Note* 116. Copán, Honduras: Copán Acropolis Archaeology Project and the Instituto Hondureño de Antropología e Historia.

1995 *Notebook for the XIXth Maya Hieroglyphic Workshop at Texas.* Austin: Department of Art and Art History, the College of Fine Arts, and the Institute of Latin American Studies, University of Texas.

Schele, L., N. Grube, and F. Fahsen

1994 The Xukpi Stone: A Newly Discovered Early Classic Inscription from the Copán Acropolis. Part II. Commentary on the Text (Version 2). *Copán Note* 114. Copán, Honduras: Copán Acropolis Archaeology Project and the Instituto Hondureño de Antropología e Historia.

1995 The Tikal-Copán Connection: The Copán Evidence. Version 2. *Copán Note* 122. Copán, Honduras: Copán Acropolis Archaeological Project and the Instituto Hondureño de Antropología e Historia.

Schele, L., and C. R. Larios

1991 Some Venus Dates on the Hieroglyphic Stair at Copán. *Copán Note* 99. Copán, Honduras: Copán Acropolis Archaeological Project and the Instituto Hondureño de Antropología e Historia.

Schele, L., and M. G. Looper

1996 *Notebook for the XXth Maya Hieroglyphic Forum.* Austin: Department of Art and Art History, the College of Fine Arts, and the Institute of Latin American Studies, University of Texas.

References

Schele, L., and P. Mathews
1998   *The Code of Kings: The Language of Seven Sacred Maya Temples and Tombs.* New York: Scribner.

Schele, L., and M. E. Miller
1986   *The Blood of Kings: Dynasty and Ritual in Maya Art.* New York: G. Braziller; Fort Worth, TX: Kimbell Art Museum.

Schele, L., D. S. Stuart, N. Grube, and F. Lounsbury
1989   A New Inscription from Temple 22a at Copán. *Copán Note 57.* Copán, Honduras: Copán Mosaics Project and the Instituto Hondureño de Antropología e Historia.

Schortman, E. M.
1986   Interaction between the Maya and Non-Maya along the Late Classic Southeast Maya Periphery: The View from the Lower Motagua Valley. In *The Southeast Maya Periphery,* edited by P. A. Urban and E. M. Schortman, pp. 114–137. Austin: University of Texas Press.

Schultes, R. E., and A. Hofmann
1992   *Plants of the Gods: Their Sacred, Healing and Hallucinogenic Powers.* Rochester, VT: Healing Arts Press.

Sedat, D. W.
1996   Etapas tempranas en la evolución de la Acrópolis de Copán. *Yaxkin* 14:19–27. Tegucigalpa.

Sedat, D. W., and F. López
2004   Initial Stages in the Formation of the Copan Acropolis. In *Understanding Early Classic Copan,* edited by E. E. Bell, M. A. Canuto, and R. J. Sharer, pp. 85–99. Philadelphia: University of Pennsylvania Museum.

Sedat, D. W., and R. J. Sharer
1997   Evolución de la Acrópolis de Copán durante el clásico temprano. *Los Investigadores de la Cultura Maya* 5:383–389. Campeche, Mexico: Universidad Autónoma de Campeche.

Segovia Pinto, V.
1969   Kohunlich. *Boletín del Instituto Nacional de Antropología e Historia* 37:1–8. Mexico, D.F.
1981   Kohunlich: una ciudad maya del clásico temprano. In *Kohunlich: una ciudad maya del clásico temprano,* pp. 211–297. Mexico: San Angel Ediciones.

Serrano Sánchez, C.
1993   Funerary Practices and Human Sacrifice in Teotihuacan Burials. In *Teotihuacan: Art from the City of the Gods,* edited by K. Berrin and E. Pasztory, pp. 108–115. New York: Thames and Hudson.

Sharer, R. J.
1977   The Maya Collapse Revisited: Internal and External Perspectives. In *Social Process in Maya Prehistory: Studies in Honour of Sir Eric Thompson,* edited by N. Hammond, pp. 531–552. London: Academic Press.

1988	Quirigua as a Classic Maya Center. In *The Southeast Classic Maya Zone*, edited by E. H. Boone and G. R. Willey, pp. 31–65. Washington, DC: Dumbarton Oaks.
1989	The Olmec and the Southeast Periphery of Mesoamerica. In *Regional Perspectives on the Olmec*, edited by R. J. Sharer and D. C. Grove, pp. 247–271. Cambridge: Cambridge University Press.
1994	*The Ancient Maya*. 5th ed. Stanford, CA: Stanford University Press.
1996	Los patrones del desarrollo arquitectónico en la Acrópolis de Copán del clásico temprano. *Yaxkin* 14:28–34. Tegucigalpa.
2003a	Founding Events and Teotihuacan Connections at Copán, Honduras. In *Teotihuacan and the Maya: Reinterpreting Early Classic Interaction*, edited by G. E. Braswell, pp. 143–165. Austin: University of Texas Press.
2003b	Tikal and the Copan Dynastic Founding. In *Tikal: Dynasties, Foreigners, and Affairs of State. Advancing Maya Archaeology*, edited by J. A. Sabloff, pp. 319–353. Santa Fe, NM: SAR Press.
2004	External Interaction at Early Classic Copan. In *Understanding Early Classic Copan*, edited by E. E. Bell, M. A. Canuto, and R. J. Sharer, pp. 297–317. Philadelphia: University of Pennsylvania Museum.

Sharer, R. J., and M. A. Canuto
2002	Before the Classic: Issues of Organizational and Ethnic Diversity in the Copan Valley. Paper presented at the 101st Annual Meeting of the American Anthropological Association, New Orleans.

Sharer, R. J., W. L. Fash, D. W. Sedat, L. P. Traxler, and R. V. Williamson
1999	Continuities and Contrasts in Early Classic Architecture of Central Copan. In *Mesoamerican Architecture as a Cultural Symbol*, edited by J. K. Kowalski, pp. 220–249. New York: Oxford University Press.

Sharer, R. J., and D. C. Grove
1989	*Regional Perspectives on the Olmec*. School of American Research Advanced Seminar Series. Cambridge: Cambridge University Press.

Sharer, R. J., J. C. Miller, and L. P. Traxler
1992	Evolution of Classic Period Architecture in the Eastern Acropolis, Copan. *Ancient Mesoamerica* 3:145–159.

Sharer, R. J., L. P. Traxler, D. W. Sedat, E. E. Bell, M. A. Canuto, and C. Powell
1999	Early Classic Architecture beneath the Copan *Acropolis: A Research Update*. *Ancient Mesoamerica* 10:3–23.

Sheehy, J.
1991	Structure and Change in a Late Classic Maya Domestic Group at Copan, Honduras. *Ancient Mesoamerica* 2:1–19.

Sheets, P. D.
1992	*The Ceren Site: A Prehistoric Village Buried by Volcanic Ash in Central America*. Fort Worth, TX: Harcourt Brace Jovanovich.

References

Sherbondy, J. E.
1982 El regadío, los lagos y los mitos de origin. *Allpanchis* 20:3–32.
1992 Water Ideology in Inca Ethnogenesis. In *Andean Cosmologies through Time: Persistence and Emergence*, edited R. V. H. Dover, K. E. Seibold, and J. H. McDowell, pp. 46–66. Bloomington: Indiana University Press.
1994 Water and Power: The Role of Irrigation Districts in the Transition from Inca to Spanish Cuzco. In *Irrigation at High Altitudes: The Social Organization of Water Control Systems in the Andes*, edited by W. P. Mitchell and D. Guillet, pp. 69–98. Publication 12. Washington, DC: Society for Latin American Anthropology, American Anthropological Association.

Shimkin, D. B.
1973 Models for the Downfall: Some Ecological and Culture-Historical Considerations. In *The Classic Maya Collapse*, edited by T. P. Culbert, pp. 269–299. School of American Research Advanced Seminar Series. Albuquerque: University of New Mexico Press.

Shorkley, G.
1892– Peabody Museum Honduras Expedition, Copan, 1892–93. Notes taken
1893 by G. Shorkley. Central American Expedition Records, 93-27A, Peabody Museum, Harvard University, Cambridge, MA.

Siemens, A. H., and D. E. Puleston
1972 Ridged Fields and Associated Features in Southern Campeche: New Perspectives on the Lowland Maya. *American Antiquity* 37:228–239.

Sigal, P. H.
2000 *From Moon Goddesses to Virgins: The Colonization of Yucatecan Maya Sexual Desire*. Austin: University of Texas Press.

Skinner, M., and A. H. Goodman
1992 Anthropological Uses of Developmental Defects of Enamel. In *Skeletal Biology of Past Peoples: Research Methods*, edited by S. R. Saunders and M. A. Katzenberg, pp. 153–174. New York: Wiley-Liss.

Smith, A. L.
1950 *Uaxactun, Guatemala: Excavations of 1931–1937*. Publication 588. Washington, DC: Carnegie Institution of Washington.

Spinden, H. J.
1913 *A Study of Maya Art: Its Subject Matter and Historical Development.* Memoirs of the Peabody Museum of American Archaeology and Ethnology, vol. 6. Cambridge, MA: Harvard University.

Squier, E. G.
1853 Ruins of Tenampua, Honduras, Central America. Proceedings of the Historical Society of New York, October.
1870 *Honduras: Descriptive, Historical, and Statistical*. London: Trubner & Co.

References

Stark, B. L.
1999 Commentary: Ritual, Social Identity, and Cosmology: Hard Stones and Flowing Water. In *Social Patterns in Pre-Classic Mesoamerica*, edited by D. C. Grove and R. A. Joyce, pp. 301–317. Washington, DC: Dumbarton Oaks.

Starratt, H. E.
2001 Excavations in El Cementerio, Group 10L-2, Copán, Honduras. Ph.D. diss., Department of Anthropology, Tulane University, New Orleans.

Starratt, H. E., and W. F. Doonan
2001 How the Other Half Lived: The Distribution of Artifacts in Group 10L-2, Copán, Honduras. Paper presented at the 66th Annual Meeting of the Society for American Archaeology, New Orleans.

Stephens, J. L.
1841 *Incidents of Travel in Central America, Chiapas, and Yucatán*. 2 vols. New York: Harper.

Stierlin, H.
1970 *Angkor*. Fribourg, Switzerland: Office de Livre.

Stone, A. J.
1989 Disconnection, Foreign Insignia, and Political Expansion: Teotihuacan and the Warrior Stelae of Piedras Negras. In *Mesoamerica after the Decline of Teotihuacan, A.D. 700–900*, edited by R. A. Diehl and J. C. Berlo, pp. 153–172. Washington, DC: Dumbarton Oaks.
1995 *Images from the Underworld: Naj Tunich and the Tradition of Maya Cave Painting*. Austin: University of Texas Press.

Stone, D. K., A. Morales, and R. V. Williamson
1996 Sacrificios y iconografía de guerra en el grupo principal de Copán. In *Visión del pasado maya: Proyecto Arqueológico Acrópolis de Copán*, edited by W. L. Fash and R. Agurcia Fasquelle, pp. 203–213. San Pedro Sula, Honduras: Asociación Copán.

Storey, R.
1992 The Children of Copan. *Ancient Mesoamerica* 3:161–167.
1997 Individual Frailty, Children of Privilege, and Stress in Late Classic Copan. In *Bones of the Maya: Studies of Ancient Skeletons*, edited by S. L. Whittington and D. M. Reed, pp.116–126. Washington, DC: Smithsonian Institution Press.
1998 The Mothers and Daughters of a Patrilineal Civilization: The Health of Females among the Late Classic Maya of Copan, Honduras. In *Sex and Gender in Paleopathological Perspective*, edited by A. L. Grauer and P. Stuart-Macadam, pp. 133–148. Cambridge: Cambridge University Press.
1999 Late Classic Nutrition and Skeletal Indicators at Copán, Honduras. In *Reconstructing Ancient Maya Diet*, edited by C. D. White, pp. 169–179. Salt Lake City: University of Utah Press.

Strömsvik, G.
1952 *The Ball Courts at Copán.* Publication 596. Washington, DC: Carnegie Institution of Washington.

Stuart, D. S.
1986 The Chronology of Stela 4 at Copán. *Copán Note* 12. Copán, Honduras: Copán Mosaics Project and the Instituto Hondureño de Antropología e Historia.
1987 Ten Phonetic Syllables. *Research Reports on Ancient Maya Writing,* no. 14, pp. 1–52. Washington, DC: Center for Maya Research.
1989a Comments on the Temple 22 Inscription. *Copán Note* 63. Copán, Honduras: Copán Acropolis Archaeology Project and the Instituto Hondureño de Antropología e Historia.
1989b The "First Ruler" on Stela 24. *Copán Note* 7. Copán, Honduras: Copán Acropolis Archaeology Project and the Instituto Hondureño de Antropología e Historia.
1992 Hieroglyphs and Archaeology at Copan. *Ancient Mesoamerica* 3:169–184.
1993 Historical Inscriptions and the Maya Collapse. In *Lowland Maya Civilization in the Eighth Century A.D.,* edited by J. A. Sabloff and J. S. Henderson, pp. 321–354. Washington, DC: Dumbarton Oaks.
1997 Hiéroglyphes et histoire de Copán. In *Les mayas au pays de Copán,* coordinated by A. S. Riotti and C. R. Reina, pp. 101–110. Milan: Skira.
1998 "The Fire Enters His House": Architecture and Ritual in Classic Maya Texts. In *Function and Meaning in Classic Maya Architecture,* edited by S. D. Houston, pp. 373–425. Washington, DC: Dumbarton Oaks.
2000 "The Arrival of Strangers": Teotihuacan and Tollan in Classic Maya History. In *Mesoamerica's Classic Heritage: From Teotihuacan to the Aztecs,* edited by D. Carrasco, L. Jones, and S. Sessions, pp. 465–513. Boulder: University Press of Colorado.
2004 The Beginnings of the Copan Dynasty: A Review of the Hieroglyphic and Historical Evidence. In *Understanding Early Classic Copan,* edited by E. E. Bell, M. A. Canuto, and R. J. Sharer, pp. 215–247. Philadelphia: University of Pennsylvania Museum.

Stuart, D. S., and S. D. Houston
1989 Maya Writing. *Scientific American* 261:82–89.
1994 *Classic Maya Place Names.* Studies in Pre-Columbian Art and Archaeology, no. 33. Washington, DC: Dumbarton Oaks.

Stuart, D. S., S. D. Houston, and J. Robertson
1999 *Recovering the Past: Classic Mayan Language and Classic Maya Gods.* Workbook for the 23rd Linda Schele Forum on Maya Hieroglyphic Writing. Austin: Department of Art and Art History and the Institute of Latin American Studies, University of Texas.

References

Stuart, D. S., and L. Schele
1986   Yax-K'uk-Mo', the Founder of the Lineage of Copán. *Copán Note* 6. Copán, Honduras: Copán Mosaics Project and the Instituto Hondureño de Antropología e Historia.

Stuart, G. E.
1997   The Royal Crypts of Copan. *National Geographic* 192(6):68–93.

Stuart, G. S., and G. E. Stuart
1993   *Lost Kingdoms of the Maya.* Washington, DC: National Geographic Society.

Stuart-Macadam, P.
1985   Porotic Hyperostosis: Representative of a Childhood Condition. *American Journal of Physical Anthropology* 66:391–398.

Tambiah, S. J.
1977   The Galactic Polity: The Structure of Traditional Kingdoms in Southeast Asia. In *Anthropology and the Climate of Opinion,* edited by S. A. Freed, pp. 69–97. New York: New York Academy of Sciences.

Tanner, J. M.
1978   *Foetus into Man: Physical Growth from Conception to Maturity.* Cambridge, MA: Harvard University Press.

Tate, C.
1982   The Maya Cauac Monster: Dynastic Contexts. In *Selected Readings in Pre-Columbian Art History,* edited by A. Cordy-Collins, pp. 33–54. Palo Alto, CA: Peek Publications.

Taube, K. A.
1992   *The Major Gods of Ancient Yucatan.* Studies in Pre-Columbian Art and Archaeology, no. 32. Washington, DC: Dumbarton Oaks.

2000   The Writing System of Ancient Teotihuacan. Ancient America, 1. Barnardsville, NC: Center for Ancient American Studies.

2004   Structure 10L-16 and Its Early Classic Antecedents: Fire and the Evocation and Resurrection of K'inich Yax K'uk' Mo'. In *Understanding Early Classic Copan,* edited by E. E. Bell, M. A. Canuto, and R. J. Sharer, pp. 265–295. Philadelphia: University of Pennsylvania Museum.

Taylor, D.
1979   The Cauac Monster. In *Tercera Mesa Redonda de Palenque, Vol. IV,* edited by M. G. Robertson and D. C. Jeffers, pp. 79–89. Palenque, Chiapas, and Monterey, CA: Pre-Columbian Art Research.

Thompson, E. H.
1897   *The Chultunes of Labna, Yucatan.* Memoirs of the Peabody Museum of American Archaeology and Ethnology, vol. 1, no. 3. Cambridge, MA: Harvard University.

Thompson, J. E. S.
1944 *The Fish as a Maya Symbol for Counting and Further Discussions of Directional Glyphs.* Theoretical Approaches to Problems, no. 2, Division of Historical Research. Washington, DC: Carnegie Institution of Washington.
1951 Aquatic Symbols Common to Various Centers of the Classic Period in Meso-America. In *The Civilizations of Ancient America. Selected Papers of the XXIXth International Congress of Americanists*, edited by S. Tax, pp. 31–36. Chicago: University of Chicago Press.
1962 *A Catalog of Maya Hieroglyphs.* Norman: University of Oklahoma Press.
1970 *Maya History and Religion.* Norman: University of Oklahoma Press.

Tozzer, A. M., ed. and trans.
1941 *Landa's Relación de las Cosas de Yucatán.* Papers of the Peabody Museum of American Archaeology and Ethnology, vol. 18. Cambridge, MA: Harvard University.

Traxler, L. P.
1994 A New Discovery at Copán. *Expedition* 35(3):57–62.
1996 Los grupos de patios tempranos de la Acrópolis de Copán. *Yaxkin* 14:35–54. Tegucigalpa.
2001 The Royal Court of Early Classic Copan. In *Royal Courts of the Ancient Maya. Volume 2: Data and Case Studies*, edited by T. Inomata and S. D. Houston, pp. 46–73. Boulder, CO: Westview Press.
2004a Evolution and Social Meaning of Early Classic Architecture at Copan, Honduras. Ph.D. diss., Department of Anthropology, University of Pennsylvania, Philadelphia.
2004b Redesigning Copan: Early Architecture of the Polity Center. In *Understanding Early Classic Copan*, edited by E. E. Bell, M. A. Canuto, and R. J. Sharer, pp. 53–64. Philadelphia: University of Pennsylvania Museum.

Trigger, B. G.
1974 The Archaeology of Government. *World Archaeology* 6:95–106.
1990 Monumental Architecture: A Thermodynamic Explanation of Symbolic Behaviour. *World Archaeology* 22:119–132.

Trik, A. S.
1939 *Temple XXII at Copan.* Contributions to American Anthropology and History, vol. 5, no. 27, pp. 81–103. Publication 509. Washington, DC: Carnegie Institution of Washington.

Turner, B. L. II
1974 Prehistoric Intensive Agriculture in the Mayan Lowlands. *Science* 185:118–124.
1978a The Development and Demise of the Swidden Thesis of Maya Agriculture. In *Pre-Hispanic Maya Agriculture*, edited by P. D. Harrison and B. L. Turner II, pp. 13–22. Albuquerque: University of New Mexico Press.

References

1978b   Ancient Agricultural Land Use in the Central Maya Lowlands. In *Pre-Hispanic Maya Agriculture*, edited by P. D. Harrison and B. L. Turner II, pp. 163–183. Albuquerque: University of New Mexico Press.

1983   *Once Beneath the Forest: Prehistoric Terracing in the Rio Bec Region of the Maya Lowlands.* Boulder, CO: Westview Press.

Turner, B. L. II, W. Johnson, G. Mahood, F. M. Wiseman, and J. Poole

1983   Habitat y agricultura en la región de Copán. In *Introducción a la Arqueología de Copán, Honduras, tomo I*, edited by C. Baudez, pp. 35–142. Tegucigalpa: Secretaría de Estado en el Despacho de Cultura y Turismo.

Urban, P. A., and E. M. Schortman

1987   Copan and Its Neighbors: Patterns of Interaction Reflected in Classic Period Western Honduran Pottery. In *Maya Ceramics: Papers from the 1985 Maya Ceramic Conference*, edited by P. M. Rice and R. J. Sharer, pp. 341–395. BAR International Series 345 (ii). Oxford: British Archaeological Reports.

Urton, G.

1981   *At the Crossroads of the Earth and the Sky: An Andean Cosmology.* Austin: University of Texas Press.

Valdés, J. A.

1991   Los mascarones del grupo 6C-XVI de Tikal: análisis iconográfico para el clásico temprano. *Estudios de Cultura Maya* 18:233–262. Mexico, D.F.

Valdés, J. A., and F. Fahsen

1995   The Reigning Dynasty of Uaxactun during the Early Classic. *Ancient Mesoamerica* 6:197–219.

Valdés, J. A., and L. E. Wright

2004   The Early Classic and Its Antecedents at Kaminaljuyu: A Complex Society with Complex Problems. In *Understanding Early Classic Copan*, edited by E. E. Bell, M. A. Canuto, and R. J. Sharer, pp. 337–355. Philadelphia: University of Pennsylvania Museum.

Viel, R.

1983   Evolución de la cerámica en Copán. Resultados preliminares. In *Introducción a la arqueología de Copán, tomo I*, edited by C. Baudez, pp.471–549. Tegucigalpa: Secretaría de Estado en el Despacho de Cultura y Turismo.

1993a   Copán Valley. In *Pottery of Prehistoric Honduras: Regional Classification and Analysis*, edited by J. S. Henderson and M. P. Beaudry-Corbet, pp. 12–18. Institute of Archaeology Monograph 35. Los Angeles: University of California.

1993b   *Evolución de la cerámica de Copán, Honduras.* Tegucigalpa: Instituto Hondureño de Antropología e Historia.

1999a   El período formativo de Copán, Honduras. In *XII simposio de investigaciones arqueológicas en Guatemala, 1998*, edited by J. P. Laporte, H. L. Escobedo, and A. C. Monzón de Suasnávar, tomo 1, pp. 99–104. Guatemala: Museo Nacional de Arqueología y Etnología.

1999b   The Pectorals of Altar Q and Structure 11: An Interpretation of the Political Organization at Copán, Honduras. *Latin American Antiquity* 10:377–399.

Viel, R., and C. D. Cheek

1983   Sepulturas. In *Introducción a la arqueología de Copán, Honduras, tomo I*, edited by C. Baudez, pp. 551–609. Tegucigalpa: Secretaría de Estado en el Despacho de Cultura y Turismo.

Viel, R., and J. Hall

1997   El período formativo de Copán en el contexto de Honduras. *Yaxkin* 16:40–48. Tegucigalpa.

Vogt, E. Z.

1956   An Appraisal of *Prehistoric Settlement Patterns in the New World*. In *Prehistoric Settlement Patterns in the New World*, edited by G. R. Willey, pp. 173–182. Viking Fund Publications in Anthropology, no. 23. New York: Wenner-Gren Foundation for Anthropological Research.

1969   *Zinacantan: A Maya Community in the Highlands of Chiapas*. Cambridge, MA: Harvard University Press.

1981a   Some Aspects of the Sacred Geography of Highland Chiapas. In *Mesoamerican Sites and World-Views*, edited by E. P. Benson, pp. 119–142. Washington, DC: Dumbarton Oaks.

1981b   *Tortillas for the Gods: A Symbolic Analysis of Zinacanteco Rituals*. Cambridge, MA: Harvard University Press.

1983a   Some New Themes in Settlement Pattern Research. In *Prehistoric Settlement Patterns: Essays in Honor of Gordon R. Willey*, edited by E. Z. Vogt and R. M. Leventhal, pp. 3–20. Albuquerque: University of New Mexico Press; Cambridge, MA: Peabody Museum of Archaeology and Ethnology, Harvard University.

1983b   Ancient and Contemporary Maya Settlement Patterns: A New Look from the Chiapas Highlands. In *Prehistoric Settlement Patterns: Essays in Honor of Gordon R. Willey*, edited by E. Z. Vogt and R. M. Leventhal, pp. 89–114. Albuquerque: University of New Mexico Press; Cambridge, MA: Peabody Museum of Archaeology and Ethnology.

Volwahsen, A.

1969   *Living Architecture: Indian*. New York: Grosset and Dunlap.

Wagner, E.

1995   When the Torch Went Marchin' In: Written Evidence for the Intentional Destruction of Buildings at Copán. Unpublished paper.

REFERENCES

Wanyerka, P.
1996   The Carved Monuments of Uxbenka, Toledo District, Belize. *Mexicon* 18(2):29–35.

Webster, D. L.
1977   Warfare and the Evolution of Maya Civilization. In *The Origins of Maya Civilization*, edited by R. E. W. Adams, pp. 335–372. School of American Research Advanced Seminar Series. Albuquerque: University of New Mexico Press.

1985   Surplus, Labor, and Stress in Late Classic Maya Society. *Journal of Anthropological Research* 41:375–399.

1989a   The House of the Bacabs: Its Social Context. In *The House of the Bacabs, Copan, Honduras*, edited by D. L. Webster, pp. 5–40. Studies in Pre-Columbian Art and Archaeology, no. 29. Washington, DC: Dumbarton Oaks.

1989b   The Original Location, Date, and Possible Implications of Altar W'. In *House of the Bacabs, Copan, Honduras*, edited by D. L. Webster, pp. 108–111. Washington, DC: Dumbarton Oaks.

1992   Maya Elites: The Perspective from Copan. In *Mesoamerican Elites: An Archaeological Assessment*, edited by D. Z. Chase and A. F. Chase, pp. 135–156. Norman: University of Oklahoma Press.

1995   Maya Shaman-Kings: Some Evolutionary Implications. *Cambridge Archaeological Journal* 5:120–122.

1998a   Classic Maya Architecture: Implications and Comparisons. In *Function and Meaning in Classic Maya Architecture*, edited by S. D. Houston, pp. 5–47. Washington, DC: Dumbarton Oaks.

1998b   Warfare and Status Rivalry: Lowland Maya and Polynesian Comparisons. In *Archaic States*, edited by G. M. Feinman and J. Marcus, pp. 311–351. Santa Fe, NM: SAR Press.

1999   The Archaeology of Copán, Honduras. *Journal of Archaeological Research* 7:1–53.

2001   Spatial Dimensions of Maya Courtly Life: Problems and Issues. In *Royal Courts of the Ancient Maya. Volume 1: Theory, Comparison, and Synthesis*, edited by T. Inomata and S. D. Houston, pp. 130–167. Boulder, CO: Westview Press.

2002   *The Fall of the Ancient Maya: Solving the Mystery of the Maya Collapse*. London: Thames and Hudson.

Webster, D. L., ed.
1989   *The House of the Bacabs, Copan, Honduras*. Studies in Pre-Columbian Art and Archaeology, no. 29. Washington, DC: Dumbarton Oaks.

Webster, D. L., B. W. Fash, R. Widmer, and S. Zeleznik
1998   The Skyband Group: Investigation of a Classic Maya Elite Residential Complex at Copan, Honduras. *Journal of Field Archaeology* 25:319–343.

References

Webster, D. L., W. L. Fash, and E. M. Abrams
1986   Excavaciones en el conjunto 9N8: Patio A (Operación VIII). In *Excavaciones en el Area Urbana de Copán, tomo 1*, edited by W. T. Sanders, pp. 155–317. Tegucigalpa: Instituto Hondureño de Antropología e Historia.

Webster, D. L., and A. Freter
1990a   The Demography of Late Classic Copan. In *Precolumbian Population History in the Maya Lowlands*, edited by T. P. Culbert and D. S. Rice, pp. 37–61. Albuquerque: University of New Mexico Press.
1990b   Settlement History and the Classic Collapse at Copán: A Redefined Chronological Perspective. *Latin American Antiquity* 1:66–85.

Webster, D. L., A. Freter, and N. Gonlin
2000   *Copán: The Rise and Fall of an Ancient Maya Kingdom*. Case Studies in Archaeology Series. Fort Worth, TX: Harcourt Brace.

Webster, D. L., A. Freter, and D. Rue
1993   The Obsidian Hydration Dating Project at Copán: A Regional Approach and Why It Works. *Latin American Antiquity* 4:303–324.

Webster, D. L., A. Freter, and R. Storey
2004   Dating the Maya Collapse at Copán. In *The Terminal Classic in the Maya Lowlands*, edited by A. Demarest, P. M. Rice, and D. S. Rice, pp. 231–259. Boulder: University of Colorado Press.

Webster, D. L., and N. Gonlin
1988   Household Remains of the Humblest Maya. *Journal of Field Archaeology* 15:169–190.

Webster, D. L., and J. Kirker
1995   Too Many Maya, Too Few Buildings: Investigating Construction Potential at Copán, Honduras. *Journal of Anthropological Research* 51:363–387.

Webster, D. L., W. T. Sanders, and P. van Rossum
1992   A Simulation of Copan Population History and Its Implications. *Ancient Mesoamerica* 3:185–197.

Weiss, A., and L. P. Traxler
1991   Computer-Assisted Surveying, Mapping, and Analysis of Architectural Development at Copán. Paper presented at the 56th Annual Meeting of the Society for American Archaeology, New Orleans.

Whittington, S. L.
1989   Characteristics of Demography and Disease in Low-Status Maya from Classic Period Copán, Honduras. Ph.D. diss., Department of Anthropology, Pennsylvania State University, University Park.
1999   Caries and Antemortem Tooth Loss at Copán: Implications for Commoner Diet. In *Reconstructing Ancient Maya Diet*, edited by C. D. White, pp. 151–167. Salt Lake City: University of Utah Press.

References

Whittington, S. L., and D. M. Reed

1997   Commoner Diet at Copán: Insights from Stable Isotopes and Porotic Hyperostosis. In *Bones of the Maya: Studies of Ancient Skeletons*, edited by S. L. Whittington and D. M. Reed, pp. 157–170. Washington, DC: Smithsonian Institution Press.

Willey, G. R.

1953   *Prehistoric Settlement Patterns in the Virú Valley, Perú*. Smithsonian Institution, Bureau of American Ethnology, bulletin 155. Washington, DC: U.S. Government Printing Office.

1956   Problems Concerning Prehistoric Settlement Patterns in the Maya Lowlands. In *Prehistoric Settlement Patterns in the New World*, edited by G. R. Willey, pp. 85–197. Viking Fund Publications in Anthropology, no. 23. New York: Wenner-Gren Foundation for Anthropological Research.

1962   The Early Great Styles and the Rise of Pre-Columbian Civilizations. *American Anthropologist* 64:1–14.

1976   Mesoamerican Civilization and the Idea of Transcendence. *Antiquity* 50:205–225.

1977   The Rise of Maya Civilization: A Summary View. In *The Origins of Maya Civilization*, edited by R. E. W. Adams, pp. 383–423. School of American Research Advanced Seminar Series. Albuquerque: University of New Mexico Press.

1980   Towards an Holistic View of Ancient Maya Civilization. *Man* (NS) 15:249–266.

Willey, G. R., W. R. Bullard, J. B. Glass, and J. C. Gifford

1965   *Prehistoric Maya Settlements in the Belize Valley*. Papers of the Peabody Museum of Archaeology and Ethnology, no. 54. Cambridge, MA: Harvard University.

Willey, G. R., W. R. Coe, and R. J. Sharer

1976   Un proyecto para el desarrollo de investigación y preservación arqueológica en Copán (Honduras) y vecindad 1976–1981. *Yaxkin* 1:10–29. Tegucigalpa.

Willey, G. R., and R. M. Leventhal

1979   Prehistoric Settlement at Copan. In *Maya Archaeology and Ethnohistory*, edited by N. Hammond and G. R. Willey, pp. 75–102. Austin and London: University of Texas Press.

Willey, G. R., R. M. Leventhal, A. A. Demarest, and W. L. Fash

1994   *Ceramics and Artifacts from Excavations in the Copan Residential Zone*. Papers of the Peabody Museum of Archaeology and Ethnology, vol. 80. Cambridge, MA: Harvard University.

Willey, G. R., R. M. Leventhal, and W. L. Fash

1978   Maya Settlement in the Copan Valley. *Archaeology* 31(4):32–43.

Willey, G. R., and P. Mathews, eds.
1985   *A Consideration of the Early Classic Period in the Maya Lowlands.* Publication 10. Albany: Institute for Mesoamerican Studies, State University of New York.

Willey, G. R., and J. A. Sabloff
1993   *A History of American Archaeology.* 3d ed. New York: W. H. Freeman.

Willey, G. R., and D. B. Shimkin
1974   The Collapse of Classic Maya Civilization in the Southern Lowlands: A Symposium Summary Statement. In *The Rise and Fall of Civilizations: Modern Archaeological Approaches to Ancient Cultures. Selected Readings,* edited by C. C. Lamberg-Karlovsky and J. A. Sabloff, pp. 104–118. Menlo Park, CA: Cummings.

Williamson, R. V.
1996   Excavations, Interpretations, and Implications of the Earliest Structures Beneath Structure 10L-26 at Copan, Honduras. In *Eighth Palenque Round Table, 1993,* edited by M. G. Robertson, M. J. Macri, and J. McHargue, pp. 169–175. San Francisco: Pre-Columbian Art Research Institute.

1997   Los orígenes de la complejidad social en Copán: excavaciones debajo de la Estructura 10L-26 en Copán, Honduras. *Yaxkin* 16:31–48. Tegucigalpa.

Wingard, J. D.
1988   Honduran Subsistence Agriculture: A Case Study. M.A. thesis, Department of Agricultural Economics, Pennsylvania State University, University Park.

1992   The Role of Soils in the Development and Collapse of Classic Maya Civilization at Copan, Honduras. Ph.D. diss., Department of Anthropology, Pennsylvania State University, University Park.

1996   Interactions between Demographic Processes and Soil Resources in the Copán Valley, Honduras. In *The Managed Mosaic: Ancient Maya Agriculture and Resource Use,* edited by S. L. Fedick, pp. 207–235. Salt Lake City: University of Utah Press.

Winning, H. von
1947   A Symbol for Dripping Water in the Teotihuacan Culture. *El México Antiguo* 6:333–341.

Wisdom, C.
1940   *The Chorti Indians of Guatemala.* Chicago: University of Chicago Press.

Wiseman, F. M.
1983a   Analysis of Pollen from the Fields at Pulltrouser Swamp. In *Pulltrouser Swamp: Ancient Maya Habitat, Agriculture, and Settlement in Northern Belize,* edited by B. L. Turner II and P. D. Harrison, pp. 105–119. Austin: University of Texas Press.

References

1983b   Subsistence and Complex Societies: The Case of the Maya. In *Advances in Archaeological Method and Theory*, vol. 6, edited by M. B. Schiffer, pp. 143–189. New York: Academic Press.

Wittfogel, K. A.

1957   *Oriental Despotism: A Comparative Study of Total Power.* New Haven, CT: Yale University Press.

1974   Developmental Aspects of Hydraulic Societies. In *The Rise and Fall of Civilizations: Modern Archaeological Approaches to Ancient Cultures. Selected Readings*, edited by C. C. Lamberg-Karlovsky and J. A. Sabloff, pp. 15–25. Menlo Park, CA: Cummings.

Wood, J. W., G. R. Milner, H. C. Harpending, and K. M. Weiss

1992   The Osteological Paradox: Problems of Inferring Prehistoric Health from Skeletal Samples. *Current Anthropology* 33:343–370.

Index

Please note: f indicates figure, t indicates table

Abrams, E. M., 31, 58, 69, 427, 440, 475
Acbi-Coner transition: burials, 294–295; ceramics, 258; structures, 282
Acbi phase: burials, 294, 295; ceramics, 150, 158, 207, 282; construction, 396; Group 10L-2, 244, 246–248, 252; population, 84–85; water management, 115–116
Acropolis: adornment, 142, 159, 160; area of, 198, 199; continuity, 412; cross-section, 203f; dating, 142, 143t, 144, 144t, 199; desecration of, 417; iconography, 95t; investigation techniques, 145–147; perspective reconstruction, 141f; plan, 95t, 154f, 155f, 164, 178f, 187f; sacred center of, 195; significance of, 150; skeletal samples, 317–322; Teotihuacan influences, 195–196, 399; water management, 116, 137. *See also specific structures*
Acropolis construction history, 27, 140–145, 151, 152t, 153–155, 195, 197–198, 358, 396, 398; K'inich Yax K'uk' Mo', 157–165, 159f; origins, 150; predynastic, 152t, 156–157; Ruler 2, 165–176, 167f, 169f, 170f, 172f, 400; Rulers 3-5, 176–177, 178f, 179–182; Rulers 6-7, 182, 183f,

184–185; Ruler 8, 185–191, 187f, 188f; Ruler 9, 191–192; Rulers 10-11, 192; Ruler 12, 27–28, 378; Rulers 12-16, 192–196; Ruler 13, 28
Acropolis Project, 21, 22–23
Adams, R. E. W., 427
Aeschlimann, B., 446
Age, concept of, 324–325
Agrarian economy: containment, 37; droughts, 15–16, 71, 418–419; ecological degradation, 31, 41; non-subsistence crops, 64; population pressure on, 58, 59, 415, 416; producers, 35–36; productivity losses, 52. *See also* settlement model; soil model
Agrarian management: by elite, 55, 57–59, 60, 61–64, 67, 70–71, 311, 406–407; Rulers 11-12, 59–60; Rulers 13-14, 60–61; Rulers 15-16, 61–64; techniques, 34–36, 50, 51, 69. *See also* water management
Agurcia Fasquelle, R., xiv, 427–428; collapse, 419; Copán Sculpture Museum, 23; investigations, 22, 25, 398; Rosalila, 190, 224; Stela P, 207, 209; three mountain site, 406
Altar A', 358, 359f
Altar de Sacrificios, 334
Altar F', 285
Altar F', 285, 286f, 414
Altar G', 297
Altar G', 285
Altar G", 288
Altar I", 288
Altar I", 288

Altar L, 304
Altar Q, 216f; authenticity of rulers, 17; construction, 214–215; half-quatrefoil motif, 121f; historical information, 148–149; iconography, 138, 234–237; Ruler 12 and, 393; Teotihuacan influences, 376, 377
Altar T, 90–91, 358–359, 359f
Altar U, 90–91, 360, 360f
Altar W (Group 9N-8), 120f, 288
Alvarez González, P., 434
Amarillo Structure, 179
Ancestor cartouches, 267, 269
Ancestors, 131
Andean cultures, 113–114
Andrews, E. W., 428, 440, 445; ceramics, 397; collapse, 101, 419; Group 10L-2, 312; ideological resources, 93–94; investigations, xiv, 22; Late Classic Acropolis, 185; non-Maya population, 76, 77; public ritual, 97; status of residents, 136
Andrews, E. W. IV, 136, 428
Andrews, E. W. V, 432
Andrews, G. F., 428
Angulo, V. J., 428
Anovitz, L. M., 429, 459
Ante Structure, 27, 186, 188–189, 188f, 190, 191
Aoyama, K., 304, 408, 419, 429
Argurcia Fasquelle, R., 440
Ariki, 55
Armelagos, G. J., 443, 453
Arthritis, 336, 337t
Ashmore, W., 429, 450

479

Index

Astronomy, 365
Aulie, E. W. de, 429
Aulie, H. W., 429
Aveni, A. F., 429
Aztec iconography, 107–108
Azul Substructure, 204–205, 207, 209f, 218, 220–221, 220f, 224, 229

Baker, J. L., 462
Ball Court IIb, 120f
Bardsley, S., 292–293, 429
Bassie-Sweet, K., 118, 131, 430
Bastarrachea Manzano, J. R., 429
Baudez, C., 13, 14, 223, 226, 430
Beach, T., 430, 437, 438
Beans, 38
Beaubien, H. F., 440
Becker, M., 462
Becker, M. J., 14, 146, 430
Beetz, C. P., 431
Bell, E. E., 397, 431, 459, 466
Benson, E. P., 137, 431
Berdache, 331
Bey, G. J. III, 431
Bierhorst, J., 431
Big-polity model, 61–62
Bijac Phase, 78, 80, 244, 248
Bilingualism, 398
Bill, C. R., 93–94, 97, 304, 419, 431
Binford, L. R., 431
Bird glyphs, 167, 168–169, 222, 223f. See also macaw imagery
Bishop, R. L., 459
Blackless, M., 432
Boucher, S., 434
Braswell, G. E., 65, 419, 432
Brenner, M., 447
Bricker, H. M., 432
Bricker, V. R., 432
Bridges, P. S., 432
Brito Sansores, W., 429
Broda, J., 432
Bronson, B., 432
Brown, J., 433
Buikstra, J., 25, 330, 433
Bullard, W. R., 476
Burgh, J., 10
Burials: desecration of, 31, 295; Early Classic, 316, 318–319, 322–323; Early Preclassic offerings, 395; elite, 83, 87–88, 90, 249, 292, 316–322, 338–339; evolution of, 93; Galindo Tomb, 192; Group 9N-8, 336, 338–339; Group 10L-2, 246–249, 250f, 251, 283, 284, 292, 294–295, 317–318, 322; human sacrifices, 195, 326–328, 329f; Jaguar Paw of Calakmul, 339–340; juvenile, 274; K'inich Yax K'uk' Mo', 26, 27, 83, 160–161, 165, 173, 195, 196, 199, 202, 204, 249; K'inich Yax K'uk' Mo', wife of, 83, 176, 249, 400; Margarita Tomb, 172–173, 172f; Motmot, 163, 328–332; 95-1 offerings, 171; pathology of corpses, 313, 337t; revisitation rituals, 249, 319–320, 321, 322, 323–324, 325, 330, 338–340; royal, 321f, 322–326, 324, 325f; Ruler 8, 189–190, 192, 322–324, 330; Ruler 12, 193, 324–326, 374, 378; settlement patterns, 62; Structure 10L-32, 259f; Structure 10L-36, 282; Teotihuacan influences, 26, 27, 83, 171, 173, 195–196, 329, 399; Tikal, 334; Uaxactun, 88; V-4, 320–321; Yax Pasaj, 31, 252–253, 265, 301, 303. See also Rosalila Structure
Burton, J., 433
Butz Chan. See Ruler 11

Calakmul, 339–340, 357, 407–408
Canuto, M. A., 431, 433, 466; collapse, 419; construction style, 397; drainage, 397; Los Achiotes, 85–86; postdynastic occupation, 422
Caracol, 34, 339
Carballal Staedtler, M., 433
Carballo, D. M., 433
Carlson, J., 138, 433
Carmack, R. M., 278, 433

Carnegie Institution, xiii, 10–11, 294–295
Carneiro, R. L., 106, 434
Carrasco, D., 432, 434
Carrasco Vargas, R., 434
Carrelli, C. W., 58, 431, 434
Carsten, J., 434
Caso, A., 434
Catherwood, F., 8–9
Cave imagery: ecological context, 116–123; royal power and, 134–135, 403; Structure 10L-29, 269; Structure 10L-41, 275, 277. See also half-quatrefoil motif
Celeste Substructure, 204–205
Celestial Monster, 229
Central Mexican influences. See Teotihuacan influences
Ceramics: Acbi-Coner transition, 258; Acbi phase, 150, 158, 207, 282; Bijac Phase, 80; Classic period, 396; collapse and, 64–65, 302, 419–422; Coner phase, 60, 64–65, 209, 210, 214–215, 274, 282, 302, 419–422; Ejar phase, 65–66, 422; Group 10L-2, 244, 249, 258, 295–296; imports, 196; non-Maya and, 91, 396–397; postdynastic, 264, 304–306; Teotihuacan influences, 195; Ulua polychrome, 93
Cerro Chino, 86
Cerro Palenque, 111
Chak, 257, 285, 286f, 287, 294, 312–313, 414
Chalchuapa, 397
Chamberlain, R. S., 434
Charuvastra, A., 432
Chase, A. F., 339, 340, 434
Chase, D. Z., 339, 340, 434
Cheek, C. D., 14, 78, 278, 430, 434–435, 473
Chilan Structure, 173, 177
Children: burials, 274; elite, 334, 340, 341; health and lifestyle, 136, 333–334, 335, 336, 340, 415–416
Chiment, J., 449
Chinchilla Floor, 156

480

INDEX

Clan organization, 55
Clavel Structure, 167–168
Cobalto Structure, 168, 169
Coe, M. D., 435
Coe, W. R., 11–12, 435, 476
Coggins, C. C., 435
Cohen, A., 435
Cole, D. R., 429, 459
Collapse, 15–16, 31–32, 414–415; areawide, 417–419; commoners and, 94; council house and, 404; dating, 303–306; ecological degradation, 31, 52, 101, 416; elite and, 31, 94, 96–101, 342–343; Group 10L-2 and, 300–302, 308; population and, 15, 65–66, 302, 304–306, 308, 415–417, 419–423; sacred and, 70; stages, 96; violence, 408, 417; of water management, 136. See also Coner phase
Commercial system, 16
Commoners, 4–5, 35–36, 55–56, 94
COMPASS system, 147
Coner phase: burials, 294, 295; ceramics, 60, 64–65, 209, 210, 214–215, 274, 282, 302, 419–422; El Cementerio, 300; Group 10L-2, 246–249
Connolly, R. P., 462
Conservation, 22, 25
Construction, 152t; early, 26; by K'inich Yax K'uk' Mo', 157–165, 159f, 195; pattern of, 93, 202, 203f; Protoclassic period, 397; by Ruler 2, 27, 165–176, 167f, 169f, 170f, 172f, 198, 242, 400; by Rulers 3-5, 176–177, 178f, 179–182; by Rulers 6-7, 182, 183f, 184–185; by Ruler 8, 185–191, 187f, 188f, 198, 252, 377–387; by Ruler 9, 191–192; by Ruler 10, 192; by Ruler 11, 192, 370; by Ruler 12, 27–28, 193, 242, 365–371, 366f, 368f, 378, 423–424; by Ruler 13, 28,

193, 242, 379, 381, 424; by Ruler 14, 29, 193, 242, 260; by Ruler 15, 29, 193, 242, 384–385, 387, 424; by Yax Pasaj, 30–31, 193–194, 214–216, 242, 253–255, 256f, 257–258, 259f, 260–261, 261f, 262f, 263, 264, 274, 275, 292, 301, 308, 358. See also specific structures
Consumers. See elite class
Copán, map, 13f
Copán Acropolis Archaeological Project (PAAC), xiii, 22–23, 241, 425
Copán Association for Pre-Columbian Studies, 23
Copan Ceramics (Longyear), 10
Copán Mosaics Project, 20, 21, 202, 425
Copán Notes (Schele and Stuart), 21
Copán pocket, 51–52, 53, 62, 66, 77f
Copán River. See Río Copán
Copán Sculpture Museum, 23–24, 24f
Copán Tomb 1 (Group 10L-2), 248–249, 251, 283
Copán Tomb 2 (Group 10L-2), 248, 249, 284
Copán Valley, 5f, 16, 40f
Corporate groups, 62, 240, 291, 300, 405
Cortés Hernández, J., 435
Council house: construction history, 193; destruction, 302; elite competition, 99–100; establishment, 403–404; fish glyph, 127, 258, 260, 411; population stress, 416–417; role, 121, 133; of Ruler 14, 29; tradition, 138
Court 2B (Northeast Court Group), 186, 188–190, 192, 193
Courtyard A (Group 9N-8), 252
Courtyard A (Group 10L-2), 243; activities, 97, 283, 295–296, 298, 309; con-

struction history, 244, 245–246, 299, 411, 412; destruction, 302; as fish place, 258, 260; plan, 309; structures in, 252. See also specific structures
Courtyard B (Group 10L-2), 281f; activities, 243, 269, 270, 277–278, 280, 282, 283, 295–296, 298, 309; construction history, 244, 245–246, 270, 272, 299, 411, 412; destruction, 302; drainage, 284; plan, 274–275, 279–282, 309
Courtyard C (Group 10L-2), 282
Cranial modifications, 319, 321, 322, 327, 328
Creation imagery, 117, 119
Crocodile imagery, 82, 88
Cross-dressing, 331
Cross Group, 346, 347f, 348f, 349–350, 350f
Cueva, J. A., 11, 435
Culbert, T. P., 67, 435–436
Curtis, J. H., 447
Cyphers, A., 436

Dating, 15, 142, 143t, 144, 144t, 199. See also obsidian-hydration dating
Davis-Salazar, K. L., 115, 401–402, 436, 440
Day of the Cross ceremony, 110
Death imagery, 93, 233–234, 237
Deer sacrifice, 329
Deforestation, 31, 43, 49
Deities: Altars T and U, 91; dynasty patrons, 204, 218, 220–223, 220f, 223f, 224, 226, 231–232, 257, 285, 286f, 287, 294, 312–313, 402, 414; gender, 331; God D, 222; impinged-bone glyph, 349–353, 351f, 352f, 356, 358–371, 359f, 361f; kun, 349–358, 405–406; Maize, 351–353, 352f; monkey-man, 268, 269; Rosalila, 218, 220–223, 224, 226, 231–232; shrines dedicated to, 291;

481

Index

Tzultacah, 116–117, 122–123, 131; water, 116–117
Demarest, A. A., 20, 74, 84, 409, 436–437, 450, 476
DeMenocal, P. B., 437
De Montmollin, O., 436
Dental modifications, 319, 321, 322, 327, 328
Derryck, A., 432
Diamanti, M., 437
Diamond, J., 34, 437
Diet: components, 38–39, 313; food distribution, 35, 37; quality, 328, 333–334, 335; of rulers, 323; soil model, 42; stress on, 63–64, 415–416; trade and, 61–62, 408
Disease, 336, 337t; collapse and, 15–16, 415–416; elite, 313; endemic, 63; water management and, 136
Dixon, B. M., 47, 437
Dobkin de Rios, M., 437
Don Carlos, L., 454
Doonan, W. F., 295–296, 428, 437, 468
Droughts, 15–16, 71, 418–419
Dunning, N. P., 430, 437–438
Dynamic model, 74, 87, 409
Dzul Góngora, D., 429

Earle, T. K., 438
Early Classic period: Acropolis, 151, 153–155, 154f, 178f, 182, 183f, 184, 187f, 198, 400; burials, 316, 318–319, 322–323; destruction of sites, 401–402; elite residences, 91; foreign influences, 407; health, 336; iconography, 424; population, 76, 401
Early Copán Acropolis Program (ECAP), 140, 146–147
Early Formative Horizon, 26, 76
Early Preclassic period, 395
East Court (Acropolis), 201–202, 252
Ecology: collapse and, 15–16, 31, 52, 101, 416; deforestation, 31, 43, 49; degradation and health, 63; erosion, 41, 47, 48–49, 48f, 51, 60, 63; natural disasters, 68; natural landscape, 37, 39, 41, 49; ritualized management of, 107; settlement pattern determinants, 104
Edmonson, M. S., 438
Ejar phase, 65–66, 305, 422
Elam, J. M., 429, 459
El Bosque, 297, 311
El Cementerio (Group 10L-2), 244, 247, 295–296, 300, 309–310
Elite class: acquisitiveness of, 84, 87–88; agrarian management, 55, 57–59, 60, 61–64, 67, 68–69, 70–71, 311, 406–407; bias of investigations toward, 6, 8; burials, 83, 87–88, 90, 249, 292, 316–322, 338–339; as change agents, 35; children, 334, 340, 341; competition among, 31, 54, 56, 63, 94, 96–101, 409, 414, 416; control of resources, 35, 37, 70, 74, 342–343, 416; development of states and, 75; economic stratification of, 68; in Hawaiian model, 55–56, 62; health and lifestyle, 313, 319, 321–322, 337t, 338, 340–343, 415–416; iconography, 133–135; in lineage model, 54, 56, 62; marriage alliances, 291; origins, 392, 398; postdynastic, 65–66; power of, 292–293; residences, 62, 91, 96–99, 126–132, 128f, 130f, 196, 310 (see also Group 9N-8); in satellite centers, 98–99; status, 92, 299, 404–405, 423–424; Teotihuacan influence on, 84, 410; trade by, 78; water management, 118–120, 122–123
Elo, I. T., 438
El Raizal, 86

Erosion, 41, 47, 48–49, 48f, 51, 60, 63, 415
Esmeralda Structure, 28, 186, 193
Ethnohydrology, 117
Everson, G. E., 428

Fahsen, F., 438, 444, 463, 464, 472; Acropolis Project, 22; Copán Tomb 1, 251; impinged-bone glyph, 355; Motmot marker, 362; Xukpi Stone, 362
Farriss, N. M., 36, 37, 75, 111, 438
Fash, B. W., 428, 438–439, 440, 475; collapse, 419; Copán Sculpture Museum, 23; council house, 403–404; Group 8N-11, 257; Group 10L-2, 312; Hieroglyphic Stairway, 25, 382; investigations, xiv, 20, 21; Papagayo, 174–175; Rosalila, 217, 224, 229, 402; satellite centers, 100; Stela 63, 174–175; Structure 10L-16, 232; Structure 10L-25, 212; Structure 10L-29, 267, 269; Structure 10L-32, 254, 288; Structure 10L-41, 275, 277, 277f, 278; Temple Inscription, 387; three mountain site, 406; water management, 88, 257, 401–404, 414
Fash, W. L.: Acropolis, 398, 400; collapse, 15, 300, 419; Hieroglyphic Stairway, 381–382, 409–410; investigations, xiv, 20, 21, 427, 438, 439–441, 450, 466, 475, 476–477; nonkinship political organization, 260; Papagayo, 181; period designations, 245; political organization, 17, 400–401; population, 45, 401, 406, 416–417; rise, 409; settlement patterns, 108–109; three mountain site, 406; water-hole groups, 403; water lily imagery, 124–125
Fausto-Sterling, A., 432

Fauvet, Marie-France, 14
Fedick, S. L., 441
Feinman, G., 441
Fertility faction, 92
Fertility imagery, 117, 119, 122, 229, 277
Fialko, C. Vilma, 450
Fish glyph: Group 10L-2, 126–127, 128f, 258, 260; royal council house, 411; Structure 10L-31, 265; Yax Pasaj, 292
Flannery, K. V., 441
Flinn, M. W., 441
Flooding, 246, 401
Flores Hernández, M., 433
Foias, A. E., 84, 437
Folan, W. J., 441
Founder king. *See* K'inich Yax K'uk' Mo'
Fox, J. A., 441
Fox, R. G., 74, 442
Franco Torrijos, E., 442
Freidel, D., 84, 229, 365, 442, 463
Freter, A., 17, 45, 47, 419–420, 442, 457, 475
Fry, R. E., 436

Galactic polity model, 74–75, 84, 87, 94, 100, 112–113, 409
Galindo, J., 192
Gallagher, J., 8
Galloy, J., 442
García de Palacios, Diego, 8, 32
García Moreno, R., 434
García Vierna, V., 434
Geertz, C., 74, 87, 89, 442
Gelles, P. H., 442–443
Gender, 330–332
Gerry, J. P., 38, 443
Gerstle, A. I., 92–93, 443
Gifford, J. C., 476
Gill, R. B., 443
Gillespie, S. D., 413, 443, 448
Glascock, M. D., 421, 432
Glass, J. B., 476
Glyphs: approach to, 4; founder's, 263, 264, 377; hieroglyphic benches, 96–97, 292, 405; Hieroglyphic Stairway, 30, 380–387, 381f, 384f, 394,

410; historical ideologies and, 374–375; as historical record, 18–19; Las Sepulturas, 404; Stela C, 394; Teotihuacan style, 387–391, 388f, 410. *See also specific glyphs*
God D, 222
Gonlin, N., 45, 443, 475
Goodman, A. H., 443, 453, 454, 467
Gordon, G. B., 9, 112, 249, 380, 394, 443
Gordon Platform, 179–180
Graham, I., 137, 444
Gran Corniza Platform (Acropolis), 174–175
Great Plaza, 97
Group 8N-11, 121f, 126, 257, 404
Group 9J-4 (Cerro Chino), 86
Group 9N-8: burials, 87–88, 318, 336, 338–339; courtyard, 88–89, 89f; destruction, 303; early occupations, 87; glyphs, 120f, 404; population increase and, 85; storage, 89. *See also specific structures*
Group 10K-4, 292
Group 10L-2, 411–414; boundaries, 296–297; building types, 240; burials, 246–249, 250f, 251, 283, 284, 292, 294–295, 317–318, 322; ceramics, 244, 249, 258, 295–296; construction history, 242, 245t, 299, 307; dating, 241–242, 294, 296; desecrated, 417; destruction, 302; dynastic decline, 300–302, 308; flooding, 246; hieroglyphic monuments, 255, 256, 284–285, 286f, 287–289, 287f, 289f, 290f, 291–294, 297, 301; iconography, 118f, 121f, 126–127, 128f, 258, 260; plan, 240, 241f, 242–244, 252–253; postdynastic occupation, 302, 304–306, 308; purpose, 413; residents, xv, 240,

251–252, 298, 299–300, 306–308, 412; ritual areas, 97, 243, 275, 280–282, 284–285, 286f, 287–289, 287f, 289f, 290f, 291, 297, 298, 309–310; use patterns, 252, 283–284, 296, 412–413; water management, 126–132, 128f, 130f, 284, 414. *See also* Courtyards A, B and C (Group 10L-2); *specific structures*
Group 10L-18, 242, 413
Group 10L plan, 7f
Group of the Cross, 346, 347f, 348f, 349–350, 350f
Grove, D. C., 444, 466
Grube, N., 444, 454, 463, 464, 465; Acropolis Project, 23; Azul text, 207; collapse, 303–304; Copán Tomb 1, 251; half-quatrefoil motif, 120; impinged-bone glyph, 346, 348–349, 351, 353, 371; kun deities, 349; Motmot marker, 362; shrines, 269, 289; Stela J, 361–362; warfare imagery, 278; Xukpi Stone, 362
Guilderson, T., 447
Guillemin, G. F., 14, 146, 444–445
Guillet, D., 455
Günther, D., 446

Half-quatrefoil motif: interpretations, 120, 121f, 122, 134–135; Structure 10L-29, 265, 269; Structure 10L-41, 275, 277, 277f, 278. *See also* cave imagery; mountain imagery
Hall, D. G. E., 445
Hall, J., 24, 77–78, 397, 445, 473
Hammond, N., 445
Hansen, R. D., 445
Hanson, C. A., 431
Harpending, H. C., 478
Harris, G., 462
Harrison, P. D., 445
Harvard University, xiii, 9, 253, 272, 282, 285, 288, 294–295

Index

Hasemann, G., 25
Haug, G. H., 446
Haviland, W. A., 334, 436, 446
Hawaiian model, 54–56, 60, 62, 63, 94, 406
Health and lifestyle: of children, 136, 333–334, 335, 336, 340, 415–416; diet and, 38; of elite, 313, 319, 321–322, 335–336, 337t, 338, 340–343; of rulers, 323; socioeconomic status and, 332–333, 340–341; stresses on, 63, 415–416
Hellmuth, N. M., 221, 228, 446
Helms, M. W., 84, 446
Hendon, J. A., 89, 298, 446–447
Hensz, J. D., 462
Hertz, R., 320, 339, 447
Heyden, D., 447
Hieroglyphic benches, 96–97, 292, 405
Hieroglyphic Stairway, 29–30, 148; chronology of usage, 79–80; conservation, 25; construction history, 28, 29, 162, 193, 376–387, 381f, 394, 424; dating, 9–10; historical ideology and, 375, 384f, 409–410; iconography, 120f, 237; Palenque influence, 407; Teotihuacan influence, 30
Hieroglyphic Stairway, Naranjo, 355–356, 356f
Hieroglyphic Stairway, Tamarindito, 356, 357f
Hieroglyphic Stairway Project, 21
Highland Mexico, 376, 399
Hillson, S. W., 447
Historical ideologies, 19–21, 373–375, 391–393, 409–410, 423–424. *See also* Hieroglyphic Stairway
Historical record, 19–20, 147–151
Hodell, D. A., 447
Hofmann, A., 465
Hohmann, H., 447
Holland, W. R., 131, 447

Honduran Institute of Anthropology and History, xiii
Hopkins, N. A., 92, 398, 448
Hornik, R., 447
House model, 72, 94
House of the Bacabs. *See* Structure 9N-82 (Group 9N-8)
House of the Scribes. *See* Structure 9N-82 (Group 9N-8)
Houston, S. D., 447, 448, 469–470; impinged-bone glyph, 345; investigations, 22; Ux Witik, 358; water and place names, 109
Hughen, K. A., 446
Hugh-Jones, S., 434
Human sacrifice, 195, 228, 318, 326–328, 329f, 337t. *See also* sacrifice imagery
Hunal Structure, 27, 159–161, 159f, 164, 176, 202, 204
Hunal Tomb, 26, 27, 160–161, 173, 195, 196, 199
Hydraulic societies, 105, 403
Hypoplasias, 333–334, 337t, 338, 340
Hyslop, J., 448

Iconography: Acropolis, 95t; Altar Q, 138, 234–237; Aztec, 107–108; Azul Substructure, 218, 220f, 224, 229, 231–232; of cross-dressing, 331; Early v. Late Classic, 403, 424; of elite influence, 133–135; Group 10L-2, 118f, 121f, 126–127, 128f, 258, 260, 403; Hieroglyphic Stairway, 120f, 237; of independence, 98–99; of K'inich Yax K'uk' Mo', 27; Las Sepulturas, 120f, 123–126, 124f, 129, 404; Margarita, 168–169, 169f, 204, 221; Motmot marker, 82–83, 329; Papagayo, 83; Rosalila, 93, 217–218, 219f, 220–232, 223f, 225f, 227f, 228f, 377–378, 402, 405;

Structure 10L-16, 204, 217–218, 232–237, 235f;
Structure 10L-22, 229;
Structure 10L-26, 237;
Structure 10L-32, 254–255, 257; Structure 10L-41, 277–278; Teotihuacan, 30, 392; of water management, 88, 118–120, 127f, 134–135, 257, 403; Yehnal, 204, 221
Ideological resources: architecture as, 145 (*see also* ritual areas); collective memory, 89–90; construction rate of, 93; elite control of, 74; impinged-bone glyph, 346–349; Motmot Structure, 80–81, 88–89; non-Maya populations, 92–93, 114; political organization and, 106; Rosalila, 93, 231–232, 423; rulers and, 100, 101, 106, 393, 423–424; Structure 10L-16, 202; symbols, 268–269; usage through time, 93–94; water, 104, 105–107, 110–114, 115, 118–120, 122–123, 129, 131, 133, 134–136, 137; of Yax Pasaj, 294; Yax Structure, 88–89. *See also* sacred geography
Impinged-bone glyph: allographs, 347f; contexts of, 349–358, 351f, 352f, 353f; deciphering, 345–349; royal legitimacy, 405–406; sacred seats and platforms, 351, 358–371, 359f, 360f, 361f
Inca, 113–114
Incense burners, 208f, 230, 306
Indigo Structure, 116, 117f
Indonesia, 112–113
Inomata, T., 448
Investigations: Acropolis techniques, 145–147; blueprint, 11–12; focus, 6; history of, xiii–xiv, 8–15, 19–25, 253, 272, 275, 282, 285, 288, 294–295; recent, 425

484

Irrigation, 43, 57, 64, 71
Isaac, B. L., 462
Itzamná, 222

Jackson, S., 98, 125, 405, 414, 448
Jaguar imagery, 214, 216f, 221, 237, 249, 251, 251f
Jaguar Paw of Calakmul, 339–340
Johnson, J. L., 428, 448
Johnson, W., 110–111, 246, 472
Jones, C., 448
Jones, G. D., xiv, 448
Jones, J. G., 438
Jones, L., 434
Josserand, J. K., 92, 398, 448
Joyce, R. A., 111, 448
Justeson, J. S., 441

K'ak' Joplaj Chan K'wail. *See* Ruler 14
K'ak' Tiliw Chan Yopat, 28, 101
K'ak' Yipyaj Chan K'awil. *See* Ruler 15
Kaminaljuyu, 196, 320, 376, 397, 407
Kampen, M. E., 448
Kaplan, R. D., 448
Kaufman, T. S., 449
Kennedy, K. A. R., 449
Kidder, A. V., 52, 449
K'inich Ahau/ Ahaw. *See* Sun God
K'inich Kan B'alam II, 349
K'inich K'an Hoy Chitam II, 356
K'inich Yax K'uk' Mo', 398; accession, 150, 383, 384f, 398; Altar Q, 236; burial, 26, 27, 83, 160–161, 165, 173, 195, 196, 199, 202, 204, 249; construction by, 152t, 157–165, 159f, 195; founder's glyph, 263, 264, 377; iconographic personifications, 223, 224, 237; origins, 26, 195, 196, 376–377, 391, 399; reign, 152t, 165; Rosalila and, 402; Structure 10L-16, 391–392; Structure 10L-26, 391; successors and,
165–166, 234–236; as Sun God, 232; Teotihuacan connections, 27, 264, 269, 376–377, 391–392
K'inich Yax K'uk' Mo', wife of: burial, 83, 176, 249, 400
Kinship groups, 54, 55, 62, 298, 299–300, 406
Kirch, P. V., 449
Kirker, J., 69, 475
Kohunlich, 221
Koontz, R. A., 449
Kosakowsky, L. J., 436
Kowalski, J. K., 449
Kramrisch, S., 449
Krueger, H. W., 38, 443
Kun, 349–358, 405–406
Kurjack, E. B., 449

Labor: access to, 57, 59, 61, 62, 87; demand for, 58, 64; organization, 104
La Canteada. *See* Río Amarillo (La Canteada)
Land, 33, 55, 58, 59, 61, 67, 111, 114
Lane, S., 438
Language, 398
Lansing, J. S., 137, 449, 462
Laporte, J. P., 449–450
Larios, C. R., 438, 441, 450, 464; Acropolis Project, 22; Hieroglyphic Stairway, 381–382; Mosaics Project, 19–21; serpent imagery, 229
Las Sepulturas: erosion, 63; hieroglyphic benches, 292; iconography, 120f, 123–126, 124f, 129, 404; residents, 298; water management, 133
Late Classic period: Acropolis, 400; burials, 316, 322–323, 327; destruction of sites, 401–402; Group 10L-2, 243, 244, 252–253, 296; health, 336, 340; iconography, 403; population, 401, 417–418
Late Formative period, 78
Late Preclassic period, 78–79
Laughlin, R. M., 450

Lauzanne, K., 432
Lawrence, D. L., 450
LeCount, L. J., 450
Lee, E., 432
Lenca, 114, 306, 397
Lentz, D., 38, 450
Leventhal, R. M., 12, 96, 450, 476–477
Lineage groups: agriculturally based, 126, 132, 133, 403; lifestyle and, 342; power of, 405; residences, 278, 300; shrines, 269
Lineage model, 54, 56, 62, 63, 68, 94
Livi-Bacci, M., 450
Long, K. Z., 440
Longyear, J. M. III, 451; collapse, 15; Group 10L-2, 244; non-Maya ceramics, 91; non-Maya population, 10, 78; population chronology, 10; rise, 17
Looper, M. G., xiv, 348–349, 405, 451, 464
López, F., 158, 381, 465
López Austin, A., 451
López Luján, L., 135
Lord of the West. *See* K'inich Yax K'uk' Mo'
Lorenzen, K. J., 138, 451
Loro Structure (Acropolis), 179, 180
Los Achiotes, 85–86
Los Higos, 96, 99
Lounsbury, F., 23, 465
Lovejoy, C. O., 454
Low, S. M., 450
Lowenthal, D., 393, 451
Lucero, L. J., 451
Lunardi, M. F., 451
Luzzadder-Beach, S., 438

Mabry, J. B., 451
Maca, A. L., 397, 452
Macaw imagery: Ante, 189; K'inich Yax K'uk' Mo' and, 237; Margarita, 204; Motmot marker, 82–83; Rosalila, 222, 223
MacLeod, B., 313, 345–346, 357, 452
Magee, C. E., 440
Magennis, A. L., 453
Mahood, G., 472

Index

Maize: creation and fertility, 117, 122, 277; deity, 351–353, 352f; importation, 61–62; production, 43, 50, 59, 72; significance of, 38, 313, 415–416; soil model, 42; Structure 9N-82, 125–126, 125f
Manahan, T. K., 432, 440, 452; collapse, 419; postdynastic occupation, 305, 306, 422; valley, 16
Mani province, 72
Manzanilla, L., 452
Maravilla Structure, 169–170, 171, 176–177, 179
Marcus, J., 3, 441, 453; dynamic model, 74, 87, 409; historical record, 18–19; investigation approach, 20; military defeats, 394; satellite centers, 96, 98–99; shrines, 291; state formation, 17; state size, 401
Margarita Structure: construction history, 170–171, 176, 193; dating, 204; iconography, 168–169, 169f, 204, 221; Teotihuacan influences, 195; Tomb, 172f
Marriage alliances, 291
Martin, D. L., 453
Martin, S., 351, 361–362, 453–454
Mascarones Structure, 184, 186, 193
Matheny, R. T., 105–106, 454
Mathews, P., 430, 465, 477
Matos Moctezuma, E., 432
Maudslay, A. P., xiii, 9, 90, 213, 306, 454
May, R. L., 454
Maya highlands influences, 196
McAnany, P. A., 300, 454
McFarlane, W. J., 433
Meindl, R. S., 454
Mensforth, R. P., 454
Merbs, C. E., 454
Michaels, J. W., 461
Michell, G., 454
Middle Preclassic period, 395–396

Millard, A. V., 454
Miller, A. G., 454
Miller, J. C. , 454–455, 466
Miller, M. E., 134, 455, 465
Millon, R., 20, 455
Milner, G. R., 478
Mitchell, W. P., 455
Mitzil Platform, 177, 179, 181
Moholy-Nagy, H., 446
Monkey-man deity, 268, 269
Moon Jaguar, 152t, 192
Morales, A., 455, 468
Morley, S. G., 6, 455; astronomy, 372; centers predating Principal Group, 90; dynasty founding, 17; Hieroglyphic Stairway dating, 9–10; non-Maya population, 10, 78, 397; Río Amarillo, 85; S10L-32 altars, 288
Mosaics Project, 20–22
Motmot marker, 82f, 170f; burial beneath, 195–196, 328–332; buried, 174; construction, 162, 164; described, 163; iconography, 82–83, 120f, 329; offerings, 81–82, 88; text, 168, 169, 171, 362–363, 363f, 364
Motmot Structure, 80–83, 88–89, 162, 164, 174
Mountain imagery, 107–108, 114, 228–229, 405. *See also* half-quatrefoil motif
Murdy, C., 455
Murillo, S., 146, 156, 455
Murillo Floor, 157–158
Murtha, T., 34, 456

Nahm, W., 353
Nakamura, S., 25
Naranjo, 351, 355
Natural disasters, 68
Navarrete, C., 442
Neely, J. A., 456
Negara kingdoms, 74, 75, 84, 87, 89, 94, 100, 101, 112–113
Newsome, E. A., 456
Nicholson, H. B., 456
Non-Maya populations: early, 10; evidence, 76, 78, 79,

91, 396–398; ideological resources, 92–93; postdynastic, 306; water management, 404
Norman, W. M., 449
Northeast Court Group (Acropolis): burials, 321–322; construction history, 153, 161–162, 165, 174–176, 179–181, 182, 184–185, 198; successors, 186, 188–190
Northwest Platform (Structure 10L-1), 78, 79
Nuñez Chinchilla, J., 11, 456
Nutrition. *See* diet

Obsidian, 408, 422
Obsidian-hydration dating: Acropolis, 142, 144t, 199; collapse, 15, 305, 419–421; Group 10L-2, 296; population decline, 16
Olmec, 107, 108
Origin myths, 114
Ortiz, P. C., 456, 460
Ortner, D. J., 456
Outsider king. *See* K'inich Yax K'uk' Mo'
Owens, J. G., 282, 380, 456
Ox Witik, 229

Pahl, G. W., 456
Paine, R. R., 51, 68, 457
Palenque: ancestor cartouches, 267; Group of the Cross, 346, 347f, 348f, 349–350, 350f; rulers, 349; Temple of the Inscriptions, 394; Teotihuacan influence, 392; ties, 407; warfare against, 356
Palerm, A., 457
Palka, J., 441
Papagayo Structure (Acropolis): buried, 193; dating, 174–175; iconography, 83; step altar, 363–364, 364f; usage, 181, 184, 185–186
Parfit, M., 457
Parker, J., 365, 442
Parsons, J. R., 461
Parsons, L. A., 457
Pasztory, E., 457

Index

Patio 5B (Northeast Court Group, Acropolis), 161, 162
Patio 5C (Northeast Court Group, Acropolis), 161–162
Pato Structure (Acropolis), 179, 180
Peabody Museum. *See* Harvard University
Peccary skull offerings, 251
Pendergast, D. M., 457
Pennsylvania State University, 19, 401
Perico Structure (Acropolis), 179, 180
Period of Exploration and Discovery, 8
Peten, 10, 26, 149, 166, 196, 397–398, 399
Peterson, L. C., 446
Phenice, T. W., 457
Piedras Negras, 66, 392
Piehl, J. C., 415–416, 457
Place names, modern, 132
Place of Cattails, 392
Plummer, T., 449
Pohl, M. D., 38, 457–458
Political organization: Acropolis expansion, 197; big-polity model, 61–62; chiefdom, 78; council house, 121, 133, 138, 193, 403–404; decline, 301–302, 308, 418; diarchal, 92; geographic extent, 4; Hawaiian model, 54–56; ideological resources, 106; instability of, 62–63, 99–101; nonkinship, 260; origins and development, 17, 20–21, 74–75, 86–87, 194–195, 400–401; patronage, 292–293; population and, 68, 401, 416–417; predynastic, 90, 91; during reign of Ruler 12, 60; settlement patterns and, 197; Teotihuacan influence, 392; trade and, 408; water management, 104, 108, 132–136, 403, 404. *See also* dynamic model; galactic polity model
Poole, J., 472

Po'ot, O. Dzul de, 432
Poot Tzul, D., 429
Po'ot Yah, E., 432
Popenoe, D. H., 458
Popol nah/otot. *See* council house
Population: agriculture and, 52, 58, 59; chronology, 10, 406; decline, 16, 48–49, 51, 64–66, 76, 77, 418, 419–420; distribution, 45–47, 50, 59, 60, 61; Group 10L-2, 298, 307–308, 412; growth, 52–53, 68, 72, 84–86, 94, 415–417; immigration, 60, 72; Mani province, 72; non-Maya, 10, 76, 78, 79, 396–398, 404; peak, 4, 51–52; political organization and, 68, 401, 416–417; postdynastic, 65–66, 302, 304–306, 308, 419–423; of residential compounds, 297–298, 299–300; seed, 42, 47, 50; settlement model, 44f, 45, 46–49, 46f, 48, 49, 50, 51–53, 62, 65, 66; soil model, 41, 42–43, 43f, 45–49, 50, 51, 66; water management and, 135; Yucatan, 72. *See also* commoners; elite class
Porotic hyperostosis, 33, 336, 337t, 338, 340
Potbelly sculpture, 78–79
Powell, C., 466
Preclassic Period, 395–398
Preston, S. H., 438
Price, B. J., 20, 461
Price, D., 433
Principal Group, 7f, 9, 85, 90, 115–116, 120
Producers. *See* commoners
Proskouriakoff, T., 10–11, 278, 458
Protoclassic period, 78, 396–398
Proyecto Arqueológico Acrópolis Copán (PAAC), 22, 140, 146, 202
Proyecto Arqueológico Copán II, 14–15, 298, 401
Proyecto Arqueológico Copán (PAC), 12–14, 19,

115
Puleston, D. E., 104, 117, 122, 458, 467
Puleston, O. S., 104, 458
Purple Platform, 182, 184, 185
Purpura, 209–210, 211f
Putschar, W. G. J., 456

Quatrefoil motif, 119–120, 120f, 135
Quelepa, 306
Quetzal imagery, 222
Quiriguá: founded, 196, 399; hegemony over, 28, 378, 401; independence, 96, 99, 101; stelae, 99, 354, 355f; warfare with, 28–29, 384, 385, 386f, 394, 407–408

Ramos, J., 397, 428
Rands, R. L., 458
Reed, D. M., 38, 459, 476
Reents-Budet, D., 459
Reilly, F. K. III, 459
Reservoirs, 108, 115–116, 129
Residential compounds: access to, 309; demographic composition, 297–298, 299–300; elite, 62, 91, 96–99, 310 (*see also* Group 9N-8); lifestyle in, 342–343; lineage groups, 278, 300; postdynastic occupation, 65–66, 302, 304–306, 308, 422–423; predynastic, 156; royal. (*see* Group 10L-2); in satellite centers, 98–99
Reyes Mazzoni, R., 12
Rice, P., 437
Rice, D. S., 437, 459
Riciputi, L. R., 429, 459
Ricketson, E. B., 459
Ricketson, O. G., 459
Riese, B., 14, 459–460
Ringle, W. M., 431
Río Amarillo (La Canteada), 85–86, 96, 99, 306
Río Copán: access, 177, 182; destruction by, 180, 184, 186, 194, 243, 246, 396, 401; levels, 37; potability, 404
Ritual areas: expansion of,

487

411; Group 10L-2, 97, 243, 275, 280–282, 284–285, 286f, 287–289, 287f, 289f, 290f, 291, 297, 298, 309–310; Group of the Cross, 346, 347f, 348f, 349–350, 350f; status and, 405–406, 423–424; Structure 10L-25, 212; Structure 10L-29, 269; Structure 10L-30, 261, 263; Structure 10L-32, 253–254; Structure 10L-43, 280–282. *See also* altars; Rosalila Structure; Structure 10L-26

Rituals: burial revisitation, 249, 319–320, 321, 322, 323–324, 325, 330, 338–340; impinged-bone glyph, 360–364, 361f, 367–368; structure termination, 209, 210f; water, 105–107, 110–114

Rivera, F., 217
Robertson, M. G., 460
Robertson, J., 346, 469–470
Robicsek, F., 460
Rodríguez, M. del Carmen, 456, 460
Romano Pacheco, A., 442
Rosalila Structure, 27, 190, 205f; adornment, 206–207, 217, 230; burial of, 205–206, 209, 210f; burial offerings in, 208f, 210f; iconography, 93, 217–218, 219f, 220–232, 223f, 225f, 227f, 228f, 377–378, 402, 405; as ideological resource, 93, 231–232, 423; investigations, 217; location, 191; plan, 206–207, 206f; purpose, 377, 409; replica, 24f, 218f, 402; significance, 209, 228–229, 230–232. *See also* Structure 10L-16
Roscoe, W., 331, 460
Ross, S. P., 462
Roys, R. L., 72, 74, 460
Rue, D. J., 427, 460, 475
Rulers: authenticity of, 17, 194–195; burials, 318–319, 322–326, 325f; Calakmul,

357; ceremonial role, 100, 101; construction by, 152t; diarchal, 92; domain extent, 4; health and lifestyle, 323, 326; ideological resources and, 106, 393, 405–406, 423–424; lineage group, 54; name changes, xv; Palenque, 349, 356; physical requirements of, 335; portraits, 226, 228, 228f; predynastic, 90, 91, 149; Quiriguá, 28; reigns, 152t; 382–383; residence. *See* Group 10L-2; sources of power of, 84; succession, 405, 413–414; Teotihuacan and, 399; water management and, 118–120, 122–123. *See also specific rulers*

Ruler 1. *See* K'inich Yax K'uk' Mo'
Ruler 2: construction by, 27, 152t, 165–176, 167f, 169f, 170f, 172f, 198, 400; reign, 152t
Rulers 3-5, 152t, 176–177, 178f, 179–182
Rulers 6-7, 152t, 182, 183f, 184–185
Ruler 8: burial, 189–190, 192, 322–324, 330; construction by, 152t, 185–191, 187f, 188f, 198, 252, 377–387; reign, 152t
Rulers 9-10, 152t, 191–192
Ruler 11, 59, 152t, 192, 370
Ruler 12: burial, 193, 324–326, 374, 378; construction by, 27–28, 152t, 193, 242, 365–371, 366f, 368f, 378, 423–424; reign, 28, 59–60, 152t; Structure 10L-26 and, 391–392
Ruler 13: construction by, 28, 152t, 193, 242, 379, 381, 424; death, 29; Hieroglyphic Stairway, 379, 381, 385, 386; Papagayo, 186; reign, 60–61, 152t
Ruler 14, 29, 60–61, 152t, 193, 242, 260
Ruler 15: construction by, 29, 152t, 193, 242,

384–385, 387, 424; reign, 61–64, 152t; water lily imagery, 123, 124f
Ruler 16. *See* Yax Pasaj Chan Yopat

Sabloff, J. A., 8, 428, 477
Sacred geography: Acropolis, 195; impinged-bone glyph and, 349–354, 351f, 352f, 353f, 358–371, 359f, 360f, 361f; Maya view of, 116; pyramids, 107, 114; royal legitimacy, 405–406. *See also* ritual areas
Sacrifice imagery, 93, 233–234, 237
Sahlins, M., 460
Sampeck, K. E., 428
Sanders, W. T., 460–461, 475; Group 10L-2, 412; investigations, 14–15; Las Sepulturas, 298; population, 71–72; regal-ritual center, 408; settlement model, 45, 50; social organization, 17; Structure 9N-82, 96–97; Teotihuacan, 20
Santley, R. S., 461
SAR seminars methodology, xiv–xv
Satellite centers, 31, 96, 98–100, 101. *See also specific polities*
Satterthwaite, L., 431, 448
Saturno, W. A., 85, 99, 461
Saul, F. P., 334, 461
Scarborough, V. L., 438, 461–462
Schele, L., 438, 442, 444, 455, 462–465, 470; Altar FN, 285; Altar Q, 235–236; astronomy, 365; Azul text, 207; cave imagery, 134; Chak, 313; collapse, 303–304; Copán Tomb 1, 251; founder's glyph, 263; Group 10L-2, xv, 289; half-quatrefoil motif, 120; impinged bone glyph, 346, 348–349, 351; investigations, xiv, 21, 23; lineage shrines, 269; Motmot marker, 362; royal legitimacy, 405; serpent

of Yax Pasaj, 414; Teotihuacan influence on elite, 410; Tikal dynasty, 399; tun motif, 137; Ux Witik, 358; water and place names, 109; water lily imagery, 125; Yax Kamlay shrine, 289
Stuart, G. E., 470
Stuart, G. S., 470
Stuart-Macadam, P., 470
Study of Maya Art, A (Spinden), 9
Sub-Jaguar Tomb, 189–190, 192, 322–324, 330
Substructure 10L-16-2nd, 209–210, 211f
Substructure 10L-16-2nd (Principal Group), 209–210, 211f
Sun God: Azul substructure, 218, 220–221, 220f; Rosalila, 223f, 225f, 231–232, 402; Yehnal, 204

Tamarindito, 356, 357f
Tambiah, S. J., 87, 470
Tanner, J. M., 470
Tartan Structure (Acropolis), 174
Tate, C., 470
Taube, K. A., 223, 230, 232, 439, 470
Taylor, D., 470
Temple Inscription, 374, 387–391, 388f, 410
Temple of the Inscriptions, Palenque, 394, 407
Temple of the Inscriptions, Tikal, 394
Temples. *See* ritual areas
10L-26-Sub Group (Acropolis): construction history, 162–165, 174–175, 181, 184, 185–186, 193; location, 153
Teotihuacan: historical ideologies, 391–393; K'inich Yax K'uk' Mo', 27, 264, 269, 376–377, 391–392; rise, 20; Tikal, 399
Teotihuacan influences, 407; Acropolis, 195–196, 399; Altar Q, 236; burials, 26, 27, 83, 171, 173, 195–196,

329, 399; ceramics, 195; on elite, 84, 410; founder's glyph, 263–264; Group 10L-2, 307; Hieroglyphic Stairway, 30; Hunal Tomb, 26, 27; Structure 10L-16, 232–233, 235f, 236, 377; Structure 10L-26 , 387–391, 388f, 410; Structure 10L-33, 263, 264; Structure 10L-41, 277–278; Yax Pasaj and, 295
Terminal Classic settlement patterns, 343
Terminal Preclassic Period, 149
Terraces, 57–58
Theater states, 74, 97, 112–113
Thompson, E. H., 470–471
Thompson, E., 94
Thompson, J. E. S., 116–117, 260, 345, 471
Three mountain site, 405–406
Tiesler Blos, V., 434
Tikal influences: burials, 334; dynasty founding and, 407; fish glyph, 128f; Hombre de Tikal statue, 159; impinged bone glyph, 347f, 350–353, 351f, 352f, 353f, 354; investigation techniques, 145; K'inich Yax K'uk' Mo', 26; Marcador, 347f, 354–355, 356f; predynastic links, 10, 196; residential compounds, 298; Temple of the Inscriptions, 394; Teotihuacan and, 399; warfare against, 354–355, 356f; Yehnal, 166
Tlaloc imagery: Altar Q, 236; in burials, 171, 173; Structure 10L-16, 232–233, 235f, 236; Structure 10L-33, 263, 264; Structure 10L-41, 277–278; Yax Pasaj and, 295
Tollan, 392
Tombs. *See* burials; *specific structures*
Toniná Monument 122, 356, 357f

Tooth modifications, 319, 321, 322, 327, 328
Tozzer, A. M., 471
Trade, 78, 87–88, 408
Transgendered persons, 330–332
Traxler, L. P., 161, 197, 413, 431, 459, 466, 471, 475
Trigger, B. G., 471
Trik, A. S., 471
Triple Alliance, 20
T-shaped stepped niche. *See* half-quatrefoil motif
Tulane University, 282
Tun motif, 117–119, 118f, 137, 221
Turban imagery, 226, 228, 228f
Turner, B. L. II, 14, 60, 110–111, 445, 471–472
Tzapah Platform, 170–171
Tzultacah, 116–117, 122–123, 131

Uapala ceramic sphere, 397
Uaxactun, 88, 145
Uir phase, 244
Ulua polychrome, 93
Upland zones: colonization, 47, 49, 50–51, 60; soils, 39, 41; terraces, 57–58
Uranio Structure, 168
Urban, P. A., 472
Urton, G., 472
Uxbenka Stela 11, 354
Ux Witik, 358, 405
U Yak' Chak. *See* Chak

Valdés, J. A., 14, 428, 472
Valdez, F., Jr., 438
Van Rossum, P., 45, 50, 71–72, 475
Vásquez Negrete, J., 434
Vega de Zea, L., 450
Venus glyphs, 277
Vermont Salas, R., 429
Viel, R., 445, 472–473; Altar Q, 138; ceramic sequence, 13; collapse, 15, 64–65, 419; dating, 59, 245; diarchal rulers, 92; Group 10L-2, 244; investigations by, 24–25; landscape conditions, 37; Late Formative period, 77–78; royal acces-

491

Index

sion, 405; water management, 397, 401–402, 404; water shrines, 110–111; Yax Structure, 80
Vogrin, A., 403, 447
Vogt, E. Z., 104, 110, 125, 131, 137, 473
Volwahsen, A., 473
Von Euw, E., 444

Wagner, E., 303–304, 474
Wanyerka, P., 474
War faction, 92
Warfare: collapse and, 16; human sacrifices, 318; imagery, 233–234, 237, 278, 295, 303–304, 352–353; against impinged-bone places, 351, 354–358; against Quiriguá, 28–29, 384, 385, 386f, 394
Water: as ideological resource, 104, 105–107, 110–114, 115, 118–120, 122–123, 129, 131, 133, 134–136, 137; land deeds, 111; place names references, 109, 110; settlement patterns and, 108–109
Water-hole groups, 109–111, 126, 133, 403
Water imagery: Aztec, 107–108; ecological context, 116–123; Indigo Structure, 117f; Principal Group, 116; Structure 10L-32 (Principal Group), 130f, 257; Structure 10L-41, 131, 277; water-hole groups and, 403; water lilies, 122–126, 124f, 128–129, 128f, 137, 138
Water management: collapse, 136; development of, 107; flooding, 246, 401; Group 10L-2, 126–132, 128f, 130f, 284, 414; iconography of, 88, 118–120, 127f, 134–135, 257, 403; Las Sepulturas, 133; non-Maya, 107, 108, 113–114, 397, 404; political organization and, 104, 108, 132, 133–136, 403, 405; population stress, 136; Río Copán access, 177, 182; sacred landscape, 114; significance, 107, 401–404; social organization and, 109–114, 123–132, 133–136; soil model, 43; Southeast Asia, 112–113; strategies, 57–58, 105, 112, 114–116, 284, 397; strategies, irrigation, 43, 57, 64, 71; strategies, reservoirs, 108, 115–116, 129. *See also* water
Waxaklajun Ub'ah K'awil. *See* Ruler 13
Webster, D. L., xiv, 457, 461, 474–475; agrarian economy, 71, 406–407; collapse, 419, 421; elite demands, 69; Group 10L-2, 412; historical record, 19; investigations, 15; Las Sepulturas, 298; population, 71–72, 401, 421; regal-ritual center, 408; rise, 17; settlement model, 45, 50; social organization, 17, 406–407
Weiss, A., 475
Weiss, K. M., 478
West Court (Acropolis), 201–202
Whittington, S. L., 38, 63, 475–476
Widmer, R., 475
Willey, G. R., 6, 8, 11–12, 19, 96, 450, 476–477
Williamson, R. V., 440, 441, 466, 468, 477
Wil Ohl K'inich. *See* Ruler 8
Wingard, J. D., 477; erosion, 47; irrigation, 64; soil model, 39, 41–43, 43f, 45–50, 51–53, 406
Winning, H. von, 477
Wisdom, C., 109, 403, 477
Wiseman, F. M., 34, 472, 477–478
Witik Platform, 168–170, 171, 175–176
Wittfogel, K. A., 478
Witz Monster mask, 228–229
Wood, J. W., 478
Wright, L. E., 433, 472

Xukpi Stone, 171–173, 172f; construction, 175; impinged-bone glyph, 358; offerings beneath, 168; remains of, 204; reset, 151, 176; translating, 362

Yaeger, J., 450
Yahaw Chan Ahbak, 414
Yaxchilán, 267, 353f, 354
Yax Kamlay, 289, 414
Yax Pasaj Chan Yopat: accession, 294, 307–308; Altar Q, 234–236; burial, 31, 252–253, 265, 301, 303; collapse and, 304; construction by, 30–31, 152t, 193–194, 214–216, 242, 253–255, 256f, 257–258, 259f, 260–261, 261f, 262f, 263, 264, 274, 275, 292, 301, 308, 358; death, 308; K'inich Yax K'uk' Mo' and, 234–236; origins, 291–292, 407; patron deity, 257, 414; personal hieroglyphic monuments, 255, 256, 284–285, 286f, 287–289, 287f, 289f, 290f, 291–294, 297, 301; reign, 62–64, 134, 152t, 297, 311; residential compound, xv, 243, 253, 254f, 256–257, 274, 309, 310, 411–413; water lily imagery, 123
Yax Structure, 80, 83, 88–89
Yax Substructure (10L-26-Sub Group), 162, 164
Yehnal Structure, 166–167, 167f, 176, 204, 221
Yucatan, 72, 111–112, 398
Yune Platform, 158–159, 159f, 164, 166–168, 175–176, 199

Zeleznik, S., 475
Zinacantan, 109–111

School of American Research Advanced Seminar Series

PUBLISHED BY SAR PRESS

CHACO & HOHOKAM: PREHISTORIC REGIONAL SYSTEMS IN THE AMERICAN SOUTHWEST
Patricia L. Crown & W. James Judge, eds.

RECAPTURING ANTHROPOLOGY: WORKING IN THE PRESENT
Richard G. Fox, ed.

WAR IN THE TRIBAL ZONE: EXPANDING STATES AND INDIGENOUS WARFARE
R. Brian Ferguson & Neil L. Whitehead, eds.

IDEOLOGY AND PRE-COLUMBIAN CIVILIZATIONS
Arthur A. Demarest & Geoffrey W. Conrad, eds.

DREAMING: ANTHROPOLOGICAL AND PSYCHOLOGICAL INTERPRETATIONS
Barbara Tedlock, ed.

HISTORICAL ECOLOGY: CULTURAL KNOWLEDGE AND CHANGING LANDSCAPES
Carole L. Crumley, ed.

THEMES IN SOUTHWEST PREHISTORY
George J. Gumerman, ed.

MEMORY, HISTORY, AND OPPOSITION UNDER STATE SOCIALISM
Rubie S. Watson, ed.

OTHER INTENTIONS: CULTURAL CONTEXTS AND THE ATTRIBUTION OF INNER STATES
Lawrence Rosen, ed.

LAST HUNTERS–FIRST FARMERS: NEW PERSPECTIVES ON THE PREHISTORIC TRANSITION TO AGRICULTURE
T. Douglas Price & Anne Birgitte Gebauer, eds.

MAKING ALTERNATIVE HISTORIES: THE PRACTICE OF ARCHAEOLOGY AND HISTORY IN NON-WESTERN SETTINGS
Peter R. Schmidt & Thomas C. Patterson, eds.

SENSES OF PLACE
Steven Feld & Keith H. Basso, eds.

CYBORGS & CITADELS: ANTHROPOLOGICAL INTERVENTIONS IN EMERGING SCIENCES AND TECHNOLOGIES
Gary Lee Downey & Joseph Dumit, eds.

ARCHAIC STATES
Gary M. Feinman & Joyce Marcus, eds.

CRITICAL ANTHROPOLOGY NOW: UNEXPECTED CONTEXTS, SHIFTING CONSTITUENCIES, CHANGING AGENDAS
George E. Marcus, ed.

THE ORIGINS OF LANGUAGE: WHAT NONHUMAN PRIMATES CAN TELL US
Barbara J. King, ed.

REGIMES OF LANGUAGE: IDEOLOGIES, POLITIES, AND IDENTITIES
Paul V. Kroskrity, ed.

BIOLOGY, BRAINS, AND BEHAVIOR: THE EVOLUTION OF HUMAN DEVELOPMENT
Sue Taylor Parker, Jonas Langer, & Michael L. McKinney, eds.

WOMEN & MEN IN THE PREHISPANIC SOUTHWEST: LABOR, POWER, & PRESTIGE
Patricia L. Crown, ed.

HISTORY IN PERSON: ENDURING STRUGGLES, CONTENTIOUS PRACTICE, INTIMATE IDENTITIES
Dorothy Holland & Jean Lave, eds.

THE EMPIRE OF THINGS: REGIMES OF VALUE AND MATERIAL CULTURE
Fred R. Myers, ed.

DREAMING: ANTHROPOLOGICAL AND PSYCHOLOGICAL INTERPRETATIONS
Barbara Tedlock, ed.

THE ANASAZI IN A CHANGING ENVIRONMENT
George J. Gumerman, ed.

CATASTROPHE & CULTURE: THE ANTHROPOLOGY OF DISASTER
Susanna M. Hoffman & Anthony Oliver-Smith, eds.

Published by SAR Press

Uruk Mesopotamia & Its Neighbors:
Cross-Cultural Interactions in the
Era of State Formation
 Mitchell S. Rothman, ed.

Tikal: Dynasties, Foreigners,
& Affairs of State: Advancing
Maya Archaeology
 Jeremy A. Sabloff, ed.

Remaking Life & Death: Toward an
Anthropology of the Biosciences
 Sarah Franklin & Margaret Lock, eds.

Gray Areas: Ethnographic
Encounters with Nursing Home
Culture
 Philip B. Stafford, ed.

American Arrivals: Anthropology
Engages the New Immigration
 Nancy Foner, ed.

Law & Empire in the Pacific:
Fiji and Hawai'i
 *Sally Engle Merry &
 Donald Brenneis, eds.*

Anthropology in the Margins
of the State
 Veena Das & Deborah Poole, eds.

Pluralizing Ethnography:
Comparison and Representation in
Maya Cultures, Histories, and
Identities
 John M. Watanabe & Edward F. Fischer, eds.

Violence
 Neil L. Whitehead, ed.

The Archaeology of Colonial
Encounters: Comparative
Perspectives
 Gil J. Stein, ed.

Published by Cambridge University Press

Regional Perspectives on the Olmec
 Robert J. Sharer & David C. Grove, eds.

The Chemistry of Prehistoric
Human Bone
 T. Douglas Price, ed.

The Emergence of Modern Humans:
Biocultural Adaptations in the
Later Pleistocene
 Erik Trinkaus, ed.

The Anthropology of War
 Jonathan Haas, ed.

The Evolution of Political Systems
 Steadman Upham, ed.

Classic Maya Political History:
Hieroglyphic and Archaeological
Evidence
 T. Patrick Culbert, ed.

Turko-Persia in Historical
Perspective
 Robert L. Canfield, ed.

Chiefdoms: Power, Economy, and
Ideology
 Timothy Earle, ed.

Reconstructing Prehistoric Pueblo
Societies
 William A. Longacre, ed.

Published by University of California Press

Writing Culture: The Poetics
and Politics of Ethnography
 *James Clifford &
 George E. Marcus, eds.*

Published by University of Arizona Press

The Collapse of Ancient States and Civilizations
  Norman Yoffee &
  George L. Cowgill, eds.

Published by University of New Mexico Press

New Perspectives on the Pueblos
  Alfonso Ortiz, ed.

Structure and Process in Latin America
  Arnold Strickon &
  Sidney M. Greenfield, eds.

The Classic Maya Collapse
  T. Patrick Culbert, ed.

Methods and Theories of Anthropological Genetics
  M. H. Crawford & P. L. Workman, eds.

Sixteenth-Century Mexico: The Work of Sahagun
  Munro S. Edmonson, ed.

Ancient Civilization and Trade
  Jeremy A. Sabloff &
  C. C. Lamberg-Karlovsky, eds.

Photography in Archaeological Research
  Elmer Harp, Jr., ed.

Meaning in Anthropology
  Keith H. Basso & Henry A. Selby, eds.

The Valley of Mexico: Studies in Pre-Hispanic Ecology and Society
  Eric R. Wolf, ed.

Demographic Anthropology: Quantitative Approaches
  Ezra B. W. Zubrow, ed.

The Origins of Maya Civilization
  Richard E. W. Adams, ed.

Explanation of Prehistoric Change
  James N. Hill, ed.

Explorations in Ethnoarchaeology
  Richard A. Gould, ed.

Entrepreneurs in Cultural Context
  Sidney M. Greenfield, Arnold Strickon,
  & Robert T. Aubey, eds.

The Dying Community
  Art Gallaher, Jr. &
  Harlan Padfield, eds.

Southwestern Indian Ritual Drama
  Charlotte J. Frisbie, ed.

Lowland Maya Settlement Patterns
  Wendy Ashmore, ed.

Simulations in Archaeology
  Jeremy A. Sabloff, ed.

Chan Chan: Andean Desert City
  Michael E. Moseley & Kent C. Day, eds.

Shipwreck Anthropology
  Richard A. Gould, ed.

Elites: Ethnographic Issues
  George E. Marcus, ed.

The Archaeology of Lower Central America
  Frederick W. Lange &
  Doris Z. Stone, eds.

Late Lowland Maya Civilization: Classic to Postclassic
  Jeremy A. Sabloff &
  E. Wyllys Andrews V, eds.

Photo by Katrina Lasko

Participants in the School of American Research advanced seminar "Copán: The Rise and Fall of a Classic Maya Kingdom," Santa Fe, New Mexico, October 11–15, 1994.
Standing from left: Robert J. Sharer, Linda Schele, Grant Jones, Ricardo Agurcia Fasquelle, Barbara W. Fash, David L. Webster.
Seated from left: E. Wyllys Andrews, David Stuart, Rebecca Storey, William L. Fash, Jr.

www.ingramcontent.com/pod-product-compliance
Lightning Source LLC
Chambersburg PA
CBHW030514230426
43665CB00010B/608